Environmental Problems in an Urbanizing World

Finding Solutions for Cities in Africa, Asia and Latin America

Jorge E Hardoy, Diana Mitlin and David Satterthwaite

Earthscan Publications Ltd, London and Sterling, VA

First published in the UK and USA in 2001 by
Earthscan Publications Ltd

ISBN: 1 85383 719 9 paperback
        1 85383 720 2 hardback

Typesetting by PCS Mapping & DTP, Newcastle upon Tyne
Printed and bound by Creative Print & Design, Wales (Ebbw Vale)
Cover design by Susanne Harris
Cover photo © Janet Jarman

For a full list of publications please contact:
Earthscan Publications Ltd
120 Pentonville Road
London, N1 9JN, UK
Tel: +44 (0)20 7278 0433
Fax: +44 (0)20 7278 1142
Email: earthinfo@earthscan.co.uk
http://www.earthscan.co.uk

22883 Quicksilver Drive, Sterling, VA 20166–2012, USA

Earthscan is an editorially independent subsidiary of Kogan Page Ltd and publishes in association with WWF-UK and the International Institute for Environment and Development

A catalogue record for this book is available from the British Library

Library of Congress Cataloging-in-Publication Data
Hardoy, Jorge Enrique.
    Environmental problems in an urbanizing world : finding solutions in Africa, Asia, and
    Latin America / Jorge E Hardoy, Diana Mitlin, and David Satterthwaite.
        p. cm.
    Rev. ed. Of: Environmental problems in Third World cities, 1992.
    Includes bibliographical references and index.
    ISBN 1-85383-720-2 (hardback) – ISBN 1-85383-719-9 (pbk.)
        Environmental policy – developing countries. 2. Developing countries – Environmental
    conditions. 3. Cities and towns – Developing countries. 4. Sustainable development –
    Developing countries. I. Mitlin, Diana. II. Satterthwaite, David. III. Hardoy, Jorge Enrique.
    Environmental problems in third World cities. IV. Title.

GE190.D44.H37 2001
363.7'009172'4–dc21

                                                                                2001018764

Contents

Tables, figures and boxes   *vi*
Acronyms and abbreviations   *x*
Preface – David Satterthwaite   *xi*
About the authors   *xiv*

1   A New Environmental Agenda for Cities?   1

     Introduction   1
     Environmental goals for cities   2
     Urban change and environmental problems   4
     A new environmental agenda   8
     The structure of the book   14
     Diversities and commonalities   17
     The environmental opportunities provided by cities   20
     An urbanizing world   24

2   Environmental Problems in the Home, Workplace and
     Neighbourhood   37

     Introduction   37
     The indoor environment at home   38
     The workplace   73
     The neighbourhood environment   75
     The importance of the home environment for well-being and child
        development   84

3   The City Environment   87

     The range of problems   87
     Air pollution   89
     Water pollution and scarcity   107
     Road accidents   111
     Toxic/hazardous wastes   112
     Export of toxic wastes or polluting industries   116
     Natural and human-induced hazards   119
     Noise pollution   125
     The environment and well-being   126
     Environmental problems in smaller cities   132
     Environmental transitions, transformations and transfers   142

4 Who Bears the Environmental Costs in Cities?   149

The correlations between incomes and hazards   149
Differentials in environmental risk   151
Vulnerability and susceptibility   152
Groups within the population that face higher risks   158
Conclusions   169

5 The Rural, Regional and Global Impacts of Cities   172

Cities' regional impacts and rural–urban interactions   172
Cities and the global commons   196

6 Tackling Environmental Health Problems   209

Introduction   209
Water, sanitation and drainage   211
Upgrading   219
Refuse collection and cities' waste economies   225
The role of privatization   235
Key roles for NGOs and CBOs   242
Different models of NGO support   250
An institutional framework to support local action on
    environmental health   267

7 Tackling City-wide Problems   270

Tackling city-wide pollution   270
Urban agriculture   280
City-wide planning and management   287
City-wide environmental indicators   302
The institutional constraints on effective action   308
The role of international agencies   313

8 Sustainable Development and Cities   336

Introduction   336
Why is sustainable development important for cities?   339
How a concern for sustainable development arose   340
Emphasizing sustainability; forgetting development   345
The ambiguities in what is to be sustained   348
Emphasizing human activities; forgetting ecological sustainability   350
A framework for considering sustainable development and cities   352
Building synergies, avoiding conflicts?   365
The national framework for city action on sustainable development   368
Enabling local action   371
Implementing sustainable development in cities   372
The global context for sustainability and development   374

9   Conclusions   380
    Introduction   380
    Environmental problems; political solutions   382
    Institutional change and the role of aid agencies   384
    From urban management to improved governance   386
    A new framework of support for citizens' groups and NGOs   389
    Linking environment improvement with poverty reduction   393
    A city-specific environmental agenda   398
    New professional attitudes   400
    City problems within a global perspective   402

References   *407*
Further Reading   *433*
Subject Index   *440*
Cities Index   *446*

Tables, Figures and Boxes

TABLES

1.1 Trends and projections in urban populations by region, 1950–2010   25

1.2 The distribution of large cities by region, 1950–1990   26

1.3 The distribution of the population between settlements of different sizes, 1990   33

2.1 The most serious water-related infections with estimates of the burden of morbidity and mortality they cause and the population at risk   40

2.2 Differentials in the cost of water (ratio of price charged by water vendors to prices charged by the public utility)   48

2.3 The relative importance of different interventions related to water and sanitation for the prevention or control of different diseases   62

2.4 The proportion of the urban population apparently having 'access to safe water' and 'access to sanitation' in selected countries, latest available estimate, 1990–1996   64

3.1 The most common urban air pollutants and their effects on health   94

3.2 Environmental impacts of selected industries   96

3.3 Air quality guidelines   98

3.4 Typical environmental problems for urban centres of different sizes and within nations with different levels of income   144

5.1 Possible major types of health impact of climate change and stratospheric ozone depletion   203

6.1 Typical range of capital costs of different sanitation systems (1990 prices)   213

6.2 Different NGO approaches   252

6.3 Government–community partnerships in addressing health risks in urban areas   260

7.1 Farming systems common in urban areas   284

7.2 OECF lending to urban development, 1987–1998   321

7.3 World Bank lending to urban development, 1981–1998   323

7.4 Asian Development Bank lending to urban development, 1981–1998   325

9.1 The different roles for external agencies working to address low-income groups' needs within the different extremes in terms of government structures   390

9.2   Examples of how environmental actions can help to reduce
      poverty or the deprivations associated with it   396

FIGURES

1.1   Distribution of the world's urban population between regions, 1995   25
1.2   Distribution in the number of the world's 'million cities' by region,
      1990   26
1.3   Average size of the world's 100 largest cities   27
6.1   Examples of different solid-waste collection vehicles used by micro
      and small enterprises and cooperatives in Latin America   229
7.1   The distribution of infant mortality among districts in Buenos
      Aires, 1991   305
8.1   The multiple goals of sustainable development as applied to cities   354
8.2   Contrasts in commercial energy use per person in 1996 between
      regions and between selected nations   359
8.3   Contrasts in carbon dioxide emissions per person in 1996 between
      regions and between selected nations   361

BOXES

1.1   The environmental impact of urban development   5
1.2   The main links between health and the environment   9
1.3   Some definitions   12
1.4   Environmental economies of urbanization   22
1.5   What is an urban centre and a city?   28
2.1   Examples of the inadequacies in cities' water supply and sanitation
      in Asia   44
2.2   The deterioration in water supplies in East African urban areas,
      1967–1997   52
2.3   Examples of the inadequacies in cities' water supply and sanitation
      in Africa   54
2.4   Examples of the inadequacies in cities' water supply and sanitation
      in Latin America and the Caribbean   60
2.5   The Year 2000 Global Assessment of Water and Sanitation   67
2.6   The impact of tuberculosis on health and its association with housing   70
2.7   Examples of the quality and extent of garbage collection from
      households   80
2.8   Some health implications of urban expansion   83
3.1   Health-threatening pollutants   91
3.2   Examples of air pollution   99
3.3   Factors that influence the public's level of risk from exposure to
      air pollution   102
3.4   Cubatão   105
3.5   Water pollution   108

3.6 Two examples of India's most polluted rivers 110
3.7 Examples of toxic chemicals, their sources and their potential health effects 114
3.8 Water, sanitation and waste-collection services in small African urban centres 134
3.9 The deterioration in the quality of municipal water supplies in Iganga (Uganda) 136
3.10 Examples of water and sanitation provision in smaller urban centres in India 137
3.11 Examples of provision for water and sanitation in Amazonian frontier towns in Brazil 138
4.1 Examples of intra-city differentials in health indicators linked to environmental hazards, access to resources and public services, and environmental hazards 153
4.2 Low-income households' adaptation to flooding in Indore, India 162
4.3 Occupational hazards faced by working children 166
5.1 The politics of land conversion on the rural–urban interface: the case of Cavite in the Philippines 178
5.2 Firewood in the cities 180
5.3 Regional impacts of Jakarta 182
5.4 Meeting Dakar's water needs 184
5.5 The impact of air pollution on agriculture 190
5.6 The ecological footprint of cities 194
5.7 The lack of an association between urban poverty and environmental degradation 199
5.8 The impact of sea-level rise and other human-induced changes on Alexandria, Egypt 205
6.1 Barrio San Jorge, Argentina 226
6.2 Solid-waste collection and disposal in Karachi 231
6.3 Examples of recyclers' cooperatives or federations 234
6.4 The Orangi Pilot Project in Karachi, Pakistan 244
6.5 Different options for government spending of US$20 million on improving housing and living environments 246
6.6 The Urban Community Development Office (UCDO) 249
6.7 Community exchanges 255
7.1 Four steps to sustainable industrial production 272
7.2 Public transport and other environmental initiatives in Curitiba, Brazil 276
7.3 Mexico City's Clean Air Policy 278
7.4 Citizen action for pollution control 281
7.5 Household and courtyard farming in urban areas in China 285
7.6 The range of techniques that can contribute towards environmental planning and management 290
7.7 Agenda 21's stress on environmental problems in cities in Africa, Asia and Latin America 294
7.8 Examples of Local Agenda 21s 298
7.9 The Peruvian Cities for Life Forum 301

7.10 The underestimation of the scale and nature of urban poverty   315
8.1   The Trump index for assessing the differentials in individuals'
      contributions to ecological unsustainability   347
8.2   The five different dimensions of environmental equity   363
8.3   Combining ecological and health considerations for city sanitation 367
9.1   The most important aid project characteristics from two different
      viewpoints   387
9.2   A city-based fund for community initiatives   394
9.3   Gender aspects of environmental improvement in cities   403

Acronyms and Abbreviations

CBO   community-based organization
DANCED   Danish Cooperation for Environment and Development
DFID   Department for International Development
GDP   gross domestic product
IIED   International Institute for Environment and Development
NGO   non-governmental organization
OECD   Organization for Economic Cooperation and Development
OECF   Overseas Economic Cooperation Fund[1]
OPEC   Organization of Petroleum Exporting Countries
SDC   Swiss Agency for Development and Cooperation
Sida   Swedish International Development Cooperation Agency
TB   Tuberculosis
UN   United Nations
UNCHS   United Nations Centre for Human Settlements
UNDP   United Nations Development Programme
UNEP   United Nations Environment Programme
UNICEF   United Nations (International) Children's (Emergency) Fund
USAID   United States Agency for International Development
WHO   World Health Organization

---

1 In 1999 this became part of the Japan Bank for International Cooperation.

Preface

This volume is a revised, updated and somewhat expanded edition of our 1992 Earthscan book *Environmental Problems in Third World Cities*. It ended up being rather more revised and expanded than we originally conceived because of the wealth of new material that has been published since the first edition. I fear that I must take the blame for any errors or omissions in that I took primary responsibility for the new edition. Diana Mitlin was on leave from the International Institute for Environment and Development (IIED), working with the South African NGO The People's Dialogue on Land and Shelter during the period when this new edition was produced, although she still had a very active role, rewriting and updating certain sections and commenting on my draft revisions for other sections.

For those people who knew Jorge E Hardoy and who also know that he died in 1993, it may be surprising to see a book published in 2001 in which he is a co-author. The text of this edition is much changed from the original that he wrote with Diana Mitlin and me. The title of the book which in the first edition was called *Environmental Problems in Third World Cities* has also been changed. With the demise of the 'Second World' (the term used for the Soviet bloc), so the term 'Third World' has become less used. But the book's structure and its main themes and conclusions have not changed much, and so many of the key insights for the first edition came from Jorge Hardoy that it seemed inappropriate to drop him from the list of authors. It is also difficult for me to disentangle the relative contributions of Jorge from those of Diana and myself. Even if I could, much of my own contribution would come from what I learnt working with Jorge from 1978 until 1993. While I have been very fortunate in having had the opportunity to work with many remarkable people – and this book draws on their knowledge and insights – it is from Jorge Hardoy that I learnt most. It was also from him that I learnt the joy of working in partnerships with researchers and activists from around the world.

Since the research programme within which I work (set up by Jorge Hardoy in 1977) has always been based on partnerships between my institute and other individuals or institutions, this book is also a synthesis of what has been learnt from these partnerships. Working in partnerships means collective learning – and it is difficult to remember from where (or from whom) many of the key ideas represented in the text of this book came. This book draws on the work we have undertaken with a great range of individuals and institutions over the last 20 years – and although we try to reference all the sources from which we draw, this does not do justice to our partners.

Our partners tend to fall into one of three groups. The first consists of those who work in NGOs with a direct engagement with low-income groups, and Chapters 6 and 9 draw much on their work. Special mention should be made of Jorge Anzorena (SELAVIP), Joel Bolnick and other friends at the People's Dialogue for Land and Shelter, Shack Dwellers' International and the South African Homeless People's Federation, Somsook Boonyabancha and other friends within the Asian Coalition for Housing Rights, Ana Hardoy and other friends at IIED-América Latina, Arif Hasan and staff at the Orangi Pilot Project, and Sheela Patel and other friends at SPARC and the National Slum Dwellers Federation in India.

The second group is our colleagues in IIED, especially in the Human Settlements Programme. Gordon McGranahan deserves special mention, not only because the manuscript was much improved by the quality and detail of his comments and suggestions, but also because it draws considerably on the work he undertook when he was at the Stockholm Environment Institute. Special thanks are also due to Sheridan Bartlett, Nazneen Kanji and Cecilia Tacoli who commented on various sections of the manuscript; the material in this book on children also draws heavily on Sheridan's work. Special mention should also be made of Åsa Jonsson who worked part-time in our research programme before she joined ESCAP in Bangkok. She contributed greatly to Chapter 2, especially with her careful review of the literature on water and sanitation provision in urban areas. Some non-IIED staff also helped to improve the manuscript, and thanks are due to Emma Grant and Trudy Harpham at South Bank University and to Caroline Hunt and Sandy Cairncross at the London School of Hygiene and Tropical Medicine.

The third group on which this volume draws are those who are actively engaged in urban environmental issues both in the UK and in Africa, Asia and Latin America. They include Anil Agarwal and Sunita Narain (Centre for Science and Environment, India), Graham Haughton (University of Hull), Michaela Hordijk and Liliana Miranda (Ecociudad, Lima) and Luz Stella Velasquez (IDEA, Manizales).

The revision and updating of this book also benefited much from our work with four other groups: the working-group developing environmental guidelines for the OECD Development Assistance Committee with support from the Department for International Development (DFID); the joint research programme on Urban Governance, Partnerships and Poverty, also funded by DFID, undertaken with the University of Birmingham, the University of Wales, the London School of Economics and nine city-based teams; the Panel on Urban Population Dynamics of the US National Academy of Sciences; and work with the Intergovernmental Panel on Climate Change. The material on climate change and cities draws heavily on the work of Michael J Scott.

Special thanks are due to Janet Jarman who provided the photographs both for the cover and within this book, and to the Earthscan staff who, as in previous books, helped to transfer our original manuscript into this final book.

The book was made possible only through the generous support of various donors. Special thanks are due to the Danish Cooperation for Environment and Development (DANCED) who provided us with a grant to help cover the time needed to prepare this revised and expanded edition. Special thanks are also due to the Swedish International Development Cooperation Agency (Sida), DFID and the Swiss Agency for Development and Cooperation (SDC) who have long helped to support our work, as well DANCED and the European Union who have also helped to fund our work.

Finally, an apology must go to those who are put off by the length of this book. It would have been much shorter if we had simply referred to examples and referenced them rather than include details – for instance, the long boxes with details of the inadequacies in cities' water and sanitation. We could have also referred the reader to other work that told of the innovations in Manizales and Ilo, and the participatory methods used in Buenos Aires, Lima, Durban and Mumbai, but the text would have been rather dull without these examples. Perhaps more to the point, these examples are needed to highlight both the scale and nature of the problems, and the ingenuity with which some citizen groups, NGOs, municipal authorities and national governments have success-fully addressed such problems.

David Satterthwaite
Human Settlements Programme
International Institute for Environment and Development
July 2000

About the Authors

Jorge E Hardoy. Prior to his death in 1993, Jorge E Hardoy was President of the Instituto Internacional de Medio Ambiente y Desarrollo (IIED-América Latina), an international non-profit NGO based in Buenos Aires, which he had also founded. He was also President of the National Commission for Historic Monuments in Argentina and Editor of the journal *Medio Ambiente y Urbanizacion*. Qualifying as an architect in 1950 with a Masters and PhD from Harvard University in city and regional planning, he wrote widely on both historical and contemporary urban issues. Among his former publications with Earthscan are *Squatter Citizen: Life in the Urban Third World* (with David Satterthwaite), published in 1989, and *The Poor Die Young, Housing and Health in Third World Cities* (edited with Sandy Cairncross and David Satterthwaite), published in 1990. He served as President of the Inter-American Planning Society, was twice a Guggenheim Fellow and served on the Board of the International Development Research Centre (IDRC) in Canada. He was an adviser of the World Commission on Environment and Development (the Brundtland Commission) and also advised the World Health Organization (WHO) on the links between health and environment in cities.

Diana Mitlin is an economist with the Human Settlements Programme of the IIED in London, a member of the editorial board of the journal *Environment and Urbanization* and Editor of HiFi News, a newsletter on innovations in housing finance. With a first degree in economics and sociology from Manchester University and a Masters in economics from Birkbeck College (University of London), she has a special interest in the role of NGOs and voluntary organizations in housing and environmental action. She recently returned from a secondment in South Africa where she worked with the People's Dialogue on Land and Shelter, a South African NGO that supports a number of community and local development activities including local environmental improvements. She is a trustee of International Technology and was a member of Homeless International's Council of Management from 1991 to 1998.

David Satterthwaite is Director of the Human Settlements Programme at the IIED and Editor of the journal *Environment and Urbanization*. He also teaches at the Development Planning Unit, the Institute of Latin American Studies at the University of London and at the London School of Economics (LSE). A development planner by training, with a PhD in social policy from the LSE, he has been working at IIED on issues related to housing and the urban environment since 1974. Recent publications include *The Earthscan Reader in Sustainable Cities* (editor), Earthscan Publications, London, 1999, *An Urbanizing World: Global Report on Human Settlements 1996*, Oxford University Press (editor and principal author) and *The Environment for Children*, Earthscan Publications, 1996 (principal author). He has advised various agencies on urban environmental issues including the Brundtland Commission, WHO, UNICEF, UNCHS, the Department for International Development and Sida and is currently serving as one of the lead authors in the chapter on human settlements for the Intergovernmental Panel on Climate Change.

Chapter 1

A New Environmental Agenda for Cities?

**Children playing in an informal settlement in Nuevo Laredo, a rapidly
growing industrial city on the Mexican border with the US**

INTRODUCTION

In the week when this book was being completed, landslides in Manila and in
Mumbai (formerly Bombay) killed dozens of people and injured many more. In
Manila, the landslide occurred at one of the city's main rubbish dumps, when a
large rain-soaked mountain of rubbish collapsed to cover a densely populated
settlement of people, most of whom made a living out of waste picking. A week
after the event, 205 bodies had been recovered, 2900 people had been displaced
and there were still many people missing (VMSDFI 2000). In Mumbai, a hillside
gave way and the informal homes perched on it were swept away. In both cities,
heavy rain contributed to the landslides, however, the real causes were due to the

fact that the low-income groups could find no land site that was safe and still close to income-earning opportunities and to the failure of government to ensure a safer site or to take measures to make existing sites safer.

We only learn about these disasters because they are 'big' enough to be reported as international news. Thousands of other urban dwellers died and tens of thousands were seriously injured in this same week in Africa, Asia and Latin America (and in every week since) from 'smaller' disasters that received no international media coverage.[1] In most large cities and in many smaller ones in these regions, it is so common for people living in an informal settlement to be killed in an accidental fire or a flood or during a storm that it hardly makes the national press, let alone the international press.

In this same week (and in every week since), in the towns and cities in these regions, several thousand people (mostly infants and children) died of diarrhoeal diseases, several thousand more died of acute respiratory infections and several hundred died of diseases spread by insect vectors such as malaria or dengue fever. Several thousand adults died of tuberculosis or some other infectious disease. Several thousand people died of accidents on the roads, at work or within their home, with tens of thousands seriously injured. Most of the families in which an adult dies prematurely face serious economic problems because of the drop in income.

What is important about all of these deaths and injuries is first, that virtually all could have been prevented, most of them at low cost, and second that good environmental management is an important part of doing so.

ENVIRONMENTAL GOALS FOR CITIES

Cities can provide healthy, safe and stimulating environments for their inhabitants without imposing unsustainable demands on natural resources, ecosystems and global cycles. A successful city, in this sense, is one that meets multiple goals. Such goals include:

* healthy living and working environments for the inhabitants;
* water supply, provision for sanitation, rubbish collection and disposal, drains, paved roads and footpaths, and other forms of infrastructure and services that are essential for health (and important for a prosperous economic base) available to all; and
* an ecologically sustainable relationship between the demands of consumers and businesses and the resources, waste sinks and ecosystems on which they draw.

Achieving such multiple goals implies an understanding of the links between the city's economy and built environment, the physical environment in which they are located (including soils, water resources and climate) and the biological

---

1 The figures for injuries and premature deaths in these paragraphs are based on World Health Organization figures; Chapters 2 and 3 have more detailed discussions of these.

environment (including local flora and fauna) and how these are changing. Such an understanding is essential if environmental hazards are to be minimized, and environmental capital not depleted.[2] The growing realization of the environmental (and other) costs that global warming will (or may) bring adds another urgent environmental agenda to cities, but again, the above goals can be achieved with levels of greenhouse gas emissions that reduce risks.[3]

There are many other important environmental goals whose achievement would make city environments more pleasant, safe and valued by their inhabitants. These usually include a sense among the inhabitants that their culture and history are a valued part of the city and are reflected in its form and layout. They certainly include city environments that are more conducive to family life, child development and social interaction. It is difficult to be precise about such aspects since their preferred form will vary according to culture and climate. They will also vary within any one city – for instance well-managed public spaces and facilities become more important in densely populated areas with overcrowded housing. The precise nature of the interaction between environmental factors and human well-being also remains poorly understood. But all city environments should include a range of public or community facilities such as open spaces within or close to residential areas where young children can play and socialize, under adult supervision. All urban neighbourhoods need community centres that serve the particular needs of their inhabitants (for instance as meeting places, organization points for negotiations with external agencies, mother and child centres, places for child activities and where social events can be organized). Sites are also required in all residential areas where adolescents and adults can gather, socialize, relax, play sports and the like; these also need to be accessible, safe and maintained. Cities need parks, beaches (where these exist) and sites of natural beauty that preserve the character of a city's natural landscape and to which all citizens have access. In hot climates, open spaces with trees can provide welcome relief from the heat, especially when combined with lakes, streams or rivers that can contribute to more comfortable micro-climates (Douglas 1983). All these sites also need adequate provision for maintenance and management.

Achieving these different goals while also responding to the needs of different groups requires a political and administrative system through which the views and priorities of citizens can influence policies and actions within the district or neighbourhood where they live and at city level. It also requires legal systems that safeguard citizens' civil and political rights to basic services as well as rights not to

---

2 Environmental capital (or natural capital) is the stock of natural assets that includes renewable resources (living species and ecosystems), non-renewable resources (for instance fossil fuels) and the waste-assimilation capacities of ecosystems and of the whole planet. As Chapter 8 will discuss in more detail, some care is needed in the use of this concept in that characterizing ecological resources as a form of capital highlights only their economic value for production. But ecosystems and natural cycles provide many functions that are difficult to value, including those that are essential life-support systems or that provide protective functions and contribute to resilience (see for instance Rees 1995 and Hanley and others 1997).

3 The key point that will be developed in later chapters is that it is possible to envisage cities with high standards of living and quality of life with much lower greenhouse gas emissions per person than is currently common in high-income nations.

face illegal and health-damaging pollution in their home, work or the wider city, and government institutions that are accountable to public scrutiny. Thus, it is about 'good governance' with the term governance understood to include not only the political and administrative institutions of government (and their organization and interrelationships) but also the relationships between government and civil society (McCarney 1996, Swilling 1997, Devas 1999). Good governance both at neighbourhood and city levels is critical for successful cities. It provides the means through which the inhabitants reach agreement on how to progress towards the achievement of multiple goals and how limited public resources and capacities are best used. It is also the means by which lower-income groups or other disadvantaged groups can influence policies and resource allocations. City government also has to represent the needs and priorities of its citizens in the broader context – for instance in negotiations with provincial and national governments, international agencies and businesses considering investments there.

URBAN CHANGE AND ENVIRONMENTAL PROBLEMS

Rapid urban change need not produce serious environmental problems. Cities such as Curitiba and Pôrto Alegre in Brazil have been among the world's most rapidly growing cities in recent decades and each has much less serious environmental problems than virtually all the cities that have grown far more slowly. And as described in more detail later, some of the most serious environmental problems are found in smaller cities (or towns), including many that have not had rapidly growing populations. However, environmental problems become particularly serious where there is a rapid expansion in urban population and production with little or no consideration for the environmental implications nor for the political and institutional framework that is needed to ensure that such environmental problems are addressed. In most low- and middle-income countries, the expansion in their urban population has occurred without the needed expansion in the services and facilities that are essential to an adequate and healthy urban environment. It has usually occurred with little or no effective pollution control, and with forms of urban governance that cannot begin to meet their multiple responsibilities. It has also taken place with little regard to the environmental implications of rapid urban expansion, including the modifications to the earth's surface (and to the local ecology), the changes wrought in the natural flows of water, and the demands made on the surrounding region for building materials as a result of the construction of buildings, roads, car-parks, industries and other components of the urban fabric (see Box 1.1).

Urban expansion without effective urban governance means that a substantial proportion of the population faces high levels of risk from natural and human-induced environmental hazards. This can be seen in most major cities in Africa, Asia and Latin America, where a significant proportion of the population lives in shelters and neighbourhoods with very inadequate provision for water and the safe disposal of solid and liquid wastes. Provision for drainage –

Box 1.1 *THE ENVIRONMENTAL IMPACT OF URBAN DEVELOPMENT*

Urban development directly transforms large areas of the earth's surface. Hillsides may be cut or bulldozed into new shapes, valleys and swamps may be filled with rocks and waste materials, water and minerals may be extracted from beneath the city, and regimes of soil and groundwater modified in many ways. The construction of buildings, roads and other components of the urban fabric modifies the energy, water and chemical budgets of the affected portions of the earth's surface. As cities expand, they not only alter the earth's surface but create new landforms (as in the case of reclaimed land).

Urban developments greatly affect the operation of the hydrological cycle, including changes in total run-off, an alteration in peak-flow characteristics and a decline in water quality. As such, they also greatly affect the processes of erosion and sedimentation. To these changes must be added the network of pipes and channels for water collection, treatment, transmission, regulation and distribution, and the culverts, gutters, drains, pipes, sewers and channels of urban waste-water disposal and stormwater drainage systems. Urbanization affects stream channels and flood-plains, often causing water to flow through cities at a high velocity.

Temperatures in urban areas are affected by many factors including the way in which the walls and roofs of buildings and the concrete or roadstone of paved areas behave in terms of high conductivity, heat capacity and the ability to reflect heat, as well as having a higher heat-storage capacity than natural soils. Also important are: the input of artificial heat generated by machinery, vehicles, heating and cooling systems; the way in which a large extent of impervious surface sheds rainwater rapidly, altering the urban moisture and heat budget; and the ejection of pollutants and dust into the urban atmosphere. The urban heat balance affects rain-producing mechanisms and the rate of snow melt over and within cities.

The creation of the city involves massive transfers of materials into the cities and within the city, and back out of the city again. These include major earth-moving activities that involve modifications to the hydrological cycle and modifications to the weight of materials on the ground surface. This redistribution of stresses in the urban area alters the natural movement of groundwater and dissolved matter within the city area. The process of building the city changes the nature of the land cover both temporarily and permanently, and induces changed relationships between the energy of falling rainwater and the amount of sediments carried into streams. This leads in turn to an increase or decrease in the sediment in the water supply to stream channels. This will affect the stability of those stream channels and the consequent pattern of downstream channel erosion.

This rearrangement of water, materials and stresses on the earth's surface as a result of urban development and its consequences requires careful assessments, as the impacts are often felt off-site, down-valley, downstream or downwind. The terrain for urban development requires careful evaluation as legacies of past colder, warmer, wetter or drier geomorphic conditions may become unstable if they are disturbed by ill-planned earthworks. Each type of geomorphic process has special limitations for urban construction, but previous phases of urban land use may leave unstable fills, poorly drained valley floors and weakly consolidated reclaimed land. Urban sediment requires special control measures.

Source: Drawn from Douglas, Ian (1986), 'Urban Geomorphology' in P G Fookes and P R Vaughan (editors), *A Handbook of Engineering Geomorphology*, Surrey University Press (Blackie & Son), Glasgow, pp 270–283 and Douglas, Ian (1983), *The Urban Environment*, Edward Arnold, London.

including that to cope with storm and surface run-off – is often deficient. A large proportion of the urban population live in poor quality housing – for instance whole households live in one or two rooms in cramped, overcrowded dwellings such as tenements, cheap boarding-houses or shelters built on illegally occupied or subdivided land. Many people live on land that is subject to periodic floods, landslides or other serious hazard.

It may also be that an increasing proportion of the urban population in Africa, Asia and Latin America is coming to live in regions or zones where the ecological underpinnings of urban development are more fragile. A considerable proportion of the rapid growth in urban population has taken place in areas that were sparsely settled only a few decades ago. In recent decades, many of the world's most rapidly growing urban centres have been those that developed as administrative and service centres in areas of agricultural colonization or mining or logging in what were previously uninhabited or sparsely populated areas. For instance in Latin America, only in the last few decades has urban development spread to the hot and humid regions in the interior of Brazil, Bolivia, Paraguay and Venezuela, Central America and Mexico, and to the Chilean and Argentinian Patagonia region. Among the reasons why most of these regions had remained sparsely populated were the greater environmental hazards or soils that were less suited to sustained commercial exploitation (di Pace and others 1992).

Urban development without effective urban governance means that environment-related diseases and injuries cause or contribute much to disablement and premature deaths among infants, children, adolescents and adults. In many cities and in most districts in which low-income households are concentrated, environment-related diseases and injuries are the leading cause of death and illness. In many poor city districts, infants are 40–50 times more likely to die before the age of one than in Europe or North America and virtually all such deaths are environment-related. When preparing a review of the state of health in urban areas in 1990 with Sandy Cairncross (from the London School of Hygiene and Tropical Medicine), we estimated that over 600 million urban citizens in Africa, Asia and Latin America live in 'life and health threatening' conditions because of the environmental problems that are evident in their shelters and neighbourhoods such as unsafe and insufficient water, overcrowded and unsafe shelters, inadequate or no sanitation, no drains and inadequate rubbish collection, unstable house sites, and the risks of flooding and other environment-related factors (Cairncross and others 1990). The numbers faced with life- and health-threatening risks have probably increased since then, as urban populations have grown faster than the expansion of the infrastructure and services that reduce these risks. And as later chapters will show, most of the diseases and injuries that arise as a result of such life- and health-threatening environments are preventable at a low cost.

Addressing such environmental problems can also mean large cost savings, in addition to improvements to health. They can bring a great saving to poorer groups in terms of time and effort. Regular supplies of water piped into the home mean that the people no longer have to fetch and carry large volumes of water from public standpipes or kiosks (and queue each time they do). Readily available supplies of water and the means to heat water make laundry, personal hygiene and many household tasks easier, more convenient and less time-consuming. Better public transport means that low-income groups no longer have to walk long distances to and from work or shops and reduces the amount of time spent travelling. More accessible healthcare centres improve health but also eliminate the need for long journeys to and from distant hospitals. Healthier children mean that adults (usually women) gain much extra time that would otherwise have been spent nursing the sick. For tens of millions of city dwellers living in areas that each year are subject to floods, basic site drainage and flood protection can remove not only the health risks of flooding but also the disruption to daily life and work that floods always cause.

There are also the environmental problems around the city. In most cities and many smaller urban centres, there is serious environmental degradation in their surrounds and damage to natural resources – for instance to soils, crops, forests, freshwater aquifers and surface water and fisheries. These arise from the demands for natural resources, changes brought to water flows and the air, and water pollution and solid wastes generated by urban enterprises and consumers. Most of such environmental degradation can also be prevented or much reduced at relatively low cost.

The scale and severity of environmental problems in cities reflect the failure of governments. In most nations, both national and urban governments have failed in three essential environmental actions: to enforce appropriate legislation (including that related to environmental health, occupational health and pollution control); to ensure adequate provision for water supply and solid and liquid waste collection and treatment systems to all homes and neighbourhoods; and to ensure the adequate provision of health care which not only treats environment-related illnesses but which implements preventive measures to limit their incidence and severity. City governments have also failed to implement land-use policies that ensure that sufficient land is available for housing developments for low-income groups. As later chapters will discuss in more detail, it is not so much a failure of the public provision of water, sanitation, drainage, house sites and healthcare, but a failure to provide the framework that ensures that provision, by community-based organizations (CBOs), non-governmental organizations (NGOs), private enterprises and other organizations, as well as by public agencies.

The policies and actions that governments take with regard to the urban environment have profound implications for the health and well-being of urban citizens and, in the longer term, for the ecological sustainability of cities and the urban and regional systems of which they are a part. The extent to which good environmental quality is achieved in cities may be one of the most revealing indicators of the competence and capacity of city and municipal government, and of the extent to which their policies respond to the needs and priorities of their population.

A NEW ENVIRONMENTAL AGENDA

A new environmental agenda is needed in cities that centres on enhancing the capacity of the city governments, professional groups, NGOs and community organizations to identify and address their environmental problems. This is to address the environmental problems that underpin ill-health and premature death and to limit the damage arising from city-based demands and city-generated wastes on the local, regional and global environment.[4] It is also to permit agreements to be reached about how each city can become a safer, more convivial place in which to live and work. The last few years have brought some signs of such an agenda. This can be seen in a growing volume of literature on the subject and in new policies or projects by certain governments and development assistance agencies, including some innovative Local Agenda 21s as described in Chapter 7. But this emerging urban environmental agenda remains weak. It is also not underpinned by any significant initiative from the world's richest nations to relieve the economic stagnation and debt burdens in so many low- and many middle-income nations which hardly provides the context for the stable, competent and democratic governance so much needed in their urban centres.

The new environmental agenda has to be rooted in more representative, transparent government structures and in locally determined priorities. The growing interest in urban environmental problems in Africa, Asia and Latin America is often too based on perceptions and precedents drawn from Europe and North America. This can lead to questionable priorities – for instance a greater attention to ambient air pollution than to biological agents in water, food, air and soil, including those responsible for diarrhoeal diseases, dysentery and intestinal parasites. It often means that critical environmental problems such as the control of disease vectors that spread malaria, dengue fever, filariasis and yellow fever are forgotten, since these are no longer central aspects of environmental policies in high-income nations. As the 1992 report by the World Commission on Health and the Environment points out, it is biological pathogens in the human environment plus the high proportion of people who lack access to fresh water and other essential natural resources that represent far more serious environmental problems than chemical contamination, both in urban and in rural areas (see Box 1.2).

---

4 Here, it is important that a distinction is drawn between environmental hazards and environmental degradation (see Box 1.3 for more details).

Box 1.2 *THE MAIN LINKS BETWEEN HEALTH AND THE ENVIRONMENT*

The most immediate environmental problems in the world are the ill-health and premature death caused by biological agents in the human environment: in water, food, air and soil. Each year they contribute to the premature death of millions of people (mostly infants and children) and to the ill-health or disability of hundreds of millions more. The problems are most acute in low- and middle-income nations where:

- 4 million infants or children die every year from diarrhoeal diseases, largely as a result of contaminated food or water;
- 2 million people die from malaria each year and 267 million are infected;
- hundreds of millions of people suffer from debilitating intestinal parasitic infestations.

In addition, all countries have serious environmental health problems, affecting:

- hundreds of millions of people who suffer from respiratory and other diseases caused or exacerbated by biological and chemical agents in the air, both indoors and outdoors;
- hundreds of millions who are exposed to unnecessary chemical and physical hazards in their home, workplace or wider environment.

Health also depends on whether people can obtain food, water and shelter and over 1000 million people lack the income or land to meet such basic needs.

Source: WHO (1992a), *Our Planet, Our Health*, Report of the WHO Commission on Health and the Environment: Summary, WHO/EHE/92.1, Geneva.

The insufficient attention given by governments and aid agencies to biological pathogens in the urban environment and to people's access to natural resources (especially fresh water and safe land sites for housing) underlie millions of preventable deaths every year. They contribute to serious ill-health or disablement for hundreds of millions. These are the environmental problems that deserve a high priority in most urban centres. The pressure for environmental action coming from many international research and activist groups and international donor agencies from Europe and North America is giving too little attention to the 'environmental health' agenda that low-income groups need. Measures to prevent or limit the transmission of diarrhoeal diseases, typhoid, cholera and other waterborne, water-washed or water-based diseases and acute respiratory infections, tuberculosis and vector-borne diseases such as malaria, dengue fever and yellow fever have critical environmental components. So too do measures to reduce injuries from physical hazards in the home, workplace and outside (especially on roads). These must be pushed higher up the urban environmental agenda.

Most environmental problems have political roots. They arise not from some particular shortage of an environmental resource (eg land or fresh water) but from economic or political factors that prevent poorer groups from obtaining them and from organizing to demand changes. In most cities, poorer groups' lack of piped water supplies is not the result of a shortage of freshwater resources (or, in most instances, of their incapacity to pay) but the result of governments' refusal to give a higher priority to water supply and the competent organizational structure that its supply, maintenance and expansion requires. The same is true for land: most cities or metropolitan areas have sufficient unused or underutilized land sites within the current built-up area to accommodate most low-income households currently living in very overcrowded conditions.

Too little attention has been given by governments and international agencies to strengthening democratic processes within each city and city district through which environmental problems and their causes can be identified, their relative importance assessed and choices made about how limited resources are best used to address them. For instance, too much attention is given to describing individual environmental problems and to particular technical solutions with little support for enhancing the capacity of city governments to act effectively and democratically. Very little support is channelled by governments and international agencies direct to low-income groups and their organizations for community initiatives to improve environmental conditions. Yet in most cities, the homes and neighbourhoods developed by lower-income groups (often illegally) remain the main source of new housing. The homes and neighbourhoods built by such groups usually house more than a quarter of all city dwellers, and often a much higher proportion. There is something wrong with a legal and institutional system that deems illegal the ways by which most new housing is built, including virtually all the housing that is affordable by low-income households. The capacity of low-income groups to build, to work collectively in addressing common problems and to negotiate effectively with local, city and (often) national government will continue to have the greatest influence on the quality of their living environment. Since they make up a high proportion of the population of most cities, the quality of their housing and living environments will be a major influence on the quality of the whole city's environment.

The long-term solution to any city's environmental problems depends on the development within that city of a competent, representative local government. Democratic structures do not necessarily ensure that the environmental priorities of lower income groups are addressed but they do provide a context within which their needs and demands are more likely to be addressed.[5] They

---

5 This point was elaborated so clearly by Jockin of the National Slum Dwellers Federation in India, in discussions with community organizers from South Africa. In South Africa, there was an assumption among urban poor groups that the transition from the apartheid state to a fully democratic state in the early 1990s would mean new government policies that would allow them to obtain good quality housing. It was contact with urban poor groups in India that emphasized that this was unlikely; India had had several decades of democratic government which had delivered very little for urban poor groups. But democratic government provides more possibility of supportive response to organized demands by organizations and federations of low-income households. In many countries, such organizations and federations have developed and are demonstrating new ways in which good quality homes and neighbourhoods can be developed to meet the needs of low-income households (see Chapter 6 for more details).

remain among the best checks on the misallocation of resources by city and municipal governments. Without effective local institutions, outside support is often ineffective. Outside agencies – whether national ministries or international agencies – often misunderstand the nature of the problem and the range of options from which to choose the most appropriate solutions. External agencies can bring knowledge, expertise, capital and advice, but they cannot solve most environmental problems without effective local institutions.

In addition, decisions have to be made with incomplete knowledge. The particular problems that are documented may not be the most serious problems in terms of their impact on health or local ecosystems but simply those that are more easily documented or those that a particular research project or institution chose to document. One example is the fact that there is often more data on ambient air pollution levels for cities for (for instance) sulphur dioxide than on the extent to which city populations are served by sewers (or other effective sanitation systems) and storm and surface drains. Yet the current health impact of inadequate sanitation and drainage is much greater than the health impact of the current levels of sulphur dioxide. There is also a tendency for authors writing about environmental problems in cities in Africa, Asia and Latin America to extrapolate from their knowledge of cities in Europe and North America. One example of this was a paper suggesting that tropospheric ozone reduction should receive a high priority in cities in Africa, Asia and Latin America because of the evidence of its health impact in Los Angeles (Edgerton 1990). Very few cities in these regions are likely to have a concentration of ozone at ground level that constitutes one of their most serious environmental problems, not least because only a handful have a comparable concentration of population and industrial production to Los Angeles, none have a comparable concentration of automobiles and most have enormous deficiencies in such basic facilities as water supply, sanitation and drainage, and healthcare.

Most of the general literature on environmental problems in cities in Africa, Asia and Latin America is written by authors from Europe or North America. Although there is an increasing wealth of literature on environmental problems in individual cities in these regions written by specialists from these cities, such authors rarely write about more than the problems within their own cities or nations. In addition, detailed documentation about the scale and nature of environmental problems exists for only a small proportion of all urban centres – and almost certainly, a highly unrepresentative sample. Despite this fact, generalizations about the most serious environmental problems in the cities of 'developing countries' or 'the Third World' or 'the South' are routinely made.

The growing pressure for action on urban environmental problems must be exerted in all urban centres. The growing enthusiasm among many governments and some aid agencies for urban issues (including the role of urban economies in national development and a greater attention to urban environmental problems) has given too much attention to the largest cities. Most of the urban population in Africa, Asia and Latin America live in urban centres with less than a million inhabitants; in many countries, half or more of the urban population live in urban centres with fewer than 100,000 inhabitants.

Box 1.3 SOME DEFINITIONS

The Environment. Various definitions can be used for this term. 'The environment' may refer to all that is external to humans (Einstein is reported to have defined the environment as 'everything that is not me' (O'Riordan 1999) or used in a more restricted sense to refer to, for instance, 'wilderness areas' or the 'natural' environment. We use the term to refer to all that is external to humans, including those environmental factors created or influenced by human activities. The impact of environmental factors can then be compared or contrasted with 'non-environmental' factors that include each individual's own biology, lifestyle and the quality of healthcare. However, there are areas of ambiguity. For instance, an individual's decision to engage in risky behaviour (for instance driving a motor vehicle too fast) may not be considered environmental for that person but such behaviour constitutes an environmental risk for others. Similarly, most causes of violence are not environmental, yet high levels of violence affect urban environments and some environmental stressors can contribute to violence. In addition, healthcare may not be considered 'environmental' but as this volume describes, a well-functioning healthcare system provides people with protection against many environmental hazards and reduces the health impact of such hazards when they cause illness or injury. This book's focus on environmental issues means that its discussion of health problems focuses on those in which the environment has a primary role.

The Urban Environment. In this book, this is taken to mean the physical environment in urban areas, with its complex mix of natural elements (including air, water, land, climate, flora and fauna) and the built environment, ie a physical environment constructed or modified for human habitation and activity encompassing buildings, infrastructure and urban open spaces (Haughton and Hunter 1994, OECD 1990). Its quality is much influenced by:

- its geographical setting;
- the scale and nature of human activities and structures within it;
- the wastes, emissions and environmental impacts that these generate; and
- the competence and accountability of the institutions elected, appointed or delegated to manage it.

Environmental Hazards and Environmental Degradation. The most serious environmental problems for the inhabitants in most urban centres in low- and middle-income nations are environmental hazards, ie environmental factors that pose a threat to their health. Most arise from biological disease-causing agents that cause infectious and parasitic diseases, physical hazards such as houses built on dangerous sites and made of inflammable materials and chemical pollutants, especially in the home and workplace. These are not the same as environmental degradation which implies the depletion or degradation of some resource or ecosystem – for instance a depletion of soils, forests, fresh water and fisheries, or the emissions of wastes or pollutants with serious local, regional or global ecological consequences. Much of the literature that discusses the links between poverty and the environment confuses environmental hazards with environmental degradation and so incorrectly states (or implies) that poverty is strongly associated with environmental degradation (or even that poverty is a major cause of poverty). Ironically, most urban poverty is associated with very low levels of environmental degradation and it is the consumption patterns of the wealthier groups and the production systems that meet their demands that are far more associated with environmental degradation – see Chapter 8 for more details.

Environmental hazards may arise from factors that are independent of human action (for instance earthquakes), influenced by human action (for instance urban development creating new possibilities for insects which transmit diseases to breed) or arise from human action (for instance the creation of hazardous chemical wastes).

A theme to which this book will constantly return is that each city and urban centre has its own unique range of environmental problems, and effective action demands local capabilities to identify problems and their causes and decide the best use of limited resources. In many societies, this will need far more support channelled directly to citizen and community action. This not only delivers immediate benefits to poorer groups more cheaply and effectively than most state actions, but it can also contribute to strengthening civil society by reinforcing democracy and participation, and by developing partnerships between CBOs, NGOs and municipal governments – in effect, building municipal governance from the bottom up.

Many local and a few international NGOs have pioneered new, more participatory approaches to working with low-income groups and their community organizations in improving environmental health and installing infrastructure and services. Some have achieved remarkable cost-reductions when compared with conventional projects – for instance Orangi Pilot Project in Karachi and its support for sewage systems (see Chapter 6). There is tremendous potential in new partnerships between local governments, local NGOs and local community organizations. Most national governments and international agencies have failed to fully recognize this. It is also rare to find national institutions and international agencies that know how to support and work with low-income groups and their organizations in ways that ensure their environmental (and other) priorities are addressed.

There is also a need for new attitudes among architects, planners, engineers and other professionals whose training should equip them to work cooperatively with low-income households and the community organizations they form. If more support is to be channelled to citizen directed community-level initiatives, professionals need to learn how to work cooperatively at community level. New tools and methods are needed for community-based actions that guide professionals in how to work with low-income groups and their community organizations in identifying problems and their underlying causes and developing appropriate solutions. Perhaps as importantly, they need to teach professionals not to impose their solutions and schedules.

If international agencies are to give more support to addressing the environmental problems described in this volume, it must have the long-term goal of building the capacity within each society to identify, analyse and act on their own environmental problems. Working together on the most immediate and serious environmental problems including those in cities would lay an appropriate foundation for joint action on protecting the global commons.

THE STRUCTURE OF THE BOOK

This book reviews the scale and scope of environmental problems in cities and their surrounds in Africa, Asia and Latin America, and draws some conclusions on the priorities for action. Box 1.3 outlines the meaning given to the terms 'the environment' and the 'urban environment'. This chapter seeks to set the context for the whole book. The sections after this one discuss the differences and shared traits among cities, the potential opportunities within cities for good environmental practices and the scale and nature of urban change. Chapter 2 describes the environmental problems and their consequences at two different geographic scales: the house and workplace and their immediate surrounds; and the wider neighbourhood or district environment. Chapter 3 describes the environmental problems of cities in general such as air and water pollution.[6] Both Chapters 2 and 3 include a discussion of natural disasters and the extent to which their incidence and the severity of their impacts are linked to human-induced changes with Chapter 2 considering such disasters at district level and Chapter 3 at city level. Chapter 4 discusses who within the urban population bears the environmental costs, including who is most vulnerable or susceptible to environmental hazards.

Chapter 5 considers the environmental impacts of cities on their wider regions and on the global commons. This includes a consideration of the resource and waste flows between the city and its region and the contribution of city-based production and consumption to environmental degradation worldwide and to climatic change, especially global warming.

Chapters 6 and 7 discuss how these problems might be resolved, with a particular emphasis on the political and institutional structures and processes that can achieve this, rather than on the technical solutions needed in each instance. Chapter 6 concentrates on addressing environmental problems at the

---

6 We have been using these geographic categories of home and workplace, district or neighbourhood, city, city-region, and global for many years to highlight the particular way in which an environmental agent impacts on human populations in cities. Ian Douglas (1989) suggested four similar but slightly different scales through which to consider the interactions between cities' physical form and flows of energy, water and materials: the micro-, meso-, macro- and megascale.

home and neighbourhood level with Chapter 7 focusing on city-wide policies and on the supports needed from national governments and international agencies.

Broader issues regarding the impact of urban-based production and consumption on global climate and global natural resource endowments are discussed in Chapter 8. This includes a consideration of the implications for cities of achieving the sustainable development goals outlined by the World Commission on Environment and Development (World Commission on Environment and Development 1987). It highlights contradictions that need to be resolved, including the contradiction between local and global sustainability and between development and sustainability goals. It also discusses the national and international frameworks that will be needed to resolve such contradictions and to encourage the pursuit of global and local sustainability goals, as well as development goals, within each city and municipal government. Chapter 9 draws some conclusions and returns to the points raised in this chapter regarding a new environmental agenda within each urban centre and region that responds to the specifics of that particular area and the needs of all its citizens.

A comment about why we chose to organize the discussion of environmental problems in this way. To help to understand and manage them, environmental problems can be grouped into various categories. The different ways of doing so reflect different professional disciplines or priorities. The basis for categorizing them can be:

- the nature of the problem (or the hazard it presents to people), eg biological pathogens, chemical pollutants and physical hazards, and lack of access to resources (for instance fresh water);
- the context within which the environmental problems occur, eg housing, workplace, city-wide problems, city-region interactions;
- the 'sector' into which the problem falls and/or the division of institutional responsibilities for their resolution (eg solid-waste management, air pollution control);
- (for infectious and parasitic diseases) the biology of the disease-causing agent or based on the media through which infection takes place (air, food, water, soil, animals, insects or other organisms that are disease vectors or carriers); and
- the kind of pollutant, the concentration and whether it arises from point or non-point sources.

This book chooses to look at the range of environmental problems by the context within which the environmental problems occur at different geographic scales (the home and workplace, the neighbourhood, the city, the city-region and the whole planet) and by the nature of the problem or the hazard it presents. Classifying environmental problems in this way helps to highlight the environmental actions that 'prevent' the problems. The types of policies and initiatives that are needed to prevent problems also tend to vary with geographic scale. This classification system also helps to make clear the distinction between the local problems that tend to affect people's health directly and the regional or global problems where it is ecologies, life-support systems and eventually future generations that are affected.

We considered organizing the discussion of environmental problems by sectoral categories such as water and sanitation, housing and health services, since these are the kinds of sectors that are common within the organizational structures of governments and many international agencies. But using conventional sectoral categories can mean:

- That the environmental aspects of problems are less clear; so too are the environmental measures that can help in prevention and how these cross sectoral and jurisdictional boundaries.
- Confusion as to what environmental problems fall into what sector (for instance a discussion of the health impacts of air pollution would have to be divided between transport, energy, health, pollution control and shelter/the physical environment).
- The omission of some important environmental issues that fall outside traditional sectors – for instance occupational exposures and environmental cost-transfers both within and between cities.
- A tendency in a sectoral classification system to imply that environmental problems have to be resolved by the direct intervention of public agencies. A sectoral view can also hide the extent to which environmental problems need coordinated actions by different groups. Combining 'the context' and 'the nature of the problem' highlights the extent to which many problems are best addressed by supporting prevention-oriented actions at household and neighbourhood levels.

One potential disadvantage of focusing on contexts and on particular environmental problems is that it can miss the scale and nature of some system-wide impacts, including ecosystem disruptions that need to be considered from the point of view of the cumulative impact of many different human activities (including those that take place outside of Africa, Asia, Latin America and the Caribbean). Moreover, ecosystems that initially are resilient to external pressures, can deteriorate suddenly and radically in response to continued pressure. Chapter 8 seeks to cover the relevant global issues.

Some comment is also needed on why we focus on urban areas. The fact that this book concentrates on environmental problems in urban areas should not be taken to imply that there are not very serious environmental problems in rural areas. Indeed, as Chapter 5 will elaborate, it is difficult to separate urban and rural environmental issues since many of the environmental problems in one impact so much on the other. Nor should this book be interpreted as a request to necessarily divert limited resources from rural to urban areas. Much of this book is about building or strengthening capacity for governance at local and city level so that more appropriate actions can be taken, using existing resources. Implementing existing environmental legislation to reduce pollution, more effective controls on occupational health problems, meeting the demands of poorer groups for improved water, drainage and sanitation with cost-effective solutions and increasing the capacity of city and municipal governments to raise their own revenues are among many measures recommended that do not need a large increase in funding. The belief that it is a lack of funds that inhibits local and city actions has drawn attention away from more important issues of governance, accountability, participation and the right of all citizens to protection under the law from enterprises that pollute their home, work and city environment.

DIVERSITIES AND COMMONALITIES

In one sense, the scope of this book can be considered to be too ambitious. It is about a great range of environmental problems in a large and diverse range of cities (and smaller urban centres) in over 140 countries. Within the tens of thousands of urban centres in the regions under consideration are some with good quality environmental management and many with little or none. At one extreme are cities such as Pôrto Alegre which has virtually all its population served with piped water and regular rubbish collection and most with good provision for sanitation (Menegat and others 1998). Its rubbish collection service includes a separate collection of recyclables which are sorted and sold by cooperatives of urban poor groups, most of whom previously worked sorting refuse at the city dump. The city has a democratically elected city government and one that through developing 'participatory budgeting' has strengthened local democracy and given citizens a more direct involvement in setting municipal priorities (Abers 1998). The city's inhabitants have an average life expectancy of 74.4 years (similar to that in high-income nations) with infant mortality rates below 20 per 1000 live births (Menegat and others 1998). At the other extreme are the hundreds of urban centres where only a small proportion of the population has piped water and adequate provision for sanitation and where the urban authorities have very little capacity to address any environmental problems. In many such urban centres, a high proportion of the population has no sanitation facilities, and defecate in the streets or other open spaces. It is common for water provision to be so poor that hundreds of people have to share each standpipe or well. The supply of water to communal standpipes is often irregular and of poor quality. Life expectancies in such urban centres can be 30 or more years less than in Pôrto Alegre while infant mortality rates are at least five times higher; it is common for more than one infant in ten to die before the age of one. And this variation is not just between countries but also within countries. For instance, there are Brazilian cities that have life expectancies 20 years lower than Pôrto Alegre (Mueller 1995). And within most cities, there is also great variation between different areas within the city boundaries.

This volume seeks to cover cities in Africa, Asia and Latin America (and also to include some examples of cities from the Caribbean), yet it would be difficult in one volume to adequately describe the scale and scope of environmental problems in cities in just one of these regions. Indeed, seeking to cover all cities in just one region might itself be too ambitious as an understanding of the environmental problems in any city and their causes have to be rooted in

the particulars of the local context. For instance, the large, complex and sophisticated African cities such as Johannesburg, Dakar or Cairo have little in
common with the hundreds of small urban centres with a few thousand inhabitants that are administrative headquarters within predominantly agrarian
employment structures that are found throughout most of Africa. There are
also a growing number of studies of particular cities that show how the scale
and nature of the environmental problems and who is most affected by them is
strongly influenced by a complex interplay of international, national and local
factors.[7] The ineffectiveness of international agencies (and often national or
provincial governments) in addressing environmental (or other) problems is so
often linked to their failure to understand and work within the particulars of
each location and its society. One worry about this volume is that it might help
to produce or reinforce another set of invalid generalizations about environmental problems in what international agencies still refer to as 'developing
countries'.[8]

But within this understanding of diversity, there are obvious characteristics
that all cities share. All cities combine concentrations of human populations
(and their homes and neighbourhoods) and a range of economic activities.
They develop as centres of production for goods and services (and for the
resource use, waste and pollution that such production brings) because they
serve the interests of those who own the production units. The size, spatial
form and environmental impact of cities are much influenced by where production units choose to locate – both directly in their environmental impacts and
indirectly in the environmental impacts of their workforce (and dependents)
and the other enterprises on which they draw (including subcontractors and
service units). The development of all cities imposes a new built environment
on natural landscapes, resource flows and ecosystems.

All cities also require some form of government to ensure adequate quality
'environments' for their inhabitants and to protect key resources in and around
the city – for instance to regulate land use, to protect watersheds, to set limits
on the generation of wastes/pollution and how they can be disposed of, to

---

7 See the 12 city studies in the journal *Environment and Urbanization*. Vol 12, No 1 (2000) on
poverty reduction and urban governance; also Hasan 1999.
8 It would have been convenient to slip into the United Nations' terminology of 'developing
countries' in this book but we have always tried to avoid this term, in part because it is inaccurate
(many 'developing' countries did not 'develop' for much of the 1980s and 1990s) and in part
because it implies that such countries are inferior to 'developed' countries. Such terminology is
also rooted in conceptions of 'development' from the 1960s that have long been shown to be
inaccurate. In the first edition of this book, we used the term 'Third World' but changed this
because of the confusion surrounding the term. With the political changes within the former
Soviet Union and East Europe, there is no longer a clear 'Second World' and some high-income
Asian and Latin American countries might now be considered part of the 'First World'. In
addition, many people consider the term 'Third World' as having pejorative implications, even if
its original use (especially by the non-aligned nations) and its origins (the term being based on the
'third estate' since Third World countries contained most of the world's population) never had
this intention. We considered using the term 'the South' as shorthand for the countries that are
the focus of this book – low- and middle-income countries in Africa, Asia, Latin America and
the Caribbean. But this term also confuses many people because many countries from 'the South'
are in the northern hemisphere while Australia and New Zealand are part of 'the North'.

ensure adequate provision of all the goods and services that are essential for environmental health (water, sanitation, drainage, etc) and to ensure the infrastructure and services that all cities need (roads, paths, drainage networks, provision for electricity, schools, etc). Ensuring good quality environments becomes increasingly complex, the larger the population and the scale and range of their daily movements, and the more industrial the production base. City governments are also needed to manage the draw that city dwellers and enterprises make on natural resources and on natural sinks for their wastes – again a task that becomes more complex the larger the city and its production base and the higher its inhabitants' consumption levels.

In all cities, environmental management is an intensely political task, as different interests (including very powerful interests) compete for the most advantageous locations, for the ownership or use of resources and waste sinks, and for publicly provided infrastructure and services. In the absence of good environmental management, many such interests contribute to the destruction or degradation of key resources. This is widely recognized, as can be seen in the shift in growing interest in the literature on urban development from 'government' (where the concentration is on the role, responsibilities and performance of government bodies) to 'governance' (which also encompasses the relationship between government and civil society).[9]

As if good environmental management within city boundaries was not complex enough, now 'good urban governance' must extend to environmental management in the regions around the city (addressing both regional and national goals) and to global goals (such as minimizing greenhouse gas emissions and protecting biodiversity). Thus, all cities (and smaller urban places) need to develop a governance structure that meets a multiplicity of needs. This structure has to provide the means by which satisfactory compromises are reached between competing interests, in which the needs of the least powerful groups receive adequate attention. It must ensure 'care and maintenance' of the productive and protective functions of the ecosystems within which the city is located. It must ensure no depletion of key natural (and other) assets, if the needs of future generations are to be safeguarded.

Thus, there are strong commonalities in the environmental problems that have to be addressed to ensure a healthy, well-functioning city. As this book draws on the experiences of a wide range of cities from such diverse countries, it helps to highlight the difficulties of developing governance structures that function effectively in these various tasks. It also highlights innovative ways in which different city or municipal authorities, CBOs or NGOs have addressed these tasks. This book also highlights the need for more detail and more analysis about the specificities of good environmental performance for individual cities, which locates the description of environmental problems and the constraints on addressing them within an understanding of each city's unique social, economic and political structure (and how and why it evolved). Indeed, the preparation of this volume, which updates, expands and revises what we wrote ten years ago has been much helped by many detailed studies of particu-

---

9 See Chapter 5 of UNCHS 1996.

lar cities published in the last ten years. The book stresses how much the solution to the most serious environmental problems in cities depends on 'good' local governance and the importance of locally driven knowledge of the 'state of the environment' within each city. It also points to the kinds of supports that are needed from higher levels of government and international agencies for such 'good' local governance.

THE ENVIRONMENTAL OPPORTUNITIES PROVIDED BY CITIES

Before describing cities' many environmental problems, it is worth noting the environmental opportunities that the concentration of production and population in any city provides. The quality of governance within any city determines the extent to which advantage is taken of these opportunities and the potential disadvantages avoided. By concentrating people, enterprises and their wastes – and increasingly motor vehicles – cities can be (and often are) very hazardous places in which to live and work. It is often assumed that cities' environmental problems are made worse by the number of people and their high concentration. But this same concentration provides many potential opportunities, as summarized below (and considered in more detail in later chapters).

Economies of scale and proximity for infrastructure and services. The concentration of population and enterprises in urban areas greatly reduces the unit costs of providing each building with piped water, sewers, drains, all-weather roads and footpaths and electricity. This concentration reduces unit costs for many services such as rubbish collection, public transport, healthcare and the provision of schools, pre-school centres and child development centres. It reduces the cost of providing emergency services – for instance fire-fighting and emergency medical services whose rapid response to acute illness or injury can greatly reduce the health burden for the people affected. But even in tenement areas and informal settlements with high population densities, the densities are rarely too high to pose problems for the cost-effective provision of infrastructure and services, especially if provision for these had been made in advance of the settlement's development.[10] What is often more expensive and time-consuming is installing infrastructure and services in densely populated illegal or informal settlements, after they have developed. These often grew without sufficient space being left for access roads, public space and community facilities, and without a site plan which makes it easier and cheaper to install piped water, drains and other infrastructure. But this high cost is not because of high population densities but because provision for infrastructure and services of an adequate standard for such population densities was not made prior to the

---

10 Many squatter settlements are densely populated, but in part this is due to the fact that so few of the buildings are more than one storey high. In terms of the number of residents per hectare, they often have a lower density than many high-quality residential areas in European cities with three- to five-storey terraced housing. If squatters can obtain legal tenure, it is often possible to develop their shelters into two- or three-storey dwellings (which can greatly reduce overcrowding within the housing stock) while also making it easier to find the space to improve access roads or paths.

settlement's development. In addition, as Chapter 6 will describe in more detail, there are many examples of community-directed programmes that have installed good quality infrastructure and provided services within existing high-density settlements at relatively low cost.

Reducing risks from natural disasters. Economies of scale or proximity also exist for reducing risks from most natural disasters – for instance in the per capita cost of measures to lessen the risks (eg better watershed management or drainage to reduce the scale of floods), to reduce the risks when they occur (eg buildings better able to withstand floods or earthquakes and early-warning systems to allow special measures to be taken) and to respond rapidly and effectively when a disaster is imminent or happens (International Federation of Red Cross and Red Crescent Societies 1998). There is generally a greater capacity among city dwellers to help to pay for such measures, if they are made aware of the risks and all efforts are made to keep down costs. However, in the absence of good practice, cities can be particularly hazardous as large (usually low-income) settlements develop in hazardous sites (eg on flood-plains or slopes at risk from landslide) because no other sites are available to them and as the needed prevention, mitigation and response measures are not taken.

Water reuse or recycling. The close proximity of so many water consumers within cities gives greater scope for recycling or directly reusing waste waters – and the techniques for greatly reducing the use of fresh water in city homes and enterprises are well-known, where freshwater resources are scarce (Rocky Mountain Institute 1991) although it is agriculture, not cities, that dominate the use of fresh water in most nations.[11] Many nations also have a long urban tradition of making efficient use of rainwater or of storing it for use during dry seasons or periods that contemporary patterns of water management have ignored (see for instance Agarwal and Narain 1997 for India).

Land. Cities concentrate populations in ways that usually reduce the demand for land relative to population. Although as later chapters will describe, valuable agricultural land is being lost to urban expansion, in most nations the area taken up by cities and towns is less than 1 per cent of their total surface area. The world's current urban population of around 3 billion people would fit into an area of 200,000 square kilometres – roughly the size of Senegal or Oman – at densities similar to those of high-class, much valued inner city residential areas in European cities (for instance Chelsea in London).[12] This is a reminder of how some of the world's most desirable (and expensive) residential areas have high densities, including densities that suburban developers and municipal

11 See Table 22.1, pages 330–331 in World Resources Institute 1990.
12 The example of Chelsea was chosen because it combines very high-quality housing, very little of which is in high rises (and most of which is pre-20th century) with a diverse economic base, large amounts of open space and among the best educational and cultural facilities in London. With a population density of around 120 persons per hectare for the whole district (and with three to four times this density in some of its more desirable residential districts), it is an example of how relatively high density need not imply overcrowding or poor quality living environments.

Box 1.4 ENVIRONMENTAL ECONOMIES OF URBANIZATION

In general, the costs per household of installing most forms of infrastructure and supplying most kinds of service fall with increasing population density – ie economies of proximity. For instance, the cost of installing pipes for water, sewers and drains and for building roads is cheaper because less pipe (and less digging to install it) or less road is needed per house served. For many forms of infrastructure and services, there are also economies of scale because unit costs fall as larger populations are served – for instance, for water-treatment plants, schools and many medical services. Providing more specialized medical and educational services, including those for particularly vulnerable or disadvantaged groups, can also become cheaper per person served with larger population concentrations. Higher capital expenditures per person for infrastructure and service provision in urban areas is more a reflection of higher quality provision than higher costs; this only becomes a public expenditure bias towards urban areas if the beneficiaries do not pay the full cost. However, increasing population density can also require that higher standards have to be provided – for instance, well-designed and maintained pit latrines can often provide hygienic and convenient forms of sanitation in rural settlements and in urban areas where population densities are not too high – but more expensive systems are usually needed in higher density or larger urban settlements. The costs of infrastructure and services may also rise with city size, if the costs of acquiring land for their provision is a significant part of the total cost. So too will labour costs, if the costs of housing, transport and other necessities rise with city size (which they often do). The need for more complex and sophisticated pollution controls may also rise with increasing population size. For instance, effluents from sewers and storm drains from a small urban centre usually do not need as complex and expensive a treatment system as those from larger cities. There are also the costs to the public authorities of formulating and implementing environmental legislation which may rise with city size (Linn 1982, World Bank 1991).

In discussing the 'economies' of scale, proximity and agglomeration, it is important to be clear in regard to who benefits (and who does not). Private enterprises benefit from many economies of scale, proximity and agglomeration in urban areas; indeed, one major reason why they choose to concentrate in urban areas is because it lowers their production costs (including infrastructure and finance, and access to cheaper and more diverse services and labour). But part of this may arise from the fact that they negotiate highly subsidized infrastructure and services or other subsidies. Part of their cost reductions often arise from their capacity to pay below subsistence wages or to externalize costs, to the detriment of their workforce (substandard occupational health and safety standards) or wider populations (through inadequate pollution control and waste management).

authorities regard as 'too high' even though many such 'high density' areas also have good provision for parks, a diverse employment structure and good cultural facilities. There are also examples of increasing populations in the central districts of certain cities, as governments controlled private cars, improved public transport and encouraged a rich and diverse street life (UNCHS 1996). The fact that cities also concentrate demand for fresh fruit, vegetables, fish and dairy products also means considerable potential for their production in the area around a city, especially if their promotion is integrated with a city-wide and region-wide plan to protect watersheds, control urban sprawl, encourage urban or peri-urban agriculture and ensure adequate provision for open space (Smit and others 1996). In many cities, this would support existing practices as a significant proportion of the food consumed by city inhabitants is grown within city boundaries or in areas immediately adjacent to the built-up areas, often with city wastes being used to fertilize or condition the soil (ibid).

Reduced heating. The fact that cities concentrate production and residential areas also means a considerable potential for reducing fossil fuel use in heating. For space heating, there are often untapped possibilities for the use of waste process heat from industry or thermal power stations to provide space heating for homes and commercial buildings. Certain forms of high-density housing such as terraces and apartment blocks also considerably reduce heat loss from each housing unit, when compared with detached housing. There are also many measures that can be taken to reduce heat gain in buildings to eliminate or greatly reduce the demand for electricity for air conditioning, although this applies to all buildings, not just those in urban areas.

Reduced motor vehicle use. With regard to transport, cities have great potential for limiting the use of motor vehicles, which also means reducing the fossil fuel consumption, greenhouse gas emissions and air pollution that their use implies. This might sound contradictory, since most of the world's largest cities have serious problems with congestion and motor-vehicle generated air pollution. But cities ensure that many more trips can be made by walking or bicycling. They also reduce travel distances, which is one of the reasons why cities developed. They make possible a much greater use of public transport and make economically feasible a high quality service. Thus, although cities tend to be associated with a high level of private car use, cities and urban systems also represent the greatest potential for allowing their inhabitants quick and cheap access to a great range of locations, without the need to use private cars.

Pollution control and management. Industrial concentration in cities cheapens the cost of enforcing regulations on environmental and occupational health and pollution control. It cheapens the cost of many specialized services and waste-handling facilities, including those that reduce waste levels or that recover materials from waste streams for reuse or recycling.

Funding environmental management. The concentration of households and enterprises in cities makes it easier for public authorities to collect taxes and charges for public services, while in prosperous cities, there is a larger revenue base, a greater demand and a greater capacity to pay for services.

Governance. The concentration of people in cities can facilitate their full involvement in the election of governments at local and city level and their active participation in decisions and actions within their own district or neighbourhood. Later chapters include various examples of community–municipal authority partnerships that contributed much improved city environments.

Greenhouse gas emissions. For most nations, a high (and growing) proportion of their greenhouse gas emissions is released within cities. If major limitations on such emissions prove necessary to mitigate climate change and its deleterious consequences, some of the most cost-effective means of achieving this goal will be found in its cities, largely through the measures noted above for reducing fossil fuel and motor vehicle use.

Only in the absence of effective governance, including the institutional means to ensure the provision of infrastructure and services and the control of pollution, are urban environmental problems greatly exacerbated. Measures taken now to promote healthy, resource-efficient, minimum-waste cities in Africa, Asia, Latin America and the Caribbean can also ensure a good quality of life, without the high (and probably unsustainable) levels of resource use and waste generation currently associated with most urban centres in Europe and North America. There is also considerable potential for employment generation in most of the measures to ensure more healthy, resource-conserving, waste-minimizing cities (Mitlin and Satterthwaite 1996, UNCHS 1996). These multiple potential opportunities of cities must thus be borne in mind, as the text concentrates on describing the very serious environmental problems that are evident in so many cities and smaller urban centres. Later chapters also point to the growing number of cities where some of these opportunities have been realized.

AN URBANIZING WORLD

Most of the world's urban population is now in the regions on which this book concentrates: Africa, Asia, Latin America and the Caribbean (see Table 1.1 and Figure 1.1). Between 1950 and 1995, the urban population in these regions grew more than fivefold from 346 million to 1.8 billion. Although Asia and Africa still have more rural than urban dwellers, they both have very large urban populations. Asia alone has close to half the world's urban population, although more than half of this population resides in just two countries, China and India. Africa now has a larger urban population than North America; as does Latin America and the Caribbean, which also has close to three-quarters of its population living in urban centres. When data become available from the new round of censuses held in 2000 or 2001, they are likely to show that the urban population of Africa, Asia, and Latin America and the Caribbean is nearly three

Table 1.1 *Trends and projections in urban populations by region, 1950–2010*

Region	1950	1965	1980	1995	2010*
Urban population (millions of inhabitants)					
Africa	33	66	130	251	458
Asia	244	426	706	1192	1816
Latin America and the					
Caribbean	69	133	233	350	463
Rest of the world	404	559	685	781	849
Percentage of population living in urban areas					
Africa	14.6	20.7	27.3	34.9	43.6
Asia	17.4	22.4	26.7	34.7	43.6
Latin America and the					
Caribbean	41.4	53.4	64.9	73.4	78.6
Rest of the world	55.3	64.1	70.5	74.2	78.0
Proportion of the world's urban population living in					
Africa	4.4	5.6	7.4	9.8	12.8
Asia	32.5	36.0	40.3	46.3	50.6
Latin America and the					
Caribbean	9.2	11.2	13.3	13.6	12.9
Rest of the world	53.9	47.2	39.0	30.4	23.7

* This is projected and the most recent population data for most countries are from censuses held around 1990 and it will take at least until 2002 before there is new census data from enough countries to have an accurate idea of the scale of urban change during the 1990s. There is also a group of countries (mostly in Africa) for which there is no census data since the late 1970s or early 1980s so all figures for their urban (and rural) populations are based on estimates and projections. Rest of the world includes all countries in Europe, North America and Oceania.

Source: Drawn or derived from figures in United Nations (1998), *World Urbanization Prospects: The 1996 Revision*, Population Division, New York.

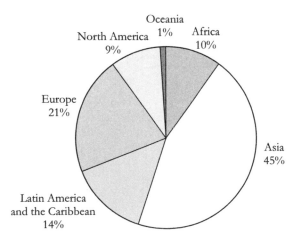

Figure 1.1 *Distribution of the world's urban population between regions, 1995*

Table 1.2 *The distribution of large cities by region, 1950–1990**

Region	1800	1900	1950	1990
Number of 'million cities'				
Africa	0	0	2	27
Asia	1	4	26	126
Latin America and the Caribbean	0	0**	7	38
Rest of the world	1	13	45	102
Number of the world's 100 largest cities				
Africa	4	2	3	6
Asia	64	22	32	44
Latin America and the Caribbean	3	5	8	16
Rest of the world	29	71	57	34
Average size of the world's 100 largest cities for different years				
Number of inhabitants	187,000	724,000	2.1 million	5.3 million

* 1990 is still the latest year for which there are statistics based on census data for most of the world's large cities. As noted earlier, it will take at least until 2002 before new census data is available from enough countries to have an accurate idea of the scale of urban change during the 1990s, and thus also the populations of the world's largest cities. There are projections for the populations of each of the world's largest cities up to 2015 (and beyond) but their validity is questionable. A city's population growth rate is much influenced by its economic performance, but it is difficult to make long-term forecasts for the economic performance of each city. Estimates for a city's future population are made by projecting past trends, yet circumstances often change, so the speed with which a city grew in its most recent intercensus period often proves to be inaccurate as a guide to its growth in the next intercensus period.
** Some estimates suggest that Rio de Janeiro had reached 1 million inhabitants by 1900 while other sources suggest that it had just under 1 million.

Sources: The statistics for 1950 and 1990 were taken or derived from data in United Nations (1998), *World Urbanization Prospects: The 1996 Revision*, Population Division, New York, but adjusted as new census data became available. The data on the distribution of the world's 100 largest cities is an updated version of a table taken from Satterthwaite 1996 which drew on the IIED cities database that combines the data on city populations from 1950 to 1990 from United Nations 1998 with recent and historic data drawn from around 250 censuses and from Chandler and Fox 1974 and Chandler 1987.

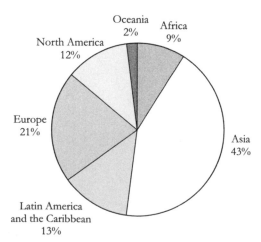

Figure 1.2 *Distribution in the number of the world's 'million cities' by region, 1990*

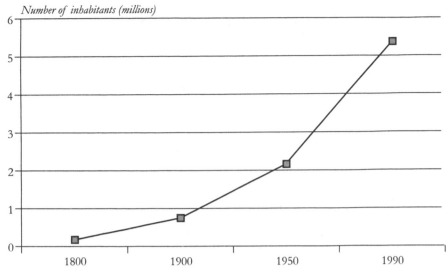

Figure 1.3 *Average size of the world's 100 largest cities*

times the size of the urban population of the rest of the world. United Nations (UN) projections also suggest that urban populations are growing so much faster than rural populations that 80 per cent of the growth in the world's population between 1990 and 2010 will be in urban areas and virtually all this growth will be in Africa, Asia and Latin America (United Nations 1998).

Two aspects of this rapid growth in urban population have been the increase in the number of large cities and the historically unprecedented size of the largest cities (see Table 1.2). Just two centuries ago, there were only two 'million-cities' worldwide (ie cities with 1 million or more inhabitants) – London and Beijing (Peking). By 1950 there were 80 and by 1990 there were 293. A large (and increasing) proportion of these million-cities are in Africa, Asia and Latin America. Many have populations that grew more than tenfold between 1950 and 1990, including Abidjan, Amman, Bhopal, Curitiba, Dar es Salaam, Dhaka, Harare, Khartoum, Kinshasa, Lagos, Nairobi, Lusaka, Maputo and Seoul. Brasilia, the federal capital of Brazil, did not exist in 1950 and now has more than 2 million inhabitants.

The average size of the world's largest cities has grown dramatically over the last 200 years (see Figure 1.3). In 1800, the average size of the world's 100 largest cities was less than 200,000 inhabitants but by 1990 it was over 5 million inhabitants.[13] This is no doubt the result of the growing number of very large cities – for instance those exceeding 5 million or even 10 million inhabitants.

By 1990, there were 34 urban agglomerations throughout the world which had more than 5 million inhabitants and which collectively accounted for around 15 per cent of the world's urban population. They included 18 in Asia,

13 Martin Brockerhoff rightly cautioned us in the use of any estimate as to the average population size of the world's 100 largest cities in 1800 and 1900, given that virtually all figures for city populations for 1800 and most for 1900 are estimates. However, the basic point that there has been a very large increase in the average size of the world's largest cities is beyond dispute.

BOX 1.5 *WHAT IS AN URBAN CENTRE AND A CITY?*

There is no general agreement among governments as to how to define 'a town', an 'urban centre' and 'a city'. In virtually all nations, urban centres include all settlements with 20,000 or more inhabitants but governments differ in what smaller settlements they include as urban centres – from those that include all settlements with a few hundred inhabitants as urban to those that only include settlements with 20,000 or more inhabitants. This greatly limits the accuracy of international comparisons, as most nations have a large part of their populations living in settlements with populations in this range. For instance, most of India's rural population lives in villages with between 500 and 5000 inhabitants and if these were classified as 'urban', India would suddenly have a predominantly 'urban' population rather than a predominantly 'rural' population.

Another factor that limits the accuracy of international comparisons is differences in the ways that urban boundaries are set, especially for large cities. In some countries, urban boundaries are set that correspond to the urban centre's built-up area (and these may be out of date, so the actual urban population is larger than the official figure, as part of it is outside the official boundary). Others use more extended boundaries that may include large areas of agriculture (and many rural households) and also settlements at some distance from the built-up area where a significant proportion of the workforce work in agriculture or commute to the central city. For very large cities, their total population can vary by several million inhabitants, depending on the criteria used for setting their boundaries.

Most governments define urban centres in one of four ways: through size thresholds (for instance all settlements with 2000 or more inhabitants are urban); through size thresholds combined with other criteria (for instance for density or for the proportion of the economically active population in non-agricultural activities); through administrative or political status (for instance all settlements designated as national, provincial or district capitals are urban centres); or through lists of settlements named in the census being 'the urban centres'. Our analysis of the urban criteria used by 147 nations that had more than half a million inhabitants in 2000 showed that 21 per cent used population size thresholds, 34 per cent used population size thresholds combined with other criteria, 31 per cent used administrative or political criteria and 12 per cent simply specified which settlements were 'urban centres'. There were some interesting regional variations – for instance in Africa and Latin America, a higher proportion used administrative and political criteria while among high-income countries, a higher proportion used population thresholds (usually combined with other criteria). Among nations with less than half a million inhabitants in 2000, it was more common for particular settlements to be specified as 'the urban centres', including some where the only urban centre was the national capital.

Among the nations that use population thresholds within their urban definitions, most set these at between 1000 and 10,000 inhabitants with 2000, 2500, 5000 and 10,000 being the most commonly used thresholds.

For most nations, figures for their current urban populations are projections. Figures for urban populations rely on censuses, and very few nations have had a census in the last few years; most had their last census around 1990 while many have not had a census since the early 1980s. Many nations are holding censuses during 2000 or 2001 but it will probably take until 2002 or 2003 until the new census data on urban populations is widely available.

The term 'city' and 'urban centre' are often used interchangeably, and there is no consensus as to the definition of a city and how it might differ from the definition of an urban centre. But few people would consider that settlements with 1000 or 2000 inhabitants are cities. There are thousands of settlements in Africa, Asia and Latin America that have only a few thousand inhabitants and are considered by their governments as urban, which lack the economic, administrative or political status that would normally be considered as criteria for classification as a city. In countries with long urban histories, there may be many historic 'cities' which achieved city status many decades or centuries ago because of their importance at that time (for instance by being political capitals or religious centres or key trading centres) and are still considered as cities, even though they are relatively small within their national urban system.

The term 'town' implies a small urban centre and might be taken to include all urban centres that were not cities, but again, there is no consensus on this and in some discussions, towns are assumed not to be urban centres. However, for those nations with national definitions of urban centres which include all settlements with a few hundred or 1000 inhabitants as 'urban', it is difficult to see how towns are not urban centres.

6 in Latin America and 2 in Africa. Although historically, there have long been cities with more than 1 million inhabitants (although very few of them), the first city to have more than 5 million inhabitants was London and it only reached this size in the late 19th century. In 1950, there were only 8 cities worldwide with 5 million or more inhabitants including only 2 in Asia and 1 in Latin America. There is also the phenomenon of the so called 'mega-cities'. By 1990, there were 12 'mega-cities' with 10 million or more inhabitants: 7 in Asia, 3 in Latin America and 2 in the United States.

These statistics give the impression of very rapid urbanization that is primarily focused on large cities. But some care is needed when generalizing about global urban trends, since there is such diversity in the scale and nature of urban change between nations and within nations over time, and also, for the larger and more populous nations, such diversity in urban trends between different regions. In addition, certain general points need to be highlighted:

More than half the world's population does not live in cities. Indeed, according to the most recent UN statistics (United Nations 2000), more than half the world's population does not live in urban centres and the world's urban population will only come to exceed its rural population around 2007. The proportion of people living in cities is considerably below the proportion living in urban centres as a significant proportion of the urban population lives in urban centres that are too small to be called cities (see Box 1.5). The world is less urbanized and has far fewer people concentrated in very large cities than had been anticipated during the 1970s and 1980s.

Less urbanized populations, smaller cities. Most of the urban population in Africa, Asia, Latin America and the Caribbean (and in other regions) live in urban areas with less than 1 million inhabitants. 'Mega-cities' with 10 million or more inhabitants had less than 3 per cent of the world's population in 1990. Even in Latin America with its unusually high concentration of population in mega-cities, more than four times as many people live in urban areas with less than 1 million inhabitants than in mega-cities. The slower population growth rates shown by most of the world's mega-cities during the 1980s and the more decentralized patterns of urban development evident in many nations from their last census suggests that the proportion of the world's population living in mega-cities will be smaller than most predictions, when new census data become available showing urban growth trends for the 1990s. Mega-cities can only develop in countries with large non-agricultural economies and large national populations; most nations have too small a population and too weak an urban-based economy to support a mega-city. Close to 50 independent countries in Africa, Asia, and Latin America and the Caribbean had no urban centre that had reached 500,000 inhabitants in 1990.

Although the size of the world's largest cities is historically unprecedented, most of the world's largest cities in 2000 are significantly smaller than had been expected. For instance, Mexico City is likely to have around 17 million people in 2000, not the 31 million people predicted 20 years ago (United Nations 1980). Calcutta is likely to have less than 13 million inhabitants in 2000, not the 40–50 million people that had been predicted during the 1970s (Brown 1974). Rio de Janeiro is likely to have around 10 million in 2000, rather than the 19 million predicted 20 years ago. Most very large cities experienced slow-downs in their population growth rate in the last intercensus period for which there are data, with many having more people moving out than moving in (including Calcutta, Buenos Aires, São Paulo, Mexico City and Rio de Janeiro). Among the 20 largest cities in Africa, Asia and Latin America, the most recent UN figures (United Nations 1998) suggest that only two had a population growth rate that exceeded 5 per cent a year during the 1980s – Dhaka and Lagos – and the figure for Lagos' growth rate is probably too high (the 1991 Nigerian census suggested a much lower population growth rate).

A range of factors help to explain the slower population growth rates for many large cities. For most, one key reason was slow economic growth (or economic decline) so fewer people moved there; this helps to explain slower population growth rates for many cities in Africa and Latin America during the

1980s. A second, particularly evident in (for instance) Mexico and Brazil, was the capacity of cities outside the very large metropolitan areas to attract a significant proportion of new investment. In the many nations that have had effective decentralization, urban authorities in smaller cities have more resources and capacity to compete for new investment.[14] Trade liberalization and a greater emphasis on exports have also increased the comparative advantage of many smaller cities. And advances in transport and communications have lessened the advantages for businesses in locating in the largest cities. A third factor, evident in many cities, was lower rates of natural increase, as fertility rates came down. However, there are also large cities whose population growth rates remained high during the 1980s – for instance Dhaka (Bangladesh) and many cities in India and China – and strong economic performance by such cities seems to be the most important factor in explaining this. China has many examples of cities with very rapid population growth rates which is hardly surprising, given the very rapid economic growth rates sustained over the last two decades. For instance, the city of Shenzhen close to Hong Kong has grown from a small border town to a metropolis of more than 3 million inhabitants in the last 20 years. In other regions, especially in sub-Saharan Africa, there are also some cities whose population growth was boosted by the movement there of people displaced by wars, civil strife or drought, but in many instances, this is largely a temporary movement, not a permanent one.

The concentration of large cities in large economies. There is an economic logic to the location of the world's largest cities. In 1990, the world's five largest economies (USA, China, Japan, Germany and the Russian Federation) had half of the world's mega-cities (with 10 million plus inhabitants) and more than a third of its 'million-cities'; when figures become available for 2000, the world's largest cities may be even more concentrated in its largest economies.[15] In 1990, all but one of the world's other mega-cities were in the next ten largest economies which also concentrated close to a quarter of the world's 'million-cities' (Satterthwaite 1996). In 1990, within Africa, Asia, and Latin America and the Caribbean, the largest cities were concentrated in the largest economies (which also tend to be among the most populous countries): Brazil and Mexico in Latin America, China, India, Indonesia and the Republic of Korea in Asia. These nations had all but one of the mega-cities' in these regions and nearly half of all the 'million-cities'. And despite the speed of change in urban populations, there is a (perhaps surprising) continuity in the location of important urban centres. Most of the largest urban centres in Latin America, Asia

---

14 Although most nations have had some form of decentralization over the last 10–15 years, the extent to which decentralization will help to underpin more decentralized patterns of urban growth will depend on the extent of this decentralization, including the extent to which resources and the capacity to raise revenues and invest in infrastructure have been decentralized from national or provincial/state authorities to urban authorities.

15 Figures for 1998 show that India had replaced Russia within the list of the world's five largest economies (GDP at purchasing power parity) which suggests a higher concentration of the world's largest cities in the five largest economies than in 1990 – World Bank figures quoted in *The Economist*, 13 May 2000, page 146.

and North Africa today have been important urban centres for centuries. More than two-thirds of the 'million-cities' in these regions had been founded by 1600 AD; more than a quarter have histories stretching back more than 1000 years (ibid).

The association between a nation's per capita income and its level of urbanization is well known – ie that in general, the higher the per capita income, the higher the level of urbanization. Most of the nations with the most rapid increase in their level of urbanization between 1960 and 1990 were also the nations with the most rapid economic growth (UNCHS 1996).

Beyond a rural–urban division. Perhaps too much stress is given to the fact that the world is soon to become predominantly urban, because of the imprecision in defining 'urban' and 'rural' populations as described in Box 1.5 and the large differences between countries in the criteria used. These differences limit the validity of intercountry comparisons. For instance, it is not comparing like with like if we compare the 'level of urbanization' (the percentage of population in urban centres) of a nation that defines urban centres as all settlements with 20,000 or more inhabitants with another that defines urban centres as all settlements with more than 1000 inhabitants. The comparison is particularly inaccurate if a large section of the population lives in settlements of between 1000 and 19,999 inhabitants (which is the case in many nations). Any nation can also increase or decrease its level of urbanization considerably, simply by changing the definition of an urban centre. The proportion of the world's population living in urban areas could be increased or decreased by several percentage points simply by China, India or a few of the other most populous nations changing their urban definition. *Thus, the proportion of the world's population currently living in urban centres is best considered not as a precise percentage (ie 47 per cent in 2000) but as being between 40 and 55 per cent, depending on the criteria used to define what is an 'urban centre'.*

There is a tendency in the discussions of urban change to concentrate too much on changes in the levels of urbanization and too little on the economic and political transformations that have underpinned urbanization – on a global scale, the very large increase in the size of the world's economy and the changes in the relative importance of different sectors and of international trade – and how this has changed the spatial distribution of economic activities, and the social and spatial distribution of incomes. The distinction between 'rural' and 'urban' populations has some utility in highlighting differences in economic structure, population concentration and political status (as virtually all local governments are located in urban centres) but it is not a precise distinction. In many areas, large sections of the 'rural' population work in non-agricultural activities or derive some of their income from such activities or commute to urban areas. Distinctions between rural and urban areas are also becoming almost obsolete in and around many major cities as economic activity spreads outwards – for instance around Jakarta (McGee 1987), around Bangkok and within Thailand's Eastern Seaboard, around Mumbai (and the corridor linking it to Pune), in the Pearl River Delta in China and in the Red River Delta in Vietnam (World Bank 1999a).

Table 1.3 *The distribution of the population between settlements of different sizes, 1990*

Region	Proportion of the total population living in					
	Rural areas	Urban areas with populations of				
		less than 1 million	1–2 million	2–5 million	5–10 million	10 million plus
Africa	67.9	22.6	4.2	2.7	2.6	–
Asia	68.1	20.2	3.1	3.2	2.4	2.9
Latin America and the Caribbean	28.9	43.1	6.0	7.7	4.7	9.4
Rest of the world	27.1	48.4	7.4	10.2	4.3	2.7

Source: Drawn primarily from data in United Nations (1998), *World Urbanization Prospects: the 1996 Revision*, Population Division, New York, adjusted when new census data became available.

In many urban centres, a considerable proportion of the workforce work in agriculture or provide goods or services for agricultural populations. Indeed, in cities with boundaries set for large metropolitan areas, 20 per cent or more of the economically active population can work in agriculture.[16] In addition, discussing 'rural' and 'urban' areas separately can ignore the multiple flows between them in terms of (among other things) people, goods, income, capital and information (Tacoli 1998). Many low-income households draw goods or income from urban and rural sources. And as Chapter 5 will describe in more detail, the quality of natural resource management in rural areas is much influenced by urban demands. Thus, an interest in poverty reduction or environmental management in urban areas implies a need to understand rural–urban linkages. It also implies a need to recognize how imprecise the distinction between rural and urban areas can be, and to avoid assumptions that people's livelihoods or economic activities or any use of resources are exclusively 'rural' or 'urban'.

Box 1.5 also noted how comparisons of city populations can be imprecise as well, as the criteria used to define city boundaries can vary so much. For some cities, their boundaries correspond to their built-up area; for others, it corresponds to much larger areas that encompass the population in surrounding rural areas and nearby urban centres. Most large cities have at least three population figures, each with validity based on different criteria – one for the central city, one for the metropolitan area and one for a wider planning region (which may also be defined to include settlements where much of the working population commute to the city). The population growth rate of such cities is also much influenced by which boundaries are chosen. For instance, it is possible to say that the population of Buenos Aires and Mexico City (or London, Los Angeles and Tokyo) declined in recent years; it is also possible to say that it expanded considerably in recent years. Both are correct but based on the use of different boundaries. So the number of 'mega-cities' and the proportion of the

16 Satterthwaite 2000 includes a table bringing together statistics for many cities, showing how common it is for 5 per cent of a city's economically active population to work in agriculture with much higher percentages evident in many cities in low-income nations, especially those with extended boundaries.

world's population living in mega-cities could also be increased or decreased, simply by changing the basis for defining boundaries for some of the world's larger cities. Thus, although international comparisons of urban populations, city populations and the speed of urban change are interesting, their precision is always limited.

The world's largest cities are not the world's fastest growing cities. Very large cities never have been among the fastest city population growth rates. The calculation of any city's population growth rate is based on dividing the increase in its population by its population at the beginning of the period under consideration.[17] If a city already has a large population at the beginning of the period under consideration, this keeps down the population growth rate. An analysis of such growth rates among all the urban centres in a country between two recent censuses often shows that several urban centres had population growth of between 6 and 14 per cent a year, especially in nations with rapid economic growth. But it is very rare for cities with several million inhabitants to have growth rates of as much as 5 per cent a year and most are much lower than this. Virtually all the world's largest cities today had their most rapid population growth many decades ago when their populations were relatively small. For some, including São Paulo and Buenos Aires, it was back in the late 19th or early 20th century. The world's most rapidly growing cities in terms of population both now and in the past are or have been relatively small cities. For instance, many small cities double their population in ten years when they first achieve economic success but this has never happened for cities of 5 million or more inhabitants. It is rare for cities that have reached 1 million or more inhabitants to double their population in ten years (although many might have done so when they were much smaller).

If the speed with which cities are growing is measured by the average increment in the population by year, rather than its growth rate, then many of the largest cities figure among the world's fastest growing cities. For instance, during the 1980s, at least seven cities had more than a quarter of a million people added to their populations each year – Tokyo, São Paulo, Mumbai/Bombay, Jakarta, Delhi, Karachi and Dhaka (although for several of these, this figure is for their metropolitan area, not 'the city').

It might also come as a surprise to many readers that while the populations of many cities in Africa, Asia, Latin America and the Caribbean have grown very rapidly, their growth rates are not unprecedented and that many of the world's fastest growing cities during the 20th century have been in the United States.[18]

In addition, one of the main reasons why the population growth rates of the largest cities in sub-Saharan Africa in recent decades appear so high in

---

17 A more sophisticated formula is used for calculating annual average growth rates (or exponential growth rates), but the denominator is still based on the city's population at the beginning of the period under consideration.

18 For instance, over the last 100 years, Los Angeles has grown far more rapidly than Calcutta while Dallas has grown at around the same pace as Lagos; Nairobi and Miami both had hardly any population in 1900 but Miami now has a much larger population than Nairobi. So too does Phoenix which was only a small town in 1900 (see Satterthwaite 1996).

comparison to the largest cities in other regions is that they began from a much smaller base. Among the 18 cities in sub-Saharan Africa that had more than a million inhabitants in 1990, half had less than 200,000 in 1950 while 5 of them (Abidjan, Maputo, Nairobi, Dar es Salaam and Conakry) had less than 100,000. Because they began from such a small base, their population growth rates from the 1950s onwards are much higher than for major cities in most other regions which already had much larger populations by the 1950s. One of the main reasons why sub-Saharan African cities grew from such a small base was that the European colonial powers had deliberately kept down their populations by imposing restrictions on the rights of their national populations to live and work in urban centres. Thus, one of the reasons why their populations grew so rapidly just before or after the ending of colonial rule was the removal or weakening of the colonial apartheid-like controls on population movements, and this allowed women and children to join their partners who were working in the city, whereas previously they had been forced to live separated, with the women and children in rural areas (Bryceson 1983; Potts 1995). Another reason why the population of many sub-Saharan African cities grew so rapidly during the 1960s and 1970s was the achievement of political independence for the nations in which they were located and the development in these cities of institutions associated with an independent state as well as the development of a higher education system that had been so undeveloped under colonial rule. A third reason was the division of what under colonial rule had been one 'country' into two or more, with each new country needing a capital (Bairoch 1988). If much of the in-migration into sub-Saharan Africa's largest cities over the past few decades can be explained by the movement of women and children to join their partners, by the expansion of higher education and the institutions associated with independent nation-states, it cannot be said that this was 'urbanization out of control'. And no sub-Saharan African city appears in the world's 20 'fastest growing cities' during the 1950s, 1960s or 1970s, if measured in terms of annual average increment in population over each decade.[19]

An uncertain urban future. Most publications discussing urban change predict or assume that the world will continue to urbanize far into the future, even if many now admit that the speed of the change and the size to which the largest cities are likely to grow has been overstated. In its most recent projections, which considerably reduce the scale of urban growth predicted up to 2025 compared with previous projections, the UN suggests that the world will have 59 per cent of its population living in urban areas by the year 2025 (United Nations 1998). Africa is predicted to have some 52 per cent of its population living in urban areas by then. But such projections should be viewed with caution. Given the historic association between economic growth and urbanization, a steady increase in the level of urbanization in less urbanized nations is only likely to take place if they also have steadily growing economies. While stronger and more buoyant

---

19 Lagos would be included in this list for the 1960s and 1970s if the United Nations estimate for its population in United Nations 1998 is used, but not if the figure of 5 million suggested by the 1991 Nigerian census is accepted.

economies for the world's lower-income nations should be a key development goal, the current prospects for most such nations are hardly encouraging, within the current world economic system. Many of the lowest-income nations have serious problems with political instability or civil war, and most have no obvious 'comparative advantage' on which to build an economy that prospers and thus urbanizes.

There are also grounds for doubting whether a large proportion of the world's urban population will come to live in very large cities. As noted above, many of the largest cities have slow population growth rates and much new investment is going to particular medium-sized cities well located in relation to the largest cities and to transport and communications systems. In addition, in regions with advanced transport and communications systems, rural inhabitants and enterprises can enjoy standards of infrastructure and services and access to information that historically have only been available in urban areas. Thus, both low- and high-income nations may have smaller than expected increases in their urban populations, although for very different reasons.

Chapter 2

Environmental Problems in the Home, Workplace and Neighbourhood

Sisters bathe next to their home in a *colonia* (low-income settlement) on the outskirts of Matamoros, Mexico
Photo © Janet Jarman, all rights reserved

INTRODUCTION

This chapter concentrates on three kinds of environmental problem in relation to the home, workplace and neighbourhood:

1   Disease-causing agents (pathogens) or pollutants in the human environment (in the air, soil, food or water) which can damage human health.
2   Shortages of natural resources essential to human health (for instance insufficient fresh water).

3   Physical hazards (for instance accidental fires or flooding for housing built
     on flood-plains or mudslides or landslides for housing built on steep
     slopes).

These are all environmental problems that can be reduced or eliminated by
human intervention. Although many of the examples given in this and subsequent chapters reveal very serious environmental problems in terms of the
scale of the ill-health, injury and premature death they cause or the damage
done to natural resources, these may not be the 'worst cases' since many of the
worst cases are unlikely to have been documented. Few nations have the range
of NGOs and citizen groups working on environmental issues comparable to
those in West Europe, North America and Japan. Within the world's high-
income countries, it was largely through the efforts of individual activists,
citizen groups and NGOs that attention was drawn to environmental problems
and public opinion mobilized to demand that these were addressed. Although
governments in these countries were often slow to react, the fact that more
effective environmental policies developed despite the opposition of powerful
vested interests is a demonstration of democratic processes at work. Such
democratic processes are controlled or repressed in many low- and middle-
income nations.

THE INDOOR ENVIRONMENT AT HOME

The fact that a high proportion of the urban population in Africa, Asia, Latin
America and the Caribbean live and work in very poor conditions is too well
known to need much elaboration. In most urban centres, between one-third
and two-thirds of the population live in housing units that are of poor quality.
Houses are often made of temporary materials which provide inadequate
protection against the elements and against extreme temperatures. There is
usually insufficient space (relative to the number of people living there) and
inadequate provision for piped water supplies, the removal of excreta and
household liquid and solid wastes, drainage, and all-weather roads and
footpaths.
    In any city, there is usually a range of housing submarkets used by low-
income groups – for instance the single rooms rented by households in
tenements or illegal settlements, the beds rented by individuals in boarding-
houses or the houses or shacks that households build on illegally occupied or
subdivided land.[1] Despite the diversity (and the differences between cities in
the range and relative importance of different housing types for lower-income
groups) almost all the housing used by low-income groups share three characteristics that contribute to poor environmental health:

---

1 For a general discussion of what influences the range and nature of housing submarkets used
by lower income groups, see Hardoy and Satterthwaite 1989. For various case studies, see
Environment and Urbanization, Vol 1, No 2, 1989. For several case studies of tenant submarkets,
see *Environment and Urbanization*, Vol 9, No 2, 1997. For city case studies, see Yapi-Diahou 1995,
and Beall and others 2000a.

- The presence within the home and its immediate surrounds of disease-causing agents (pathogens) because of a lack of basic infrastructure and services – for instance no sewers, inadequate provision for drainage and irregular or no services to collect solid wastes and safely dispose of them.
- Inadequate supplies of safe water.
- Overcrowded, cramped living conditions that increase the transmission of airborne infections and those passed by human contact and increase the risk of accidents. Each of these is described in more detail below.

The health problems associated with inadequate water and sanitation

A lack of readily available water, of sewers (or other systems to safely dispose of human wastes), of drainage systems, rubbish collection and basic measures to prevent disease and provide healthcare result in very large health burdens from easily prevented diseases. They also result in high levels of infant and child death.

Many health problems are linked to water – its quality, the quantity available, the ease with which it can be obtained and the provisions made for its removal, once used. The health links with sanitation are also obvious; human excreta is an extremely hazardous substance. At any one time, close to half of the urban population in Africa, Asia and Latin America is suffering from one or more of the main diseases associated with inadequate provision for water and sanitation (WHO 1999). These diseases account for a high proportion of infant and child deaths. Improved water and sanitation can bring great benefits not only in terms of reducing infant and child mortality and improved health, but also in reduced expenditures (on water purchased from vendors or kiosks and on treatment for diseases), higher real incomes (because of less time off work for illness) and much reduced physical effort (especially for those who have to collect and carry water from standpipes or other sources far from their shelters). Table 2.1, drawn from a WHO report, lists the water-related diseases and estimates of their impact on mortality and morbidity and, where information is available, the size of the population at risk.[2] As this report notes, the health effects of these diseases are heavily concentrated in Africa, Asia and Latin America and, within these regions, among the lower-income urban and rural households within the lower-income countries.

Table 2.1 classifies the water-related diseases by the mechanisms by which the disease is transmitted: water-borne, water-washed, water-based and water-related insect vector. David Bradley developed this classification because it was more easily understood by and relevant to non-health professionals than the conventional classification systems used by doctors where diseases are classified according to the nature of the pathogens that cause them (Cairncross and Feachem 1983). This classification system also highlights the environmental pathways by which the diseases infected humans, and so helps to identify the extent to which they can be addressed by preventive measures.

---

2 These figures are for rural and urban populations; statistics for urban areas only were not found.

Table 2.1 *The most serious water-related infections with estimates of the burden of morbidity and mortality they cause and the population at risk*

Disease (common name)	Name	Morbidity	Mortality (number of deaths per year)	Population at risk
1 Water-borne (and water-washed*; also food-borne)				
Cholera	Cholera*	More than 300,000	More than 6000	
Diarrhoeal diseases	This group includes salmonellosis*, shigellosis*, Campylobacter*, E coli, rota-virus amoebiasis* and giardiasis*	700 million or more people infected each year, 1.8 billion episodes a year	More than 3 million	More than 2000 million
Enteric fevers	Paratyphoid	500,000 cases; 1 million infections (1977–78)	25,000	
	Typhoid			
Infectious jaundice	Hepatitis A*			
Pinworm	Enterobiasis			
Polio	Poliomyelitis	204,000	25,000	
Roundworm	Ascariasis	800–1000 million infected; 214 million with clinical symptoms	60,000	
Leptospirosis	Leptospirosis			
Whipworm	Trichuriasis	133 million cases		
2 Water-washed				
a Skin and eye infections				
Scabies	Scabies			
Impetigo	Impetigo			
Trachoma	Trachoma	6–9 million people blind; 13 million infected;		500 million
Leishmaniasis	Leishmaniasis	400,000 new infections per year	197,000	350 million
b Other				
Relapsing fever	Relapsing fever			
Typhus	Rickettsial diseases			

Table 2.1 *continued*

Disease (common name) Name	Morbidity	Mortality (number of deaths per year)	Population at risk
3 Water-based			
a Penetrating skin			
Bilharzia Shistosomiasis	200 million infected	Over 200,000	500–600 million
b Ingested			
Guinea worm Dracunculiasis	Over 10 million infected		Over 100 million
4 Water-related insect vector			
a Biting near water			
Sleeping sickness African trypanosomiasis	20,000 new cases per year	55,000	50 million
b Breeding in water			
Filaria Filariasis (lymphatic)	100 million people infected		900 million
Malaria Malaria	267 million infections a year; 107 million clinical cases a year	2 million (more than half children under five)	2100 million
River blindness Onchocerciasis	18 million infected (over 300,000 blind)	35,000	85–90 million
Yellow fever Yellow fever	200,000 new cases a year	30,000	
Breakbone fever Dengue fever	Millions of cases each year with 500,000+ people needing hospital treatment	23,000	

Source: Adapted from WHO (1992a), *Our Planet, Our Health*, Report of the World Commission on Health and Environment, Geneva. The structure of the table was drawn from Cairncross, Sandy and Richard G Feachem (1983), *Environmental Health Engineering in the Tropics: An Introductory Text*, John Wiley & Sons, Chichester; and White , G F, D J Bradley and A U White (1972), *Drawers of Water: Domestic Water Use in East Africa*, University of Chicago Press, Chicago. Figures for morbidity, mortality and population at risk from WHO (1991), *Global Estimates for Health Situation Assessment and Projections 1990*, Geneva, April, with figures updated from WHO (1995), *The World Health Report 1995: Bridging the Gaps*, World Health Organization, Geneva.

Among the many water-related diseases, *water-borne diseases* – mostly diarrhoeal diseases – are the most common.[3] Diarrhoeal diseases account for a high proportion of infant, child and adult illnesses, and for most water-related infant and child deaths.[3] When combined with undernutrition (as they often are), they can also so weaken the body's defence that diseases such as measles and pneumonia become major causes of death (WHO 1992a). Where water supplies and provision for sanitation are inadequate for much of a city's population, water-borne diseases can remain one of the most serious health problems within city-wide averages.[4] Overcrowding and inadequate food hygiene exacerbate the risks from contaminated water and poor sanitation (Rossi-Espagnet and others 1991). There are also water-borne intestinal worms that cause severe pain and undermine the nutritional status of hundreds of millions of urban dwellers, but only a small proportion of those infected will die of them (WHO 1990). Many case studies in low-income settlements have shown that a high proportion of the population have debilitating intestinal worm burdens.[5]

The *water-washed* diseases are associated with a lack of water supplies for washing. These include various skin and eye infections such as scabies and trachoma. The number of people who can be affected and the extent to which lower-income groups face greater problems (largely because of poorer quality provision for water) is illustrated by a study of 1103 primary school students in the urban district of Bamako (Mali's capital and largest city). This found the overall prevalence of scabies among the pupils to be 4 per cent, ranging from 1.8 per cent at the school with the highest socio-economic level to 5 per cent at primary schools serving poorer areas (Landwehr and others 1998). Most water-borne diseases are also 'water-washed', as their incidence is associated with inadequate water supplies as well as with contaminated water.

Diseases spread by *water-related insect vectors* are among the most pressing environmental problems in many cities. These include malaria. Although commonly considered a 'rural' disease, there are severe problems with malaria in urban areas in large parts of Africa, Asia and Latin America (Rossi-Espagnet and others 1991). In many cities or in particular poor peripheral city districts, malaria is one of the main causes of illness and death (ibid). The *Anopheles* mosquitoes that are the vector for malaria breed in standing water, so good drainage is a critical part of malaria control.

Other kinds (or genera) of mosquito can be the vectors for other serious diseases. The diseases spread by *Aedes* mosquitoes (which include dengue, dengue haemorrhagic fever and yellow fever) are serious health problems in many cities. Containers used for storing water in houses lacking regular piped supplies (pots and jars, small tanks, drums and cisterns) can provide breeding habitats for these mosquitoes. Many households with piped supplies are also at risk because of intermittent supplies of water in the piped system, so they store water in tanks, when water is available. Later sections of this chapter will highlight how water is only available in piped systems for a few hours a day (or

---

3 See for instance Songsore and McGranahan 1993; Misra 1990, and Adedoyin and Watts 1989.
4 See for instance Songsore and McGranahan 1993, and Surjadi 1988.
5 Many of these are summarized in Bradley and others 1991. See also Mahfouz and others 1997, and Misra 1990.

less) which means that water storage in the home becomes essential. Small pools of clean water within residential areas in, for instance, discarded tin cans and rubber tyres can also be breeding grounds (Cairncross and Feachem 1993). Reliable, steady piped water supplies (so households do not need to store water) and good rubbish collection can greatly reduce the risk of diseases spread by *Aedes* mosquitoes. *Culex* mosquitoes, which can be one of the vectors for bancroftian filariasis (a debilitating disease affecting millions of people), can breed in open or cracked septic tanks, flooded pit latrines and drains but can be controlled through measures as simple as polystyrene balls in septic tanks and latrines (Cairncross and Feachem 1993). Even where mosquitoes do not pose health threats, they are often a severe nuisance and low-income households may spend a significant proportion of their income on insecticides or repellents.

Disease vectors also have an important role in the transmission of many water-borne or water-washed diseases including diarrhoeal diseases (cockroaches, blowflies and houseflies), hepatitis A (houseflies, cockroaches), relapsing fever (body lice and soft ticks), scabies (scabies mites), trachoma (face flies) and typhus (body lice and fleas) (Schofield and others 1990, WHO 1992a). Many disease vectors thrive when there is poor drainage and inadequate provision for rubbish collection, sanitation and piped water supplies. There are also case studies showing the health impact on urban populations of schistosomiasis which is normally considered a rural disease, since it is usually caught through contact with irrigation water or stored water in which the aquatic snails that are host to the schistosome worms live. But there is evidence of schistosomiasis infections in Belo Horizonte (Brazil) where infection was probably through swimming and playing in water (Firmo and others 1996) and Ibadan (Nigeria) where infection probably took place as a result of swimming, fetching water and cleaning clothes (Okoli and Odaibo 1999).

The inadequacies in provision for water[6]

Hundreds of millions of urban dwellers do not have piped water supplies and have no alternative but to use contaminated water, or at least water whose quality is not guaranteed. As one specialist commented, 'those not served are obliged to use water from streams or other surface sources which in urban areas are often little more than open sewers, or to purchase water from insanitary vendors. It is little wonder that their children suffer frequently, often fatally, from diarrhoeal diseases' (Cairncross 1990, page 109). Hundreds of millions more may have 'access to piped supplies' but do not have a piped supply into their home or yard and thus have to rely on standpipes or other communal or public supplies to which access is often difficult and time-consuming. Large numbers of those with piped supplies only receive water through the pipe intermittently and the quality of the water is often poor. Boxes 2.1–2.4 give examples of the inadequacies in provision for water, sanitation and drainage in cities in Africa, Asia and Latin America and the Caribbean.

---

6 This and some subsequent sections draw on Jonsson and Satterthwaite (2000), a background paper prepared for the US National Academy of Sciences' Panel on Urban Population Dynamics for its forthcoming report on urban change.

Box 2.1 *EXAMPLES OF THE INADEQUACIES IN CITIES' WATER SUPPLY AND SANITATION IN ASIA*

Bangalore (India). In this city of some 6 million inhabitants, it is estimated that more than half depend on public fountains, but these often have broken taps or pipes and damaged platforms (TARU 1998). Almost a third of the population has partial or no access to piped water. The lack of provision is particularly acute in peripheral areas within the metropolitan area where a large and increasing proportion of the population live. Private tankers supply a very large population in the intermediate and peripheral zones. In 1991, for a population of 4.5 million, there were only 183,000 house connections and 4320 street taps. In a study of 5 'slums', 2 had no water supply, 1 was supplied by bore-wells and 2 had to depend on public fountains where between 1 and 2 bore-wells and 1 tap served a population of between 800 and 900. Residents of the 4 'slums' had to walk from 20 metres to 1 kilometre to fetch water. With regard to sanitation, 113,000 households are reported to have no latrine at all. In a study of 22 'slums', 9 with a total population of 35,400 had no latrine facilities. In another 10, there were 19 public latrines serving 102,000 people. Defecation in the open is common (Benjamin 2000 and Benjamin and Bhuvaneshari 1999, drawing on TARU 1998, Achar and others, forthcoming, and Sanbergen, forthcoming).

Baroda (India). A survey in 1991 found that only 70 per cent of households had access to adequate drinking water, with 53 per cent having individual bathrooms and 60 per cent having individual toilets. One-third of households were not connected to sewers. A 1992 survey of 400 households drawn from different 'slums' found that almost all had water available to them but only 12 per cent had an independent source. In all but one 'slum', most households depended on taps and hand pumps provided by the municipality. Only 9 per cent had their own latrines. In many localities, community toilets had been provided by the municipality but people did not use them because they were not regularly cleaned or there was no water supply. Drainage facilities were equally poor; 87 per cent of the households in 12 slums reported that there was no provision (Ghosh and others 1994).

Calcutta (India). For Calcutta Municipal Corporation, only around 25 per cent of the population are served by single-tap connection into their homes. About half the population that live in the slum or squatter colonies collect water from stand-posts. The rest of the population do not have access to the municipal water supply and have to make their own arrangements – for instance relying on handpumps drawing from tube wells. Some 70 per cent of the population (and 50 per cent of the area) have sewerage and drainage facilities. For the larger Calcutta Metropolitan Area population, only half have sewer connections and drainage facilities (Hasan and Adil Khan 1999).

Cebu (Philippines). In 1990, only 15 per cent of households had their own individual household connection to a piped water supply with another 24 per cent relying on a shared faucet. Most others rely on wells (often shared) or purchase from vendors. Only 45 per cent of households had access to water-sealed toilets (and many of these shared such toilets) with 18 per cent relying on pit latrines and 36 per cent having no toilets at all. There is a lot of open defecation or what is termed locally as 'wrap and throw' (Etemadi 2000, drawing on 1990 census data).

Colombo (Sri Lanka). Virtually all permanent residents have access to piped water but some 30 per cent rely on public taps with 40–50 persons per tap on average. There is low pressure and irregular supplies in some areas. Two different figures are given for the proportion of residents served by the city sewerage system: 60 per cent and 78 per cent. A 1994 demographic survey showed that 46 per cent of the housing units in Colombo either share toilets or have no access to toilets. Open defecation is common. A high proportion of the population live in places with 50 or more persons per toilet. There are serious problems with flooding, linked to inadequate drainage in many parts of the city, in part because many waterways are not maintained adequately and so debris collects, blocking the free flow of water. Poor drainage is also a major cause of filariasis of which there are 700–2000 cases annually (Fernando and others 2000).

Chittagong (Bangladesh). Around a quarter of the population of 1.6 million is served by individual house connections, 200,000 are served by 588 street hydrants and the rest collect water from other sources such as natural springs, canals, ponds and rainwater catchments (Kaneez Hasna 1995). For sanitation, a 1993 survey found that nearly three-quarters of the metropolitan 'slum' population relied on bucket or pit latrines (Bangladesh Bureau of Statistics 1996).

Dhaka (Bangladesh). According to the 1995 Study of Urban Poverty in Bangladesh, 99 per cent of poor households in urban Bangladesh had access to 'safe' drinking water but if 'access' is defined as the availability of water within 100 metres, the proportion counted as having 'access' would be much lower (Islam and others 1997). A survey found that for half the population in 'slum' areas, it takes more than 30 minutes to collect water.[7] In regard to sanitation, in Dhaka, 13 per cent of the poor had a connection to a sewerage system, 13 per cent used a septic tank, 19 per cent had a sanitary/latrine and 42 per cent a pit or open latrine, 2 per cent of the urban poor had no fixed arrangement, and 2.7 per cent used an open field (Islam and others 1997). Another source suggested that over 90 per cent of the 'slum' population in Metro Dhaka rely on pit latrines or bucket (or 'hanging') latrines, which also served 35 per cent of the 'non-slum' population (Bangladesh Bureau of Statistics 1996).

Faisalabad (Pakistan). Some two-thirds of the city's 2 million inhabitants live in largely unserviced areas. Over half have no piped water supply and less than a third have sewers (Alimuddin and others 2000).

---

7 Survey by the International Centre for Diarrhoeal Disease Research, cited in UNICEF–Bangladesh and others 1997.

Kabul (Afghanistan). The most common type of toilet used both in planned and unplanned housing is the raised drop latrine. It consists of a raised squatting slab, often of wood and mud built over a box structure with its base approximately at street level, usually built of stone or concrete. This box has a small outlet directly to the street. Even in two- or three-storied buildings, sewage from higher floors reaches the outlet box by a drop chute. Some sections of the community separate the urine and the faeces, with the faeces passing through to the receptacle and the urine down a tube to the outside of the house. This causes a pile of fresh faeces to build up under the slab until somebody removes it. In many areas there is no way to mechanically collect the faeces due to the steep terrain and narrow streets. When the latrine is not manually emptied, fresh faeces pass out into the street. Defecation in the open is also common practice. Kabul has an extensive network of surface drains for carrying rainwater but the Municipality cannot afford to maintain them. Refuse and nightsoil are often dumped into the drains forming blockages which restrict water flow. This results in the formation of hundreds of large pools of standing water forming breeding sites for disease vectors. In the rainy season, this inadequacy in drainage leads to flooding and the formation of large pools of sewage in the flatter areas, where the water collects and mixes with the excreta from the latrines (Safi, 1998).

Jakarta (Indonesia). Residents face a great variety of problems in regard to water, sanitation and drainage. Microbial contamination of household water supplies is pervasive; almost nobody drinks unboiled tap or well water voluntarily. A household survey drawing on five households from 211 census areas found that the government's piped drinking water supply system only reached 18 per cent of households. Private wells were the primary source of drinking water for 48 per cent of households, with 22 per cent using water vendors (who charged about ten times the price of the piped water tariff). Many of those using wells faced problems; salination of groundwater, possibly fuelled by excessive abstraction, has rendered wells in the northern part of the city impotable even after boiling. Many residents face supply interruptions – for instance 9 per cent of respondents had suffered from periods of at least a week in the past year when there were regular interruptions to their drinking water supply. Regarding sanitation, the city has no sewer system. Seventy-three per cent of households had private lavatories in their homes which were not shared with 16 per cent having shared private toilets and 12 per cent using public toilets. There were high levels of dissatisfaction among those who used public toilets with the most common complaint being having to wait too long, although many households complained of the dirt, damage or problems with flushing. Of the 851 household toilets observed, more than half had no hand washing basin in the vicinity. A third of respondents reported that some people in their neighbourhood sometimes defecated outside the toilet – this was mostly children and the most common sites were drains and gutters. Problems of flooding are common in many parts of the city and accumulations of water provide the breeding ground for insect vectors including the dengue bearing mosquito (Surjadi and others 1994).

Karachi (Pakistan). More than half of Karachi's 12 million inhabitants live in *katchi abadis.* The most recent figures available (for 1989) show that only half the katchi abadis have piped water and only 12 per cent have provision for sanitation, compared with the planned areas where more than four-fifths have piped water and sanitation. For the whole city, only 40 per cent of the population is connected to the official sewer system (Hasan 1999).

Madras/Chennai (India). With a metropolitan population of about 5 million inhabitants, Madras has the lowest per capita supply of any metropolitan centre in India – an average of 70 litres per day. A household survey in 1996 found that 42 per cent of households in the city and 70 per cent of households in the rest of the metropolitan area were not connected to the piped water supplies. For the whole metropolitan population, 18 per cent of households had no water source within their premises while 29 per cent relied on shallow wells. Statistics for 1991 suggested that the sewage system serves 31 per cent of the metropolitan population and raw sewage flows freely into the Metropolitan Area's natural watercourses at many points (Anand 1999).

Ludhiana (India). This is one of India's richest cities; its population grew from 154,000 in 1951 to over 1 million by 1991 and it is likely to be close to 2 million today. Two-fifths of the population are without regular water supplies and half live in areas with no sewage system. Provision for drainage is very inadequate and low-lying areas get flooded during the rains. There are serious problems of groundwater contamination from sewage and industrial effluents yet large sections of the population depend on it, because of the inadequacy of the piped water network. Concentrations of chromium, zinc and cyanide in water drawn by handpumps were found to be many times the official permissible limits (Agarwal and others 1999a).

Visakhapatnam (India). The Water Supply Department claims that 90 per cent of the city's population has access to clean drinking water, although other sources suggest that it is between 60 and 70 per cent. Official figures suggest that 48 per cent of residents have piped water supplies to their home while 42 per cent rely on public fountains with an average of 150 residents to each fountain (Kumar and Amis 1999, Amis and Kumar 2000). A 1996 case study on 170 slums in Visakhapatnam reports that few slum households in the city have private tap water, and only half of the slums have public tap water (Abelson 1996). The water is supplied twice a day, for one-and-a-half hours in the morning and one hour in the evening. For sanitation, the underground sewage system only covers one block. Close to two-thirds of 'slum' dwellers have private toilets linked to septic tanks. A large section of the 'slum' population has to rely on public toilets (Kumar and Amis 1999). As a result of inadequate provision for sanitation, large sections of the population defecate in the open.

Table 2.2 *Differentials in the cost of water (ratio of price charged by water vendors to prices charged by the public utility)*

City	Price ratio of water from private vendors:public utility
Abidjan	5:1
Bangkok	Up to 5:1
Dhaka	12:1 to 25:1
Istanbul	10:1
Jakarta	Up to 10:1
Kampala	4:1 to 9:1
Karachi	28:1 to 83:1
Lagos	4:1 to 10:1
Lima	17:1
Lome	7:1 to 10:!
Nairobi	7:1 to 11:1
Nouakchott	Up to 10:1*
Surabaya	20:1 to 60:1
Tegucigalpa	16:1 to 34:1

* Can rise to 40:1 when there is a water shortage.
Sources: Bangkok, and Asian Development Bank (1997), *Second Water Utilities Data Book Asian and Pacific Region*, edited by Arthur C McIntosh and Cesar E Yñiguez, ADB, Manila. Nouakchott: Azandossessi, A. (2000), The struggle for water in urban poor areas of Nouakchott, Mauritania, *WATERfront*, Issue 13, January, UNICEF, New York. The rest: World Bank (1988), *World Development Report* 1988, Oxford University Press, page 146.

The quantity of water available to a household and the price that has to be paid can be as important to a family's health as its quality (Cairncross 1990). The cost of water and the time needed to collect it influence the quantity used. Where the official water companies (whether public or private) provide no water supply – as is common in informal or illegal settlements – households often obtain water from private vendors, at a cost per litre that is much higher than the cost paid by those with piped supplies. Thus, low-income households can pay many times the cost per litre paid by richer groups with piped supplies (see Table 2.2). The differentials in the cost per litre vary a lot from city to city and from neighbourhood to neighbourhood within cities. Factors that often influence the scale of this differential include the extent of competition between vendors for customers, the ease with which vendors can obtain their supplies, and the distance and physical accessibility of their customers.

It is clear that a large proportion of urban dwellers rely on water vendors although most households will purchase water from vendors for use only in cooking and drinking, and rely on poorer quality but cheaper water sources for, for instance, washing and laundry. Fifteen years ago, John Briscoe (1986) estimated that water vendors probably serve between 20 and 30 per cent of the urban population. It is difficult to estimate whether this proportion has fallen but we do not know that in some places, it has increased, as described in Box 2.2.

It is not unusual for poor households reliant on water vendors in major cities to spend 5–10 per cent of their total income on water. There are examples of low-income households paying a much higher proportion than this. For instance, in Nouakchott, the purchase of water is estimated to absorb 14–20 per cent of the budget for most low-income households (Azandossessi 2000). A case study in Karton Kassala (Khartoum) found that 35 per cent of household income went on payments to water vendors (Cairncross 1990). As this case study noted, payments for water come out of the household's food budget, exacerbating the prevalence of malnutrition and so contributing to high levels of child mortality. However, households served by vendors would generally be even worse off without these supplies and vendors usually operate in a competitive market, where the high cost of the water they supply reflects the high costs they face in obtaining the water and/or in travelling with the water to supply the low-income households (ibid).

The examples in Boxes 2.1–2.4 illustrate how common it is for a high proportion of those registered as having access to piped water to have access only to public standpipes. Where water is only available at a public place – for instance a communal well or public standpipe – the quantity used by each household will be influenced by the time and energy needed to collect and carry water back to the home. Where water provision is through public standpipes, collecting water can be very time-consuming. There is often a great shortage of taps, so there is only one tap per several hundred persons, and obtaining water usually means a long queue. It is common for there to be 200 to 500 persons per standpipe and for government agencies to regard this as 'adequate'. In one part of Dakar, a survey in the late 1980s found that there were 1513 persons per tap (Ngom 1989). In Nouakchott, only 179 standpipes were installed to cover the entire urban area which meant an average of only one standpipe for around 2500 inhabitants (Azandossessi 2000). In many areas of Luanda, there is one stand-post for 600–1000 persons (Development Workshop 1995).

For those reliant on standpipes, the difficulties in getting water are often much increased by the fact that water is only available in the piped system a few hours a day, or water pressure is very low, so it takes a long time to fill up each person's water containers. The time that has to be spent queuing and then filling the water containers is a particularly unwanted extra burden, especially since low income people often work very long hours. Queuing for water when long waits are necessary and supplies are uncertain is also a source of tension and can precipitate fights.[8] Queuing at a tap and carrying water from the tap to the home takes away from time that could be used in earning an income. In some communities, people have to queue for hours each day – for instance in Shajahmal within the Indian city of Aligarh, where the only water available is from a municipal tubewell (Agarwal and others 1999a). Interviews with a range of households in 16 sites in 9 urban areas in Kenya, Uganda and Tanzania in 1997 found that those without piped supplies spent an average of 92 minutes each day collecting water (Thompson and others 2000). This represents a more than threefold increase compared with the late 1960s when the average time collecting water in these same sites was 28 minutes a day (ibid, White and others 1972). In 1997, those using kiosks were spending almost two hours a day collecting water (see Box 2.2).

---

8 Moser, Caroline O N, personal communication.

The persons within a household who are allocated the responsibility of collecting water (generally women or children) often have to get up very early. Water is also very heavy to carry any distance and requires much physical effort so the amount of water used will be influenced by the distance that it has to be carried. If a household keeps its water consumption down to only 120 litres a day (and many use more than this) this translates to the equivalent of 12–16 full buckets of water that have to be collected each day. This means carrying a total weight of 120 kilos of water each day from the standpipe, well or kiosk to the home. Not surprisingly, those who have to fetch and carry water (usually women) often suffer severe back problems. Limited quantities of water mean inadequate supplies for washing and personal hygiene, and for washing food, cooking utensils and clothes. Eye and ear infections, skin diseases, scabies, lice and fleas are very difficult to control without sufficient supplies of water. So too is maintaining a good standard of personal hygiene. Thus, if governments or the water agencies they supervise find that providing piped connections to each household is too expensive or beyond their institutional capacity, they have to ensure a much better level of quality, reliability and accessibility in public provision than is generally the case.

Many piped water systems do not have water in them for much of the time, as illustrated by many examples in the boxes. For instance, in Zaria (Nigeria), a survey in 1995 found that 11 per cent of those who had piped water received water one day in two while 4 per cent received it once a week or once a fortnight and 12 per cent rarely or never received water (CASSAD 1995). In Mombasa (Kenya), very few parts of the city have a continuous supply (on average water is available for only 2.9 hours a day) and some parts of the city have had no water in the pipes for several years (Rakodi and others 2000). The availability of water supplies in several Indian cities, including Madras (or Chennai) and Hyderabad, deteriorated during the long drought of the early 1990s to the point where water was available for only 2 hours in every 48. In Madras the situation deteriorated further in 1993 to one where water was only available every third day (Giles and Brown 1997). Even in India's capital city, Delhi, water supplies are intermittent for large sections of the population, including one-fifth that receive water for less than four hours a day (Giles and Brown 1997). Data on water provision from water utilities in 50 cities in Asia and the Pacific during the mid-1990s highlighted how many provided water for a few hours a day including Karachi (4 hours), Madras/Chennai (4 hours), Mumbai/Bombay (5 hours), Bandung (6 hours), Kathmandu (6 hours) and Faisalabad (7 hours) (Asian Development Bank 1997). In 26 of the 50 cities, the utilities claimed to provide water 24 hours a day but consumer surveys, drawing from 100 randomly selected customers in each city, suggested that the water utilities overstated the time for which water was available (ibid).

In many urban centres, provision for water supply has not only not improved but it has actually deteriorated. This is illustrated by a study of domestic water use in 1997 that included 16 urban sites in Kenya, Uganda and Tanzania. Since these were sites in which domestic water use was also researched in 1967, this allowed a comparison of conditions in 1997 with 1967. The findings of this work are summarized in Box 2.2. These highlight how for households with piped supplies in 1967 and 1997 there was:

- A dramatic decline in water use per person.
- A significant decline in the reliability of piped water supplies.
- Increasing reliance on alternative sources.

For households lacking piped supplies, the main findings show:

- A very large increase in the time needed to obtain water and the increased distances that had to be walked to collect it.
- A greater reliance on higher-cost sources.

Governments and international agencies generally assume that households with piped supplies are adequately served. A study in a Palestinian camp in Amman highlights just how inadequate piped supplies can be. This found that although the houses were connected to the piped water system, due to a government-directed conservation measure for saving water, people received water only once a week, and only for several hours (usually at night). There had also been times when two or three weeks had passed without water. Even when water was available, it was difficult to get enough, because of low pressure. And here, as in most other piped water systems where water is only available intermittently, there were high levels of water contamination, as waste water (including sewage) got into the piped system when there was no water in it (Arar 1998).

Although official statistics tend to assign only one water source to each household, it is common for households to use multiple sources. In many instances, those with piped supplies are forced to do so because of the unreliability of piped supplies. In addition, households without piped supplies will, where possible, avoid having to use the more expensive water sources for anything more than cooking and drinking. Thus, they may purchase water for drinking and cooking from vendors or a water kiosk but get water for washing and laundry from a nearby river. For example, focus group discussions in one neighbourhood in Jakarta showed a high level of detail in local knowledge about different water sources (and their relative costs and qualities) and the extent to which different water sources were drawn on for different uses (Surjadi and others 1994).

In many of the larger, wealthier cities in Latin America, there has been considerable progress in increasing the proportion of households with water piped to their home. For instance, in Pôrto Alegre (Brazil), by the mid-1990s, 99 per cent of the population was served by the piped water system and 80 per cent by sewers (Menegat 1998). In São Paulo, by 1991, 96 per cent of the population in the Metropolitan Region had piped water and 80 per cent were connected to the sewer system or septic tanks (Mueller 1995). In Santiago de Chile, by 1992, 89 per cent of the population had water piped into their home and were connected to sewers (Rodriguez and others 1999). In Mexico City Metropolitan Area, most of the population had access to piped water by 1990 (although as noted in Box 2.4, many still did not have household connections). However, for large cities, even impressive levels of coverage can still mean large numbers of households inadequately served; for a city of 10 million inhabitants, a coverage of 90 per cent still means a million people lacking adequate provision.

BOX 2.2 *THE DETERIORATION IN WATER SUPPLIES IN EAST AFRICAN URBAN AREAS, 1967–1997*

One of the largest and most influential studies of water use was carried out in rural and urban areas in Kenya, Uganda and Tanzania in 1967. Its results were published in the book *Drawers of Water* (White and others 1972). A research programme entitled *Drawers of Water II* returned to the same sites in 1997. This box reports on findings from the 16 urban sites (in 9 different urban centres), focusing on the changes in domestic water use by households when comparing 1967 with 1997.

Declining water use for those with piped supplies. For households with piped water, average per capita use declined from 124 litres a day in 1967 to 64 litres a day in 1997. In the 14 sites with piped water, all but three had much lower consumption levels in 1997 compared with 1967. In some, the decline was dramatic, as in Iganga (Uganda) from 79 to 34 litres per day and in Moshi (Tanzania) from 95 to 41 litres per day. Although the more affluent study sites such as Parklands in Nairobi and Oyster Bay and Upanga in Dar es Salaam experienced decreases in water use levels, the mean daily water use still remained well above the average while those with relatively low household incomes, water use was well below it. Many low-income households had such unreliable piped water supplies that their water use had fallen to levels similar to many households that did not have piped supplies.

Declining reliability of piped supplies. Different factors contribute to this, including lack of system maintenance and the stress on existing network capacity from increasing urban populations. In 1967, virtually all the households interviewed who had piped supplies received 24-hour service; by 1997, only 56 per cent did so with around a fifth receiving only 1–5 hours of service a day. Again, the more affluent sites were generally the ones that had the most reliable water supplies. There had been a huge increase in the proportion of households who store water at home – from 3 per cent in 1967 to 90 per cent in 1997. In some sites, all those interviewed in 1997 collect water from various sources and store it at home to ensure adequate supplies because the piped system is so unreliable. The single most important change in the nature of secondary water supplies is the introduction of private sources such as kiosks and vendors. By 1997, these were used by almost 40 per cent of piped sample households. Private sources are particularly important in many low-income areas such as Changombe and Temeke in Dar es Salaam (Tanzania) and in Iganga (Uganda) where over 60 per cent of piped households use vendors as their primary source. By 1997, private water vending through kiosks or vendors had become a booming business in many of the low- and middle-income study sites, despite the fact that the water they sell frequently costs considerably more per litre than the public supplies. Researchers encountered several instances of public supplies being sabotaged.

Changes in water sources used by unpiped households. In 1997, a smaller proportion of unpiped households drew on protected or improved sources (wells, standpipes and hydrants) than had been the case in 1967. In 1967, more than three-quarters of unpiped sample households obtained water from protected or improved sources, with almost 100 per cent of households drawing from these in Mathare Valley (one of the largest informal settlements in Nairobi), and in the towns of Moshi and Dodoma in Tanzania. Thirty years later, only 56 per cent of unpiped households used protected or improved sources. In part this is because more are serviced by private vendors and kiosks, and these are particularly important in Mathare Valley and in Moshi and Dodoma where over half the sampled unpiped households view these as their primary source of water. Many households also use more than one water source, and by 1997, some 60 per cent of unpiped households regularly used a secondary source for water that is some distance from their home.

The increase in the time taken to obtain water. The average distance that unpiped households walked to obtain their water did not change much between 1967 (an average of 222 metres) and 1997 (an average of 204 metres) but distances to unprotected water sources had increased. The number of trips to collect water had increased from an average of 2.6 a day in 1967 to 4.0 in 1997. On average, unpiped urban households were walking 1 kilometre each day to and from water sources (up from 0.6 kilometres a day in 1967). *But the total time spent collecting water each day increased more than threefold from an average of 28 minutes in the late 1960s to an average of 92 minutes in 1997.* Households using private sources such as kiosks report the highest time collecting water. By 1997, on average, those using kiosks were spending almost two hours a day collecting water.

The higher cost of water. In 1997, piped supplies were less than a quarter of the cost per litre of supplies from vendors (the only other water source that delivers to the household). Water from kiosks was nearly twice the cost of piped supplies, but as noted above, getting this water was also time-consuming. Getting water from a neighbour or from a protected or improved source was less costly than kiosks but more costly than piped supplies.

Sources: White, Gilbert F, David J Bradley and Anne U White (1972), *Drawers of Water: Domestic Water Use in East Africa*, University of Chicago Press, Chicago and Thompson, John, Ina T Porras, Elisabeth Wood, James K Tumwine, Mark R Mujwahuzi, Munguti Katui-Katua and Nick Johnstone (2000), 'Waiting at the tap: changes in urban water use in East Africa over three decades', *Environment and Urbanization*, Vol 12, No 2, October.

Water utilities in several Asian cities report 100 or close to 100 per cent coverage (Asian Development Bank 1997) but it is clear that for some of these this includes those inadequately served by communal standpipes.

Box 2.3 EXAMPLES OF THE INADEQUACIES IN CITIES' WATER SUPPLY AND SANITATION IN AFRICA

Accra (Ghana). Interviews with 1000 households undertaken in 1991 found that only 35 per cent had water piped into their house. Most of the rest relied on private or community standpipes or vendors although a small percentage have to rely on open waterways, rainwater collection and wells. Over 80 per cent of the lowest income quintile had to fetch their water, compared with 10 per cent of the wealthiest group (Songsore and McGranahan 1993). The water distribution system to low-income areas is more vulnerable to contamination, and the water quality in low-income areas is generally worse that in those areas with indoor plumbing (Amuzu and Leitmann 1994). A survey of 558 households in 1997 found that only 45 per cent had drinking water from an inside tap (Morris and others 1999). For sanitation, 36 per cent of the 1000 households interviewed in 1991 had flush toilets with 41 per cent using pit latrines, 20 per cent using pan or bucket latrines and about 4 per cent having no access to toilet facilities. Nearly three-quarters of the lowest income quintile shared toilet facilities with more than 10 people (Songsore and McGranahan 1993). Users of public toilets generally find them unsatisfactory with regard to cleanliness, convenience and privacy. Those using public toilets pay the equivalent of around US$1 per head per month. Those with pit latrines in the house paid about US$4 monthly to a private individual for emptying. There is a sewer system in Accra's central business district but only 1 per cent of the city's population is connected (Amuzu and Leitmann 1994). Open defecation is a common practice with people using various means, including the wrapping of human excreta in polythene bags (commonly referred to as 'precious package') for disposal. With no usable toilets in the home or conveniently located nearby, many Accra residents have no choice but to defecate along beaches, water courses and gutters (Bogrebon 1997).

Addis Ababa (Ethiopia). Around 30 per cent of residential dwellings in Addis Ababa use open fields for defecation. In peri-urban and urban centres outside Addis Ababa, about 46 per cent of families have no sanitary facilities (Tadesse 1996).

Dar es Salaam (Tanzania). From a survey of 660 households drawn from all income levels in 1986–87, 47 per cent had no piped water supply either inside or immediately outside their houses while 32 per cent had a shared piped water supply. Of the households without piped water, 67 per cent bought water from neighbours while 26 per cent drew water from public water kiosks or standpipes. The average water consumption was only 23.6 litres a day. Of the 660 households, 89 per cent had simple pit-latrines (and most of Dar es Salaam continues to rely on pit latrines). Only 4.5 per cent had toilets connected to septic tanks or sewers. Most households have to share sanitary facilities. Overflowing latrines are a serious problem, especially in the rainy season and provision to empty septic tanks or latrines is very inadequate (Kulaba 1989). A study conducted during 1997–1998 in six low-income wards found that in most sites, water supplies were sporadic, often unsafe and expensive, where the sole water source was vendors. Where people had access to water from government wells, the wells were generally poorly managed. In some instances, newly installed pumps were stolen within weeks of being installed. In all the areas visited, pit latrines were the only form of sanitation (CARE-Tanzania 1998).

Ibadan (Nigeria). Only 22 per cent of the population are served by the municipal water supply system. The city has no sewer system. City inhabitants rely on pit latrines and latrines connected to septic tanks (UNICEF-Nigeria 1997).

Khartoum (the Sudan). A report in 1989 described how the systems of water supply and sewage disposal were inadequate both in coverage and in maintenance of the service. For water supply, coverage was poor, with low-income groups in squatter settlements paying the most for water, often bought from vendors. Breakdown and cuts in the supply system were common. The municipal sewage system served only about 5 per cent of the Khartoum urban area. Even that system was susceptible to breakdowns when waste is discharged either directly into the river or on to open land. For most people in the low-income areas, there was no system of sewage disposal (El Sammani and others 1989).

Kumasi (Ghana). Three-quarters of the population are served with piped water but large numbers only have access through shared taps or standpipes, and long waits and queues are common. Only 10 per cent of households have indoor plumbing. Even when an area has a piped network, water pressure is often inadequate and the service not continuous. Those who depend on vendors have to pay high prices. Water provision is particularly poor on the urban periphery where there is rapid urban growth. For sanitation, only 30 per cent of households have satisfactory arrangements in their homes. Some 15 per cent of the population rely on bucket latrines; 7 per cent on pit latrines; 8 per cent on open defecation; 25 per cent on a WC and septic tank, and 7 per cent on sewers. Nearly 40 per cent rely on 400 public latrines scattered around the city; long waits are common and most latrines are poorly maintained. In Atoinsu, for example, there are only two public toilets with 14 squat holes each to serve 10,000 inhabitants. Many people relieve themselves in plastic bags which are put into the community refuse skips or disposed of indiscriminately. In regard to drainage, there is no comprehensive storm drainage system, and flooding, with related building damage and loss of property, is a common occurrence during the rainy season. Usually the poor are affected most because they have settled the least desirable locations in low-lying areas adjacent to drains and watercourses (Korboe and others 2000, Devas and Korboe 2000).

Luanda (Angola). Three-quarters of the population (estimated at 2.8 million inhabitants) has no access to the formal water supply system. Depending on where they live, the poor pay from 800 to 8000 times more for untreated water than the official rate for piped water in the city core. In 1994, there were less than 50 functioning standpoints for over 2 million people – by the end of 1997, this had increased to about 220 standposts. Each stand-post provides treated water for about 600–1000 persons. A 1996 study in one of the municipalities in Luanda (Sambizanga) found that only half of all families had on-site sanitation (Development Workshop 1999).

Mombasa (Kenya). Although the majority of households are said to 'have access to' piped water, a 1993 estimate suggested that only 29 per cent had their own connection. Very few parts of the city receive a continuous supply and some have had no water in their pipes for several years. On average, water is available for only 2.9 hours a day. In a sample survey of 182 poor households in 1986, 92 per cent experienced water shortages, about half all the time, and half occasionally. Regarding sanitation, the 1989 census showed that only 10 per cent of Mombasa's households were served by a conventional sewerage system. The great majority of households (68 per cent in the mid-1990s and 81 per cent of poor households) use pit latrines. Shortages of water and capital funds have delayed extensions to the sewage system and repairs to the non-functioning treatment works, with the result that untreated sewage runs into the sea. Those lacking sewers face particular problems disposing of their domestic waste water (grey-water) (Rakodi and others 2000; the results of the household survey came from the African Medical Relief Fund (AMREF) and Office of the Vice-President/Ministry of Planning and National Development 1997. Other data was drawn from Gibb (Eastern Africa) Ltd 1995).

Nairobi (Kenya). A report in 1994 described how 55 per cent of Nairobi's population lived in informal settlements which are squeezed on to less than 6 per cent of the city's land area. Only 12 per cent of plots in these settle-ments have piped supplies. Most people have to obtain water from kiosks. Water shortages are common; a survey found that 80 per cent of house-holds complained of water shortages and pipes often running dry. With regard to sanitation, this same survey suggested that 94 per cent of the inhabitants of informal settlements do not have access to adequate sanita-tion. Only a minority of dwellings have toilets. Significant proportions of the total population have no access to showers and baths, and in most areas, drainage is inadequate (Alder 1995). Kibera is the largest low-income urban area in Nairobi, covering an area of 225 hectares and an estimated popula-tion of 470,000. Traditional pit latrines are the only excreta disposal system available and a high proportion of households have no toilet within or close to their home. There are often up to 200 persons per pit latrine. Pits fill up quickly and emptying is a problem due to difficult access. Space to dig new pits is often not available (Water Newsletter 1996).

Owerri (Nigeria). A 1995 study found that 83 per cent of the sampled residents had access to a piped water supply; the rest relied on other sources which were often contaminated. More than half of those with access to piped water did not have private connections in their homes; they either shared with neighbours or used public taps near their houses. With regard to regularity, 45 per cent of respondents only received free flowing water a few hours in the day while 15 per cent had water flowing every alternate day, 2.5 per cent had water once a week, and 8.5 per cent rarely had water. When tap water was not available, most households used water from streams. Some 27 per cent of respondents had a bathroom in the home; 67 per cent had one in the compound; and 6.5 per cent had 'no bathroom at all'. For sanitation, water closets were the most common (69 per cent) followed by pit latrines (15 per cent); 16 per cent of respondents had no toilet at all (CASSAD 1995).

Sanitation

Removing and safely disposing of excreta and waste water is also a critical environmental health need. Yet many governments and international agencies have concentrated on improving provision for water and not on sanitation and on ensuring the safe removal of waste water. For sanitation, the key is to ensure no human contact with excreta, and also safe excreta disposal so, for instance, the excreta does not contaminate water or allow the parasitic worms in excreta to survive, develop and re-infect humans. Most of the diseases associated with contaminated water including all the waterborne diseases listed in Table 2.1, are excreta-related. Among the other common diseases that are excreta-related are schistosomiasis, hookworm, beef and pork tapeworms and filariasis (Cairncross and Feachem 1993).

There are no accurate statistics on the proportion of the urban population in Africa, Asia, and Latin America and the Caribbean that have adequate provision for sanitation. Perhaps as many as two-thirds of this population have no hygienic means of disposing of excreta and an even greater number lack the adequate means to dispose of waste waters (Sinnatamby 1990). Most urban centres in Africa and many in Asia have no sewers at all. This is not only the smaller urban centres; many major cities with a million or more inhabitants have no sewer system. Pit latrines and bucket latrines, often shared between many people, are among the most common response, along with defecation in open spaces. Ditches, gullies, streams, canals and rivers are where most human excrement and waste water ends up, untreated. For those cities with sewer systems, rarely do they serve more than a small proportion of the population – typically the richer residential, government and commercial areas. Boxes 2.1, 2.3 and 2.4 provide many illustrations of the inadequacies in provision for sanitation. They also highlight how most of the inhabitants in many major cities are affected – for instance in major cities such as Bangalore, Dar es Salaam, Dhaka, Faisalabad, Jakarta, Kabul, Khartoum, Kinshasa, Kumasi, Luanda, Madras/Chennai and Ouagadougou.

Official statistics for the national coverage of sanitation often understate the problem because they do not distinguish between households with a toilet within their home and those that rely on communal or public provision. Many also assume that if a household has some toilet facility, that it is adequate. It is common for many (or even most) households that in national statistics are said to have provision for sanitation to only have access to a latrine shared with many other people for which maintenance is a problem, and within which there is little or no provision for anal cleaning and hand washing. It is common for a considerable proportion of low-income households in African cities to have no toilets within their home, as illustrated by the profiles of Accra and Kumasi in Box 2.3. In a low-income settlement in Nairobi (Mukuru village), before two public latrine blocks were constructed in 1996, there was only one latrine per 1000 persons (Wegelin-Schuringa and Kodo 1997). In a low-income settlement in Kumasi, Atoinsu, there are 360 persons per squat hole (Devas and Korboe 2000). In most Indian cities, a considerable proportion of low-income households have no provision for sanitation in their home, as illustrated by the profiles of Ahmedabad, Bangalore, Baroda and Visakhapatnam. A survey in Pune (India) found that in the worst served settlements, there was just one toilet stall per 2500 inhabitants (Shelter Associates 1999). Tenements, cheap boarding-houses or other forms of cheap rented accomodation often have the worst provision for sanitation or no provision. It is difficult to get landlords to invest in sanitation, especially where their tenants have very low incomes and the landlords' profits come from squeezing as many tenants as possible into rooms within shacks that required very little investment to build.

Households with no provision for individual or shared sanitation within their homes have only three possibilities – public toilets, defecation outside, or defecation into some container which is then thrown away (what in some cities is called 'wrap and throw' or 'flying toilets'). Provision for public toilets is often so inadequate (or non-existent) that large sections of the urban poor have to defecate outside or 'wrap and throw'. As shown in Boxes 2.1, 2.3 and 2.4, among the cities where open defecation is reported to be common are Accra, Addis Ababa, Ahmedabad, Bangalore, Cebu, Colombo, Dhaka, Kingston, Kumasi and Ouagadougou.

The extent to which low-income urban households have to rely on open defecation and the problems they face is probably best documented in India. Defecating in the street, park or some other open space is common practice since a significant proportion of the urban population has no latrine of any kind. For instance, in Ahmedabad, an estimated half a million people defecate in the open (Dutta 2000). In Delhi, a 1990 survey showed that the 480,000 families in 1100 'slum' settlements had access to only 160 toilet seats and 110 mobile toilet vans (Chaplin 1999). Studies in Indian cities other than those summarized in Box 2.1 have also shown that large sections of the population in other cities have to defecate in the open – for instance a United Nations (International) Children's (Emergency) Fund (UNICEF) survey of several Indian cities in 1995–1996 (UNICEF 1996). A survey across 141 Indian cities found that less than 40 per cent of the urban poor living in 'legal slum settlements' had access to toilets; the proportion lacking access to toilets is probably much higher in unauthorized/unrecognized illegal settlements (NIUA 1997).

Some consideration needs to be given to what it implies for a family to have to rely on open defecation. An article on India's urban areas discussed this. As it states, open spaces are becoming more scarce as cities grow and all available land is used for building. With no secluded open space available to them, those who have to rely on open defecation have to wait for darkness, especially girls and women, since there is less chance of attracting men. Even where communal toilets are available and of good quality, unless they are close by, many will not use them. As a study in one low-income settlement in Kanpur showed, many did not use a community toilet because mothers did not have time to accompany their children and young girls to use it, and they were also afraid to use it at night because of the distance (NIUA 1997). A study in Bangalore showed how women or girls often face particularly severe problems of harassment and risk of rape when they defecate outside.[9] Chapter 6 will include some examples of well-managed public toilets with washing facilities but these serve only a small proportion of the urban households who have no provision for sanitation in their homes.

There are also the costs of sanitation that have to be considered. The use of public toilets may be costly for low-income households; again in Kumasi, the fee for the use of a latrine may seem reasonable but based on a five-person household, with each person using the latrine only once a day, paying this fee can use up 10–15 per cent of the main income-earner's wages (Korboe and others 2000). In Accra, families have to pay the equivalent of several dollars a month for access to public toilets (see Box 2.3). Pit latrines are used by a large proportion of low-income households (and higher-income households in cities with very poor provision for sanitation). But pit latrines have to be emptied, and this can also be expensive, especially where it is difficult or impossible to get a vacuum truck or handcart close enough to do this work or where there is no efficient emptying service (Muller 1997, Kirango and Muller 1997).

Table 2.3 emphasizes how different aspects of improved water and sanitation influence the control of different water or excreta-related diseases. It also emphasizes how it is not only improved water quality that is important but also more regular and convenient supplies (so more is available to allow improved personal and domestic hygiene and food sanitation) plus provision for the disposal of excreta and waste water.

The scale of the problem for water and sanitation, and the inaccuracies and exaggerations within official statistics

Official statistics suggest that problems with the provision for water and sanitation in urban areas are less serious than that described above. For instance, statistics for 1994 suggested that only 300 million urban dwellers were not

---

9 See for instance Sanbergen (forthcoming), quoted in Benjamin and Bhuvaneshari 1999 which found that in a survey of 22 'slums', in 12, women face harassment, particularly from drunken men, in 15 they feel very uncomfortable and in 9, women feel it takes too long before they can reach open space.

Box 2.4 *EXAMPLES OF THE INADEQUACIES IN CITIES' WATER SUPPLY AND SANITATION IN LATIN AMERICA AND THE CARIBBEAN*

Brazilian cities. In general, there has been a large increase in the proportion of the urban population with piped water and adequate provision for sanitation. For the wealthier cities in the South and Southeast, by 1991 close to 90 per cent of the population in their metropolitan area had piped water (for São Paulo it was 96 per cent). Provision for sanitation was not so good – typically between a fifth and a third of the population of most cities still had inadequate sanitation in 1991. The proportion of populations adequately served was less in the poorer cities of the North and Northeast – for instance more than a quarter of the population of Belem, Fortaleza and Salvador lacked piped water connections in 1991 while between a half and a third had inadequate sanitation (census data quoted in Mueller 1995).

Cochabamba (Bolivia). Only 60 per cent of the urban area and 53 per cent of the population are connected to water systems either inside or outside the home and only 23 per cent of those connected receive a 24-hour supply of water. The water network provided by SEMAPA (Servicio Municipal de Agua Potable y Alcantarillado) has not been able to keep up with the growth of the city, and it is estimated that 100,000 people are not connected to the system. Industrial, commercial and wealthier residential areas have the highest rates of connection – reaching 99 per cent in Casco Viejo. Yet half the homes in Cochabamba are located in the northern and southern suburbs, and in some districts in these areas, 1992 data indicate that less than 4 per cent of homes had potable water connections; 18 per cent had access to water outside the house; and 80–90 per cent obtained water supplies from cistern trucks. Only 46 per cent of the population have a connection to a sewerage network. There is insufficient water provision to meet existing levels of demand (Marvin and Laurie 1999).

Guayaquil (Ecuador). Of a population of 1.6 million dwellers 35 per cent do not have access to adequate and reliable water supplies and the whole city suffers from chronic and absolute water shortages. The sewerage system is on the verge of collapse. Approximately 400 tankers service 35 per cent of the total urban population; these water merchants buy the water at a highly subsidized price and can charge up to 400 times the price per litre paid by consumers who receive water from the public water utility. There is sufficient supply available to be able to reach each inhabitant with an average daily consumption of 220 litres. Compared with the internationally accepted standard of 150 litres per person per day, Guayaquil is in the position to provide every citizen with a sufficient supply of potable water. The problem is thus clearly one of distribution (Swyngedouw 1995).

Kingston (Jamaica). Official estimates suggest that 35–40 per cent of the population in Kingston Metropolitan Area are served by sewers. Other estimates suggest that only 18 per cent are served by sewers with 27 per cent having soak-away pits, 47 per cent using pit latrines and 8 per cent with no facilities at all. The sewers in the inner city are very old, and often blocked (Robotham 1994). 'A significant percentage of the Kingston Metropolitan Area population, especially in low-income communities, defecate in open lots, in abandoned buildings or in plastic shopping bags which are then thrown into gully courses to be washed down into the city' (ibid page 39).

Mexico City. In 1990, 36 per cent of households in the Mexico City Metropolitan Area still lacked water piped into their homes; the proportion lacking this had fallen very little since 1970, although the proportion having access to a piped water source outside their home increased substantially. In some of the poorer districts, most houses were without water piped into them (National Census Data 1990, quoted in Connolly 1999).

Montego Bay (Jamaica). Over 90 per cent of households have access to good quality piped water for drinking but in informal settlements, a much smaller percentage have connections to their house. Two-thirds of the population (many in informal settlements) rely on pit latrines or septic tank systems or have no sanitation. The densest settlements often have only a few pit latrines to serve residents. Pit latrines are often little more than holes in the ground about 1–1.5 metres deep. Possibly 5 or even 10 per cent of those living in informal settlements put their faeces in plastic bags and throw these into nearby gullies or bushes (Ferguson 1996).

Port-au-Prince (Haiti). Although local groundwater around Port-au-Prince is more than sufficient to supply all 2 million of the city residents with water, only 10 per cent of families have water connections in the home. The public water service, CAMEP, is heavily in debt and has stopped maintaining many of the city's public water taps. A vast clandestine system of water distribution has sprung up to meet the needs of 90 per cent of the city's population. The operators of this system rely on private wells and distribution trucks that provide water to private tank owners. The tank owners then sell small amounts of water to individuals and families at prices that range from US$3–$5 per cubic metre, compared with 50 cents per cubic metre that CAMEP bills its customers. Residents in 'slums' not only paid the highest prices for water, they also carried it for long distances in areas with no paved roads (Constance 1999).

Santo Domingo de los Colorados (Ecuador). About 70 per cent of the water entering the supply system is tapped illegally (compared with 30–40 per cent for most South American cities). Approximately 60–80 per cent of households receive running water, but only for a few hours a day (Ferguson and Maurer 1996).

Table 2.3 *The relative importance of different interventions related to water and sanitation for the prevention or control of different diseases*

Disease	Water quality	Water quantity or convenience	Personal and domestic hygiene	Waste water disposal or drainage	Excreta disposal	Food sanitation
Diarrhoea						
a) Viral diarrhoea	medium	high	high	–	medium	medium
b) Bacterial diarrhoea	high	high	high	–	medium	high
c) Protozoal diarrhoea	low	high	high	–	medium	medium
Poliomyelitis and hepatitis A	low	high	high	–	medium	medium
Worm infections						
a) Ascaris, trichuris	low	low	low	low	high	medium
b) Hookworm	low	low	low	–	high	–
c) Pinworm, dwarf tapeworm	–	high	high	–	medium	low
d) Other tapeworms	–	low	low	–	high	high
e) Schistosomiasis	low	low	–	low	high	–
f) Guinea-worm	high	–	–	–	–	–
g) Other worms with aquatic hosts	–	–	–	–	medium	high
Skin infections	–	high	high	–	–	–
Eye infections	low	high	high	low	low	–
Insect transmitted						
a) Malaria	–	–	–	low	–	–
b) Urban yellow fever, dengue	–	–	low*	medium	–	–
c) Bancroftian filariasis	–	–	–	high	high	–
d) Onchocerciasis	–	–	–	–	–	–

The degree of importance of each intervention for each particular disease is ranked as 'high', 'medium' and 'low'; a dash means that it has negligible importance.

* Vectors breed on water-storage containers.
Source: WHO (1983) *Maximizing Benefits to Health: An Appraisal Methodology for Water Supply and Sanitation Projects,* unpublished WHO Report ETS/83.7, WHO, Geneva, quoted in WHO (1986), *Intersectoral Action for Health – The Role of Intersectoral Cooperation in National Strategies for Health for All,* Background Document for the Technical Discussions, 39th World Health Assembly, May, Geneva, page 104.

served by water supplies for Africa, Asia, Latin America and the Caribbean (WHO/UNICEF 1994), which implies that 80 per cent of the urban population was served. The United Nations Development Programme's (UNDP) Human Development Report 1996 states that by the early 1990s, 87 per cent of the urban population of 'developing countries' had access to 'safe' water and 72 per cent had access to sanitation (UNDP 1996). This same source also included a table, showing that a considerable proportion of low- and middle-income countries had 80–95 per cent of their urban populations adequately served both by safe water and sanitation (see Table 2.4). It even suggested that

63 per cent of sub-Saharan Africa's urban population had safe water and that 56 per cent had provision for sanitation.

Official statistics also suggest that there has been considerable progress in improving provision, especially for water, and that urban inhabitants are far better served than rural inhabitants. Although there has been great progress in some countries (and particular cities) in improving provision and there are some cities in Latin America and Asia where virtually all households have water piped into their home, unfortunately, official statistics greatly overstate the extent and quality of provision.

There are two main reasons why they do this. The first is the use of inappropriate criteria to define what is 'adequate'. The second is that governments provide inaccurate statistics and it is difficult for international agencies who publish these statistics to question their accuracy. International agencies such as the World Bank, the WHO or the UNDP are 'intergovernmental bodies' with governing boards made up of representatives of national governments. This makes it difficult (or impossible) for them to publicly question the validity of what their member governments say. It was staff from the WHO who alerted us to the inaccuracies in the water and sanitation statistics that their member governments supplied to them.

With regard to the criteria used for assessing provision, for a water supply to be 'adequate', it must be of good quality, readily available, piped to the house (or at least very close-by) and affordable. But official statistics of people 'adequately' served often include all households with access to public standpipes (or with some form of water supply infrastructure within 100 metres of their home). So among those classified as 'adequately served' are the inhabitants of settlements where hundreds of people have to share each standpipe. They remain classified as adequately served, even if the public standpipes are poorly maintained (and contain contaminated water). They are still classified as served by piped systems, even if water is only available in the piped system intermittently. For instance, no doubt the households in Mombasa who have water pipes to their homes but who have seen no water in these pipes for years (Rakodi and others 2000) are still classified as adequately served. So are the many households who only get water through their pipes for one or two hours a day, or even only once a week or fortnight, as highlighted earlier.

Perhaps the strongest evidence for the inaccuracies in official statistics comes from comparing official statistics for provision in urban areas with data from detailed city studies such as those summarized in Boxes 2.1–2.4. Table 2.4 has figures for the proportion of some nations' urban populations apparently having access to safe water and access to sanitation drawn from the UNDP's *Human Development Report 1996* and the World Bank's *World Development Indicators 2000*. According to the UNDP Report, 99 per cent of the urban population of Zimbabwe and Bangladesh had safe water by the early 1990s; for Pakistan, it was 96 per cent, for India 85 per cent, for the Philippines 93 per cent. The World Bank's *World Indicators 2000* suggests more modest figures for urban Bangladesh and Pakistan but gives similar figures for Zimbabwe, the Philippines and India. Both publications also suggest that many African nations other than Zimbabwe have urban populations that are relatively well served, as can be seen in Table 2.4.

Table 2.4 *The proportion of the urban population apparently having 'access to safe water' and 'access to sanitation' in selected countries, latest available estimate, 1990–1996*

Country	Statistics from the UNDP Human Development Report 1996		Statistics from the World Bank's World Development Indicators 2000	
	% of urban population with access to safe water	*% of urban population with access to sanitation*	*% of urban population with access to safe water*	*% of urban population with access to sanitation*
Bangladesh	99	75	47	77
Burkina Faso	na	42		78
Ethiopia	91	97	90	na
Ghana	70	53	70	53
India	85	70	85	46
Indonesia	79	73	78	73
Jamaica	na	100	92	89
Nigeria	63	40	63	61
Pakistan	96	62	77	53
Philippines	93	79	91	88
Sudan	84	79	66	79
Tanzania	67	74	65	97
Uganda	47	94	47	75
Zimbabwe	99	99	99	99

Note: The World Bank figures are said to be the most recent year available in the period 1990–1996.

It is difficult to reconcile the figures for India in Table 2.4 with the profiles of the provision for water and sanitation in Box 2.1 which covers Ahmedabad, Bangalore, Baroda, Calcutta, Madras/Chennai and Visakhapatnam. Detailed statistics for many other cities in India show that much less than 85 per cent of their population is adequately served with 'safe water' and much less than 70 per cent has adequate sanitation (UNICEF 1996). To prove beyond any doubt that the national statistics were wrong would require detailed profiles of provision for water and sanitation in many other urban areas since India has over 4000 urban centres. Most of the water and sanitation profiles in Box 2.1 are for relatively large cities. The proportion of India's total urban population that is adequately served would be boosted if provision was much better in smaller urban centres, but it is difficult to believe that provision is better in smaller and less well-known cities than in the larger, more successful and more politically powerful cities, and where statistics are available for smaller urban centres, these generally show very inadequate provision. Similarly, it is difficult to reconcile the official statistic of 96 per cent of Pakistan's urban population with safe water in the UNDP Report (or the lower figure of 77 per cent in the World Bank report) with the description of water provision for Karachi and Faisalabad in Box 2.1 since these two cities contain a sizeable chunk of Pakistan's total urban population. Again, provision for water and sanitation may be much better in Pakistan's many other urban centres, but this is unlikely. It is difficult to see how 70 per cent for Ghana's urban population can have had access to safe water in the early 1990s if the descriptions of water provision in Kumasi and Accra in Box 2.3 are accurate.

One particular example of false statistics comes from Kumasi, Ghana's second largest city. The official figures for Kumasi suggest that 99 per cent of the population are adequately served with water.[10] It is difficult to reconcile this with a recent report on Kumasi which states that although three-quarters of the population are served with piped water, large numbers only have access through shared taps or standpipes and long waits and queues are common. Even where there is a piped network in an area, water pressure is often inadequate and the service not continuous. The report also notes that only 10 per cent of households have indoor plumbing and that water provision is particularly poor on the urban periphery where there is rapid urban growth (Korboe and others 2000).

Thus, it is certain that tens of millions (and perhaps hundreds of millions) of urban dwellers classified in official statistics as having 'safe water' still face great difficulties in obtaining clean water and sufficient water for good health.

A comparable gap between reality and official statistics is also evident for sanitation. Official statistics suggest that by 1994, more than half the urban population in Africa had adequate provision for sanitation, as did two-thirds of the population of Asia and close to three-quarters of the urban population of Latin America and the Caribbean (WHO/UNICEF 1994). To return to the statistics in the UNDP's *Human Development Report 1996*, how can Jamaica be said to have had 100 per cent of its urban population with sanitation by the early 1990s when a report on Kingston, Jamaica's largest city, suggests that only 18 per cent of the population are connected to sewers, with 27 per cent having soak-away pits, 47 per cent using pit latrines and 8 per cent reporting no sanitary facilities at all and a report on Montego Bay, the second largest city (Ferguson 1996), reveals that provision for sanitation is even worse and again a significant proportion of the population 'wrap and throw' their faeces (see Box 2.4 for more details)? One also wonders whether the provision for sanitation was really so good by the early 1990s in Zimbabwe (99 per cent of its urban population with sanitation), Uganda (94 per cent) and Ethiopia (97 per cent). Recent studies of the provision for sanitation (and water) in particular settlements within Harare (Zimbabwe's capital and largest city) or among particular urban poor groups suggest that far more than 1 per cent of the nation's urban population lack safe water and provision for sanitation (see Mupedziswa and Gumbo 1998, and Henderson 2000).

Many of the sanitation statistics in the World Bank's *Environmental Indicators 2000* are the same as those in the UNDP report – for instance it also lists Zimbabwe as having 99 per cent of its urban population with sanitation and the Sudan as having 79 per cent. In some countries, it suggests higher levels of coverage for the early 1990s than the UNDP report – for instance 97 per cent of Tanzania's urban population and 88 per cent of the Philippines' urban

---

10 Living standards survey quoted in Devas and Korboe 2000.

population is said to have had access to sanitation by the early 1990s. This statistic for Tanzania obviously assumes that access to pit latrines represents access to sanitation. But reports on the provision for sanitation in Dar es Salaam (see Box 2.3) which contains a considerable proportion of the whole country's urban population hardly suggests that these provide effective sanitation. This statistic for the Philippines cannot be reconciled with reports on the provision for sanitation in Manila and Cebu, and it is unlikely that most other urban centres in the Philippines have much better provision than these two cities – one the national capital, the other the most economically successful of the nation's major cities.

One possible reason why official statistics exaggerate the extent of provision for sanitation is because they classify any household that in the census or any other household survey is said to have access to a latrine as having 'access to sanitation'. In many cities, official statistics for the proportion of inhabitants having access to sanitation must include the people who have to rely on public latrines. Thus, they include those who have to compete with 100 or more other people for access to each latrine and where the maintenance and cleaning of public latrines is so poor that using the latrine itself is a major health hazard and many people avoid using it. For instance, it is likely that the 40 per cent of Kumasi's population that are served so inadequately by public latrines (see Box 2.3) are officially classified as served with sanitation, even if many defecate in the open because they cannot afford the wait or the fee or they avoid the use of such poorly maintained facilities. It may also be that many households with very inadequate facilities in their home – for instance a poorly maintained, overflowing pit latrine – are said to have access to sanitation. This is not to say that pit latrines are necessarily inadequate; in locations with suitable ground conditions, on sites that do not flood and when well designed and maintained, they can provide 'adequate sanitation'. Where house plot sizes are not large enough to allow new pits to be dug, when the existing pit is full, there also needs to be good provision to empty them (and an easily available service to do so). One survey in Kumasi found that many householders preferred improved pit latrines to WCs, because they did not use water and some were concerned about higher water bills or were worried about the fact that a WC would not function if the water system broke down (Whittington and Lauria 1990).

Thus, there are strong grounds for doubting the accuracy of official statistics on the provision for sanitation in urban areas, as well as for water. If our concern is to significantly reduce the health burden associated with the inadequate provision for water and sanitation, then the criteria used by governments and international agencies as to 'what is adequate' needs to be changed. There are some studies on which this can draw – for instance a study of the association between health and provision for water and sanitation in Betim (Brazil) which emphasized how it was not only the availability of water and sanitation infrastructure that influenced health but also water quality, per capita consumption, regularity of supply, extent of indoor plumbing and provision for drainage (Heller 1999). There are some moves in this direction, as in the arrangements made for the latest global assessment of water and sanitation (see Box 2.5).

Box 2.5 *The Year 2000 Global Assessment of Water and Sanitation*

The WHO/UNICEF Joint Monitoring Programme (JMP) of water supply and sanitation is in the process of completing the Year 2000 Global Assessment. This follows on from previous JMP reports by providing national, regional and global water supply and sanitation coverage figures. This JMP differs considerably in its approach to those of previous years in that the data are primarily from consumer-based sources, largely from household surveys. For the first time there has been a move away from accepting 'official' government figures, towards the use of nationally representative sample surveys.

There are still many difficulties involved in this approach, such as:

- the use of definitions that vary widely across both time and space;
- the fact that many countries do not have either household survey data or recent census data, leaving the traditionally used provider-based data as the main source of information;
- the nature of survey data collection means definition is based on technology type alone from which adequacy is inferred – eg in-house piped water supply as a technology tells us nothing of the quality of the service such as how many hours a day water is available;
- although the sample surveys used (including Demographic and Health Surveys and UNICEF's Multiple Cluster Survey) are designed to be nationally representative, it is questionable whether they really do represent the poorest people within a country. This will depend in part on the sampling frame used and if it includes people in informal settlements for instance.

Despite these problems, the Assessment is an improvement on previous monitoring at this level in the sector. It has also found some surprising results. Sanitation for instance, has been found to be higher than expected. This suggests that many households have provided their own sanitation that has not been identified within the traditional provider-based monitoring. The Year 2000 Global Assessment Report is due to be published jointly by the WHO and UNICEF in November 2000. Beyond the report, the WHO and UNICEF are planning to set up a joint website on which all of the national data reported (including detailed breakdowns of technology and source of information) will be shown. This should ensure the continued discussion and improvement of national level water supply and sanitation coverage data.

Source: Caroline Hunt, London School of Hygiene and Tropical Medicine, personal communication.

There also needs to be more possibilities for questioning the accuracy of official statistics. The inaccuracy of official statistics on urban provision also means that the 'rural–urban' comparisons so often given by international agencies (as in the table noted above from the *Human Development Report 1996* which is called 'rural–urban gaps') should be questioned. Data on the provision for water and sanitation in urban and rural areas is often used as evidence of urban bias in government investments since official statistics generally show that a higher proportion of urban populations are served than rural populations. If official statistics greatly overstate the extent of the provision for urban populations, the extent of these gaps may be much less. In addition, among both rural and urban populations that lack provision for sanitation, urban populations may face a significantly higher health burden because higher densities and larger populations make it more difficult to dispose of excreta and waste water in ways that ensure no possibility of human contact, and it is also more difficult to safeguard local water sources from contamination. Urban populations may face much greater difficulties than rural households in getting access to a communal standpipe 50 metres from their home because there are far more people competing with them for access. Urban households are less likely to be able to access safe water sources or latrines free. Defecation in the open may be less problematic in rural areas, as places are available for open defecation that limit the risk of human contact with the excreta and that pose less threat of harassment to women as they defecate. Urban populations may be more willing and able to pay for improved provision, in part because many have higher monetary incomes, and in part because of the large direct and indirect costs of inadequate provision, in part because efficient water and sanitation providers can use economies of scale in provision to bring down the costs of individual house connections. But the discussion of priorities for water and sanitation should not turn into a fight between rural and urban proponents (as it often does). It is clear that the provision for water and sanitation is also very inadequate for large sections of the rural population. It may be that official statistics for rural areas also exaggerate the quality and extent of provision. What needs to be recognized are key differences in rural and urban contexts and thus in the forms of provision for water and sanitation that best meet people's needs while minimizing the health risks.

Overcrowding

Another characteristic that is common to most of the homes of low-income groups in cities is crowded, cramped conditions. Many health problems affecting poorer groups are associated with overcrowding, including household accidents, acute respiratory infections (of which pneumonia is perhaps the most serious), tuberculosis and other airborne infections (WHO 1992a). In the predominantly low-income residential areas in cities, there is often an average of four or more persons per room and in some instances less than 1 square metre of floor space per person.[11] Diseases such as tuberculosis, influenza and

---

11 For detailed examples, see Aina 1989 and Murphy 1990.

meningitis are easily transmitted from one person to another. Their spread is often aided by low resistance among the inhabitants due to malnutrition and by frequent contact between infective and susceptible people.

Acute bacterial and viral respiratory infections account, with tuberculosis, for some 5 million deaths annually; tuberculosis is responsible for more than half of these deaths (WHO 1992a). Box 2.6 describes the impact of tuberculosis on health and its association with housing. A child who contracts bronchitis or pneumonia in low- and middle-income nations is 50 times more likely to die than a child in Europe or North America (Pio 1986). A WHO report summarized the problem:

> *Acute respiratory infections tend to be endemic rather than epidemic, affect younger groups, and more prevalent in urban than in rural areas. The frequency of contact, the density of the population and the concentration and proximity of infective and susceptible people in an urban population promote the transmission of the infective organisms. Poorer groups ... are much more at risk because of the greater proportion of younger age groups, limited health and financial resources, and over-crowded households in congested settlements with limited access to vaccines and antibacterial drugs* (WHO 1992a, page 204).

Acute respiratory infections were responsible for some 3.5 million deaths in 1998, more than half of these being children under five. Pneumonia kills more children than any other infectious disease and 99 per cent of these deaths occurred in low- and middle-income nations. Most of the health burden from acute respiratory infections is linked to environmental factors such as chilling, overcrowding and indoor air pollution (WHO 1999).

The vaccine-preventable 'childhood' diseases such as measles, diphtheria and whooping cough also spread more rapidly in overcrowded urban areas. While measles holds few worries for children in richer households, among low-income households it is often one of the most common causes or contributory factors to infant and child death. Meningococcal meningitis is another airborne infection whose transmission is partly due to overcrowding (WHO 1992a). Overcrowding increases the risk of transmission for these and for other infectious diseases; it also increases the risk of multiple infections, the risk of infection early in life (when immune systems are still immature) and the risk of severe infection (UNCHS 1995). However, overcrowding will have less significance as a risk factor where the population (especially children) are protected by immunization programmes and by healthcare services that provide rapid and appropriate treatment for acute respiratory infections.

Few studies have sought to isolate the health impacts of overcrowding. A study in the city of Bissau (Guinea Bissau) found that many persons per bed and many children under five within a family were among a range of risk factors for childhood mortality while in a low-income settlement in Jakarta, persons per room and the number of children under five per room were significant factors for diarrhoea and respiratory diseases (UNCHS 1995).

BOX 2.6 *THE IMPACT OF TUBERCULOSIS ON HEALTH AND ITS ASSOCIATION WITH HOUSING*

About 20 million people worldwide have active cases of pulmonary tuberculosis, a contagious chronic disease of the lungs caused by a bacterium transmitted through the air when infected people cough or sneeze. If untreated, the fatality rate is close to 50 per cent, mostly among young adults. Around 2 million people die each year from tuberculosis (TB), more than from any other infectious disease, and it is the world's single largest cause of adult death. Virtually all these deaths are in low- and middle-income nations, over 60 per cent of them in Asia and over 20 per cent in Africa. Of the very small proportion of all deaths from TB that occur in high-income nations, most occur among the elderly, ethnic minorities and immigrants.

Each year, there are 8 million new cases of TB, 4 million of which are infectious. Countries with the largest number of TB cases are Bangladesh, Brazil, China, India, Indonesia, Nigeria, Pakistan, the Philippines and Vietnam. Sub-Saharan African countries tend to have the highest proportion of their population infected.

One of the main reasons for the rapid increase in the number of TB cases in many nations is the spread of infection with the human immunodeficiency virus (HIV); when people infected with TB are also infected with HIV, TB is likely to become more active. The time it takes for HIV to develop into AIDS is shortened dramatically in people with TB. Around 30 per cent of all AIDS deaths result directly from TB and by 2000, HIV infection is estimated to cause an additional 1.5 million cases of TB annually.

Household members living with an infectious case are at greatest risk. The high incidence of TB tends to be among populations living in the poorest areas where families are usually large, housing inadequate and overcrowded, nutrition levels low and health care limited or unavailable. Household, social or work contacts are at greatest risk from infection as the number of infective cases increases; high population densities also accelerate transmission rates. Overcrowded housing conditions and poor ventilation often means that TB infection is transmitted to more than half of family members.

Source: WHO (1992), *Our Planet, Our Health*, Report of the WHO Commission on Health and Environment, World Health Organization, Geneva, 282 pages; WHO (1999), 'Creating healthy cities in the 21st Century,' Chapter 6 in David Satterthwaite (editor), *The Earthscan Reader on Sustainable Cities*, Earthscan Publications, London, pages 137–172.

Food-borne or food-related diseases

There are many opportunities for food contamination during food preparation and storage within overcrowded, poor quality domestic environments (Bryan 1992, quoted in Birley and Lock 1998). Most diarrhoeal diseases and many other water-borne diseases (including cholera and hepatitis A) can be transmitted by food as well as water. Contaminated or undercooked food are also the cause of some of the most widespread intestinal worms such as ascariasis (roundworm), trichinosis (whipworm) and taeniasis (beef and pork tapeworm). Crowded cramped conditions, inadequate water supplies and inadequate facilities for preparing and storing food greatly exacerbate the risk of food contamination:

> ... *microbially contaminated food contributes to a high incidence of acute diarrhoea in Third World countries and food borne diseases including cholera, botulism, typhoid fever and parasitism ... microbial activity generally contributes to food spoilage while unsafe chemicals may deliberately be added to retard or disguise spoilage ... food contamination is intimately linked to the sanitary conditions of food preparation, processing and even production* (McGranahan 1991, page 24).

In addition, bacterial multiplication is extremely rapid in warmer climates, making the risk of contamination and spoilage all the greater, especially for households lacking a refrigerator (ibid).

Within poor quality housing that lacks basic infrastructure, it is difficult to separate out the health impact of inadequate water, inadequate sanitation, inadequate refuse collection and inadequate facilities to safely prepare, cook and store food. There are numerous interconnections and interactions within the home among water, sanitation, flies, animals, personal hygiene and food that are responsible for diarrhoea transmission (Esrey and Feachem 1989). For instance, one important source of food contamination is inadequate hand-washing after defecation which in turn is linked to inadequate water supplies. One reason for the lack of success in achieving declines in morbidity from acute infant diarrhoea is the inadequate attention given to improving food safety, which for infants is linked to contaminated complementary foods (Kaferstein 1997).

Many environment-related diseases are significant contributors to under-nutrition, including intestinal worm infections and diarrhoeal diseases. Micro-nutrient deficiencies in food supplies for particular regions are also a serious and widespread problem – for instance iodine and vitamin A deficiencies have a very large health impact each year. However, while the immediate cause of many micro-nutrient deficiencies may be environmental, these often can be addressed by ensuring a greater intake by the population – for instance through supplying iodized salt and vitamin A capsules or promoting dietary modifications – and the cost of doing so is generally very low.

Accidents in the home

Accidents within the home are among the most serious causes of injury and accidental death in most urban areas (WHO 1991). Their health impact is particularly large in cities or city districts where a high proportion of the population live in overcrowded housing – for instance where it is common for people to live in accommodation with three or more persons to each room in a shelter made from temporary (and inflammable) materials with open fires or stoves used for cooking, and (where needed) heating and candles or kerosene/paraffin lamps used for lighting. It is almost impossible to protect occupants (especially young children) from burns and scalds in such circumstances. However, there has been relatively little research on this. A study in 1986 found that accidents were one of the five leading causes of death in an analysis of the causes of mortality in ten nations (Manciaux and Romer 1986). A study of injuries in urban squatter settlements in Karachi found that most severe injuries were due to falls, burns and cuts; falls mostly affected pedestrians while many of the cuts and burns were suffered by women who were cooking (Rabbani 1999).

One paper looking at fuel use in informal settlements in Cape Town (South Africa) provides an insight into the hazards associated with the use of paraffin for heating, cooking and lighting (Mehlwana 1999). It suggested that burns resulting from the use of domestic energy sources (mainly paraffin) are one of the main causes of injury and mortality for those under the age of 14. It also highlights the very large social and material costs that fires bring for low-income groups. In one settlement (Joe Slovo), seven major fires were recorded between March 1996 and January 1997 in which 153 shacks were burned and 498 people displaced (South African Red Cross Society, quoted in Mehlwana 1999). The causes of the fires were thought to be faulty paraffin stoves and candles overturning. Civic committees in these kinds of settlements have tried to lessen the risk of fires by for instance banning the use of candles and requiring that persons found guilty of causing fires have to pay for the damage, however, this often leads to harsh punishments, high costs or even eviction for persons blamed for causing fires.

Overcrowded conditions also increase the risk of accidental poisonings as it is so difficult to prevent children from coming into contact with harmful chemicals used in the household (for instance bleach or kerosene) or to keep medicines in a secure place when whole families live in one or two rooms. The health impact of accidents is much increased by a lack of a healthcare service, especially one that can provide rapid responses to emergencies outside of the health clinic's opening times, followed by longer-term treatment and care (WHO 1991). Tetanus remains a major health problem, as tetanus spores enter the human body through a cut or wound, but this can be addressed by immunization.

Indoor air pollution

The health impacts of indoor air pollution for those households who use open fires or stoves indoors for cooking and/or heating with inadequate venting for the smoke and fumes have probably been much underestimated (WHO 1992a). The smoke or fumes from burning coal, wood or other biomass fuels can cause or contribute to serious respiratory and eye problems. The (limited) research on indoor air pollution from biomass fuels suggests that concentrations of total suspended particulates are 10 to 100 times higher than the typical health-related standards (Saksensa and Smith 1999). Chronic effects include inflammation of the respiratory tract which in turn reduces resistance to acute respiratory infections, while these infections in turn enhance susceptibility to the inflammatory effects of smoke and fumes (WHO 1992a). Exposure to carcinogens in emissions from biomass fuel combustion has been confirmed in studies in which exposed subjects wore personal monitoring equipment. Women who may spend two to four hours a day at the stove must be at risk. Infants and children may be heavily exposed because they remain with their mothers; the added exposure to pollutants combined with malnutrition may retard growth, leading to smaller lungs and greater prevalence of chronic bronchitis (ibid). In South Asia, indoor air pollution from solid fuels burned in open stoves probably accounts for a larger total exposure than outdoor sources (Smith and Akbar 1999).

This is a problem that is generally concentrated among low-income households, since higher-income households generally choose fuels that generate less indoor air pollution (such as kerosene), much less indoor air pollution (natural gas) or virtually no indoor air pollution (electricity). This has been described as an 'energy ladder' as low-income households use dung, crop residues and wood while those with higher incomes use kerosene and those with the highest incomes use natural gas or electricity (Smith and others 1994). If a low-income household's income rises, they will generally move up the 'energy ladder' to cleaner fuels but changes in income or availability of other resources may force them back down it (Smith 1990).

THE WORKPLACE

Environmental hazards arising in the workplace are also a major problem and are evident in workplaces from large factories and commercial institutions down to small 'backstreet' workshops and people working from home. They include dangerous concentrations of toxic chemicals and dust, inadequate lighting, ventilation and space, and lack of protection for workers from machinery and noise. One global estimate suggests that there are 32.7 million occupational injuries each year with about 146,000 deaths (WHO 1990). Environmental hazards in the workplace are made all the more serious by the lack of social security; there is little or no provision by most employers for sick pay or compensation if workers are injured or laid off. Many industries have long been associated with high levels of risk for their workforce from toxic chemicals – for instance in factories extracting, processing and milling asbestos, chemical industries, cement, glass and ceramics industries, iron and steel industries, factories making rubber and plastics products, metal and non-ferrous metal industries and textile and leather industries (WHO 1992b). Some of the most common environment-related occupational diseases are silicosis, byssinosis, lead and mercury poisoning, pesticide poisoning, noise-induced hearing loss and occupational skin diseases (WHO 1990).

Various case studies show how a high proportion of the workers in particular industries or industrial plants have serious health problems from workplace exposures. For instance, a study of Egyptian pesticide factories found that 'about 40 per cent of the workers had problems related to pesticide poisoning, ranging from asthma to enlarged livers' (Pepall 1992). In most countries, the scale of occupational injuries and diseases is almost certainly greatly under-reported. For instance, the Mexican Social Security Institute reported an average of 2000–3000 cases of work-related illnesses across the country in 1988 but a study in just one large steel mill found 4000–5000 cases alone, with more than 80 per cent of the workers exposed to extreme heat, noise and toxic dust (Castonguay 1992). A paper on Bangkok's environmental problems noted that a remarkable number of Thai workers are exposed to poor working environments but that the number of workers suffering from occupational diseases appeared small. However, this may simply reflect the difficulties of linking disease to working conditions rather than revealing a satisfactory condi-tion (Phantumvanit and Liengcharernsit 1989). This point has wider relevance since people's long-term exposure to dust, excessive noise, inadequate lighting and pollutants in the workplace often contributes much to ill-health, disable-ment and premature death, but it is difficult to prove the link, if compensation is being sought. There are many examples of industrial workers being killed or permanently injured by chemicals they handle or inhale at work (see for instance Centre for Science and Environment 1985) but the health impacts that take longer to become apparent are more worrying in that these affect such a large number of industrial workers.

There is also an increasing number of studies documenting serious health problems from environmental hazards in small workshops. One example is the informal enterprises in Jamaica that recycle and repair lead-acid batteries, result-ing in the exposure of both workers and the wider public to lead (Matte and others 1989). Many people working in informal enterprises use chemicals that should only be used under carefully controlled conditions with special safety equipment. One example is the rise in leukaemia among leather workers in Turkey after the introduction of a cheaper benzene-containing glue in making leather goods; over 50 deaths were documented and many thousands of leather workers were put at risk (Aksoy and others 1976). The number of occupational health hazards found in small-scale industries has probably been underesti-mated. In many countries, small-scale enterprises are legally exempt from labour regulations including health and safety (Barten and others 1998). In addition, occupational and environmental health problems of workers are often particu-larly serious in the informal sector (ibid). One example of this is the serious occupational health problems within the lead-battery breaking and lead-smelt-ing units in Calcutta (Dasgupta 1997).

A review of occupational health issues in Latin America, after listing many examples of serious health problems affecting high proportions of the workforce of particular industries, commented that:

> Few health standards are applied to limit work-place exposures; in most of the region's countries, the standard-setting process is either just beginning or has not yet begun. In those nations where standards regulating work practices or toxic exposure do exist, the standards are often not enforced, either for political or economic reasons or because of a lack of trained inspectors (Michaels and others 1985, page 538).

It is also appropriate to consider environmental problems associated with work in 'the home' in that many poor city-dwellers use their homes as a workshop to produce goods for sale or as a store for goods sold on the street, or as a shop, bar or café. Environmental problems here are too diverse to be covered in a short summary, but briefly, there are often problems with levels of light and ventilation, as well as major problems arising from the use of toxic or flammable chemicals in the home as part of the work done there. One common way in which this happens is through outworking; here, well-organized (and often large) enterprises commission people (usually women) working in their homes to fabricate some product – for instance, sandals or articles of clothing. These enterprises will often supply the outworkers with raw materials and chemicals and collect the finished articles. Many of these chemicals are a serious fire hazard and should be used in carefully controlled conditions in factories with special provisions to limit inhalation or skin contact and to guard against fire hazards. The advantages of such home-workers to the enterprise are obvious: low wages, no costs involved in building and running factories, no costs for social security and few problems with labour unrest since the workforce is too scattered to allow them to organize.

Certain groups are particularly at risk from occupational hazards, especially working children, as described in Chapter 4.

THE NEIGHBOURHOOD ENVIRONMENT

Added to health risks associated with the presence of toxic substances or pathogens inside the home are those that arise from the sites on which many poorer households live. The two are not easily separated since deficiencies in environmental protection in one will impact on the other. For example a lack of sewers to remove excreta and waste water from each house results in open drains which then present hazards for the whole neighbourhood. But four problems are worth emphasizing within the neighbourhood environment – dangerous sites, no collection of household refuse, disease vectors, and inadequate provision for drainage and other forms of infrastructure.

House sites

Tens of millions of urban inhabitants in Africa, Asia and Latin America live on hazardous land sites, either because of natural hazards or risks from human activities, or a combination of the two. It is easy to see which areas are at risk from natural hazards in most cities – for instance, the clusters of illegal housing on steep hillsides, flood-plains or desert land. Large concentrations of poor settlements can be seen on hills prone to landslides in Rio de Janeiro (Brazil), La Paz (Bolivia) and Caracas (Venezuela); or in deep ravines (Guatemala City); or in sandy desert as in Lima (Peru) and Khartoum (the Sudan); or on land prone to flooding or tidal inundation or under water as in Guayaquil (Ecuador), Recife (Brazil), Monrovia (Liberia), Lagos and Port Harcourt (Nigeria), Port Moresby (Papua New Guinea), Delhi (India), Bangkok (Thailand), Jakarta (Indonesia), Buenos Aires and Resistencia (Argentina), Accra (Ghana) and many others.

Densely populated residential areas also develop on sites that, as a result of human actions, are hazardous – for instance around solid-waste dumps, beside open drains and open sewers or close to quarries or particular factories with high levels of air pollution. Many settlements with a high proportion of low-income households develop on sites subject to high noise levels, close to major highways or airports.

Children and youth are particularly at risk, because of the lack of provision for the public space and facilities they need for play, sport and social life. Roads, rubbish tips and other hazardous places become their playgrounds, in the absence of any better alternative. They are particularly at risk from road vehicles, pathogens or toxic substances – from the problems of (say) contracting diarrhoea because their hands become contaminated with the faecal matter that contaminates the land on which they play (with food that they handle and eat with dirty hands causing its ingestion) to coming into contact with some toxic chemical in a nearby stream or dumped on a land site nearby to being hit by a motor vehicle. Arif Hasan's recent book on *Understanding Karachi* (Hasan 1999) provides an illustration of how provision for public space is eroded in low-income city districts, as no public policy ensures the provision or protection of such space. The book describes how government land set aside for parks, playgrounds, educational institutions, medical facilities and roads is often acquired and built on by developers with support from politicians and bureaucrats. Developers are able to violate bye-laws and zoning regulations and even build on natural drainage channels and land reserved for infrastructure. They often get government land or properties very cheaply, far below their market value. Hasan's book includes an example of a district in Karachi where all the land reserved for public amenities has been converted into residential and commercial developments, with the loss of over 300 hectares of amenity space, including some 80 hectares that had been allocated for parks and playgrounds. The book also has a case study, drawn from the Urban Resource Centre in Karachi,[12] of the struggle by the community organization in Mujahid Colony first to keep ten plots in the centre of their settlement as a park (and to prevent informal land developers from selling it for housing) and then to develop it as a park. Maria Elena Foronda's case study of environmental problems in Chimbote also includes details of the residents' fight to stop a much-used park being sold (Foronda 1998).

In most cities, there is a complex interaction between natural hazards and human actions – human actions can often greatly reduce or eliminate environmental hazards but they may also act to make them more frequent or increase the scale and severity of risk (Douglas 1983). For instance, in Caracas, where

12 The Urban Resource Centre in Karachi was set up in 1989 to serve NGOs and community organizations and urban planning related professionals and teachers. It serves not only as a resource centre with information about Karachi but also undertakes research and critically reviews proposed urban development projects, especially with regard to how they will affect low-income groups and their community organizations. It also organizes many forums and public discussions. It works in close association with Orangi Pilot Project and the Department of Architecture and Planning at the Dawood College of Engineering and Technology. It publishes various reports and monographs, including a monthly publication *Facts and Figures*.

close to 600,000 persons live on slopes with a high risk of landslide, most slope failures were associated with earthquakes until the 1960s (Jimenez Diaz 1992). From the 1970s onwards, they have been increasingly associated with rains and with areas where low-income barrios have developed; it is the changes introduced in the slopes through their development for housing that has increased the likelihood that rainfall can trigger the slope failure (ibid). Many of those who died in the catastrophic floods in Venezuela in December 1999 were low-income urban households living on unstable hill-slopes.

The vast majority of those who live on such hazardous sites are low-income groups. Rarely do they live here in ignorance of the dangers; such sites are chosen because their location and low monetary cost meet more immediate and pressing needs. Poorer groups need to minimize the cost and time taken getting to and from work (or to and from places where incomes can be earned); most also need to pay as little as possible for housing. Hazardous sites are often the only places where poorer groups can build their own house or rent accommodation. The sites are cheap or can be occupied without payment because the environmental hazards make them unattractive to alternative users. Such sites are often publicly owned and may have been designated as parks. Polluted sites next to industries or on steep hillsides or on outcrops of rock or valley slopes close to city centres are close to jobs. If the land is unsuitable for commercial developments, the possibility of avoiding eviction from such sites is greater.

To the hazards inherent in the site are added those linked to a lack of investment in infrastructure and services. For instance, most new residential developments do not include storm and surface water drains while many make no provision for sanitation. The introduction of water supplies with no provision for draining away waste water may add significantly to the risk of slope failure for houses on steep hillsides. There may also be a lack of knowledge among the settlers as to how to reduce risks – for instance minimizing the amount of vegetation cleared from a slope as it is developed for housing, which can reduce the risk of land-mudslides (Greenway 1987). Or the knowledge may be there, but without the collective organizations to permit its effective use. For instance, those who have settled on a slope may be powerless to prevent new housing developments or a new road development at the base of the slope which puts the whole hillside at risk (Douglas 1986). However, it should also be noted that many illegal settlements located on steep slopes have developed cheap and effective ways of minimizing the risks, which may indeed be more cost-effective than those recommended by external specialists.

The impact of unsuitable sites on health is often the result of a mix of everyday risks, risks in particular seasons (for instance the rainy season for those on steep slopes or areas subject to flooding) and occasional but high risks from particular natural events. Sites subject to flooding are often damp with pools of stagnant water for large portions of the year and damp housing can contribute significantly to poor health. The risk of contracting malaria may vary a lot – for instance as the rainy season provides many more breeding grounds for the Anopheles mosquitoes. Poorer groups living on hillsides usually have to transport the goods they use (from groceries to building materials) up the hill, which can represent a major drain on their time and energies. Hillsides lacking drainage, steps and paved roads are also hazardous, especially when wet, and younger and older age groups may have particular difficulties avoiding accidental falls and subsequent injuries.

Disasters that arise because of unsafe house sites are common. The disasters on the Manila waste dump and on the hillside in Bombay/Mumbai were noted at the beginning of this volume. For instance, if we focus only on Latin America, hundreds of low-income urban dwellers lost their lives in floods and landslides during Hurricane Mitch in 1998 and during heavy rains in Venezuela in December 1999. There were also the accidental deaths (although on a more modest scale) during heavy rains in Central America in October 1999, Colombia in May 2000 and Guatemala in June 2000.[13] When we were preparing the first edition of this book in 1991, there were hundreds of people killed or seriously injured and thousands made homeless by mudslides in Medellin in 1987, Rio de Janeiro in 1988, and Caracas in 1989. In each of these, there were also the large numbers of schools, health centres, roads, bridges and other structures that were destroyed or severely damaged and a large number of households who lost their livelihoods.

There are also far more smaller 'disasters' that do not get reported. In most cities where there have been large-scale disasters, there are many 'small' disasters each year where some people get killed and rather more get injured and have their homes damaged or destroyed. Most of the deaths, injuries and loss of property in these large and 'small' disasters could have been prevented because there are relatively cheap and effective ways by which the public authorities can greatly reduce the risks in such sites (for instance by paving access roads, installing drains, helping to stabilize slopes and other safeguards). They can also reduce the loss of life, injury and damage to property through disaster preparedness. The conventional approach of seeking to evict all those living on hazardous sites is hardly realistic, unless the public authorities have the capacity to offer all those displaced safer sites that meet their own needs and priorities. A more realistic approach – and one very rarely seen – is for public authorities to work with those living in hazardous areas in mapping the sites and shelters most at risk and in implementing household and community-level interventions to reduce the likelihood of a disaster or its severity when it happens and ensure plans for rapid action, if or when it takes place.

Waste

There is the additional problem of inadequate or no collection of household waste. An estimate made in the early 1980s suggested that it is common for 30–50 per cent of solid wastes generated within urban centres to remain uncol-

---

13 This should not be taken to imply that it was only low-income urban dwellers that suffered. Hurricane Mitch and the floods in Venezuela in particular caused enormous devastation, damage and death over large areas. Hurricane Mitch and the flooding and landslides that its very high winds and very heavy rains caused are reported to have killed over 10,000 people in Central America. It also caused billions of dollars in damage and made some 2 million people homeless. Around 30,000 people are reported to have died during the floods in Venezuela with another 600,000 severely affected. More than 20,000 houses were destroyed and more than 60,000 houses were damaged. See www.disasters.org

lected (Cointreau 1982); in most cities in low-income nations, this estimate is probably still valid. Of course, the proportion of the population served by a regular collection service varies greatly from city to city; in some, most or nearly all inhabitants have a regular waste collection service – for instance in Cebu, Pôrto Alegre and Johannesburg and Santiago (see Box 2.7). At the other extreme, as Box 2.7 shows, there are many cities where more than half the population is not served or has irregular and inadequate services. In Lusaka, Zambia's capital, only 10 per cent of the wastes generated by households are collected.

It is generally the responsibility of the local city or municipal authority to provide a regular house-to-house waste-collection service and to keep roads and public spaces clean, although many contract out some or all of the collection to private enterprises. Where public authorities are unable to provide house-to-house collections, they often resort to providing communal skips to which households have to transport their wastes. But there are usually too few skips per household; as the example given of Kumasi in Box 2.7 shows, communal skips are meant to be within 400 metres of households but they can be up to 1.5 kilometres away. Where government agencies provide communal skips, it is rare for the service emptying the skips to be adequate or regular, so the skips overflow and the site in which they are located becomes a large waste dump. Where assessments of waste-collection services are available, they usually emphasize the lack of funding for equipment and serious problems with collection trucks out of use because of a lack of spare parts (UNCHS 1996).

The environmental and other problems faced by residential neighbourhoods with no regular service to collect household wastes are obvious. Without a collection service, households generally dump their wastes on any available empty site or in nearby ditches or lakes or simply along streets, sometimes to the point where it actually blocks roads (see for instance Izeogu 1989). Problems include the smells, the disease vectors and pests attracted by rubbish (including rats, mosquitoes and flies) and the drainage channels clogged with waste and overflowing as a result. Since provision for sanitation is also so often deficient, many households dispose of toilet wastes into drains so when drains overflow, they also spread excreta around the site. Alternatively, human wastes are included in the dumped waste – for instance, as noted earlier, the common practice for people to defecate into plastic bags where there is no toilet in their home, with these bags included in rubbish piles.

Uncollected waste is obviously a serious health hazard, especially for children playing in and around their homes (and for many playing with items drawn from uncollected rubbish) and for any persons sorting through the rubbish, looking for items that can be reused or recycled (Cointreau 1982). Flies and cockroaches feeding on such waste can also subsequently contaminate food (ibid). Piles of dumped rubbish are also a fire hazard, as the gases from decomposing waste can catch fire or spontaneously ignite. It is also common practice for households to burn their wastes if there is no service to collect them, and this adds to the air pollution (McGranahan 1991, Yhdego 1991). Leachate from decomposing waste can also contaminate local water sources (UNCHS 1988).

Box 2.7 *EXAMPLES OF THE QUALITY AND EXTENT OF GARBAGE COLLEC-TION FROM HOUSEHOLDS*

Addis Ababa (Ethiopia). Only about 60 per cent of the solid waste generated is collected. The remaining 40 per cent is dumped in open sites, streets, ditches and drainage channels until it is eventually washed away by floods during the rainy season. During the rains it clogs drainage channels (Shenkut 1998).

Ahmedabad (India). The Municipal Corporation claims to cover the entire city with waste collection services including slums on private lands for which it has no functional responsibility. However, the quality of service is poor in many slum areas. A survey of 1200 members of the Self-Employed Women's Association (SEWA) in 12 wards where members were concentrated found that waste collection services were only available to 65 per cent of respondents of which only 40 per cent were satisfied because of the irregular nature of the service (Dutta and Batley 2000).

Baroda, Bhilwara, Sambalpur and Siliguri (India). A survey of 400 households in each of the four cities' 'slums' pointed to the great inadequacies in the provision for rubbish collection, as well as for water, sanitation and drainage, as summarized in previous boxes. In Baroda, rubbish disposal facilities were available to only 1 per cent of the households, while 95 per cent reported that they either threw their wastes on to the street or somewhere else outside the house. In Bhilwara, 36 per cent threw their rubbish out on the streets and 56 per cent disposed of it outside their house. In Sambalpur, 98 per cent of households reported that they threw rubbish out in the open and that there was no rubbish bin available in the area (Ghosh and others 1994).

Kumasi (Ghana). Estimates suggest that only some 30 per cent of refuse generated in residential areas is collected. The only service available for most of the population is through skips placed in various transfer stations around the city to which they have to carry their wastes. Although each house is meant to have a skip within 400 metres, some residents have to travel 1.5 km to reach them. Skips are often not emptied, and some residential areas have no communal skips. In peripheral areas, households dump wastes in small depressions. In other areas, they heap their refuse at selected points and set it on fire at the end of the day. A small group of wealthy households receive regular house collections, twice a week, for which they pay very little (Devas and Korboe 2000).

Latin America. About 70 per cent of the population in large Latin American cities (with one million plus inhabitants) have waste collection services; in smaller cities, this coverage is estimated to range between 50 and 70 per cent. It is normally the high- and middle-income areas that enjoy regular service while low-income neighbourhoods can count only on erratic services any at all. In many capital cities including Tegucigalpa, Managua, San Salvador, Caracas, Lima and Asuncion, waste-collection coverage remains below 40 per cent for the low-income areas (Arroyo Moreno and others 1999).

Lusaka and other urban centres in Zambia: 90 per cent of the 1400 tonnes of solid waste generated by Lusaka's inhabitants is not collected because the local authority has too few staff, funds and equipment (Agyemang and others 1997 cited in Clarke 1999). A household survey in 1996 found that only 10 per cent of urban households across the country had their waste collected; 52 per cent used a pit for disposal and 37 per cent just dumped their rubbish (Central Statistics Office 1997).

Mombasa (Kenya). The Municipal Council is responsible for solid-waste management but only 40 per cent of households had a regular waste-collection service in 1993 and only half the waste generated was collected because of supervisory staff and equipment shortages and charges that are well below costs. By the end of 1998, the council was only providing a service for the island, since it had privatized services in all the mainland areas. However, higher charges confined the services provided by private operators to high-income households and formal sector businesses, with many low-income households unable to afford the charges. In the absence of legal backing to ensure that private contractors collect from all households (and operate a cross-subsidy if appropriate) the Corporation had no option but to collect the refuse dumped along roadsides in low-income areas and informal settlements itself (Rakodi and others 2000).

Montego Bay (Jamaica). Waste is meant to be collected from residential areas twice a week but the actual frequency varies from twice a week in formal sector residential neighbourhoods to never in some of the largest informal settlements. The main reasons include lack of road access to large areas of informal settlements, lack of cooperation by residents, density and inadequate finance (Ferguson 1996).

Nairobi (Kenya). A report written in 1994 noted that the Nairobi City Council had been unable to provide a regular waste-collection service to all areas of the city for some years. In the informal settlements (which house 55 per cent of the city's population), the City Council does not collect waste on a regular basis and limits collection to clearing large piles of refuse when they become a health hazard. Even this is not undertaken regularly. Areas in most settlements are littered with refuse and are contaminated with rotting waste with the attendant health risks (Alder 1995).

Ouagadougou (Burkina Faso). About 30 per cent of the refuse generated daily is collected (Ouayoro 1995).

It is the poorer areas of the city that generally have the least adequate waste-collection service or no service at all. Many informal settlements are also on land sites to which access by motor vehicles (especially large conventional refuse trucks) is difficult or impossible and local authorities make little or no attempt to develop waste-collection services that are suited to such sites. Most poor households also have very limited space in or around their homes (especially in tenements and high-density illegal settlements) which makes waste storage difficult, and they also face great difficulty in transporting rubbish to a supervised dump site.

Disease vectors

A large range of disease vectors live, breed or feed within or around houses and settlements. The diseases they cause or carry include some of the major causes of ill health and premature death in many cities, especially malaria (*Anopheles* mosquitoes) and diarrhoeal diseases (cockroaches, blowflies and houseflies). But there are also many other diseases caused or carried by insects, spiders or mites, including bancroftian filariasis (*Culex* mosquitoes), Chagas' disease (*Triatomine* bugs), dengue fever (*Aedes* mosquitoes), hepatitis A (house-flies, cockroaches), leishmaniasis (sandfly), plague (certain fleas), relapsing fever (body lice and soft ticks), scabies (scabies mites), trachoma (face flies), typhus (body lice and fleas), yaws (face flies), and yellow fever (*Aedes* mosquitoes) (WHO 1992a, Schofield and others 1990).

Although some of these remain predominantly rural, many have long been urban problems (for instance, malaria is among the most common causes of infant and child death in many low-income settlements). Others have become urban problems. For instance, Chagas' disease with an estimated 18 million people infected in Latin America primarily affects poor rural households, as the insect vector rests and breeds in cracks in house walls. But it is increasingly an urban problem too both through the migration of infected persons to urban areas (there is no effective treatment for the disease) and through the peri-urban informal settlements where the insect vectors are evident (Gomes Pereira 1989, Briceno-Leon 1990). Leptospirosis outbreaks have been associated with flooding in São Paulo and Rio de Janeiro, the disease passing to humans through water contaminated with the urine of infected rats or certain domestic animals (WHO 1992a).

Urban expansion may also change the local ecology in ways that favour the emergence or multiplication of particular disease vectors (WHO 1992a). For instance, *Aedes aegypti*, the mosquito vector for dengue fever and yellow fever, is often found to breed in polluted water sources such as soak-away pits and septic tanks. Anopheline mosquitoes generally shun polluted water but certain species have adapted to the urban environment and now breed in swamps and ditches in or close to urban areas. Box 2.8 gives more details.

Drainage

Drainage is simply the removal of unwanted water from urban communities; this includes stormwater, external floodwater (for instance from rivers that top

---

Box 2.8 SOME HEALTH IMPLICATIONS OF URBAN EXPANSION

Urban expansion may be associated with new diseases. The expansion of the built-up area, the construction of roads, water reservoirs and drains together with land clearance and deforestation can effect drastic changes to the local ecology. Natural foci for disease vectors may become entrapped within the suburban extension and new ecological niches for the animal reservoirs may be created. Within urban conurbations, disease vectors may adapt to new habitats and introduce new infections to spread among the urban population. For instance in India, where the vector of lymphatic filariasis is a peridomestic mosquito, there has been a rapid increase in the incidence of the disease and in the vector population associated with the steady increase in the growth of human populations in these endemic areas. Anopheline mosquitoes generally shun polluted water yet *A stephensi*, the principal vector for urban malaria, is also reported in India and the Eastern Mediterranean region to have adapted to survive in the urban environment and other species of anophelines have also adapted to breed in swamps and ditches surrounding urban areas in Nigeria and Turkey. *Aedes aegypti*, the vector of dengue and urban yellow fever proliferates in tropical urban settlements and has been frequently found to breed in polluted water sources such as soak-away pits, septic tanks and other breeding sites that have been found to contain a high amount of organic matter. *Aedes albopictus* was introduced to the Americas from Asia around 1986 and within five years, it had spread in the United States to 160 counties in 17 states. It was also introduced into Brazil where it is reported to be present in four states. This species is a peri-domestic species like *A aegypti* and an excellent vector of dengue and other mosquito-borne viruses.

Source: WHO (1992), *Our Planet, Our Health*, The report of the World Commission on Health and Environment, Geneva, 282 pages.

---

their banks), marshwater, sullage, and toilet wastes (Cairncross and Ouano 1990). It is appropriate to consider problems arising from the lack of provision for drainage in urban neighbourhoods after considering environmental hazards from house sites and disease vectors since improved drainage can also help to control certain water-related or water-based diseases or disease vectors, as well as to reduce flooding.

Stagnant water in urban areas can provide a breeding place for schistosomiasis snails, and as noted earlier, malarial mosquitoes and mosquitoes that serve as the vector for dengue, yellow fever and bancroftian filariasis may breed in standing water (Kolsky 1992). Good drainage can also help to prevent waste water from contaminating local surface water bodies or shallow aquifers. It also greatly reduces the problem of flooding that is so evident in many low-income areas of cities. And in the absence of sewers – and very few low-income areas of cities have sewers – the drainage system ends up as the system that takes away waste water, including waste water with excreta. So an effective drainage system often has great importance for reducing human exposure to excreta.

Problems with drainage are less serious where there are effective sewers, since these deal adequately with households' waste water (sullage) as well as toilet wastes. Excreta may also be disposed of safely in other kinds of sanitation system – for instance in pit latrines or toilets connected to septic tanks – but there are still the other liquid wastes noted above that must be disposed of. The need for drainage also increases, as water supplies improve. Many low-income urban communities consider drainage to be their most urgent need because they occupy land sites subject to flooding or steep hillsides subject to erosion and landslides (Cairncross and Ouano 1990).

THE IMPORTANCE OF THE HOME AND NEIGHBOURHOOD ENVIRONMENT FOR WELL-BEING AND CHILD DEVELOPMENT

The last ten years have brought increasing evidence of the degree to which lower-income groups' lives are dominated by ill health, disablement or premature death and the extent to which environmental factors in the home and neighbourhood are major causes or contributors. This is especially so for infants and children (Satterthwaite and others 1996). Ten years ago, the WHO stated that in many illegal or informal settlements in cities in low-income nations, a child is 40 to 50 times more likely to die before the age of five than a child born in a high-income nation (WHO 1990). This is still likely to be true in many cities. However, there are still few detailed studies looking at the impact of ill-health on the lives of low-income urban households, with the work of Jane Pryer (1989, 1993) being a notable exception. A few other studies give an idea of the disruption caused by constant illness – for instance a study in three secondary cities in Benin found that diarrhoeal diseases were so common among children under five that they caused their mothers to lose seven to ten work days per month (Yacoob and Kelly 1999).

Work on global disease burdens undertaken during the 1990s has highlighted the much larger disease burdens per person in the lowest income regions. For instance:

- The disease burden per person in 1990 was nearly five times higher in sub-Saharan Africa than in the world's wealthiest countries.
- For 0–4-year-olds, the disease burden was more than 40 times higher per child in sub-Saharan Africa, compared with the world's wealthiest nations; in India it was more than 20 times higher.
- The disease burden per person from diarrhoeal diseases was 200 times higher per person in sub-Saharan Africa than in the world's wealthiest nations; in much of Asia and the Middle East, it was 80 to 120 times higher (World Bank 1993, Murray and Lopez 1996).

These figures give some indication of how much larger the average health burden per person is in low- and middle-income nations compared with high-income nations. But they do not show the health burden associated with low-income households within these nations or the health burden associated with having a low income in urban contexts. The larger health burden suffered by the urban poor (compared to the urban non-poor) is highlighted more by studies of specific diseases – for instance of diarrhoeal diseases, TB or intestinal parasites (see Bradley and others 1991, and Harpham and Molyneux 2000) – but few studies consider the implications for poor households of these disease burdens. Studies of the health problems faced by poorer groups point not only to the higher rates of infant and child deaths but also to higher rates of death, disablement and serious injury from household accidents, and high proportions of people in each age group suffering from ill health for substantial proportions of their lives. The studies also suggest that it is in the house and its immediate surrounds that most injuries and diseases are contracted. Chapter 4 will return to the issue of the differentials between groups in urban areas in terms of environmental health risk and health impact.

The impact of diseases, accidental poisonings, burns, cuts, scalds and other injuries contracted in and around the home is further magnified by a lack of first aid provision within the neighbourhood. In addition, sick or injured people cannot be rapidly transported to hospitals. A lack of paved roads and the fact that the houses are on sites that are difficult to reach with motorized vehicles (eg steep hillsides, waterlogged sites) also means that in the event of fires, neither fire engines nor ambulances can reach the settlement, at least not without long delays (Goldstein 1990, WHO 1992a).

In discussing the different environmental hazards evident within the home and neighbourhood environment of a large proportion of the urban population in Africa, Asia and Latin America or the incidence of specific diseases, one can miss the fact that safe and secure housing with adequate infrastructure and services not only reduces ill health, injury and premature death but also supports well-being. Safe, secure housing has a particularly significant influence on the well-being of young children who spend most of their time within or close to the home. As a recent book *Cities for Children* notes:

> *Reliable housing supports not only physical health, but also emotional security, stability, and the comfort of daily routines. Children can become deeply attached to familiar surroundings, and this, like their human attachments, is a wellspring for their trust in the world (Chawla 1992). This security is challenged when housing is vulnerable to flooding, mudslides or other disasters; or when tenure is insecure... Home is the primary environment for children's early social and intellectual development. If they are well cared-for and have had adequate loving human contact, most of their energy in early years will be focussed on interaction with features of the physical environment – with objects and settings that invite exploration, manipulation, and imaginative experimentation, both together and with others (Valsiner 1987, Heft 1987). But the living conditions of many poor urban children deny them access to safe, stimulating, varied play environments, and can deprive them of the opportunities they need to develop as socially competent and intellectually curious beings (Bartlett and others 1999, page 68).*

This book also stresses the importance of a good quality neighbourhood environment for children:

> *Ideally, a neighbourhood should be a place where children can play safely, run errands, walk to school, socialize with friends and observe and learn from the activities of others. When neighbourhoods provide a secure and welcoming transition to the larger world, children can gradually test and develop their competence before confronting the full complexity of city life* (ibid, page 122).

Thus, there are important issues regarding the quality of the home and neighbourhood environment that go beyond the avoidance of ill health and that are easy to miss, when concentrating on describing specific environmental problems.

Chapter 3

The City Environment

**A young boy returns home from school in La Oroya, Peru, where indus-
trial activities have contaminated nearby rivers and turned surrounding
mountainsides into what some describe as a lunar landscape**

THE RANGE OF PROBLEMS

The environmental problems most commonly associated with cities in high-
income nations such as high levels of air and water pollution and large volumes
of solid wastes (including some highly toxic or otherwise hazardous wastes)
might be assumed to be less important in Africa, Asia and Latin America for
two reasons. The first is that a smaller proportion of their population lives in
cities (although this is no longer true for Latin America). The second is that
these regions are less industrialized and despite having more than three-quarters
of the world's population, they still have a relatively small proportion of the

world's industry. Rural and agricultural environmental problems such as deforestation, soil erosion and floods may seem more urgent even if, as described
later, some of these have important linkages with cities.

However, close to half of all low- and middle-income nations with more
than 1 million inhabitants have a quarter or more of their gross domestic
product (GDP) derived from industry, including many which rely on industry
for between a third and a half of GDP (World Bank 1999a). These countries
include hundreds of cities or city-regions with high concentrations of industries. Nations such as China, India, Mexico, Brazil and South Korea figure
prominently among the world's largest producers of many industrial goods.
Not surprisingly, cities or city-regions with high concentrations of industries
(especially heavy industries) suffer comparable industrial pollution problems to
those currently or formerly experienced in cities in Europe, Japan and North
America. In many cities, industrial pollution is far more serious. Industrial
production has often increased very rapidly in the absence of an effective
planning and regulation system. More than 35 low- and middle-income nations
recorded average growth rates for industrial value added of 5 per cent or more
a year between 1965 and 1980; even during the 1980s, when so many nations
had stagnant or contracting economies, more than 20 had average growth rates
of 5 per cent or more a year for industrial value added, while more than 25
sustained such growth rates for 1990 to 1998 (World Bank 1999a). China, India,
Indonesia, South Korea, Malaysia, Pakistan, Thailand and Turkey are among
the countries that had growth rates averaging more than 5 per cent a year for
the whole period 1980–1998. China's growth rate was particularly spectacular,
producing a more than eightfold increase in industrial value added in these 18
years, which helps to explain why air and water pollution levels are so high in
many Chinese cities.[1] The more rapid the growth in industrial production, the
more serious the environmental problems related to industrial pollution are
likely to be since time is required to identify and act on problems, to develop
the legislative basis for pollution control and develop the institutional structure
needed to implement it. In addition, there are usually powerful vested interests
that oppose the implementation of pollution control and political circumstances often slow or halt such implementation. Until the 1990s, few
governments showed much interest in controlling industrial pollution.
Governments' concern to foster job creation usually meant that when a new
factory or mine was proposed – by local, national or international businesses –
little attention was given to likely environmental impacts.

A second reason why industrial pollution can be particularly serious is the
concentration of industry in relatively few locations; in most nations, industrial
production is heavily concentrated in one or two of their cities or 'core regions'.
For instance, the metropolitan areas of Bangkok, Dhaka, Johannesburg, Lima,
Mexico City, Manila and São Paulo include a high proportion of their nation's

---

1 China's National Environmental Protection Agency estimated that industrial pollution accounts
for 70 per cent of all organic water pollution, 72 per cent of sulphur dioxide emissions, 75 per
cent of flue dust (a major component of suspended particulate matter) and 87 per cent of solid
wastes (Dasgupta and others 1997).

industrial output; the same is also true in less industrialized countries – for instance Nairobi and Port-au-Prince contain a high proportion of their nation's total industrial output.

Industrial pollution is not the only cause of air and water pollution. The high proportions of households and businesses not served by sewers, drains and solid-waste collection add greatly to land and water pollution problems. A lack of sewage treatment adds greatly to water pollution, for cities with sewer systems. In cities where many households use solid fuels in inefficient heaters and cookers, these contribute much to air pollution. The often rapidly growing numbers of motor vehicles, congested roads and a high proportion of inefficient and poorly maintained motor vehicle engines add greatly to air pollution. Air pollution from vehicles might be assumed to be less of a problem than in Europe, North America or Japan because low- and middle-income nations have fewer cars per person. But this is not so in many major cities in middle-income nations that have as many cars per person as many cities in many high-income nations. Even where the ratio is lower, a combination of narrow congested streets and old and poorly maintained vehicles with higher levels of polluting emissions can still result in serious air pollution problems.

As later sections will describe in more detail, local conditions can also exacerbate the problem. Many cities have long periods in the year with very little wind to help to disperse air pollution; where there is also a high concentration of road vehicles and an abundance of sunshine, photochemical smog has become an increasing problem. For water pollution, problems are much increased where there are serious shortages of water, since this limits the extent to which local water bodies can break down or dilute the industrial effluents and other wastes that enter them.

AIR POLLUTION

The main pollutants and their sources

Most outdoor air pollution in urban areas comes from the combustion of fossil fuels (oil or oil-derived fuels, coal and natural gas) for heating and electricity generation, and in industrial processes and motor vehicles (WHO 1992a). (Many cities also have significant natural sources – for instance wind-blown dust which is often made more serious by poor land management and many unpaved roads.) The use of fossil fuels in each of these tends to increase with economic growth;[2] so too does air pollution unless measures are taken to promote efficient fuel use, the use of the least polluting fuels (for instance natural gas rather than coal with a high sulphur content for domestic and industrial use, and unleaded petrol for motor vehicles) and the control of pollution at source (World Bank 1992).

---

2 The extent of this growth obviously varies between countries depending on, for instance, the scale and nature of industrial growth (there are very large variations in the energy intensity of different industries relative to the value of their output) and the climate which influences demand for space heating and for air-conditioning.

In many cities, the concentrations and mixes of air pollutants are already high enough to cause illness in more susceptible individuals and premature death among the elderly, especially those with respiratory problems (WHO 1992a). Air pollution is likely to be impairing the health of far more people. The WHO (1999) estimates that worldwide, 1.5 billion urban dwellers are exposed to levels of ambient air pollution that are above their recommended maximum levels (and most of these will be in low- and middle-income countries). For instance, India has had a very rapid increase in the number of industries and motor vehicles in the last decade, bringing a dramatic deterioration in urban air quality in most regions of the country, as statistics given later in this chapter will show (Agarawal and others 1999a).

Box 3.1 describes the main air pollutants while Table 3.1 outlines their effects on health. Until relatively recently, most urban air pollution came from the burning of coal or heavy oil by industry, power stations and households. This produces a mix of sulphur dioxide, suspended particulates and inorganic compounds. These were the source of the infamous London 'smogs' of the 1950s and although in most cities in Europe and North America sulphur dioxide concentrations have fallen considerably, they remain the main source of air pollution in many cities in Africa, Asia and Latin America. For instance, in Asia, levels of smoke and dust are generally twice the world average and more than five times as high as in most high-income nations (Asian Development Bank 1997). Without effective control measures for sulphur dioxide, emissions are likely to more than triple within the next 12 years (Clarke 1999).

In many cities, especially within city cores, road transport is becoming the dominant source of many of the pollutants that affect the health of urban residents (Elsom 1996). Largely as a result of growing car use, there has been a growing contribution of what are termed photochemical ('oxidizing') pollutants to air pollution in many cities (although industry can also be a major source). Among these, the oxides of nitrogen are particularly important. It is usually not stationary sources (industries, power stations, household stoves) but petrol-fuelled motor vehicles that are the major source. Hydrocarbons are another important pollutant; most of them come from petrol evaporation and possibly leaks in gas pipes and emissions from petroleum industries. Secondary reactions in the air between nitrogen dioxide, hydrocarbons and sunlight cause the formation of ozone, which is present in photochemical smog along with other hazardous chemicals. Ozone can have serious health impacts when in high concentrations in or close to cities, while by contrast, the ozone layer in the stratosphere has an essential role in maintaining health since it absorbs the fraction of ultraviolet rays coming from the sun which can damage human health and other living organisms (WHO 1992a).

Carbon monoxide is also a common air pollutant, formed by the incomplete combustion of fossil fuels; the main danger in cities is high concentrations in particular areas, from motor vehicle emissions. Lead is also a common air pollutant in urban areas, with high concentrations often evident where lead compounds are still widely used as additives in petrol. Airborne lead can also contaminate the soil and dust near busy roads, affecting crops grown in gardens or other open spaces (WHO 1992a). There may also be small concentrations of

Box 3.1 *HEALTH-THREATENING POLLUTANTS*

Sulphur Dioxide. Most comes from the combustion of sulphur-containing coal and lignite in power stations or industries while some also comes from sulphur-containing heavy fuel oil. In some cities, the burning of coal with a high sulphur content in domestic stoves and small-scale industries can be a major source. In China, although total fuel combustion by households is small by comparison to industry and power stations, 'the burning of raw coal in millions of small inefficient stoves is a very burdensome air pollution source through the colder half of the nation' (Smil 1984). Diesel-engined vehicles emit significant amounts of sulphur dioxide and emissions from diesel buses, trucks and cars can be a major cause of poor air quality.

Suspended Particulates. These include a great range of substances and particle sizes. They include naturally generated particles (for instance soil particles) and particles released during the combustion of fossil fuels associated with power generation, home heating and cooking, motor vehicles and a wide range of industrial processes including waste incineration. The size of the particle determines how deeply they penetrate into people's lungs. Large inhalable particles are usually trapped in the nose and throat while particles that are 5–10 µg across reach the upper parts of the lungs and smaller particles (less than 5 µg diameter) penetrate deeply into the respiratory system. Finer particles tend to come from combustion sources and to be more harmful to health. Thus, the control of particulates now includes not only an interest in controlling 'total suspended particulates' (TSP) but also those particulates that are smaller than 10 µg (often referred to as PM_{10}) and those that are smaller than 2.5 µg ($PM_{2.5}$). Recent studies show that in general, $PM_{2.5}$ is a better predictor of health effects than PM_{10} and that the constituents of $PM_{2.5}$ such as sulphates and strongly acidic particles are sometimes better predictors of health effects than $PM_{2.5}$.

Acid Aerosols. High concentrations of sulphur dioxide are often accompanied by high concentrations of acid aerosols (sulphates and sulphuric acid aerosols) and suspended particulates that make it difficult to separate out the health impacts (and other effects) of individual pollutants and the nature of any synergistic effects. The health effects of acid aerosols and fine particles within winter smogs have probably been underestimated. Sulphate aerosols are also produced during warm sunny weather when sulphur dioxide is oxidized during photochemical episodes. The main health effect may be caused by sulphuric acid which occurs when both sulphate and ozone levels are high.

Carbon Monoxide. An odourless and colourless gas produced by the incomplete combustion of carbon-based fuels, mostly by motor vehicle engines. It is formed when oxygen is scarce and fuel does not burn properly, so it is a greater problem in high-altitude cities and during cold conditions. Carbon monoxide emissions from motor vehicles are greatest when an engine is first started from cold and when the engine is idling, as at traffic lights and during traffic jams. The busy roads of most major cities experience high carbon monoxide concentrations during the rush hours.

Nitrogen Oxides. These are generated when fuel combustion occurs at high temperatures; most emissions in urban areas come from motor vehicles.

Volatile Organic Compounds (VOCs). These include a wide range of chemicals that exist as vapour in the air. Most come from incomplete fuel combustion or evaporation of petrol from vehicle fuel tanks and carburettors or from leakage during the transport, storage and distribution of fuel to petrol stations. Leakage from natural gas distribution networks also adds to VOCs; so too do various domestic sources such as many paints and solvents and various consumer products, adhesives and fuel combustion. VOCs contribute to the formation of photochemical oxidants such as ozone, although there are major differences between the various VOCs in their potential to do so. Some such as benzene are also carcinogens.

Ozone. This is a 'secondary' pollutant formed through photochemical reactions between nitrogen oxides and VOCs (and involving carbon monoxide) in sunlight. The photochemical reactions also create other oxidants and fine particulates that give photochemical smogs a hazy appearance. During stable weather conditions, large quantities of the chemicals that allow the formation of ozone often become trapped under a low-level temperature inversion allowing time for ozone to be formed.

Airborne Lead. The combustion of petrol with lead additives is the main source of lead in the urban atmosphere.

Source: Drawn principally from Elsom, Derek (1996), *Smog Alert: Managing Urban Air Quality*, Earthscan, London.

certain organic chemicals in the air with worrying health implications – for instance benzene which is a known carcinogen (UNEP 1991).[3]

Table 3.2 summarizes the environmental impacts of selected industries in terms of their contributions to air, water and soil/land pollution. This highlights the range of air pollutants that different kinds of industries emit – and most contribute both to the 'traditional' mix of suspended particulates and sulphur dioxide and to the pollutants that contribute to photochemical smog (although the amount of pollution generated varies greatly according to the technology used in production and the extent to which pollution controls are installed and maintained). Many industries also emit smaller amounts of more hazardous air pollutants.

3 Agarawal and others 1999a report on a study in Delhi which showed worrying benzene concentrations and the discussions within India about its implications.

Air quality

For most air pollutants, different air quality standards are set that depend on the period of exposure. For instance, for sulphur dioxide and suspended particulates, standards may be set not only for the maximum permitted concentration for the annual average but also a less stringent standard which is permitted for less than seven days each year or for one day. For air pollutants such as carbon monoxide, ozone and nitrogen dioxide, with much more immediate health impacts, air quality standards are set for much shorter exposures. For carbon monoxide, since the health effects are immediate (the reduction in the oxygen-carrying capacity of the blood with impacts on the central nervous system and the heart), different air quality guidelines are set for 15 minutes, 30 minutes, 1-hour and 8-hour exposures. Air quality guidelines for nitrogen dioxide usually have a 1-hour average maximum permitted concentration; for ozone, the guidelines are for an 8-hour average maximum permitted concentration. Table 3.3 gives air quality guidelines, drawn mainly from the WHO.

Box 3.2 gives examples of cities in which concentrations of sulphur dioxide and total suspended particulates (or PM_{10}) far exceed safe standards. In many of the largest cities in the more wealthy nations, emissions from road vehicles and the concentration of secondary pollutants (such as ozone) to which they contribute may be more of a problem than the traditional (reducing) pollutants from coal/heavy oil combustion which are the main problem in many Indian and Chinese cities.

There is less data for concentrations of nitrogen oxides and carbon monoxide. Too few cities monitor these and among those that do, few have data showing trends over time. There are isolated examples of documentation on particular cities with problems. For instance, in India, data for 1990 to 1996 on nitrogen oxides showed that most major cities have average annual concentrations below the WHO guidelines. But there are exceptions. Howrah had concentrations that were five times the WHO guidelines for 1995 and 1996. Several other cities had concentrations well above the WHO guidelines for one or more years between 1990 and 1996. In Delhi, the trend was upwards and the 1995 figure of 47 µg/cubic metre was above the WHO guidelines (data from the Central Pollution Control Board, Delhi, reported in Agarwal and others 1999a).

High concentrations of carbon monoxide (virtually all coming from motor vehicles) have been recorded in particular locations (usually alongside busy roads or in central areas) – for instance in Kuala Lumpur (Sani 1987) and Bangkok (Wangweongwatana 1992). Motor vehicles are the major source of carbon monoxide in locations where short-term exposure levels routinely exceed the accepted standard.

High ozone concentrations are a particular problem in Mexico City and ozone levels reached 1200 µg/cubic metre in the southwest in November 1992 – ten times the guideline figure set by the WHO. Ozone concentrations well above the WHO guidelines have also been recorded in many parts of Delhi (Agarwal and others 1999a). The examples given in Box 3.2 may not be among the 'worst' examples since many cities have very inadequate or no provision for monitoring air pollution.

Table 3.1 *The most common urban air pollutants and their effects on health*

Pollutant	Action	Effect
1 Traditional ('reducing') pollutants from coal/heavy oil consumption		London Smog Complex
Smoke/suspended particulates (some contribution from diesel traffic too)	Can penetrate to lungs; some retained: possible long-term effects. May also irritate bronchi	*Short-term effects:* sudden increases in deaths, hospital admissions and in illness among bronchitic patients. Temporary reductions in lung function (patients and some healthy people)
Sulphur dioxide	Readily absorbed on inhalation: irritation of bronchi, with possibility of broncho spasm	*Long-term effects:* increased frequency of respiratory infections (children). Increased prevalence of respiratory symptoms (adult and children). Higher death rates from bronchitis in polluted areas
Sulphuric acid (mainly a secondary pollutant formed from sulphur dioxide in air)	Hygroscopic; highly irritant if impacted in upper respiratory tract. Acid absorbed on other fine particlesmay penetrate further to promote broncho spasm	
Polycyclic aromatic hydrocarbons (small contribution from traffic also)	Mainly absorbed on to smoke; can penetrate with it to lungs	*Possible carcinogenic effects:* may play some part in the higher incidence of lung cancer in urban areas
2 Photochemical ('oxidizing') pollutants from traffic or other hydrocarbon emissions		Los Angeles Smog Complex
Hydrocarbons (volatile: petrol etc)	Non-toxic at moderate concentrations	*Short-term effects:* primarily eye irritation. Reduced athletic performance. Possibly small changes in deaths, and hospital admissions
Nitric oxide	Capable of combining with haemoglobin in blood but no apparent effect in humans	

Nitrogen dioxide and ozone (mainly secondary pollutants formed in photochemical reactions)	Neither gas is very soluble: some irritation of bronchi but can penetrate to lungs to cause oedema at high concentrations. Urban concentrations too low for such effects, but evidence of reduced resistance to infections in animals	*Longer-term effects*: increased onsets of respiratory illnesses (children), increased asthma attacks (adults). No clear indication of increased bronchitis
Aldehydes, other partial oxidation products, peroxyacetylnitrate	Eye irritation, odour	

3 Others from traffic

Carbon monoxide (other sources contribute – smoking an important one)	Combines with haemoglobin in blood, reducing oxygen-carrying capacity	Possible effects on central nervous system (reversible unless concentrations are very high). Some evidence of effects on perception and performance of fine tasks at moderate concentrations
Lead (some industrial sources contribute to air lead; human intake often dominated by lead in food and drink)	Taken up in blood, distributed in soft tissues and some to bone	Possible effects on central nervous system (longer time-scale that in the case of CO and not necessarily reversible). Indications of neuropsychological effects on children within overall environmental exposure range, but role of traffic lead uncertain

Source: Waller, Robert E (1991), 'Field investigations of air' in W W Holland, R Detels and G Knox (editors), *Oxford Textbook of Public Health*, Volume 2 (second edition), Oxford University Press, Oxford and New York, pp 435–450.

Table 3.2 *Environmental impacts of selected industries*

Sector	Air	Water	Soil/land
Chemicals (industrial inorganic and organic compounds, excluding petroleum products)	Many and varied emissions depending on processes used and chemicals manufactured Emissions of particulate matter, SO_2, NO_x, CO, CFCs, VOCs and other organic chemicals, odours Risk of explosions and fires	Use of process water and cooling water Emissions of organic chemicals, heavy metals (cadmium, mercury), suspended solids, organic matter, PCBs Risk of spills	Chemical process wastes disposal problems Sludges from air- and water-pollution treatment disposal problems
Paper and pulp	Emissions of SO_2, NO_x, CH_4, CO_2, CO, hydrogen sulphide, mercaptans, chlorine compounds, dioxins	Use of process water Emissions of suspended solids, organic matter, chlorinated organic substances, toxins (dioxins)	
Cement, glass, ceramics	Cement emissions of dust, NO_x, CO_2, chromium, lead, CO Glass emissions of lead, arsenic, SO_2, vanadium, CO, hydrofluoric acid, soda ash, potash, specialty constituents (eg chromium) Ceramics emissions of silica, SO_2, NO_x, fluorine compounds	Emissions of process water contaminated by oils and heavy metals	Extraction of raw materials Soil contamination with metals and waste-disposal problems
Mining of metals and minerals	Emissions of dust from extraction, storage and transport of ore and concentrate Emissions of metals (eg mercury) from drying of ore concentrate	Contamination of surface water and ground water by highly acidic mine water containing toxic metals (eg arsenic, lead, cadmium) Contamination by chemicals used in metal extraction (eg cyanide)	Major surface disturbance and erosion Land degradation by large slag heaps
Iron and steel	Emissions of SO_2, NO_x, hydrogen sulphide, PAHs, lead, arsenic, cadmium, chromium, copper,	Use of process water Emissions of organic matter, tars and oil, suspended solids, metals, benzene,	Slag, sludges, oil and grease residues, hydrocarbons, salts, sulphur compounds, heavy metals, soil

Industry	Air emissions	Water	Land / waste
	mercury, nickel, selenium, zinc, organic compounds, PCDDs/PCDFs, PCBs, dust, particulate matter, hydrocarbons, acid mists; Exposure to ultraviolet and infrared radiation, ionizing radiation; Risks of explosions and fires	phenols, acids, sulphides, sulphates, ammonia, cyanides, thiocyanates, thiosulphates, fluorides, lead, zinc (scrubber effluent)	contamination and waste disposal problems
Non-ferrous metals	Emissions of particulate matter, SO_2, NO_x, CO, hydrogen sulphide, hydrogen chloride, hydrogen fluoride, chlorine, aluminium, arsenic, cadmium, chromium, copper, zinc, mercury, nickel, lead, magnesium, PAHs, fluorides, silica, manganese, carbon black, hydrocarbons, aerosols	Scrubber water containing metals; Gas scrubber effluents containing solids, fluorine, hydrocarbons	Sludges from effluent treatment, coatings from electrolysis cells (containing carbon and fluorine), soil contamination and waste-disposal problems
Coal-mining and production	Emissions of dust from extraction, storage and transport of coal; Emissions of CO and SO_2 from burning slag heaps; CH_4 emissions from underground formations; Risk of explosions and fires	Contamination of surface water and ground water by highly saline or acidic mine water	Major surface disturbance and erosion; Subsidence of ground above mines; Land degradation by large slag heaps
Refineries, petroleum products	Emissions of SO_2, NO_x, hydrogen sulphide, HCs, benzene, CO, CO_2, particulate matter, PAHs, mercaptans, toxic organic compounds, odours; Risk of explosions and fires	Use of cooling water. Emissions of HCs mercaptans, caustics, oil, phenols, chromium, effluent from gas scrubbers	Hazardous waste, sludges from effluent treatment, spent catalysts, tars
Leather and tanning	Emissions, including leather dust, hydrogen sulphide, CO_2, chromium compounds	Use of process water; Effluents from the many toxic solutions used, containing suspended solids, sulphates, chromium	Chromium sludges

Source: Drawn from Table 2.3 in *World Resources 1998–99* which, itself, was adapted from World Health Organization (1997), *Health and Environment in Sustainable Development: Five Years After the Earth Summit*, WHO, Geneva, Table 3.10, page 64.

Table 3.3 *Air quality guidelines*

Air pollutant	Average ambient air concentration (microgram or μg/cubic metre)	Guideline value (μg/cubic metre)	Averaging time
Carbon monoxide	500–7000	100,000	15 minutes
		60,000	30 minutes
		30,000	1 hour
		10,000	8 hours
Lead	0.01–2.0	0.5	1 year
Nitrogen dioxide	10–150	200	1 hour
		40	1 year
Ozone	10–100	120	8 hours
Sulphur dioxide	5–400	500	10 minutes
		125	24 hours
		50	1 year
Particulates Total suspended particulates		75	1 year
PM_{10}		50	1 year
		150	24 hours
$PM_{2.5}$		15	1 year
		65	24 hours

Note: High-income countries are setting their targets for PM_{10} much lower than that suggested in the above table. The guidelines for suspended particulates are from the USA. The WHO's Guidelines for Air Quality state that available information does not allow a judgement to be made of concentrations below which no effects would be expected and presents graphs showing links between the increase in daily mortality as a function of PM concentration, per cent change in hospital admissions assigned to PM_{10} and sulphates and change in health endpoints as a function of PM_{10} concentration from which guidelines can be derived.
Source: Schwela, Dietrich (1999), 'Local ambient air quality management', in Gordon McGranahan and Frank Murray (editors), *Health and Air Pollution in Rapidly Developing Countries*, Stockholm Environment Institute, Stockholm, pages 57–75; WHO (2000), *Guidelines for Air Quality*, World Health Organization, Geneva (available from www.who.org).

The scale of the pollution, the relative importance of different pollutants and the relative contribution of the different sources varies greatly from city to city and often from season to season within cities. Existing evidence suggests that city-wide air pollution problems are most serious in industrial cities with inadequate pollution control, in cities where solid fuels are widely used for cooking and heating in homes and small-scale industries, and in large cities with a high concentration of motor vehicles where local conditions inhibit the dispersal of air pollutants. More localized problems with air pollution occur, in and around particular industries or roads or particular hot-spots created by particular combinations of emissions and weather conditions. The concentrations of air pollutants may vary greatly throughout a day.

The extent to which particular air pollutants (or a particular mix of pollutants) constitutes a threat to human health will depend much on the city site and on weather conditions. For instance, in cities such as Bangkok and Buenos

BOX 3.2 *EXAMPLES OF AIR POLLUTION*

Indian Cities. The annual mean concentrations of ambient PM_{10} in Indian cities is more than six times the US urban mean (AMIS 1998 quoted in Smith and Akbar 1999). For many cities or particular city districts, it is many times the WHO guideline of 50 µg/cubic metre. For instance, in the mid-1990s, it was between 300 and 550 for residential, commercial and industrial areas in Calcutta and above 200 for Lucknow (city-wide), New Delhi (commercial, industrial and residential areas) and Kanpur and Jaipur (industrial areas) (ibid). Several cities had average annual concentrations of sulphur dioxide that were well above the WHO guideline of 50 µg/cubic metre for more than one year between 1990 and 1996 including Gajroula, Howrah and Surat (Central Pollution Control Board Delhi, reported in Agarawal and others 1999a). Figures for 1995 also showed a list of residential areas in cities such as Howrah, Surat, Ahmedabad and Baroda with mean concentrations above the WHO guidelines (ibid). There are also serious problems with carbon monoxide, oxides of nitrogen and hydrocarbons emitted by motor vehicles in central areas and alongside major roads or intersections in many Indian cities (Sharma and Roychowdhury 1996).

São Paulo. Between 1987 and 1994, air quality standards for suspended particulate matter were regularly exceeded on both a daily and a yearly basis. Daily and yearly standards were also regularly exceeded with regard to smog and carbon monoxide. During periods unfavourable to pollutant dispersion, the concentration of particulates regularly exceeded 375 µg/cubic metre – the lowest 'alarm' level (Jacobi and others 1999).

Bangkok. The annual average for total suspended particulates exceeded the official standards (and the WHO guideline level) at all ambient air quality monitoring stations in Bangkok city. Short-term 24-hour averages near the main streets were also often far above official standards (and WHO guideline levels). Carbon monoxide concentrations were generally below standards although in certain locations (typically streets with heavy traffic, narrow streets and tall buildings on both sides), short-term (8-hour average) concentrations sometimes exceed official standards. Airborne lead was not a city-wide problem but concentrations of lead in particular roadside stations exceeded WHO guidelines – in some instances by several times. Other air pollutants do not seem to be a problem (Wangwongwatana 1992).

Ilo (Peru). This city with around 60,000 inhabitants in 1999 has one of the world's largest copper foundries and a copper refinery close-by, operated by The Southern Peru Copper Corporation. The city has had one of the world's highest levels of air pollution, since the foundry began operating in the early 1960s, largely because of the sulphur dioxide emissions. Dark toxic clouds can gather over the town. In May 1995, peak levels of sulphur dioxide of 15,000 μg/cubic metre were registered, 30 times the WHO 10-minute guideline. Although emissions have come down, largely as a result of sustained community pressure, the foundry still emits 1400 metric tonnes of sulphur dioxide into the atmosphere each day, as well as suspended particulates that include heavy metals. Despite this, over the last 18 years, Ilo has developed one of the most successful environmental management programmes, as described in Chapter 7 (Follegatti 1999, Díaz and others 1996, Boon and others 2001).

Cities in China. Some of the highest levels of sulphur dioxide concentration occur in cities in southern China because of the widespread burning of coal with a high sulphur content, particularly in domestic stoves and small-scale industries. Annual average concentrations in Chongqing in 1994 were 330 μg/cubic metre, more than six times the WHO guideline; in Beijing they were twice the WHO guideline (WHO 2000). Many cities also have very high concentrations of total suspended particulates. Although the ambient total suspended particulate concentrations have been declining, in 1995, they still averaged around 400 μg/cubic metre in cities in the North and 300 μg/cubic metre in coastal cities (World Bank 1999). Guangzhou has had averages of more than 300 μg/cubic metre in recent years (WHO 2000).

Kathmandu (Nepal). Daily mean concentrations of sulphur dioxide were in the range of 273–350 μg/cubic metre in residential areas during September–December 1993; in monitoring sites close to main roads, the reported range was 310–875 μg/cubic metre (Sharma 1997, quoted in WHO 2000).

Mexico City. Although there have been significant reductions in the concentration of most air pollutants since the early 1990s and also a lowering of the peaks in ozone and particulates, levels still exceed the official acceptable limits much of the time (Connolly 1999). Ozone concentrations exceeded the WHO guidelines for 8 hours in over 300 days a year in 1994–1996 (WHO 2000). During 1997, the average ozone concentration was 1.7 times the official acceptable limit (ibid).

Aires, the location on or close to the coast on a flat plain means that a prevailing wind helps to disperse pollutants. A combination of topography, particular climates and weather conditions can help to trap pollutants in or over a city. For cities in valleys (such as Mexico City and Chongqing) or surrounded by mountains (as in Santiago de Chile), particular weather conditions help to trap pollutants for substantial parts of the year. Many cities suffer from thermal inversions where a mass of warm air well above a city helps to trap pollutants in the cool air underneath it.

Air pollution's health impacts

It is difficult to establish the precise health impact of the air pollutants introduced by human activities into urban air. For instance, it is difficult to isolate
the impact of one particular pollutant from others, and some health impacts
are the result of combinations of air pollutants or of synergistic interactions
between them. There is also the difficulty of distinguishing between the health
impacts of ambient pollution from indoor air pollution. Many factors can influence the level of risk – these are summarized in Box 3.3 – consequently there
are large differences in the exposure of each person to air pollutants and the
extent to which the exposure is likely to impair their health. There are particular groups within the population who are more susceptible to air pollution,
including people with asthma, those with existing health and lung diseases, the
elderly, infants and pregnant women and their unborn babies (Elsom 1996).
Particular circumstances can also increase exposure – for instance those who
spend longest in or close to busy roads, including drivers and passengers in
cars, cyclists and pedestrians walking along pavements beside the road. Drivers
and passengers in cars in congested driving conditions face much higher pollution levels than those outside the car (Elsom 1996). However, there is a growing
literature that seeks to quantify the health impacts of air pollution in Latin
America, Asia and Africa.[4]

Worldwide, it is estimated that around half a million additional deaths each
year can be attributed to particulate matter and sulphur dioxide in the ambient
air (WHO 2000). One estimate for Latin America suggests that over 2 million
children suffer from chronic coughs as a result of urban air pollution and that
air pollution means an excess of 24,300 deaths a year in Latin America. This
same source estimated that some 65 million person days of workers' activities
were lost to respiratory-related problems caused by air pollution. While the
authors emphasize that these are rough estimates, they give an idea of the size
of the problem (Romieu and others 1990). An estimate for India suggests that
air pollution is causing 40,000 premature deaths a year in cities and contributes
to a far larger number of hospital admissions and illnesses that require medical
treatment (Brandon and Homman 1995). An estimate for China suggested that
10,000 people die prematurely each year from particulate pollution in just four
of its largest cities – Chongqing, Beijing, Shanghai and Shenyang (World Bank
1996b). Another estimate for China suggested that smoke and small particles
from burning coal cause more than 50,000 premature deaths and 400,000 new
cases of chronic bronchitis a year in 11 of its largest cities (World Bank 1997).
A report on Bangkok estimated up to 1400 deaths a year and between 9 and 51
million days per year of restricted activity for respiratory reasons as a result of
particulate matter (US AID 1990). Although there are cities with notable
improvements in air quality in recent years, it is likely that air pollution is
increasing in many (or most) urban centres.

There is also growing concern about the health impact of the smallest particles within particulate matter. Initially, the concern for controlling particulate

---

4 See section 3.4 of WHO 2000.

Box 3.3 *FACTORS THAT INFLUENCE THE PUBLIC'S LEVEL OF RISK FROM EXPOSURE TO AIR POLLUTION*

The extent to which air pollution poses a risk to the general public depends on a number of factors including:

- The hazard of the compound released or of derivatives formed by chemical processes occurring within the air (for instance the formation of secondary pollutants such as ozone and acid sulphates), including the stability and persistence of the agent within the environment and its ability to penetrate indoors.
- The amount of pollutant released and the height at which it is released; tall chimney stacks tend to protect local people but disperse the pollutant over a wider area.
- The atmospheric conditions leading to dilution and dispersal of the pollutant, including worst-case inversion conditions and geographical considerations; local topographical and climatic conditions can exacerbate the situation as in Mexico City where thermal inversions trap pollutants within the valley in which the city is located.
- The person's distance from the source.
- The composition, activities and location of the general public in relation to the time of release (eg they might be exercising; children might be present).
- The presence of particularly susceptible individuals in the exposed groups.

Source: WHO (1992), *Our Planet, Our Health,* Report of the Commission on Health and Environment, Geneva.

---

matter concentrated on setting and enforcing standards for 'total particulate matter'; subsequently in recognition of the larger health impact of small particles, standards were set for particles that were smaller than 10 microns – so-called PM_{10}. More recently, standards began to be set for even smaller particles – those that were smaller than 2.5 microns – so-called $PM_{2.5}$. The associations between concentrations of airborne particulate matter and rates of mortality and morbidity in city populations generally get stronger, if the measure goes from total suspended particulate matter to PM_{10} to $PM_{2.5}$ (Lippmann 1999). The smallest particles include several chemically distinctive classes of particles that may have more serious health impacts, including those that are emitted in the exhausts from diesel engines and those formed during photochemical reactions (Lippmann 1999).

The concern is not only about the health impact of the particles but also about the potentially toxic pollutants present in much smaller concentrations, some of them bound to particles of smoke. For instance, analyses of the chemical composition of particulate matter from Beijing and Tianjin show the presence of relatively high levels of organic compounds, including the carcinogen benzo-pyrene (UNEP and WHO 1988). Although much uncertainty remains as to the precise nature and scale of the health impacts, estimates suggest that between 300,000 and 700,000 premature deaths a year could be averted in low- and middle-income countries if all urban centres brought suspended particulate matter concentrations down to those considered safe by WHO; this is equivalent to between 2 and 5 per cent of all deaths in the urban centres in which this kind of pollution is a problem (World Bank 1992). Chronic coughs in urban children would also be much reduced; so too would the probability of permanent respiratory damage (ibid). One estimate for Delhi suggested that an annual reduction of 100 $\mu g/m^3$ in total suspended particulates could be associated with a reduction in 1400 premature deaths a year (Cropper and others 1997, quoted in Romieu and Hernandez 1999).

Airborne lead remains a particular concern, especially for infants and children because of the evidence that relatively low concentrations of lead in the blood can have a damaging effect on their mental development with an effect that persists into adulthood (Needleman and others 1991). Some city studies have shown how a considerable proportion of the child population is suffering from impairment of learning ability, intelligence (including their IQ lowered by several points) and fine motor coordination and behavioural problems because of exposure to lead (WHO 1999). Their exposure to lead comes not only from the exhausts of petrol-engined motor vehicles but also from lead water piping (especially where water supplies are acidic), paint, some industrial emissions (see Table 3.2 for examples) and food (WHO 1992a). Traffic-related levels exceed the WHO guideline value of 0.5 $\mu g/m^3$ in many cities and in extreme cases are between 1.5 and 2 $\mu g/m^3$ (WHO 2000). Studies in the USA have also highlighted the huge savings to be made in medical and special educational costs if blood lead levels are reduced (WHO 1999).

A study in Bangkok which sought to rank urban environmental problems on the basis of their health risks suggested that lead should be ranked with airborne particulates and biological pathogens (primarily acute diarrhoea, dengue fever, dysentery and intestinal worms) as the highest risk environmental problems (USAID 1990). Studies in South Africa found that large numbers of inner-city (and some other) children have unacceptably high blood lead levels (von Schirnding and others 1999). Hasan 1999 reported on the very high levels of lead found in the blood of school children in the Saddar area of Karachi. A study in Mexico City in 1988 found that over a quarter of the newborn infants had lead levels in their blood that were high enough to impair neurological and motor-physical development (Rothenburg and others 1989). Exposure to lead may also contribute significantly to higher risks of heart attacks and strokes in adults. One major reason for such high concentrations of lead is the high lead content in petrol permitted by most governments (McGranahan 1991), although there is a growing awareness that the concentration of lead additives can often be cut and that a substantial proportion of petrol-engined vehicles can use unleaded petrol with little or no modification to their engines.

With regard to ground-level ozone, studies in Mexico City where ozone levels often exceed the WHO guidelines by a large margin have shown an increase in asthma-related emergency visits and an increase in respiratory symptoms in asthmatic children (Romieu and others 1997, quoted in Romieu and Hernandez 1999).

In many cities, air pollution levels can be sufficiently high to show demonstrable health impairment for the population in general or for particular groups. For instance, in Cubatão (Brazil) during the 1980s, as Box 3.4 describes, air pollution levels were linked to reduced lung functions in children (Hofmaier 1991). Non-ferrous metal smelters are often major contributors to air pollution and although we found no well-documented example in Africa, Asia or Latin America, a study in the Katowice district in Upper Silesia (Poland) shows the links between high air pollution levels from non-ferrous metal industrial plants and elevated lead and cadmium concentrations in the blood of 20 per cent of children. Some of those tested were also found to exhibit the early detectable symptoms of toxic lead effects (Jarzebski 1991).

A more common indicator of the health impacts of air pollution comes from comparisons between the health of people in highly polluted areas within cities against those in less polluted areas. These generally show a strong association between the incidence of acute respiratory infections and pollution levels. They may show associations between pollution levels and other health problems – for instance heart problems or certain kinds of cancers. If, for example, the incidence of cancers and respiratory diseases is drawn on a city map, this often pinpoints certain areas where residents suffer most from air pollution, and these are usually directly linked to one industry or one industrial complex. However, causal relationships between urban air pollution levels and cancer rates are difficult to establish, because of the difficulties in separating the contribution of ambient air pollution as distinct from occupational exposures, indoor air pollution, tobacco smoking, or socio-economic status (WHO 1992a).

In cities where acute air pollution episodes occur at particular times (for instance when high emissions coincide with particular meteorological conditions), the link between air pollution and health can often be seen in increased mortality among particularly vulnerable groups – for instance the elderly (WHO 1992a). Acute air pollution episodes occur regularly in cities such as Mexico City, Santiago de Chile, São Paulo and many cities in Southern China.

Cubatão in Brazil remains one of the most dramatic examples of unchecked industrial pollution and its impact on human health (Box 3.4). What is difficult to assess is whether the levels of industrial pollution permitted in Cubatão during the 1970s and early 1980s are an extreme example, or representative of what has happened and what continues to happen in many industrial complexes in other locations. It is perhaps revealing that only with the removal of media censorship and the return to free direct elections in Brazil did the scale and nature of the pollution in Cubatão (and in many other cities in Brazil) become widely known and was action taken to address it (Lemos 1998). Under the military government, there had been restrictions on all press reports on Cubatão, up to 1978. It was local citizen organizations (including the AVPM, the Association of the Victims of Pollution and Bad Living Conditions) that helped to document and publicize the problem, and helped to set up a system to monitor emissions from certain factories (ibid). AVPM also

Box 3.4 *Cubatão*

The city of Cubatão in Brazil, close to São Paulo and to the major port of Santos, was long known as the 'Valley of Death'. The city contains a high concentration of heavy industry that developed rapidly under Brazil's military government from 1964, including 23 large industrial plants and dozens of smaller ones. These included a steel plant, a pulp and paper plant, a rubber plant and several metallurgical, chemical and petrochemical industries. Most were Brazilian owned (including five owned by the federal government) although they included some multinational plants, for instance a Union Carbide fertilizer factory and a plant owned by the French Rhodia company.

There was little or no attempt on the part of the government or the companies to control pollution. High levels of tuberculosis, pneumonia, bronchitis, emphysema and asthma, and a high infant mortality rate were all associated with the very high levels of air pollution. In 1984, the concentration of fine particulate matter (PM_{10}) was more than three times the WHO guideline figure. At certain times, it also became common for young children to go, almost daily, to a hospital to breathe medicated air. There was a much above average incidence of infants born with serious birth defects and of a workforce suffering from certain occupational health-related diseases. The Cubatão river was once an important source of fish but industrial pollution severely damaged this. Local crabs came to contain too high a level of toxic chemicals to be safe to eat. Toxic industrial wastes were dumped in the surrounding forests, contaminating surface and ground water which was drawn on for human consumption (drinking and cooking). Vegetation in and around Cubatão suffered substantially from air pollution and from acid precipitation arising from locally generated air pollution to the point where landslides occurred on certain slopes as vegetation died and no longer helped to retain the soil. Many of those who came to work in the rapidly growing city lived in illegal settlements built on stilts above swamps; by building their homes on swamps, the inhabitants had a better chance of avoiding eviction, since the land had little commercial value. Around a hundred of the inhabitants of one such settlement (Vila Socó) were killed in late February 1984 after a pipeline carrying gasoline leaked into the swamp under the settlement and then caught fire; some 600 shacks were burnt and some 2000 people were displaced. In September 1984, an atmospheric inversion, combined with the high level of polluting emissions, led to the state governor declaring an emergency; the state's environmental agency ordered nine industries to close down and also an evacuation. Some months later, the release of ammonia from a ruptured pipe at a fertilizer factory led to the evacuation of 6000 residents.

For many years, there was little or no protection for the workers in many of the industries and many came to suffer from serious occupational diseases or disabilities arising from their exposure to chemicals or waste products while at work. Until the late 1970s, 'attempts to enforce environmental regulations met with great resistence from the industries, local government, and economic sectors of the state of São Paolo government' (Lemos 1998, page 80). The industries in Cubatão also sought to avoid the installation of pollution-control equipment by demanding the relocation of settlements most affected by the pollution, including one of the largest informal settlements (Vila Parisi).

Conditions in Cubatão have improved but as Lemos (1998) describes, driven largely by a strong citizen movement and progressive technocrats within the state government's environmental protection agency and by the political changes that permitted them to act, including the removal of press censorship in 1978 and the return to elected state governments. In 1983, the State of São Paulo's environmental protection agency, Cetesb, began to impose environmental controls and fined many industries while closing down others because they contravened the environmental regulations. The volume of industrial effluents disposed of in local rivers and solid wastes placed in local landfills was cut substantially. The average concentration of PM_{10} halved between 1984 and 1998, although in 1998 it was still 80 µg per cubic metre, well above the WHO guideline of 50 µg per cubic metre. Sulphur dioxide emissions were reduced, with average concentrations falling from 50 µg per cubic metre in 1984 to below 10 by 1995. The number of 'air pollution alerts' decreased from an average of 15 per year in 1984–1985 to 4 per year in 1986–1988 to less than 1 in 1989–1993. Emissions of other industrial air pollutants such as hydrocarbons, ammonia and hydrogen sulphide were also reduced by the large petrochemical and fertilizer industries.

Some companies in Cubatão subsequently publicly committed themselves to a more responsible attitude to the local environment, as they substantially reducing emissions and support local initiatives to improve conditions in and around the city. The local authorities have sponsored a project to help poorer households to move to a more healthy site and to build good quality housing for themselves. But for many people, this is too late, since they are already permanently disabled or a member of their family has died. The longer-term impact on health of pollutants already in the local rivers or leaking into ground water is also uncertain.

Sources: This box draws from various sources, although the primary source is Lemos, Maria Carmen de Mello (1998), 'The politics of pollution control in Brazil: State actors and social movements cleaning up Cubatão', *World Development*, Vol 26, No 1, pages 75–87. This paper includes not only details about Cubatão but also a discussion of how and why the environmental problems came to be addressed and, in particular, the key role of the AVPM (and the support they attracted from influential groups) and of progressive technocrats within the state's environmental agency. The figures for the reduction of pollution come from World Bank 1999b. Other sources: Leonard 1984, Landin 1987, Pimenta 1987, World Bank 1989, Bartone 1990, Hofmaier 1991, World Bank 1992.

demanded that the state environmental protection agency (Cetesb) keep them informed about each step in the implementation of the pollution control programme (Lemos 1998). Public pressure and a government that was more responsive to environmental issues and citizen concerns have produced sufficient improvement for Cubatão to be held up as a success story (see for instance World Bank 1999b). But perhaps it is more appropriate as a cautionary story of what companies and corporations can get away with, especially under the protection of a repressive political system.

One final issue to stress with regard to air pollution is the reminder that people's exposure to air pollution includes exposure indoors (at home or at work) or within neighbourhoods with particularly high levels of air pollution, as described in Chapter 2. This means that the measures of outdoor air pollution are not necessarily reliable indicators of total exposure (Smith and Akbar 1999).

WATER POLLUTION AND SCARCITY

Water pollution

In most cities, there are serious problems with water pollution. This not only damages water bodies (and aquatic life within them including fisheries) but also contaminates freshwater sources that then cause health problems for those who subsequently use them. There are few rivers or lakes in or close to major cities that are not heavily polluted. For instance, in Asia, rivers typically contain 4 times the world average of suspended solids and 20 times the levels common within high-income nations and levels of suspended solids have almost quadrupled since the late 1970s (Asian Development Bank 1997). Asia's rivers also contain three times the world average for bacteria from human wastes and more than 10 times the guidelines of the Organization for Economic Cooperation and Development (OECD) (ibid). The reported median faecal coliform count is 50 times higher than the WHO's guidelines (ibid).

Table 3.2 highlights the kinds of water pollutants that different industries discharge. Within each industrial sector, environmental impacts can vary considerably between the best and the worst performers. For instance, pulp and paper production in Asia generates many times more water pollution (in terms of total suspended solids) per unit output that in North America (Grieg Gran and others 1996). An industry's performance is driven by many factors, including (obviously) the form of environmental regulation and the extent to which it is enforced, company size, location, profitability and the availability of clean technologies.

Although no city or smaller urban centre can exist without reliable sources of fresh water, very few urban authorities have paid sufficient attention to safeguarding freshwater sources and preventing water pollution. This often means an increasing number of people drawing on polluted sources (for instance using polluted rivers, streams, lakes and ground water); Chapter 2 emphasized just how large a proportion of the population in many cities have no access to protected piped water supplies. It also means the depletion of the

Box 3.5 *WATER POLLUTION*

Most water pollution falls into one of three categories: liquid organic wastes; liquid inorganic wastes; and waterborne or water-based pathogens.

Liquid organic wastes. These can be termed 'oxygen-demanding' wastes since when disposed of into water, bacteria and other micro-organisms combine with oxygen dissolved in the water to break them down. The biochemical oxygen demand (BOD) of such wastes is a measure of how much oxygen dissolved in the water they will need to be broken down and as such, is one of the most widely used indicators of pollution. Liquid organic wastes include sewage, many liquid wastes from industries (especially industries processing agricultural products) and run-off from rains and storms that pick up organic wastes from land, before flowing into streams, rivers, lakes or seas. Too great a volume of organic wastes can overload the capacity of the water's bacteria and other micro-organisms to the point where all dissolved oxygen becomes exhausted. As the concentration of dissolved oxygen decreases, so fish and aquatic plant life suffer or die. Some portions of rivers or lakes that receive large volumes of organic wastes can have all their dissolved oxygen used up and thus lose their ability to break down these kinds of wastes and become black and foul smelling.

Liquid inorganic wastes. Most inorganic liquid wastes come from industry; these are not broken down in water in the same way as organic wastes but for most, their dilution in large water bodies renders them harmless. Many such wastes kill animal and plant life unless diluted sufficiently. Some inorganic wastes can become concentrated up the food chain to fish or through other freshwater or seawater products (shellfish, seaweed) to the point where they can kill or cause severe damage to the health of humans who eat them. Wastes that include certain chemical elements known as the heavy metals (including cadmium, chromium, mercury, arsenic and lead) or some of their compounds can be particularly dangerous. Many of the pollution incidents that have resulted in the largest number of deaths and serious injuries from water pollution have arisen from human ingestion of fish or crops contaminated with heavy metal compounds.

Water-borne or related pathogens. Many pathogens (disease-causing agents including bacteria, viruses and worms) are spread in water, either through human ingestion of contaminated water or through water providing the habitat for intermediate hosts. Much the most common and widespread problem is pathogens from human excreta which contaminate water supplies. Typhoid, diarrhoeal diseases and cholera are among the diseases spread by contaminated water. Contaminated water also has a central role in the transmission of many intestinal worms (see Chapter 2 for more details).

chcapest and most convenient sources, especially the overuse of groundwater resources. This usually implies much higher costs if water supplies are to be improved, as more expensive, distant sources have to be tapped (Bartone and others 1994).

There are usually four main sources of water pollution: sewage, industrial effluents, storm and urban run-off and agricultural run-off (Lee 1985). Agricultural run-off is often an 'urban' problem since water sources from which an urban centre draws may be polluted with agricultural run-off and contain dangerous levels of toxic chemicals from fertilizers and biocides. Box 3.5 describes the most common kinds of pollution arising from these sources.

Most cities in low- and middle-income nations have much more serious 'non-point' sources of water pollution than cities in high-income nations because large sections of their population are not served by sewers, drains or solid-waste collection services. A sewage and storm-drainage system that serves the whole city makes it much easier to control water pollution since the wastes collected by this system can be treated, before being returned to rivers, lakes, estuaries or the sea. A comprehensive solid-waste collection and disposal system greatly limits the amount of solid waste that is washed into water bodies. In the absence of such systems, much of the liquid wastes from households and businesses (and often industries) and a considerable proportion of the solid wastes end up in the nearest streams, rivers or lakes, greatly increasing the biochemical oxygen demand. The advantage of point sources is that treatment plants can be easily added, although in most cities, in the absence of adequate treatment, most 'point' sources (liquid wastes coming from sewers and industrial waste pipes) receive minimal or no treatment and are also major sources of water pollution.

Most rivers running through cities in low- and middle-income countries are literally large open sewers. Take the case of India, as documented in the series of reports on *The State of India's Environment* produced by a network of Indian NGOs coordinated by the Centre for Science and Environment. The most recent, *The Citizen's Fifth Report* (Agarwal and others 1999a), includes detailed descriptions of India's most polluted rivers and a discussion of the limitations in the measures taken to address the problems. Box 3.6 is drawn from this report and gives two examples.

Water shortages

A shortage of water adds greatly to the problem of disposing wastes, especially liquid wastes from industries and sewage. Large volumes of water dilute wastes and can render them much less dangerous; in addition, as noted above, bacteria and other micro-organisms in the water can break down organic wastes, if these wastes' biochemical oxygen demand is not too high relative to the water's dissolved oxygen. For instance, river pollution in many Indian cities has been made much more serious by the much reduced volume of water, due to overextraction of water upstream, usually for irrigation (Agarwal and others 1999a).

Mexico City is just one of many large cities that has outgrown the capacity of its locality and surrounding region to provide adequate, sustainable supplies.

BOX 3.6 *TWO EXAMPLES OF INDIA'S MOST POLLUTED RIVERS*

The Yamuna. The Yamuna river is the source of drinking water for some 57 million people, including Delhi, Agra and various other towns and cities. It is also the sink for sewage and run-off from industries, urban centres and a vast agricultural hinterland. The water quality of the Yamuna begins to deteriorate almost as soon as it enters the plains. Along its course, fresh water is abstracted while large volumes of polluted water are returned to it, ensuring a constant deterioration in its quality. There are serious problems with a range of micro-pollutants coming from pesticides and industrial effluents. A 1996 study of the Yamuna noted that Delhi's water-treatment plants often have to be closed because of high pollution levels to let the polluted band of water flow past the intake points, resulting in less water supplies for a day or two. In January 1997, high levels of ammonia detected in the river from industrial effluents led to major cuts in the water supply. Delhi is the largest polluter of the river. Some 1700 million litres of untreated sewage flow into the river each day. Industrial waste from 20 large, 25 medium and about 93,000 small-scale industries located in Delhi also flows into the river. After Delhi, there is a 490-kilometre section of the river which is called the 'eutrophicated' segment.

The Damodar. The Damodar river is one of the most polluted rivers in India, due largely to the industries that have developed on its banks and the minerals, mine rejects and toxic effluents that flow into it from coal mines. More than half the industries are coal mining, coal washing and coke over plants and the easy availability of coal has attracted thermal power stations and steel plants. The river is so polluted that the water is unfit even for agriculture, let alone for human consumption. Yet the river is the main source of drinking water for numerous rural and urban centres located along its banks. There is hardly any aquatic life in the river for 300 km between Giridih and Durgapur. Many stretches of the river and its tributaries resemble large drains carrying black water. Total suspended solids at most places along the upper and middle stretches of the river are 40 to 50 times the permissible limit. There are also high concentrations of oil and grease and toxic substances (including phenolic compounds and heavy metals).

Source: Agarwal and others (1999a), *State of India's Environment: The Citizens' Fifth Report,* Centre for Science and Environment, New Delhi.

But as Connolly 1999 describes, Mexico City is actually relatively well endowed with water resources. It has an average annual rainfall of 1000 mm and very large groundwater resources on which the city and its wider metropolitan area still depend for more than half its water. However, since the city is located in a closed basin, as water-use exceeded the supply that could be drawn from local resources, first its water supply was supplemented by water from the Lerma Valley, 60 kilometres away and then by the Cutzamala aqueduct, bringing water from 150 kilometres away and having to pump this water up nearly 1000 metres. Meanwhile, the depletion of the aquifer underneath the city has caused it to sink unevenly damaging the infrastructure and causing substantial leakage of piped water. As Connolly (1999) remarks, this is an absurd water system where a very large and expensive drainage system is needed to take waste water out of the closed basin while increasing volumes of water have to be pumped in, drawing from ever more distant sources, at great cost, including high energy costs. Despite the very high costs of drawing water from outside the valley and the high costs of managing the very large volume of wastes that then have to be pumped out of the valley, little effort has been made to increase the efficiency of water use, or to encourage water conservation, where appropriate, the reuse of waste water (Connolly 1999).

Chapter 5 will discuss the problem faced by cities that have outgrown the capacity of their locality to supply water and thus have to draw on more distant sources. It will highlight the particular problems faced by cities in arid areas or in areas where rainfall has declined. However, some care is needed in assuming that there is a link between the inadequate provision for safe water and a scarcity of freshwater resources. The growing literature on water scarcity often states or implies that this is so. But many cities and smaller urban centres where much of the population suffer from very inadequate provision have more than adequate freshwater resources. In addition, water shortages are often caused more by inadequate water management than by a lack of freshwater resources.

ROAD ACCIDENTS

Deaths and injuries from motor vehicle accidents have become an increasingly significant component of all premature deaths and injuries in urban centres, especially those where the contribution of infectious and parasitic diseases have been successfully reduced. Worldwide, over the last 50 years, the world's motor vehicle fleet has grown fifteenfold (Walsh 1999) and a large and growing proportion of these motor vehicles are in low- and middle-income countries. As noted earlier, some of the wealthier cities in Latin America have as many or more motor vehicles per person as many cities in Europe. However, as Newman 1996 shows, there is great variation among high-income nations in the number of cars per person and in their use, and Asian cities such as Tokyo, Singapore and Hong Kong, with good quality public transport that have much lower levels of motor vehicle use than cities in North America with comparable per capita incomes.

The rate of increase in recent years in the number of motor vehicles in many cities is dramatic. For instance, in Visakhapatnam, a successful port and industrial city in India, the total number of motor vehicles increased more than tenfold between 1980 and 1981 and 1993 and 1994 while the population doubled (Amis and Kumar 2000). Between 1982 and 1996, the vehicle population increased more than fivefold in Hyderabad and Chennai (formerly Madras) and more than fourfold in Delhi and Bangalore (official statistics quoted in Agarwal and others 1999b). Statistics for individual cities outside of India are rare but national figures show the scale of change (since most motor vehicles will be used in urban areas). In Sri Lanka, the total stock of petrol and diesel vehicles increased more than tenfold between 1974 and 1996.[5] For nations that have some economic success, the numbers are likely to rise rapidly, especially for those that start from a low base. In Beijing, the capital of China, estimates suggest that the motor vehicle population will double between 2000 and 2010 (Walsh 1999).

An estimate for 1993 suggested that there were 885,000 accidental deaths from motor vehicles worldwide (WHO 1995) and for every accidental death, there are likely to be several hundred accidental injuries (Manciaux and Romer 1986). In India alone, between 50,000 and 65,000 people have been reported killed in road accidents each year between 1989 and 1995 (official statistics quoted in Agarwal and others 1999b). This means that in the early 1990s, there were more deaths from road accidents in India than in the United States, even though India had less than a twentieth of the road vehicles of the USA. This shows how even in cities where there are fewer road vehicles, road accidents can still be a serious problem, because the number of fatalities and serious injuries per road vehicle is very high (UNCHS 1996). For instance, in Kenya, in 1991, the number of deaths from road accidents per 100,000 vehicles was 30 times that in the safest European nations (Odero 1996).

Despite the large and usually growing contribution of road accidents to serious injuries and premature death in many urban centres, there is relatively little research on this. Sheridan Bartlett, in reviewing the literature on the impact of accidents on children, suggests that road accidents are often the cause of the most critical injuries among the accidents that children suffer and that they tend to be more common for older children (Bartlett 2000). A hospital-based study in Kumasi (Ghana) found that pedestrian road accidents were the single largest cause of injuries (Abantanga and Mock 1998). Risks from road traffic are particularly serious in many illegal settlements because they developed next to major roads or highways and there has been little or no public provision for pedestrian crossings or bridges or for setting or enforcing speed limits.

TOXIC/HAZARDOUS WASTES

In cities in Africa, Asia and Latin America, as in Europe and North America, one sees the familiar list of solid and liquid pollutants: heavy metals (which include lead, mercury, arsenic, cadmium and chromium and their compounds), waste oils, suspended particulates, polychlorinated biphenyls (PCBs), nitrates, cyanide, as well as various organic solvents and asbestos. Some of these and certain other industrial and institutional wastes are categorized as 'hazardous' or 'toxic' because of the special care needed when handling, storing, transporting and disposing of them, to ensure they are isolated from contact with humans and the natural environment. Most come from chemical industries although others such as iron and steel plants, non-

---

5 Estimates made by the Sri Lankan Transport Sector Planning Centre quoted in Ellepola 1999.

fcrrous metal plants, oil refineries and industries producing petroleum products, pulp and paper industries, transport and electrical equipment industries, and leather and tanning industries also produce significant quantities of hazardous wastes. So too do many mines. Table 3.2 includes details of the main pollutants arising from the industrial groupings responsible for most toxic/hazardous wastes.

There are many different kinds of hazardous wastes. Some are highly inflammable, as in many solvents used in the chemical industry. Some are highly reactive and can explode or generate toxic gases when coming into contact with water or some other chemical. Some have disease-causing agents; sewage sludge or hospital wastes often contain bacteria, viruses and cysts from parasites. Some wastes are lethal poisons – for instance cyanide and many heavy-metal compounds. Many are carcinogenic (ie cancer inducing), including asbestos, arsenic, nickel and benzene. Some cause serious diseases of, for instance, the kidney (eg cadmium and mercury), the central nervous system (organic solvents, mercury, manganese), the cardiovascular system (including cobalt and chlorinated solvents), the blood-forming organs (lead, benzene), the reproductive organs (probably lead and some solvents) and the liver (some organic solvents (WHO 1992c). Many hazardous chemicals are extremely persistent; many also bio-accumulate causing much higher concentrations as the substance moves up the food chain (Budd 1999). Many are so toxic that even small quantities are enough to cause serious health or environmental damage. Many are associated with birth defects (see Chapter 4). Box 3.7 gives some examples of toxic chemicals, their sources and their potential health impacts.

Only in the last two decades has the scale of the problem of hazardous wastes and the potential risk to people's health been widely recognized (WHO 1992a). It is worth reflecting on the experience in high-income nations. The United States provides an example of the high costs that build up as industry expands in the absence of adequate controls on hazardous waste disposal or of their enforcement. The United States industrialized rapidly, giving little consideration to the regulatory aspects of hazardous wastes until the late 1970s. By the early 1990s, it was faced with the problem of some 50,000 land sites where hazardous wastes may have been dumped without control, and without provision to ensure that the wastes do not pollute the ground water. The costs of dealing with many years of inadequate control ran into tens of billions of dollars. It is also dangerous for any nation to tighten regulations governing hazardous wastes without the institutional capacity to enforce it; the greater the costs that have to be borne by the polluter, the greater the incentives for illegal dumping or other forms of evasion.

In most urban centres in Africa, Asia and Latin America, there are few or no measures taken to stop toxic or otherwise hazardous wastes being disposed of without treatment (Clarke 1999). They are disposed of as liquid wastes that run untreated into sewers or drains or directly into rivers, streams or other nearby water bodies. Or they are placed on land sites with few safeguards to protect those living nearby or prevent nearby water sources from contamination, or they are simply dumped down wells where they often contaminate ground water.

Box 3.7 *Examples of toxic chemicals, their sources and their potential health effects*

Examples of sources		*Health effect*
Arsenic	Pesticides, some medicines, variety of industrial air and water emissions, some mining processes	Toxic, dermatitis, muscular paralysis, damage to liver and kidney, cancer risk
Asbestos	Mining and milling, manufacture of asbestos products, asbestos products (eg roofing, insulation, brake lining)	Various cancers, chronic respiratory disease/asbestosis, chromosomal damage in exposed workers
Benzene	Petrochemical and leather industries, gasoline (especially unleaded), some other industries	Serious risk of leukemia, cancer risk, possible risk of heart disease
Cadmium	Zinc refining, electroplating, plastics, pigments, some fertilizers, some batteries, some coal burning	Kidney damage, emphysema, renal dysfunction, possibly carcinogenic, teratogenic & mutagenic
Chromium and chromates	Metal and various other industries, cement production, use of fossil fuels, waste incineration	Sensitization of skin and respiratory tract, various cancers
Lead	Some water pipes, some batteries and paints, emissions from various industries (including printing, mining milling and smelting, plastics), gasoline additive, lead-glazed pottery	Intoxicant that can result in acute poisoning and death, neurological impact in lower concentrations producing behaviour disorders and mental retardation, probably causing hypertension.
Mercury and compounds	Chloralkali cells, fungicides, wastes from various industries	Irreversible neurological damage, kidney damage
PCBs	Use in electric transformers and electric equipment, also in numerous products (eg paints, fire retardants).	Possibly carcinogenic, nerve, skin and liver damage, reproductive and immune system disorders
Vinyl chlorides	Plastics, organic compound synthesis, vinyl chloride production	Systemically toxic, carcinogenic

Note: This is by no means a complete list. WHO (1992c) also highlights the health effects of polycyclic aromatic hydrocarbons (PAHs), chlorinated fluorocarbons, fluorides, radon (and its decay products), nickel, maldorous reduced sulphur compounds, dioxins and formaldehydes, as well as some of the air pollutants discussed earlier in this chapter.
Sources: WHO (1992c), *Report of the Panel on Industry*, WHO Commission on Health and Environment, WHO/EHE/92.4, WHO, Geneva; Anandalingam, G and M Westfall (1987) 'Hazardous Waste Generation and Disposal: Options for Developing Countries', *Natural Resources Forum* Vol 11, No 1, February.

Few nations have effective government systems to control the disposal of hazardous wastes. In many, there are no regulations dealing specifically with such wastes (or even the legal definition of toxic wastes), let alone the system to implement them; in others, the problem is less the regulatory framework and more the lack of enforcement. The control of hazardous wastes needs a competent, well-staffed regulatory authority with the ability to make regular checks on each industry that is likely to be using or generating such wastes, and with the power to penalize offenders. This authority needs the backing of central government and the courts. For the effective control of hazardous wastes, industries must keep rigorous records of the kinds and quantities of waste and the dates and methods by which these are disposed of. Businesses that specialize in collecting and disposing of these wastes must be very carefully monitored; so too must the specialized facilities that need to be created to handle hazardous wastes. Since the safe disposal or incineration of toxic wastes is extremely expensive, there are enormous incentives to cheat any regulatory system.

One indicator of a failure to control the disposal of hazardous wastes are the many reports of problems with heavy metal pollution. Perhaps the best known and most dramatic example is that of Minamata in Japan. Although Japan has long been one of the highest-income nations, the example has relevance because it illustrates the scale of damage that can be done (in this case by a single industry) and the costs this brings. The industry discharged mercury-contaminated waste water into Minamata Bay and the mercury was biologically concentrated in fish and shellfish that were then consumed by people living around the Bay. As of 1990, 2248 people had been recognized as suffering from Minamata disease and of these 1004 had died (WHO 1992a). It is likely that far more had their health impaired, but were unable to prove this. The costs of dredging the bay to reclaim mercury and of compensation ran to the equivalent of hundreds of millions of US dollars. This illustrates the enormous cost in human life and health and in the costs of seeking to compensate for the damage done, if environmental regulations are not enforced.

Table 3.2 highlights how many industrial groupings can have heavy metals in their waste water, including chemical, glass and ceramic, mining, iron and steel, non-ferrous metals, petroleum refining and leather and tanning industries. The problem of mercury-contaminated wastes or of other heavy metal-contaminated wastes being discharged into water bodies has been noted in many cities. The Global Environment Monitoring System of the United Nations Environment Programme found heavy metal contamination in several rivers in Chile, China, Japan, Mexico, Panama, the Philippines and Turkey (UNEP 1991). Significant build-ups of compounds of mercury, lead, cadmium, copper and chromium have been reported in recent years in almost every industrializing nation in Southeast Asia (Jimenez and Velasquez 1989). On the south-east Pacific coast of Latin America, heavy metals have been detected in practically all areas that receive industrial and municipal wastes and worryingly high concentrations of mercury, copper and cadmium have been found in some fish species (Escobar 1988). Thirteen children were reported to have died of mercury poisoning in Jakarta in 1981 after eating fish caught in the waters of Jakarta Bay

tributary, while mercury concentrations in the water polluted by nearby factories were found to have reached dangerously high levels (Leonard 1984). Jakarta Bay remains the source of much of the fish consumed in the city; for a sample of fish and shellfish caught in the bay, 44 per cent exceeded the WHO's guidelines for lead, 38 per cent those for mercury and 76 per cent those for cadmium (World Bank 1992). Reports from China in 1980 and 1981 noted 'some astonishingly high cadmium and mercury concentrations in rivers and underground waters'; concentrations in water and in fish were found to be many times the level considered safe (Smil 1984) – in some rivers, the concentration is hundreds or even thousands of times the maximum recommended concentration within the European Commission. Conditions may have improved in China since then as a result of a stricter enforcement of regulatory standards for water pollutants (Dasgupta and others 1997).

One kind of hazardous waste that deserves special attention is radioactive wastes. The problems are illustrated by an accident in Goiania, Brazil, where a scrap-metal dealer broke up an abandoned cancer therapy machine releasing the radioactive caesium-137 from inside it. Because the powder and some of the metal glowed in the dark, the scrap dealer and his family and friends handled it. Around 240 people were contaminated and several people had died by 1988; many of those who survived will probably develop cancer (Anderson 1987, Consumer Information and Documentation Centre 1988). Even for nations with no nuclear power stations, radioactive chemicals are widely used in other activities.

Wherever governments seek to develop waste-disposal sites for these or other toxic wastes, local citizens are likely to mount strong protests. For instance, there was a long battle in Papan, Malaysia, between the Asian Rare Earth Company (which was partly owned by the Japanese Mitsubishi Chemical Company) and local residents (aided by environmental groups) because the company was disposing of radioactive thorium wastes on an open site, close to the town (Consumer Information and Documentation Centre 1988, Castleman 1987). Citizen action against this took place not only in Malaysia but also in Japan where a coalition of citizen groups denounced the Mitsubishi Chemical Company (Castleman 1987).

EXPORT OF TOXIC WASTES OR POLLUTING INDUSTRIES

In general, there appears to have been less relocation of 'dirty industries' from high-income to low- and middle-income nations than had been feared (Pearson 1987). As regulations on air and water pollution and on the management of wastes (including toxic or otherwise hazardous wastes) increased in high-income nations in the early 1970s, there was a fear that there would be a large-scale transfer of polluting industries to low- and middle-income nations, because of costs saved through less stringent environmental and occupational health controls (ibid). However, there was some transfer during the 1970s – for instance many industries manufacturing asbestos transferred from the United States to Latin America, with Brazil and Mexico as the most frequently noted recipients (Castleman 1979). There was also some transfer of production within 'dirty industries' during the 1970s by Japanese and North American subsidiaries with Taiwan, South Korea, the Philippines and Thailand being among the recipients (Castleman 1979, El-Hinnawi 1981).

The 'world map' of dirty industries is also likely to have changed as the proportion of world production from most such industries declines in high-income nations and increases in certain low- and middle-income nations. In part this is because of rapid industrial growth in many low- and middle-income nations to meet domestic demand, in part it is because production for international markets is cheaper in many such nations. Barry Castleman (1987) documented a large number of instances of multinational corporations with industries in low- and middle-income nations with serious problems of pollution or occupational health or both. Most of these cases arose in asbestos-related industries, pesticide industries or chemical industries.

Another indication of this shift comes from a study examining whether the exports of the products of dirty industries increased faster than imports in low- and middle-income nations while doing the reverse in high-income nations (Mani and Wheeler 1998, World Bank 1999b). There is evidence of a greater concentration of production in low- and middle-income nations in five particularly polluting sectors: iron and steel, non-ferrous metals, industrial chemicals, pulp and paper, and non-metallic mineral products. For Japan, the import/export ratio in these products fell from 1963 to the mid-1970s (ie as exports of the products of these polluting sectors grew more rapidly than imports) and then increased rapidly from the mid-1970s until 1990, reflecting tighter environmental controls and the high costs needed to meet them if production remained in Japan. Trends in what were then the 'newly industrialized economies' of the Republic of Korea, Taiwan, Singapore and Hong Kong were the reverse, as the ratio of imports to exports of the products of polluting industries increased from 1963 to1970 and then fell rapidly from 1970 to 1981 (ie as they increasingly produced and exported the products of dirty industries). The same pattern is evident in mainland China and other countries in East Asia, but later with the ratio of imports to exports of the products of polluting industries increasing from 1970 to the early 1980s, then falling to 1990. However, the authors of these studies emphasize that the import/export ratios stabilized at levels greater than one in both sets of nations and they remain net importers of pollution-intensive products from high-income nations. Similarly, in the United States and Canada, the import/export ratio for the products of polluting industries grew from 1963 to the late 1980s (after which it reversed) while Latin America had a steady decrease from 1973 to the late 1980s (ie as local production increased) with the import/export ratio levelling off at around one by the 1990s (ibid).

There are many examples of 'dirty industries' in cities in low- and middle-income nations with serious local health and ecological impacts. There are also examples of the export to low- and middle-income nations of outdated industrial technology which has serious environmental implications, as in the case of an industry in Indonesia utilizing an outdated mercury cell process for the production of caustic soda resulting in leaks of mercury to the environment per unit of output exceeding by several thousand times the acceptable standards (Anderson 1992). But there is little idea of whether this is a common trend or a relatively isolated example, or whether it is a problem that has become less common. The World Bank's recent report on Greening Industry tells the story of an Indonesian pulp and paper mill that imported an outdated factory for its mill in Sumatra in 1984 that dumped its wastes into the local river after minimal treatment. Local inhabitants working with local and national NGOs organized to demand pollution control and compensation, and the national pollution control agency mediated an agreement between them and the company. The company subsequently installed new technology which met national regulations (World Bank 1999b).

We suspect that the problems arising from the expansion of production from 'dirty industries' in many low- and middle-income nations combined with lax or non-existent enforcement of pollution controls and occupational health and safety regulations, are under-estimated. The lessons learnt in high-income nations on the enormous health costs associated with occupational exposures in particular industries that were not controlled and with the uncontrolled disposal of toxic wastes by certain industries do not seem to be heeded by governments in many low- and middle-income nations. They are also often being ignored by the industrial sector.

There is also the issue of the 'export' of hazardous wastes from high-income to low- and middle-income nations. Ten years ago, in the first edition of this book, this was a particularly important issue. There were many examples of European or North American businesses or municipal authorities that were transporting toxic wastes to particular low or middle income nations with little or no consideration as to the possible consequences for local populations. The local authorities at the disposal site were often unaware of the composition of the wastes and of the hazards that they presented (WHO 1992a). In the late 1980s, it also became evident that the volume of such exports was likely to grow very rapidly, unless steps were taken to curb this trade. The cost of transporting toxic wastes to low-income nations where they can be dumped without treatment and without sophisticated, safe storage facilities is only a small fraction of the cost of safely treating, incinerating or storing them in high-income nations and meeting government regulations in doing so. In addition, both companies and public authorities in high-income nations were also facing rising public opposition to the opening of new waste-disposal sites. The previous edition of this book included examples of toxic wastes that had been exported to Thailand, Nigeria, Mexico and Venezuela, and examples of companies that were negotiating with the governments of several Latin American nations and of Benin and Guinea-Bissau to export large volumes of toxic wastes there.[6] The example from Nigeria showed just how serious the problem could be. In this instance, 3800 tons of European chemical wastes were dumped by Italian ships in the southern port of Koko on the Niger river with a payment to the landowner of the equivalent of around $100 a month; the

---

6 IIED-AL, CEA and GASE 1992, Consumer Information and Documentation Centre 1988, Kone 1988, Phantumvanit and Liengcharernsit 1989, Secrett 1988.

cost of disposing of these in Europe would be of the order of $350–1750 a ton. The wastes were stored in 45-gallon (c200-litre) drums, many of them leaking and most in poor condition. Many drums had volatile chemicals that, in a hot climate, present a serious risk of a spontaneous fire or explosion.

The concern about the growth in this international trade prompted action and resulted in a number of countries prohibiting the export of hazardous wastes. The Italian government took the responsibility of addressing the problems caused by the dumping of toxic wastes in Koko, Nigeria, even though it had been carried out without their knowledge (WHO 1992a). International measures were also taken to limit this problem – for instance through the Basel Convention on the Control of Transboundary Movements of Hazardous Wastes and their Disposal. However, continuous vigilance is needed as in, for instance, the export of 'non-hazardous wastes' from high- to low-income countries (which is permitted) to ensure that no toxic wastes are included within the exported 'non-hazardous wastes'.

NATURAL AND HUMAN-INDUCED DISASTERS[7]

All cities face risks from a range of natural and human-induced disasters, including disasters arising from extreme weather events, fires, epidemics and industrial accidents. Most cities face risks from floods and many from earthquakes. Disasters are considered to be exceptional or unusual events that suddenly result in large numbers of people being killed or injured or large economic losses, and as such, they are distinguished from the environmental hazards that were discussed in Chapter 2 and in earlier sections of this chapter that are common or constant. This is a useful distinction but it has its limitations. For instance, far more urban dwellers die from easily prevented illnesses arising from environmental hazards in their food, water or air than from 'disasters', yet the death toll from disasters usually gets greater attention in the press and other media. If 100 people are killed by a flood, earthquake or industrial explosion in a large city, such a disaster is reported around the world. The fact that ten times as many people die each year in that same city from traffic accidents or (as in many larger cities) 100 times as many children die each year from diseases or injuries that are easily prevented or cured, or even (as in some cities) 1000 or more people are murdered each year is not considered a disaster. The same is true for illness and injury. While disasters can critically injure thousands of people, over time, their contribution to all illness and injury is usually relatively small. This is why it is becoming more common to integrate an understanding of risk from disasters (and who is most vulnerable) with risk from other hazards, especially environmental hazards.

The disasters most commonly associated with urban areas are cyclones/hurricanes, earthquakes, floods, landslides and industrial accidents. Droughts, famines, fires and epidemics are often not listed among urban disas-

---

7 This section draws on a background paper on this topic prepared for the 1999 World Disasters Report by David Satterthwaite with assistance from Ben Wisner and Terry Cannon.

ters, perhaps because a high proportion of the deaths they cause are on too small a scale to be considered 'disasters'. More details of each of these are given below. It should be noted that in many nations in recent decades, wars/civil strife have killed far more people than all these and other 'natural' disasters put together (International Federation of Red Cross and Red Crescent Societies 1998).

Drought/famine. Urban populations should be less vulnerable to drought/famine than rural populations whose livelihoods and assets are depleted or destroyed by drought or some other disaster. But many famines arise because poorer groups cannot afford to purchase sufficient food rather than from a shortage of food. Falling food supplies and rising prices put low-income urban families at risk. Hundreds of millions of urban dwellers have insufficient food intakes outside of any 'disaster' and, as noted in Chapter 2, their nutritional status is so often also compromised by diarrhoeal diseases, large intestinal worm burdens and/or micro-nutrient deficiencies.

Cyclones/high winds/storms. These have probably caused more deaths in urban areas than other 'natural' disasters in recent decades. It is not only the high winds that are hazardous but the heavy rainfall (which in turn may cause flooding, landslides and mudflows) and, in low-lying coastal areas, the storm-surge flooding that they often bring. The urban areas most at risk are heavily concentrated in coastal areas of the tropics where there are thousands of urban centres, including many large cities. The small island states in the Pacific and Indian Oceans and in the Caribbean are particularly at risk. A combination of disaster-preparedness (including specially strengthened homes or public buildings where people can shelter during the event), advance warning and good emergency response can greatly reduce the number of persons killed or injured.

Earthquakes. Earthquakes have caused many of the biggest urban disasters since many large and dense cities lie on earthquake belts. Collapsed buildings and infrastructure are the main causes of death, injury and damage, although secondary effects including fires and landslides can also be serious. Unlike cyclones and floods, earthquakes are difficult to predict. Keeping down fatalities and injuries is largely through a combination of adopting earthquake-resistant designs in all buildings and in roads, bridges and dams, avoiding the use of the most hazardous sites and having well-prepared emergency services.

Floods. Most floods arise from natural causes – heavy rainfall or snowmelt, exceptionally high tides and storm surges.[8] Most of the deaths, injuries and loss of property they cause in urban areas are human-induced, both because protective measures were not taken and from inaction in flood warning, flood preparation and post-disaster response. In cities where flooding is common, it

---

8 Human-induced climate change as a result of greenhouse gas emissions may come to contribute much to flooding because of its impact on sea-level rise and on the frequency and severity of extreme weather events; see Chapter 5 for more details.

is generally low-income households who are most affected as they have settled on flood-plains, river banks or other areas most at risk. Flood disasters affect many more people than cyclones and earthquakes but kill fewer people. However, large numbers of flood-related deaths in urban areas may go unrecorded or are not classified as 'disasters' because most occur within illegal or informal settlements. It may have become so common for 'a few people' to die from floods in these settlements that the deaths are never included in disaster statistics, although in aggregate, around the world, there is a large annual total of deaths from 'non-disaster' floods.

Landslides. Landslides can take the form of mudflows, rockfalls or avalanches. They are often triggered by storms, waterlogged soils and heavy construction but they may also be triggered by earthquakes or volcanic eruptions. Many major cities and thousands of smaller urban centres have high concentrations of people living on or below steep slopes and cliffs. Most are low-income households with limited possibilities of finding land for housing elsewhere and limited means to make their shelters safer. Official statistics suggest that landslides cause far fewer deaths and injuries than floods, cyclones and earthquakes but, as with floods, this may be because of undercounting as deaths from landslides become so common that they are not considered as disasters.

Fires. Historically, many of the greatest urban disasters have been caused by fires, although with modern materials and urban designs and fire-fighting responses, this is no longer the case. Measures to limit the risk of large-scale fires were also among the first examples of 'disaster prevention'. Some large-scale fires arise from other disasters – for instance the fires from ruptured gas pipes in the 1995 Kobe earthquake. However, there are far more deaths and injuries from accidental fires that are too small to be considered 'disasters'. People living in informal settlements with high population densities, homes built mainly of inflammable building materials, widespread use of open fires or kerosene stoves and lamps (or candles) are particularly at risk. The risk is much exacerbated by the lack of fire-fighting services and of rapid treatment for those who are burnt.

Epidemics. Historically, the impact of epidemics has probably been greater than all other disasters, but modern control measures have greatly reduced this. However, there are still serious epidemics, as in the outbreak of a new strain of cholera in Bangladesh in 1993 that accounted for over 1400 deaths and the cholera epidemic in Peru that began in 1991 and caused at least 2600 deaths (and spread to most countries in Latin America). Although the health impact of epidemics has been much reduced, as noted already, less progress has been made on reducing the impact of 'non-disaster' (endemic) infectious and parasitic diseases. As with accidental fires and probably floods, the number of deaths from 'non-disaster' diseases that can be easily prevented or cured greatly exceeds the number of deaths from epidemics. However, epidemics often occur after a period of deteriorating conditions or lax management (for instance of water sources) and should serve as signals of deeper problems. They can also serve to mobilize action, as in the greater attention given to water and sanitation in many Latin American cities to combat the spread of cholera and the actions taken in Surat (India) after the outbreak of plague there (Robins and Kumar 1999).

Industrial accidents. These include chemical and nuclear accidents, industrial explosions and the spillage of hazardous chemicals. The fact that industries are usually located in cities greatly increases the number of people at risk. Over 3000 people died in Bhopal after an industrial accident in 1984 released methyl iso-cyanate and another 200,000 fell ill (Agarwal and others 1999a). Other examples include the natural gas explosion in Mexico City in 1984 (over 1000 dead, 4200 injured, over 200,000 evacuated) and the explosion of explosives in Islamabad (Pakistan) in 1988 (over 100 dead, some 3000 injured) (UNEP 1991). The risk of industrial disasters is obviously increased if governments fail to ensure compliance by industries of environmental and occupational health and safety regulations.

Others. Volcanic eruptions and tsunamis (sea waves generally caused by earthquakes or volcanic events out to sea or under it) are among the other most prominent causes of disasters in urban areas. Some volcanic eruptions take a very heavy toll, as in the volcanic eruption and mudflow in Amero (Colombia) in 1985 that killed most of the town's 25,000 inhabitants. The disaster in Amero is also a reminder of how many of the worst urban disasters affect smaller urban centres whose governments are often less able to take the measures needed to reduce risks.

The possible influence of global warming. Global warming will increase the frequency and severity of many 'natural' disasters in urban areas. For instance, the threat of flooding will be particularly serious for many port cities from the rise in sea level and the increased frequency and severity of storms. Rising sea levels and the increased scale and frequency of floods also bring disruptions to sewers and drains, and may undermine buildings and increase the risk of seawater intrusion into freshwater aquifers. Changes in rainfall regimes may reduce the availability of freshwater resources or bring an increased risk of floods and landslides. This is a subject covered in more detail in Chapter 5.

Although 'natural' disasters are distinguished from 'human-induced' disasters, for cities, most of the deaths and injuries from the natural disasters are not 'natural' in that they occur because of inadequate attention to disaster-prevention, disaster-mitigation and disaster-preparedness. Most 'natural' disasters would not be disasters if people and institutions were prepared for them. Virtually all of the deaths and injuries each year in urban areas from floods, landslides and fires, and most of the deaths and injuries from earthquakes and tropical cyclones could be prevented. So too could the deaths and injuries from industrial accidents. There are also many instances of 'natural' disasters contributing to 'human-induced' disasters, as in the fires that often occur after 'natural disasters' or chemical contamination as tanks holding industrial chemicals or wastes are ruptured. The difference between disasters and other environmental hazards also becomes less clear when these other hazards are particularly serious. As noted earlier, accidental fires, landslides and floods that are too small-scale to be considered disasters and 'endemic' diseases and undernutrition that are not considered 'epidemics' or 'famines' underlie far more premature death, injury and serious illness than 'disasters'. In addition, pollution levels may fluctuate between 'disaster' and 'non-disaster', as illustrated by examples given earlier in this chapter. Air pollution levels vary according to the season and/or weather conditions and in many cities, they can become so bad for particular periods that they are declared 'a disaster' with special measures taken to reduce them. Without effective air pollution control, the intensity and frequency of such 'disasters' can increase and what was originally an occasional 'disaster' level for air pollution may become sustained for long periods. The air pollution produced by forest fires in Southeast Asia during 1997 was a disaster affecting tens of millions of people, including the inhabitants of cities far from the fires, but this is not a new problem. What made it a 'disaster' in 1997 was its scale and severity.

The way in which urban expansion and urban development is managed strongly influences the extent of risk from disasters and who is most at risk. As described in Chapter 1, city development involves massive modifications to the natural site including the reshaping of hill-slopes, the extraction of ground water and (often) the filling of valleys and swamps (Douglas 1983). The extraction of ground water, perhaps combined with the compaction of soil, may also increase the risk of floods and seriously interfere with natural or human-made drainage systems. The exposure of soil during the development of roads or new residential, industrial or commercial developments often leads to the erosion of surface soil which then increases silt loads of streams by as much as 50–100 times, blocking drains and raising the bed of rivers and streams, greatly exacerbating the scale of floods (Douglas 1986).

It has also become common for cities that were originally located on relatively safe sites to outgrow them. Most cities in Latin America, Asia and North Africa and many in sub-Saharan Africa were founded in what were considered safe and convenient sites centuries ago. Most of the world's largest cities and metropolitan areas are relatively ancient foundations. For instance, in Latin America, virtually all the capital cities and cities with 500,000 or more inhabitants were founded by the Spaniards and Portuguese during the 16th and 17th centuries, while a few had pre-Columbian precedents (Hardoy 1975). Most major cities in India, Indonesia, Pakistan and China (which between them contain a large proportion of the world's largest cities) have even longer histories. The same is true for many of the largest cities in Northern Africa and in Nigeria, the most populous country in sub-Saharan Africa. The many cities that owe their foundation and early development to indigenous civilizations were often developed by cultures with great experience in the ecological advantages and disadvantages of different sites. But city locations, then as now, are also influenced by economic and political factors. Sites with major advantages for defence, transport and political considerations were often developed as cities, despite the fact that the site (or certain locations within the site) were at risk from natural hazards.

For most cities, population growth was slow for much of their history. When relatively small, there was no need for urban development to take place on steep hillsides or over flood-plains or in areas with unstable soil conditions. It is the vast expansion of the urban population and the subsequent demand for space that has done more to increase the scale and severity of risk. Most major cities had sites that served them well until recent decades; they were either relatively free from natural hazards, within their national context, or measures were taken to limit the risks. But city sites that can ensure relatively safe sites for tens of thousands or even hundreds of thousands of people often cannot do so when populations expand to millions. Large cities today have long since reached a size far beyond what their founders could have imagined as possible.

Growing cities often exceed the availability of safe sites, or at least the price of safe sites become so high that poorer groups can no longer find accommodation there. For instance, for most of Caracas' history, the entire population was easily accommodated in the valley surrounded by hills. In recent decades, with the large expansion in the population and highly commercialized land markets that exclude poorer groups from good quality sites, poorer groups have been pushed in increasing numbers into settlements on steep hillsides with high risks of landslides (Jimenez Diaz 1992). Many cities that grew beside rivers, lakes or estuaries, where once the urbanized area was confined to sites with little risk of flooding, have now expanded on unsafe sites. Again, commercialized land markets exclude poorer groups from all possibility of developing housing on safe, legal sites. Thus, illegal settlements developed on land subject to flooding represent the best possibility for housing that is easily accessible to jobs.

The question arises as to why, if a particular city outgrows its site, it does not stop growing with new urban investments going elsewhere. One reason is the scale and influence of the city by the time the environmental hazards become apparent. When countries (and their economies) began to urbanize rapidly, the economic and political power concentrated in the major cities ensured a high concentration of population there, whether or not local physical and climatic conditions were well suited to the vast expansion of population and production located there. The scale of investments and the multiplicity of vested interests within any major city ensure an inertia against change which usually ensures a slow response. And even with severe environmental problems, the economies of scale in concentration for powerful groups may still exceed the costs. A second reason why city populations continue to grow over hazardous sites is simply that it is usually the poorer groups that bear most of the environmental costs. For instance, in the earthquake that hit San Salvador in 1986, causing some 2000 deaths and 10,000 serious injuries, most of those who were killed or injured and who lost their homes were low-income groups (Cuny 1987, Barraza 1987, Lungo 1987, Lungo 1988). In the floods that hit Resistencia (Argentina) in 1982–1983 which affected most of its population (and flooded half of the urbanized area), most of those who lost their homes were low-income households.

Many of the world's largest cities now find they are on sites ill-suited to the scale and concentration of pollutants generated there; the high levels of air pollution in Mexico City, Santiago de Chile and Chongqing and the particular characteristics of their site (and weather patterns) that inhibit their dispersal contribute much to this problem and have been described already. Other cities have developed on sites at risk from flooding, but the combination of much increased numbers concentrated there and a failure to limit the negative impacts of human-induced changes in the hydrological cycle have greatly increased the number of people at risk and the risk of flooding. Others have developed on seismic zones where again, the combination of much increased numbers and a failure to implement measures to limit the impact of an earthquake when it occurs has also meant a large increase in the number of people at risk.

Certain disease epidemics may be associated with natural disasters, especially floods that can contaminate all available water supplies and be associated with epidemics of dysentery or other water-borne and water-washed diseases. Outbreaks of leptospirosis (usually caused by drinking water infected by rat urine) have been associated with floods in Rio de Janeiro and São Paulo, and those living in poor-quality settlements at risk of flooding with high levels of overcrowding and inadequate provision for waste collection (or living close to rubbish dumps) are particularly at risk (WHO 1992a).

Integrating an understanding of disasters within other environmental hazards also shows the extent to which human intervention can greatly reduce risks. Many disasters may have natural triggers that cannot be prevented but their impact can generally be greatly reduced by understanding who within the city population is vulnerable to such disasters and by acting to reduce this vulnerability, before the disaster occurs. There are also important overlaps between 'the culture of prevention' for everyday hazards and for disasters. For instance, a city with a good sewage, drainage and waste-collection system is also a city much better able to reduce the risk of flooding. Good quality housing greatly reduces risks from physical hazards and, with appropriate building and settlement design, also reduces risks in the event of earthquakes, floods or cyclones. Good emergency services for 'non-disaster' accidents and acute illnesses can also serve as the basis for rapid and effective emergency responses when disasters occur.

NOISE POLLUTION

The health impacts of noise on city inhabitants is now being given more serious attention, even if the precise health and environmental effects are not fully known (Lee 1985). Temporary or permanent hearing loss is the best known health impact, although high noise levels are also known to be one of the critical stress factors that influence mental disorders and social pathologies (WHO 1992a). The most intense, continuous and frequent exposure to high noise levels is generally within particular jobs in particular industries (ibid). In the wider urban environment there are usually four principal sources of noise: aircraft, industrial operations, construction activities and highway traffic (Lee 1985).

Large areas of many cities have high levels of noise from aircraft landing and taking off in nearby airports; for instance, in Latin America, many major airports are in the middle of densely populated areas (the international airport of Mexico City and airports in Lima, Bogota, Quito, Guayaquil, Buenos Aires, Port-au-Prince and Santiago de Chile). Noise from major roads or highways is a serious problem, especially since few governments have instituted effective noise-control programmes on road vehicles, as in Europe and North America. In Shanghai, the average noise volume was reported as being as high as 62 decibels with noise levels reaching an average of 75 decibels at rush hour and 90 decibels in certain locations (Zhongmin 1988). Noise levels in central Karachi vary between 72 and 110 decibels (Hasan 1999). In Bangkok, noise pollution is considered a serious problem. Noise from trucks, buses and motor-cycles mean noise levels greater than 70 decibels in many locations although research suggests that outdoor noise levels should be kept under 65 decibels to comply with desirable limits indoors (Phantumvanit and Liengcharernsit 1989). Motorboats that are widely used in Bangkok frequently exceed the noise standard of 85 decibels at a distance of 7.5 metres set by the Harbour Department and an examination of motorboat operators found that 80 per cent had hearing loss (WHO 1992a). While noise pollution remains a major problem in Western nations, at least there are regulations, institutions to enforce them and democratic procedures through which protests can be organized; one or more of these is lacking in virtually all low- and middle-income nations.

ENVIRONMENT AND WELL-BEING

Good health is more than an absence of disease. As the WHO has long emphasized, it is also a sense of well-being and security (WHO 1992a). Thus, it is important to consider the large and varied range of environmental measures that not only reduce the risk of illness but also make cities, neighbourhoods and shelters more pleasant, safe and valued by their inhabitants. And by doing so, these measures will reduce the stress that contributes to both physical and mental ill health.

Good quality housing and living environments reduce stress and make life more pleasant through providing sufficient indoor and outdoor space with few personal hazards, minimum noise, a location close to family and friends, and easy access to desired services, recreation and facilities for safe play for children (WHO 1992a). Within the wider neighbourhood in which each shelter is located, it is clear that a sense of security, good quality infrastructure (eg roads, pavements, drains, street lights) and services (eg waste collection, street cleaning), the availability of emergency services and easy access to educational, health and other social services, as well as cultural and other amenities, also contribute to good mental health/well-being (Ekblad and others 1991, Schaeffer 1990). It is difficult to be precise about what environmental measures need emphasis, both because the interaction between environmental factors and human well-being is poorly understood, and because individuals and social groups have different needs and priorities. For instance, they vary considerably between different age groups and different cultures. What makes a neighbourhood environment safe, stimulating and supportive of social interaction for 5-year-olds is not the same as that for 15-year-olds.

Our understanding of the importance of environmental factors for well-being has been enhanced by the fact that so many psychosocial disorders are associated with poor quality housing and living environments. Among the most serious psychosocial disorders are depression (and other forms of mental ill-health), drug and alcohol abuse, suicide, and violence of different kinds such as child and spouse mistreatment and abuse and target violence, such as teacher assault and rape (WHO 1992a). Households constantly at risk from floods, landslides or other natural hazards are also more at risk from psychosocial disorders; the dislocation to their lives in the event of a disaster will also have health impacts.

Of course, psychosocial disorders are also associated with many non-environmental factors, for instance inadequate or insecure incomes, indebtedness, oppression, racism and other forms of discrimination, insecure tenure (especially for those who are squatters or unprotected tenants) and negative life events such as the death of a member of the immediate family, loss of employment, separation from a partner, etc (Cohen and Swift 1993, Harpham 1994, Harpham and Blue 1995, Wilkinson 1996). It is important not to overstate the influence of environmental factors. Acting to directly reduce the underlying causes of psychosocial disorders (for instance reducing discrimination or developing community-responses to reduce drug and alcohol abuse and domestic violence) and to reduce non-environmental risk factors are often more effective than improving the environment. But it is difficult to separate environmental and non-environmental factors as most are so closely interrelated. For example, for most households in most cities, their level of income and assets are the primary influence on the quality of their living environment – the house, the supporting infrastructure and services and the extent of secure tenure. As later chapters will describe in more detail, governments are often able to increase the quality and availability of secure housing with good quality infrastructure and services to lower-income groups and thus help to provide a larger proportion of the population with some of the key underpinnings of good mental health (as well as physical health). In addition, many negative life-events are largely the result of the poor quality, dangerous, insecure home and neighbourhood environment, including the death of infants or children and serious injury to one or more family member.

A concern for well-being within cities certainly requires more attention to psychosocial and chronic diseases. For instance, psychosocial and chronic diseases are among the most important causes of death in cities as diverse as Shenyang and Rio de Janeiro (Bradley and others 1991). Among the psychosocial disorders, two need emphasis: mental ill-health and violence. Only relatively recently has the first of these, mental ill-health, begun to receive the attention it deserves, in terms of its contribution to ill-health and of the number of people affected (see for instance Harpham 1994). As Blue (1996) notes: '...it is a problem that affects a large number of people, creates a great deal of suffering and produces a considerable burden on health services and society as a whole' (page 92). It is common for 10 to 20 per cent of those who visit primary care facilities to be suffering from mixed anxiety-depression, even though many sufferers do not seek help from such facilities (Harpham 1994). Blue's study of mental health in three subdistricts of São Paulo highlights how the prevalence of probable cases of mental disorder were highest in the poorest subdistrict with the worst environmental conditions. Discussions with women from this subdistrict also highlighted how much the poor quality of the housing and the deficiencies in the physical infrastructure contributed to stress (Blue 1996).

The women from this subdistrict also emphasized the lack of safety. One critical aspect of well-being in any urban (or rural) setting is a low risk of violence, within the home, the neighbourhood or the wider city. Violence is a major health threat in many cities in low- and middle- (and high-) income countries. A study undertaken in the late 1980s and early 1990s found that in selected cities in Africa and South America with more than 100,000 inhabitants, around one person in three was the victim of violence over a five-year period – the violence including assault, mugging, aggravated theft, grievous bodily harm and sexual assaults (UNICRI 1995, quoted in Vanderschueren 1996). This was twice the rate in cities in Europe and close to three times that in the cities of Asia (ibid). The trend seems to be upward in most cities.

One aspect of the increase in violence is the increase in murders or homicides. Homicides alone have come to be among the main causes of death in many cities in Latin America (Vanderschueren 1996). Murder rates (usually given as number of murders a year per 100,000 population) vary by a factor of at least 50 between the most and the least safe countries or the most and the least safe cities. A safe city should have a murder rate below 2 per 100,000 inhabitants but many Latin American cities have rates of 30 and some have rates of between 50 and 100 (UNCHS 1996), although others have very low rates. Aggregating murder rates for whole city populations obscures the fact that it is particular groups that are most at risk. For instance, young men are generally most at risk in Latin American cities. In São Paulo, in 1992, violence (mostly homicides) accounted for most deaths in boys aged 15 to 19 and for more than half of the deaths among boys aged 5 to 14 (Stephens and others 1994). And for every murder, there are many times more non-fatal assaults. But in other contexts, there are other groups particularly at risk – for instance in Maharashtra, the Indian state in which Mumbai is located, young brides burnt to death for not bringing enough dowry figure as one of the main victims of murders (Rai 1993).

A consideration of the scale and nature of violence, the causes and the means by which different forms of violence can be reduced highlight once again the difficulty of separating environmental and non-environmental factors. The underlying causes of most violence are not environmental, although environmental stressors can be important contributors to some forms of violence. But the risk of violence (or what people perceive to be the risk) is a major influence on city environments. Perceptions of personal safety influence women's and men's use of urban space. As Cohen and Swift 1993 point out, an awareness of violence within a city determines where people prefer to live, where they shop, how they respond to strangers on the streets, where they walk and drive and how late at night they can stay outside their home. A high risk of violence can be particularly problematic for people who are dependent on public facilities, as is illustrated by homeless women in Calcutta who cited rape and domestic violence as a major 'environmental problem' and explained how using communal toilets or public washstands at night was particularly risky (Stephens and Gupta 1996).

High risks of violence or of crime in general also helps to reshape cities as those with the means to do so choose new residential locations, forms and modes of transport. Teresa Caldeira's (1996) study of São Paulo shows how the increase in violence, insecurity and fear have changed the city's environment, including the landscape, the patterns of daily life, people's movements and the use of public transport, as crime and violence discourages people from using the streets and public spaces altogether. Streets where children used to play, where neighbours used to congregate and where it was common for people to stroll are now much less used. Increasingly, higher income groups are living, working, shopping and taking their leisure in what are essentially fortified enclaves and are no longer making use of streets or public spaces which are abandoned to the homeless and the street children (ibid). Similar developments are evident in many cities around the world as middle- and upper-income groups move to fortified residential enclaves, or barrios cerados, and journey by private vehicle between these or apartment complexes, shopping centres or malls and office complexes, each with sophisticated security systems and their own secure car parks. So there is little or no necessity to walk on the streets or to use open spaces. High levels of crime and fear of violence have helped to push shopping centres, office complexes and leisure activities to suburban areas and in some cities, this has reached the point where it is increasingly rare for middle- and upper-income groups to visit the city centre.

High levels of crime can have a very serious impact on the economy and the environment of a neighbourhood or city centre:

> *The abandonment of neighbourhoods by the most positive elements, the decrease in traffic and the risks of break-ins and armed robbery drive business out. House values drop, and buildings deteriorate. Urban services departments spend less and less to maintain and upgrade ageing and vandalized infrastructures. Industries opt for other sites because these areas no longer have the labour force they are looking for and the physical conditions they need to operate. Tourists are very careful to avoid venturing into these areas* (International Centre for the Prevention of Crime 1995).

Violence generally hits the poor hardest. For instance, in São Paulo in 1992, death rates from homicides were 11 times higher for adolescent boys in deprived areas than for those living in non-deprived areas (Stephens and others 1994). High levels of violence not only erode the physical and human capital of communities including the quality of open space, transport systems, schools and healthcare centres (and whether, how and when they can be used 'safely'), but also the social capital, including the ability of communities' formal and informal social institutions to address problems (Moser and McIlwaine 1999).

As with the measures to address most other psychosocial health problems, violence-prevention strategies usually centre on non-environmental strategies, although such strategies often lead to improved environments or include important environmental components. A study in São Paulo in regard to homicides highlights the many factors that influence the higher rates of homicides in low-income areas:

> *... concentrated poverty, urban deterioration, racism and other forms of social discrimination, lack of opportunities of employment and formal education, lack of policing... emphasis on violent behaviour as a way of resolving personal conflicts... easy access to fire arms, the increasing consumption of drugs (such as crack and marijuana) and alcohol abuse... The correlation between living conditions and structural violence (violence arising from a social system that produces gender, race and age discrimination as well as inequalities of social class) is not a linear or mechanical relation... (also involved are) cultural traits and aspects of personal relationships in some segments in the population* (Barata et al 1998, page 7, quoted in Harpham and Molyneux 2000).

Thus, it is clear that poor quality living environments can contribute to the stress that underlies many diseases. Many physical characteristics of the housing and living environment can influence the incidence and severity of psychosocial disorders through stressors such as noise, overcrowding, inappropriate design, poor sanitation and waste collection and inadequate maintenance (WHO 1992a). A poor quality living environment can also serve as a constant reminder of the lack of any sense of having a place in a community and of one's social exclusion (Wilkinson 1996).

When considering the possible impact of the physical environment on people's psychosocial health, Ekblad and others 1991 suggests the need to focus on three aspects:

1   The dweller's level of satisfaction with the house and its neighbourhood and its location within the urban area.
2   The dwelling's physical structure (eg the amount of space, state of repair, facilities, which may influence the level of privacy, the possibilities for meeting relatives and friends and child-rearing practices).
3   The neighbourhood, including the quality of services and facilities, and the level of security. Many characteristics of urban neighbourhoods that are not easily identified or defined may have important influences on an individual's level of satisfaction and on the incidence of crime, vandalism and interpersonal violence (Jacobs 1965, Newman 1972).

The use of participatory techniques has also highlighted the range of environmental and non-environmental priorities that residents have for improving conditions and the role that they choose to take in implementing them or monitoring those who do implement them. It is clear that the extent to which any individual or household has the possibility of modifying or changing their housing environment and working with others in the locality to effect change in the wider neighbourhood is also an important influence on their sense of well-being. Many critiques of public housing and of urban planning in cities in low- and middle-income nations (especially 'slum' and squatter clearance and redevelopment) have centred on the loss of individual, household and community control that they cause (Turner 1976). There is also the importance for the physical and mental health of individuals and communities of being able to command events that control their lives (WHO 1992a, Duhl 1990). Medical doctors and psychiatrists are increasingly recognizing the importance of such a link (Duhl 1990).

There are also the multiple influences of the built environment on child development. Poor physical environments can inhibit or permanently damage a child's mental development as well as their physical development (Myers 1991). Children are especially vulnerable to deficiencies in the provision for play and for informal learning from their peers, with the particular needs also varying considerably at different ages. In most poor districts in cities, there is little or no formal provision for playgrounds for young children that are both safe (eg free from faecal contamination) and stimulating. The needs of older children and adolescents are also rarely met, for easily accessible indoor and outdoor space for games, sports and socializing. Yet the importance of safe and stimulating play in, for instance, the evolution of a child's motor skills and communication skills, problem solving, logical thinking, emotional development and social and socialized behaviour is increasingly recognized (Hughes 1990).

Infants and children often suffer not only from a poor physical environment in the sense of overcrowded and hazardous housing and inadequate provision for play (including dangerous and unsuitable play sites) but also from the psychosocial disorders that deficiencies in the physical environment and the stressors associated with them promote in their parents or carers. Among the key psychological and social development needs of children are a need for interaction (to provide stimulation and reaction to the child), the need for consistency and predictability in their care-giving environment and a need to explore and discover (Myers 1991). It is easy to see how a poor physical environment makes these more difficult to provide, although perhaps a more important (non-environmental) factor is that in many low-income households, all adults work long hours to obtain sufficient income to survive, and providing child supervision, care and stimulation are very difficult.

The precise linkages between different elements of the physical environment and people's sense of well-being are difficult to ascertain and to separate from other influences. There are also other influences that can promote or prevent the process that might lead to disease (Kagan and Levy 1975) – for instance 'strong social networks and a sense of community organization in many rundown inner city districts ... and squatter settlements ... might help explain the remarkably low level of psychosocial problems' (WHO 1992a). The importance of such networks can also be seen in the increase in physical and mental ill health among populations relocated from inner city tenements or illegal settlements to 'better quality' housing, partly because such networks became disrupted (Turner 1976). One key conclusion seems to be that people's capacity to choose housing and neighbourhoods whose built and natural environment meets their environmental and non-environmental needs has considerable importance for their physical and mental well-being. Another is that good quality, well-managed schools, health centres, public transport and emergency services and supportive policing (including an emphasis on prevention) contribute much to good mental as well as physical health.

ENVIRONMENTAL PROBLEMS IN SMALLER CITIES

Their demographic dominance within urban populations

Given that in most countries, a significant proportion of urban dwellers live in relatively small urban centres, there is a remarkable lack of documentation on environmental problems other than those in large cities. Virtually all the examples given of environmental problems so far in this book are for urban centres with more than one million inhabitants. Yet most of the urban population lives in urban centres with less than a million inhabitants. In Africa and Asia, more than three-fifths of the urban population lives in urban centres with less than a million inhabitants; even in Latin America, for 1990 (the last date for which reliable statistics are available for most countries), three-fifths of the urban population lived in cities with less than a million inhabitants.[9] Close to 50 independent nations have no city that has reached 500,000 inhabitants (United Nations 1998).

All urban centres (whether large or small cities or urban centres too small to be called cities) need:

- Water supply systems which protect water sheds and ensure uncontaminated water is easily available to all households.
- Provision for the disposal of household and human wastes (including excreta, household's waste waters, storm and surface run-off and solid wastes).
- Preventative and curative health services and basic environmental management (for instance to protect water sources, to minimize breeding and feeding grounds for disease vectors).

Growing urban centres need land-use management to ensure sufficient land for housing (and other uses) while protecting valuable land and avoiding settlement over hazardous land. Small urban centres with polluting industries need the implementation of pollution control legislation. All urban centres need local authorities with the competence and capacity to ensure that these are provided and the accountability to their citizens to ensure that they do so.

Water, sanitation and waste collection

The limited information available about provision for water, sanitation and waste collection in smaller cities suggests that most have serious environmental problems. It would be surprising if this was not the case, given that most larger cities are also more prosperous and by being seats of national or

---

9 See Chapter 1 for more details.

provincial/state governments, obtain more government resources and attention. But Box 3.8 illustrates the lack of any capacity by local authorities to ensure adequate provision for water, sanitation and waste collection in the smaller African urban centres. Note how most or none of the population in Kabale, Mbandjock, Aliade, Igugh, Ugba, the smaller towns in Mwanza Province and two of the three towns in Benin had access to a piped water system. Most small African cities and smaller urban centres also have no public provision for sanitation. This is not just the lack of a sewer system but also the lack of a system to serve a population reliant on pit latrines – for instance there is no service to advise on pit-latrine construction (so they function effectively and do not pollute ground water) and no equipment to empty them. What case studies of such centres make clear is local authorities' lack of any investment capacity for installing or expanding basic infrastructure and the inadequacy in the basic capital equipment. For instance, in the example of Kabale in Uganda given in Box 3.8, in 1991, when the study was undertaken, the entire population of some 28,000 people relied on one working tractor and trailer to collect wastes (Amis 1992). However, even when some capital investment has taken place, the capacity to manage or maintain it is often very limited. For instance, even though two of the smaller towns in the Mwanza region in Tanzania had a network of pipes in place and functioning piping stations, water was rarely delivered to the network because the fuel allocation could only meet the requirements of a few weeks' operation per year (Zaba and Madulu 1998).

Given that some of the studies reported in Box 3.8 were undertaken eight to ten years ago, conditions may have improved since then, but one cannot assume that this is the case. Box 2.2 showed how provision for water had got worse in many urban sites in East Africa over the last 30 years. Box 3.9 presents another example from a small urban centre in Africa, but this time it gives a picture of how provision for water has changed over the last three decades.

In Asia too, there is far more documentation of the environmental problems in large cities. In part, this is because census data about the quality of housing and of provision for water, sanitation and drainage is never published (or made available) for individual urban centres. It is usually independent research studies that provide evidence of the serious environmental problems in smaller cities, as in Box 3.10 which gives examples of the inadequacies in provision for water, sanitation and drainage in smaller cities in India. These examples also illustrate a problem that appears to be particularly common in smaller urban centres in Africa and Asia – the high proportion of low-income households who have no provision for sanitation and so defecate in open spaces.

In Latin America, there are also case-studies of particular smaller cities showing the inadequacies in provision for water, sanitation and drainage. For instance, Foronda (1998), while describing the innovative Local Agenda 21 developed by a coalition of groups in Chimbote (Peru), also highlights the main environmental problems: the inadequacies in provision for water and sanitation with two-fifths of the population lacking piped water and connection to sewers, the lack of a regular waste-collection system in most residential areas and the many informal settlements at high risk from floods.

Box 3.8 *Water, sanitation and garbage services in small African urban centres*

Kabale (Uganda). With 27,905 inhabitants in 1991, this is a market town in an extremely fertile and high-density rural area. For water supply, there were just 217 connections to the piped water system and on average, water was supplied for four hours in the morning and two hours in the evening. Estimates suggest that less than 16 per cent of the population had access to water from this system. Provision for sanitation was also very deficient. Refuse collection relies on one working tractor and trailer that collects wastes from 20 areas marked with signposts where refuse may be deposited by the public. It is estimated that around 10–20 per cent of the daily refuse is collected (Amis 1992).

Mbandjock (Cameroon). Only about 20 per cent of the population (estimated at 20,000 in 1996) have access to piped water; the rest rely on wells and springs for their water supply but tests found that all spring and well waters presented evidence of faecal contamination from human and/or animal origin. Data from the city hospital show that gastro-intestinal and diarrhoeal diseases are among the most prevalent diseases in the community (after malaria and onchocerciasis). The city has no sewer system and the only method of sewage disposal is by pit latrines or septic tanks (Tchounwou and others 1997).

Mwanza Province (Tanzania). According to the 1988 census, over 90 per cent of households in Mwanza town used a piped water supply for drinking, but the situation in smaller towns nearby was much worse. Only 20–30 per cent of households living in the other two towns on the lakeshore had piped drinking water, and in the inland towns only 1–5 per cent. The main problems in providing a piped supply in urban areas was maintenance and the installation of infrastructure, and obtaining fuel for pumping (the overriding problem for smaller towns). Even though two of the smaller towns in the Mwanza region had a network of pipes in place and functioning piping stations, water was rarely delivered to the network because the fuel allocation could only meet the requirements of a few week's operation per year. In the smaller towns, virtually all households that report using piped water supplies are dependent on public standpipes. In Mwanza town, around 20 per cent of households have water piped into the home or their yard, and 10 per cent have full plumbing facilities including flush toilets. In urban Mwanza, on average, migrant households had to walk 750 metres, and resident households 600 metres, to obtain water (Zaba and Madulu 1998).

Aliade, Igugh and Ugba (Nigeria). Each of these urban centres had an estimated population between 6000 and 8000 in 1980. Two of them have no piped water system and in the third, only a small number of households have access to treated water (from the state rural water supply scheme).

Most households obtain water from compound wells that are the responsibility of the compound owner; the next most common sources of water are streams, ponds and rivers. The State Water Boards in Nigeria are responsible for providing water supplies to urban centres but piped water schemes are rarely available to small urban centres. There is no public provision for sanitation; most households use pit latrines although some households have no access to a latrine. About half of the households using such latrines share them. Refuse collection and disposal is, in theory, a local government responsibility but 67 per cent of households dump refuse in their back yard while most of the rest burn or bury it. Only in one of the three urban centres was there neighbourhood collection and disposal and this was organized on a small scale (Meekyaa and Rakodi 1990).

Benin City (Nigeria). Families in the informal-housing sector in Benin City normally use pit latrines. A 1995 survey found that 74 per cent of households relied on these and most were of questionable quality. Household water is mainly piped from outside the housing premises (from another compound, the street or other neighbourhoods) or obtained from a water vendor or from a rain harvester underground tank (Ogu 1998).

Small cities in Benin. A study of three secondary cities in Benin found that in two of them, the vast majority of the population lacked running water and latrines so most people defecated in the 'bush' (Yacoob and Kelly 1999).

Another set of examples of the inadequacies in provision for water, sanitation and drainage (and in the capacity and competence of local authorities) comes from Brazil from a book entitled *Rainforest Cities* (Browder and Godfrey 1997). This includes case studies of 'boom cities' on the agricultural/forest frontier and is a rare example of careful documentation of the environmental (and other) problems of the new cities that grow up within areas where forests are being logged and land is being cleared for cultivation. One of the authors, while telling the story of his visit to Rolim de Moura in 1984, recounts the comments of the municipal prefect who

> ... *wasted no time reciting a long list of hardships endured by his fellow citizens, who numbered, he believed, somewhere between 10,000 and 20,000. Rolim de Moura suffered from no running water or plumbing, no electricity, malaria and dysentery of epidemic proportions, terrible communications, daily homicides, prostitution, runaway inflation and choking dust. The prefect blamed these problems, all customary trademarks of frontier urban life in the Amazon, on a 'governo que não vale' (a worthless government)* (Browder and Godfrey 1997, page 161).

Box 3.11 gives examples of the inadequacies in provision for water and sanitation in Rolim de Moura and in some other frontier cities. In the three towns

Box 3.9 *THE DETERIORATION IN THE QUALITY OF MUNICIPAL WATER SUPPLIES IN IGANGA (UGANDA)*

A study of domestic water supplies in Iganga in 1967 found that all sample households received adequate supplies of water 24 hours a day. A study in 1997 that returned to the same sites found that for the households interviewed, the municipal water system had deteriorated to the point that only 13 per cent of them received piped water and even for these, water only trickled out of pipes a few hours each day. Some households reported being without piped water for up to three years.

One respondent explained: 'During the 1960s and early 1970s, the situation was good but from the late 1970s, the supply of water began to deteriorate. The situation worsened in the 1980s when water pumps and most of the distribution lines broke down. Of the four pumps operating in the 1960s, only one was still working by 1980.' The water storage tanks and the distribution lines were also rusty and leaking. One urban water officer reported that 'most of the revenue collected from water bills is spent on repairing the pipes and pumps. Moreover, since the water pumps run off electricity that are subject to frequent power cuts, water supply is unreliable. It is really beyond our control.'

By the late 1980s, in an attempt to compensate for these problems, alternative sources were developed. Private individuals began to drill boreholes and establish their own water kiosks. In 1998, these private sources were supplemented with kiosks built by the Iganga Town Council.

Per capita water use had increased for unpiped households, although not very much from an average of 15 litres per person per day in 1967 to 24 litres in 1997.

Source: John Thompson, Ina T Porras, Elisabeth Wood, James K Tumwine, Mark R Mujwahuzi, Munguti Katui-Katua and Nick Johnstone (2000), 'Waiting at the tap: changes in urban water use in East Africa over three decades', *Environment and Urbanization*, Vol 12, No 2, October, and White, Gilbert F, David J Bradley and Anne U White (1972), *Drawers of Water*, University of Chicago Press, Chicago and London.

from Para, more than three-quarters of the residents interviewed were not connected to piped water systems and drew their water from surface sources that were easily contaminated – shallow wells, local creeks and open springs. Browder and Godfrey 1997 describe in some detail the public health problems suffered by the inhabitants; for these three towns, around half of all heads of household interviewed had had malaria and more than a fifth of households had had one or more member who had suffered from diarrhoea in the previous year; 4 per cent had had one member contracting hepatitis in the previous year. Environmental problems are always likely to be particularly serious in cities that grow very rapidly in newly settled areas (whether on the agricultural frontier or in response to some new economic activity such as mines) since it is rare for there to be any government institution able to manage the rapid growth and to

---

Box 3.10 *EXAMPLES OF WATER AND SANITATION PROVISION IN SMALLER URBAN CENTRES IN INDIA*

A survey of 400 households drawn from different 'slums' in each of three cities found the following:

Bhilwara. Most housholds surveyed had access to water through taps and hand pumps but many mentioned their distance from a water source as a major problem. Only 25 per cent had a water source inside their house, and the proportion of households with water inside their house rose with income, from 10 per cent for those with monthly incomes of less than 500 rupees to 48 per cent for those with incomes above 2000 rupees. Three-quarters of surveyed households had no toilet, and most defecated in some open space or nearby fields. There were no public or community toilets.

Sambalpur. Of the households surveyed 95 per cent depended on a community source and in most slums, the number of such sources was inadequate. Only 56 per cent had access to the municipal piped water supply, and the supply was irregular. In 4 of the 12 sample slums there was no source of piped water at all. Most of the 'slums' had grown up around a tank or a pond that was initially a major source of water, but these became unusable because they were not kept clean and many of them had dried up completely. The municipality does not take responsibility for cleaning these ponds. More than three-quarters of the 400 households reported that they had no provision for any type of toilet facility and no drainage facility around the house. Of the 24 per cent of households reporting any type of drainage, 43 per cent said that these were not cleaned regularly.

Siliguri. Half the households surveyed had an independent water source while the rest used a common source. Most houses had water supplies nearby and 87 per cent thought that the water was fit for drinking and nearly all of them were satisfied with the supply. Three-quarters of the houses had an independent toilet (most built by the municipalities against a deposit of Rs 150 by the beneficiary) and 18 per cent used communal toilets. Two-fifths of the households had no provision for drainage with the rest having open drains that were rarely cleaned.

Source: Ghosh, A, S S Ahmad and Shipra Maitra (1994), *Basic Services for Urban Poor: A Study of Baroda, Bhilwara, Sambalpur and Siliguri*, Urban Studies Series No 3, Institute of Social Sciences and Concept Publishing Company, New Delhi.

---

ensure adequate provision for environmental health (or government interest, at a higher level, to ensure this happens).

Thus, it is not only in the smaller urban centres in the lower-income nations of Latin America and the Caribbean that there are serious problems, as examples drawn from Argentina and Brazil show. Indeed, a substantial propor-

---

Box 3.11 EXAMPLES OF PROVISION FOR WATER AND SANITATION IN
AMAZONIAN FRONTIER TOWNS IN BRAZIL

Two small towns in Rondonia:
Rolim de Moura is one of hundreds of frontier towns that grew in the
Amazon over the last 20 years. Founded in 1976, it developed as a service
centre for the logging of mahogany; by 1984, it was known as the world
capital of mahogany. Its economic base contracted after the mahogany
boom collapsed in 1985 but its population continued to grow, reaching
around 30,000 in 1990. A survey of 419 households found that 44 per cent
had an informal water supply (either from a private well without a pump or
hand-carried water from the local river) and 67 per cent had informal sanitation (lack of septic tank or connection to a sewer and reliance on outhouses
or defecation outside).

Santa Luiza d'Oeste is a town that grew close to Rolim de Moura as a
service centre for settlement and then for the agriculture that developed
close-by. With a population estimated at 6000 in 1990, a survey of 208
households found that 52 per cent relied on an informal water supply and
80 per cent relied on informal sanitation.

Three small towns in Southern Pará:
Xinguara, Ourilândia do Norte and Tucumã are the principal towns within
the Xingu settlement corridor and they grew rapidly as migrants came
seeking land or employment based on the extraction of timber, gold and
other natural resources.

Xinguara: the town mushroomed from a small cluster of housing to a
population of 8000 between 1976 and 1978 at the juncture of a new road.
Local interests managed to get it declared an independent municipality in
1982. Despite the exhaustion of local timber and mineral resources, the
town benefited from the expansion of resource extraction west along the
Xingu corridor. A survey of 410 households found that 72 per cent relied
on an informal water supply and 86 per cent on informal sanitation.

Tucumã: originally the headquarter town for a vast private colonization
scheme, it sought to keep out the northeastern migrants but these developed their own settlement outside the project (what later became
Ourilândia do Norte). After the migrants also invaded land within the
colonization scheme, the corporation withdrew and sought compensation
from the government. The town's economy depends on many local miners
and logging. A survey of 320 households found that 69 per cent relied on
informal water supply and 86 per cent on informal sanitation.

Ourilândia do Norte: a spontaneous settlement to the west of Xinguara
that formed close to Tucumã (see above), this had 10,893 inhabitants by
1991. A survey of 173 households found that 95 per cent relied on informal water supply and informal sanitation (typically an outhouse or
defecating outdoors).

Source: Browder, John D and Brian J Godfrey (1997), *Rainforest Cities: Urbanization, Development
and Globalization of the Brazilian Amazon*, Columbia University Press, New York and
Chichester.

tion of the population in some of the wealthiest smaller urban centres may still have serious environmental problems, as illustrated by the case study of San Carlos de Bariloche by Abaleron (1995). This is a very successful tourist city with 81,000 inhabitants in 1991, located with an area of exceptional natural beauty. But in 1991, 19 per cent of households still lacked water piped into their homes and 11 per cent lacked access to public water networks. A considerable proportion lacked adequate provision for sanitation and 30 per cent had inadequate housing, which is particularly serious due to the harsh climate during the winter months. However, there had been considerable progress in reducing the proportion of the population with unmet basic needs between 1980 and 1991 (ibid).

These examples suggest that smaller urban centres are likely to have a much lower proportion of their populations served by piped water systems and by sewage systems (or other systems providing adequate quality sanitation) than larger cities, although it is rare to find statistics comparing the provision for water and sanitation by city size. Vaclav Smil suggests that the problems with water quality found in most urban areas of China are especially serious in rural towns and medium-sized cities (Smil 1995). Data on Argentina from the 1980s shows that the smaller the urban centres, the higher the proportion of households lacking piped water and connections to sewers. The average for urban centres with between 200,000 and 500,000 inhabitants was around 18 per cent lacking piped water and 60 per cent lacking connection to sewers. The average for urban centres with between 5000 and 10,000 inhabitants was for over 40 per cent of households to lack piped water with more than 90 per cent lacking connection to sewers (Zorrilla and Guaresti 1986). For instance, in Noetinger, a small agricultural town in the Pampas, there is no piped water system and no sewer system. The inhabitants obtain their water from tanks and individual wells from which water is pumped – and many draw water from the first aquifer from which there is a growing risk of contamination from excreta because most households dispose of their excreta through septic tanks or simply deep holes (di Pace and others 1992).

Other environmental problems

Many smaller urban centres have serious environmental problems other than those related to water, sanitation, drainage and solid waste. Although most have little or no industry, there are still many that developed as centres for particular industries where there are serious problems from industrial pollution. Cubatão, whose environmental problems were described earlier in this chapter is one example. Cubatão is one of many small cities that developed because of a concentration of industries there, close to a major metropolitan centre. Most large metropolitan centres have one or more small cities close-by with high concentrations of industries. Other small cities develop as industrial centres because of some particular resource based there (for instance coal, copper or large quantities of fresh water) or because of economic incentives (for instance duty-free export processing zones) or because of some political advantage (eg powerful politicians steering industries there). The very high levels of air pollution suffered by the inhabitants of Ilo in Peru as a result of the copper mine and refinery were noted earlier. In Chimbote, there are serious air and water pollution problems from canneries, fishmeal industries and a steel plant owned by the government (Foronda 1998, Miranda and Hordijk 1998). In Cerro de Pasco in Peru, there are very serious problems of lead contamination affecting most of the population as a result of the operation of the government-owned mine (Miranda and Hordijk 1998). Browder noted the very high air pollution levels of the frontier town Rolim de Moura coming from the lumber mills there when he visited it in 1984 (Browder and Godfrey 1997).

The chapter on urban areas in the most recent State of India's Environment report (Agarwal and others 1999a) concentrates on small and medium-sized urban centres. As it states, most discussions about urban environmental problems are for the largest cities, not the thousands of small- and medium-sized urban centres where most of India's urban population lives. The Centre for Science and Environment which published this report undertook studies in four industrial towns (Ludhiana, Jetpur, Tiruppur and Rourkela) and four non-industrial urban centres (Aligarh, Bhagalpur, Kottayam and Jaisalmet). These studies highlight the very poor state of the urban centres' environments ranging from the inadequacies in the provision for water, sanitation, drainage and waste collection to failures to control industrial pollution. They also highlight the absence of any organized civic effort to address this problem. Case studies such as that of Jetpur highlight how serious industrial pollution can be even in small towns; Jetpur had only 30,000 people in the last census (1991) but estimates for 1997 suggest a population of more than 100,000. It is a very successful centre for dyeing and printing saris. There are around 1200 dyeing and printing units, with another 400–500 ancillary industries such as those involved in chemicals, dyes and screen manufacturing. But with little pollution control, both the local river (Bhadar) and the ground water are heavily polluted. The residents of the town of Dhoraji, 16 km downstream of Jetpur, have been complaining about the pollution of their river by the industries in Jetpur for nearly 30 years. Tiruppur is another example of a small successful industrial city with serious environmental problems. It grew rapidly as its knitted and other garment manufacturing base became very successful but it also has a great multiplicity of environmental problems including serious levels of air and water pollution. Residents complain of respiratory diseases but there is no monitoring of air pollution. The Noyyal river is heavily polluted with effluents from factories; so too are many fields in low-lying areas into which many dyeing and bleaching units discharge their waste water which flows into the Noyyal or seeps into ground water (Agarwal and others 1999a).

Small cities usually have even less effective pollution control and land use planning (for instance to ensure polluting industries are downwind and downstream of the inhabitants) than larger cities. It also does not need a heavy concentration of industry to bring serious pollution problems. Just one or two agricultural processing factories or chemical, pulp and paper or beverage factories can seriously pollute a river. Just one cement plant can create serious air pollution problems.

We suspect that there are hundreds of smaller cities with highly polluting industries (and probably also with serious cases of occupational exposure for their workforces) that remain undocumented. When the Indian government's Central Pollution Control Board began publishing the ten locations in India with the highest annual mean concentrations of sulphur dioxide, nitrogen oxides and suspended particulate matter, the list included some smaller cities. For instance, in 1992, Gajroula, a small town in Uttar Pradesh, had the highest recorded levels of sulphur dioxide and of oxides of nitrogen and the sixth highest level of suspended particulate matter (Central Pollution Control Board statistics quoted in Agarawal and others 1999a). Dehradun, also in Uttar Pradesh, figures among the urban centres with the highest levels of suspended particulate matter for 1992, 1993 and 1994 (ibid). The problem of small urban centres with highly polluting industries is likely to be particularly serious in countries such as China with its very rapid industrial development and with a significant proportion of the industrial development taking place in smaller cities and towns. One wonders what China's pollution record would be if its citizens were allowed to compile *State of the Environment Reports* with the comprehensiveness, detail and regularity of those compiled by the Centre for Science and Environment in India.

One final example of the scale and range of environmental problems in urban centres other than the largest cities is drawn from Bamenda in the Cameroon. A case study of Bamenda by Acho-Chi shows the scale and range of environmental problems evident in this rapidly growing city (Acho-Chi 1998). Bamenda's population expanded more than tenfold between 1965 and 1993 to reach around 270,000 in 1993. Human settlements have expanded up hill slopes and on to wetlands because land is very cheap (land can be 300–400 times more expensive within the urban district compared with the very steep slopes and wetlands) but it is difficult (and expensive) to build stable safe homes there. Around 20 per cent of Bamenda's population live on flood-plains and around 7 per cent live in informal settlements on steep slopes. There are great inadequacies in provision for water, sanitation, schools, health posts, roads and drainage. Land clearance for settlement and for quarrying and sand-mining along with other land-use changes caused by urban expansion have created serious problems of soil erosion, with the soil that is washed down the hills blocking drainage channels and changing peak water flows. These have exacerbated problems with floods, although flooding has long been a problem in Bamenda. Acho-Chi's case study points to Bamenda's need for an environmental strategy that addresses both the environmental health problems of the inhabitants and the broader environmental problems caused by unregulated urbanization. It also points to the difficulties of achieving this, especially in the absence of capacity and skills within the local authority (further exacerbated by the cuts in salaries) and the economic crisis. But as he states, it is not possible to meet the population's needs if the supporting ecosystems (water, soil and forest) are being damaged.

ENVIRONMENTAL TRANSITIONS, TRANSFORMATIONS AND TRANSFERS[10]

It has become obvious from the discussions in this and the preceding chapter that there are very large differences between cities in the scale, range and relative importance of different environmental problems. Chapter 5 will amplify this by highlighting the variation between cities in the scale and range of their environmental impacts on their wider region and on global systems. Table 3.4 illustrates this by contrasting the range and relative importance of different environmental problems between four categories of urban centre. The first category has urban centres in which the environmental problems are those associated with poor environmental health and not with high levels of industrial pollution, resource use and waste. Most urban centres in most low-income and many middle-income nations fall into this category. At the other extreme are cities in high-income nations where the main environmental problems are no longer within the city but in the collective impact of the consumption and waste produced by city inhabitants and city businesses on regional and global resource bases and systems. The other two categories fall within these two extremes. Of course, most urban centres do not fall neatly into one of these categories, but the table does highlight the way in which the scale, nature and relative importance of environmental problems differ between cities of different size and wealth.

The last ten years has brought a growing interest in studying how urban environmental problems differ in relation to the wealth of nations. This includes a considerable debate about whether pollution levels follow a 'Kuznets' (inverted U) curve, ie that they rise, level off and then fall as income levels increase. It is clear that some environmental problems are generally much less serious in urban centres in high-income nations, as Table 3.4 highlights. In addition, there is evidence that certain urban environmental problems do stop increasing and then decrease, as nations or cities get wealthier, for instance sulphur dioxide concentrations in the air. This can easily lead to a suggestion or assumption that countries can grow out of pollution or even that economic growth is the solution for pollution control. But as Banuri (1997) notes, in criticizing this assumption, environmental degradation is not a technical process determined by relationships between production and pollution but a political process dependent on the ability of the powerful to transfer their costs to others and the capacity (or otherwise) of the weak to defend themselves against such transfers. The very high pollution levels in Cubatão in the late 1970s and early 1980s were not the result of low per capita income but of industries failing to comply with environmental legislation and a government failing to enforce it while also repressing the citizens' right to protest. Indeed, Cubatão had one of the highest per capita incomes of any city in Brazil (Lemos 1998). The extent of occupational exposure to environmental hazards also depends heavily on the competence and capacity of public agencies setting and enforcing health and safety in the workplace and on the rights and capacities of workers to demand good practice from their employers.

---

10 This section draws on Satterthwaite 1997a.

In addition, if we consider the full range of environmental problems within cities, many do not follow a 'Kuznets' curve. Some environmental problems are generally less serious, the higher the per capita income – for instance the quality and extent of provision for water and sanitation in urban areas is generally better, the higher a nation's per capita income. However, this is not simply a relationship between per capita income levels and the extent of provision since the quality and extent of provision is also strongly influenced by the quality of government, as some cities in relatively low-income nations are well served and some cities in nations with much higher incomes are not. Some environmental problems increase with per capita incomes, especially greenhouse gas emissions and solid-waste levels per person (although with considerable variation in the levels between countries with comparable per capita incomes as Chapter 5 will describe). Some environmental problems are generally more serious, the higher the per capita income but the increase can be moderated, halted or even reversed by government regulation – for instance traffic accidents and air pollution from motor vehicles. Much of the literature on how environmental problems change with income levels gives too little attention to the extent to which the environmental problems are related to the competence and capacity of government in setting and enforcing environmental and occupational health regulations and in ensuring the adequate provision of environmental infrastructure, especially for water, sanitation and drainage. (Or beyond this of the extent to which citizens' groups can hold governments or polluting industries to account, and demand and get action.) Too little attention is also given to the influence of income distribution. The scale of environmental health problems in any city is obviously influenced by the proportion of the city population unable to afford to 'buy' their way out of some of the most serious environmental health problems, such as affording fuels that generate less indoor air pollution, and affording housing that is less crowded and better served with environmental infrastructure.

There is also the issue of whether environmental problems are actually less serious in wealthier cities (or generally within urban centres in wealthier nations) or whether environmental problems are simply being transferred to other people, other ecosystems or into the future. One of the key insights into how environmental problems in cities change in relation to their size and income is the comment by Gordon McGranahan and Jacob Songsore that as cities get larger and the residents wealthier, so they can transfer their environmental problems away from their homes and neighbourhoods to other people and regions. They also transfer responsibility for these problems to someone else:

> ... *many environmental services such as piped water, sewerage connections, electricity and door to door garbage collection not only export pollution (from the household to the city) but also shift both the intellectual and practical burdens of environmental management from the household to the government or utility* (McGranahan and Songsore 1994, page 41).

Chapter 5 will describe these transfers of environmental problems in more detail, and this issue is discussed more fully in McGranahan and others 2001.

Table 3.4 *Typical environmental problems for urban centres of different sizes and within nations with different levels of income*

Environmental problems	Category 1: Most urban centres in most low-income nations and many middle-income nations	Category 2: More prosperous cities in low- and middle-income countries, including many that have developed as industrial centres	Category 3: Prosperous major cities/ metropolitan areas in middle- and upper-middle-income countries	Category 4: Cities in high-income countries
Environmental hazards within the human environment				
1 Those linked mainly to inadequate provision for: • water supply and sanitation • drainage • solid-waste collection • primary health care	Many or most of the urban population lacking water piped into the home and adequate sanitation. Lack of public or private service for water and any form of sanitation for most households. Also many or most residential areas lacking drainage so such areas often having mud and stagnant pools. Many residential areas at risk from flooding. Many or most residential areas also lacking services for solid-waste collection and healthcare, especially the poorer and more peripheral areas	Piped water supplies and relatively hygienic forms of sanitation reaching a considerable proportion of the population but most low-income households not reached, especially those in illegal or informal settlements on the city periphery. For those that are reached, often it is only through communal provision (eg standpipes and shared latrines) of poor quality. Solid-waste collection and healthcare usually reaching a higher proportion of the population than in category 1 but still with 30–60 per cent of the population unserved	Generally acceptable water supplies for most of the population. Provision for sanitation, solid-waste collection and primary healthcare also much improved, although 10–30 per cent of the population still lacking provision (or adequate provision). The proportion of people lacking adequate services generally smaller than in category 2 but in very large cities, this can still mean millions who lack basic services. In large metropolitan areas, service provision often least adequate in the weakest, peripheral municipalities	Provision of all four services for virtually all the population

2 Those linked to physical and chemical hazards in the home and workplace	The main hazards associated with poor quality and overcrowded living and working environments, and evident in the large health impact of domestic and workplace accidents. There may be serious occupational hazards among certain small-scale and household enterprises; also for much of the workforce in many smaller industrial and mining centres	A great increase in the problems with occupational health and safety at all levels and scales of industry. Government often not giving occupational health and safety adequate priority. A high proportion of low-income households living in illegal or informal settlements with high risks of accidental injuries, especially if they settle on dangerous sites	Improved government supervision or worker organization to ensure improved occupational health and safety. Often, a decline in the proportion of the population working in hazardous jobs. A rise in the contribution of traffic accidents to premature death and injury. Improved provision of water, sanitation, drainage and healthcare lessening physical hazards in residential areas	Road accidents remaining one of the most serious health threats. Occupational health problems lessened through much better health and safety standards. Active programmes usually promoting injury reduction for homes and on the roads
3 Those linked to air pollution	Often serious indoor air pollution, where coal or biomass fuels used as domestic fuels – especially where indoor heating is needed. Small industrial or mining centres can also have very high levels of air pollution	Often severe problems from industrial and residential emissions. Indoor air pollution in many households lessened as those who can afford to do so switch to cleaner fuels	Increasingly important contribution to air pollution from motor vehicles. Perhaps less from industry as the city's economic base becomes less pollution intensive and as measures begin to be taken to control industrial emissions	Motor vehicles becoming the major source of air pollution. Little or no heavy industry remains in the city and the control of air pollution becomes a greater priority for citizens
Renewable resource use				
1 Land/soil	Urban expansion taking place with few or no controls, or where controls	Urban expansion continuing to take place with few or no land-use controls; often	More controls imposed on urban expansion but these often prove ineffective as	Where there is concern for agricultural land loss, land use often tightly regulated.

Table 3.4 *continued*

Environmental problems	Category 1	Category 2	Category 3	Category 4
	exist, they are largely ignored	rapid growth in illegal or informal settlements, including illegal land subdivisions; loss of farmland to expanding urban areas, to demand for building materials and aggregate, and often to land bought up by speculators	illegal residential developments continue, in the face of a considerable section of the population unable to afford to buy or rent the cheapest 'legal' land site or house. Different groups often in conflict over use of best located undeveloped land sites or of use of agricultural land for urban purposes	perhaps to the point where house prices begin to rise as land supplies for new housing become constrained. Where there is little concern, often large loss of agricultural land to suburban or ex-urban developments
2 Freshwater	Generally, the wealthier the city, the larger the use per capita with large wealthy cities also having to draw on the water resources of an increasingly large area. Certain industries often have a particularly high demand for water. A strong emphasis on water conservation can considerably reduce per capita consumption in wealthy cities.			
Non-renewable resource use	Generally, the wealthier the city, the higher the consumption of fossil fuels and other mineral resources, although again, there are very large variations between cities with comparable per capita incomes. A strong citizen and government commitment to reducing motor car dependence, waste reduction and to reuse, reclamation and recycling can keep down per capita consumption figures in wealthy cities			
Generation of biodegradable and non-biodegradable wastes				
1 Water pollution	The main 'pollution' problems arise from a lack of provision for	Most local rivers and other water bodies polluted from industrial and urban	Severe problems from untreated or inadequately treated industrial and	Much improved levels of treatment for liquid wastes from homes and productive

sanitation and waste collection, except in industrial or mining centres	discharges and storm and surface run-off	municipal liquid wastes that are usually dumped without treatment in local water bodies	activities. Concern with amenity values and toxic wastes
2 Solid waste disposal	Open dumping of the solid wastes that are collected; many wastes not collected	Mostly uncontrolled open land dumps; mixed wastes	A proportion of landfills controlled or semi-controlled	Controlled sanitary landfills, incineration, some recovery
3 Hazardous waste management	No capacity but also volumes generally small	Severe problems; limited capacities to deal with it	Growing capacity but often still a serious problem	Moving from remediation to prevention
4 Household generation of non-biodegradable wastes (including greenhouse gas emissions)	Very low levels per capita	Generally low levels per capita	Generally intermediate levels per capita	Generally high levels per capita, although large variations between cities with comparable per capita incomes linked to number of cars per person and their use, density, commitment to energy efficiency, fuel prices, etc
Other environmental hazards	No provision by public authorities for disaster preparedness; disasters (floods, storms, etc) often common with severe damage and loss of life. In cities with an industrial base, inadequate provision to guard against industrial disasters and to act to limit the damage and loss of life		Some provision for disaster preparedness	Increasingly sophisticated disaster preparedness

Source: This is a modified version of a table in Bertone, Carl, Janis Bernstein, Josef Leitmann and Jochen Eigen (1994), *Towards Environmental Strategies for Cities; Policy Considerations for Urban Environmental Management in Developing Countries*, UNDP/UNCHS/World Bank Urban Management Program, No 18, World Bank, Washington DC.

Thus, in concluding the discussion of environmental problems in cities and smaller urban centres for both this and the preceding chapter, it is the quality of governance that has such importance for reducing environmental problems, especially for low-income groups (as Chapter 4 will describe). Obviously, the higher the per capita income of city inhabitants, the more potential for good environmental quality as city inhabitants can afford to pay more for environmental infrastructure and services, and as government has a larger resource base on which to draw. But as Chapters 6 and 7 will emphasize, 'good governance' can ensure much improved environmental quality even in cities and smaller urban centres with relatively low per capita incomes. And as Chapter 8 will emphasize, 'good governance' can also check the environmental problems associated with high-income societies.

Chapter 4

Who Bears the Environmental Costs in Cities?

A young boy works in a garage shop in Bangalore, India
Photo © Janet Jarman, all rights reserved

THE CORRELATIONS BETWEEN INCOMES AND HAZARDS

Perhaps the least surprising point arising from the review of environmental problems in Chapters 2 and 3 is that it is generally lower-income groups that bear most of the ill-health, injury or premature death and other costs of environmental problems. They are the least able to afford accommodation that protects them from environmental hazards – good quality housing in neighbourhoods with piped water, and adequate provision for sanitation, waste collection and drains. Low-income groups' capacity to live where housing or land for housing is cheaper – ie at considerable distances from the main economic centres – is constrained by the costs in time and money of going to and from the places where they earn an income and, often, by poor provision for public transport.

If there was sufficient information available to construct city-wide maps, showing the level of risk from all environmental hazards in all areas, in most cities, the neighbourhoods with the highest risks would also be the neighbourhoods with a predominance of low-income groups. The correlations between income levels and environmental risks would be particularly strong with regard to the risks arising from poor quality, overcrowded housing, inadequate provision for household water supply, sanitation, drainage and solid-waste collection; also with regard to the level of risk from natural disasters – for instance floods or landslides; the reasons for this have already been discussed in some detail but they centre on the fact that housing and land markets price low-income groups out of safe, well-located, well-serviced housing and land sites (and also the absence or inappropriateness of government responses to address this). In many cities, there will be a strong correlation between indoor air quality and income since low-income groups use more polluting fuels and more inefficient stoves (or open fires) because they are cheaper, but this brings a much worse air quality indoors. The fact that low-income groups also live in much more cramped and over-crowded conditions obviously exacerbates this, and also the transmission of infectious diseases and the risk of accidents. In most urban centres, a high proportion of low-income groups live in shacks made of inflammable materials such as wood and cardboard; the risk of accidental fires is much increased when households also use open fires or portable stoves for cooking and/or heating and have no electricity, so kerosene lights or candles are used for lighting. Neighbourhoods with a predominance of low-income groups will generally have the least provision for playgrounds, parks and other open spaces that are managed for public use and where hazards like faecal contamination, rubbish and waste water are avoided. There is also the tendency for polluting industries, waste dumps and waste-management facilities to concentrate in low-income neighbourhoods, a tendency that is also evident in high-income nations, as the literature on environmental racism has helped to document (Wing and others 1996).

The correlations between low-income levels and high levels of outdoor air pollution may not be so precise. In certain 'hot-spots' such as in areas close to quarries, cement factories and industries with high levels of air pollution in their immediate surrounds, the correlation is likely to be strong. Air pollution levels in low-income areas may also be particularly high because many households are using polluting fuels. The burning of rubbish can be a significant source of air pollution in settlements where there is no regular waste-collection service (see for instance Surjadi 1993). But the correlations are less clear when an entire city suffers from air pollution or when prevailing winds help to disperse the pollution (reducing risks in the areas where the pollution is generated but perhaps increasing risks in certain 'downwind' areas). In addition, particular 'hot-spots' for air pollution have often developed relatively recently, and if they persist and are well defined, they will probably be reflected in housing and land prices as higher-income groups move out, prices fall and lower-income groups move in.

It is not only that low-income groups generally face higher levels of risk but also that most have less possibility of getting rapid and appropriate medical treatment, if they are injured at work or at home, or fall ill from some environmental hazard. They have the least possibility of affording effective treatment and medicines and of taking time off to recover from sickness or injury because they cannot afford the loss of income and do not have jobs that allow for sick-leave or that are covered by health insurance. Many low-income households have little or no asset base that can be rapidly converted to cash to allow food to be afforded when an income-earner is sick or injured and cannot work, or to pay for treatment that could hasten their recovery. Low-income groups are generally at much higher risk of suffering from psychosocial health problems because they have to live and work with much higher levels of environmental stressors – for instance higher noise levels, higher levels of overcrowding, less security and less services. They also have to cope with the stresses caused by much higher levels of ill-health and injury, and of infant and child death within their households, to which environmental factors contribute so much.

DIFFERENTIALS IN ENVIRONMENTAL RISK

There is little available data on the extent of people's exposure to environmental hazards relative to their income level. Our knowledge of differentials in environmental risks is mostly through data on the differentials between districts within a city in, for instance, environmental hazards or access to environmental resources (for instance fresh water) or in health outcomes that are much influenced by environmental conditions. The differentials become apparent as data are compared between the different neighbourhoods, districts or municipalities that make up the city (see Box 4.1). The differentials between high- and low-income groups become apparent as the data from high-income areas are compared with the data from low-income areas. But this is less precise than comparisons between income groups since each district has some mix of income groups. The size of the differential between high- and low-income groups is also masked when data are only available for relatively large areas, for instance for the municipalities that make up a major city. Most data on the extent of service provision or on health outcomes for particular low-income districts are also only available as averages for the whole district's population that can obscure the more serious health problems suffered by the poorer groups within that district. This was demonstrated by a study in a low-income settlement in Khulna (Bangladesh) that showed the sharp differentials in workdays lost to illness or injury among the inhabitants when comparing (within the context of the settlement) the 'wealthier' households with the poorer households. It also showed how in the poorer households, such illness or injury often meant growing indebtedness and undernutrition for all family members (Pryer 1989 and 1993).

Perhaps the most dramatic evidence of differentials in environmental risk between income groups comes from data or studies on the differentials in infant or child mortality rates between city districts (see Bradley and others 1991, Stephens 1996). Infant mortality rates are often four or more times higher in poorer areas than in richer areas (or even ten times higher – see Stephens

1996), with much larger differentials often apparent if the poorest district is compared with the richest district. Large differentials between rich and poor districts are also common in the incidence of many environment-related diseases – for instance tuberculosis, malaria and typhoid. Differentials in the number of people dying from certain environment-related diseases are also often very large; for instance many more deaths in poorer communities are likely to come from diarrhoeal diseases and acute respiratory infections such as pneumonia and influenza. Statistics for water consumption often reveal large differentials between richer and poorer areas of a city. It is also common for urban poor groups to pay much higher prices per litre for water than richer groups, as described in Chapter 2.

Box 4.1 gives some examples of differentials between different areas of a city in environmental hazards, access to resources and public services and health indicators. Many of the examples given are actually from cities where differentials are likely to be relatively low; there is generally better documentation of intra-city differentials in such indicators as infant mortality rates from relatively wealthy and well-run cities. Some of the statistics come from relatively old studies – for instance that for Bombay/Mumbai coming from 1977 and that from Port-au-Prince coming from 1983. This reflects the lack of such studies, especially in cities and smaller urban centres where environmental conditions are particularly bad. The examples of the inequality in access to land in Nairobi, Manila and Surabaya are a reminder of how low-income groups are generally heavily concentrated in a relatively small proportion of the city.

There are also the many aspects of inequality noted earlier that are not recorded in statistics such as these, including access to medical treatment, availability of emergency services and the level of risk from physical hazards in the home or workplace.

VULNERABILITY AND SUSCEPTIBILITY

The presence of an environmental hazard (for instance a pathogen, pollutant, physical hazard or psychosocial stressor such as high noise levels) does not necessarily mean that it will harm someone. This also depends on the characteristics of the individual, household or social group exposed to the hazard. Certain individual or group characteristics can also influence the severity of the health impact.

Certain people or households are more at risk from environmental hazards because they are:

1   Less able to avoid them (eg living in a settlement lacking provision for protected water, sanitation and drainage).
2   More affected by them (eg infants at much greater risk of death from acute respiratory infections than older groups).
3   Less able to cope with the illness, injury or premature death they cause (eg persons who cannot afford to go to a doctor or pay for medicine).

Box 4.1 *EXAMPLES OF INTRA-CITY DIFFERENTIALS IN HEALTH INDICA-TORS LINKED TO ENVIRONMENTAL HAZARDS, ACCESS TO RESOURCES AND PUBLIC SERVICES, AND ENVIRONMENTAL HAZARDS*

a Differentials in health indicators linked to environmental hazards
Buenos Aires (Argentina). In 1990, infant mortality rates within local government areas (municipalities and the central federal district) vary from a low of 15 in the federal district to a high of 30 in San Fernando and Tigre (Arrossi 1996).

Cape Town (South Africa). Infant mortality rates in 'deprived areas' were more than four times higher than in non-deprived areas. The relative risk from TB was more than 20 times greater for the deprived, compared with the non-deprived population (Stephens 1996 quoting from Yach and Harrison 1996).

Jakarta (Indonesia). Official estimates suggest an infant mortality rate for the whole city of 33 per 1000 live births while estimates for some of the poorer areas suggest rates of four to five times the city average (Harpham and others 1990).

Karachi (Pakistan). Surveys in six *katchi abadis* (informal settlements in which half of Karachi's population live) and one middle-lower-middle income area during the 1980s found that infant mortality rates varied from 33 (in the middle-lower-middle income area) to 209 per 1000 live births. In all but one of the katchi abadis, they were over 100.[1]

Port-au-Prince (Haiti). In the early 1980s, one in five infants died before their first birthday in the 'slums', while another one in ten died between their first and second birthday; this was almost three times the mortality rates in rural areas and many times the rate in the richer areas of Port-au-Prince where infant and child mortality rates were similar to those in urban areas of the USA (Rohde 1983).

Porto Alegre (Brazil). Infant mortality rates in squatter settlements were 75.5 per 1000 compared with 25 per 1000 in non-squatter areas in 1980 (Guimaraes and Fischmann 1985); in 1996, infant mortality rates for the municipality averaged 18 per 1000 live births but an analysis of how they differed between the 83 districts found that they varied from 60 to under 5 (Menegat and others 1998).

São Paulo (Brazil). Infant mortality rates in the different municipalities that make up Greater São Paulo in 1992 vary from 18 (in São Caetano do Sol)

---

1 Surveys by the Community Health Department of the Aga Khan University, quoted in Hasan 1999.

to 60 in Biritiba-Mirim. All areas have seen substantial falls in infant mortality rates since 1980; the average infant mortality rate for Greater São Paulo in 1992 (25.5) was half the rate in 1980 (51.8), and in 1980, five municipalities had rates of over 100. In addition, differentials have fallen; in 1980, the best performing municipality had a rate of 29.3 while the worst had a rate of 152 (EMPLASA 1994). When the subdistricts of São Paulo municipality are classified into four categories, according to social, economic and environmental criteria, mortality rates from infectious diseases for children under four years of age living in the worst of the four categories were more than four times higher than children living in the best of the four categories. There was also close to a fourfold difference between these zones in death from respiratory diseases (Stephens and others 1994).

Tianjin (China). A study of environment-related morbidity and mortality in the different subdistricts of the city found large variations. For instance, the average for a subdistrict's infant mortality rate was 13 but it reached as high as 31 in one district. TB prevalence in the subdistricts averaged 172 per 100,000 people with the highest subdistrict figure being 347 and the lowest just 54. There were also major differences in mortality rates for lung cancer and cervical cancer (Bertaud and Young 1990).

b Differentials in environmental hazards
Bombay/Mumbai (India). A study in 1977 compared the health of residents in two districts with heavy concentrations of industries, with those in a district with very little industry. People in the industrialized districts suffered a much higher incidence of diseases such as bronchitis, TB, skin allergies, anaemia and eye irritation, and there was a notable rise in deaths from cancer in one of the industrialized districts (Centre for Science and Environment 1982).

Caracas (Venezuela). An estimated 574,000 people live in illegal settlements on slopes with a significant risk of landslides; most of the areas continuously affected by slope failures have been low-income settlements (Jimenez Diaz 1992).

c Differentials in access to public services
Accra (Ghana). In the high-class residential areas with water piped to the home and water closets for sanitation, water consumption per capita is likely to be well in excess of the recommended figure of 200 litres per person per day. In slum neighbourhoods such as Nima-Maamobi and Ashiaman where buying water from vendors is common, the water consumption is about 60 litres per capita per day (Songsore 1992).

Dar es Salaam. A 1997 study of domestic water use in four sites, all with piped supplies, found large differentials in water use and reliability. The average per capita water use for households interviewed in Oyster Bay (a high-income area) was 164 litres a day. It was much less in two lower-income settlements: in Changombe it was 44 litres a day and in Temeke, 64 litres a day. In Oyster Bay 70 per cent of the households interviewed received a 24-hour supply compared with 10 per cent of households in Temeke and 11 per cent in Changombe. The unreliability of the piped water supplies in Changombe and Temeke meant that more than 60 per cent of the inter-viewed households with piped supplies use vendors as their primary source, despite the higher costs (Thompson and others 2000).

Guayaquil (Ecuador). In 1990, average daily consumption ranged from 307 litres/inhabitant in the well-to-do parts of the city to less than 25 litres/inhabitant for those supplied by the private water-sellers (Swyngedouw 1995).

Monterrey (Mexico). The proportion of houses with running water varied from 49 per cent to 93 per cent among the eight municipalities that made up the metropolitan area in 1990, while the proportion with drainage varied from 35 to 96 per cent (Garza 1996, drawing on official statistics). Garza 1996 also includes a more detailed analysis, based on 710 areas (rather than 8 municipalities) which shows the variations within each municipality and the limitations in using boundaries with such large and diverse populations to study inequality.

Nairobi (Kenya). Average daily water consumption varies from between 20 and over 200 litres per person per day, depending on the quality of provi-sion for water (Lamba 1994).

Surabaya (Indonesia). The wealthiest 20 per cent of the population are reported to consume 80 percent of the public services, including those essential to a healthy environment (Douglass 1992).

d Differentials in access to land
Nairobi. In Nairobi, the informal and illegal settlements that house more than half the city's population occupy less than 6 per cent of the land area used for residential purposes. The city has a relatively low density – some 20 persons per hectare in 1989 – but in many informal settlements includ-ing some of the largest (Langata/Kibera), average densities exceed 1000 persons per hectare (Alder 1995).

Manila. In Metro Manila, more than two-fifths of the population live in illegal or informal settlements that cover less than 6 per cent of the land area (ANAWIM 1990).

Surabaya. An estimated 63 per cent of Surabaya's inhabitants live in kampungs although these informal settlements cover only 7 per cent of the city area (Silas 1992).

Such individuals or households are generally termed vulnerable. But to ensure a more precise understanding (from which more appropriate responses can be developed), it is worth distinguishing between susceptibility (where the increased risk is related to endogenous factors such as a person's nutritional status, the state of their immune system or their genetic make-up) and vulnerability (where it is external social, economic or cultural conditions that increase the risk – for instance through an increased likelihood of exposure to environmental hazards or less capacity to cope with or adapt to an illness or injury).[2]

The characteristics that influence a person's susceptibility to environmental hazards include:

- For many biological pathogens, weak body defences (some a function of age and of nutritional status, some a function of acquired immunity as in the protection given against certain diseases by vaccines).
- For physical hazards, limited mobility, strength and balance (as is evident for young children and for many older people and people with physical disabilities).
- For exposure to chemicals: age and health status at the time of exposure. Micro-nutrient deficiencies are likely to enhance the adverse effects of air pollution exposure (Romieu and Hernandez 1999). There are also certain susceptible groups such as asthmatics and the elderly with chronic respiratory diseases who are particularly susceptible to certain air pollutants. Genetic factors may influence sensitivity to some chemicals.

The characteristics that influence a person's vulnerability to environmental hazards include:

- *Income and assets* which influences the individual's or household's ability to afford good quality housing (which minimizes environmental hazards) and healthcare and emergency response (which minimizes their health impact), including purchasing the most effective medicines, and taking time off to recuperate when sick or injured.
- *Economic or social roles which increase exposure to environmental hazards* (for instance particular occupations such as picking through rubbish or particular tasks such as disposing of human excreta).
- *The extent of public, private and community provision for healthcare*, including emergency response to accidental injuries or acute diseases.
- *Individual, household or community coping mechanisms* once a hazard has caused illness or injury; for instance, knowing what to do, who to visit and how to rearrange individual/household survival strategies.[3]

---

2 We are grateful to Tony McMichael at the London School of Hygiene and Tropical Medicine for his advice on this distinction.
3 This list draws from Chambers 1989, Corbett 1989 and Pryer 1989. The literature on rural poverty was the first to develop a detailed understanding of what underpins vulnerability for poorer groups, but this encouraged urban researchers to also develop vulnerability frameworks – see for instance Moser 1996, 1998.

The key role that assets have in helping low-income individuals or households to avoid deprivation is now more widely recognized. However, the discussion of the role of assets in helping low-income groups to avoid deprivation has generally concentrated on those that are important for generating or maintaining income or for helping low-income people to cope with economic stresses or shocks. Too little attention has been given to the role of good quality housing, infrastructure and services in reducing low-income groups' vulnerability by reducing their exposure to environmental health hazards and the role of healthcare services and emergency services in reducing their health impact. In this sense, it is the quality of housing and basic services that is the asset, regardless of whether the house is owned, rented or borrowed. The discussions of housing as an asset tend to concentrate on its capital value or its potential income-earning possibilities (through providing space for income-earning activities or for renting out space) rather than its potential role in helping its inhabitants to avoid environmental hazards.

The distinction between vulnerability and susceptibility is perhaps clearest when considering infants and young children since they are all particularly susceptible to a wide range of environmental hazards compared with most other age groups, but those who live in poor quality housing are far more vulnerable. They are particularly susceptible to many diseases from their birth onwards, until their immune system has developed (and, for many serious childhood diseases, strengthened through vaccines). Young children are particularly susceptible to physical hazards from the time they begin to crawl, because (among other reasons) of their lack of knowledge of the dangers they face from (for instance) falls and hot surfaces, and because of their desire to explore and experiment. However, as a later section in this chapter describes, their vulnerability to the environmental hazards to which they are particularly susceptible is much increased by poor quality housing that lacks adequate provision for water, sanitation, drainage and waste removal, and as such also lacks safe indoor and outdoor living and play environments.

It has become more common for governments to try to identify 'vulnerable' groups and to draw on this in designing interventions to reduce their vulnerability. The definition of vulnerability is broader than that discussed here, as it includes not only vulnerability to environmental hazards but also to other hazards or economic shocks or stresses. It is often difficult to separate vulnerability to environmental hazards from these other aspects as both are underpinned by inadequate incomes and assets. Once one begins to examine who is most affected by environmental hazards, the interaction between environmental hazards and social, economic, political and demographic factors becomes much clearer. 'Health outcomes are not only influenced by environmental conditions but also by the inputs of health services, by the characteristics of the population and by the socio-economic conditions in which people live' (Stephens and Harpham 1992). Virtually all environmental health problems in urban areas have a social, economic or political underpinning in that it is these factors that determine who is most at risk and who cannot obtain the needed treatment and support, when illness or injury occurs (see for instance Douglass 1992). To give but one example, the high incidence of diseases associated with contaminated food and water in most low-income urban communities is an environmental problem in that the disease-causing agents infect humans through the water or food they ingest, but this high incidence can also be judged to be a political problem since nearly all governments and aid agencies have the capacity to greatly reduce current levels of morbidity and mortality by improved provision of water, sanitation and drainage, and by increasing the possibilities for low-income groups to find better quality housing. This makes it difficult to isolate the impact of environmental factors on health from other (non-environmental) factors.

GROUPS WITHIN THE POPULATION THAT FACE HIGHER RISKS

In any city population, there are particular groups within the low-income population that face particularly high levels of risk from environmental hazards. For instance, there are:

- Those who work in particularly dangerous occupations, or occupations where environmental risks are much increased because regulations on occupational health and safety are not enforced.
- The inhabitants of particularly dangerous settlements such as those most at risk from disasters or those with very high air pollution levels.
- Particular groups that face most difficulty getting access to water and washing and bathing facilities such as pavement dwellers or those who sleep in open spaces, parks and graveyards.

The disposal of wastes from urban households or enterprises often puts particular groups at risk – for instance as rivers or lakes are contaminated, affecting the health of those inside and outside the city that use the water. There is also the differentiation in risk levels within low-income groups caused by demographic, health or social characteristics. This is illustrated by the sections below that look in more detail at vulnerability to disasters, and the particularly high risks faced by infants, children and women. However, an interest in establishing who is most susceptible or vulnerable to environmental hazards would also have to consider the particular problems of other groups – for instance the elderly, those with physical disabilities, and those groups within the population that face discrimination in obtaining access to good quality housing and environmental services because of their ethnicity, skin colour or the fact that they are immigrants.

Vulnerability to disasters

Chapter 3 included a description of the different kinds of disasters that are common in urban areas. The growing interest in achieving a better understanding of who is vulnerable to environmental hazards in urban areas also includes an interest in who is vulnerable to disasters (Sanderson 1997, International Federation of Red Cross and Red Crescent Societies 1998). This is spurred by the fact that the death toll from disasters of a comparable type and scale can vary greatly from place to place; in a wealthy, well-managed city, it is rare for many people to die from a hurricane, flood or earthquake, but large death tolls are much more common in poorly managed cities. The differences in the number of deaths and injuries are much influenced by how much action had been taken beforehand to reduce people's vulnerability to the disaster. For instance, it became clear after the earthquake in Turkey in 1999 that most of the deaths, injuries and building collapses were related to the fact that so many buildings had not incorporated earthquake-resistant features (which by law they were required to). The health impact was also increased by the slow and inadequate response of the emergency services (Özerdem 1999).

It is rare for the social impact of disasters to be documented, especially the long-term impact and who is most affected by it. After counting the number of people killed, injured and missing (presumed dead) and moving the injured, evaluations of disasters usually reveal the vulnerability of the thousands of people who were affected. For instance, in most disasters, most of those who lose their homes are relatively low-income households who had developed the site and built the shelter themselves. They lose their homes and belongings because the design and technology used in constructing the house could not resist an earth-tremor or because the site where the people built their shelter was flooded or destroyed by a landslide. They may lose their source of income because they are relocated, usually under the direction of some public or international agency, to a place distant from their job or where they had previously earned an income. They lose most or all of their physical 'capital' including the improvements they had made in the house and the infrastructure within their settlement to which they had contributed their time and savings – for instance the improvements to the water system or the construction of a nursery, health centre or footpath. And in many instances, they are forced to move to a new site where they lose many key social contacts (family, friends and contacts important to finding paid work).

Analyses of vulnerability to disasters also make clear how much vulnerability can be reduced by competent and effective urban authorities. Drawing on the framework noted above for identifying what causes vulnerability and applying it to disasters, people can be vulnerable in at least three different aspects:

1 *Living or working in places at high risk from disasters* such as land sites more at risk from flooding, landslides or earthquakes, buildings not designed to withstand floods or earthquakes, and neighbourhoods lacking protective infrastructure such as storm drains able to rapidly channel floodwaters away.
2 *Being more affected by the lack of rapid response to the disaster* because of slow or ineffective emergency services.
3 *Being less able to cope with the consequences*, for instance losing all capital assets or sources of income or being unable to afford needed medical treatment.

There are also the groups within the population that are more susceptible, for instance young children or older people less able to rapidly move to safer sites when a flood, fire, landslide or earthquake occurs.

Analyses of who is most vulnerable to disasters make clear why it is generally low-income households that are most affected. In most urban areas, it is low-income groups that are heavily concentrated in the sites most at risk from disasters – flood-plains, steep slopes, sites around heavy industry, and sites most at risk from earthquakes. Low-income groups inevitably have less money to spend on building or renting a house designed to avoid or limit damage in the event of a disaster and it is also generally the low-income neighbourhoods that have the least provision for protective infrastructure.[4] Low-income groups also have the least resources on which to call, when some disaster damages or destroys their housing.

Such analyses also make clear the different ways in which vulnerability can be reduced. For instance, for the inhabitants of a settlement at risk from flooding, their vulnerability may be reduced by:

- *Reducing the risk of flooding*, which may be achieved 'upstream' through better watershed management.
- *Offering them a safer site and help in moving there*, although as Box 4.2 shows, hazardous sites often serve the needs of low-income households well in all other aspects so it may be difficult to find a less hazardous site that will serve their needs.
- *Helping to make their homes and neighbourhood better able to cope with floods*, for instance structural modifications to buildings, improved storm and surface drains (but tenants often face particular problems because landlords are reluctant to invest or to allow tenants to alter their homes – see for instance Pelling 1997).
- *Developing an effective early warning system to warn when floods are likely* (so people can take protective measures or temporarily move away).
- *Ensuring emergency services are ready to respond rapidly in the event of a flood.*
- *Having in place the supports the inhabitants need to cope with their losses, after the flood.*

There is often considerable overlap in the means to reduce people's vulnerability to disasters and to reduce their vulnerability to 'everyday' hazards. But Box 4.2 is included as a reminder of how low-income households' economic needs often conflict with their environmental needs. In this case study in Indore (India), the inhabitants of a low-income settlement at high risk of flooding had developed their own temporary and permanent adaptations to flooding and were unwilling to move to safer sites because these would not be so well located with regard to income-earning opportunities (Stephens and others 1996). This does not mean that low-income households living on dangerous sites will not move but it does mean that measures to relocate them must fully involve such households in choosing alternative locations and

---

4 See Pelling 1997 for a detailed discussion of what determines vulnerability to floods in Georgetown (Guyana) where close to 50,000 people experience regular flooding and another 50,000 experience occasional flooding. This includes a comparison between four different settlements that are at high risk of flooding to look in more detail at the factors that influence vulnerability.

setting the terms under which the new sites are acquired and provided with infrastructure and services.[5]

As external agencies have learnt to work in more participatory ways with 'vulnerable' groups, the analyses of hazards and vulnerabilities have also come to include analyses of local capacities to identify and act – see for instance the work in Caqueta Ravine in Lima to map not only the hazards and vulnerabilities but also the local inhabitants' and local organizations' capacities to address these (Sanderson 1997).

Infants and Children[6]

Children are particularly at risk from many environmental hazards, compared with most other age groups, from the time of their conception through their development in the womb, their birth, infancy and early and late childhood. Age-related risk factors include weak body defences, susceptibility to particular chemicals and, for younger children in particular, inadequate or no understanding of how to avoid hazards. But the quality of the environment is the main influence on whether this susceptibility to environmental hazards results in serious illness, injury or death. In a city with a well-managed environment, less than one in a hundred children dies before the age of five and very few such deaths are the result of environmental factors; in cities with inadequate provision for environmental infrastructure and services, it is common for between one child in four and one child in ten to die before the age of five and environmental hazards are the main causes or contributory factors in most such deaths. Similarly, in a well-managed city, the differences in mortality rates between the lowest income areas of the city and higher income areas for children aged one to four is not very large; in a badly managed city they can vary by a factor of 10 or even 20 or more.

Even in the relatively sheltered environment of their mother's womb, the developing embryo is strongly influenced by external factors, including environmental factors. Perhaps the most important environmental influences are those that affect the health and nutritional status of the mother – for instance the high levels of risk for mothers from diarrhoeal diseases and intestinal worms in most low-income settlements and from malaria in many. Pregnant mothers suffering from protein and calorie undernutrition or micro-nutrient deficiencies face a greater risk of giving birth to low birth-weight babies; such babies

---

5 See Patel and Sharma 1998 for a discussion of this in relation to the relocation of 'slum' communities living along Mumbai's railway tracks to allow the rail system to function more effectively. Around 25,000 households live along the railway tracks, some with their shacks being within 1 metre of the tracks. As a result, people are killed or seriously injured nearly every day and the railways' safety commissioner requires trains to greatly reduce their speeds when houses are within 9 metres of the track. The households living along the tracks are prepared to move to other sites or to move their shacks away from tracks and have shown how this can be done in pilot projects, but it has been difficult for their organizations and the NGOs with whom they work to get agreement from the state government, the railways board and the World Bank (which has given a loan to help finance the improvement of the railways).

6 This section draws heavily on Satterthwaite and others 1996, and Bartlett and others 1999. The discussion of physical hazards also draws on Bartlett 2000.

Box 4.2 *Low-income Households' Adaptation to Flooding in Indore, India*

In many low-income communities in Indore, flooding is perceived as a natural, seasonal event and households take steps to limit the damage it does. Those who live on land sites adjacent to small rivers that are also key storm drains are particularly at risk. But these sites have the advantage of a central city location. They have economic advantages because they are close to jobs or to markets for the goods these households produce or collect (many earn a living collecting waste). The land is cheap and because it is in public ownership, they are less likely to get evicted. These sites have social advantages because they are close to health services, schools, electricity and water. Most inhabitants have strong family, kinship and community ties with other inhabitants. Some residents noted that the sites are considered safer for children because narrow streets made them inaccessible to motor vehicles.

Households and small enterprises made both temporary and permanent adaptations to flooding. These include raising plinth levels and paving courtyards, using landfill, using materials that resist flooding, choosing furniture that is less likely to be washed away and ensuring that shelving and electric wiring are high up the walls, above expected water levels. Roofing may not be attached to a house so it can be quickly removed if the structure is in danger of being swept away. Many households also have suitcases ready, so valuables can be carried away.

Residents had also developed flood prediction and protection systems and contingency plans for evacuating persons and possessions. In one settlement (Shekha Nagar), the residents' first response to the threat of severe floods was to move the elderly, children and animals to higher ground. Then they moved electrical goods such as televisions and radios, followed by other lighter valuables and cooking utensils, with clothes being moved last as these are more easily replaced and not damaged by flooding. The more established residents have also learnt how to use the state system of compensation for flood damage and this can provide a perverse incentive for residents to build houses in the most vulnerable and dangerous areas.

Source: Stephens, Carolyn, Rajesh Patnaik and Simon Lewin (1996) *This is My Beautiful Home: Risk Perceptions Towards Flooding and Environment in Low-income Urban Communities: A Case Study in Indore, India*, London School of Hygiene and Tropical Medicine, London.

---

are also more likely to die in infancy. Malaria contracted by pregnant mothers is often associated with still-births or low birth-weight and maternal mortality. The mother may also be exposed to chemical pollutants, some of which can cause cancer or birth defects in the foetus or kill it; examples of chemicals that are known to harm the foetus through being transferred through the placenta are lead, methyl mercury, certain pesticides, PCBs and carbon monoxide (UNEP and UNICEF 1990).

The quality of the environment into which an infant is born exerts a powerful influence on whether she or he will survive their first birthday and, if they do, their subsequent physical and mental development. Infants and young children are at greater risk of dying from many environment-related diseases than older children or adults – for instance diarrhoeal diseases, malaria, pneumonia or measles (UNICEF 1992, WHO 1992a). Infections and parasites arising from contaminated food or water can contribute much to undernutrition which, in turn, retards children's growth and lowers their immunity. Infants are also more at risk than adults from various chemical pollutants such as lead (in food, water and air) and high nitrate concentrations in water. The transfer of infants and young children from exclusive reliance on breast milk to powdered milk and semi-solid and solid foods is often particularly hazardous for those living in housing that lacks safe water and the facilities needed for hygienic food preparation and storage.

Once infants and young children become mobile – first crawling, then walking and running – safety becomes an increasing concern:

> *They are driven by the desire to investigate and to extend their skills by crawling, climbing, exploring and putting objects in their mouths. In conditions of urban poverty, excreta, broken glass, crawling insects, plastic bags, rotted food and burning coals are common hazards. Children of this age have the highest incidence of intestinal disease as they make intimate contact with the numerous pathogens in their environment* (Bartlett and others page 78).

Mobile infants and children are particularly at risk from various hazards commonly found in low-income areas – for instance, open fires or stoves or kerosene heaters/cookers, which means a high risk of burns and accidental fires. In households with high levels of indoor air pollution, infants and young children may be heavily exposed, because of the amount of time they spend indoors – for instance strapped to their mother's back when fires are being tended and cooking done. When they are exposed to these irritant fumes and develop respiratory tract infections, their reduced resistance can lead to repeated episodes of acute respiratory infections, paving the way for the early onset of chronic obstructive lung disease (WHO 1992a). Reducing indoor air pollution from very high to low levels could halve the incidence of children's pneumonia (World Bank 1993).

The increasing mobility of the infant and young child to walk and their natural curiosity and desire to explore can also expose them to other environmental hazards, especially where space and facilities are lacking, both indoors and outdoors. For instance, in poor and overcrowded dwellings, it is difficult to keep chemicals used in the home (for instance bleach and pesticides) out of their reach. Where provision for safe play sites is deficient, children will play on roads, rubbish tips or local open spaces where, in the absence of good sanitation and waste collection, faecal matter and household rubbish is dumped. They also often play in construction sites and in their own homes which have dangerous areas, such as unprotected roofs.

Most documentation about children's injuries is based on hospital records but there are good reasons to believe that these provide a very incomplete record. One reason for this is the number of children's injuries that are not treated in hospitals – in part because of the expense and the lack of emergency transport to get them to hospitals. Community-based studies point more precisely to the context and frequency of various kinds of injuries and can take into account the large number of injuries that are not seen in hospitals. A study in Ibadan (Nigeria) documented 1236 injuries involving 436 children over three months involving puncture wounds, lacerations, sprains and dislocations; none were major injuries and less than 1 per cent were treated in formal health facilities (Edet 1996).

Falls appear to be the most common cause of injury in most instances and are especially common for younger children. Burns are often the most common for children under four and most occur within the home. These include burns from hot water or other hot fluids and accidents with open fires or kerosene appliances. Children (especially girls) often begin helping with cooking and heating water at an age when they are too young to safely do so, including handling unstable or dangerous cooking equipment and heavy, hot pots. A study of fuel-use in the shack areas of Cape Town which highlighted how common accidental fires were in these areas also noted that children as young as seven or eight handle cooking with little or no adult supervision and have to work with dangerous kerosene/paraffin stoves (Mehlwana 1999). Poisonings are also common, especially for one- to three-year-olds, most often from kerosene, household products (for instance bleach) and medications, although pesticides can also be involved. Road accidents are often among the most common causes of serious injury, and this too is related to the lack of provision for safe and stimulating play space. In South Africa, traffic accidents were found to be the leading cause of death for children over one year of age (Kibel and Wagstaff 1995). In a study in the early 1980s, motor accidents were found to be the leading cause of death for 5- to 14-year-olds in the state capitals of Brazil (PAHO 1988).

A study in a Brazilian squatter settlement in 1989 focused on 600 children under five, drawing on interviews with mothers. The mothers reported that in the two weeks prior to the interview, 30 per cent of the children had had at least one accident and 12 per cent of these were serious enough to have required care in a clinic or hospital. Falls accounted for 53 per cent of these accidents followed by cuts (17 per cent) and burns (10 per cent). Many of the falls were linked to the settlement's rough topography (Reichenheim and Harpham 1989). The age of the child was an important determinant of accidents and peaks in accidents were in the second or fifth year of life.

The quality of any child's home and neighbourhood environment also has a profound, direct influence on her or his physical, intellectual, social and emotional development. This influence begins from the day that they are born. The home and its wider neighbourhood are the physical and social environment in which they play. It is largely through play that they further their own development. Through their intense interaction with the environment and people around them, they acquire the physical, social and mental skills they need as they grow older. They learn so much through their manipulation of objects – mud, sand, water, pieces of wood, waste materials. They learn about the property of different substances and the principle of cause and effect. They learn about their own capacity to create, and to affect and transform their environment. Through play with other children, they learn about social roles and relationships – sharing materials, agreeing on rules, learning from others.

Infants and children often suffer not only from a poor physical environment in the sense of overcrowded and hazardous housing and inadequate provision for play (including dangerous and unsuitable play sites) but also from the stress and possible psychosocial disorders that deficiencies in the physical environment promote in their parents or carers. Among the key psychological and social development needs of children are a need for interaction (to provide stimulation and reaction to the child), the need for consistency and predictability in their care-giving environment and a need to explore and discover (Myers 1991). It is easy to see how a poor physical environment makes these more difficult for parents to provide although perhaps a more important factor is that in many low-income households, all adults work long hours to obtain sufficient income to survive; ensuring child supervision, stimulation and care is particularly problematic in such circumstances. Children are also more susceptible to psychological damage arising from the loss of their home through a disaster or eviction, especially if the family and their social networks are broken up.[7]

Certain occupations in which it is common for children or youths from low-income households to work are associated with particular environmental risks – for instance, those who make a living from picking through rubbish (Furedy 1992, Hunt 1996, Huysman 1994) or those working in particularly hazardous industries (Lee-Wright 1990). Many industries in Asia and Latin America make widespread use of child labour, with such children exposed to high levels of risk from dangerous machinery, heat, toxic chemicals and dust. Box 4.3 gives more details.

Children in low-income households may also have domestic responsibilities which can be hazardous – for instance carrying heavy loads of water from wells or standpipes, or taking domestic wastes to dump sites, or helping with cooking and heating water. Many street children face particular environmental hazards in their work – for instance dodging traffic on major highways, or selling goods to passing motorists. Street children who have been abandoned by their families (or who have run away from home)[8] often have no adult to whom to turn when they are sick or injured. They generally have very poor

---

7 See Dizon and Quijano (1997) of the Urban Poor Associates in Manila who recorded the experiences of children in evictions.
8 It is useful to distinguish between children who work in the street but live in a stable home, usually with their parents, and children who live and work on the streets. UNICEF has suggested three categories. The first is 'children on the street' which is much the largest category of 'street children'; these are children who work on the streets but have strong family connections, may attend school and, in most cases, return home at the end of the day. The second category is 'children of the street'; these see the street as their home and seek shelter, food and a sense of community among their companions there. But ties to their families exist, even if they are remote and they only visit their families infrequently. The third category is 'abandoned children'; these are difficult to distinguish from children of the street since they undertake similar activities and live in similar ways. However, these children have no ties with their families and are entirely on their own.

Box 4.3 OCCUPATIONAL HAZARDS FACED BY WORKING CHILDREN

Working children are subject to all the occupational hazards and diseases faced by adults, but they are frequently more at risk because of their growing bodies, their lower threshold for toxic chemicals and their more limited size and strength.

Children from low-income families are likely to be poorly nourished and in precarious health to begin with, and the demands of work create an additional health burden. Children working long hours suffer from excessive fatigue, and may have inadequate time for meals. Their run-down state can make them especially susceptible to infectious diseases.

In some occupations, children are exposed for long hours every day to toxic fumes or industrial waste. Others do work that strains and damages their eyesight. Children frequently perform work that is too demanding for their size and strength. This, combined with the effects of repetitive actions, can result in musculo-skeletal damage that is permanently distorting. Some work situations expose children to unprotected machinery, the risk of explosions and industrial accidents. An International Labour Office survey in the Philippines found that 60 per cent of working children were exposed to hazardous conditions in their work and of these, 40 per cent had experienced serious injury or illness (ILO 1996).

Unsuitable and hazardous work has many direct effects on developing children, but it also harms them indirectly by depriving them of positive experiences. Time spent working is time taken away from the education, play, and rest necessary for their optimal development. When children's work prevents them from making use of opportunities for learning and growth, it reduces their chances in life.

Source: Bartlett, Sheridan, Roger Hart, David Satterthwaite, Ximena de la Barra and Alfredo Missair (1999), *Cities for Children: Children's Rights, Poverty and Urban Management*, Earthscan, London.

---

quality accommodation (often sleeping in the open or in public places) and they have great difficulty in finding places to wash and defecate and to obtain drinking water and health services (Patel 1990). In addition, many children and youths imprisoned for crimes or vagrancy or placed in corrective institutions may not only have to live in a very poor quality environment but also be deprived of the child–adult relationships and stimulation that are so important for child development (Bartlett and others 1999, Bibars 1998). There are also other children in especially difficult circumstances who face particular environmental risks. For instance, a study by the Indian NGO SPARC in Bombay/Mumbai identified children of pavement dwellers and construction workers and 'hotel boys' as particularly vulnerable, along with street children (Patel 1990). The children of construction workers who live on site lack access to schools, day care, health facilities, water and sanitation; living on construction sites also poses particular hazards for children (ibid).

Women[9]

Women are more vulnerable than men to many environmental hazards because of gender relations (ie as a result of the particular social and economic roles that women have, determined by social, economic and political structures). They are also particularly susceptible to many environmental hazards when pregnant since the reproductive system is particularly sensitive to adverse environmental conditions. 'Every stage of the multi-step process of reproduction can be disrupted by external environmental agents and this may lead to an increased risk of abortion, birth defects, fetal growth retardation and perinatal death' (WHO 1992b, page 21).

Every year, more than half a million women die of causes related to pregnancy and childbirth (UNICEF 1991) while 23 million suffer serious complications with childbirth and 15 million suffer long-term morbidity (WHO 1994). These half a million deaths each year leave around one million children without mothers (UNICEF 1991). Inadequate contraception, unsafe abortion, lack of sanitation and inferior healthcare are some of the main reasons why the risk of dying in childbirth is over 100 times greater among poor women in low- and middle-income countries, than among women in high-income countries (WHO 1995). The absence or very poor quality of health services for child-bearing women is the main cause (Germain and others 1994) but environmental factors are also important, especially the water-related, airborne or food-borne diseases associated with poor quality housing and a lack of basic services that contribute to undernutrition and ill health. A woman's health and nutritional status substantially affects her capacity to cope with difficulties during pregnancy, childbirth and the post-partum period, to produce a strong healthy baby and to breastfeed and care for it (World Bank 1990).

The risk for a mother of dying during pregnancy or childbirth in a poor urban district can be 1000 times or more than for a mother from a wealthy household living in a healthy environment with good quality health services and antenatal and post-natal care. This susceptibility during pregnancy, childbirth and the period just after childbirth is biologically determined, but the high rates of maternal mortality are not, since they are the result of the low priority given by governments and international agencies to addressing their causes.

Women are generally far more severely affected than men by poor-quality and overcrowded housing conditions, and by the inadequate provision of water, sanitation and health care (and also schools and nurseries) because they take most responsibility for looking after infants and children, caring for sick family members and managing the household.[10] It is generally women who are responsible for the disposal of human wastes when provision for sanitation is inadequate and this exposes them to diseases associated with contact with human excreta. It is generally women who are responsible for disposing of household wastes when there is no regular waste-collection service from each household. The fact that women take most responsibility for child-care means

---

9 This section is drawn largely from WHO 1999.
10 See for instance Beall and Levy 1994; Moser 1987; Lee-Smith and Trujillo 1992. See also Songsore and McGranahan 1998 for a detailed analysis of this for Accra.

that they also have to cope with most of the illnesses and injuries from which infants and children suffer. Caring for the sick and handling and laundering soiled clothes are particularly hazardous tasks when water supplies and sanitation and washing facilities are inadequate (Sapir 1990).

The people within a household who are responsible for water collection and its use for laundry, cooking and domestic hygiene also suffer most if supplies are contaminated and difficult to obtain, and these people are generally women or girls. Women often suffer more than men from chronic back pain because they have to collect water from wells or public standpipes. Policymakers almost always have piped water systems in their homes and they forget just how heavy water is and the immense physical effort needed to fetch and carry enough water for a household's needs even from standpipes 20–30 metres from a house.

Tuberculosis is a particularly serious problem among low-income urban dwellers living in overcrowded conditions and suffering from undernutrition. Women seem to be most vulnerable to TB in their early and reproductive years and the biological changes that occur in those years may make women more likely to progress to TB once infected. Tuberculosis is also an indirect or contributory cause to many maternal deaths.

A study of household environmental management in Accra noted that:

> *Household and neighbourhood level environmental problems do not receive the attention they deserve in environmental debates and this probably reflects, at least in part, a form of gender discrimination: once the water has left the tap, the fuels have been purchased, and more generally the environmental problems have entered the home, they are considered less important 'private' problems. But since 'private' environmental problems tend also to be 'women's' problems, the seemingly rational emphasis on 'public' problems can easily mask a lack of concern for women's problems* (Songsore and McGranahan 1998, page 409).

A large proportion of urban households use coal, wood or other smoky fuels for cooking and, where needed, heating in open fires or poorly vented stoves. It is generally women (or girls) who take responsibility for tending the fire and doing the cooking and who inhale larger concentrations of pollutants over longer periods (WHO 1992a). It is usually women who take responsibility for firewood gathering and subsistence crop and livestock production in the millions of urban households where these are important components of households' livelihoods; rarely, if ever, do urban housing schemes make allowances for these activities and urban land use and zoning regulations usually discriminate against such tasks (Lee-Smith and Trujillo 1992).

> *The main reason why household energy management, indoor air pollution and other health consequences of unsafe kitchens are receiving so little attention is that the managers of energy resources in households are almost always women. In all cultures women's status tends to be lower than men's, which often means that neither women's household problems nor the technical expertise they can*

bring to bear on these problems are taken seriously enough. Moreover, house-
hold work everywhere is unpaid, invisible, low-status work which is not
included in national economic statistics. Yet the enormous amount of time it
takes a woman to do this work has significant implications for the health of
her entire family (Crewe 1995, pages 94–95).

This section has sought to highlight how women often face higher levels of
environmental risk than men in many urban settings. But as the discussion of
maternal health issues made evident, these environmental risks have to be
understood within a broader context. For instance, one of the reasons that
women have difficulty finding better quality housing with the basic services
that greatly reduce environmental hazards is the discrimination they face in
obtaining employment, in what they are paid when they do find work, in
purchasing or renting housing and in obtaining credit. Many problems also
arise from a complex combination of environmental and non-environmental
factors. For instance, domestic violence which is a serious and often growing
problem to which women and children are particularly vulnerable may arise
from, or be much increased by, poor quality and overcrowded housing and
living environments. Such housing environments also contribute to a higher
incidence of mental disorders and social pathologies and obviously, the adults
who spend most of their time in the home looking after children (generally
women) are most at risk (WHO 1992a, Blue 1996).

CONCLUSIONS

In most urban areas of Africa, Asia and Latin America, low-income groups
have very little chance of obtaining a healthy legal house or apartment within a
neighbourhood where environmental risks are minimized, ie one with sufficient space, security of tenure, services and facilities, and on a site not prone to
flooding, waterlogging or landslides. Many also have the constant fear of
eviction from their homes; this is a permanent worry for most tenants, temporary boarders in cheap rooming houses, those in illegal settlements and 'land'
renters.

  If an individual or household finds 'minimum standard' accommodation
too costly, they have to make certain sacrifices in the accommodation they
choose so they can afford it. They usually make sacrifices in environmental
quality. Although this means health risks and much inconvenience, these are
less important for their survival than other items. For instance, expenditure on
food or children's education or on (say) purchasing a second-hand sewing-
machine to allow a member of the family to earn additional income are more
important than 'minimum standard' accommodation. Each low-income individual or household will have their own preferred trade-offs in terms of the size
of the accommodation, the terms under which it is occupied, the suitability of
the site, housing quality, location and access to infrastructure and services. For
example, to bring down housing costs, a household of five persons might sacrifice space and live in one room, or sacrifice secure tenure and access to piped

water and live in a self-constructed house on illegally occupied land. To understand the possibilities for improving the housing environment of such people,
one must understand their diverse needs and priorities.

Low-income groups may even choose particular locations where pollution
levels are highest because these are the only locations where they can find land
for their housing close to sources of employment without fear of eviction. It
was the high concentration of low-income residents around the Union Carbide
Factory in Bhopal that contributed to so many deaths and injuries, when the
accidental release of the toxic chemicals occurred. Large waste dumps often
have high concentrations of low-income groups living close-by, despite the
environmental hazards and the poor quality environments because they derive
their income from picking, processing and trading materials gathered from the
wastes.

The dangerous living and working environments of low-income people
reflect the failure of government in a number of tasks:

- The failure to invest in basic services and infrastructure which can generally only be undertaken cost-effectively either by government or with their
  support.[11]
- The failure to implement pollution control.
- The failure to ensure that employers conform to occupational health and
  safety standards.
- The failure to ensure that low-income groups can get access to shelters that
  are not so dangerous or to the resources that allow them to build these
  themselves.

The large health-burden faced by low-income groups is also linked to the failure
of government to ensure provision for the community-based healthcare and
emergency services that can do so much to prevent illness or injury and to limit
its impact.

This is not to say that government agencies have to provide the housing or
all the infrastructure and services. As later chapters will emphasize, community,
NGO or private sector provision is often more effective, or simply the only
possibility because of the weakness of local government. But ensuring that
these failures are addressed usually needs a supportive public framework. For
instance, increasing the supply and reducing the cost of good quality, secure
housing requires support for increased supplies of legal land site for housing –
on a scale to have a downward pressure on land prices – within a planning
framework that also guarantees sufficient open space and minimizes infrastructure costs.

Analyses of environmental hazards can point to the very large health (and
economic) benefits of addressing them and it has become more common for
estimates to be made of the benefits from doing so. But what such estimates

---

11 Chapter 6 includes some examples of community-based provision which are exceptions but it
is very difficult for large-scale community provision without a broader framework of water
supply, sewers, drains and solid- waste management systems into which community-based provision can integrate.

often miss, as later chapters will discuss in more detail, is that addressing these brings most benefits to low-income groups and usually implies higher costs for powerful vested interests – for instance industries that are forced to meet existing regulations on pollution control and occupational health and safety, and the enterprises and households that are well-served with public infrastructure and services who have to pay more realistic prices for these. Once again, one returns to the issue of the quality of governance – in this instance in the ability of public authorities to stop enterprises from transferring environmental costs to its workforce or to city residents, and to ensure that all residents have safe homes with basic services (whether through public, private, NGO or community provision). *One of the best indicators of 'good governance' in any city or metropolitan area is the scale of the differentials between its various districts or neighbourhoods in environmental hazards, basic service provision (which reduces the hazards) and health indicators.*

Chapter 5

The Rural, Regional and Global Impacts of Cities

A pool of oil left by oil companies in the Amazon region in Ecuador

CITIES' REGIONAL IMPACTS AND RURAL–URBAN INTERACTIONS

Introduction

Cities transform environments and landscapes not only within the built-up area but also for considerable distances around them. This includes environmental impacts in the region around the city which usually includes large areas defined as (or considered) rural. The inhabitants, environment and natural resource base of this wider region are usually affected by:

- The expansion of the built-up area and the transformations this brings – for instance land surfaces are reshaped, valleys and swamps filled, large volumes of clay, sand, gravel and crushed rock extracted and moved, water sources tapped, and rivers and streams channelled (Douglas 1983, 1986).

• The demand from city-based enterprises, households and institutions for the products of forests, rangelands, farmlands, watersheds or aquatic ecosystems that are outside its boundaries.

• The solid, liquid and air-borne wastes generated within the city and transferred to the region around it which have environmental impacts, especially on water bodies where liquid wastes are disposed of without adequate treatment and on land sites where solid wastes are dumped without the measures to limit their environmental impact.

Cities require a high input of resources – fresh water, fuels, land and all the goods and raw materials that their populations and enterprises require. The more populous the city and the richer its inhabitants, the greater the demand on resources and, in general, the larger the area from which these are drawn, although at any one time, each particular type of natural resource may have its own particular area of supply.[1] The more valuable and lighter natural commodities such as fruit and vegetables, wood and metals may be drawn from areas hundreds of kilometres away or imported from other countries. So may cheaper foods and other natural resources, if these are not easily produced locally. But the more bulky, low-value materials will usually come from close-by; as Ian Douglas (1983, page 26) notes, 'the physical structure or fabric of the city, the buildings, the roads, railways, airports, docks, pipe and conduit systems require large quantities of materials for their construction' and 'the bulk of the structures are derived from locally available clay, sand, gravel and crushed rock'. This can be seen in the brickworks, quarries, claypits, sand and gravel pits in and around most cities, all of which have environmental impacts.

Cities are also usually major centres for resource degradation. Water needed for industrial processes, for supplying residential and commercial buildings, for transporting sewage and for other uses is returned to rivers, lakes or the sea at a far lower quality than that originally supplied. Solid wastes collected from city households and businesses are usually disposed of on land sites in the region around the city while much of the uncollected solid waste generally finds its way into water bodies, adding to the pollution. Air pollutants generated by city-based enterprises or consumers are often transferred to the surrounding region through acid rain. These can be termed regional impacts. We look first at the environmental impact of cities' physical expansion, then at the demand for resources from the wider region (the 'inputs') and then at the impact of wastes generated by city-based activities (especially waste disposal) on the wider region (the 'outputs'). This is followed by a discussion of how to measure cities' 'ecological footprints' (to draw on the term and concept developed by William E Rees) and to assess their draw on global resources and systems.

---

1 See Chapter 3 of Douglas 1983 for more details and also examples of maps showing the locations for sources of food or materials for different cities.

Cities' physical expansion

In the absence of any effective land-use plan or other means to guide and control new developments, cities generally expand haphazardly, determined by where different households, residential areas, enterprises and public sector activities locate, legally and illegally. Uncontrolled physical growth impacts most on what might be termed an immediate hinterland around a city; much of this cannot be described as urban or suburban and yet much of it is no longer rural. If the city has been designated a 'metropolitan centre', much or all of this hinterland may fall within the metropolitan boundaries.

Within this area, agriculture may disappear or decline as land is bought up by people or companies in anticipation of its change from agricultural to urban use and of the (often very large) increases in land value that this brings, as the city's built-up area and transport system expands. There is usually a lack of effective public control of such changes in land use or on the profits that can be made from them, even when it is public investment (for instance the expansion of road networks) that creates much of the increment in land value. Around prosperous cities, it is also encouraged by the scale of profits that can be made, and it is difficult to develop governance structures that prevent politicians and powerful vested interests from being the prime beneficiaries. In many cities, it is also encouraged by a lack of other domestic high-return investment opportunities.

Unplanned and uncontrolled city expansion produces a patchwork of different developments, including businesses and many high-density residential settlements, interspersed with land that remains undeveloped, in anticipation of speculative gain. Development occurs through legal and illegal action by various landowners, builders, developers and real-estate firms in an adhoc way, producing an incoherent urban sprawl. There are usually many legal subdivisions in this hinterland for houses or commercial and industrial buildings that have been approved without reference to any city-wide plan. Many cities have a considerable range of new factories and other businesses developing in surrounding 'rural' areas, although their functioning and markets are intimately tied to the city (Jones 1983, McGee 1987). In more prosperous cities, many new low-density, high-income residential neighbourhoods may also develop here, along with some commercial developments and leisure facilities for higher-income groups (for instance country clubs and golf courses). In many cities, especially those with high levels of crime and violence, there are often many residential developments enclosed within walls developing around the cities (usually close to major highways) that are protected by private security firms – the 'walled cities' or barrios cerados. There are usually many unauthorized subdivisions as well and where regulation is lax, these may cater for middle- and upper-income developments too. There are usually illegal squatter communities too, that originally located here because the inaccessibility, lack of infrastructure and poor quality of the site gave more chance of not being evicted. In many cities (including Buenos Aires, Delhi, Santiago, Seoul and Manila), this hinterland also contains settlements formed when their inhabitants were dumped there, after being evicted from their homes by 'slum' or squatter clearance.[2] The inhabitants of these settlements may again find themselves under threat of eviction as the physical expansion of the urban area and its road network increases the value of the land on which they live.

There may be no city-wide plan and in many larger cities, responsibility for land-use planning and development control is held by many individual municipal or other local authorities with few if any mechanisms to ensure some coordination between them. Some local authorities may seek to attract new business by lax environmental controls. One interesting case study of this is in Colombia where the cities of Villamaria and Manizales share an ecosystem and both rely on various natural resources but the local authorities had very different attitudes to environmental management (Vélasquez and Pacheco 1999). Manizales is well known for the quality of its environmental management and its innovative Local Agenda 21 (as Chapter 7 will describe), but neighbouring Villamaria sought to attract new enterprises by keeping down taxes (for instance on petrol) and having more lax controls on land development and pollution, although there are now institutional measures in place to ensure better joint management of shared resources between the two municipal authorities (ibid).

The uncontrolled and unregulated physical expansion of a city's built up area usually has serious social and environmental consequences, including problems of soil erosion and its contribution to the silting of drainage channels and the segregation of low-income groups in the worst located and often the most dangerous areas. The haphazard expansion of settlements can also bring greatly increased costs for providing basic infrastructure as new developments that need connection to networks of roads, water mains, sewers and drainage pipes spring up far from existing networks. It is also more expensive to provide public transport and social services. In viewing the area around cities, one often sees the paradox of extreme overcrowding, serious housing shortages and acute shortages of infrastructure and services in particular areas, and yet large amounts of land left vacant or only partially developed with all that this implies in terms of increasing the cost of providing infrastructure and services. Illegal or informal settlements are often concentrated on land sites subject to flooding or at risk from landslides or other natural hazards, especially where these offer well-located sites on which low-income settlers have the best chance of establishing a home and/or avoiding eviction. But these are also land sites to which it is more difficult and expensive to extend basic infrastructure.

It is not only around the major cities that uncontrolled urban expansion produces these kinds of serious social and ecological impacts, as can be seen in Acho-Chi's study of Bamenda in Cameroon, noted in Chapter 3 (Acho-Chi 1998). In Bamenda, settlements expanded up the steep hill-slopes of the Bamenda escarpment with no public provisions to ensure that the more unstable areas were avoided or to minimize soil erosion when sites were cleared. Flooding has become a particular problem, as land clearance-induced erosion contributes to the silting of stream beds or other drains and more rapid water

2 See for instance Asian Coalition for Housing Rights 1989; Makil 1982; Shrivastav 1982; Hardoy and Satterthwaite 1989.

run-off. The impact of the floods is made more serious by the expansion of settlements over flood-plains and the inadequate provision for drainage, along with the expansion of paved or otherwise impervious surfaces. The main reason for the expansion of settlements up these fragile slopes is that land here is very cheap and low-income households cannot afford the much more expensive but safer sites. But as Acho-Chi points out, it is also very expensive to extend basic services to those living on the steep slopes so a failure to manage urban expansion brings high social as well as ecological costs.

The loss of agricultural land, forests or other land sites with valuable ecological functions (for instance wetlands) is another consequence of uncontrolled city growth. Cities often expand over some of their nation's most productive agricultural land since so many cities grew up within highly fertile areas. Most cities in Latin America, Asia and North Africa were important urban centres before the development of motorized transport.[3] At that time, no major city could develop too far from the land that produced its inhabitants' daily food and fuel requirements. In addition, many cities first developed as market centres to serve the prosperous farms and farming households around them. For example, almost all the large cities in the nations around the Pacific were established on lowland delta regions and continue to expand into their nation's most fertile agricultural land (Douglass 1987).

This loss of agricultural land can usually be avoided or minimized if government guides the physical expansion and ensures that vacant or underutilized land is fully used. In most cities, the problem is not a lack of vacant land but a lack of appropriate government action to guide new developments on land other than the best farmland. In Egypt, more than 10 per cent of the nation's most productive farmland has been lost to urban encroachment in recent decades, much of it through illegal squatting or subdivision while at the same time prime sites within cities remain undeveloped (Kishk 1986), although Egypt is unusual in having such a small proportion of its national surface as cultivatable since more than 95 per cent of the country is desert. The urban area of Delhi (including New Delhi) has grown more than 13-fold since 1900, eating into surrounding agricultural areas and absorbing more than 100 villages. However, some care is needed in assuming that urban expansion necessarily means reduced agricultural output or impoverishment for villagers, as shown by Johan Bentinck's study of changing patterns of land use and livelihood on Delhi's fringe (Bentinck 2000). Although this documents serious environmental and social problems, it also shows how the inhabitants of villagers that become engulfed by Delhi's expansion improve and diversify their livelihoods and that agricultural decline is only partial. 'Many of the agricultural fields that are left are used for intensive agriculture and horticulture. Combined with the added value derived from transporting crops to the city this brings good revenues for enterprising farmers'(ibid, page 150).

---

3 Although much of the general literature on urban change in Africa, Asia and Latin America talks about an urban explosion and a mushrooming of cities, most cities in North Africa, Asia and Latin America have a long history as significant urban centres. There are very few major cities in these regions that do not pre-date the motor car.

Urban land markets can also disrupt agricultural production and the livelihoods of those who depend on it for areas that stretch far beyond sites developed for urban use. There are also conflicts over land-use priorities between urban-based demands and ecological services; examples include the loss of agricultural lands and of forests, wetlands and other undeveloped sites to industrial estates and residential developments or to golf courses and country-clubs. These conflicts generally involve social conflicts too as the livelihoods of those who depend on the agricultural lands or forests are threatened by urban-based demands (see for instance Douglass 1989 and Kelly 1998). Box 5.1 describes these conflicts in the highly productive agricultural zone to the south of Manila and how national, local and personal forces ensure that land for residential, industrial or other urban developments are favoured over the protection and continued use of highly productive farmland.

Uncontrolled physical expansion also destroys natural landscapes in or close to cities that should be preserved as parks, nature reserves, historic sites or simply as areas of open space for recreation and children's play. The need to preserve or develop such areas might seem less urgent than, say, land for housing. But once an area is built up, it is almost impossible (and very expensive) to remedy a lack of open space. In addition, the richer groups suffer much less. Their residential areas usually have plenty of open space. Their homes often have gardens. They are much more mobile and so can travel more easily out of the city. And they can afford to become members of the country clubs, sports clubs and golf courses that have become common on the outskirts of many cities, and so can enjoy walks, playgrounds and facilities for sport.

Inputs into urban areas – the demand for resources

It is difficult to draw up any 'balance sheet' regarding the environmental (and other) benefits and costs of urban-based demand for rural resources. This chapter concentrates on the environmental costs. But urban-based demand for rural resources is also an important (and often the most important) basis for rural incomes and livelihoods, and the rural incomes produced by urban demand may form the basis for prosperous, well-managed farms, fisheries and forests. This is a point to which we will return in a later section on rural–urban relations.

The demand for rural resources from city-based enterprises and households may limit their availability for rural households. For instance, in cities where wood and charcoal are still widely used for cooking and heating (mostly by lower-income households), city-based demand may pre-empt supplies formerly used by rural inhabitants. Where once poor rural inhabitants gathered wood from what was regarded as common land, now they may be barred from doing so, as the wood is harvested for sale. Common land once used for gathering wild produce and grazing can be taken over by mono-culture tree plantations where such gathering or grazing is no longer permitted (Agarwal and Narain 1992, Lee-Smith and Trujillo 1992). High demand for fuelwood from cities may be a prime cause of deforestation (and the soil erosion that usually accompanies it) and this may be taking place at considerable distances from the city. Box 5.2 gives some examples. However, some care is needed in

Box 5.1 *THE POLITICS OF LAND CONVERSION ON THE RURAL–URBAN INTERFACE: THE CASE OF CAVITE IN THE PHILIPPINES*

In the province of Cavite, just to the south of Manila, agricultural land and the rural livelihoods and staple food this supports are being lost to urban and industrial development. Official figures show that 1840 hectares of agricultural land in Cavite were converted to non-agricultural use between 1988 and 1995, more than half for residential developments with most of the rest for industrial and institutional developments. Most land conversions are on irrigated rice lands. But these figures almost certainly understate the land taken out of agricultural production since they do not include land that is lying idle because the owners have removed the tenant farmers but not yet developed it or land that has been converted without the knowledge of the authorities.

The land conversion displaces the farming population; the biggest losers are the landless agricultural labourers since at least the tenant farmers receive disturbance compensation.

In terms of environmental impact, farmers in Cavite complain that irrigation canals have been silted up with eroded material from local building sites. In other cases, the water supply is also blocked by household wastes as new residents respond to inadequate waste-collection services by discarding these in nearby canals. Farmers have also complained that crop pests have become an increasing problem with the development of residential areas in the midst of farmland.

Despite an agrarian law which is meant to protect rice and corn lands and support the transfer of land to the tenant farmers who work it, various factors at national, local and personal levels ensure a continued loss of agricultural land:

- Landlords keen to avoid losing their land can circumvent the agrarian reform law by converting it to other crops or to non-agricultural uses. In many cases, tenant farmers have been removed and the land has been left idle because leaving a farmer to cultivate rice would make it difficult to obtain a non-agricultural zoning from the local government. In addition, the longer a tenant is allowed to farm land, the higher the compensation that has to be paid. But if land is left idle, after a few years, the owner can claim that the land is 'non-productive' and therefore eligible for conversion.
- The government under President Ramos emphasized industrial development and although this was meant to include agro-industrialization, this came to mean industrial development located in agricultural areas rather than the formation of functional linkages between agriculture and industry.
- The legal setting for land conversion has various measures to protect agricultural land but few provisions for punishing offenders and numerous opportunities for evasion. Various laws also undermine the

control of land conversion by the Department of Agrarian Reform. In addition, the political climate has been one in which industrial development is aggressively promoted while agricultural land is seen as expendable when it conflicts with other priorities. Those with the means and good connections can circumvent the land conversion regulations relatively easily.

- At local level, many towns have no precisely defined or publicly available zoning maps so local officials (especially mayors) have great scope for land reclassification. As a result, Cavite's municipal mayors have become the province's leading real-estate agents and brokers (Sidel 1995). In part, this is because municipal revenues increase with residential and industrial growth, but local politicians generally have a more direct stake in land conversion. Since local councils are also in charge of law enforcement, pressure can be brought to bear on farmers who resist a decision to convert farmland. Provincial governments can also become involved, although technically they have little power to influence land-conversion decisions. However, the governor of Cavite in the early 1990s was reported to have ordered the bulldozing of homes and engineered the destruction of irrigation canals so land was cleared of 'squatters' and tenant farmers and made available for Manila-based or foreign companies for 'development' into industrial estates (ibid).
- At the level of personal relations, there is little basis for equality as tenant farmers negotiate with landlords who have high social status, sufficient resources to bribe officials and access to legal counsel. This negotiation also takes place within a cultural context of patron–client ties that preclude farmers from asserting their legal rights.

Land has long been the key source of power and conflict in the Philippines but in the past, the struggle has focused on the control of agricultural land as the basis for wealth, patronage and dominance. Now it is the potential of agricultural land for urban–industrial uses that motivates the will to control it in areas such as Cavite.

Source: Kelly, Philip F, 'The politics of urban–rural relationships: land conversion in the Philippines', *Environment and Urbanization*, Vol 10, No 1, 1998, pages 35–54.

---

assuming that city markets necessarily cause large-scale deforestation. Studies in various African countries showed little evidence of large-scale deforestation associated with urban-based demand for wood and fuelwood (Leach and Mearns 1989).

A study of the long-term impact that Jakarta may have on its wider region provides an example of the complex rural–urban interactions taking place between a city and its surrounding areas and shows how serious the environmental impacts on the surrounding areas can be (Douglass 1989). As Box 5.3 describes in more detail, the expansion of the urban area and urban activities pushes farmers from agricultural land; productive agriculture is replaced by

---

Box 5.2 *FIREWOOD IN THE CITIES*

To meet demand for firewood in Delhi, 12,423 railway wagons of firewood arrived at Tughlakabad railway siding during 1981–82 – some 612 tons a day. Most of this wood comes from Madhya Pradesh, nearly 700 kilometres away. The Shahdara railway siding also receives firewood daily from the forests in the Himalayan foothills in Assam and Bihar, although in smaller quantities. In addition, the forested area and trees within Delhi yield thousands of tons annually. Yet Delhi has a relatively low per capita consumption of firewood because of the ready availability of kerosene, coal and liquid petroleum gas (which are much preferred as fuel if they can be afforded). In Bangalore, an estimated 440,000 tonnes of commercial firewood are consumed each year, far more than in Delhi, even though Bangalore has around half the population of Delhi. Most of it arrives by road – an average of 114 trucks a day. Most firewood comes from private farms and forests within 150 kilometres of Bangalore but 15 per cent comes from government forests, 300 to 700 kilometres away.

Source: Centre for Science and Environment (1985), *The State of India's Environment 1984–5: The Second Citizens' Report*, New Delhi.

---

urban developments or by commercial ventures for tourism and recreation. Agriculture is pushed on to land that is less suited to such use in hill and upland areas. Soil erosion there often lowers agricultural productivity and causes siltation of water reservoirs, flooding after heavy rains plus reduced flows in rivers during dry periods. Meanwhile, the government must seek new sources of water to supply Jakarta since the shallow aquifers from where most households draw their water are saline. The supply of water will need to multiply considerably, especially if rising demand from a growing population and expanding productive base is to be combined with improvements in the supply of piped water to city households. But many of the lowland river and water courses nearby have high concentrations of organic chemicals and heavy metals from agricultural biocides that are not broken down by natural processes, and this limits their possible use for human consumption.

Depletion of freshwater resources. Many urban centres face similar difficulties to Jakarta's in obtaining sufficient fresh water and this is even the case in cities where half or more of the population are not adequately served with safe, sufficient supplies. Many cities have outgrown the capacity of their locality to provide adequate water supplies, as all nearby surface water sources have been tapped and/or as groundwater resources are being drawn on much faster than the natural rate of recharge; or they face acute problems during particular periods of low rainfall.

There are also often problems with water quality. Surface water sources on which cities draw are often of poor quality – for instance they are saline because of the return water from irrigation and are contaminated with agricultural

Box 5.3 REGIONAL IMPACTS OF JAKARTA

The Jakarta metropolis now ranks as one of the world's largest urban agglomerations. By 1980, most of the growth in population was taking place on the periphery of the metropolis with the population in previously low-density areas such as Depok and Cibinong growing at rates of 10 per cent a year. A significant proportion of population growth has occurred through the attraction of migrants from other regions of Java.

The first major planning study to deal solely with the spatial dimension of environmental degradation in the Jakarta metropolitan region in 1983 identified problems such as severe water pollution from both urban and agricultural uses, unnecessary loss and degradation of prime agricultural land through urban expansion, potentially serious erosion problems developing in the uplands, extensive loss of natural habitation and severe threats to the remaining areas of natural forest, coastlands and marine ecosystems. Other studies of environmental conditions in Jakarta have noted the existence of mercury poisoning in Jakarta Bay and the absence of concrete government measures to deal with the mounting levels of toxic wastes. These problems are not simply the result of either a unidirectional spread of urbanization into agricultural lands or the movement of rural households into ecologically critical uplands. Rather they are the outcome of the negatively reinforcing impacts of both the rapid urbanization and rapid expansion of rural land use in coastal, upland and forest areas in the region reaching beyond the Jakarta agglomeration and along the Jakarta–Bandung corridor.

As the metropolis has expanded, the negative environmental impacts of one activity have been magnified by those of another. Industrial pollution of the water systems has occurred alongside that caused by the excessive use of fertilizers, pesticides and herbicides in agriculture which feed into the same water system.

In a region such as Jakarta, environmental problems go beyond the categories of simple negative externalities and threaten the very sustainability of development. One example is the extraction of ground water at an accelerating rate by a multiplicity of users. Sea water has intruded 15 kilometres inland, creating a zone of salinized ground water reaching to the centre of the city.

The expanding population and economic activities have brought about land-use changes within the region. As the zone of urban land expands, agriculture is pushed outward and upward toward less suitable agricultural land in hill and upland areas. In upland areas, soil erosion is a particular concern; besides generally lowering agricultural productivity, it also has potentially severe downstream impacts including the siltation of reservoirs, flooding through loss of upland capacity to retain water after heavy rains, and a reduced flow in other seasons which would exacerbate downstream pollution and reduce water availability for agriculture.

There is a major dilemma to be faced by efforts to improve the quality of life in metropolitan core regions in Asia. This centres on the fact that the major parameters that need to be guided are neither contained within Jakarta nor are subject to substantial manipulation by the spatial allocation of infrastructure in the capital city region. Mechanization of agriculture and a decline in public spending on rural construction are both working to accelerate rural-metropolitan migration. So too are the fall in the prices of outer-island exports, import-substitution and, more recently, export-oriented manufacturing policies that have worked to polarize manufacturing employment within the Jakarta agglomeration.

It is already evident that land-use management within the region must be dramatically improved if the negative impacts of land-use changes and conflicts are to be reduced to allow for an environmentally sustainable development process. At present there are three main obstacles to land-use policy implementation: the failure to effectively coordinate the programmes of government bureaus responsible for various aspects of land-use control; the absence of sufficient incentives to guide land-use changes by the private sector away from environmentally sensitive areas; and the absence of a clear political will to implement existing policies and regulations.

Source: Douglass, Mike (1989), 'The environmental sustainability of development: coordination, incentives and political will in land use planning for the Jakarta metropolis', *Third World Planning Review*, Vol. 11, No 2, pages 211–238.

chemical and human and livestock wastes or heavily polluted by industries or other users 'upstream'. Groundwater resources are also often contaminated, especially if industries have been disposing of their wastes down deep wells. In many cities, local water resources have been over-used or otherwise mismanaged so these are no longer available, for instance, in many coastal cities, local aquifers that have been over-pumped, resulting in saltwater intrusion.

Problems of water scarcity are particularly acute in the many urban centres in relatively arid areas. Hundreds of urban centres that developed in relatively arid areas have grown beyond the point where adequate supplies can be tapped from local or even regional sources. Many of the coastal cities in Peru (including Lima), La Rioja and Catamarca in Argentina and various cities in Northern Mexico are among the many cities with severe constraints on expanding freshwater supplies. Many urban centres in Africa's dryland areas face particularly serious problems because of a combination of rapid growth in the demand for water and unusually low rainfall in recent years, with the consequent dwindling of local freshwater resources. These and many other cities face problems in financing the expansion of supplies to keep up with demand, as the cheapest and most easily tapped water sources have been tapped or polluted, and drawing on newer sources implies much higher costs per unit volume of water (Bartone and others 1994).

In Dakar (Senegal), as in many other cities, water supplies have to be drawn from ever more distant sources (White 1992). This is both because local groundwater supplies are fully used (and polluted) and local aquifers are over-pumped, resulting in saltwater intrusion; a substantial proportion of the city's water has to be brought in from the Lac de Guiers, 200 kilometres away (see Box 5.4).

Rural–urban interactions

For most urban centres, an examination of the resource flows into them reveals a scale and complexity of linkages with rural producers and ecosystems within their own region and beyond which implies that they cannot be considered separately.[4] The rural–urban linkages can be positive in both developmental and environmental terms. For instance, demand for rural produce from city-based enterprises and households can (and often does) support prosperous farms and rural settlements, where environmental capital is not being depleted – for example as local producers invest in maintaining the quality of soils and water resources. Increasing agricultural production can support rising prosperity for rural populations and rapid urban development within or close to the main farming areas, the two supporting each other.[5] Many of the most rapidly growing urban centres in Africa and Latin America in recent years have been those within or close to agricultural areas growing high-value added crops (for instance fruit, tea or coffee). Here are also many examples of organic solid and liquid wastes that originate from city-based consumers or industries being returned to the soil.

There are generally many 'rural' households for whom urban incomes are important components of total incomes. This often includes large numbers of low-income households who live in rural areas around cities and are considered rural inhabitants but who have one or more member who works in the city or commutes there. There is also the large and growing evidence of the importance for livelihoods and for urban consumers of food production in areas close to the built-up area.[6]

The scale and nature of migration flows to urban centres from the regions around them will be influenced by the extent to which government policies support rural livelihoods and good environmental management. Ironically, many governments claim to want to slow migration to cities yet they do little to support rural livelihoods, protect agricultural land and prevent resource degradation in the areas around cities, as was evident in the case study of land conversion just outside Manila (Box 5.1) and around Jakarta (Box 5.3). Similarly, as the next section will describe, a lack of attention to controlling the pollution of local water bodies so often means damage to or destruction of productive local fisheries that previously supported many jobs and often provided cheap high quality protein. This is not to say that urban expansion (and the conversion of land) has to be

---

4 This section draws on the findings of the IIED's research programme on rural–urban interactions, especially from Tacoli 1998 and on Satterthwaite and Tacoli forthcoming.
5 See Chapter 9 of Hardoy and Satterthwaite 1989, and Satterthwaite and Tacoli forthcoming.
6 See for instance Stren 1986, Lee-Smith and others 1987 and the early work of Jac Smit which were among the first to highlight this; see Smit and others 1996 for the most comprehensive overview (a new edition of this overview of urban agriculture is also being completed).

Box 5.4 MEETING DAKAR'S WATER NEEDS

In 1961, on the eve of independence, Dakar was a city of approximately 250,000 people. It occupied a peninsular site, open to cooling winds and scoured by ocean currents. Most of the drinking water was drawn straight from the basalt aquifer on which the city was built. By 1988, the population of Dakar had reached 1.5 million.

As the city expanded, it overran and polluted the local groundwater supplies, while overpumping of the aquifer resulted in saltwater intrusion. As the basalt aquifer became inadequate, supplies were drawn from sedimentary aquifers 80 kilometres distant. Later, as these were unable to keep up with demand, water was drawn from sedimentary strata further north. As these too were surpassed a pumping station was established in the Lac de Guiers, a shallow reservoir created in a fossil river valley, 200 kilometres from Dakar. By 1978 the Lac de Guiers was providing approximately 20 per cent of Dakar's water supply, although this figure varied greatly according to the amount of water in the lake. In the late 1970s plans were made for the doubling and tripling of the capacity of the water pipes from the Lac de Guiers to Dakar. The money was never found to finance these schemes. A much larger plan is now on the drawing board, to bring water from the southern end of the Lac de Guiers by an open canal, known as the Canal de Cayor. There is virtually no recycling of water; it is widely believed that there would be serious cultural objections to such a proposal.

An important effect of the overall lack of water is that the sewage and waste-water canals and drains are inadequately flushed. To reduce the amount of household waste dumped in the canals, some have been cemented over, hiding a growing problem. Sewage and semi-liquid waste are usually the first to have visible negative impacts on the urban system, resulting in increased coliform counts,[7] beaches closed for swimming and reduced catches from the inshore fishery. In 1986 the Senegalese Department of the Environment put into operation its first (mobile) water quality laboratory. It carried out coliform counts for the beaches around the city and it presented the results in the annual (September) warning regarding storms and dangerous tides, which was published in the national newspaper. The results were appalling; for some samples the coliforms were too numerous to count. In the meantime the combination of household and industrial wastes has polluted the Baie de Hann so badly that algal growths have killed off the inshore fishery. Few local fishermen have the equipment to fish further from the shore. From simply being a nuisance, environmental decline has now begun to undermine the local economy beginning with fishery and tourism.

Source: White, Rodney R (1992) 'The international transfer of urban technology: does the North have anything to offer for the global environmental crisis?', *Environment and Urbanization*, Vol 4, No 2, pages 109–120.

---

7 A coliform count is a good indicator of water quality since faecal coliform bacteria are found in human and animal wastes. Although coliform bacteria themselves do not cause disease, their presence can indicate the presence of bacteria that cause typhoid, cholera, dysentery and other waterborne bacterial diseases. A faecal coliform bacteria count gives the number of bacterial colonies per 100 ml of water and a sample with less than 100 is considered safe to drink while a sample with less than 200 is considered safe for swimming.

halted; prosperous urban centres need more land and constraining the land available for housing pushes up house prices, which so often means that lower-income groups face worse, more overcrowded conditions and/or resort to illegal developments. City-based demand can also stimulate and support a considerable range of new 'rural' enterprises and occupations. For instance, many farmers around Mexico City have benefited from the expanded demand for high-value agricultural produce and from tourist demand (Losada and others 1998). Many farmers around Yogyakarta have benefited from urban demand and more accessible markets (Douglass 1998). Agricultural production may find new opportunities to respond to external demand as urban expansion improves farmers' access to roads, ports, airports, credit and information about market opportunities. Although it is obviously the land owners who stand to gain most, either by meeting demand for higher value crops or by converting their land for non-agricultural use, urban expansion may also bring better livelihood opportunities for lower-income groups. The study of changing patterns of land use and livelihoods on Delhi's fringe mentioned earlier (Bentinck 2000), while documenting the serious social and environmental problems, also notes that many villagers have benefited through improved and diversified livelihoods, including many that now work in the city (and commute) or work in newly developed non-agricultural activities, and some who benefit from renting property to tenants or entrepreneurs. The study is also unusual in that it considers the benefits and costs to different income groups and it shows how it is not only the landowning villagers who have benefited but also the lower caste villagers, including those who previously owned little or no land (ibid). Here, as in the regions around many other expanding cities, there is evidence of large and diverse non-agricultural economic activities developing, although as noted earlier, from an environmental perspective, care is needed to ensure that the more environmentally damaging enterprises do not relocate there because environmental regulations are less strict or less enforced than within the city. The fact that it is common for a diverse range of residential, commercial and industrial developments to develop in the region around cities can bring higher incomes and a more robust livelihood base for many rural dwellers. But measures are needed to limit their environmental impacts and to protect rural resources. This includes avoiding the enhanced possibilities for disease vectors to breed, as noted in Chapter 2. It includes the need to guard against the potential for intensive agriculture or livestock production to pollute water sources. Care is also needed to ensure that a greater concern for protecting the environment is not socially regressive. Large 'green belts' or other means of preventing new urban developments on large areas of land may drive up housing prices, by restricting land supplies for housing, and encourage more dispersed, car-dependent patterns of urban expansion. High-income localities or residential areas have long used 'environmental' arguments or measures to keep out 'lower-income groups'.

The above examples help to show the difficulty in considering 'urban' and 'rural' problems separately. The impoverishment of rural people in a region and the movement of many of them to cities may be considered a rural problem, but it may be largely the result of the commercialization of agricultural land markets and crop production because of city-based demand.

Deforestation may be considered a rural problem but it may be intimately linked to urban-based demand – for instance for agricultural products, which makes it profitable for those who own or control forests to clear them for agriculture or for timber, fuelwood or charcoal. The soil erosion linked to deforestation may be destroying rural inhabitants' livelihoods, with the result that they migrate to the city. The environmental impacts of large hydro-electric dams (eg the loss of agricultural land and the introduction or exacerbation of water-borne or water-related diseases) are usually considered rural even if most of the electricity will be consumed in urban areas. Other examples include the environmental effects of agricultural or mining operations that produce raw materials for city-based activities or poorly designed and located bridges, highways and roads linking smaller settlements with cities, which might contribute to problems of flooding. But an expanding city can also be seen as having great potential to increase incomes and fund good environmental management in its surrounding region, although there are usually strong political and administrative constraints on doing so, not least because of the difficulties in getting the different local authorities to work together.

City outputs – solid, liquid and gaseous wastes

Liquid, gaseous and solid wastes generated by city-based enterprises and consumers often have significant impacts in the region surrounding the city. Each is considered here.

Disposal of liquid wastes. The contamination of rivers, lakes, seashores and coastal waters is an example both of the impact of city-generated wastes on the wider region and of governments' negligent attitude to protecting open areas. Untreated waste water and sewage from both households and commercial and industrial enterprises are usually discharged into nearby rivers or lakes.[8] This often leads to serious health problems for large numbers of people whose water supply is drawn from these water sources. In cities on or close to coasts, untreated sewage and industrial effluents often flow into the sea with little or no provision to pipe them far enough out to sea to protect the beaches and inshore waters. Most coastal cities have serious problems with dirty, contaminated beaches and water so there is a major health risk to bathers. Oil pollution often adds to existing problems of sewage and industrial effluents. Pollution may be so severe that many beaches have to be closed to the public. It is usually the most accessible beaches that are most polluted and in many cities, these are among the most widely used recreational areas by lower-income groups. Richer households suffer much less; those with cars can reach more distant, less accessible and less polluted beaches.

The possibilities for improvement vary greatly. In many of the largest cities in Europe and North America that are located on rivers or by lakes, great improvements have been achieved in reducing water pollution, mostly through stricter controls on industrial emissions and more sophisticated and compre-

---

8 See for instance details of this in China in Changhua and others 1998.

hensive treatment of sewage and water run-off collected in drains. Rather less success has been achieved in reducing polluting discharges to the sea. In most cities in low- and middle-income nations, the problems are not so easily addressed as they have much more serious 'non-point' sources of water pollution because of the lack of sewers and drains in many city districts and peripheral areas, and the inadequate services to collect solid wastes. A lack of solid-waste collection adds to water pollution problems since many of the uncollected wastes are washed into streams, rivers or lakes, adding to the pollution load.

Liquid wastes from city activities have environmental impacts stretching beyond the immediate hinterland. It is common for fisheries to be damaged or destroyed by liquid effluents from city-based industries, with hundreds or even thousands of people losing their livelihood as a result; among the places where major declines in fish catches have been documented are many rivers, estuaries or coastal waters in India, China and Malaysia, Lake Maryut in Alexandria, the Gulf of Paria between Venezuela and Trinidad, Manila Bay, Rio de Janeiro's Guanabara Bay, the Bay of Dakar and the Indus delta near Karachi.[9] The fish may also be contaminated, as described in Chapter 3 with regard to heavy metal pollution.

Red tides have become a major concern in several Asian countries and seem to be increasing in frequency (Clarke 1999). Red tides are caused by algal blooms that deplete oxygen in coastal waters causing the mass death of aquatic organisms; the algae may also produce toxins that cause shellfish poisonings (ibid). Large volumes of sewage, industrial effluents and agricultural run-off contribute to the nutrient-rich waters which cause algal blooms.

River pollution from city-based industries and untreated sewage can lead to serious health problems in settlements downstream. Paper and rayon factories in India are notorious water polluters and such pollution causes diseases in villagers who live downstream; it often means declining fish catches and declining water volumes as well (Gadgil and Guha 1992). *The Fifth Citizen's Report on the State of India's Environment* (Agarwal and others 1999a) has a long and detailed chapter about the high levels of river pollution in many major Indian rivers coming from industries, industrial or mining complexes or cities which then affects the health and livelihoods of those living downstream. Rivers that are heavily contaminated as they pass through cities may become unusable for agriculture downstream or particular contaminants in the water may damage crops or pose risks to human health. For instance, cadmium and lead concentrations in rivers are particular problems downstream from certain industries, and if the water is used for growing crops like rice, those regularly eating that rice can easily exceed the WHO defined acceptable daily intake (Conway and Pretty 1991). Chapter 3 included the example of the Damodar river which is so

---

9 For India, see Agarwal 1983, Centre for Science and Environment 1982, and Agarwal, Narain and Sen 1999a. For China, see Smil 1984. For Alexandria, see Hamza 1989. For the Gulf of Paria, UNEP 1988. For Manila Bay, see Jimenez and Velasquez 1989. For Rio de Janeiro, see Kreimer and others 1993. For the Bay of Dakar, Kebe 1988 and White 1992. For the Indus Delta, see Sahil 1988 and Beg and others 1984.

polluted by industries on its banks that its water becomes unfit even for agriculture, let alone for human consumption. Yet the river remains the main source of drinking water for numerous rural and urban centres that are located along its banks downstream of the industries (Agarwal and others 1999a).

This regional impact of water pollution can even extend to international water bodies. For instance, in the Persian/Arabian Gulf (a small, shallow, salty and almost landlocked sea) rapid urban and industrial growth on its shores is threatening its fragile ecosystem. While the major danger of marine pollution comes from oil, especially from tanker deballasting and tank washing, sewage from the rapidly expanding coastal cities and untreated industrial liquid wastes are also having a considerable impact, as are the concentration of desalination plants along the coast.[10] The Caribbean faces problems because of the high concentration of people living on or near the seashore, the concentration of tourist developments and the lack of effective control over coastal developments and of discharges of municipal, industrial and mining liquid wastes. Large quantities of untreated sewage are discharged directly into bays, estuaries, coastal lagoons and rivers, and 'highly toxic effluents from rapidly developing light and heavy industries … also often discharged directly into adjacent bays' (Lopez 1988, pages 30–31). Heavy metals from mining operations, metal smelting or other industrial processes pose serious problems to coastal environments in some areas – for instance the Coatzacoalcos estuary in the Gulf of Mexico and the bays of Cartagena, Guayanilla, Puerto Moron and Havana (Hinrichsen 1998). There are also problems with oil pollution from illegal discharges by tankers and other ships, offshore oilrigs and the many oil refineries within the region (ibid).

Solid waste disposal. It is still common for most of the solid wastes collected within urban centres to be dumped on some site outside the city with no site preparation to minimize the threat of pollutants within the wastes seeping or leaching into local water resources and with no provision to cover the wastes to reduce the breeding of disease vectors and uncontrolled burning. Dump sites are often ecologically valuable wetlands, as these are the most accessible, undeveloped sites. The inadequacies in the provision for handling hazardous wastes was noted earlier; it is also common for hazardous wastes that should receive special handling, storage and treatment to ensure safe disposal to be dumped on the same land sites as conventional solid wastes, with few (if any) safeguards to protect those living nearby or nearby water sources from contamination.

Acid precipitation. Consideration must be given to the impact of air pollutants from city-based activities on the wider region. The air pollutants that cause the most damage to forests, soils and agriculture are sulphur dioxide, oxides of nitrogen and ozone (and other photochemical oxidants) and, in certain instances, fluorides (see Box 5.5). Sulphur and nitrogen oxides discharged by

---

10 There is also the massive oil pollution arising from the Gulf War whose long-term effects are not known. See Hinrichsen 1998.

power stations burning high-sulphur coal or oil, and from car exhausts can make rain acid, with this acid rain falling to earth a considerable distance from the emission sources. The result can be declining or disappearing fish populations and damage to soils and vegetation. Toxic metals may also be leached from the soil into water used for animal or human consumption, or lead, cadmium or copper mobilized by acidic drinking-water supplies from piped water systems. Acid precipitation is causing concern in the areas surrounding many cities in Asia and Latin America (McCormick 1997). Within much of Asia, emissions of sulphur dioxide are rising and acidification is an emerging issue; the most sensitive areas are in south China, the southeast of Thailand, Cambodia and South Vietnam (Hettelingh and others 1995).

The most dramatic examples of damage to crops (and other flora) come in the immediate vicinity of industries with very high sulphur dioxide emissions. Metal smelters without pollution controls and tall smokestacks can cause severe damage to vegetation over areas of several hundred square kilometres. Most emissions from cities do not produce such high concentrations, although a combination of high emissions and a lack of winds to disperse them can mean evidence of damage to vegetation or falling crop yields. The problem is reported to be particularly acute in Southwestern China – for instance around cities that have high levels of sulphur dioxide emissions such as Guiyang and Chongqing (Conway and Pretty 1991).

The relative acidity (or its opposite, the alkalinity) of any substance is measured by its pH and the neutral point is a pH of 7. Rain with a pH value below 5.6 is generally considered 'acidic'. In the provinces of Guizhou and Sichuan, measurements in the late 1980s showed that some 40,000 square kilometres received rainfall with a pH of less than 4.5 (Zhao and Xiong 1988). At Guiyang itself, the pH of rainfall was reported to be less than 4 from September to January. Around Chongqing, large areas of (rice) paddy turned yellow, following rainfall with a pH of 4.5 while in Chongqing itself, vegetation has been damaged by rain with a pH of 4.1 (Conway and Pretty 1991). Professor Vaclav Smil in his review of environmental problems in China (Smil 1984) suggests that such cases are 'most certainly just the proverbial tip of the iceberg' and that regional damage to plants and livestock must also be quite considerable near coal-fired power stations, refineries and chemical works with no (or only rudimentary) controls. There may be many other city-regions where damage to agriculture is visible, although the fact that this needs a high concentration of emissions combined with particular meteorological conditions will make this unusual.

As Box 5.5 describes, urban ozone plumes can damage flora in the surrounding regions. Ozone concentrations may not reach a maximum until the urban plume of pollutants is well away from the city (Conway and Pretty 1991). For fluorides, although the damage to crops, pasture and livestock is well known, there are few reports on this outside Europe and North America, except for the serious damage reported to sericulture from fluoride emissions from small rural industries in China (Wang and Bian 1985).

Box 5.5 *THE IMPACT OF AIR POLLUTION ON AGRICULTURE*

Air pollution can cause serious losses to crops and animal husbandry, although the levels of loss under different circumstances are difficult to assess experimentally.

Acid pollution. Sulphur dioxide and the oxides of nitrogen coming from fossil fuel combustion in cities can be deposited directly from the air on to farmers' fields (dry deposition) or from rain, clouds/fog or snow acidified by these chemicals. Both can damage plants at high concentrations (causing acute damage, especially to certain species of plants that are particularly sensitive to exposure), although the concentrations needed to achieve this are rare, except in the immediate vicinity of intense sources of emissions (for instance metal smelters with no pollution controls and lacking high chimneys). At lower concentrations, both sulphur dioxide and the oxides of nitrogen are associated with reductions in yields and growth for many crops, although there are many other factors that can influence this. For acid rain, experimental reports of foliar injury are for pH values of less than 3.5, a level of acidity that rarely occurs. Soils are also at risk since in many tropical and subtropical countries, the soils are already acidic and unable to buffer any further additions in acidity. Further acidification can bring into solution potentially toxic trace elements; for instance, aluminium in acid soils disrupts the metabolic processes of roots and inhibits their growth.

Ozone. Ozone is produced by complex photochemical reactions involving air pollutants that are common over cities (oxides of nitrogen, carbon monoxide and hydrocarbons) reacting in sunlight. Temperature inversions over cities can keep the reactive chemicals in touch by inhibiting the dispersion of pollutants. Ozone continues to be generated in plumes of contaminated air originating in cities but often at a considerable distance from the source, which can make the concentration of ozone in rural areas downwind of cities higher than in the city itself. Plumes downwind of large North American cities produce ozone concentrations of between 130 and 200 parts per billion, often over distances of 100–300 km (Krupa and Manning 1988); ozone concentrations of only 60–100 ppb are sufficient to cause significant loss of yield in a wide variety of crops. The most direct impact on plants is the reduction in the amount of light caused by the photochemical smog. In many cities, ozone also causes visible leaf damage while concentrations well below those needed to cause visible injury (and also below that of most air quality standards) are also known to significantly reduce crop growth and yields for a wide range of plants, including oranges, lemons, grapes, wheat and rice.

Fluorides. These are typically emitted as hydrogen fluoride from brick, glass and tile works, steel works, potteries, aluminium smelters, phosphate factories and some other industries. Particular industries can cause acute damage over considerable distances, if no measures are taken to limit emissions. For vegetation far from emission sources, the hazard arises from long-term exposure to very low levels, so trees and perennial plants are more likely to suffer damage than annuals. Fluoride may directly damage fruits or accumulate in forage and so present a particular risk to grazing livestock.

Other air pollutants and their interactions. Soot or dust may affect plant growth by reducing the rate of photosynthesis or damaging the plant. Mixtures of pollutants may produce synergistic or antagonistic effects, or one gas may predispose or desensitize a plant to the effect of another. Gaseous pollutants may also stimulate more serious attacks by pests such as aphids or white fly.

Source: Drawn from Conway, Gordon R and Jules N Pretty, *Unwelcome Harvest*, Earthscan Publications, London 1991.

Cities' ecological impacts

The extent of the environmental changes caused by any urban centre on its surrounds and the size of the area that has been changed is much influenced by the urban centre's size and wealth (as these are key influences on the scale and nature of resource demands and waste generation), as well as the nature of its production base and of the resource endowments of the region around it. It is also much influenced by the quality of environmental management both within the urban centre and in the region surrounding it.

Two issues inhibit more effective measures to limit cities' ecological impacts. One was highlighted by Mike Douglass in his discussion of Jakarta's environmental impact on its region and by Philip Kelly in discussing competition for land around Manila – the fact that there are so many different influences on land use from local concerns (for instance the competition between agriculture and urban development for land), to regional and national concerns (the promotion of industrialization) to international concerns (for Jakarta, the fall in the price of export crops for the outer islands, reducing the attraction for migrants of areas outside Jakarta and other areas in Java). The second is the difficulty in coordinating actions in different places by different agencies and different levels of government because cities' environmental impacts are so diverse and often happen over such distances (as in the example of Delhi described in Box 5.2, with much of the firewood coming from a region nearly 700 kilometres away).

Although much of the literature on the generation and transfer of environmental costs from cities concentrates on the region around cities, the demands that the larger and wealthier cities concentrate for food, fuel and raw materials may be increasingly met by imports from distant ecosystems with much less demand placed on the region surrounding the city. This makes it easier to maintain high environmental standards in this region and, for instance, to preserve forests and natural landscapes. In addition, the goods whose fabrication involves high levels of fossil fuel consumption, water use and other natural resource use, and dirty industrial processes (including the generation of hazardous wastes) and hazardous conditions for the workforce, can be imported. The possibilities for enterprises and consumers to import such goods from a greater distance is much helped by the low price of oil (and the fuels derived from it).

Other environmental cost transfers are into the future. For instance, air pollution may be controlled with a major decline in some particular pollutants (as has been achieved in many of the world's wealthiest cities) but emissions of carbon dioxide (the main greenhouse gas) remain very high and in most cities may continue to rise – for instance because of increasing private motor car ownership and use, and with the increased use of air-conditioning where this is powered by electricity from thermal power stations. This is transferring costs to the future through the human and ecological costs of atmospheric warming. The generation of hazardous non-biodegradable wastes (including radioactive wastes) or non-biodegradable wastes whose rising concentrations within the biosphere has worrying ecological implications[11] is also transferring costs to the future. So too are current levels of consumption for the products of agriculture and forestry where the soils and forests are being destroyed or degraded and biodiversity reduced.

It is difficult to estimate the ecological costs that arise from producing all the inputs that support city production and consumption – the large and diverse range of raw materials, intermediate goods and final goods. To do so would require not only an accurate mapping of the scale and nature of resource inputs but also an assessment of the ecological impacts of their production. As noted earlier, intensive rural production for urban markets need not be ecologically damaging, while rural incomes derived from production for urban markets may be providing the means for better management of land, forests and watersheds. But the scale of the demand for resources and of the waste generation concentrated in cities has encouraged the development of new concepts to help map out and to begin to quantify the scale and nature of these interregional or international transfers.

The development of a method to calculate the 'ecological footprints' of cities (and of particular households, enterprises and nations) by William E Rees is one of these (Rees 1992, Wackernagel and Rees 1995). This makes evident the large land area on whose production the inhabitants and businesses of any city depend for food, other renewable resources and the absorption of carbon to compensate for the carbon dioxide emitted from fossil fuel use. Rees calculated that the lower Fraser Valley of British Columbia (Canada) in which Vancouver is located has an ecological footprint of about 20 times as much land as it occupies – to produce the food and forestry products its inhabitants and businesses use and to grow vegetation to absorb the carbon dioxide they produce (Rees 1992). London's ecological footprint is estimated to be 125 times its actual size, based on similar criteria (Jopling and Girardet 1996). However, care is needed in comparing the size of different cities' ecological footprints.

---

11 These are often referred to as POPs (persistent organic pollutants). See Agarwal and others 1999c for a discussion of these and of international measures that seek to control their use.

One reason is that the size of the footprint as a multiple of the city area will vary considerably, depending on where the city boundary is drawn, and this is the main reason why London's inhabitants appear to have a much larger individual ecological footprint than the inhabitants of the Fraser Valley.[12] A second reason are the differences between cities in the quality and range of statistics from which a city's ecological footprint is calculated (Levett 1998).

Wealthy and powerful cities have always had the capacity to draw resources from far beyond their immediate region. For instance, imperial Rome drew timber, grain, ivory, stone and marble from North Africa (Girardet 1992). But the scale of this capacity of consumers and producers to draw on the productivity of distant ecosystems has been greatly increased in the last few decades as incomes have risen and transport costs have declined. City-based consumers and industries in the wealthy nations have increasingly drawn on the carrying-capacity of rural regions in other nations. This separates the environmental impact of the demand for natural resources from the city itself to the point where city inhabitants and businesses have no idea of the environmental impact for which their resource use is responsible. One of the advantages of having the environmental impact in a city's own surrounds is the visible evidence of environmental damage that could spur actions to reduce it (Rees 1992).

Certain natural resources such as fresh water, food and fuel suppliesare essential to the existence of any city. Many of the economic activities on which a city's prosperity depends require regular supplies of renewable resources; if there was a diminishing supply of fresh water, agricultural goods and forest products, many cities would rapidly decline in size and have reduced employment opportunities for their residents. Many other formal and informal economic activities, although not directly linked to resource exploitation, depend on such exploitation to generate the income to support their own activities. In the past, the size and economic base of any city was constrained by the size and quality of the resource endowments of its surrounding region. The cost of transporting food, raw materials and fresh water always limited the extent to which a city could survive by drawing resources from outside its region. The high costs of transporting city-generated wastes away from the surrounding region promoted local solutions, and there was a need to ensure that such wastes did not damage the soils and water on which local agricultural production (and often fishing) depended. If local ecosystems were degraded, the prosperity of the city suffered, or in extreme cases, its viability as a city was threatened. A city's ecological footprint remained relatively local.

Motorized transport systems and electric pumps introduced the possibility of disassociating the scale of renewable resource use in cities from the productivity of its region. As noted earlier, fresh water can also be drawn from distant watersheds and even pumped hundreds of metres up hills, as long as little consideration is given to the high energy costs that this entails (usually coming from thermal power stations that also mean high levels of greenhouse gas emissions). Such technology and its high-energy requirements obscure the link

---

12 The calculation for London was based on an area of 1580 square kilometres (virtually all of which is built-up area) with a population of 7 million. The calculation for the lower Fraser Valley was for an urban–agricultural region of 4000 square kilometres with 1.8 million inhabitants.

Box 5.6 *THE ECOLOGICAL FOOTPRINT OF CITIES*

All cities draw on natural resources produced on land outside their built-up areas (eg agricultural crops, wood products, fuel) and the total area of land required to sustain a city (which can be termed its ecological footprint) is typically at least ten times or more greater than that contained within the city boundaries or the associated built-up area. In effect, through trade and the natural flows of ecological goods and services, all cities appropriate the carrying-capacity of other areas. All cities draw on the material resources and productivity of a vast and scattered hinterland.

Ecologists define 'carrying-capacity' as the population of a given species that can be supported indefinitely in a given habitat without permanently damaging the ecosystem upon which it is dependent. For human beings, carrying-capacity can be interpreted as the maximum rate of resource consumption and waste discharge that can be sustained indefinitely in a given region without progressively impairing the functional integrity and productivity of relevant ecosystems.

Preliminary data for industrial cities suggest that the per capita primary consumption of food, wood products, fuel, waste-processing capacity, etc coopts on a continuous basis several hectares of productive ecosystem, the exact amount depending on individual material standards of living. This average per capita index can be used to estimate the land area functionally required to support any given population. The resultant aggregate area can be called the relevant community's total 'ecological footprint' on the Earth.

Regional ecological deficits do not necessarily pose a problem if import-dependent regions are drawing on true ecological surpluses in the exporting regions. A group of trading regions remains within net carrying-capacity as long as total consumption does not exceed aggregate sustainable production. The problem is that prevailing economic logic and trade agreements ignore carrying-capacity and sustainability considerations. In these circumstances, the terms of trade may actually accelerate the depletion of essential natural capital, thereby undermining global carrying-capacity.

Because the products of nature can be so readily imported, the population of any given region can exceed its local carrying-capacity unknowingly and with apparent impunity. In the absence of negative feedback from the land on their economy or life-styles, there is no direct incentive for such populations to maintain adequate local stocks of productive natural capital. For example, the ability to import food makes people less averse to the risks associated with urban growth spreading over locally limited agricultural land. Even without accelerated capital depletion, trade enables a region's population and material consumption to rise beyond levels to which they might otherwise be restricted by some locally limiting factor. Ironically then, the free exchange of ecological goods and services without constraints on population or consumption ensures the absorption of global surpluses (the safety net) and encourages all regions to exceed local carrying-capacity. The net effect is an increased long-range risk to all.

This situation applies not only to commercial trade but also to the unmonitored flows of goods and services provided by nature. For example, Northern urbanites, wherever they are, are now dependent on the carbon sink, global heat transfer and climate stabilization functions of tropical forests. There are many variations on this theme, touching on everything from drift-net fishing to ozone depletion, each involving open access to, or shared dependency on, some form of threatened natural capital.

Source: Rees, William E, 'Ecological footprints and appropriated carrying capacity: what urban economics leaves out', *Environment and Urbanization*, Vol 4, No 2, October 1992, pages 121–130.

between a city's renewable resource use and the impact of this use on the ecosystem where the resource is produced. Prosperous cities also draw from the entire planet as their 'ecological hinterland' for food, fossil fuels and raw materials. If many consumers in (say) Singapore or São Paulo (and of course European and North American cities) are drawing their fruit, vegetables, cereals, meat, fish and flowers from an enormous variety of countries, how can a link be established between this consumption and its ecological consequences?

Prosperous cities can also transport their wastes and dispose of them beyond their own region. In extreme cases, they can even ship them abroad, although this is an issue that has in part been addressed by international action. Or they can 'export' their air pollution to surrounding regions through acid precipitation and urban pollution plumes with sufficiently high concentrations of ozone to damage vegetation in large areas downwind of the city. Perhaps only when the cost of oil-based transport comes to reflect its true ecological cost in terms both of a depleting non-renewable resource and its contribution to greenhouse gas emissions will a stronger connection be re-established between resource use within cities and the productive capacity of their surrounding regions.

The calculation of ecological footprints for cities should not obscure the fact that particular enterprises and richer income groups contribute disproportionately to these footprints. For example, Wackernagel and Rees (1995) calculate that the average ecological footprint for the poorest 20 per cent of Canada's population is less than a quarter that of the wealthiest 20 per cent. It is also possible to measure the ecological footprints of particular activities. For instance Wackernagel and Rees' book on Ecological Footprints considers the ecological footprint of different kinds of housing, different commuting patterns, road bridges and different goods (including tomato production and newspapers) (ibid). It is also worth noting that high-income households in rural or suburban areas generally have larger ecological footprints than those with comparable incomes living in cities.[13]

13 Middle- or upper-income city dwellers generally have fewer cars and use them less than those living in suburban or rural areas with the same per capita income. City dwellers also generally have smaller homes and have lower fossil fuel or electricity consumption for heating or air-conditioning them.

Another concept that helps to reveal the reliance of wealthy cities on non-renewable resources is through calculating the 'material intensity' of the goods consumed in that city (or what is sometimes termed these goods' ecological rucksack). The material intensity of any good can be calculated, relative to the service it provides, as a way of providing a quick and rough estimate of its environmental impact (Schmidt-Bleek 1993). This calculation can include all the energy and material inputs into any good from the extraction or fabrication of materials used to make it through its use to its final disposal. It can also include consideration of how much service that good provides, including how long it lasts so, for instance, a refrigerator or car that lasted 20 years would have less material intensity than one that lasted 10 years. It has been calculated that a home fridge designed to lower its 'material input:intensity of service ratio' could be constructed with available technologies and materials to achieve a resource productivity of roughly six times that of currently available models (Tischner and Schmidt-Bleek 1993).

There are other methods that are useful in revealing the ecological impact of human activities, including capacity studies and environmental audit procedures (see Chapter 7 for more details). There is also the long-established practice of calculating the energy-intensity of different goods which can also take into account the energy used in their fabrication, transport, preparation for sale, sale, use and disposal. Since in most instances, most or all of the energy input comes from fossil fuels, this allows an idea of how the use of this good contributes to the use of fossil fuels and the generation of carbon dioxide (the largest contributor to atmospheric warming), and perhaps also gives some idea of the air pollution implications of its fabrication, use and disposal.

While concepts such as 'ecological footprints' and 'ecological rucksacks' have helped to make apparent the extent to which modern cities can generate environmental costs far from their boundaries, it is difficult to quantify all such transfers. For instance, the long-term health and ecological consequences of many chemical wastes are unknown, including those arising from the accumulation of certain persistent chemicals. It is also difficult to estimate the scale of the health risks faced by the workers and their families who make the goods which the consumers and enterprises within wealthy cities use. It is also difficult to adjust the calculations for a city's 'ecological footprint' to take account of the goods and services that its enterprises produce for those living outside its boundaries. Measures are needed to reduce the ecological footprint of wealthy and large cities, but this must not detract from cities' key roles within the efficient, prosperous, innovative and flexible economies that all nations want to develop. As Chapter 3 stressed, prosperous cities with high-quality environments can also be highly efficient in their use of resources and generation of wastes.

CITIES AND THE GLOBAL COMMONS

No overview of environmental problems in cities would be complete without some consideration of the impacts of city-based activities on the global commons. These impacts include the depletion of non-renewable resources and emissions of 'greenhouse gases' (which contribute to global warming) and of gases which contribute to the depletion of the stratospheric ozone layer. They also include the environmental degradation to which city-based demand for goods and city-generated wastes contribute beyond the city and its surrounding region. There is also the pressing issue of the possible or probable impacts on cities arising from global climate change. This requires some discussion of the difference between the production and consumption patterns that contribute most to climate change (much of which arises outside of Africa, Asia, and Latin America and the Caribbean) and the people most likely to suffer from its direct and indirect effects. In general, low-income people and many low-income countries are likely to bear much of the costs, despite having contributed least to the problem.

The main contribution of city-based production and consumption to greenhouse gases are carbon dioxide emissions from fossil fuel combustion by industry, thermal power stations, motor vehicles, and domestic and commercial energy uses. City-based activities also contribute to emissions of other greenhouse gases – for instance of chlorofluorocarbons by certain industries or industrial products, of nitrous oxide by motor vehicle engines and of methane by city-generated solid and liquid wastes. City-based demand for fuel wood, pulp and timber also contributes to deforestation in most countries (although one could equally well treat inadequate forest management as the cause). A considerable proportion of the greenhouse gas emissions arising from rural food production (for instance methane emissions from livestock and from rice cultivation) can be attributed to the city-based consumption of such food.

There are few figures available on the scale of greenhouse gas emissions for individual cities, although those that do exist suggest relatively low levels of per capita emissions for carbon dioxide (the main greenhouse gas) for most cities in Africa, Asia and Latin America, when compared with cities in Europe and North America (Nishioka and others 1990). In general, figures available for different nations' per capita consumption of non-renewable resources and greenhouse gas emissions show much higher consumption and emission levels among high-income countries (in Europe, North America, Australasia and Japan) than elsewhere (WHO 1992a, Agarwal and Narain 1991). This suggests that cities in high-income countries have in aggregate a much higher draw, per capita, on the global commons both in terms of resource consumption and of using the atmosphere and seas as sinks for wastes. Among other evidence that would support this would be: the much lower levels of fossil fuel consumption per capita in cities in Africa, Asia, and Latin America and the Caribbean, the small proportion of the world's industrial production located there;[14] the lower number of cars per inhabitant; and the lower levels of waste generation per capita (WHO 1992a).

However, the very large differences between cities in (among other things) their production structure, per capita income (and income distribution) and

---

14 The ratio of greenhouse gas emissions to the unit value of output may be significantly higher, both because of old, inefficient equipment and, for some nations, a greater reliance on heavy industries within the industrial sector.

consumption patterns suggests enormous variations in resource use, waste generation and greenhouse gas emissions. Cities such as São Paulo with its high concentration of industry and of middle- and upper-income groups with high levels of resource use (including fuels) and waste generation will put the average per capita resource use and greenhouse gas emissions for the city far above the average for cities in low- and middle-income nations (McGranahan and others 2001). In terms of greenhouse gas emissions per capita, this may also be true for many centres of heavy industry – for instance some of China's centres of heavy industry, but here the greenhouse gas emissions derive more from the widespread use of coal in industry and for domestic and commercial heating, and less from high-consumption levels. By contrast, most cities and smaller urban centres in low- and middle-income nations are likely to have per capita greenhouse gas emissions far below the average.

The very low incomes on which such a high proportion of the urban population survive is one key reason for this. From the point of view only of sustaining the global commons, the rich nations are fortunate that the urban (and rural) poor make such a minimal call on the world's renewable and non-renewable resources, and contribute so little to the use of stratospheric ozone-depleting chemicals and to the generation of toxic wastes and of greenhouse gas emissions. With regard to the hundreds of millions of people living in urban areas with inadequate incomes and very poor housing conditions, there is no evidence that they are major contributors to environmental degradation on a global scale, despite the suggestion that poverty is a major source of environmental degradation.[15] Most of the urban poor are exposed to very high levels of environmental risk because of the hazards they face from the inadequacies in the provision for piped water, sanitation, drainage, paved roads, healthcare and emergency services (as described earlier), but this is not the same as high contributions to environmental degradation. Here, it is so important to distinguish between environmental hazards and environmental degradation. If we consider environmental degradation in terms of the loss of environmental capital, then in none of the categories of environmental capital do the urban poor have a significant role in its depletion at a global scale (see Box 5.7).

There is also the issue discussed under the earlier section on cities' ecological footprints regarding the extent to which the population and enterprises in wealthy cities can ensure high-quality environments in their surrounds by drawing most resources and goods from distant regions. The level of greenhouse gas emissions per person from within wealthy cities will be lowered by enterprises and consumers there using energy-intensive goods that are made elsewhere. Similarly, urban centres with a concentration of factories producing

15 Many international reports claim that poverty is a major cause of environmental degradation, including the World Commission on Environment and Development's report, *Our Common Future* (WCED 1987) and UNEP's Geo 2000 (Clarke 1999). There is very little evidence that this is actually the case on a global scale. The text in this chapter considers this with regard to the contribution of the urban poor to environmental degradation. For a discussion of the limited contributions of poor rural populations, see Satterthwaite 1998, Hartmann 1998 and IIED, ODI, MRAG AND WCMC 1999.

Box 5.7 *THE LACK OF AN ASSOCIATION BETWEEN URBAN POVERTY AND ENVIRONMENTAL DEGRADATION*

It is overwhelmingly the consumption patterns of non-poor groups (especially high-income groups) and the largely urban-based production and distribution systems that serve them that are responsible for most environmental degradation caused by urban populations. There is very little evidence that urban poverty is a major cause of environmental degradation.

With regard to non-renewable resource use, most of the houses in which low-income groups live (and often build for themselves) make widespread use of recycled or reclaimed materials and little use of cement and other materials with a high-energy input. Such households have too few capital goods to represent much of a draw on the world's finite reserves of metals and other non-renewable resources. Most low-income groups in urban areas rely on public transport (or they walk or bicycle), which means low average figures for oil consumption per person.[16] Low-income households on average have low levels of electricity consumption, not only because those who are connected use less but also because a high proportion of low-income households have no electricity supply. Thus, they are responsible for very little of the fossil fuel use that arises from oil, coal or gas-fuelled power stations (and most electricity is derived from such power stations).

With regard to the use of renewable resources, low-income urban dwellers generally have much lower levels of consumption than middle- and upper-income groups. They have much lower levels of use for fresh water, although this is due more to inconvenient and/or expensive supplies than to need or choice. As described earlier, they also occupy much less land per person than middle- and upper-income groups. They consume less food and generally have diets that are less energy- and land-intensive than higher income groups. There are examples of low-income populations that do deplete renewable resources – for instance where low-income settlements have developed around reservoirs into which they dump their liquid (and perhaps solid) wastes or where low-income settlements have developed on slopes that, when cleared for housing, contribute to serious soil erosion (and the clogging of drains), but these are generally problems caused by the failure of urban authorities to ensure that they have access to other residential sites. In many low-income countries, a considerable proportion of the low-income urban population use fuel wood or charcoal for cooking (and where needed heating) and this may be contributing to deforestation,

16 A small proportion of the urban centres in Africa, Asia and Latin America do have high levels of cars relative to populations; some have higher ratios of cars to population than many cities in Europe and some in North America. But an average figure for per capita fuel consumption taken across all urban centres in Africa, Asia and Latin America would produce a much lower figure than that for all urban centres in other regions.

although fears that this is so have often proved to be without foundation (see for instance Leach and Mearns 1989).

With regard to waste generation, low-income groups usually generate much lower levels per person than middle- and upper-income groups and the urban poor generally have a very positive role from an ecological perspective as they are the main reclaimers, reusers and recyclers of wastes from industries, workshops and wealthier households. If it was possible to determine who consumed most of the goods whose fabrication involved the generation of most toxic or otherwise hazardous wastes or of persistent chemicals whose rising concentration within the environment has worrying ecological and health implications, it is likely to be middle- and upper-income groups. There are examples of small-scale urban enterprises (including illegal or informal enterprises) that cause serious local environmental problems – for instance contaminating local water sources – but their contribution to city-wide pollution problems relative to other groups is usually very small. In addition, it is difficult to ascribe the pollution caused by small-scale enterprises to the urban poor when many such enterprises are owned by middle- or upper-income groups.

With regard to greenhouse gas emissions, low-income groups usually generate much lower levels per person than middle- and upper-income groups as their total use of fossil fuels, of electricity derived from fossil-fuelled power stations and of goods or services with high fossil-fuel inputs in their fabrication and use is so much lower. The only exception may be for some low-income households in urban areas where there is a need for space heating for parts of the year and a proportion of the urban poor use biomass fuels or coal in inefficient stoves or fires. This may result in these households having above average per capita contributions to carbon dioxide emissions (and also to urban air pollution), but these are exceptional cases and in general, the consumption patterns of low-income groups imply much lower greenhouse gas emissions per person than those of middle- and upper-income groups.

energy-intensive goods or materials will always tend to have above average levels of greenhouse gas emissions per person. This helps to illustrate the difficulties in seeking an 'accounting system' that penalizes locations with high emissions since it is the people who use the energy-intensive goods or materials, not the places where they are made, that should be penalized.

At present, and for the foreseeable future, the institutional means do not exist to discourage the displacement of so many of the serious environmental implications of the consumption patterns of wealthy citizens and wealthy cities to 'foreign' people and their ecosystems.[17] The need to address such issues has

17 This issue is discussed in more detail in Satterthwaite 1997a, McGranahan and others 1996, Haughton 1999a and McGranahan and others 2001.

been highlighted by 'green consumerism' and by companies that recognize the need to improve the social and environmental performance both of their own operations and of their suppliers. But there is little progress on the international agreements that could address such problems. The environmental implications of free trade worldwide will have to be addressed if this is leading to serious and sustained ecological deterioration in many low- and middle-income nations (as soils and forests are damaged or destroyed by the pressure to produce the 'cheapest' goods) and, within the world system, to increasing greenhouse gas emissions.

The low average for greenhouse gas emissions per person in all urban areas in Africa, Asia and Latin America might suggest little need to act there. But with growing urban populations and a large and increasing share of the world's population located there, the future form and content of urban development both in its built form and in its spatial organization has major implications for atmospheric warming worldwide. Many of the more prosperous cities in Asia and Latin America (or the more prosperous suburbs) already have spatial structures that build in a high dependence on private car use for all citizens who can afford this, which also implies high greenhouse gas emissions. Few countries or cities have building codes or effective incentives to encourage buildings that minimize the need for heating or air-conditioning. The extent to which middle- and upper-income groups in cities in Africa, Asia and Latin America draw on artificial heating or cooling and depend on private cars has large implications for countries' greenhouse gas emissions. In addition, the pressure on the global commons would be enormous, if meeting the needs of low-income groups implied the levels of resource use and waste generation now common among most middle- and upper-income groups. This is a point to which Chapter 8 will return when discussing sustainable development and cities.

The impacts of global warming on cities

There is still uncertainty about the possible scale of global warming in the future and its likely direct and indirect effects. But atmospheric concentrations of the most important greenhouse gases (carbon dioxide, halocarbons, methane and nitrous oxide) are increasing and the rate of increase for each of these has been particularly rapid since around 1950. There is evidence of an increase in the global average temperature over the last 120 years and many of the warmest years on record have been in the last 15 years. Glaciers in virtually all parts of the world are receding. These are consistent with global warming induced by greenhouse gases released by human activities, but there are uncertainties as to the extent to which the increase in global temperature is the result of human activities and the extent to which it will continue. For instance non-human-induced factors such as volcanic eruptions are also important. Some of the warming trend might be part of a natural variation that may reverse itself. There are uncertainties as to the extent to which increasing carbon dioxide concentrations in the atmosphere will be absorbed by increased plant growth or ocean sinks. But if global warming arising from human-induced releases of greenhouse gases does continue, which it certainly will if no action is taken to moderate such emissions, it is likely to create very serious problems for a large number of the world's settlements.

These problems can arise from:

- The direct effects of changes in temperature (including heat waves) and the changes in weather that this brings, including changes in the hydrological cycle (and thus water supplies) and altered frequency and/or intensity of extreme weather events.
- The indirect effects, as the changes in temperature and the weather induce changes in (among other things) sea levels, ecological systems and air pollution levels, with these ecological changes also having significant effects on, for instance, food production. Table 5.1 illustrates the range of possible health impacts of climate change and also of stratospheric ozone depletion.

With regard to cities, among the most immediate effects of climate change would be:

- higher global mean temperatures;
- sea level rises;
- changes in weather patterns (including those of rainfall and other forms of precipitation);
- changes in river flow arising from increased temperature (and the melting of snow and ice) and changes in precipitation with increased risks of flooding in many cities or particular city-districts;
- changes in evaporation rates;
- changes in the structure of ecosystems, for instance as a result of changes in plant growth rates and favoured species and in insect populations; and
- changes in the frequency and severity of extreme weather conditions such as storms and sea surges (Scott 1994).

The scale and nature of the consequences will obviously differ depending on the city location, the characteristics of its site and the particular changes in that region in (for instance) precipitation and humidity. There will also be very large differences in the capacity of city authorities and of city-based households and enterprises to take measures to limit an increase in risk (for instance by better drainage systems and other measures to protect against flooding) and to ensure rapid and effective responses when flooding or some other disaster occurs.

Sea-level rises will obviously be most disruptive to settlements on coastal and estuarine areas and this is where a considerable proportion of the world's population lives. One estimate suggested that 60 per cent of the world's population live within 60 kilometres of a seacoast (Scott and others 1996). Many of the world's most densely populated areas are river deltas and low-lying coastal regions in low- and middle-income nations. For instance, in the unprotected river deltas of Bangladesh, Egypt and Vietnam, millions of people live within 1 metre of high tide in unprotected river deltas (Scott 1994). The lower reaches of many major rivers that also have high population concentrations present particular difficulties – for instance on the Hwang Ho and Yangtze in China

Table 5.1 *Possible major types of health impact of climate change and stratospheric ozone depletion*

	Mediating process	*Health outcomes*
		Direct
	Exposure to thermal extremes	➤ Altered rates of heat- and cold-related illnesses and death
	Altered frequency and/or intensity of other extreme weather events	➤ Deaths, injuries, psychological disorders; damage to public health infrastructure
	Indirect	
	Disturbances of ecological systems Effects on range and activity of vectors and infective parasites Altered local ecology of waterborne and foodborne infective agents Altered food (especially crop) productivity due to changes in climate, weather events, and associated pests and diseases	➤ Changes in geographic ranges and incidence of vector-borne diseases ➤ Changed incidence of diarrhoeal and other infectious diseases ➤ Malnutrition and hunger, and consequent impairment of child growth and development
Temperature and weather changes	Sea level rise, with population displacement and damage to infrastructure	➤ Increased risk of infectious disease, psychological disorders
	Levels and biological impacts of air pollution, including pollens and spores	➤ Asthma and allergic disorders; other acute and chronic respiratory disorders and deaths
	Social, economic and demographic dislocations due to effects on economy, infrastructure and resource supply	➤ Wide range of public health consequences: mental health and nutritional impairment, infectious diseases, civil strife
Stratospheric ozone depletion		➤ Skin cancers, cataracts and perhaps immune suppression; indirect impacts via impaired productivity of agricultural and aquatic systems

Source: McMichael, A J, A Haines, R Sloof and S Kovats (1996), *Climate Change and Human Health*, WHO, Geneva.

Box 5.8 *THE IMPACT OF SEA-LEVEL RISE AND OTHER HUMAN-INDUCED CHANGES ON ALEXANDRIA, EGYPT*

Alexandria is on the northeast fringe of the Nile delta, on the Mediterranean sea. The Nile delta has a rare set of fossilized sand-dunes along its coastal fringe that provide a stable foundation for the city above the low delta plain. The Old City is as much as 12 metres above sea level and is safe from the direct effects of sea-level rise. However, the port area and newer suburbs that have been built on low land with the aid of flood defences are at risk. The low marshes and lagoons that surround the city could be lost or seriously contaminated with salt water due to sea-level rise. Ultimately, the city could become a peninsula, surrounded by the Mediterranean, only reached by bridges and causeways.

Both subsidence and coastal erosion have been enhanced by development projects, which have also increased the city's vulnerability to climate change. The control of floods on the Nile (the most important being through the Aswan High Dam completed in 1964) has produced major benefits for irrigated farming and tourism but has stopped sediment previously brought down to the coast, which has meant some dramatic erosion around the mouths of the Damietta and Rosetta river mouths. Sediment starvation may eventually erode the already fragile beaches protecting Alexandria. The control of floodwaters in the Nile has also reduced the volume of water that recharges the aquifers below the delta. This has led to the increased rates of groundwater withdrawal which in turn has increased subsidence and saltwater intrusion into freshwater aquifers. The net result is deeper extraction and more subsidence.

A sea-level rise of just 10–20 centimetres would accelerate significantly the retreat of the coastline. Rises of 30–50 centimetres would probably require expensive and extensive protection measures to reduce the risk to Alexandria (and also to Port Said). Plans to boost beach tourism would certainly be jeopardized. A relative rise of 1 metre could submerge lowlands to within 30 kilometres of the coast; engineering solutions could mitigate the flooding problem but the capital costs would be high.

Source: Turner, R K, P M Kelly and R C Kay, (1990) *Cities at Risk*, BNA International, London.[18]

(ibid). The Maldives, the Marshall coastal areas, archipelagos and island nations in the Pacific and Indian Oceans and the Caribbean are likely to lose their beaches and much of their arable land (ibid). Global warming is also likely to increase the incidence and severity of tropical cyclones and expand the areas at risk from them, bringing particular dangers to such places as the coastal areas of Bangladesh that are already subject to devastating cyclones (WHO 1992a).

---

18 This source drew on: El Raey, Nasr and Frihy 1990, El Sayed 1989, Meith 1989, and Sestini, Jeftic and Milliman 1990.

Most of the largest cities in Africa, Asia and Latin America are port cities for historic reasons linked to their colonial past. The high cost of land in the central city and/or around ports has often encouraged major commercial developments on land reclaimed from the sea or the estuary and these will often be particularly vulnerable to sea-level rises. So too will the many industries and thermal power stations that are concentrated on coasts because of their need for cooling water or as the sea becomes a convenient dumping ground for their waste (Parry 1992). Sea-level rises will also bring rising groundwater levels in coastal areas that will threaten groundwater resources, disrupt existing sewerage and drainage systems and may undermine buildings. Box 5.8 gives an example of the environmental impacts of sea-level rise on a low-lying coastal city – in this instance, Alexandria in Egypt. It also shows how other human-induced changes such as reducing sediment flow and floodwater flows in the Nile have also helped to increase the risk of flooding in the city (Turner and others 1990).

Ports and other settlements on the coast or estuaries are also most at risk from any increase in the severity and frequency of floods and storms induced by global warming. The combination of high winds, intense rainfall, higher sea levels and storm-induced tidal surges will be particularly problematic (Smit 1990, Turner and others 1990). Coastal cities whose economies benefit from tourism may have considerable difficulties protecting tourist attractions such as beaches and nearby wetlands (Turner and others 1990). There are also the impacts of changes in the availability of freshwater resources – for instance for many cities, shortfalls because of reduced precipitation levels and the difficulties in protecting groundwater resources from contamination by sea water. The drinking-water supplies of many coastal cities is already threatened by a landward shift in the interface between salt water and fresh water – for instance Dhaka (Muhtab 1989) and, as already noted, Dakar and Bangkok; sea-level rise would further compound this problem.

There will also be serious impacts for many inland cities. Virtually all cities and most smaller urban centres are on or close to rivers; many already have serious problems of flooding due to inadequate investment in drainage systems, flood control and in watershed management (see Chapters 2, 3 and 4). Global warming will mean that many cities and smaller urban centres are likely to face an increase in the scale, frequency and intensity of rainfall regimes, increasing the risk of flooding, the intensity of the floods and the number of inhabitants at risk. For instance, in Latin America, increased flooding will pose serious threats to thousands of city dwellers in many urban centres that are in the foothills of the Andes, including such major cities as Lima, Santiago, Quito and Bogota (di Pace and others 1992). Increasing rainfall or changes in its distribution over the year may seriously affect many cities built next to rivers – for instance cities such as Formosa, Clorinda, Resistencia and Goya which lie on reclaimed land beside the middle Parana and lower Paraguay rivers (ibid). In other regions, changes in rainfall regimes will reduce the availability of fresh water which will pose particular problems for cities and smaller urban centres already facing serious freshwater shortages.

Climate-induced changes in the frequency and magnitude of precipitation will increase flooding, landslides and mudslips in many places; this will bring much increased dangers to many residential sites (di Pace and others 1992, Scott and others 1996). The devastation brought to Central America by Hurricane Mitch in late October 1998 (and the flooding and landslides that its very high winds and very heavy rains caused) demonstrate the vulnerability of the region to extreme weather events. Over 10,000 people were killed and some 2 million people lost their homes; there were also several billion dollars' worth of damages. The floods in Venezuela in December 1999 also demonstrated the vulnerability of very large numbers of people to extreme weather events; around 30,000 people died and some 600,000 others were severely affected.[19] There is also the vulnerability of much of Latin America to the changes in weather when the El Niño phenomenon occurs, as shown by the deaths, injuries and very large economic losses it causes, perhaps especially during 1997–98 (although the negative impacts of previous El Niños had also been very severe).

Much of Latin America and large parts of Asia have always been vulnerable to storms and other extreme weather events but their frequency and intensity is likely to increase with global warming.[20] In addition, in many coastal areas, sea-level rises will also make the impact of 'normal' extremes such as high tides, storm surges and seismic sea waves (tsunamis) more severe (Scott and others 1996). As Chapter 4 described, the impacts of disasters often fall particularly heavily on low-income groups because so many of them can only find land for housing in the areas that are most vulnerable to extreme weather events and because they lack the resources to minimize the risk and the damage and to help them cope in the event of a disaster.

Global warming will also mean increased human exposure to exceptional heat waves. The elderly, the very young and those with incapacitating diseases are most at risk from these (WHO 1992a). Low-income groups will generally be more vulnerable because their housing is less suited to moderating extreme temperatures and they lack air-conditioning (McMichael and others 1996). Those living in cities or those parts of cities that are 'heat islands' where temperatures remain significantly above those of the surrounding regions will also be particularly at risk. High relative humidity will considerably amplify heat stress (WHO 1992a). One study of China suggested that future warming may affect mortality markedly, especially in mid-latitude cities such as Shanghai. Two categories of potentially stressful air masses were identified in Shanghai: the first characterized by hot clear and dry conditions, the second by humid, maritime tropical conditions. Although these two air masses occur for less than a third of the time during the summer, they account for 94 per cent of the top 50 mortality days in Shanghai. These air masses are likely to occur much more frequently with climate change (McMichael and others 1996).

Increased temperatures in cities are also likely to aggravate air pollution problems. For instance increased temperatures can increase the concentrations of ground-level ozone (whose health effects were discussed earlier), as it increases the reaction rates among the pollutants that form ozone (Gupta 1990).

---

19 The examples in this paragraph are drawn from reports on www.disasters.org.
20 The Intergovernmental Panel on Climate Change's Third Assessment Report due for publication in early 2001 will include detailed regional sections.

Warmer average temperatures permit an expansion in the area in which 'tropical diseases' can occur – for instance global warming is likely to permit an expansion of the area in which the mosquito types that are the vectors for malaria, dengue fever and filariasis can survive and breed (WHO 1992a). The same is true for the aquatic snail that is the vector for schistosomiasis and also for the vectors of leishmaniasis and Japanese encephalitis (WHO 1992a). Rodent populations are likely to increase and with them the increased risk of the many infectious diseases in which rodents are involved (McMichael and others 1996).

Climate-change induced reductions in water supply or increased floods (which also contaminate water supplies) could increase the incidence of water-borne and water-washed diseases. Precise predictions are difficult because climate change will bring changes to so many factors that influence disease-causing agents and vectors, including temperature, humidity, precipitation, flora, fauna, predators and competitors (McMichael and others 1996).

The more indirect routes by which global warming affects settlements such as through disturbances to crop production will probably have as dramatic an impact on urban areas as the more direct effects. These include:

- The changes in rural production caused by the increasing temperatures and changes in weather patterns and their impacts on ecosystems which then impact on the livelihoods of those who exploit or rely on natural resources for their livelihoods. Changes in rural production will include disruptions to production destined for cities and to rural incomes spent in cities.
- The changes in resource availabilities for urban enterprises (for instance from changes in rural production or changes in freshwater availabilities).

There are also the broader ecological changes within which these fall. The physical damage, habitat loss and species depletion currently suffered by marine and terrestrial ecosystems such as pastoral lands, ocean fisheries and wetlands may be exacerbated by climate change (McMichael and others 1996). The additional cost of meeting global food demand has been estimated to be up to 10 per cent of the world's GDP (IPCC 1990).

Many cities and smaller urban centres will have increased in-migration of people who have lost their homes and livelihoods as a result of the direct or indirect effects of global warming. The economic base of many villages, towns and cities will be altered by the changes brought to agricultural production and productivity from changes in temperature and precipitation, and this will affect existing patterns of regional, national and continental urban development. In some cities and regions, opportunities will increase and incomes rise while other areas will experience economic decline. Both traditional and modern agricultural practices may be vulnerable to the relatively rapid changes in temperature, rainfall, flooding and storms that global warming can bring. Forests and fisheries may also be subject to rapid change. Reduced rainfall in the Sahel has already increased population growth considerably in urban centres in the region, as pastoralists deprived of their livelihood move there. The problems are likely to be most serious in the countries or areas where the inhabitants are already at the limits of their capacity to cope with climatic events; for instance populations in low-lying coastal areas and islands, subsistence farmers, and populations on semi-arid grasslands (Scott 1994).

A considerable range of manufacturing and service industries will also be affected. For example, reductions in the availability of water will jeopardize those industries that use large volumes of water, while changes in agricultural production will affect food-processing industries, and changes in the weather will impact on the tourist industry.

One other aspect of global warming is difficult to predict – the capacity and readiness of societies to respond to the changes that warming and its associated effects will bring. All societies have evolved a range of measures to reduce risk from natural hazards, including long-established traditions through which house design and settlement layout include measures to limit loss of life and property from earthquakes or storms. There are also those that have passed into law and statute books that can be seen in building and planning codes and in health and safety regulations, and the institutional measures developed to enforce them. Where these are appropriate to that particular society and its resources,[21] and where they are followed, they reduce risk and ensure that the built environment can cope with high winds, accidental fires or sudden heavy rainstorms. Their effectiveness can be seen in the great reductions achieved in accidental death and injury. For instance, even as late as the last century, it was common for accidental fires to destroy large areas of cities in Europe and North America.

This complex set of institutional measures and the built environment that they have influenced will have to change to reflect new hazards or a much increased scale of existing hazards. There is the vast stock of buildings, roads, public transport systems and basic urban infrastructure that were built without making allowance for the changes that global warming will bring (Scott and others 1996). Modifying or replacing these will be expensive and time consuming, and particularly difficult in low-income countries with weak and under-resourced city authorities, where there are still large deficits in basic infrastructure that need addressing.

---

21 In many countries, they are not, because they are based on old colonial codes or on inappropriate imported models (see Hardoy and Satterthwaite 1989).

Chapter 6

Tackling Environmental Health Problems

A young boy manoeuvres his bicycle through a ditch full of rubbish behind his house in Nueva Era, a colonia located in Nuevo Laredo, Mexico
Photo © Janet Jarman, all rights reserved

INTRODUCTION

The idea that environmental quality and the control of pollution are expensive luxuries that governments need only pursue when a country is rich enough is slowly being eroded, at least with regard to industrial pollution. Attitudes regarding the safe collection and disposal of household and human wastes and the provision of safe, sufficient, water supplies have proved harder to change. It has taken 30 years for many governments to accept that illegal settlements are not a threat to established order but a symptom of the lack of alternative means for low-income people to secure housing. Most new urban housing and urban neighbourhoods in Africa and most of Asia and Latin America are developed through informal processes, often with no legal basis. While most governments still seek to prevent or inhibit such processes, it is now less common for them to try to 'bulldoze' them away. But let us hope that it does not take another 30 years for governments to learn how to work with the inhabitants of these informal settlements to tackle their environmental health problems, and to understand how much improvement can be made at relatively low cost.

One reason for the inadequacies in government action in addressing environmental problems is that the health impacts of the most serious problems are largely confined to lower-income groups as described in Chapters 2, 3 and 4. It is common for the residential areas of middle- and upper-income groups and the main commercial and industrial concerns in a city to receive good quality water supplies, sewers, drains, electricity supplies and regular services to remove solid wastes while 30 per cent or more of the city population in the poorer residential areas receive little or nothing.[1] The middle- and upper-income households are often subsidized in the publicly provided infrastructure and services they receive, since they are not charged a price that reflects the total costs of supply (World Bank 1988).

National and city governments frequently claim that extending piped water, sewers, drains and regular waste-collection services to households in low-income areas is too expensive. But this claim is generally based on the cost of systems in Europe and North America. Such systems are convenient and have contributed much to better health but they are also expensive and bring with them disadvantages in resource use. They do little to moderate the very large throughput of resources with the used resources becoming wastes that have to be collected and disposed of. Large volumes of solid wastes have to be collected from households and businesses and are usually disposed of in landfills. Large volumes of liquid wastes are collected by sewers and drains and dumped in the nearest convenient water body, generally after some treatment. These systems also require sophisticated management to keep them functioning effectively. There are two key questions:

- Are there alternative ways to address the environmental health problems associated with the inadequacies in provision for water, sanitation, drainage and waste collection that are cheaper, less wasteful of resources, and better matched to the institutional constraints evident in most cities and smaller urban centres in low- and middle-income countries?
- Is there a sufficient range of alternatives to match the diversity between urban centres (or districts within cities) in terms of needs, preferences and capacities to pay on the part of citizens and institutional capacities to invest, install and maintain on the part of the providers?

---

1 Where government capacity to provide infrastructure and services is very weak, it is common for wealthy households and businesses to have developed their own solutions either through private provision in particular districts or industrial sites (for instance for solid-waste collection and disposal and street cleaning) or through individual provision (for instance sinking their own well for water).

WATER, SANITATION AND DRAINAGE

The good news is that significant improvements in the provision for water, sanitation and drainage are possible in most low-income urban areas at low cost and often with good possibilities of cost recovery. The last 20 years have shown the many ways in which provision can be improved to those inadequately served. These include not only different technologies but also innovations in institutional arrangements, installation methods and payment procedures. It is more often innovations in how water, sanitation and drainage systems are planned, installed and paid for that have brought greater benefits to low-income groups than technological innovations, as examples given later in this section will illustrate. The bad news is that achieving these improvements on a large scale depends on the public or private companies responsible for water and sanitation (and the international agencies that fund them) being more flexible in what they can do and being more able to work in real partnership with community organizations and (where appropriate) local NGOs.

The best means to improve the provision for water, sanitation and drainage within limited budgets (and where possible with costs covered by user charges) will vary considerably from settlement to settlement because of:

- *Technical issues* related to the cost of supply (eg a settlement's distance from existing water mains, sewers and drains, topography, soil structure, settlement layout, the possibilities of tapping local water resources).
- *Demand and affordability* (the priorities of the inhabitants, income levels).
- *Land tenure and official attitudes to illegal land occupancy.* The possibilities for improving provision are obviously greater in informal settlements where the inhabitants are not occupying the land illegally (for instance in illegal subdivisions) and where there are well-established community organizations. It is difficult for any water agency to provide house connections and obtain regular payments in settlements where it is not clear who owns what plot and where houses have no official address.[2]
- *Institutional capacity to plan and manage new systems.* Many successful projects have been the result of innovative local NGOs or municipal authorities or community organizations with the capacity to organize and represent the needs of all inhabitants; many informal settlements lack any of these.

There is a growing recognition that companies or agencies responsible for water, sanitation and drainage need to be able to offer a range of options (and prices) to households. For many of the lower-income settlements or settlements within the weakest local authorities, this will often include support for community provision (for instance the agency providing piped water and sewer or drain connections to the site and the inhabitants organizing the installation and maintenance of the systems within their settlement) and community

---

2 There is an interesting discussion of the many factors influencing the most appropriate solutions by Lyonnaise des Eaux, a French company that has won contracts to manage water and sanitation systems in various countries in the South (see Lyonnaise des Eaux 1998).

management (for instance of communal water taps and shared sanitation and washing facilities). There is also a need to act on sanitation and drainage, not just water supply. It has been all too common for agencies responsible for water and sanitation to extend only improved provision for water to low-income areas because it is cheaper and easier and because payment is easier to collect (since water supplies can be cut off if bills are unpaid but it is difficult or impossible to block non-payers' use of sewers and drains). Improving water supply may not improve public health if there is no provision to remove waste water. In part this is because improved sanitation is also needed to reduce diarrhoeal and other water-borne diseases. The safe disposal of households' waste water (sullage) is also important because this contains some disease-causing agents, or when not removed, it provides a breeding ground for disease-carrying insects or facilitates the development of soil-based parasitic worms such as hookworm.

For excreta disposal, there is a wide range of alternatives far cheaper than conventional sewers and sewage treatment plants, but far more effective and hygienic than pit or bucket latrines. World Bank research involving field studies in 39 communities in 14 nations found a wide range of effective household and community systems. Within this range were options that could be implemented to match the particular physical conditions and economic resources in each locality and the social preferences of its inhabitants. Several options had costs per household of between one-tenth and one-twentieth that of conventional sewerage systems (see Table 6.1). Most needed far lower volumes of water while some demanded no water at all (although of course household water needs for drinking, cooking, washing and laundry have to be met). It is also possible to install one of the lower cost technologies initially and then upgrade it in a series of steps (Kalbermatten and others 1980). However, in large and high-density residential areas, the cost of sewer systems per household may be comparable with 'on-site' systems (such as pit latrines) and much preferred by the inhabitants because these also remove waste water and do not need emptying.

The last 30 years has brought a wealth of experience in implementing the alternatives to conventional sewer systems and in learning about their relative strengths and weaknesses. It has also brought a better understanding of the need to involve low-income households and their community or neighbourhood organizations in decisions about the most appropriate design and about how new facilities can be maintained and repaired (Warner and Laugeri 1991). Among the options for improving sanitation are a range of methods for safe, good quality 'sewerless' sanitation,[3] often called on-site sanitation. These include ventilated improved pit latrines (VIP latrines) and pour-flush twin-pit latrines. On occasion, significant improvements have been achieved at low cost; for instance, a simple ventilation pipe used with the VIP latrine can greatly reduce the smells associated with pit latrines while covering the vent pipe with a gauze screen can greatly reduce the number of flies (Sinnatamby 1990). On-site sanitation also includes more conventional flush toilets connected to

3 For more details on non-sewer sanitation options, see Winblad and Kilama 1985, Pickford, 1995 and Esrey and others 1989.

Table 6.1 *Typical range of capital costs of different sanitation systems, 1990 prices*

Type of system	US$ per household
Twin pit pour-flush latrine	75–150
Ventilated improved pit latrine	68–175
Shallow sewerage	70–325
Small-bore sewerage	120–500
Conventional septic tank	200–600
Conventional sewerage	600–1200

Note: Capital costs alone should not be used as the only basis for determining the cost of a system since some systems are more expensive than others to operate and maintain. For example, pit latrines and septic tanks need services to empty them regularly. It is important to determine the total discounted capital, operation and maintenance cost per household for each system. From this, one can calculate the charge that would have to be levied to obtain full cost recovery, and from this, to establish whether households can afford and are prepared to pay this amount. Many low-cost sanitation alternatives are affordable even by the poorest urban communities. The convenience of off-site systems may also mean that low-income households are prepared to pay more for these.

Source: Sinnatamby, Gehan (1990), 'Low cost sanitation' in Jorge E Hardoy, Sandy Cairncross and David Satterthwaite (editors), *The Poor Die Young: Housing and Health in Third World Cities*, Earthscan Publications, London. The lower range of the costs of shallow and small bore sewers has been reduced, reflecting project costs in some Asian and Latin American cases.

household or community septic tanks. Many countries have large-scale programmes already implemented in urban areas in pour-flush latrines and VIP latrines, and a knowledge of where these are or are not appropriate.

Some caution is needed regarding the growing enthusiasm among many environmental groups and international agencies for sewerless sanitation. Their environmental advantages are obvious. They need far less water than conventional flush toilets connected to sewers; some, such as pit latrines, need none at all. They can be installed without increasing demand for fresh water, which is particularly valuable in cities where freshwater resources are in short supply. They also greatly reduce the problem of water pollution as they no longer generate large volumes of excreta-laden waste water. Some designs for on-site sanitation also make possible the use of the decomposed excreta as a fertilizer/soil conditioner.

But they are rarely as healthy or convenient as toilets connected to sewer systems. They require more maintenance, and where support for improved sanitation is for sewerless sanitation, too little attention is paid to ensuring there is an effective service to collect and dispose of the solid sludge from the pits or septic tanks. Households with pit latrines or septic tanks need an efficient and affordable service. Manual emptying of pit latrines is a very unpleasant and hazardous job (Muller 1997). It is common to find septic tanks overflowing because they need desludging. On-site sanitation can also be particularly hazardous in settlements that flood regularly, as overflowing latrines spread excreta everywhere. It is also common to find much overused and poorly maintained latrines for communal or public use or within institutions (for instance schools), as noted in Chapter 2. Emptying and maintenance may be particularly difficult in dense settlements, especially where there are no roads or lanes through which the pumping equipment can get close enough to houses to empty their tanks (although there are now smaller pumps that can fit down lanes and footpaths). Latrines and septic tanks can be efficient breeding grounds for *Culex* mosquitoes (see Chapter 2).

There is also the issue of whether people will use new latrines. There is little point in investing in improved sanitation if a significant proportion of the population still defecate outside. Where improved provision is through public toilets, if these are inconvenient (for instance with long queues), too far away from homes, poorly maintained or expensive, they will not be used. One of the best tests of the suitability of provision for sanitation in any area is whether children use it. Well-maintained communal solutions for sanitation may work well for most residents but remain impractical for children who may be pushed out of queues by impatient adults and who may have difficulty, when very young, in controlling their bowels and bladders while waiting in line. Young children may also resist using latrines that they find dark and frightening and fearing that they will fall through large pit openings designed for adult bodies.

One of our main worries is that the pressures to keep down costs for improving sanitation and pressures from environmental groups to avoid sewer-based systems mean that on-site sanitation systems are being installed when sewer-based systems are more appropriate, in terms of household preferences and public health. Sewer systems have three great advantages: they eliminate the need for anyone to handle or manage human excreta and they remove the excreta from the residential area (which is a huge health benefit); they need less maintenance at the toilet end (since there is no pit or septic tank that has to be emptied); and they remove households' waste water. Settlements with piped water and on-site sanitation systems often have difficulties getting rid of the waste water. Sewer systems are also better suited to heavily used toilets where there is limited provision for maintaining them – for instance communal, public or institutional toilets (including those in schools). Many of the economic and environmental disadvantages of conventional sewer systems can also be avoided. For instance, there are many shallow sewer or small bore sewer systems functioning successfully that proved much cheaper than conventional sewers (Sinnatamby 1990) and require much lower volumes of water per person to function. (Chapter 3 also discussed how the 'scare' that cities are running out of freshwater resources is overstated, but this scare is often used to justify sewerless sanitation systems). In addition, the environmental disadvantages of city-wide sewer systems, as they concentrate very large volumes of excreta-laden water that need treatment, can also be avoided by having district- or neighbourhood-based sewer systems, each with its own treatment system. There is also more scope for sewage treatment that uses natural processes for district-level systems.

The discussion above is not meant to be 'pro-sewer' solutions but pro-effective, convenient and cost-efficient solutions for low-income households. What is needed in each city is the knowledge and experience to permit appropriate choices to be made within each settlement or district – choices in which low-income households have influence, and which include provision for maintenance and repair. This also allows key local factors to be taken into account – for instance inadequate and intermittent water supplies might make sewered systems unattractive because there is insufficient water to keep them unblocked. Changes in national or municipal rules and regulations may also be needed since these will be contravened by many of the most effective and appropriate sanitation systems.

Improvements in the quality of water and its availability are also often possible at relatively low cost and with good possibilities of cost recovery, especially if optimal use is made of local resources and knowledge (Cairncross 1990). In many cities, largely self-financing water supply systems can reach poorer groups with much improved levels of service. A piped water system can often be installed to replace water vendors and provide customers with a larger, safer and more convenient supply for the same price that they previously paid to vendors. A thriving informal market for water is evidence of a demand unsatisfied by official providers. It is also evidence of the money value that poorer groups give to the time they would have to spend obtaining water from the nearest available source if they did not buy from vendors and is therefore indicative of how much they would be willing to pay for an adequate conventional water supply, were it made available to them (Cairncross 1990). Involving residents in decisions about the level of service and payment often surprises professionals as to what 'poor people' are prepared to pay; widely used guidelines often underestimate the value they place on the saving in time and energy provided by water piped to their home or yard in comparison to collecting water from a public standpipe. There is also the obvious but often overlooked point that different persons within households place different values on improved water and sanitation. It is usually women and children who fetch water and women who manage the disposal of excreta and waste water, and who will value most the time and effort saved through more convenient provision. When planning for improved provision, the perspective of young children's care-givers must be considered. A distance to a standpipe that may seem reasonable to some community decision-makers may be too far for anyone looking after small children and may prevent them from collecting the quantities of water needed for good health.

Where cities face shortages of freshwater supplies, better management and maintenance of existing water systems may increase available supplies more cheaply and quickly than increasing capacity. Many water supply systems lose 40 to 60 per cent of their water to leaks in the pipes (Cairncross 1990). In Bangkok, 43 per cent of water is lost in distribution (due to leaking pipes and unmetered use), which is one reason why demand far outstrips supply (Daniere 1996). In Karachi, leakage is about 40 per cent (Rahman and others 1997). Reducing the leakage rate from 60 per cent to 12 per cent (the typical figure for well-managed systems) would more than double the amount of water available for use. Often, just 20 per cent of the leaks account for 80 per cent of the water losses (Bachmann and Hammerer 1984). In São Paulo, the proportion of water leaking out of the system was reduced by some 50 per cent over a ten-year period (Cairncross 1990). There is also a large range of techniques and technologies that reduce the volume of water that large water consumers need with the additional capital cost being rapidly repaid, either to the water company because no new investment is needed to expand the water supply or to the consumer through lower water bills or to both (Rocky Mountain Institute 1991). There are also many ways of making better use of existing resources. Agarwal and Narain (1997) describe the many historic and contemporary systems for freshwater management in India, including the ingenuity with which water is (or was) harvested in arid and semi-arid areas (including its storage during rainy periods for use during dry periods or seasons). Although this work focuses mainly on water supplies for villages and for their inhabitants' livelihoods, it includes examples showing the potential of rainwater harvesting to better meet urban needs, including harvesting at household level (for instance through roof tanks) and at neighbourhood and city level (including provision to better use or store water from periods of intense rainfall and greater attention to the protection of urban lakes, tanks and wetlands).

In many regions where cities are running out of new, cheap freshwater sources, a combination of improved water management, better use of rainwater, better maintenance of water supply systems and greater efficiency in water use encouraged among the largest users can often greatly increase the volume of available fresh water. Many commercial, industrial and recreational water uses can also be served by waste water from urban sewers or drains, with some minimal treatment within the city area.

The approach needed is one that analyses local problems and assesses which combination of actions best utilizes local resources. Sandy Cairncross (1990) has pointed out that various approaches considered 'unconventional' by Western-trained engineers may be the cheapest and most effective in certain localities. For instance, where capital to extend piped water systems is lacking, a government programme to make water vendors more efficient and their water of better quality might be the most cost-effective option. In others, making use of local ground- or surface-water sources for small independent networks for particular city areas may be more cost-effective than extending the water mains system. In areas with sufficient rainfall, financial support to households to install guttering and rainwater tanks may be a cheap way of improving supplies. Where piped systems are to be installed, modifications to official standards can produce major cost savings with little or no reduction in performance; the minimum depth set for laying sewage pipes hardly needs to be to a depth to protect it from 40-ton trucks if the pipe is being installed in a high-density, low-income settlement (Sinnatamby 1990). Standards appropriate to local circumstances do not always mean lower standards; higher standards may be appropriate in some cases to compensate for lower levels of maintenance (Gakenheimer and Brando 1987).

The particular nature of infrastructure means that it is often more cost-effective to provide shared infrastructure. To take an extreme example, it is expensive to run individual water pipes from a water source to each house and much cheaper to use a larger pipe from the water source to the settlement and then run individual house connections from this. Some infrastructure investment is also a 'public good'. Once the initial investment is made, another household or individual can use it without anyone else having a reduction in the value of the service that they obtain from it. In the case of a road or footpath, for example, it is no loss to the person using it if another person uses it. If it becomes so heavily used that there is serious congestion, there is a problem, but up to that point everyone can use it with no loss to another.

For water and sanitation, there are economies in provision if these are provided for a whole street or neighbourhood, with the costs split between households. Virtually all households prefer their own individual water connection and their own latrine or sewer connection, when these are available at a price they can afford. But in the absence of a competent external agency able to offer households access to piped water and sanitation systems at a price they can afford, it is difficult for individual households to organize settlement-wide provision and so benefit from the potential economies in doing so.

Later in this chapter, details will be given about the long-established community-based programme to install sewers in one of Karachi's largest informal settlements, Orangi, supported by a local NGO, Orangi Pilot Project.[4] Perhaps the greatest challenge this NGO faced was to convince the households who shared a lane (between 20 and 40) that in the absence of a competent external agency able to provide them with sanitation, only by organizing themselves to work together could they get the economies of scale that made good quality sanitation affordable (Hasan 1997).

In many low-income urban settlements in India, the focus is on improving toilet provision for shared, communal or public use. In part, this is because the homes are so small that there is little room for individual facilities, or because of the impossibility of installing a toilet (for instance in a pavement dweller's hut). In part it is to reduce costs. As Chapter 2 noted, large sections of India's urban population have no toilet provision in their homes and defecate in the open because public or communal provision is so inadequate. Many Indian NGOs have become involved in communal or public toilet provision – for instance Sulabh International which has helped to provide pour-flush toilets in one million households and has built over 3000 community toilets (Pathak 1999). Community organizations have also become interested in developing their own communal toilets. The women's groups (Mahila Milan) working with the Indian NGO SPARC are developing their own communal toilets. These women (living on the pavements and in the designated 'slum' areas in Mumbai and other Indian cities) recognize that there is a need to strengthen their local organizations. They see collective toilet provision as a means to do this, as well as getting better quality, more appropriate toilet and washing facilities. In Mumbai, the municipal corporation is also seeking to provide public toilets (or improve provision) in 'slums' and recognizes that the conventional public toilets do not work well. SPARC, the National Slum Dwellers Federation and Mahila Milan have built a community toilet in Mumbai with a community hall for meetings and to hire out for other functions (with the money raised going to the toilet management fund) and room for the Mahila Milan groups to use for

---

4 Orangi Pilot Project developed into four autonomous institutions in 1988 – OPP-Research and Training Institute, Orangi Charitable Trust, Karachi Health and Social Development Association and the OPP Society which channels funds to these institutions (see Hasan 1997).

managing their savings schemes (Patel and Mitlin 2001). In Lucknow too, communities are developing their own communal toilet blocks. The land and finance are provided by local authorities and the construction and maintenance are undertaken by residents. Women organize the cleaning, management and up-keep of the toilet. The National Slum Dwellers Federation is building communal toilet blocks in Bangalore, much cheaper than contractors. Similar arrangements for community development and management have been developed for public toilets in Pune, supported by local NGOs, although, as Hobson 2000 explains when describing the work of Shelter Associates in this, it is difficult for NGOs to work in ways that are participatory and accountable to community members while also meeting the timetables set by supportive bureaucrats and coping with the slow responses of local bureaucracies.

Another example of an approach to limit sanitation costs is provided by some of the apartment blocks that the National Slum Dwellers Federation are constructing in Mumbai; Mahila Milan groups proposed toilets that are shared among several apartments since this helps to strengthen local organization, saves space and forms a disincentive to these apartments' capture by middle-income groups (SPARC 2000a). Below are examples of different measures that show how it is not only technological innovations that can improve provision and cut costs.

Technological innovations. Table 6.1 illustrates the variation in capital costs for different sanitation options. The cost of sewers can be cut by using smaller pipes and shallower trenches, shallower gradients and interceptor tanks.

Institutional innovations. Tariff structures with a low price per unit volume of water up to a certain consumption level can make piped water supplies more affordable for low-income groups. In settlements where it is too expensive or too difficult institutionally to provide piped water connections to each house or yard, there are a range of measures to improve provision, many of which can also recover costs. Where people rely on communal water points and water vendors, well-managed water kiosks (including those managed by community organizations) may improve service levels, reduce the distance that water has to be carried and reduce prices while also recovering costs. But if water is scarce and if those who operate the water kiosks are not answerable to the users, they can get away with over-charging.

Water connections to each house or plot remain the ideal because these provide health benefits that more distant sources do not. These are the preferred option of low-income households, if they can be afforded. Connection charges can be a major constraint – for instance in Buenos Aires, connection charges in expansion areas in 1998 were US$500 for a water connection and US$1000 for a sewer connection (Lyonaisse des Eaux 1998). There are often ways in which water agencies can support such connections rather than providing them themselves. For settlements where the inhabitants lack the income to afford connection charges, the water agency can provide connections to water mains and trunk sewers at the settlement's boundary with the inhabitants organizing the systems within their settlements. For water agencies seeking to reach low-income households with affordable piped supplies, costs can be reduced by selling the water 'wholesale' to a community with the community collecting payments from households. For instance, using a community water meter means the agency avoids the cost of individual house meters (which are expensive to install and to get read). Comparable measures can also be used for communities that are too distant from water mains to be connected – for instance, a water agency might deliver bulk water to a large community tank with the community organization taking on the task of piping the water into each household and collecting payments.

Innovations in installation. The costs of installing pipes for water and/or sanitation can be reduced if households and/or community organizations are prepared to dig the ditches and ensure that houses are prepared for connections. A strong focus on keeping down costs as in the NGO-supported construction of sewers in Orangi in Karachi may allow good quality 'expensive' solutions to be installed for low-income households with costs fully recovered (Hasan 1997). For settlements to which it is expensive to extend mains water, tapping local water resources or bulk delivery to a community tank may be cheaper.

Payment procedures. The difficulties that low-income households face in paying connection charges for piped water or sewers can be reduced by allowing this to be paid over a number of months, with the payment integrated into service charges or through providing loans. Connection charges in La Paz (Bolivia) and Buenos Aires (Argentina) were reduced for households who contributed labour to the installation and made more affordable by allowing repayment over a five-year period (Lyonaisse des Eaux 1998).

Micro-finance. Loans available to low-income households can allow them to afford better provision – for instance through affording connection charges or by paying for better provision within their home (eg installing a well-designed latrine) or through allowing them to buy or build a better quality home. There are many examples of successful community-based savings and loans schemes that have done this with high levels of cost recovery (Mitlin 1997).

UPGRADING

The importance of upgrading

'Upgrading' is the term usually given to projects or programmes that seek to improve conditions in particular areas of cities characterized by poor-quality housing and the inadequate provision of infrastructure and services. Upgrading projects are often titled 'slum upgrading', as the areas to be upgraded are categorized by governments as 'slums' (or at least labelled as such). Others are called 'squatter upgrading', because the settlement being upgraded was originally developed by households who built their homes on land they occupied illegally.

Upgrading projects or programmes have particular importance for environmental conditions since they are the primary means by which governments and international agencies fund environmental health improvements in low-income areas. Most upgrading programmes include improved provision for piped water, sanitation, drainage, roads and paths. Some include provision of social services – for instance of healthcare, schools and day-care centres. Some include support to the households to improve the quality of their homes – for instance through making loans available for rebuilding, improving or extending houses and technical advice. Some include other components such as support for micro-enterprises or income-generation schemes. Since such a high proportion of low-income urban dwellers live in settlements developed on illegally occupied land, many upgrading programmes also have provision to transfer the tenure of the land to the occupiers. Moreover, being multi-sectoral, upgrading has more potential to respond to the priorities of residents than programmes or projects that are limited to specific improvements such as water, waste collection or healthcare.

Although the success of upgrading initiatives has been varied, many upgrading projects have delivered real benefits for large sections of the low-income urban population. For instance, an evaluation of the upgrading programme in Visakhapatnam (India) showed that upgrading can help to address multiple deprivations, through, for instance, improved health, more secure tenure, and reduced impact of external shocks (eg flooding). Improved infrastructure was much appreciated as it reduced flooding, making roads passable, and reduced the burden of collecting water. Street lighting increased the length of the day and pre-school play centres for young children were widely appreciated. A fifth of the households interviewed also reported that their economic circumstances had improved (Amis and Kumar 2000). In many illegal or informal settlements, a large proportion of households derive much or all of their income from home-based enterprises and these can be helped by improved provision of electricity, water, drainage and solid-waste collection (Kellett aned Tipple 2000).

Government support for upgrading is underpinned by two important principles. The first is that the inhabitants in the area to be upgraded have the right to infrastructure and services, even if there are aspects of the settlement that are illegal – for instance the land occupation or the use to which the land is being put or the buildings (or often all three). The second is that the settlements that are to be upgraded, whether they are 'slums' or 'illegal settlements', have value. Before upgrading programmes became common, official housing policies usually assigned no value to what governments regarded as 'slums and squatter settlements', even when between a quarter and a half of an entire city's population lived in them. Housing policies would, typically, calculate a 'housing deficit' based on the number of housing units that official regulations classified as substandard (or 'slum') and the number of new units needed to reduce housing densities (for instance the number of persons per room) to some officially defined acceptable standard. In doing so, the policies assumed that all units defined as 'substandard' would have to be replaced. In many cities, this meant regarding as worthless the homes and neighbourhoods that housed much of the city's labour force and a considerable proportion of all its businesses. This included many settlements where low-income dwellers had invested much in developing their own homes and neighbourhoods. Such attitudes underpinned the large-scale 'slum and squatter clearance' programmes so evident in many cities during the 1960s and 1970s.

This shift in government attitude from 'clearance' to upgrading has not been universal (there are still many large-scale 'slum' clearance programmes).[5] And upgrading programmes vary in their scale (the extent to which they reached all areas in need of upgrading), effectiveness (in improving conditions) and the extent to which the improvements are sustained. But they have become recognized as an essential part of housing policy in most countries, both by national governments and by city and municipal authorities. It was during the 1970s that upgrading programmes became more widely accepted, although there are examples of 'upgrading' programmes before this. One important international influence on this was the support for upgrading provided by the World Bank from the early 1970s. This helped to get the concept of upgrading more widely accepted by governments, although upgrading never received a high priority within the Bank and support for it fell away in the mid-1980s onwards (see Chapter 7 for more details).

Governments' acceptance of upgrading programmes

Various factors help to explain governments' acceptance of upgrading programmes. One was the widespread failure of their conventional 'public' or 'low-cost' housing programmes for poorer groups during the 1960s and 1970s which meant that the proportion of the populations living in 'slums and squatter settlements' continued to grow (Hardoy and Satterthwaite 1989). A second factor was the introduction of or return to democratic rule, including democratically elected city authorities. A significant proportion of city electorates lived in what governments had previously labelled 'slums and squatter settlements' and their inhabitants often showed themselves to be politically adept at negotiating for infrastructure, services and legal tenure, in return for votes. A third factor was that the illegal settlements did not generally threaten the most powerful landowners. When land was illegally occupied, it was generally public land or sites that were ill-suited to commercial development (for instance land on flood-plains or steep slopes) or land in peripheral locations, or, in particular instances, land whose ownership was in dispute. In Latin America, many large-scale land invasions were carefully organized at points when political circumstances were favourable to governments tolerating or ignoring them, or to form a basis for negotiating another site (see for instance Peattie 1990, Cuenya and others 1990, Arévalo T 1997, Barbosa and others 1997). Indeed, many landowners were themselves involved in the development of illegal settlements – for instance by developing and selling subdivisions illegally or even by encouraging the invasion of their land, because of the likelihood of obtaining compensation from government which was more than the value of the land before it was invaded (see for instance the example of El Mezquital in Guatemala City described in Díaz and others 2000). Low-income groups also

5 See for instance the case studies on evictions in *Environment and Urbanization*, Vol 6, No 1, 1994.

generally avoid invading land sites that were too prominent or too visible from the central city or richer neighbourhoods, since this lessens the risk of eviction by mayors or government authorities intent on 'beautifying the city'. In some instances, local politicians were also involved in supporting the formation of 'illegal' settlements to increase political support.

The limitations of upgrading programmes

Perhaps the three most serious difficulties with upgrading programmes are how to ensure sufficient 'upgrading' (in terms of quality and range of improvements), how to sustain the initial impetus (to make sure the areas remain 'upgraded') and how to expand them to the point where they reach most or all of those living in homes and neighbourhoods that need upgrading. The upgrading tries to make up for a lack of past public investment in basic infrastructure and services by a single intervention – for instance, paving roads and installing drains, water pipes and electricity. These should have been installed in the first place, and maintained and improved on a continuous basis by particular agencies – for instance the local agencies responsible for roads and drains and the public or private agencies responsible for water and electricity. An upgrading programme may install these but only rarely does it increase the capacity of the agencies or utilities that should have installed them in the first place and that are usually left to maintain them.

Upgrading programmes make up for a deficiency in these agencies' investment and implementation capacity, but there is often a conflict between scale and quality as large-scale upgrading programmes seek to keep down unit costs (so more people can be reached), but what they install is inadequate (for instance too few water standpipes for the total population and no provision for improved sanitation) and often of poor quality. Upgrading programmes rarely take into account the 'upgrading' needs of children – for instance the needs of small children for safe space to play close to home or the desire of older children for adequate space for games and sports. Agencies that implement upgrading or supervise their implementation often pay too little attention to quality control. In addition, the basic institutional deficiencies are not resolved. Upgrading programmes often avoid the institutional complexities of having to coordinate a great number of agencies by having a single agency (or private contractor) implement the upgrading, but again with no provision to ensure that the different government agencies that are given responsibility for running and maintaining the new infrastructure and services can do so. The need is also not only to maintain the newly installed infrastructure but also to continue to run the new schools, health centres or day-care centres that have been installed, where there are staffing costs and supplies that have to be purchased, as well as buildings and equipment that have to be maintained. The problem of maintenance is often made more acute by the upgrading programme – providing facilities that have to be shared – for instance shared or communal standpipes or toilets. These are used more intensively than if such facilities were provided to each house and provision for maintenance has to be institutionalized.

Different approaches to resolving these problems

One of the simplest ways to ensure better maintenance of upgraded infra-structure is to provide improved facilities to each household, so each household gets a water, sewer and electricity connection, with the household knowing which agency is responsible for provision and maintenance. This works well where the agency responsible provides a good service at a reasonable price and households can afford to pay. There are many examples of low-income settle-ments that are well supplied with water, sanitation and electricity by public and private enterprises for which the inhabitants pay. In some instances, improved provision is organized by community organizations, including some where such organizations provided a better quality and cheaper service than public or private agencies and achieved cost recovery as in the sewer construction programme in Orangi, Pakistan (Hasan 1997), and the water and sanitation system in El Mezquital, Guatemala City (Díaz and others 2000).

Some upgrading arises from the inhabitants negotiating direct with external agencies – for instance getting piped water or electricity from official providers at a 'wholesale' rate with community organizations collecting payments from all households. This approach naturally leads to a focus not on upgrading but on expanding the capacity of the agencies responsible for components of upgrad-ing to reach low-income households and communities with improvements that can be sustained and for which the communities are prepared to pay. This obviously works best in cities where low-income households are able and willing to pay full costs and where efficient agencies keep down costs and make payment easier (for instance, as noted earlier, allowing connection charges for piped water or sewers to be paid over a number of months or years, integrated into payments for water).

Another approach to this problem of maintaining the upgraded infrastruc-ture is to rely on local residents and community organizations. But this is rare in upgrading schemes. It can also be highly inequitable, since it is only in the poorer communities that the inhabitants have to take on responsibility for maintenance (which is often difficult to do) when richer areas not only receive higher quality public infrastructure and services but also have these maintained by local government or other agencies.

Some upgrading programmes that include a transfer of tenure to the inhab-itants have recovered some costs by charging households for the land title. There is a danger that this can force out lower-income households but this can be avoided by separating a right to live there from a right to sell, so all inhabi-tants are provided with a right of occupancy but those who want to acquire the land title (and have the right to sell it) have to pay for this.

There are certain key features of upgrading programmes that have made them more effective:

- The development of strong local partnerships, as public agencies work with community organizations, NGOs and, in some instances, private sector enterprises. Local authorities can use their limited funding in combi-nation with their powers to draw on underused resources (such as unused public land) and to change regulatory frameworks.

- A more comprehensive range of improvements, as an upgrading programme includes measures to involve more sectoral agencies so it is not just infrastructure that is improved but also housing, schools and health care as in, for instance, the slum-networking project in Ahmedabad (Dutta 2000), the urban basic service programme in Cebu (Etemadi 2000) and project Bairro in Rio de Janeiro (Fiori and others 2000).
- More participatory methods for planning, implementation and maintenance.
- A more explicit attempt to integrate the areas being upgraded into the wider city.
- A long-term commitment to upgrading that over time reaches most or all areas of the city in which upgrading is needed.

One measure of a government's commitment to upgrading would be the extent to which it has moved from 'upgrading projects' to supporting the institutionalizion of upgrading within city and municipal authorities. Here, the goal is to develop the capacity of local governments to work continuously with the inhabitants of low-income settlements in upgrading the quality and extent of the infrastructure and service provision, and in regularizing land tenure. In this, there are a few examples of the needed institutional restructuring. Certainly, some progress was made in this direction in Indonesia, in terms of the expansion of the Kampung Improvement Programme first started in Jakarta in 1969 which developed to reach a considerable proportion of low-income urban dwellers in a great range of urban centres, although the improvements achieved by the upgrading were often not sustained (although with notable exceptions as in Surabaya as documented by Silas 1994). Progress was also made in Sri Lanka during the Million Houses Programme, as the National Housing Development Authority supported local (urban) authorities and community development councils in developing upgrading projects, but this was not sustained, in part because of the weakness of the Community Development Councils, in part because of declining government support, and finally, because of the political change in 1995 (Russell and Vidler 2000). Here, as in so many other places, successful government initiatives to work in partnership with low-income households in upgrading stop when governments change, as the newly elected politicians cannot stand to continue supporting what their predecessors initiated; or attempts to scale up or multiply a successful initiative are stifled by the bureaucratic and institutional constraints that a small initiative was able to bypass.

The vast number of smaller upgrading schemes

Perhaps of greater significance worldwide than the large, well-known and well-documented upgrading programmes funded by international donors are the much greater number of smaller, often more ad hoc 'upgrading' schemes in which the inhabitants of a low-income settlement negotiate with a local government or some other public agency for tenure of the plots on which they live and/or with a public or private agency for some basic infrastructure and services. The significance of these schemes lies in their numbers and in the fact that they demonstrate a much wider acceptance of the concept of 'upgrading' by city and municipal authorities. Where these small 'upgrading' schemes have been documented, they often show this process to be slow and inefficient – for instance, with support for paved roads negotiated at one point, then later drains or improved water supplies when there would have been major cost savings if provision for water supply, sanitation, drainage and paved roads were combined. But their importance lies in the fact that they represent a fundamental change in the attitude of local authorities to illegal or informal settlements. If municipal authorities can acquire increased power, resources and capacities within the many decentralization programmes around the world, so too can their capacities expand to respond more effectively to these kinds of demands. One-off, ad hoc upgrading projects can then develop into continuous programmes where infrastructure and service provision is improved and partnerships developed between public agencies and resident organizations to keep down costs and ensure provision for maintenance and for further improvements. Box 6.1 gives an example of one such small-scale upgrading programme that began independently of any local government involvement. In Barrio San Jorge, in Buenos Aires, there is a long-term improvement programme, supported by an Argentine NGO, IIED-America Latina. The programme is unusual in that it began within a squatter settlement in which there was no representative community organization. Most external support for community improvement programmes are in settlements in which a community organization had already been formed, since this makes it easier for external agencies to negotiate with the inhabitants and obtain rapid implementation. After many years of indifference from most government agencies in Argentina, the Barrio San Jorge programme also helped to stimulate a much larger upgrading programme, supported by national government agencies and local authorities (Schusterman and others 1999).

REFUSE COLLECTION AND CITIES' WASTE ECONOMIES

Ensuring regular collection services

Chapter 2 pointed to the lack of a regular waste-collection service in most urban areas, especially for the lower-income areas. The conventional 'high-income country' model for refuse collection and disposal is relatively expensive, especially if all the collection trucks have to be imported, and is beyond the means of most existing urban/municipal government budgets, if they want to extend a regular service to all those within their jurisdiction. The conventional large-truck oriented house-to-house collection service can also be wasteful of resources and inappropriate for many districts where roads are too narrow for the trucks or unpassable when it rains. There are sufficient examples of alternative approaches to suggest that major improvements in service provision can be made (including regular waste collection in poor and peripheral districts) at lower costs than the conventional approach with the added advantages of greater support for employment generation and waste reduction. Cities need solid waste-management strategies that incorporate such multiple goals and build on existing informal waste recovery and recycling systems (Furedy 1992).

Box 6.1 BARRIO SAN JORGE, ARGENTINA

Barrio San Jorge is one among a large number of informal settlements in Buenos Aires in which the inhabitants survive with very inadequate incomes. It is located in San Fernando, one of the municipalities on the periphery of Buenos Aires metropolitan area and some 35 kilometres north of the city centre. It covers a flat site of less than 10 hectares, next to a heavily polluted river that often floods. Before the community development programme, it was also among the many settlements where, despite many official speeches, promises and programmes, there had been little support from government programmes. Water supply was precarious and inadequate and there were no sewers. The site was at high risk of flooding with very inadequate provision for drainage and for waste collection. The settlement had no internal paved roads or paths and the inhabitants had no support to help them to improve and extend their homes.

Since 1987, various community projects have been implemented to improve conditions, with funding raised from a variety of local, national and international sources. They include the construction and development of a mother-and-child crèche/day-care/health centre and the conversion of an existing house into a community centre (the house of the barrio), the provision of a piped water and small bore sewer system, a health education programme, a sewing and clothing workshop; and the surfacing of some internal roads. A community-managed building materials store has also been opened that has lowered prices and made it easier for inhabitants to obtain materials. The buildings material store also provides materials on credit and delivers materials to each house site. It also serves as a centre of technical advice.

When the construction of the mother-and-child centre began in September 1987, only 16 people in San Jorge (mostly women) were interested in community activities. Most inhabitants looked upon the construction of the centre with scepticism. In late 1989, residents became more interested in the activities being introduced in the barrio. Attendance at meetings increased, so too did participation in decisions about work priorities, but few people were prepared to contribute to building unless they received payment. During the first half of 1990, the consolidation of a community organization continued. In August 1990, elections were held to choose representatives from the community to join a commission that was to develop a long-range programme for the improvement and integrated development of the barrio. This programme included negotiating secure tenure for the inhabitants and obtaining an extra 7 hectares of land, adjacent to the barrio on which to resettle some of the inhabitants, reducing the overall density and moving people from areas most at risk of flooding.

The 7-hectare site was finally acquired and it is now being developed. An agreement was developed with the newly privatized water company, *Aguas Argentinas*, to take over the maintenance of the water and sewer system. Many households have improved their homes, and many good quality new houses are being built in the new 7-hectare extension. But getting official tenure has proved to be more difficult than anticipated, in part because of cumbersome bureaucratic procedures.

The experience in Barrio San Jorge and the neighbouring newly constructed settlement has many positive achievements. But it also shows the difficult relations with external agencies, especially the long negotiations and often difficult relations with the municipal authorities (although this relationship has improved greatly in recent years). It also shows the long period needed to negotiate support for basic improvements and to develop a representative community organization. And despite all the improvements, the underlying problem of very low incomes and very inadequate employment opportunities remains. However, the experience in Barrio San Jorge has encouraged other Argentine agencies and municipal authorities to develop community support programmes similar to that provided in Barrio San Jorge by the Argentine NGO IIED-America Latina.

Sources: Schusterman, Ricardo and Ana Hardoy (1997), 'Reconstructing social capital in a poor urban settlement: the Integrated Improvement Programme, Barrio San Jorge', *Environment and Urbanization*, Vol 9, No 1, April, pp 91–119; Schusterman, Ricardo, Florencia Almansi, Ana Hardoy, Cecilia Monti and Gastón Urquiza (1999), Reducción de la pobreza en acción; planificación participativa en San Fernando, *Medio Ambiente y Urbanizacion*, No 54, December.

There is now a greater recognition of the need to develop local solutions that match local needs and possibilities. One reason for this is that conditions vary so much from city to city in (among other factors) the scale and type of refuse generation, the amount residents can afford and are prepared to pay for refuse collection, the type of vehicles needed to get to each building in different settlements, local possibilities for recycling or reclaiming part of the refuse, local traffic conditions, the availability for land sites for city dumps and the resources available to local authorities for collection and disposal.

A recent study in Latin America (Arroyo and others 1999) highlighted the key role of micro-enterprises, small enterprises and cooperatives in solid-waste collection and management. Drawing on research in 89 enterprises in 7 countries, it shows how small enterprises or cooperatives serve substantial proportions of the population in many cities. These generally provide a moderately priced service and are often the only service available in low-income neighbourhoods. These enterprises include:

- Those developed with the approval of municipal authorities by groups of small entrepreneurs to offer urban waste-management services to the public.
- Informal sector waste-pickers who have organized themselves into cooperatives or small enterprises to protect their livelihoods and to obtain official contracts.
- Collection enterprises formed by entrepreneurs with the support of community organizations.

- Collection organizations created by (usually low-income) communities in response to their own needs.
- Enterprises or cooperatives supported by local or international NGOs.
- Enterprises/cooperatives created by the municipal authorities and operating with their support.

Figure 6.1 shows the range of collection vehicles used by these enterprises. While these enterprises are best known for providing waste-collection services, many operate in other areas such as the recovery of recyclables, street sweeping, cleansing of canals and storm drains, maintenance of parks and other public spaces, and management of disposal sites (ibid). Although many of these enterprises or cooperatives were founded without any involvement of the municipal authorities and continue to operate outside the framework of official solid waste-management programmes, some national, city and municipal authorities have created new opportunities for them and allowed them to compete for public contracts (ibid).

One example of an NGO-managed approach that operates on a large scale is Exnora International, an NGO based in Chennai (formerly Madras) in India (Anand 1999). This promotes the formation of neighbourhood associations that set up their own Civic Exnoras to manage primary waste collection. Each neighbourhood association appoints and trains someone to collect the wastes and provides them with equipment – usually a tricycle waste-collection cart. Wastes are collected from each household and taken to a municipal bin or transfer station. Each household pays a monthly fee to their local Civic Exnora which covers the collector's salary and helps to pay for their equipment. By 1996, there were 1500 Civic Exnoras providing services to 450,000 people. Many have also taken on other tasks such as taking up civic grievances regarding problems with water supply, drainage and faulty street lighting, and promoting environmental awareness and tree planting. However, as Anand 1999 discusses, they can only function where there is a secondary waste-collection system into which they can feed.[6] One returns to the fact that community-based or neighbourhood-based solutions need a supportive city-wide framework, if they are to be effective on a large scale. Most community-based waste-collection systems cannot manage the transport of the wastes to distant dumps and the final disposal, just as community-based piped water, sewers and drains need the water mains and trunk sewers and drains into which they integrate.

Integrating collection with resource recovery

In wealthy societies, on average, each person generates between 300 kilos and 1 tonne of solid waste a year; in low-income countries, it is generally between 100 and 220 kilos per person per year with middle-income countries usually having figures of between 180 and 330.[7] As the figures suggest, in general, the higher

---

6 Anand 1999 also discusses some of the problems of relying on such a system and the fact that it only developed because of the failure of the municipal government to meet its responsibilities.
7 Drawn from Cointreau 1982 with the ranges of waste generation extended, reflecting new data on municipal waste generation in different cities.

1 Equipment used by the street sweeping micro-enterprise in the district of Miraflores, Lima, Peru.
2 Hand cart used for household waste collection by a micro-enterprise in La Paz, Bolivia.
3 Collection cart used in El Salvador.
4 Collection cargo tricycle used in Peru.
5 Pick-up truck used for collection in various countries.
6 High-sided truck used in various countries for collection.
7 Farm tractor and trailer used in Costa Rica and Cajamarca, Peru. A mini-tractor is used in Niteroi, Brazil.

8 Cart used by the waste pickers in Brazil and Colombia.
9 Three-wheeled cart used for collection in Cochabamba, Bolivia.

Source: Arroyo Moreno, Jorge, Francisco Rivas Ríos and Inge Lardinois (1999), *Solid Waste Management in Latin America: The Role of Micro- and Small Enterprises and Cooperatives*, IPES, ACEPESA and WASTE.

Figure 6.1 *Examples of different solid-waste collection vehicles used by micro and small enterprises and cooperatives in Latin America*

the per capita income, the larger the average weight of waste per person. The differences are not only between countries with different per capita incomes but also between households within cities as high-income households usually generate much more waste per person than low-income households. Higher-income cities and higher-income households also tend to generate higher proportions of inorganic wastes (including more potentially reclaimable and recyclable materials).

The fact that household 'wastes' and wastes from commercial and industrial enterprises include valuable resources that can be reused or recycled is shown by the large 'waste economies' of many cities in low- and middle-income countries. Most are not the result of government action but of long-established systems that grew and evolved, in response to changing waste patterns and changing demands for what can be reclaimed, reused or recycled. From a 'green' perspective, these waste economies bring many advantages – much less waste (and so much less need for landfills or other forms of disposal), usable waste products, including compost derived from organic wastes that returns nutrients to the soil, less use of natural resources (as metals and glass drawn from waste are fed back into production streams) and generally less fossil fuel use and pollution (as using metals and glass from waste streams within production systems is less energy- and pollution-intensive than drawing on natural resources). For municipal authorities, their budgets benefit greatly from the individuals, households and informal groups who separate recyclables from their own wastes and collect them from other waste streams (for example paper, metals and glass) since this reduces waste volumes and in large cities, the cost of collecting and transporting solid wastes to landfill sites and the development of new landfill sites is a major part of total solid waste-management costs. For instance, in Bangalore, one of India's most prosperous cities, in the mid-1990s, the municipal authorities were having to dispose of only 335 tonnes of solid waste a day because around 2700 tonnes was being recovered daily for reuse or recycling by waste-pickers, households themselves and the municipal collectors (Furedy 1994, Huysman 1994). In addition, since most inorganic wastes (including glass and tins) are taken out of domestic waste streams, what is left has a high proportion of organic waste which can be composted (ibid). Similarly in Karachi, the volume of solid waste is much reduced by resource recovery (see Box 6.2). Ironically, over the last 25 years, nine major internationally funded studies have been prepared for Karachi to suggest how to improve solid-waste management, but none recognized the crucial role of the recycling industry that provides a livelihood for some 55,000 families, recovers and recycles or reclaims a large volume of resources and greatly reduces the amount of waste that has to be disposed of (Hasan 1999).

These waste economies also provide substantial economic benefits: the livelihoods of several million urban dwellers in Asia depends on wastes, including workers in small industries that use plastics, tin cans, bottles, bones, feathers, intestines, hair, leather and textile scraps (Furedy 1990a). Numerous businesses are part of the waste economy – itinerant buyers who collect or purchase certain kinds of wastes direct from households or businesses, waste-pickers who recover materials for sale from the streets, dump-pickers who recover

---

BOX 6.2 *SOLID-WASTE COLLECTION AND DISPOSAL IN KARACHI*

Karachi generates some 6000 tones of solid waste every day. Some 800 tons are removed at source within households (glass, plastic, metal and paper) and sold to some 15,000 *kabaris* who pick this up from people's homes. Another 700 tons (mostly paper, rags, plastic, metal, glass and bones) are collected from neighbourhood rubbish dumps and from streets and markets by some 21,000 waste pickers. Some 350 tons of solid waste and building material debris is used each day for landfill, as Karachi Metropolitan Council staff deposit this in locations where informal developers are reclaiming land. Around 400 tons of organic waste are used by pottery kilns as fuel or burnt to extract metal from it. Waste from high-income localities (where waste-pickers are not allowed) are taken to 'scavenger colonies' where all recyclable materials are removed.

The recycling industry transforms waste paper into paper board, glass into bottles, plastic into toys, utensils and electric conduits, bones into ornaments and poultry feed, and various types of metals into utensils, steel bars and machinery items. Rags are used for upholstery. There are 435 recycling factories in Karachi. The recycling industry provides employment for over 55,000 families.

Source: Hasan, Arif (1999), *Understanding Karachi: Planning and Reform for the Future*, City Press, Karachi. This drew from Ali, Mansoor (1997), *Integration of the Official and Private Informal Practices in Solid Waste Management*, unpublished thesis and from studies by the Karachi Urban Resource Centre.

---

materials from city dumps, small waste shops, second-hand markets, dealers, transporters and the various recycling industries (Furedy 1992). In Calcutta, an estimated 40,000 people make a living from recovering and using (or selling) resources picked from wastes, and many thousands more make a living from intensive farming using composted household wastes and fish-rearing in ponds fertilized by city sewage (Furedy 1990b). In Manila, some 30,000 people are involved in informal waste recycling (UNCHS 1993). In Karachi, as noted in Box 6.2, the waste economy provides livelihoods for over 50,000 households. But it is not only in the poorer Asian cities where the reclamation and recycling of wastes are important sources of employment; in Bogota, the capital of Colombia, an estimated 30,000–50,000 people earn a living, including cart drivers, small-scale waste dealers, people reclaiming materials from street waste and the employees of the municipal waste-disposal and street-cleaning department (Pacheco 1992). Waste dumps often have a large and varied employment base around them that depends on the materials recovered from the dump-site; for instance, around 4000 waste-picker families live around the Payatas dump in Manila (Vincentian Missionaries 1998).

This intensive use of city resources and wastes also brings major environmental benefits and cost savings for national economies. Margarita Pacheco has highlighted the major savings to Colombia, for instance, from the energy saved in the recycling of glass, cardboard, paper and plastics (Pacheco 1992). Recycling cardboard and paper reduces the paper industry's demand for trees and thus reduces deforestation. However, these large and complex 'waste economies' are also driven by poverty and include within them some of the most serious forms of poverty and exploitation. This has been highlighted by Christine Furedy who has been documenting these informal waste economies for more than 20 years; her observation for Asian cities that the poorer or less equal the society, the greater the range and volume of wastes that have value and are reused or recycled (Furedy 1990a), has validity for cities in other regions. The individuals or households who use or collect resources rarely obtain an adequate return relative to the number of hours worked. They undertake this work since, in the absence of a better alternative, it provides a livelihood. It is common for some of the poorest and most disadvantaged groups to be involved in this work – for instance particular castes or outcaste groups or street children. During an economic recession, more people seek incomes from picking through wastes to recover goods for sale (Furedy 1990a). Such work is usually unpleasant and has many health risks – for instance injuries from broken glass and the sharp edges of cans for those sorting by hand and excreta-related diseases from excreta-contaminated wastes that are so common in cities where households do not have convenient sanitation. They are also at risk from disease vectors that feed or breed in waste or rubbish dumps. In many cities, hazardous wastes become mixed with household wastes – for instance toxic wastes from industries and hospital wastes (Cointreau 1982). Given all these hazards, one common official response is to ban waste-picking activities, yet this simply removes the livelihoods of large sections of the poorest population. A more appropriate response is to consider how the great environmental advantages of informal resource recovery and utilization can be kept (and enhanced) while income levels and working conditions are improved and health risks reduced for the individuals, households and enterprises engaged in this process.

There are many examples of initiatives taken by local NGOs or CBOs to improve conditions and returns for waste-pickers, but many suffer from the difficulties that most small, voluntary initiatives face (Furedy 1992). In particular, they are too small and only reach a small proportion of those in need. In response to this, some NGOs and grassroots organizations have sought to demonstrate to the responsible authorities what should be done and then work with them to develop workable models. For example, the Indian NGO SPARC is working in one district in Mumbai (formerly Bombay) on a waste-recycling scheme run by street children. The district council provided the land in exchange for the money it saved from not having to drive trucks that it could not afford to run to a landfill some distance from the district. In Khon Khan in Thailand, local community organizations have founded a centre that local recyclers can use without being cheated. Having developed the centre, the community is now in discussions with the municipality to see how they can support other such initiatives. In other instances, waste-pickers have organized themselves into cooperatives or federations, as in the examples given in Box 6.3. One of the recurring concerns raised by waste-pickers and recyclers in different cities is the very poor prices they receive from 'middle-men' or from industries who purchase their materials. Forming cooperatives or developing their own recycling depots are often means by which they can negotiate better prices.

As in actions on water, sanitation and drainage, the kinds of actions needed from government will vary greatly, depending on local circumstances. They may include providing healthcare for waste-pickers, and washing and sanitation facilities for their use at city dumps; or simply providing a platform at the dump site to allow waste-pickers to sort waste as it was unloaded from trucks. A better solution is illustrated by an initiative in Pôrto Alegre (Brazil). The waste-pickers who previously picked through the waste after it had been dumped on a landfill site now manage a waste reclamation and recycling depot to which the official house-to-house waste-collection service delivers the bags into which households have put recyclables (and thus separated these from non-recyclable wastes). The scheme also includes housing next to the recycling depot, so the former waste-pickers also received better quality housing. And by having their own depot and being able to supply much larger quantities of separated wastes, they can also obtain better prices.[8]

Obviously, the most efficient way to separate out reusable or recyclable wastes is at the point where the wastes are generated – the household or enterprise. Many recycling schemes encourage households and enterprises to separate out their recyclables for a separate collection – as in the Pôrto Alegre example noted above. But it is not easy to get high levels of household compliance, especially for the more complex schemes that require most work by households – for instance separate packages for different recyclables, each with a different collection date. Compliance drops off if the collection of the recyclables is not regular and convenient. The economics of official collection schemes may be undermined by the fact that many households already collect and sell their recyclables to informal collectors.[9] Or the collection service may expect households to bring out their recyclables as the collectors pass through the neighbourhood, yet they come at a time when many households have no-one at home. It is also particularly inconvenient for households living in very cramped conditions to store their recyclables.

If there is no separation of recyclables by households, the sooner they can be sorted, the better since the less mixed and compacted the wastes, the easier and safer this separation. Items that can be reused are also less damaged. It may be appropriate to have neighbourhood or district level transfer points for solid wastes where reusable or recyclable materials can be separated before the wastes are taken to the city dump (Puerbo 1991). Such district level separation can also guard against the mixing of toxic and hazardous wastes from industries or commercial institutions with residential waste.

City authorities might also consider support for decentralized centres where recyclable material can be collected. In many peripheral low-income settle-

---

8 Personal visit to the cooperative and their recycling site and housing project in June 1999.
9 See Hernández and others 1999 for a report on the success and limitations of a pilot recycling scheme in Quito (Ecuador) that discusses in detail the factors that encouraged and discouraged households to separate their wastes and support the pilot scheme.

Box 6.3 *EXAMPLES OF RECYCLERS' COOPERATIVES OR FEDERATIONS*

Bogota (Colombia). An estimated 12,000 families are involved in waste-recycling activities in Bogota, many of them organized into associations, cooperatives and community enterprises. One example is the Rescatar Recyclers Cooperative. It has 150 recyclers and most of its work comes from the collection of source-separated recyclables from offices, industries, hotels and other commercial entities. It is also involved in public cleansing services and household waste collection. Its members had to struggle to gain recognition for their work and in the past, they had to overcome internal difficulties, government agencies whose promise of support was not realized and falls in the price of recyclable materials.

Medellin (Colombia). Recuperar, a cooperative specializing in waste management was formed in 1983 when the municipality closed the Moravia dump where 320 informal waste-pickers worked. The initial proposal to create a cooperative was only of interest to 23 waste-pickers but within two years, it was generating employment for all 320. By the end of 1995, the cooperative had 917 workers, mostly engaged in the separation of recyclables at source and recovery. In 1995, almost 5000 tonnes of recyclables were sold. About 70 per cent of the material gathered by the cooperative is recovered by its associates through the Source Separation Programme that serves industries, businesses and public and private institutions. It has contracts with various enterprises and hotels to collect their wastes. It has also begun to offer other environmental services that have produced more jobs and higher incomes.

Manila (Philippines). The Patayas dump site, the largest dump site in Metro Manila, provides a home and a livelihood for some 4000 households. These include waste-pickers who supply recyclable materials to established waste-recovery and recycling businesses and home-based micro-enterprises engaged in the recovery, recycling and reuse of solid waste materials – for instance using wastes to make wall decorations, tin crafts, laundry brushes and dust pans. A local NGO, the Vincentian Missionaries Social Development Foundation, has worked with the waste-pickers and recyclers since 1991 and, with other local NGOs, has supported a community development programme. This has two roles. The first is to support local initiatives (for instance a micro-credit scheme, a project to improve water supplies and a housing programme). The second is to negotiate with local authorities for basic services, legal status, and a recognition of the role of the waste-pickers and recyclers. The waste-pickers have formed a Federation which in 1998 had 1200 members organized within 15 chapters, each representing a community with at least 50 households. This achieved official recognition as a legally constituted people's organization (see Vincentian Missionaries 1998 for a much more detailed description of this programme).

Sources: Arroyo Moreno, Jorge, Francisco Rivas Ríos and Inge Lardinois (1999), *Solid Waste Management in Latin America: The Role of Micro- and Small Enterprises and Cooperatives*, IPES, ACEPESA and WASTE. Vincentian Missionaries (1998), 'The Payatas Environmental Development Programme: micro-enterprise promotion and involvement in solid waste management in Quezon City', *Environment and Urbanization*, Vol 10, No 2, pages 55–68.

ments, the cost to the city authorities of a regular waste-collection service is often high, especially if access roads to the site are poor. Support for a neigh-bourhood-based centre with glass, cans and paper separated for sale and organic waste composted might be a more appropriate response (de Cuentro 1990). This would greatly reduce the volume of waste that had to be collected. The needed form of support may simply be a guarantee by the municipal authorities of a price for the compost and its use in city parks, together with its collection, and the collection of wastes that are neither recyclable nor compostable. In another approach tried in Curitiba, the public authorities 'purchased' waste from the inhabitants of squatter settlements. They received tickets for use on public transport or for purchasing agricultural and dairy produce in return for refuse brought to a central collection point. Conventional waste-collection services were often impossible for such settlements because the rubbish trucks could not reach them. In this experiment, the cost to the public authorities was equivalent to the cost of paying a private company to collect the waste (Rabinovitch 1992).

Thus, city or municipal authorities can work with decentralized waste-collection services and also with the informal 'waste economy', allowing and supporting neighbourhood-based and informal activities within their city-wide waste-management programme. This can bring cost advantages to themselves, better returns and working conditions for those who make a living from the waste and the retention, by the city, of the environmental advantages (Furedy 1992).

THE ROLE OF PRIVATIZATION

Low-income groups need safe and sufficient supplies of water. Drains are needed to remove waste water (including rainwater) and, where possible, sewers to take away excreta. Where sewers are too expensive, or on-site sanitation can work well, regular services are needed to empty pit latrines or septic tanks. Low-income groups also need healthcare services, all-weather roads and footpaths, electricity connections and regular collections for waste. Many governments and aid agencies are promoting privatization to improve provision for such basic needs. The idea that privatization alone can improve provision to low-income groups and solve the problems already outlined is generally overstated.

The main justifications for privatization advanced by its proponents are that public utilities are inefficient and that they have constraints on raising the capital needed to expand and improve provision. Their case is strengthened by the poor performance of so many public sector utilities. As a publication by one of the main international companies involved in water and sanitation privatization points out, the poor performance of many government water companies is also related to their inflexibility (linked to little dialogue with their current or potential customers) in offering only a single, standard, high-price option – a household water and sewer connection (Lyonnaise des Eaux 1998). The hope is that the private sector, if offered the opportunity, will provide the capital needed to expand and improve services and the options offered to households. The assumption is that the improved efficiency brought by the private company will allow it to perform better than a public agency in terms of coverage, quality of provision and price, despite its need to get a profitable rate of return. It is possible to see privatization better serving those households that can afford to pay for infrastructure and services but which remain unserved or inadequately served because of inefficient, inflexible or poorly managed public services. But it is difficult to see how privatization, in most instances, can provide adequate quality and coverage for low-income groups.

It is worth considering how private enterprises currently serve low-income households. There are many examples of private enterprises filling important gaps in provision to low-income groups, where public provision is inadequate or non-existent – for instance water vendors or kiosks, waste collectors, private schools, day-care centres, bus/shared taxi services and healthcare services.[10] But in most such instances, private provision only works because public provision is so poor and because there is competition between private enterprises that helps to keep down prices. The quality of provision is often poor; if the enterprises provided higher standards, they would have to charge prices that low-income groups could not afford. In most instances, these are also services that do not require much capital investment, and the capital equipment that is needed (eg the bus, medical equipment, water tanker) can be moved to another location, if insufficient profit is being generated.

Most low-income groups also use the 'private' sector to obtain housing. The private sector is generally the main provider of rental accommodation; the extent to which low-income groups depend on rental accommodation and the extent to which such accommodation is located in illegal or informal settlements has often been under-estimated (UNCHS 1996). The private sector is also generally the main provider of land for housing, although most land sales (or land renting) to low-income groups takes place outside any legal framework – for instance through the sale of land that is illegally subdivided or even the sale of land that the seller does not own. In this, the private sector can hardly be said to provide good quality goods and services for low-income groups. The lack of infrastructure and services supplied by the enterprises that develop land for sale or rent to low-income households, and the poor conditions in most rental housing that low-income groups can afford, do not support the idea that privatization will necessarily improve standards for poorer groups. However, without their provision, low-income groups would be worse off. Where there are competitive pressures in these markets – for instance a great variety of landlords or land subdividers – prices are kept down. But even with competitive pressures, the quality of provision is poor because it is impossible to combine good quality provision with prices that low-income groups can afford and profit for the provider.

---

10 The private provision of healthcare and bus/shared taxi services serving low-income groups is well documented. We have not come across much documentation of the private provision of schools and day-care centres for low-income groups although these can often be seen in low-income areas. Among the many programmes run by Orangi Pilot Project was one to help improve the quality of the very cheap private schools widely used by low-income households in Karachi.

The potential of privatization to serve low-income groups is most problematic where the capital costs of extending the infrastructure are high per person reached and where there are no competitive pressures. Many forms of infrastructure are 'natural monopolies'. Once a piped water supply, sewer system or drainage or road network is built in a particular district, it is virtually impossible for another business to compete by building another water, sewer, drainage or road system. Customers who are dissatisfied with prices or the quality of provision cannot transfer and use the roads, sewers, drains or pipes of another supplier. Thus, once the investment has been made and the supplier established, customers may be vulnerable to exploitation by a single supplier. Such natural monopolies require large capital investments to set up the supply, but once in place, the cost of extending them to more people is relatively low.

When a form of infrastructure or service that is a natural monopoly is privatized, the operation of the private company has to be carefully regulated with regard to price, coverage and quality of service. Where possible, some competitive pressures need to be brought in – for instance through competitive bidding for concessions or dividing provision within a city between different concessions. But if privatization is done because local government is so weak, how can this same weak local government regulate the private firms and adequately represent the needs of low-income citizens? For instance, for water supply, how can it fulfil its responsibility to ensure that water quality is guaranteed, that services are extended and that prices are controlled? The privatization of infrastructure and service provision does not remove the need for government intervention; it simply changes the nature of this intervention. Government remains responsible for ensuring that an adequate quality of service is maintained, that coverage is expanded and that the public are not over-charged.

For some services, a lack of information means that consumers cannot easily determine the quality of the product even if the market is competitive. Domestic water supply is the most important example because it is difficult for households to judge whether the water they use is safe to consume. If private enterprises provide water supplies, local government must not only control prices but also monitor water quality and have in place an effective deterrent system to penalize companies that fail to maintain adequate standards. Likewise transport services will also require monitoring to ensure that the vehicles are safe, adequately maintained and not overcrowded.

The enthusiasm for the 'privatization' of public companies or public assets may also pose threats to the inhabitants of many squatter settlements. In many cities, a considerable proportion of the population live in illegal settlements that developed on land that belongs to public companies (for instance railway or water companies). If the land on which the squatters live is now sold to private companies, there will be a much increased pressure to evict them. Indeed, one of the attractions for private capital of many public companies is the land they own. Similarly, poorer groups that have developed livestock rearing or agricultural production on public lands may lose this possibility if the land is sold.

The privatization of public water and electricity services, or other public utilities, may also mean the disconnection of many low-income households.

Public agencies have often tolerated (or ignored) illegal water connections or electricity connections in illegal settlements. They have often accepted that those served by communal standpipes get the water free. But no private company taking over water or electricity supplies is going to tolerate this since it cuts into their profits. Illegal connections to water mains may also be a major source of leakage. The end result is that many low-income households may be disconnected.

However, private enterprises may also be prepared to develop supplies to illegal or informal settlements that public agencies had ignored and in so doing, provide a formal market service that better serves the inhabitants' needs. The best way to avoid the disconnection of low-income households because of their illegal connections is to negotiate solutions that benefit both sides – the inhabitants who relied on illegal connections getting legal connections and better quality services, and the providers getting paid. But part of the profitability of private companies is based on providing standard solutions and keeping down staff costs, and this constrains solutions that need to be negotiated within each settlement and that use non-standard solutions to keep down prices.

There is also the problem that private enterprises will only want to provide the infrastructure and services that provide attractive returns and only provide them in the countries, cities or city districts where the costs of provision are not too high and where there is sufficient 'density of demand' for them to make a profit. To take the first of these, not all infrastructure and service provision is an attractive investment. For instance, private enterprises will not want to provide street lighting, site drainage and roads, unless the companies are paid to do so or required to do so by their contract with the government. In other cases, the lowest cost method of providing the service may require a large capital investment that the private sector is reluctant to undertake without a government guarantee that minimizes their risk. In addition, important cost savings can be lost if different forms of infrastructure are installed by different companies at different times. For instance, water supplies piped to each house require drains connected to each house, and preferably sewers. Sewers need sufficient water to keep them functioning. House sites usually need drains for rainwater. Roads and other paved areas need drains. Drains need efficient waste collection, otherwise they become blocked; so too, on occasion, do sewers. The public good is best served when water, sewers and drains are installed simultaneously. First, this brings the greatest improvement in health; if only the water supply is improved, this may increase health problems (see Chapter 2). Second, there are large cost savings if piped water, drains and sewers are installed together, along with the paving of roads and footpaths. But private companies are unlikely to want to take on the operation of water, sanitation, drainage and the paving of roads and paths. Water supply is generally the most attractive for them because people pay as they consume and often pay for the initial cost of connection. Enforcing payment is easier because households who do not pay can have their supplies cut off. Waste collection may also be attractive to private enterprises since the capital costs to set up the service need not be high and again, services can be stopped if households do not pay. But private enterprises will be less attracted to the supply of sewers, site drains, roads and paths since it is difficult to penalize households for non-payment. They will generally only be prepared to provide these if the full cost of the investment is provided up-front, either by households or by government.

Private companies may also be reluctant to extend infrastructure and services to areas with a predominance of low-income groups, especially if this requires a large investment and they are uncertain of the willingness of residents to pay for their product. The costs of provision are higher for many low-income settlements because of their location (for instance far from exist-ing water mains and trunk sewers and drains), terrain (on hillsides or flood-plains), site layout (for instance plot layouts within which it is difficult to install pipes), tenure (for instance uncertainty as to who owns each plot and to where plot boundaries are) or lack of infrastructure (for instance no paved roads to the settlement and within it). It does not cost much for a private company to see if a new bus service or the delivery of water by tanker to a squatter community is profitable. If the venture is not generating sufficient return, a different route can be tried or the bus or tanker sold. But laying water pipes or sewers and drains is a much greater risk, since these are far more expen-sive and the pipes, sewers and drains cannot be dug up and moved, if they prove unprofitable. Private sector companies will also not invest in smaller and less prosperous urban centres. To date, most private sector investment in water and sanitation has been in the more prosperous countries of Asia and Latin America. One estimate suggested that sub-Saharan Africa has received less than 1 per cent of the total private investments in water and sanitation (Johnstone and others 1999), yet its urban centres are among the world's worst served with regard to water and sanitation.

In particular cities (or parts of cities), government weakness, inefficiency or corruption may provide a strong case for the private supply of certain services or certain kinds of infrastructure. This is especially so where public companies or utilities fail to provide adequate services to businesses and house-holds who can afford such services. As Kyu Sik Lee has pointed out in his study of deficiencies in infrastructure provision in Nigeria, the failure of government to provide businesses with adequate standards of water supply, electricity, telephones and drains means that these businesses make very large investments to guarantee their own supplies, ie their own electricity generators, wells for water and microwave telephone systems. The costs to each business are enormous and any larger-scale supplier (public or private) could meet their demands far more cheaply (Lee 1988). Here, private sector provision can bring major benefits to the competitiveness of the city but not necessarily to inade-quately or unserved low-income groups.

In other services, especially those that are not a natural monopoly, private enterprises can help to improve quality and choice for the public. In city trans-port, private enterprises often provide a cheaper, more flexible service than public sector bus companies; private buses, mini-buses, shared taxis, powered rickshaws and other kinds of 'paratransit' either replace or supplement public sector buses in virtually all cities. Large companies, whether private or public, may be poorly suited to running such services because they find it difficult to provide sufficient flexibility. In some cases, the public and private sectors can cooperate effectively, with the government establishing the network and conditions for quality and cost of services with the private sector operating individual routes; this has been done in Curitiba within a public transport system that is praised for its efficiency and for the fact that it does not lose money (Rabinovitch 1992). Private companies might also improve waste collection at an affordable cost to customers with appropriate encouragement and regulation by local government. This might be particularly attractive for local governments that cannot obtain investment funds, however, the private companies may only operate in the areas where households pay enough to make the service profitable. In Mombasa (Kenya), when waste collection was privatized on the mainland, only higher-income households and formal businesses could afford the prices charged by the private contractors, so low-income areas and informal settlements were no longer served and the municipal authority had no option but to collect the refuse they dumped along roadsides (Rakodi and others 2000). In Benin City (Nigeria), the privatization of waste collection brought no significant improvements (Ogu 2000).

There is also a tendency to overlook the current and potential role of the small-scale private sector in provision for water and sanitation. Recent research has shown that tens of millions of low-income households would be worse off without their operations and that many provide good quality, low-cost services (Solo 1999). They also generally operate with no subsidy. The very high prices that low-income households often pay water vendors was noted earlier, but this often reflects the high costs that water vendors face in supplying these households (Cairncross 1990). In settlements where the combination of very low household incomes, high installation costs and a poor local government makes the installation of piped supplies impossible, water supplies should be cheaper and of better quality if different vendors compete with each other and information is available about the quality of the water they sell. Here, one option for local government would be to assist water vendors to improve services as well as regulating quality (Cairncross 1990). It may be a lack of public provision in other areas that keeps prices high, as in settlements lacking paved access roads that make it difficult or impossible for water tankers to get there. However, Tova Maria Solo has shown how small-scale entrepreneurs have successfully developed more sophisticated forms of provision, for instance in Asunción (the capital of Paraguay) where there are many enterprises providing piped water to between 50 and 2000 families including some that are developing sewers (Solo 1999).

Privatization may also allow a more rational pricing structure to develop. One reason why private companies may operate more profitably than public enterprises is their greater efficiency in collecting payments for services provided. Public utilities often subsidize richer groups through the non-collection of payments or by charging prices that are far below real costs. A public water company's failure to collect payments for piped water or to increase tariffs to reflect rising costs has the effect of subsidizing those with piped water (often not among the poorer households). This penalizes those with no piped supply since it lowers the returns to the company and thus inhibits new investment to expand the service. Reducing the proportion of households who do not pay the full cost of some service is one important way to fund better maintenance of the system and its expansion to reach previously unserved households. However, improved cost recovery may simply lead to better profits for the owners with no improvement or extension of services.

Again, one returns to the importance for privatization (and much else) of having a competent, knowledgeable, accountable local government that promotes (or safeguards) the public good. Such a local government can better negotiate a contract with private providers that brings benefits for low-income groups. It can develop models for privatization that allow low-income groups more influence over what is provided and allow independent providers to develop forms of provision that are better tailored to the needs and constraints of difficult-to-reach, low-income settlements (see Hardoy and Schusterman 2000 which discusses how this can be done, based on their experience with improving provision in Buenos Aires). Local government needs to do this while also safeguarding water supplies for the future (so freshwater resources are not depleted or degraded). It also needs to protect the environment – for instance by ensuring that private providers do not keep down costs through dumping, inadequate treatment or poor management of solid and liquid wastes. It has to have the capacity to ensure that the contract's conditions are met, and to achieve this in ways that are acceptable to the private companies.

Allowing private enterprises to provide certain services that are now inadequately provided (or not provided at all) by local government can be useful and worth considering, especially for the services that are not natural monopolies. There is now more experience to draw on, which highlights what has worked well and what has not. There is also a greater appreciation of the range of ways in which governments can use private sector provision; indeed, most local governments have long used private contractors for building some kinds of infrastructure or providing services. Privatization does not mean having to transfer public assets – for instance as private companies are awarded contracts to provide particular services or to manage public provision.

But in the services that are the main concern of this section, there will be problems with quality, price and with reaching poorer households if there is no strong, competent and accountable local government to supervise levels of private service and charges. There may be problems with quality even if there is a competent local government because of the low level of affordability by low-income groups. If local government is competent and accountable to its citizens, it may be able to provide such services more cheaply and effectively itself. There are many efficient public sector water and sanitation utilities, although the efficiency is generally related to the fact that these operate with some autonomy so, for instance, political pressures do not keep prices below costs (Johnstone and others 1999). The aim is to seek the best possible fit between guaranteeing a basic level of service to everyone, maximizing cost recovery and avoiding the transfer of costs to others. As noted earlier, new technologies and innovative institutional arrangements can considerably cheapen the cost of supplying a basic level of services, and greatly narrow the gap between the cost of provision and what poorer households can afford. They can also make it easy for households to obtain better services, once they can afford to pay more, ie bring piped water into the house rather than in the yard outside. But perhaps the key issue to address is a change in roles and responsibilities. The work of a number of NGOs and other innovative programmes have demonstrated that local and national government institutions that work in traditional ways fail to address the needs of their poorest citizens, regardless of whether they privatize or continue with public service provision.

Perhaps the argument is focused wrongly if it remains at the level of privatization. There is a deeper level of analysis that needs more consideration. Privatization generally involves a continuation of the present assumption that a Northern model of urban development should prevail (although it should be acknowledged that there are exceptions). And privatization has been promoted by certain international agencies (especially the World Bank) because international agencies need local implementors for the projects they fund and they were frustrated by the poor performance of public agencies. But the lesson from some of the more innovative and successful programmes in Africa, Asia and Latin America is that it is not privatization that is needed but a redefinition of the roles and responsibilities of the citizen and the state. At the centre of this is a reconstruction of local organizations, and of the relationship between communities and the state, be it local government or national departments. Within such a reconstruction, it may be that the private sector, be it large formal sector companies or smaller informal sector entrepreneurs, as an important role.

KEY ROLES FOR NGOS AND CBOS

In many urban areas, a more relevant debate about privatization and improving environmental health for lower-income groups has to do not with private commercial enterprises but with non-profit organizations and with organizations set up by the residents themselves. Local NGOs or organizations formed by residents (or other groups) may match (or exceed) private enterprise's record in cost recovery and provide cheaper services in ways that are more immediately accountable to their customers. This could be regarded as privatization in another form, although it may be inappropriate to call it this since control of the infrastructure and services rests largely with representatives of the 'consumers' of that service. There is tremendous potential in new partnerships between local governments, local community organizations and local NGOs. Underlying these innovations is a recognition that debates about the 'best' provider of services are often academic as no one is providing services. What is needed is a series of pragmatic alternatives with a potential to expand so all those in need can be reached.

There may be considerable possibilities for improvement without local government as is shown by the early work of the Pakistan NGO Orangi Pilot Project with low-income households and community organizations in Orangi, the largest unauthorized settlement in Karachi. This shows what can be achieved with minimal external funding and with most of the investments made by the poor households themselves (see Box 6.4). Once the local government saw the improvements that the people had made, they began to realize how they could use their limited funds to better effect through working with initiatives such as these. So what began as a small community-funded initiative, supported by a local NGO (whose approach was initially heavily criticized by a UN agency)[11] expanded to serve tens of thousands of households and to set an example that is now used by government agencies, NGOs and community-based organizations (CBOs) in other parts of Karachi and other Pakistan cities. Another example of improvements achieved without (or despite) local government is the initial development programme in Barrio San Jorge described earlier, supported by an Argentine NGO and with some foreign funding. Here too, once the programme demonstrated tangible achievements, it encouraged the local government to be more supportive, and both this and other local governments developed comparable support programmes for other low-income settlements, with the support of the federal government (Schusterman and others 1999). The comprehensive development programme within El Mezquital (Guatemala City) which included a self-managed piped water supply and sewers, and an innovative primary healthcare programme was also achieved with very little support from local government; here support from various international agencies and some national agencies was important (Díaz and others 2000).

However, the possible scope and effectiveness of programmes to tackle the most serious environmental health problems with limited resources is much increased if local government agencies can cooperate with community-based citizen groups. Joint programmes can be set up to drain stagnant pools, to reblock existing settlements so pipes, drains and access roads can be installed and space made for schools and health centres, to locate and destroy disease vectors within homes and their surrounds, to design educational programmes on health prevention and personal hygiene, to set up emergency life-saving systems through which first aid can be provided in each neighbourhood and through which seriously ill or injured persons can be rapidly transported to a hospital. One example of how much can be achieved comes from a small Peruvian city, Ilo, whose development programme will be discussed in more detail in Chapter 7, because it was city-wide in scope. But a key part of this development programme were 300 local projects financed and implemented through partnerships between the municipal government and community-level management committees that concentrated on different aspects of environmental improvement such as paving streets, developing neighbourhood parks and installing piped water (Follegatti 1999).

Box 6.5 illustrates the kind of impact that local government support for community-level initiatives can have. It outlines four different ways of spending US$20 million to improve poorer groups' housing and living conditions. Option 1, the construction of 'low-cost' housing, was the most common approach during the 1960s and part of the 1970s; its limited impact is obvious in that very few households are reached. It was also common for the 'low-cost' housing built by government programmes to be allocated to better-off households.[12] Option 2, the construction of 'serviced sites' or of core houses,

---

11 Orangi Pilot Project 1995.
12 Hardoy and Satterthwaite 1989 contains a more detailed review of case studies documenting the failings or limitations of public housing and serviced site schemes.

Box 6.4 *The Orangi Pilot Project in Karachi, Pakistan*

Orangi is a unauthorized settlement with some 1.2 million inhabitants extending over 8000 hectares. Most inhabitants built their own houses and none received official help in doing so. There was no public provision for sanitation; most people used bucket latrines that were emptied every few days, usually on to the unpaved lanes running between houses. More affluent households constructed soakpits but these filled up after a few years. Some households living near creeks constructed sewage pipes that emptied into the creeks. The effort of getting local government agencies to lay sewage pipes in Orangi was too much for local residents who also felt that these should be provided free. Believing that government should provide, they had little incentive to improve their situation.

A local organization called the Orangi Pilot Project (OPP), established in 1980 by Dr Akhtar Hameed Khan, was sure that if local residents were fully involved, a cheaper, more appropriate sanitation system could be installed. Research undertaken by OPP staff showed that the inhabitants were aware of the consequences of poor sanitation on their health and their property but they could neither afford conventional systems nor had they the technical or organizational skills to use alternative options. OPP organized meetings for those living in 10–15 adjacent houses each side of a lane and explained the benefits of improved sanitation and offered technical assistance. Where agreement was reached among the households of a lane, they elected their own leader who formally applied for technical help. Their site was surveyed with plans drawn up and cost estimates prepared. Local leaders kept their group informed and collected money to pay for the work. Sewers were then installed with maintenance organized by local groups.

OPP's research concentrated on the extent to which the cost of sanitary latrines and sewerage lines could be lowered to the point where poor households could afford to pay for them. Simplified designs and the use of standardized steel moulds reduced the cost of sanitary latrines and manholes to less than one-quarter of the contractors' rates. The cost of the sewerage line was also greatly reduced by eliminating the profits of the contractor. The average cost of the small bore sewer system is no more than US$66 per house.

Technological and financial innovations were the easy part. The difficult part was in convincing residents that they could and should invest in their own infrastructure and in changing the nature of local organizations such that they responded to these needs. OPP staff had to wait for two years before the inhabitants of a lane were prepared to organize themselves to develop their own sewage system. Gradually, the residents of other lanes, after seeing the results achieved, also sought OPP's help in developing sewers. There were problems in some lanes and money went missing or was insufficient. In general OPP staff stood back from these issues (once they had persuaded the first communities to begin). Once a lane had ensured that the finance was available, they would provide technical assistance. The first challenge was one that the communities had to realize by themselves.

The scope of the sewer construction programme grew as more local groups approached OPP for help and the local authorities began to provide some financial support. To date, close to 6000 lanes have developed their own sewer system linked to sanitary pour-flush latrines serving over 90,000 housing units, using their own funds and under their own management. One indication of the appropriateness of the model developed by OPP is the fact that some lanes have organized and undertaken lane sewerage investments independently of OPP; another is the households' willingness to make the investments needed in maintenance. The main reason why low-income households could afford this is that the work cost one-sixth of what it would have cost, if it had been undertaken by the state.

Women were very active in local groups; many were elected group leaders and it was often women who found the funds to pay for the sewers out of household budgets.

OPP understood the need to simultaneously improve technical, financial and organizational options. At the beginning they were established to provide a pilot for government. Their experience taught them that government generally had little interest in what they were trying to do. But local residents became more interested and involved, as did their elected representatives who now found they were dealing with people who had a good understanding of infrastructure investments. There are now many project level agreements between OPP, local communities and state agencies. In all of these settlements the state is doing much more than it was before, although it is working within a model of sanitation that has reduced its responsibilities.

The programme is now being replicated in other cities in Pakistan by local NGOs and community-based organizations, and in 49 other settlements in Karachi by the government agency responsible for upgrading the informal settlements, the Sindh Katchi Abadi Authority.

Sources: Hasan, Arif (1989), 'A low cost sewer system by low-income Pakistanis' in Bertha Turner (editor), (1988) *Building Community – a Third World Case Book*, Habitat International Coalition, London; Hasan, Arif (1990), 'Community organizations and non-government organizations in the urban field in Pakistan', *Environment and Urbanization*, Vol 2, No 1, April, pp 74–86; Khan, Akhter Hameed (1991), *Orangi Pilot Project Programmes*, Orangi Pilot Project, Karachi; Hasan, Arif (1999), *Understanding Karachi*, City Press, Karachi.

represents one of the most common 'new' approaches of the last 30 years; it reaches more households than a 'low-cost housing' programme, but many serviced site schemes were ineffective because they were not allocated to low-income households or were inappropriate because they ill-matched the needs of low income households – for instance by being built in locations far from income-earning opportunities. Many were also of poor quality with the chief beneficiary being the contractor that built them, not the household who obtained them. Option 3 is the conventional 'upgrading' approach and its limitations were discussed earlier, especially the limits to improving environmental health if improved water provision is only communal standpipes and no

Box 6.5 DIFFERENT OPTIONS FOR GOVERNMENT SPENDING OF US$20 MILLION ON IMPROVING HOUSING AND LIVING ENVIRONMENTS

Option 1. US$20 million spend on the construction of two-bedroom 'low-cost' housing units 'for low-income groups'. The cost of each unit is some US$10,000, once the land has been purchased, the site prepared, the contractor paid for building the units and the infrastructure and the units allocated. Thus, 2000 households or 12,000 people receive a good quality house – if we assume that on average, there are six persons per household. Cost recovery would be difficult if these were from among the poorer households.

Option 2. US$20 million is spent on a serviced site project, so that more households can be reached than in public housing projects. Knowing that poorer households need to live close to the main centres of employment, a relatively central site was purchased for US$12 million with the other $8 million spent on site preparation and installing infrastructure and services. At a cost of US$2000 per plot, 10,000 households (or 60,000 people) could benefit. It would be easier to recover some costs than in the public housing project but for the poorer households, US$2000 for a site on top of the cost of having to construct their own house would make cost recovery difficult.

Option 3. US$20 million spent on a 'slum and squatter' upgrading programme. To keep down costs and reach as many households as possible, a standard package of improvements is introduced, including the paving of roads and footpaths, the installation of surface drains, the extension of piped water to communal standpipes with provision for washing facilities, and support for the building of some community facilities. The provision of piped water and sewers to each household was not included as this is considered to be too expensive. Unit costs can be kept down to US$200 per household so 100,000 households were reached.

Option 4. A local government agency makes available to any residents' organization formed by the majority of the inhabitants of an area up to US$100,000 for site improvements. These residents' organizations have considerable flexibility as to how they choose to spend these funds and who they turn to for technical advice. For instance, they can use local NGOs for technical advice, as long as certain basic standards are met. Although what can be achieved with US$100,000 will vary greatly depending on site characteristics, local costs and the extent to which residents contribute their skills and labour free, within most informal settlements with 500 households, it should be possible to 'reblock' the site to allow better access roads and to pave them, and also to greatly improve site drainage, water supply and sanitation. Support could be given to local artisans to fabricate the materials, fixtures and fittings that are most cheaply and effectively made on site – for instance, a carpenter's cooperative to make doors and windows or cheap building-block fabrication. Of the $100,000, an average of $150 is spent per household on improved infra-structure and services, with $10,000 spent on technical advice and $15,000 on support for local businesses. The 'reblocking' of the site can also free up additional land, and allow 50 more housing plots to be developed within the existing site or on adjacent land as yet undeveloped, and the cost of providing these with infrastructure and services and of building a commu-nity health centre paid for by selling them.

With US$100,000 provided to 150 community organizations with an average of 500 households (3000 people) the total cost was $15 million and the whole programme reached 150 X 3000 people, ie 450,000 people. Since an average of 50 new housing plots were produced in each reblocking, not only did 450,000 people benefit from improved housing, infrastructure and services, but 7500 new plots with services were developed and new health centres constructed in each site. The possibility of cost recovery was much better than for the other options since it was planned from the outset with households knowing in advance what had to be repaid and under what conditions. Local savings and credit schemes made the repayment easier, so the US$200 that each household had to raise could be repaid gradually. Repayments could also be integrated into charges for water. Spending $15 million in this way still left $5 million from the original $20 million which could be used to improve some city-wide service – for instance, providing medical personnel to run health clinics or investing in the water and sewer mains to which each community could connect the water and sewer systems they installed.

Source: This box was first published in Jorge E Hardoy and David Satterthwaite (1989), *Squatter Citizen: Life in the Urban Third World*, Earthscan Publications, although the text has been modified and developed.

provision is made to improve sanitation. Option 4 represents a more effective model because it seeks to support innovation and action within many different low-income areas. It is not a 'standard package of measures' implemented by external agencies but support for diverse local development initiatives. Its effec-tiveness has been proven by the hundreds of small projects implemented by community organizations with the help of NGOs or church groups over the last 40 years. What it seeks to do is to provide the institution that can support a great range and number of community initiatives within one city.

Consider these four options in a city of one million inhabitants, growing at 5 per cent a year. Each would take several years to implement. Options 1 and 2 would do nothing to improve conditions in existing settlements. Option 1 would not produce sufficient new housing for one year's growth in population and Option 2's 12,000 units would only just do so. Option 3 would reach just over half the city's population with improved infrastructure and services but with no increase in the number of units and the limitations in improvement noted above. Option 4 would reach close to half the city's population and contribute much more than the other options to employment creation. It would increase the capacity of community organizations and support the development of local NGOs as centres of advice and support for low-income organizations and would create almost as many new units as Option 2. Furthermore, US$5 million would be left for investment in improving some city-wide service.

In addition, Option 4 has much better prospects for cost recovery than the other three. In Option 1, there is little chance of much cost recovery if the units are allocated to low-income groups. Option 2 may get some cost recovery, but most serviced site schemes have had a poor record in actually achieving this. Option 3 generally gets no cost recovery directly; most upgrading programmes rely on a quick, standard, public works programme to keep down costs, and cost recovery is considered too difficult or too complex institutionally. Option 4 has far more potential to generate cost recovery, especially if the funds recovered are recycled back into further community improvements.

Approaches like those outlined in Option 4 do not simply save money because local residents contribute labour free (many poor households lack 'free time' to do so because of long working hours). There are generally large savings arising from:

- The elimination of the (often large) profits made by contractors.
- The much reduced time needed for architects, planners, surveyors and other expensive professionals as community consultations work out and resolve such issues as how to move certain houses that stand in the way of access roads or water or drainage pipes (and ensure that the households moved get an adequate alternative) and collect funds from households to pay for the improvements.
- The use of specialized equipment and materials not only for piped water but also provision for sanitation, drainage and all-weather roads and paths (so the costs are shared between these).

The match between what is provided and the capacity to pay is much improved when local community organizations are fully involved in such decisions. Perhaps the most critical need is to ensure that there are local institutions from which community organizations can obtain loans and credits for these kinds of programmes and funds to pay for technical advice; external funding from national agencies or foreign sources could never fund the tens of thousands of such community initiatives that are needed, since even if they had the commitment to provide this, they lack the institutional structure to be able to do so. Here too, the role of local NGOs can be important. These could serve not only as technical advisers to community organizations but also as supervisors of loans or credits.

There are many ways in which a scheme like Option 4 can be realized. One example is the support that the Thai government's Urban Community Development Office provides to low-income communities, both in the forms of loans and of small grants (see Box 6.6).

Box 6.6 THE URBAN COMMUNITY DEVELOPMENT OFFICE (UCDO)

In March 1992, the Thai government approved a budget of US$50 million to initiate an Urban Poor Development Programme within the Seventh National Economic and Social Development Plan. The approval of this budget resulted in the establishment of a new organization, the Urban Community Development Office (UCDO), with responsibility for implementing the programme nation-wide.

The UCDO offers loans to community organizations in low-income urban settlements for income generation, house improvement, developing new housing and small-scale community activities. Its overall objective is to strengthen the capacity of the urban poor and those living in illegal settlements to obtain increased and more secure incomes, appropriate housing with secure tenure, and better quality infrastructure and services. The programme is unusual for the extent to which it supports community-level decision-making and management since the credit is provided to community organizations or federations of community organizations and these are responsible for ensuring loan repayments. Community organizations can draw on a range of different loans – for instance for income generation, for small revolving funds (for instance to provide individual emergency loans), for house upgrading or for developing new housing.

Increasingly the UCDO works in partnership with a range of locally-based development committees that generally include staff from the municipality, academics, religious leaders and NGOs that support the work of local community organizations. The UCDO will fund the committee for up to two years to support people-centred development processes through micro-credit activities. The committees have particular responsibility for strengthening the network of community organizations. As the committees become successful in supporting the networks, they take on more of an advisory and facilitation role.

To supplement the credit programme, the UCDO set up an Urban Community Environment Fund in 1996 that provided small grants to support community-initiated and managed environmental projects within low-income settlements in urban areas throughout Thailand. Drawing on a grant of US$1.3 million from the Danish Government agency DANCED, over a two-year period, this supported 196 low-cost environmental improvement projects – for instance for water supply, drainage, community centres, walkways and waste management. The average cost of each project was just over US$2000. The 196 projects brought benefits to 41,000 families. Although this was a fund managed by a Thai government agency, it allowed low-income communities to choose projects and to manage their implementation. It also encouraged intercommunity exchanges and, more generally, strengthening the capacity of low-income communities to negotiate and work with external agencies.

Source: Boonyabancha, Somsook (1996), *The Urban Community Development Office*, IIED Paper Series on Poverty Reduction in Urban Areas, IIED, London; Boonyabancha, Somsook (1999), 'The Urban Community Environmental Activities Project, Thailand', *Environment and Urbanization*, Vol 11, No 1, April, pages 101–115.

However, there are many institutional constraints that make it difficult to realize an Option 4-like programme. Quite apart from finding a government agency capable of supporting community-driven planning and implementation (and willing to do so), it requires strong local organizations within settlements that are not dominated by community leaders serving their own self-interest and that have a capacity for financial management. Such organizations need to be able to manage potentially divisive debates about priorities and financial obligations. They also need to ensure that all interests are represented. For instance, the priorities of children may be overlooked by even the most well-intentioned adults, unless adequate scope is given for their inclusion in planning and decision-making (Bartlett and others 1999). It is also likely to be more effective if the local authority (and other public agencies) have flexible procedures and regulations – for instance, a willingness to accept that infrastructure improvements will be partial and piecemeal, and that they will help to support the improvements that are made as needed. It requires a pool of professionals who can work with urban poor groups but not distort their priorities or impose their professionally driven agenda. It also requires local government institutions (both officials and politicians) that are willing to provide services more transparently and accountably than has previously been the case. Despite these problems, in a number of cases, NGOs and other development institutions have sought to innovate to support schemes such as these.

DIFFERENT MODELS OF NGO SUPPORT

The need is for NGOs that have the capacity to work with low-income groups and their organizations and/or have the capacity to influence the policies and the practices of local, national and international agencies so the most serious environmental problems get addressed. But the term 'non-governmental organization' is not very specific, and a very large range of organizations describe themselves as NGOs. They range in size from small voluntary organizations operating in a single location providing one service with no paid staff to large multinational organizations or federations (for instance the World Wide Fund For Nature with its many national chapters) and international non-governmental donor agencies with funding programmes of tens of millions of dollars each year. They range in ideology from those set up by powerful corporations to protect their interests (for instance the Global Climate Coalition in the United States funded by oil, coal, motor car and other corporations to play down the threats of climate change because measures to reduce this threat would reduce their profits) to radical anti-business groups or 'deep-green' environmental groups. The extent to which they are 'non-governmental' also varies with, at one extreme, organizations entirely independent of government (and with no reliance on government funding) and at the other, NGOs set up by governments and often staffed by ex-government employees.

Our interest in this chapter is in NGOs that are actively engaged in addressing the most serious environmental health problems in urban areas; Chapter 7 will discuss NGOs with a wider focus. Even within this more limited focus, there are large numbers of NGOs with considerable diversity in the roles they take. These roles are strongly influenced by the nature of government. For instance, in Latin America, from the 1960s to the mid-1980s, many NGOs concerned with urban problems were formed by academics and activists who were opposed to dictatorships, including many of the region's leading urban researchers who had been expelled from universities. Some of the region's best known urban NGOs were formed during this period, and many such NGOs worked with each other on joint programmes of research, seminars and publications. With the move or return to democracy in the region, it became far more common for NGOs to work with government. This was further supported in many countries by stronger local democracy and by decentralization. In addition, many of the urban specialists who were active in NGOs under the dictatorships went into government agencies and some helped to encourage new partnerships between government, NGO and community organizations. Some government agencies were formed or restructured to support the work of NGOs and CBOs. More international agencies recognized the potential for using local NGOs as institutions that are able to develop more effective urban programmes for low-income groups and their community organizations.

To bring out the different ways in which NGOs become active in environmental health issues or other local environmental improvements, four different approaches can be identified:

1   A market orientation, with initiatives to introduce and pay for improved housing, infrastructure and services through market-related mechanisms and local entrepreneurs. Credit often has an important role within this, as it allows low-income households to afford the capital costs of improved infrastructure (or improving their own home), and spread the repayments over time.
2   Welfare approaches with NGOs offering assistance to those in need, often fulfilling a role that government agencies should provide – for instance the provision of water or waste removal.
3   Claim-making on the state with the NGO active in the advocacy of citizen's rights and in putting pressure on local authorities or other state agencies to provide infrastructure or services to the poor.
4   Civil-society driven alternatives through programmes that involve a combination of community and state support to provide or improve housing, infrastructure and services in non-traditional ways.

All four approaches contribute to improving the urban environment in low-income settlements. Table 6.2 summarizes the different approaches, the main focus of their activities and the ways in which they attempt to address these problems.

The first two approaches are generally the most common, with the second also the one most commonly funded by international aid. But the third and fourth deserve more consideration in that they seek to improve local governance, not bypass it.

Table 6.2 *Different NGO approaches*

Approach	Typical activities	Primary focus	Attitude to government	Strategies for increasing scale
Market	Water vending; piped water provision; waste collection and recycling; credit for house improvement	Informal entrepreneurs and cooperatives; households able to repay loans	Government should encourage informal sector provision and support where possible	Improve existing activities among the poor
Welfare	Water, emergency housing, primary health care	Communities in need	Little direct contact, may campaign for better provision	Seek more external funding
Claim-making on the state	Campaigns and pilot projects for environmental justice, housing rights, better services	Decision-makers and policy-makers	Responsibility of government is to provide	Changes in government policy and action
Civil society driven alternatives	All forms of housing improvement and infrastructure and services at level of community	Communities in need	New models of governance to support greater community involvement	Community to community learning. Local partnerships with state agencies

Claim-making on the state. The lack of public recognition of and support for the needs of low-income groups lead to NGOs taking on a 'claim-making' role, arguing for improved provision in a wide range of infrastructure and services both for neighbourhood improvement and for improving access to livelihood opportunities. Success depends on a supportive political environment, especially if new or modified, more 'pro-poor' laws and regulations are to be translated into tangible progress. There are many examples of NGOs (and other civil society organizations) that focus on lobbying and advocacy for greater rights for the poor, including changes to regulations, laws and the distribution of resources. Certain city authorities have deliberately changed their policies or procedures to provide more scope for greater participation of grassroots organization in municipal plans and activities. Examples include participatory budgeting (as pioneered by Pôrto Alegre in Brazil and now also in use in many other Brazilian cities – see Souza 2001), and some Local Agenda 21s in Latin America (including Ilo in Peru and Manizales in Colombia, for which more details will be given in Chapter 7).

Civil-society driven alternatives. This approach is of particular interest in that for NGOs, it combines direct action, working with low-income groups to improve conditions, with a strong interest in improving local governance. Many creative measures to improve environmental infrastructure and services (and address other aspects of deprivation) have been initiated by local NGOs working with organized urban poor groups, based on scaling up self-help solutions.[13] They rely on community-level mobilization, action and management, and in so doing, usually greatly reduce the need for external funding. Most such initiatives start outside of formal government structures, although there are examples of government agencies set up to fund these as in the Thai government's Urban Community Development Office described earlier. Most such initiatives are relatively small, although there are a growing number that have scaled up, because of their capacity to negotiate resources to support this and to support a rapid expansion in the number of local initiatives (often underpinned by community savings and credit groups), combined with a supportive institutional environment and new partnerships with state agencies. Examples include the scale of community development in Thailand supported by the Urban Community Development Office (Boonyabancha 1996, 1999); in India, supported by the National Slum Dwellers Federation, the Indian NGO SPARC and cooperatives of women pavement dwellers (SPARC 1996, Patel and Mitlin 2001), and in South Africa, through the South African Homeless People's Federation and the supporting NGO, People's Dialogue on Land and Shelter (Bolnick 1993, 1996). Or they scaled up, simply because they responded to particular priorities of urban poor households and kept costs down to what these households could afford, as in the support provided by the Orangi Pilot Project for the construction of sewers in Karachi (Hasan 1997).

The methodology developed by the Indian NGO SPARC has particular relevance, and is one that has been followed (with local adaptations) by many other NGOs. This involves two critical components:

- Developing pilot projects with low-income groups and their community organizations to show alternative ways of doing things (building or improving homes, running credit schemes, setting up and running public toilets, organizing community-determined resettlement when low-income households have to be moved).
- Engaging local and national officials in a dialogue with communities about these pilot projects and about how they can be scaled up (or the number of such initiatives multiplied) without removing community management.

The negotiation with government agencies can be done with constant reference to what has already been achieved, and an important part of this is bringing government officials and politicians to visit the pilot projects and talk to those who implemented them. This approach inevitably includes 'claim-making on the state' but by also being able to demonstrate solutions, the engagement with the state is more productive.

---

13 See for instance Anzorena and others 1998; also different issues of SELAVIP News and of the Asian Coalition for Housing Rights newsletter.

The pilot projects also stimulate other groups to initiate comparable actions and there is a constant interchange between those involved in different community initiatives (see Box 6.7). This then leads to work to change local institutional constraints on community initiatives – for instance changing building regulations to enable housing developments to better suit the needs of low-income groups, participating in the design and realization of a new state policy for legalizing and improving housing for the poor in Mumbai, developing community designs for toilet provision and proposing and implementing schemes for the resettlement of urban communities in which the resettled people have a key role in determining the location, timing and form of their relocation (Patel and Mitlin 2001). Community exchanges also serve to stimulate and support initiatives in other cities and nations (see Box 6.7).

The direct contribution of the local communities is increasingly recognized as a key to local environmental improvement. While all four approaches listed in Table 6.2 emphasize the importance of participation and local involvement, the civil-society driven approach is the only one that centres on building local capacity to improve and install services (both for civil society organizations and government institutions). The community organizations and NGOs mentioned above that are involved in civil-society driven alternatives also recognize the heterogeneity within low-income settlements' populations and make provision to ensure that the needs and priorities of the poorer, the less organized and the less articulate groups within 'low-income groups' are addressed. In addition, in all of them, women have a central role, from the lowest level (for instance in the organization and management of savings and credit schemes) to the elected settlement representatives to the staff of the federations and the support NGOs.

NGOs that invest in developing community capacity and in helping other communities to learn from these experiences contribute to the institutional change that is required to secure improvements. The experience of a number of groups suggests that NGOs can contribute to the links between the formal and informal agencies. One of the aspects that government agencies struggle with, in their dealings with low-income communities, is the informal nature of their activities and approaches. NGOs may be important interlocutors, explaining to communities the nature of state regulations and to the state the objectives that communities are trying to achieve. Such a role increases the chance of successful government–community partnerships.

NGOs can also help to change the nature of grassroots organizations to make them more able to support and manage local environmental improvements. Many NGOs have turned to savings as a mechanism to strengthen local networks of trust and reciprocity. The Orangi Pilot Project requires groups to find the finance for improved sanitation before they provide technical assistance. Community-based savings and credit schemes have particular importance in the community organizations within the SPARC–Mahila Milan–National Slum Dwellers Federation partnership that is active in many cities in India. The People's Dialogue on Land and Shelter supports the network of autonomous savings schemes that make up the South African Homeless People's Federation and seeks to represent the needs of their members, primarily black low-income

Box 6.7 COMMUNITY EXCHANGES

One important support for increasing the scale of community-driven initiatives has been community exchanges. The Indian NGO SPARC began supporting these in 1988 with community leaders or organizers visiting other organizers in different settlements within Bombay/Mumbai and subsequently visiting groups in other cities. This was not an exchange of professional staff but of, for instance, the women among groups of pavement dwellers or the inhabitants of illegal settlements who managed their local cooperative savings and credit schemes. *Exchanges work when people who want to learn share their experiences with others facing similar problems or seeking to implement similar initiatives.* The exchanges focus on a shared attempt to solve problems. This direct interchange between community organizers has proved to be a very powerful way of developing and spreading knowledge and of supporting the formation and development of new community initiatives. Community members exchange ideas not only about what they do and how they do it, but also about the strategies that they found useful in negotiating with government and other external agencies. From these discussions, all the groups involved develop insights into how external factors affect opportunities and constraints within their settlement and city.

Community exchanges:

- Increase the confidence of the community organizers as they see what others achieve and reflect on their own achievements. They recognize that they can have a role in their own development.
- Enable learning and knowledge. For those elaborating on their own experience, this helps them to draw lessons from it. The exchange of experience about tactics and strategies with governments helps all groups to learn how to access land for housing more quickly or avoid eviction.
- Strengthen organizational capacity.
- Improve relations with other groups (particularly government agencies).
- Support the acquisition of skills (for instance in building, in building design, in the use of materials and in managing savings and credit).
- Build solidarity between different groups within a city, which helps them to work together to negotiate with a higher level of government and stops them competing with each other for external resources (and stops government playing one community off against another).
- Spread a greater sense of equality; the sharing of ideas puts in place building-blocks for a movement of the urban poor.

Among the groups who have made widespread use of such interchanges are the SPARC–Mahila Milan–NSDF alliance, the South African Homeless People's Federation and the Asian Coalition for Housing Rights. Although most community exchanges are local (for instance between groups within a city) or regional (inter-city), an international dimension also developed. For instance, the visits of community organizers from India were important in helping the development of the South African Homeless People's Federation, while community organizers from this Federation have helped to develop comparable community initiatives and federations in Zimbabwe and Namibia. International exchanges have also proved useful in that they attract the attention of politicians and civil servants, and draw them into discussions about the goals and the work being undertaken. Different organizations involved in developing civil-society driven alternatives (including those also involved in supporting local, regional and international community exchanges) have formed an international umbrella organization, Shack Dwellers International, to help support their work.

Sources: Patel, Sheela, Joel Bolnick and Diana Mitlin (2001), 'Squatting on the global highway' in Michael Edwards and John Gaventa (editors), *Global Citizen Action*, Earthscan-UK/Westview-US; Asian Coalition for Housing Rights (1999), *Face to Face*, Newsletter of the Asian Coalition for Housing Rights, Bangkok.

women. The schemes are held together by regular (daily) saving among members. The Federation has developed strategies for self-build housing and land acquisition and currently 300 groups are building and 8,000 houses have been built, about two-thirds of them partly funded by credit.[14]

However, while local (or international) NGOs can be important supporters of civil society driven alternatives, they can also act as key constraints. They often impose their agenda on communities, in part because they often obtain and control external funding, and retain management and financial control. It is also difficult for professionals to recognize and support the right of community structures and discussions to make key decisions. Or to have the patience to allow community processes to develop their capacity for planning and management. Or to ensure that their NGO is accountable to the community groups with which they work. Many NGOs, by failing to delegate power and responsibility to community organizations, inhibit the development of community capacity. NGOs can also be insensitive to political and power struggles among the inhabitants of low-income settlements. And where local NGOs are dependent on external funding, there are often many contradictions between satisfying the institutional requirements of their funders and supporting and being accountable to community processes (Anzorena and others 1998). In sum, it cannot be assumed that NGOs necessarily support community-driven processes.

Participatory tools and methods

As external agencies (from NGOs and local governments to international agencies) have sought more participatory (or collaborative) ways to work with grassroots organizations, new tools and methods have been developed to facil-

---

14 Many also draw on the government's housing subsidy. See Baumann and others 2001.

itate this. These include more participatory methods of gathering information within low-income settlements and of analysing it and drawing from it in developing responses to problems. They include more scope given to residents to define needs and priorities, and the most appropriate means to address them. More participatory methods have also been developed to evaluate projects (or other externally supported interventions) and to monitor progress. Many professionals have recognized that the use of more participatory methods of information gathering and the information gathered can become a catalyst for a greater involvement by residents and their community organizations.

There are also the constraints on participation that have to be recognized. Most settlements with a predominance of low-income groups are heterogeneous. As in other settlements, they have within them a complex mix of different interests and often power struggles for 'community leadership'. Oppression, discrimination and years of politicians' broken promises have not been conducive to the development of representative community organizations. And inhabitants' previous experience with external agencies has often been anything but participatory, so why should they expect anything different from some new external initiative? If what little support they have received from local authorities or politicians in the past has been a result of patron–client relationships, why change this? And even where municipal authorities are committed to more participatory engagements, they too have many internal constraints inhibiting their capacity to do so (Plummer 2000). There are also all the constraints that individuals face in being able to participate, as most work very long hours. And the reluctance to do so, unless it is seen to provide tangible benefits.

A growing number of case studies show different ways in which participatory tools and methods can be used to identify the main environmental (and other) problems, identify local resources and capacities, and develop more effective responses. These have particular importance for external agencies that recognize the right of low-income groups and organizations to influence their policies, programmes and projects. Or, more pragmatically, that recognize the ineffectiveness of the interventions they undertake or fund if they do not do so. But these tools and methods can also serve low-income groups and their organizations as they seek to map conditions and trends in their own settlement, independent of any external agency. However, as in more general discussions of participation, there is considerable variation in the extent to which the use of these tools and methods allows or supports participation. At one extreme, they can be used by external agencies simply to cheapen the costs of information gathering; at the other, they can be key parts of community-level mobilization, action and management.

Some of the most interesting information-gathering measures have been developed by the NGO–community organization partnerships described above such as SPARC–Mahila Milan–National Slum Dwellers Federation in India and the South African Homeless People's Federation–People's Dialogue for Land and Shelter. These include house modelling and shack counting/community censuses.

House modelling allows a low-income community to develop the kind of house design and the use of building materials that best suit their needs and their capacities to build and to pay. It begins with different community members thinking about and sketching the house that they would like to live in and refining their designs in group discussions. The groups then build a cardboard model of the design on which they agree and develop a detailed costing of how much it would cost to build. The different models then stimulate discussion and debate within the settlement regarding the most appropriate designs. Full-scale models of one or more of the most favoured designs can also be built, using simple wooden frames with cloth used to simulate walls. These full-scale models are often built by large groups of people as part of community consultations or exchanges. The models again serve as the focus for community discussions. Having the possibility of walking into and around a full-scale model house and imagining how it would function in real life often leads to further modifications (Bolnick and Patel 1994).

Community censuses or shack counting are methods by which low-income groups can develop maps and other information about their settlement. Once community leaders have agreed to undertake this, a rough map is prepared, along with a series of photographs to orient those who will undertake the shack counting. Groups of citizens then walk through different areas of the settlement, counting and numbering shacks, shops, churches and other buildings, and noting key landmarks such as rivers, hills, paths, roads, drains and electricity lines. They also talk to people as they do this. These informal discussions of squatter to squatter are very useful in identifying the feelings, frustrations and expectations of the inhabitants. As two staff members from the South African and Indian NGOs that have supported many shack counts note:

> *The informal exchanges [that take place during this count] are the very soul of the process. This simple process of dialogue and exchange only occurs when the people from communities do the counting. The informal discussions that accompany community-driven enumerations are both an outstanding method of mobilization and an exceptionally accurate way of identifying issues that people in the community regard as relevant* (Bolnick and Patel 1994, page 24).

The different groups that have undertaken the counting then return to work together to develop a detailed map of the settlement. Such maps are particularly valuable for discussions about needs and priorities. They are also useful for developing any community-driven development programme or for use in developing actions with external agencies. For instance, a detailed plan of the settlement allows discussions of how best to modify roads, paths and buildings to allow the installation of water pipes, sewers and drains.

Three other examples are given below, to illustrate different ways in which participatory tools and methods can be used:

1　To identify environmental (and other) risks in low-income areas, drawn from a case study in communities close to industries in Durban (Nurick and Johnson 1998).

2   To develop an environmental plan in a low-income settlement to serve as the basis for environmental improvements and for obtaining legal tenure, drawn from a case study in a low-income settlement in Lima (Hordijk 1999).

3   To develop indicators through which residents can assess and monitor the performance of external agencies in infrastructure and service provision and press these agencies for improved performance, based on a case study in four low-income settlements in Lucknow (Revi and Dube 1999).

The identification of environmental risks in Durban was undertaken through consultations with community groups that live close to areas of heavy industry. This was part of the development of Durban's Local Agenda 21. The consultations asked participants to identify the positive and negative attributes of their areas, including those relating to industrial impact. These consultations highlighted the range of environmental risks in each area (along with other problems) and how their range and relative importance differed from location to location. Although industrial pollution was the top concern only in areas with better housing and living conditions and lower crime rates, all groups included pollution from industries in the top half of their ranking of issues that affected their quality of life. Among the environmental issues highlighted by community consultations were high levels of air and water pollution and noise (both from industries and from the transport linked to them), the need for conservation of open spaces and local ecology, and the risk of accidents from explosions, lorries and toxic (or otherwise hazardous) wastes. Many specific examples of industrial pollution were highlighted, including the residents in three areas close to oil refineries regularly having oily deposits on their cars, roofs, washing and kitchens. The consultation process also highlighted how citizens now felt able to protest against industrial pollution when under the previous apartheid regime, any protest would have been repressed (Nurick and Johnson 1998).

The environmental plan in Lima was developed in Pampas de San Juan, a recently settled zone on the city's periphery. In this informal settlement, created by a land invasion, the inhabitants had created many communal works such as roads, staircases (as the site has many steep slopes) and communal spaces for a crèche, communal kitchen and community meetings. For the settlers to obtain legal tenure and the possibility of public provision of infrastructure, they needed to develop an urban plan. Most settlers in Lima commission professionals to prepare maps and plans but these are often inaccurate and of low quality, and this often leads to poorly designed development plans. In Pampas de San Juan, a plan was developed through a consultative process. Workshops were held where the inhabitants identified the most serious problems and suggested the most appropriate ways to address them. These led to a consultative process through which many people helped to develop plans showing the good and the bad sites (and the neighbourhood's strengths and weaknesses) and also the kind of neighbourhood environment they wanted. Asking everyone to begin by drawing their own maps allowed everyone to express their own concerns and hopes for the future, but the individual maps then served as the

Table 6.3 *Government–community partnerships in addressing health risks in urban areas*

Health risks	Action at individual and household level	Public action at neighbourhood or community level	Public action at district or city level	Action at national level
Water, sanitation, drainage and refuse collection				
Contaminated water: typhoid, hepatitis, dysenteries, diarrhoea, cholera, etc *Inadequate disposal of human wastes:* pathogens from excreta contaminating food, water or fingers leading to faecal-oral diseases or intestinal worms (eg hookworm, roundworm, tapeworm, schistosomiasis)	Protect water supply to house; promote knowledge of hygienic water storage Support for construction of easily maintained WC or latrine that matches physical conditions, social preferences and economic resources. Washing facilities to promote hand washing	Provision of water supply infrastructure; knowledge and motivation in the community Mix of technical advice, equipment installation and its servicing and maintenance (the mix is dependent on the technology used)	Plans and resources to undertake or support action at lower levels, including, where appropriate, funding to support community-directed provision for water, sanitation and drainage. Trained personnel and finances to service and maintain them	Ensure that local and city governments have the power, funding base and trained personnel to implement actions at the household, neighbourhood, district and city levels. Review and where appropriate change legislative framework and norms and codes to allow and encourage actions at lower levels, and ensure that infrastructure standards are appropriate to the needs and the resources available. Support for training courses and seminars for architects, planners, engineers etc, on the health aspects of their work
Waste water and refuse: waterlogged soil ideal to transmit diseases like hookworm; pools of contaminated standing water, conveying enteric	Provision of storm and surface water drains on house plot and spaces for storing waste that are rat-, cat-, dog- and child-proof	Design and provision of storm and surface water drains. Advice to households on materials and construction techniques to make houses less damp. Consider feasibility of community-	Regular removal or provision for safe disposal of household wastes (including support for community schemes) and plan framework and resources for improving drainage	

diseases. Waste water can provide breeding ground for mosquitoes spreading filariasis, malaria and other diseases. Waste water attracting disease vectors	level waste collection which includes recycling			
Insufficient water for domestic hygiene: diarrhoeal diseases, eye infections (including trachoma), skin diseases, scabies, lice, fleas	Adequate water supply for washing and bathing. Provision for doing laundry at household or community level	Health and personal hygiene education for children and adults. Facilities for laundry and bathing at this level, if not within each house	Support for health education and public facilities for laundry	Technical and financial support for educational campaigns. Coordination of housing, health and education ministries
House structure *Disease vectors or parasites in house structure* with access to occupants, food or water, eg rats, cockroaches, mosquitoes or other insects (including the Chagas' disease vector in Latin America)	Support for improved house structure, eg tiled floors, protected food-storage areas, roofs, walls and floors protected from disease vectors	Technical advice and information, part of adult and child education programme. Where appropriate, support for community-level savings and credit schemes	Loans for households to upgrade shelters (including small ones with flexible repayment term) or support for community-level credit schemes. Guarantee supply of cheap and easily available building materials, fixtures and fittings; support for building-advice centres in each neighbourhood	Ensure building codes and official procedures to approve house construction or improvement are not inhibiting individual, household and local government actions. Support for nationwide availability of building loans, cheap materials (where possible based on local resources) and building-advice centres. Produce technical and educational material to support this

Table 6.3 *continued*

Health risks	Action at individual and household level	Public action at neighbourhood or community level	Public action at district or city level	Action at national level
Inadequate size house and poor ventilation: helps transmission of diseases such as tuberculosis, influenza and meningitis (aerosol drops) especially when many households share premises. Risks of household accidents increased with overcrowding; impossible to safeguard children from poisons, open fires and stoves	Technical and financial support for house improvement or extension and provision of cheap sites with basic services in different parts of the city to offer poorer groups alternatives to their current shelters	Technical advice on improving ventilation and lessening indoor fumes and smoke. Education on overcrowding-related diseases and accidents	As above	As above
Air pollution *Indoor air pollution* due to open fires or poorly designed stoves and smoky fuels. These cause or exacerbate	Posters/booklets on improved stove design and improving ventilation	Ensure that availability of designs and materials to build improved designs	Consider extent to which promotion of alternative fuels would lessen problem	

Issue				
respiratory illnesses, especially in women and children *Outdoor air pollution*		Identify major sources of ambient air pollution within each neighbourhood and seek to limit their emissions	Act to control main sources of ambient air pollution	Ensure legislative framework allows urban authorities to effectively control ambient air pollution
Nutrition *Nutritional deficiencies and low income:* nutritional deficiencies can be addressed by higher incomes, better access to food and reducing diseases that rob the body of nutrients. Inadequate intake of certain micro-nutrients is a particular problem in many locations	Reduce intestinal worm burden and worm transmission. Appropriate treatment for diarrhoea and worms. Support for income-generating work within the house	Food supplements and/or meals or community kitchens where appropriate. Action to address micro-nutrient deficiencies where needed. If land is available, support food production (urban agriculture can be very effective in increasing incomes and/or increasing food intake)	Support for local enterprises and appropriate nutrition programmes; support urban agriculture where possible and relevant	Structural reforms, funds for nutrition programmes and other measures to improve poorer groups' real incomes
House sites *Children's exposure to environmental hazards:* playing in and around house site constantly exposed	Day care services to allow care and supervision for children in households where all adults work; these can also contribute much to	Provision within each neighbourhood of well-drained site, separated from traffic, kept clean and free from waste and easily	Support given to neighbourhood-level play, sport and recreation facilities	Support for city/local governments with information and advice on recreation and play, provision for child development

Table 6.3 *continued*

Health risks	Action at individual and household level	Public action at neighbourhood or community level	Public action at district or city level	Action at national level
to hazards from traffic, unsafe sites (eg slopes, open drains) or sites contaminated with pollutants or faeces	learning and health	supervised for children's play. Ensure first aid services are to hand		
House sites subject to landslides or floods as a result of no other land being affordable to lower-income groups	Regularize each household's tenure if danger can be lessened; relocation through offer of alternative sites as last resort	Action to reduce risks of floods/landslides or to reduce potential impact; community-based contingency plan for emergency. Encourage upgrading or offer alternative sites	Ensure availability of safe housing sites that lower-income groups can afford in locations accessible to work	National legislation and financial and technical support for interventions by local and city governments in land markets to support action at lower level. Training institutions to provide required personnel at each level
Illegal occupation of house site or illegal subdivision with disincentive to upgrade, lack of services and mental stress from fear of eviction	Provide secure tenure and ensure adequate provision for piped water, sanitation and storm and surface drains	Local government working with community to provide basic infrastructure and services, and incorporation into 'official city'	Support for incorporating illegal subdivisions and for providing tenure to squatter households	As above

Health services			
No or inadequate access to curative/preventive health care and advice	Widespread availability of simple primer on first aid and health in the home plus home visits to promote its use	Primary health care centre; emphasis on child health, sexual and reproductive health, preventive health and support for community action and for community volunteers	Small hospital (first referral level) and resources and training to support lower level services and volunteers	Technical and financial support for nationwide system of hospitals and health care centres. Preventive health campaigns (eg immunization) and nationwide availability of drugs and equipment Set up training system for paramedics and community health workers. Provide guidelines for setting up emergency services and planning and risk minimization in risk-prone areas to minimize injuries and damage if disaster occurs
No provision for emergency life-saving services in the event of injury or serious illness	As above, backed by educational programmes on minimizing risks Discussions with individuals and community organizations about some minimum changes to site layouts to improve emergency vehicle access and create fire-breaks	Basic equipment (eg stretchers, first aid) available at all times. Community volunteers with basic training on call and arrangements for rapid transfer of sick/injured person to hospital. Equipment to rescue/treat those saved from burning houses	Support for neighbourhood equipment plus organization of training programmes for community volunteers. Fire-fighting equipment. Ambulances. Contingency plans for emergencies	As above

basis for group discussions to develop a shared perspective. There was a surprising degree of agreement with regard to what people wanted, and it proved possible to develop an integrated plan based on these drawings and discussions. This plan was again subject to community discussion. It needed to broker agreement on potentially divisive issues such as introducing roads, stair-cases and inter-settlement connections which meant that each neighbourhood had to sacrifice some of their area. This finally produced an agreed plan that neighbourhood leaders could present to the public agency from which the inhabitants could receive official titles to the land they occupied. Once tenure was secure, various projects were begun, contributing towards the realization of the plan, including the design of a park (in whose design and realization a group of teenagers has the key role) and the construction of sports grounds and community centres (Hordijk 1999).

The initiative in Lucknow (India) used community consultations to develop a set of indicators on infrastructure and service provision which were then presented to the agencies that were meant to provide infrastructure and services. This showed the gap between what residents prioritized and the indica-tors used by external agencies to monitor their performance. It also showed the potential for developing a dialogue (and even a working partnership) between the agencies and the inhabitants of settlements with very inadequate provision of infrastructure and services, and also for developing a more appropriate set of indicators to monitor and evaluate the quality of provision (Revi and Dube 1999). This illustrates how community consultations can allow public, private or NGO service providers to learn how to make their systems for monitoring performance more participatory and more accountable to their customers. It can also help to resolve conflicts – for instance by identifying forms or methods of payment that low-income households can afford and that are also accept-able to infrastructure and service providers.

There are now a well-developed set of tools and methods that can be used to gather and analyse information about conditions, trends and resources within settlements, including:

- Collective modelling of house designs or settlement plans (as described above).
- Collective identification of resources covering such issues as income, assets and links to rural areas and also who has access, management and control of these.
- Transect walks with groups walking through settlements with a particular goal (for instance identifying the scale and scope of informal sector activi-ties or reviewing housing conditions) and discussing informally with people they meet what they are doing and drawing out their concerns.
- Wealth ranking and well-being analysis.
- Trend analysis or life histories to bring about an understanding of processes. In trend analysis, long-term residents are asked to plot, in diagrammatic form, when particular developments occurred and how populations or conditions changed over time. These can then be developed through small group discussions.

- Institutional analyses of relations with other local and external groups and organizations, which can use Venn diagramming to show the relative importance of each such group or organization to the person or group developing the analysis.
- Matrices that can include scoring and ranking to identify, analyse and compare different resources and development options, and develop priorities.
- Social dramas and role plays, acted out by local people to provoke discussion about opportunities and constraints facing community members (Mitlin and Thompson 1994).

Many of these can serve as information sources in their own right or provide the information to stimulate group discussions. Participatory research usually uses a mix of these and other tools. But research is not participatory just because it uses some of these tools; researchers using such tools have to ask themselves searching questions such as who is defining the research questions, who takes part in the research, who controls the information generated and how it is used to get action on the problems the research identified.

AN INSTITUTIONAL FRAMEWORK TO SUPPORT LOCAL ACTION ON ENVIRONMENTAL HEALTH

To end this chapter, Table 6.3 seeks to illustrate the kinds of combined actions through which different groups working at different levels can address the main environmental health risks faced by lower-income groups. The column on the left lists the most pressing health risks; other columns summarize the actions needed at different levels: individual and household; neighbourhood or community; district or city; and national. The table highlights:

- the importance of action at all levels, from individual and household to community to city and regional level;
- the importance of national authorities providing the framework that encourages and supports actions at city, neighbourhood and local levels;
- the extent to which improved health depends on better quality housing with adequate basic services for low-income groups and thus why the 'public's' health depends on programmes that inevitably fall outside 'public health agencies' – for instance programmes to ensure that low-income households can obtain land on which to construct a home and can obtain credit and other forms of support in doing so.

However, the table is only an illustration of the range of measures that contribute to good public health. The most appropriate mix of actions will vary considerably from place to place.

The cost of the actions summarized in this table are not beyond the means of most governments, but they do imply a change in the nature of governance. In discussing the political economy of urban poverty and environmental management in Asia, Mike Douglass (1992) stresses the need, above all, to increase poorer groups' access to key economic and environmental resources, and to empower households and communities to participate as active decision-makers in the use and management of resources. But, as he states, this implies significant changes in the institutional arrangements and practices underlying government–community relations; most governments in Asia (and in Latin America and Africa) remain highly centralized, even if most are less so than they were ten years ago. Many are also working actively to deny the legitimacy of political associations emerging from civil society (Friedmann 1990) and as such are actively disempowering the kinds of actions summarized in Table 6.3. The new kinds of relationships described earlier in this chapter change the nature of governance not by broadening out those participating at the top but by changing relations between the citizen and the community organization, and between the community organization and the state such that power is dispersed downwards.

In addition, few city or municipal governments have shown themselves capable of developing the means to achieve the integration between different policies and financial investments that an effective environmental policy requires. In most countries, the institutional structure for addressing environmental problems is not only weak and ineffective but also divided into different technical departments with little coordination (Douglass 1992). Ironically, the fact that resources are so scarce actually requires municipal governments in low- and middle-income countries to be more sophisticated, innovative and flexible than those in high-income countries. Ideally, each house should be provided with piped water and connection to a sewer (or other good quality provision for sanitation), and each residential area with paved pathways and access roads, electricity and storm-rainwater drainage. There should be regular collection of household wastes, nutrition programmes for vulnerable groups (where needed) and comprehensive healthcare and emergency life-saving services. But this may be too expensive and local governments in consultation with citizen's organizations must make pragmatic choices as to where limited funds should be spent and what government–citizen–NGO partnerships can make limited funding go the furthest. They need considerable sophistication and sensibility to detect the major health problems and to design and implement appropriate interventions.

However, there are many more examples of innovation by city authorities in supporting a multiplicity of community organizations and the NGOs that work with them. The urban basic services programme in Cebu (Philippines) is notable for the range of NGOs involved in it with the government providing the logistics, technical support and legislation, and NGOs managing projects and providing social services; city government has also sought to be more responsive to the demands of CBOs and coalitions (Etemadi 2000). The city authorities in Ilo (Peru) have supported a multiplicity of community initiatives to ensure much improved basic infrastructure and service provision for much of the city population (Follegati 1999), as described in Chapter 7. The 'Healthy Cities' programme in León (Nicaragua) is an example of a bottom-up, community-driven 'healthy cities' programme (Montiel and Barten 1999).

To conclude this chapter and reflect again on the role of privatization, the issue is certainly about making the suppliers of environmental infrastructure and services more responsive to consumer demands. It is about local government giving the 'private sector' a greater role in decision-making, service provision and increasing their influence in determining priorities. But this 'private sector' includes a wide range of community organizations and of non-profit professional groups that pioneer new ways of working with them and with developing community–government partnerships.

Chapter 7

Tackling City-Wide Problems

**Marisol Rodriguez and her mother Eloisa collect tins from the
municipal dump in Matamoros, Mexico**
Photo © Janet Jarman, all rights reserved

TACKLING CITY-WIDE POLLUTION

The last 20 years have shown that polluting emissions can be controlled and
solid and liquid wastes managed (and often reduced). Major improvements are
possible to urban environmental quality simply through more attention to
implementing existing pollution control and occupational health legislation,
and better use of existing infrastructure and equipment – for instance minimizing water losses in piped systems and giving more attention to maintaining
public service vehicles (whether buses, waste-collection trucks or trucks that
empty latrines and septic tanks). In many cities, air pollution levels can be
reduced substantially by ensuring that some of the largest polluters limit their

emissions. Promoting use of cleaner fuels in households, industries and motor vehicles can, over time, reduce concentrations of various air pollutants.

Towards clean industries

Measures to ensure that new industrial and power station investments use, wherever possible, new plant designs that eliminate or minimize wastes also cumulatively build a less polluting industrial sector. Numerous new industrial plant designs eliminate or reduce polluting wastes or recover and reuse process chemicals that were formerly dumped (Phantumvanit and Sathirathai 1986, Robins and Kumar 1999). For most industrial operations, a substantial reduction in pollution is possible for a small fraction of production costs and often with reduction of costs and increased profits (Schmidheiny and others 1992, von Weizsäcker and others 1997).

Wastes not amenable to elimination through changes in plant design and operation can often be used as inputs into other industries. Organic residues, usually among the most bulky of solid wastes and among the most serious sources of water pollution, can be used as feedstock for the manufacture of packing materials, chemicals and pharmaceuticals, fertilizers, fuel, food and construction materials (Vimal 1982). Wastes from many agro-processing industries can be valuable feedstock for other industrial operations. Smaller industries may find it more costly to install waste-treatment equipment, but central waste-treatment plants can often serve many medium and small companies. A central waste-treatment facility established in Vaniambaddi, India, serves a few dozen tanneries and recovers and properly disposes of chromium salts from waste waters; the industries pay 75 per cent of the costs and government the rest (Halter 1991). Box 7.1 highlights the shifts in thinking about the regulation of industrial production that move from controlling pollution to reducing wastes, to institutionalizing environmental management within production, and finally to industry taking responsibility for the environmental impacts not only of their factories but also of their suppliers and products.

The key to improving industry's environmental performance is not only appropriate legislation on air and water pollution and waste management (and its enforcement), but also measures to increase industry's accountability. An independent judiciary to which citizens and public interest groups can turn to demand the enforcement of environmental legislation or to hold enterprises or government agencies to account for damages arising from pollution is also important.[1] Other measures include requiring enterprises to disclose details of their environmental performance to the public or government agencies, publishing details of their environmental performance and measures to encourage voluntary improvements (Robins and Kumar 1999). Government agencies can also support citizens' efforts to ensure that pollution-control legislation is enforced; for instance, when political circumstances in Cubatão allowed

---

1 The latest *State of India's Environment Report* (*The Citizens' Fifth Report*, Agarwal and others 1999a) includes a chapter on the importance of the judiciary in India in getting more attention to enforcing environmental regulations, closing polluting industries and other environmental measures. It also discusses its limitations and the measures taken to address these.

Box 7.1 *FOUR STEPS TO SUSTAINABLE INDUSTRIAL PRODUCTION*

	Firm	*City*	*Nation*
Step 1: Control	End-of-pipe technology	Relocation	End-of-pipe regulation
Step 2: Efficiency	Cleaner production	Collective environmental services	Environmental assessment
Step 3: Institutionalize	Life-cycle environmental management	Eco-industrial estates	Integrated pollution control
Step 4: Restructure	Zero emissions	Carrying-capacity planning	Extended producer responsibility

Source: Robins, Nick and Rita Kumar (1999), 'Producing, Providing, Trading: Manufacturing Industry and Sustainable Cities', *Environment and Urbanization*, Vol 11, No 2, pages 75–93.

---

organized citizen protest and an elected state government, the state environmental protection agency worked with citizens' organizations that were trying to stop the pollution (Lemos 1998). Recent World Bank papers even suggest that incorporating community pressures and market forces within industrial pollution-control strategies represent a new paradigm (Afsah and others 1996, World Bank 1999b), although community pressure has a rather longer history than this implies as a key pressure on industry to reduce pollution.

One measure that has encouraged reduced industrial pollution in various high-income countries is legislation requiring companies to report publicly on their annual emissions of toxic chemicals. In the United States, such requirements (as part of the Toxic Release Inventory) encouraged many companies to take waste minimization measures while also giving inhabitants living close-by the information that allowed them to press for improved environmental performance (Robins and Kumar 1999). Egypt and Mexico have pilot 'Pollutant Release and Transfer Registers', although covering fewer chemicals than in the United States and focusing on those with relatively high hazard ratings (World Bank 1999b).

A World Bank report on 'Greening Industry' highlighted how the Indonesian government's pollution control agency has had some success in reducing industrial pollution by rating and disclosing the environmental performance of factories (World Bank 1999b). This Programme for Pollution Control, Evaluation and Rating (PROPER) classifies factories on five levels:

- Gold: clean technology, waste minimization, pollution prevention.
- Green: above standards and good maintenance, housekeeping.
- Blue: efforts to meet minimum standards.
- Red: efforts do not meet standards.
- Black: no pollution-control effort and serious environmental damage.

In a pilot programme begun in 1995, the agency rated 187 plants for the water pollution they generated. At first, public disclosure centred on publicly praising plants whose performance exceeded formal requirements, and giving those that were not in compliance six months to clean up before publishing details of their performance. There was some improvement in performance before the initial public disclosure with further improvement in the following year. The value of community pressure was also demonstrated when a plant originally praised for achieving a 'green' level of performance was demoted to black as the community reported its heavy night-time pollution. PROPER is now being expanded to cover more plants and it hopes to rate factories on air pollutants and toxic wastes as well as water pollution (World Bank 1999b). A comparable programme has been implemented in the Philippines, is being developed in Mexico and Colombia, and is planned in several other countries (World Bank 1999b).

Another important part of improved pollution control and waste minimization is voluntary action by companies. Many companies have made public commitments to improved environmental performance and there are a growing number of codes of conduct issued by industries at sectoral and national levels. This has also been encouraged by agreed international standards. The International Organization for Standardization's ISO14001 standard requires companies to have an environmental policy, to assess their environmental aspects and legal obligations, to install a management system, to carry out periodic internal audits and to publicly declare that ISO14001 is being implemented. Growing numbers of companies in China, India, South Korea, Malaysia and Thailand are certified as having met these standards, and further growth is expected as many international corporations ask their suppliers to seek certification. But companies applying ISO14001 standards do not have to commit to reducing pollution (or other aspects of improved environmental performance), only to continuous improvement of the environmental management system. ISO14001 also does not require companies to report publicly on their environmental performance (Robins and Kumar 1999).

A final noteworthy innovation is interindustry working groups or task forces within cities which can also become the means by which city authorities encourage improved environmental performance. An example comes from Surat in India. In the early 1990s, this had become one of India's most successful cities, but also one in which industrial pollution was not controlled and a basic investment in water, sanitation and solid waste-management was not made. This set the conditions for the plague which struck the city in 1994 and thereafter, state and city authorities came under pressure to address environmental problems, including enforcing pollution control laws for the many textile industries. In 1994, a waste-management group was set up by textile processors, dyestuff manufacturers and academics. This group sought to minimize waste generation and to create awareness of the benefits of pollution prevention and control. It disseminated information on the benefits and costs of environmental audits and waste minimization and prepared safety data sheets for 200 chemicals and dyes used by local textile manufacturers. It also carried out environmental impact studies for the textile industry, prepared manuals on energy and water conservation and launched waste minimization demonstration projects. Various plants within Surat found that pollution control and waste minimization brought substantial savings (Modak 1998, Robins and Kumar 1999).

Reducing air pollution

In most cities, much of the air pollution from industries comes from relatively few (often old) factories or power stations; substantial reductions are possible by improving equipment, adding pollution-control equipment, or moving or closing the worst offenders. For instance, in the mid-1980s, in Mexico City's Metropolitan Zone, of the 35,000 industrial emission points, just paint factories and one oil refinery were responsible for most industrial hydrocarbon emissions, four thermal power stations were responsible for around 30 per cent of sulphur dioxide emissions, and cement plants were responsible for a high proportion of total particulates (SPP 1984). New designs for power stations burning coal or heavy oil can greatly reduce sulphur dioxide emissions and increase the efficiency with which the fuel is converted into useful energy. Governments, utilities or private companies building power stations, or building or expanding heavy industry plants now have a wider array of 'cleaner' technologies on which to draw.

Reducing air pollution from road vehicles is also possible through more efficient engines, mandatory annual checks for all vehicles (so engines are kept properly tuned) and a move to lead-free petrol. There may also be scope for promoting better quality fuels that reduce emissions for diesel and two-stroke engines (Wangwongwatana 1992). Increasing taxes on petrol can promote more fuel-efficient vehicles while providing valuable revenue; differential tax rates can be used to promote the use of lead-free petrol by making it cheaper. The widespread availability of lead-free petrol is also essential for vehicles with catalytic converters (which can reduce up to 90 per cent of the emissions of oxides of nitrogen, hydrocarbons and carbon monoxide from car exhausts) since these cannot use leaded petrol. Combine such measures with regulations on the use of private vehicles and efficient public transport, and the problems of pollution and traffic congestion can be tackled at the same time. A judicious mix of taxes and physical restrictions on private cars, improved facilities for the other most commonly used forms of transportation (from trains and buses to communal taxis and rickshaws, to bicycles and feet) and better traffic management can reduce congestion and greatly increase the efficiency of the whole transport system at relatively little cost.[2] The Brazilian city of Curitiba's greatly improved transport system also brought lower levels of air pollution and per capita fossil fuel use, lower accident rates and a lower citizen expenditure on transport (see Box 7.2).

Many of the more modern and rapidly expanding industries such as electronics do not require the large consumption of natural resources and lack

---

2 The Sustainable Transport Action Network for Asia and the Pacific (SUSTRAN) has a regular e-mail newsletter about innovations in transport of relevance to their region; see www.geocities..com/Rainforest/Canopy/2853

the potential contribution to air, water and land pollution of, say, the steel or pulp and paper industries.[3] This has helped to cut industrial emissions in Europe and North America and may also do so in the more successful industrializing low- and middle-income nations. Service enterprises also account for a large and increasing proportion of the economic base which implies fewer problems with pollution and heavy resource consumption.

All cities need to develop their own framework for urban air-quality management which draws on an effective monitoring network and is based on an inventory of polluting emissions (Elsom 1996, WHO 2000). Such inventories should allow assessments as to the relative contributions of different sectors and sources to different pollutants, including the identification of those that are the sources of the primary pollutants and the precursors of the secondary pollutants that have the most serious health impacts. There are very large differences between cities in the scale and relative importance of the different pollutants, and considerable differences in the relative contribution of different sectors; there are also large differences in the extent to which these represent a health risk and in the people within the city who are most at risk. All cities obviously need legislation which sets air-quality standards (which may be the responsibility of national or provincial governments) and the institutional capacity to enforce them.

Many cities have instituted special measures to limit or stop short-term peaks in air pollution. When the concentration of particular pollutants (or combinations of pollutants) reaches a certain threshold, the public is warned and may be asked to limit the use of cars. When higher thresholds are reached, more stringent measures can be taken, including closing down certain industries and mandatory restrictions in car use (Elsom 1996). Some cities implement control measures for periods when pollution levels are particularly high, as in, for instance, the *Rodizio* programme in São Paulo which included a ban on the use of each private car once a week and requires more stringent testing of vehicle emissions; this improved air quality, reduced congestion and significantly increased bus speeds (Jacobi and others 1999). Such special measures are often linked to indexes of air quality that are more easily understood by the public than the full list of pollutant emissions and guidelines. For instance, Santiago de Chile's index based on measures of carbon monoxide, sulphur dioxide, nitrogen dioxide, ozone and PM_{10} results in air quality being classified as 'good', 'regular', 'bad', 'critical' or 'dangerous'. The authorities have the powers to close down particular industries and restrict motor car use, during periods or days when air quality is poor, and with industries organized into different categories according to their emissions, so more can be closed down if air quality is particularly bad (Rodriguez and others 2000). Many cities now have pollution indexes with figures published daily which can be linked to voluntary and mandatory measures to reduce emissions when air quality is getting worse. These are useful short-term measures but, as a study of the

---

3 Note should be made that parts of the electronics industry do have special pollution and waste-handling problems, but these are not on a comparable scale to traditional heavy industry and their resolution is likely to be much cheaper, relative to the value of production.

Box 7.2 *Public transport and other environmental initiatives in Curitiba, Brazil*

Curitiba's innovative public transport system is one among several initiatives to improve environmental quality and reduce resource use. The improvements in public transport also depended on complementary initiatives in planning and land-use management which are rarely included in descriptions of the city's achievements.

The public transport system, developed over the last 30 years, began with the use of express buses on exclusive busways on axes radiating out of the city centre. These proved much cheaper and less disruptive than conventional metro or light railway systems. Over the years, these axes have been further developed, helping to link the different municipalities within the broader metropolitan area, and urban growth has been encouraged along them. There are five main axes, each with its 'trinary' road system. The central road has two exclusive bus lanes in the centre for express buses and is flanked by two local roads. Each side of this central road, one block away, are high-capacity, free-flowing, one-way roads, one for traffic flowing into the city, the other for traffic flowing out. In the areas adjacent to each axis, land-use legislation has encouraged high-density residential developments, along with services and commerce. The express buses are served by interdistrict buses and conventional feeder buses.

With a more deconcentrated pattern of employment, central city areas could be pedestrianized and historic buildings protected from redevelopment. Several main thoroughfares have been closed to traffic and converted into tree-lined walkways. One important complementary action was the municipal government's acquisition of land along or close to the new transport axes, prior to their construction. This allowed the government to organize high-density housing programmes close to the transport axes; in all, some 17,000 lower-income families were located close to these.

There are now 58 km of express lines, 270 km of feeder lines and 185 km of interdistrict lines. Buses are colour coded: the express buses are red, interdistrict buses are green and the conventional (feeder) buses are yellow, and transfers and ticketing between them is fully integrated; a single fare is valid on all buses and those travelling long distances (mostly low-income groups) are subsidized by those making shorter trips. There are large bus terminals at the end of each of the five express busways where people can transfer to inter-district or feeder buses. Along each express route, smaller bus terminals are located approximately every 1,400 metres and are equipped with newspaper stands, public telephones and post office facilities. There are also 'direct' express buses, with fewer stops and where passengers pay before boarding in special raised tubular stations. These new stations (with platforms at the same height as bus floors) cut boarding and deboarding times; a rapid bus system with 'boarding tubes' can take twice as many passengers per hour or three times as many as a conventional bus operating in a normal street. Payment before boarding eliminates the need for a crew to collect fares and frees up space for more passengers.

The public transportation system is used by more than 1.9 million passengers each day. Some 28 per cent of express bus users previously travelled by car. The system has brought savings of up to 25 per cent of fuel consumption city-wide and contributed to one of the lowest levels of ambient air pollution in Brazil. Curitiba's transport policy has also contributed to one of the lowest accident rates per vehicle in the country and considerable savings for inhabitants in expenditure on transport (on average, residents spend only about 10 per cent of their income on transport which is relatively low for Brazil).

Other environmental initiatives in Curitiba include innovative waste-recycling programmes and sewage-treatment facilities, a large expansion in parks and green spaces (integrated into a flood-prevention and control programme), and the combination of environmental education and day-care provision in the low-income favelas. The city has an average of 52 square metres per person of green space. The 'Waste that is not Waste' recycling programme encourages city residents to separate organic and inorganic waste. Once a week, a lorry collects waste materials that households have sorted. By the early 1990s, over 70 per cent of the community was participating in the programme, due largely to a city-wide environmental education programme. Of the refuse collected 13 per cent is recycled and the recycling schemes are spreading to neighbouring municipalities within 'Greater Curitiba'. Since its inception, over 400,000 tonnes of refuse have been recycled; its paper recycling alone saves the equivalent of 1200 trees a day. This programme has generated other positive side effects, including support for social programmes from the income earned through the sale of the recyclable waste.

There is a 'Purchase of Rubbish' programme run in the favelas with no household waste-collection service. Many settlements lack access roads to permit trucks to enter and the residents would simply dump their rubbish in open-air pits or vacant plots. Residents can now 'sell' their bags of waste for bus fares and agricultural and dairy produce. The cost to the city is equivalent to paying a private company to collect the waste. More than 22,000 families in 52 communities are benefiting. Green exchanges also encourage people to bring recyclable rubbish that can be exchanged for food, toys and educational materials.

Sources: Rabinovitch, Jonas (1992) 'Curitiba: towards sustainable urban development', *Environment and Urbanization*, Vol 4, No 2, October; the website www.curitiba.pr.gov.br, consulted on 30 September 2000.

Rodizio programme in São Paulo points out, more fundamental measures are generally needed (Jacobi and others 1999). Such measures also need accurate pollution inventories, a widespread acceptance of the measures needed by industrial concerns and car owners, and an institutional capacity to implement them.

Box 7.3 *Mexico City's Clean Air Policy*

1982   First Federal Environmental Legislation (Ley General de Equilibrio Ecológico y Protección al Medio Ambiente) established some norms for industrial emissions. Inspections undertaken selectively by the Ministry for Health (Secretaría de Salubridad y Assistencia) but to little effect.

1986   The above legislation re-formed into the Ley General de Equilibrio Ecológico y Protección al Ambiente (LEGEEPA). The Ministry for Urban Development and Ecology now in charge of inspections. About 6000 industrial inspections carried out between 1986 and 1992.

1986   Introduction of new petrol with additive to reduce lead emissions.

1989   Introduction of unleaded petrol.
Introduction of 'HOY NO CIRCULA' banning all cars from the road in the Mexico City metropolitan area once a week, and twice weekly and at weekends when pollution reaches dangerous levels.

1990   Introduction of yearly emissions-testing for vehicles in Mexico City.

1990   First Integral Programme against Atmospheric Pollution in Mexico City Metropolitan Area (Programa Integral Contra la Contaminación Atmosférica en la ZMCM (PICCA)). The main measures arising out of this have been:

1991   Closure of oil refinery situated in central Mexico City.

1991   Obligatory catalytic converters in all new cars.

1991   Improvement of fuel by PEMEX (on-going).

1991   Prevention of vapours in petrol stations (on-going).

1991   Substitution of diesel by natural gas for industry, including main power station. By 1997, 84 per cent of industry had converted to natural gas.

1992   Creation of the Federal Prosecutor for the Environment (Procurador Federal de Protección al Ambiente (PROFEPA)). This is now in charge of inspecting industrial emissions, among other things, and prosecuting where necessary. The number of inspections between 1992 and 1997 increased to 69,076, 43 per cent of which were in Mexico City's Federal District, resulting in 2340 total or partial closures and 54,261 fines.

1992–   Conversion of commercial cargo vehicles to liquid petroleum gas.
98   (In 1998, about 30,000 commercial vehicles were powered by privately distributed propane gas.)

1994   Stricter emissions controls on all new vehicles.

1994   Frequency of obligatory vehicle emissions-testing increased to six-monthly periods.

1994   Revised and stricter industrial emissions norms.

1996   Programme to Improve Air Quality in the Mexico Valley 1995–2000 (Programa para Mejorar la Calidad del Aire en el Valle de México (PROAIRE)). Major resulting measures:

Stricter emissions-testing with three qualification levels:
1 Vehicles subjected to normal once-a-week ban plus three times a week in times of pollution emergency.
2 Vehicles only subjected to normal once-a-week ban.
3 Vehicles exempt from any restrictions (post-1993 models only).

1996 LEGEEPA re-formed, widening federal jurisdiction in industrial regulation and imposing stricter fuel and emissions standards for industry and services, especially for nitrogen oxides and volatile organic compounds.

1998 Programme to Reinforce Actions to Improve Air Quality in the Mexico Valley (Programa para Fortalecer las Acciones de Mejoramiento de la Calidad del Aire en el Valle de México). Implications for 1999:
- Stricter vehicle emissions standards (for hydrocarbons and carbon monoxide) aimed at eliminating pre-1985 models which constitute 50 per cent of all vehicles in circulation but contribute 80 per cent of the pollution).
- Exemption from six-monthly emissions-testing for two years for 1999 models that meet a more rigorous standard for oxides of nitrogen per kilometre travelled.

Stricter emissions standards for industry and revision of industrial register.

Criteria for declaring pollution emergencies changed to when:
- ozone exceeds 2.4 times the acceptable norm; or
- PM_{10} exceed 1.75 the acceptable norm; or
- ozone exceeds 2.25 and PM_{10} exceed 1.25 their acceptable norms.

Source: Connolly, Priscilla (1999), 'Mexico City: our common future?', *Environment and Urbanization*, Vol 11, No 1, April, pages 53–78.

Box 7.3 draws on Priscilla Connolly's (1999) analysis of Mexico City's environmental problems in describing the evolution of the city's clean air policy and illustrates the need for concerted action on many fronts. As she points out, although Mexico City has long had serious problems of air pollution, it has never warranted the label as the world's most polluted city. But it has had particularly serious problems with air pollution as one of the world's largest urban agglomerations, with a very large concentration of motor vehicles and industries. Its high altitude means that fuel combustion is less efficient and its valley location, surrounded by mountains of up to 5000 metres in height, limits winds that would otherwise disperse air pollution. Its altitude and subtropical location means there is plenty of sunlight which contributes to photochemical reactions, and it also experiences frequent temperature inversions during its winter season (Connolly 1999, Elsom 1996). Mexico City's clean air policy has reduced pollution levels considerably, especially those arising from industry. It is also one of a number of cities that have emergency measures brought into force when air pollution levels are particularly high, and these have virtually eliminated the high peaks of occasional extreme pollution. But even with all the measures listed in Box 7.3, ozone levels were still 1.7 times the acceptable limit in 1997 and air quality was still not meeting official norms (Connolly 1999).

But all these measures towards controlling air pollution (and other forms of pollution) are unlikely to happen without constant citizen pressure. The comment by Jockin noted in Chapter 1 is worth recalling – that democratic government provides more possibility of supportive response to organized demands by citizens, but will not do so unless these demands are organized by broad and representative coalitions or federations. Box 7.4 is a summary of the suggestions by Anil Agarwal, founder and director of India's Centre for Science and Environment, in reply to the large response he received from an article he had written in *The Hindu* in India about air pollution in Delhi.

URBAN AGRICULTURE

The importance of urban agriculture to food and fuel production and its contribution to the diet/food security and income of poor (and non-poor) urban households is underestimated by most public authorities. But this is changing, in large part due to the work of the Urban Agriculture Network, on whose work this section is based.[4] There has also been a very considerable increase in the literature available on this topic since 1992.[5]

Urban agriculture is 'an industry that produces, processes and markets food and fuel, largely in response to the daily demand of consumers within a town, city or metropolis, on land and water dispersed throughout the urban and peri-urban area, applying intensive production methods, using and reusing natural resources and urban wastes, to yield a diversity of crops and livestock' (Smit and others 1996, page 3). It is central to the lives of tens of millions of urban dwellers, and contributes to the food and livelihoods of a much larger number. It is common for between a quarter and a half of all households in African cities to be engaged in some form of urban agriculture, as documented in, for instance, Ouagadougou, Yaounde, Nairobi, Maputo and Lusaka (ibid).

In most cities, there is a great variety of different 'urban farmers' from

> ... *a woman with a family who has lived in town for several years, grows vegetables and raises small livestock to feed her family and earns income from sales within the community to wealthy producers of specialized crops for expensive restaurants and export, agribusinesses with plantations and out-grower contracts, fishermen cooperatives, 'Saturday only' part timers who grow*

---

4 This section draws heavily on Smit, Jac, Annu Ratta and Joe Nasr (1996), *Urban Agriculture: Food, Jobs and Sustainable Cities*, UNDP, New York. This is available from UN Publications, 2 UN Plaza DC-2-853, New York, NY 10017, USA. This book also has details of the Urban Agriculture Network, including the names and addresses of resource people. A new edition of this book is also due shortly.
5 See 'Further Reading', page 433.

Box 7.4 *Citizen Action for Pollution Control*

Following the huge public response to his article in the Sunday magazine of *The Hindu* published on 23 January 2000 on 'pollution is snuffing us out', Anil Agarwal (of the Centre for Science and Environment) suggested some guidelines for citizens to take up the fight against air pollution in cities.

The main points made in his letter to those who responded are reproduced below.

One thing to remember about controlling air pollution is that you and I as individuals can do precious little. What we can do is to press the government to take the necessary action. In this struggle, we have only two solutions: one, to work with the media and the courts in the best democratic traditions to put pressure on the government, and the other is to undertake *dharnas*, or other tools of mass agitation to force the government to act. Both these are legitimate strategies, but the Centre for Science and Environment (CSE) has no experience in taking recourse to the latter. We have not even organized a cycle rally. We are a knowledge-based activist organization and we constantly generate information that will challenge the government to act. We have always found the media extremely supportive, and we have always found the learned judges of the Supreme Court and the High Courts very willing to listen. Judges are not experts in pollution control. They need good advice from the petitioners on what orders to pass. We will do our best to help you regardless of the strategy you choose.

Keeping the above in mind and our own experience, I would suggest the following:

a) *First, form a small but good group of people who want to take up the cause on a voluntary basis.* This group should meet regularly and try to study and understand the nature of the air pollution problem in your city, whether the main cause is power stations, industry or vehicles or all put together. The first job would be to put together a small 15–20 page report on the *State of Air Pollution* in your city or village. This report will give an authoritative basis to your work and you can use it to get journalists to write articles about the problem. If you had some technical people, like professors in a local college, to help you, that would help you a lot. Many academics often get very excited by such efforts, and are more than willing to provide time. CSE will gladly help you with whatever information it has on your city and other relevant information, and also a general format for your report which you can modify to suit your needs.

b) *Second, you should build linkages in the society.* Find out and meet journalists interested in the problem. Tell them about your work and get them interested. Try to find out if any officials are interested and prepared to help you. Just seek an appointment and go and tell them about your work. You just might find one or two who will be prepared to give you help. Find lawyers in your city who can give you free legal advice and take up your case pro bono, if necessary. Nothing of this is difficult. It just means meeting and talking to people, and it is often more fun than frustrating. You may be surprised with the sympathy and support you get. You must also meet a lot of doctors and find out whether they are finding health effects of the air pollution like increasing asthma among children. Information on health impacts is very powerful. And doctors making statements can have a big impact.

c) *Next, you must build up informed, I repeat, informed local public opinion.* The public must come to grips with precise information rather than some generalities because they don't lend themselves to any action. Your State of Air Pollution report will help you to spread information about the precise nature of the problem and of solutions. No one can ever be perfect but it helps to be as precise as you can. I sit on an authority that has the mandate to give orders to the Central and State governments on what to do to clean up Delhi's air. None of us as yet has enough information to know how this can be done with precision, but in two years we have done our best to identify key actions with as much precision as we can. So precision will come with time. It evolves. But make every effort not to advocate sloppy decisions. Study before you write or say anything. What you don't know, admit you don't. What can you do? Give lectures in schools and colleges to rope in teachers and students, at the local rotary clubs to speak to business persons, local residents' associations, at the local chapter of the Indian Medical Association, etc. Apart from giving our information, always ask for volunteers for your campaign at these meetings. You will be amazed at the response you will get.

d) *At some stage, when you feel confident, meet the local officials and possibly the state minister as a group and prod them to take action.* Inform the press that you did this so that pressure on them increases. If the major polluter is an industry or a power station, you should also go and request its top management to cut down its pollution. Always meet the person at the top. Never waste your time with people below. They will always pass the buck. Industry requires pushing but it ultimately responds to public pressure. So keep it on.

e) *Finally, of course, if nothing happens your only option is to go to court.* Find yourself a good pro bono lawyer. We could also try to find you one if you can't, but our reach is small. But generally more and more lawyers are coming forward to help.

So tell me how you respond to the above. I am convinced that if committed citizens' groups take up the cause we will lick the problem. The biggest problem with the country is that there is very little informed citizens' action.

Source: Centre for Science and Environment (2000), *A Citizens' Guide to Fight Air Pollution*, CSE, Delhi.

cassava by the roadside and market gardeners with yearly contracts with
supermarkets and hotels (Smit and others 1996, page 4).

Plot sizes also vary enormously, from large-scale operators who may rent 10 hectares in an industrial zone, to a small-scale farmer making a living on as little as 200 square metres, to a household garden that may cover 20 square metres or less (ibid). There are also differences between the farming practices of low-income and high-income urban farmers; monocropping is more common among wealthier farmers (eg mushrooms, shrimp or flowers for export) while lower-income urban farmers tend to choose multicrop farming systems that require low capital and minimize risk. In many cities and smaller urban centres, there are easy-entry/easy-exit opportunities for urban or peri-urban farming as low levels of capital, inputs and skills are required and these make them attractive to individuals with few resources, but urban farming often evolves into a stable source of family income.

The term urban agriculture includes a great variety of products grown or livestock raised in small spaces such as rooftops, balconies and small backyards, and it is common for high-value products to be grown in these – for instance medicinal herbs grown on rooftops in Santiago de Chile, silkworms on balconies in Delhi, pigeons in Cairo, rabbits in informal settlements in Mexico City, and orchids in houses in Bangkok. Snails, ornamental fish and ornamental plants may also be grown. A visit by one of the authors to an inner city *kampung* in Surabaya in 1998 found fighting cocks and singing birds being raised as both generated more income per unit space than more conventional forms of urban agriculture. In Mexico City, demand for turf, ornamental plants and traditional foods from middle class households and tourists have helped to increase the scope for urban, suburban and peri-urban agricultural producers (Losada and others 1998). Urban agriculture often includes various forms of 'value-added' which are important for the incomes of those engaged in it – for instance many women are not only urban farmers but also engaged in processing their produce (preserves, spices, relishes, salsas and dried food) for family and for the market, and often they are also engaged in selling.

Urban agriculture is often so much part of the urban landscape that much of it may not be noticed – for instance the diverse, intensive household systems that take place within the home and backyard. Box 7.5 gives an extreme example of the productivity and diversity of a one-household system. But even outside the home, much urban agriculture goes unnoticed and unrecorded – fruit trees along streets, crops grown on slopes in low-density areas of the city or alongside roadsides and rights-of-way, and in areas not suitable for building such as flood-plains, wetlands, steep slopes, airport buffers and bodies of water. Schools, hospitals, women's groups and churches often have community gardens. Smit and others (1996) include many case studies of groups engaged in urban agriculture, including a cooperative of 100 poor women in Jerusalen, outside Bogota (Colombia's capital), who grow up to 30 different varieties of hydroponic vegetables on contract for a supermarket chain on roof-tops and other household surfaces. Hydroponics has two great advantages – it is safe from water and land pollutants, and since production is soilless, it does not depend on land space.

Table 7.1 *Farming systems common in urban areas*

Farming system	Product	Location or technique
Aquaculture	Fish and seafood, vegetables, seaweed and fodder	Tanks, ponds, streams, rivers, cages, estuaries, sewage lagoons, wetlands
Horticulture	Vegetables, fruit, compost	Home sites, parks, rights-of-way, roof-tops, containers on patios or walls, hydroponics, wetlands, greenhouses
Livestock	Milk and eggs, meat, manure, hides and fur	Zero grazing, rights-of-way, hillsides, coops, peri-urban open spaces (also back-yards and cages for small livestock such as rabbits, guinea-pigs, chicken)
Agroforestry	Fuel, fruit and nuts, compost, building materials	Street trees, home sites, steep slopes, vineyards, green belts, wetlands, orchards, forest parks, hedgerows
Other	Houseplants, medicine, beverages, herbs, flowers, insecticides	Ornamental horticulture, roof-tops, containers, sheds, beehives/cages, greenhouses, rights-of-way, urban forests

Source: Smit, Jac, Annu Ratta and Joe Nasr (1996), *Urban Agriculture: Food, Jobs and Sustainable Cities*, UNDP, New York.

The particular form that urban agriculture takes and the scope for its development varies, depending on, among other things, the nature of the city and its surrounds, the formal and informal rules governing who can use open land or water (and on what terms), the natural resource base available for its support, the economic circumstances, the time constraints on potential farmers and fish-rearers, and their knowledge of how to profitably engage in such activities. In some African and Asian cities, one influential factor is related to the colonial heritage (Douglas 1983); the lack of planning and infrastructure provision in the 'indigenous quarters' of colonial cities (usually kept strictly segregated from the residential areas of the colonial elite) permitted newly arrived rural settlers to develop urban settlements with house forms and plans similar to their rural settlements. The very limited income-earning opportunities open to most such people also encouraged indigenous food production.

In certain cities, perhaps most especially in China, the policies and attitudes of public authorities have greatly enhanced the role of urban agriculture. In China, this builds on an ancient tradition of urban agriculture that has long used sophisticated methods of crop rotation, interplanting, intersowing and the use of human and animal wastes as organic fertilizer, and has been developed and encouraged since 1949 (Honghai 1992). The remarkable scale and value of food production so often reported in Chinese cities may owe much to the fact that such production is considered within large administrative boundaries for city regions that include large amounts of rural area rather than the boundaries of the built-up area. Nonetheless, the public authorities have encouraged this synergy whereas its potential in other countries is often lost or diminished as agricultural land on city peripheries is purchased as speculative

---

Box 7.5 *HOUSEHOLD AND COURTYARD FARMING IN URBAN AREAS IN CHINA*

Fish and livestock-raising, vegetables and fruit can be grown together in small urban courtyards. One example comes from the courtyard of Yang Puzhong, located on the outskirts of Bozhou in Hebei Province. This courtyard is only 200 square metres in size. At the centre is a fish pool, 20 square metres in size and 2 metres deep where carp, black carp, grass carp, loach and turtle are raised. Around the pool is a grape trellis that produces more than 1000 kg of grapes a year. On one side of the pool is a pigeon house and a pigsty with about 40 pigeon and 8 pigs. Above the pigsty is a chicken-house with 20 chickens and on top of the chicken-house, a solar water-heater. Below the pigsty is a methane-generating pit. On the other side of the pool is a small vegetable garden that supplies the family with vegetables all year round. Chicken droppings are used to feed the pigs, nightsoil is used to generate methane for cooking and liquid from the methane pit is used to feed the fish, with the remainder used as manure for farmland or as a culture medium for mushrooms.

Intensive cultivation is also evident in many other cities. For instance, in Shanghai, China's most populous city, there are increasing numbers of backyards, roofs, balconies, walls and vacant spaces near houses being used to develop such agroforestry systems as orange tree/vegetable/leguminous plant, grapevine/gourd and melon/leguminous plant and Chinese tallow tree/vegetable/leguminous plant.

Source: Honghai, Deng 'Urban agriculture as urban food supply and environmental protection subsystems in China', paper presented to the international workshop on 'Planning for Sustainable Urban Development', University of Wales, 1992. This drew from Li Ping, 'Eco-farming on Huaibei Plain, *Beijing Review*, Vol 34, No 28, 1991, pp 8–16.

---

investments (and no longer farmed). There are also examples of public entities that have leased urban land for agriculture – for instance hospitals in Lima and the University of Manila (Smit and Nasr 1992).

In many cities in Africa, the scale of urban agriculture owes less to government policy (which may actively discourage it) and more to a combination of relatively low-density cities with open spaces suited to urban agriculture and the high proportion of households with low incomes for whom the returns from urban agriculture are attractive. For many urban dwellers in Africa, access to land on which crops can be grown is an essential part of their livelihood and food so produced is an important part of their nutritional intake.

There are important city-wide benefits from urban agriculture, in addition to the obvious benefits to those involved in urban agriculture in terms of food, fuel or income. They include the relatively low-energy intensity of the food produced, compared to conventional commercial food-production systems; they often include the intensive use of organic wastes from household refuse that reduces waste volumes and reduces (or eliminates) the need for artificial fertilizers. For instance, in Calcutta, vegetable farms developed on refuse dumps where the mixture of organic refuse, coal ash, street sweepings and animal dung have allowed intensive production and these farms, combined with farms in adjacent villages that use garbage as fertilizer, provide some 150 tonnes of vegetables each day to the city (Furedy 1990a). In many cities, peri-urban agriculture also serves as a cheap and effective means of providing treatment for sewage (Furedy 1990a, Smit and others 1996). Again, in Calcutta, fish-farms have long been functioning in the wetlands to the east of the city which are fed by the city's sewers and storm drains; the large, shallow ponds are fringed with water hyacinth (on which cows graze) and sustain several types of carp and tilapia (Furedy 1990a). In Tunisia, official policy has supported the use of waste water coming out of sewage treatment plants for urban agriculture; the crops irrigated include fruit trees, forage crops and cotton, and it is illegal to irrigate vegetables (Pescod 1992, quoted in Smit and others 1996). The potential costs – for instance the health risks for urban agricultural workers and for those consuming its products in fertilizing fields and crops with sewage can be minimized through avoiding certain crops and through good practice in waste-water use, and management and worker protection (Mara and Cairncross 1990, Birley and Lock 1998).

As Smit, Rattu and Nasr (1996) describe in more detail, urban agriculture can also bring wider environmental advantages. It can help to protect soils and so reduce erosion and sediment-laden run-off that often clogs drainage channels. Appropriate cultivation on deforested hills can prevent soil erosion and create farmable terraces. Urban agriculture can provide green spaces and improve micro-climates – for instance through a combination of provision for urban agriculture and for parks, playgrounds and other areas of open space. It can be used to transform unsightly and unused vacant plots (that so often become illegal dumping grounds for wastes). In most cities, there are examples of urban agriculture producing additional environmental benefits – for instance residents in a low-income settlement in Nairobi created a banana plantation to protect themselves from flash floods and to produce income from the sale of bananas, assisted by a local NGO. Composted household waste was also used for soil renewal (Smit and others 1996).

There are also environmental problems that can arise from urban agriculture or its products, including:

- The production of food or food products that are unsafe or contaminated.
- The production of wastes that pollute land sites or water sources, especially from livestock and from crop production with the high use of fertilizers and agricultural chemicals. Intensive livestock production can be particularly problematic, unless livestock wastes are reused as manure for soils.
- Diseases from animals.
- Freshwater resources pre-empted by urban agriculture reducing availability for other uses.
- The ecological changes brought by urban agriculture increasing risks from disease vectors (for instance for *Anopheles* mosquitoes).

- The use in urban agriculture of polluted water (although this is generally more of a problem for those working in urban agriculture than those who consume its products).
- High levels of risk for many of those working in urban agriculture. For instance, the level of risk of exposure to agro-chemicals is usually higher in intensive farming and horticulture than in traditional farming. Some farming practices can also contribute to erosion and flooding.

However, as Smit and others (1996) and Birley and Lock (1998) emphasize when reviewing these potential problems, most generally arise from inadequate or no government regulation or from inappropriate government policy. For instance, urban agriculture may increase the risk of introducing new mosquito-breeding sites but it need not do so if appropriately designed. There is a widespread belief that cereal crop production does so (which is one reason for governments trying to stop urban agriculture) but this is not so since the *Anopheles* mosquito requires sources of open and relatively unpolluted water to breed (Birley and Lock 1998).

CITY-WIDE PLANNING AND MANAGEMENT

Chapters 5 and 6 and the above sections of this chapter have outlined different components of city-wide environmental management. These include:

- ensuring the availability of infrastructure and services, with the appropriate framework to encourage, support and supervise local providers (including public and private sector enterprises, NGOs and community-based providers);
- waste management with a stress on waste-reduction and on reuse and reclamation, within a regulatory framework that ensures that businesses take responsibility for their own wastes;
- environmental regulations to control occupational exposure and air and water pollution;
- building codes and regulations that ensure good health and safety standards among homes and commercial and industrial buildings and encourage waste-reduction measures;
- managing the availability, use and development of land in ways that meet multiple goals, including ensuring that sufficient land is available for housing and economic expansion (and avoiding the expansion of settlements on land ill-suited to development), avoiding urban sprawl, ensuring sufficient land for public facilities, sport, recreation and children's play, and protecting watersheds and other land areas with important environmental functions.

There are obvious conflicts of interest within each of these, and often between them. It is the task of city-wide planning and management (and the political and institutional structures within which they operate) to reach the best possible match for these multiple goals and, obviously, to include in this the needs and priorities of those that are often excluded (low-income groups in general or particular groups, infants and children, future generations, and, in many societies, women).

The last 20 years have brought considerable innovation in the tools and methods that can help to ensure better city-wide environmental planning and management, including the needed coordination between different policies and actions; these are summarized in Box 7.6. Many were developed to make environmental planning and management more responsive to local needs, and more accountable and transparent to the local population, but their appropriate use will obviously depend on the quality of governance. Each tool also has the potential to be used in ways that protect or promote the interests of higher-income groups or exclude lower-income groups. The most appropriate mix of tools and methods will also vary greatly from city to city.

Local Agenda 21s

The importance of Local Agenda 21s

One of the most significant innovations in addressing urban environmental problems since we prepared the first edition of this book (in 1991) is the emergence of a new kind of city-wide initiative to address environmental problems – the Local Agenda 21. At base, a Local Agenda 21 is about 'good governance' for the environment and development. At its best, it is a means by which environmental issues become more integrated with development concerns within the planning and management of an urban area. It usually involves the development of a particular document – the Local Agenda 21 – but the significance of the document should be that it was developed through a broad, inclusive consultation process that helps to develop consensus between different (often conflicting or competing) interests. The consultation process with its potential to develop consensus and to secure more intersectoral cooperation is as important as the documents it produces; without it, the Local Agenda 21 cannot succeed. Local Agenda 21s have particular importance because they can help to address many weaknesses or limitations in local development planning and environmental management. They also have some potential to integrate global environmental concerns into local plans.

Local Agenda 21s can become ways of:

* Institutionalizing consultation, participation and accountability. Local Agenda 21s should be developed through consultative processes that involve all 'stakeholders'. They should be organized in such a way as to develop a broad consensus on the key problems and how these should be addressed. As such, they help to develop agreement between diverse groups in which all citizens have a real say in how resources are used. *Environmental planning moves into the public arena as it shifts from being something determined or driven by professionals to something developed, discussed and influenced by public consultation.* However, Local Agenda 21s should also draw more on the knowledge of local professionals. As will become evident in the cases discussed, knowledgeable professionals and their institutions (including universities

and NGOs) have a critical role, but more as organizers and stimulators of debate and discussion and advisers on scientific or technical issues, and less as 'planners'.

- Integrating concerns for the environment and for development. Local Agenda 21s should provide a means through which citizen concerns and priorities for environmental quality become more influential in government, both in the use of government resources and in government regulation and control of private sector development. Where significant sections of a city's population suffer serious environmental health problems – for instance from industrial pollution or lack of provision for water, sanitation, drainage and garbage collection, by being inclusive and set up to be able to be shaped by citizen pressure – the Local Agenda 21 should help to ensure that these problems receive a higher priority. By being inclusive, they should also guard against too elitist a concern for the environment.
- Ensuring that plans are inherently local as they are driven by local concerns, although they should take into account the regional concerns (discussed in Chapter 5) and national and global issues, particularly regarding resource use and waste generation (although these need guidance from higher levels of government and also international agreements as will be discussed in Chapter 8).
- Ensuring coordination and cooperation between different government agencies, as they involve the different public bodies or agencies active within any locality (including those responsible for infrastructure and service provision, land-use planning and management and environmental regulation). Effective Local Agenda 21s help to ensure coordination between these (including between sectors and between different levels of government).
- Tapping what one former US president referred to as that 'vision thing' – for instance pride in a locality's natural resources and cultural heritage, and in the quality of its governance (including its Local Agenda 21) and a commitment to protecting or enhancing things for the future.

However, there are two great limitations for Local Agenda 21s. The first is that their effectiveness depends on accountable, transparent and effective local government, although they can also become a means for making local government more accountable, transparent and effective. The second is their weakness in ensuring adequate attention to the environmental issues beyond those of environmental quality for local inhabitants – for instance the transfer of environmental costs to other people and other ecosystems, both now and in the future (although here too, some Local Agenda 21s have certainly promoted more attention to this). But before discussing these constraints, some details are given about the development of the concept and its application.

The development of Local Agenda 21s

The term Local Agenda 21 comes from Agenda 21, the document formally endorsed by the government representatives attending the UN Conference on Environment and Development (also known as the Earth Summit) in Rio de

Box 7.6 *The range of techniques that can contribute towards environmental planning and management*

Economic tools and regulatory systems. It is increasingly common for market-based tools to be used with pollution control regulations to encourage consumers, firms and governments to reduce pollution or waste. These include:

- Charging polluters with government agencies' levying charges according to the scale, nature and intensity of the pollution. (This can include the use of permits that allow firms to trade pollution rights.) This needs an effective regulatory system.
- Full-cost pricing to recover hidden costs and/or to promote conservation – for instance car taxes that cover all the indirect costs that car use brings (pollution, accidents); deposit charges repaid when wastes are returned for reuse or recycling (eg on bottles, batteries, tyres, used oil); and prices charged for water, sewers and waste collection which reflect the full cost of providing these within good environmental management. Care is needed to avoid making market, subsidy and taxation reforms socially regressive.

Land use and strategic urban planning. A range of tools can be applied to limit urban sprawl (with its many costs including loss of agricultural land, increasing infrastructure costs, contribution to car-dependent cities), promote mixed land uses (ie within each locality a mix of residential, employment, leisure, health care and education), ensure land availability for low-income households wishing to develop their own homes and prevent the development or redevelopment of inner cities and other areas simply displacing all poor groups. These tools include mixed use zoning, planning gain and, transport planning (with appropriate provision for pedestrians and cyclists whose role increases within mixed use communities where low-density sprawl is prevented). These can also be used to help to preserve a city's cultural heritage and to ensure sufficient provision for green space (including provision for urban agriculture) and trees (with their multiple environmental benefits such as noise-barriers, windbreaks and capacity to lower temperatures).

Transport planning and management. This requires city-wide measures to control pollution and integrate land-use controls and provision for public transport (as illustrated in Box 7.2 for Curitiba). In more wealthy cities, road-pricing and petrol taxes can also be used but integrated with land use and transport planning. Within each locality, measures can be taken to control car use, including speed restrictions, pedestrianization and improvements for bicycle users and pedestrians.

Site planning and building design. Encouraging environmental considerations in site and building design can bring various advantages – for instance building designs that minimize the need for heating and/or cooling, and site designs that meet needs for open space and allow water infiltration, limiting the need for expensive drainage. There is often a need to change environmental and building controls which establish unrealistically high or inappropriate standards.

Waste management. There is often considerable potential to promote waste reduction or its reuse or recycling. Waste-management frameworks should also encourage enterprises to consider the potential cost-savings from low or no-waste production systems. Supporting waste reclamation, including community-based schemes.

Demand-side management and supply-side improvement. Instead of assuming that investments must be made to meet the projected growth in demand, this explores the administrative and technical ways in which existing resources and infrastructure could be used better. One example is good transport planning, with improved public transport (supply-side improvement) combined with pricing systems for private cars and fuel use which keep down growth in road traffic and so reduce the need for new road investment. It is not only about resource conservation but about delivering appropriate, efficient, good quality services at the lowest possible price. Its stress is on improving system efficiency in parallel with extending system capacity.

Environmental Impact Assessments. Typically these are independently conducted studies commissioned to examine the likely impacts of a proposed project. They seek to identify the key environmental conditions of a site (covering the natural environment, built environment and human impacts) to assess the key aspects of damage that is likely to arise from the proposed development, including assessing alternative ways to diminish adverse impacts. Some consider the likely distributional impacts of costs and benefits; many also provide an assessment of how the proposed project links to existing land use and environmental regulatory systems.

Strategic environmental impact procedures. These developed as the limits of the site-based environmental impact assessments were recognized. These generally consider the likely environmental impacts of a range of projects or a policy or plan and consider the additive effects that these might have.

Capacity studies. These can examine the scope for introducing new forms of human activity to any area – for instance new housing or a new industrial estate. They have similarities to strategic environmental impacts but with a greater concern for mapping out the quality of a locality's environment and its carrying capacity. One key role for them is to identify critical (ie not readily replaceable or substitutable) and non-critical stocks of resources.

Environmental audit procedures. Now increasingly used by large organizations (including businesses, universities and local governments), these assess an organization's internal procedures, including purchasing policies to see the potential for changes to improve environmental performance – for instance to improve energy efficiency, minimize waste and increase recycling. These can be applied more broadly to whole corporations or to all the operations of a local government, or more specifically to a particular building (including residential dwellings).

State of the Environment Report. These are often developed as the first stage of an environmental audit for local governments as they look at the whole area under its jurisdiction. Typically such reports outline baseline conditions, attempt to set meaningful targets for improvement, assess priorities and allocate lead roles for bringing about change. Many Local Agenda 21s include State of the Environment Reports (see the section below for more details). These may also seek to clarify the links between the city and the wider regional or global environment, and incorporate concepts such as ecological footprint analysis (see Chapter 5).

Indicators of sustainable development. At their best they involve the use of readily measurable indicators of local environmental conditions which also embrace issues of social welfare and health. They should be reported on regularly and also involve considerable discussion and education. At their worst they can be technocratic, incomprehensible and useless, including long lists of indicators for which data is difficult or expensive and only readily appreciated by experts.

Statutory plan consultation. One important part of any good statutory plan-making process is public consultation at various stages of design, from initial principles and broad concepts to final suggestions. The statutory system can be adapted to make it more transparent and open, and to bring the process closer to communities and businesses – for instance through the use of visioning workshops and open meetings.

Source: This is based on a background paper prepared by Graham Haughton for the preparation of guidelines on the urban environment for the OECD Development Assistance Committee. Part of this background paper was published in Haughton, Graham (1999), 'Information and participation within environmental management', *Environment and Urbanization*, Vol 11, No 2, pages 51–62.

Janeiro in 1992. The text of Agenda 21 had been drafted in a long and complex preparatory process prior to the conference itself. It represents the most substantive document to come out of this conference. In the words of the introduction, it is intended as 'an action plan for the 1990s and well into the 21st century, elaborating strategies and integrated programme measures to halt and reverse the effects of environmental degradation and to promote environmentally sound and sustainable development in all countries'. Agenda 21 contains 40 chapters divided into 4 broad sections: social and economic dimensions; conservation and management of resources for development;

strengthening the role of major groups; and means of implementation. Box 7.7 outlines some of Agenda 21's main points that are related to environmental problems in cities.

Local Agenda 21s are seen as the means by which each locality develops its own sustainable development plan. The text of Agenda 21 recognizes that such local action plans are central to its achievement:

> *Because so many of the problems and solutions being addressed by Agenda 21 have their roots in local activities, the participation and cooperation of local authorities will be a determining factor in fulfilling its objectives. Local authorities construct, operate and maintain economic, social and environmental infrastructure, oversee planning processes, establish local environmental policies and regulations and assist in implementing national and sub-national environmental policies. As the level of governance closest to the people, they play a vital role in educating, mobilizing and responding to the public to promote sustainable development* (28.1).

Although this might overstate the actual role of most local authorities, the recognition of the role they should have in both development and environmental management is important. Local Agenda 21s are seen as the means by which most of the measures contained in the 40 chapters of Agenda 21 are to be implemented. Agenda 21 includes guidelines for developing Local Agenda 21s within a chapter entitled 'Local Authorities Initiatives in Support of Agenda 21' (Chapter 28). This lists four objectives:

1 By 1996, most local authorities in each country should have undertaken a consultative process with their populations and achieved a consensus on 'a Local Agenda 21'.
2 By 1993, the international community should have initiated a consultative process aimed at increasing cooperation between local authorities.
3 By 1994, representatives of associations of cities and other local authorities should have increased cooperation and coordination to enhance the exchange of experience and information between them.
4 All local authorities should be encouraged to implement and monitor programmes that aim to ensure that women and youth are represented in the decision-making, planning and implementation processes.

It is worth noting that these objectives are not so much on what Local Agenda 21s should include but on how they should be organized, especially the local consultation processes to ensure that all groups are involved (Lafferty and Eckerberg 1998).

The fact that virtually all national governments committed themselves to implementing Local Agenda 21s at the UN Earth Summit does not, in itself, mean much. In all the global UN conferences held during the 1970s, 1980s and 1990s, from the 1972 UN Conference on the Human Environment onwards, government representatives formally endorsed a wide range of recommendations. If these had been implemented, they would have greatly reduced poverty

Box 7.7 *Agenda 21's stress on environmental problems in cities in Africa, Asia and Latin America*

Urban environmental problems. Agenda 21 includes many aspects that are relevant to identifying and acting on environmental problems in cities. There are separate sections on urban health, health risks from environmental pollution and hazards, the provision of environmental infrastructure, and planning for human settlements in disaster-prone areas. There are also individual chapters on promoting sustainable human settlement development and environmentally sound management of toxic chemicals, hazardous wastes, and solid wastes and sewage-related issues. Some key points are highlighted below.

Urban health. Agenda 21 argues that urban growth has exposed people to serious environmental hazards and that the rate of growth has exceeded the capacity of municipal and local government to provide the environmental health services required. One of Agenda 21's objectives is to improve the health and well-being of all urban dwellers. Local authorities are identified as the key agents of change. Agenda 21 argues that better national and municipal statistics based on practical standardized indicators are required, as are methodologies to measure intraurban and interurban district variations in health status and environmental conditions.

Human settlement management. To improve conditions for people living in urban centres, Agenda 21 recognizes the need to improve the level of infrastructure and service provision in poorer areas. It argues that cities should: institutionalize a participatory approach; improve the urban environment by promoting social organization and environmental awareness, and strengthen the capacities of local governing bodies.

Environmental infrastructure. Residential densities in urban areas offer unique opportunities for the provision of sustainable environmental infrastructure, but the lack of urban investment and its poor quality is currently responsible for much ill-health and many preventable deaths. One objective of Agenda 21 is to secure the provision of adequate environmental infrastructure facilities in all settlements by the year 2025.

Waste management. Agenda 21 recognizes the need to strengthen and expand national waste reuse and recycling systems. It argues that multinational and national government institutions and non-governmental organizations should actively promote and encourage waste reuse and recycling. It also emphasizes the need to establish environmentally sound waste-disposal and treatment systems for waste that cannot be recycled or reused.

Who are the key actors? Agenda 21 recognizes the critical contributions of both non-governmental organizations and local authorities, and includes separate chapters focusing on the work of these groups. The document stresses the importance of partnerships between public, private and community sectors in improving social, economic and environmental quality, and of participation in decision-making processes by community groups and special interest groups.

and tackled many of the most serious environmental problems. But most of the recommendations that would have done most to reduce poverty and improve environmental management have hardly been implemented. Virtually all governments in Africa, Asia and Latin America made a commitment to increase the priority they gave to water and sanitation at the first UN Conference on Human Settlements (Habitat) in 1976. These were further endorsed at a special UN Conference on Water the next year in Mar del Plata and the 1980s was then designated by the UN General Assembly as the International Drinking Water Supply and Sanitation Decade. In the 1970s, 1990 was set as the target year by when virtually all rural and urban dwellers were to have adequate provision for water and sanitation. Chapter 2 revealed the huge shortfall in the achievement of this target and even included details of urban locations where provision for water and sanitation is worse now than it was in the late 1960s.

In the case of Local Agenda 21s, there is evidence of considerable innovation in urban areas in different regions, including Africa, Asia and Latin America as well as Europe[6] and North America.[7] There has also been some action in items 2 and 3 listed above – for instance the many new initiatives to encourage city governments to share their experiences (including more conferences, journals and newsletters) and the new interest in urban development showed by many international agencies (as described later in this chapter). International agencies and international events have given more importance to city mayors, in part because mayors have become more important political actors within many countries (through decentralization and the introduction or strengthening of democratic processes in many cities). The mayors of many major cities have become national or even international figures. The recognition of the important role of local authorities in achieving sustainable development goals was then further developed at Habitat II, the second UN Conference on Human Settlements in 1996 (also known as the City Summit).

But it is too soon to judge the significance of the 'Local Agenda 21' movement. Thousands of urban centres may report that they have developed a Local Agenda 21, but many are neither participatory nor effective. Some are no more than a document setting out the goals or plans of some government agency that was developed with little consultation with citizens or other groups. Many have plans and programmes for which there is little government interest or capacity to implement. Some may simply be conventional development plans renamed. Others may be the result of one or two workshops that also resulted in little action. Others may include admirable consultative processes and well-developed goals, yet founder on the very limited capacity of the city authorities to work in partnership with other groups and to plan, invest and coordinate the investments and activities of other agencies (including those of higher levels of government). One also wonders how many Local Agenda 21s have been developed and implemented, ensuring that 'women and youth are represented in decision-making, planning and implementation processes' (as the text of

---

6 See for instance Roberts 2000, Lafferty and Eckerberg 1998, Mega 1996a and 1996b.
7 See for instance AtKisson 1996, Brugmann 1997.

Agenda 21 recommends). And all city authorities, regardless of how effective they are, will have difficulties incorporating those aspects of sustainable development that respond to the needs of future generations or to limiting the environmental costs that are passed on to 'distant elsewheres' (to use William E Rees' term – see Rees 1992), a point to which we will return in Chapter 8.

Without careful, independent evaluations of Local Agenda 21s, it is difficult to gauge their effectiveness and there are few independent evaluations available. Most available case studies were produced either by those involved in their development or by international agencies that funded them. The desire among international agencies to demonstrate their effectiveness to what is often an increasingly sceptical public (who are their 'funders', directly or indirectly)[8] has encouraged some to publish and promote 'success stories' and 'best practices' whose 'success' is judged too uncritically and whose relevance to other locations can be overstated.

However, there are examples of innovative Local Agenda 21s that show the potential of the approach. They are better characterized as 'good principle' rather than ' best practice'.[9] Perhaps, more than anything else, they show the willingness of citizens, community organizations and local NGOs to 'buy in' to planning and environmental management, if these are organized in such a way as to encourage and support their participation. It is no coincidence that most of the Local Agenda 21s described in Box 7.8 are in cities with strong local democracies. Much of the innovation in Local Agenda 21s has been the result of local, not national initiatives.

Drawing from these experiences and also from some experiences in other countries (see for instance Tuts 1998 and Mwangi 2000), the following points seem relevant.

Many innovative Local Agenda 21s were possible because of some coincidence of key local and national changes,[10] especially decentralization (which gave more scope for local action, even if it often did not transfer public resources) and strengthened local democracy. This was important for Ilo, along with the emergence of political leaders with a commitment to real participation. The changes in Colombia in the early 1990s in terms of decentralization (which in this instance increased resource transfers to local governments and strengthened their revenue base) strengthened local democracy and a greater

---

8 Virtually all international agencies depend ultimately on a public perception of their effectiveness among citizens in high-income nations. Multilateral agencies such as the UN agencies and the International Development Association of the World Bank depend almost entirely on funding from the governments of high-income nations (and thus on their citizens' acceptance of this). Official bilateral aid programmes depend on funding from their governments (who in turn are influenced by perceptions of their effectiveness from voters). Charities or international non-governmental agencies rely on donations from the public (and often in part from governments). There are, however, exceptions, for instance private foundations drawing funds from companies, corporations or individuals – but they represent a very small proportion of the total funding for development.

9 John F C Turner (1996) highlighted the importance of understanding 'good principle' rather than 'best practice' in his reflections on Habitat II: the second UN Conference on Human Settlements in Istanbul in 1996.

10 See Follegatti 1999 discussing this for Ilo.

interest in the environment in central government helped to underpin and support the innovation in Manizales (Velasquez 1998).

Many Local Agenda 21s were spurred by large or powerful groups within the locality that recognized the need for local action. In some instances, this is in response to particular environmental hazards as in Ilo where all citizens wanted action on the very high levels of air pollution and the other environmental costs generated by the Southern Peru Copper Corporation (Follegatti 1999). In Chimbote, the threat to the park/tree nursery noted in Box 7.8 and the industrial pollution from a steel mill and local fishmeal-processing industries helped to mobilize citizen action which then helped to develop into the coalition that now seeks to address a wider range of environmental problems (Foronda 1998). In Manizales, one underpinning of environmental action was the need to reduce risks to the population from landslides. Local Agenda 21s can also be much strengthened if local governments and local businesses see them as part of a strategy to attract and hold new investment. For instance, the richness and diversity of the ecology in and around Manizales and the great natural beauty are obvious assets on which the city can build its tourism base. Even for cities that are seeking to attract industry, a reputation for good environmental management need not be a disadvantage and can be turned into a strong advantage, as the well-managed environment makes it attractive for all employees and as an efficient government ensures that infrastructure and services are available for enterprises and the homes of their employees. Obviously, any city authority that enforces environmental regulations can be at a disadvantage to other cities which do not on account of those industrial concerns whose profits are much increased by avoiding pollution control and good waste management, as can be seen by the attitude of the local authority next to Manizales, Villa Maria, which for a while sought to tempt enterprises away from Manizales by lax environmental controls (Velasquez and Pacheco 1999). But a large (and probably growing) proportion of industrial concerns, especially those planning to invest in new facilities, do not have serious pollution implications, or there are 'clean' production equipment and processes available that minimize them. And competent, effective local government is generally more important to the profitability of most new industrial production than ineffective local government that does not implement environmental regulations.

Many innovative experiences benefited from long-term political support, so long-term strategies were not disrupted or reversed after each election. Good long-term initiatives set in motion by one mayor are often reversed immediately or changed by their successor. Ilo's success owes much to the fact that successive mayors supported and developed the innovations first set in motion by its first elected mayor in the early 1980s. It often takes a considerable time before long-range policies begin to show their effects, especially where local authorities have limited investment capacity. Many of the Local Agenda 21s noted here were developing innovative responses to local environmental problems before the concept of a 'Local Agenda 21' had been invented, and so their achievements since 1992 must also recognize the work done before they were rebranded as 'Local Agenda 21s'.

Box 7.8 EXAMPLES OF LOCAL AGENDA 21s

Manizales (Colombia). This is a famous, historic city with around 360,000 inhabitants which developed in a rich coffee area on a mountainous site with great natural beauty. A local environmental action plan (Bioplan-Manizales) was developed with widespread consultation and this became integrated into the municipal development plan and the municipal budget. It includes measures to protect and revitalize the city's rich architectural heritage, improve public transport (partly funded by a tax on petrol), reduce the risk of landslides and relocate the population living on steep slopes that are at high risk of landslides. The relocation programme was linked to the development of eco-parks throughout the city, some on the land that had slopes that were too dangerous for permanent settlement and others with important ecological functions – for instance one integrated into the city's watershed and another focusing on conserving biodiversity. Some of the eco-parks are managed by community associations that also manage 2 community plant nurseries and 15 neighbourhood parks. Community-based environmental initiatives helped to generate jobs – for instance, managing eco-parks, running tree nurseries and increasing recycling. Community- or neighbourhood-based environmental action plans have also been developed – for instance, one for Olivares commune (one of 11 communes in Manizales and also the one with the lowest average income) identified the main environmental problems and also the areas's environmental resources on which their neighbourhood agenda could build. The city has also developed an innovative indicators programme – the 'environmental traffic lights' through which progress in each of its 11 communes are tracked with regard to social conditions, community involvement, natural resource use, energy efficiency and waste management. Data on current conditions and trends in each commune are displayed in public places. They are called traffic lights because, for each indicator, public boards show whether things are improving (green), getting worse (red) or are relatively stable (amber). The monitoring of progress is also helped by environmental observatories set up in different parts of the city (Velasquez 1998, 1999).

Chimbote (Peru). In this provincial capital and industrial fishing port with some 278,000 inhabitants in the early 1990s, a coalition of 42 public and private institutions, including grassroots organizations, NGOs, universities, professional training institutions and government bodies have formed ADECOMAPS (the Association for the Defence and Conservation of the Environment of the Province of Santa). This brings together those concerned with getting basic infrastructure and services to the informal settlements, with controlling the air pollution and water contamination arising from local industry and protecting the area's natural resources (including local wetlands and a park which a local iron and steel works had created in 1958 and which, when it was privatized, it wanted to sell).

Grassroots organizations formed by the residents of low-income settlements to fight for basic services and to organize local actions to improve environmental conditions are a central part of ADECOMAPS. ADECOMAPS has developed a Local Agenda 21 through a participatory process which includes an environmental diagnosis of the city and is developing proposals to reduce the pollution of El Ferrol Bay beside which the city developed (Foronda 1998).

Ilo (Peru). In this port city in southern Peru with around 60,000 inhabitants in 1999, the quality of the environment has been transformed over an 18-year period with major improvements in the quality of housing and in the provision of water, sanitation, waste collection, electricity, paved streets and green areas. The city has a plentiful water supply and virtually all waste water is treated in bio-stabilization ponds. Some 300 projects have been financed and implemented through partnerships between the municipal government and community-level management committees, with these also able to draw support from other institutions, including local NGOs. The projects have concentrated on different aspects of improving the immediate neighbourhood environment such as paving streets, developing parks and installing piped water and electricity. The total value of investments is equivalent to more than US$10 million. The municipal council also avoided the problem of squatting, despite the city's six-fold increase in population since 1961, by developing an urban expansion area where even low-income households could obtain a site on which to develop their own housing and receive basic infrastructure and services. A large coastal area along the seafront within the city has been reclaimed for public use (with the municipal authorities helping to move the industries, settlements and institutions that were located there) and this has transformed 3 kilometres of the coastline, which now includes a pier, tree-lined walkways, play spaces and an amphitheatre. There has been a long fight with a copper factory which generates high levels of solid waste and very high air pollution levels. Citizen pressure forced the company to stop polluting the local bay and dumping wastes on local beaches, but reducing the very high output of sulphur dioxide has proved more difficult. However, despite this limitation, the municipal authorities, working with the citizens, have transformed Ilo from a place where migrants came only to work (and then return home) to a city where residents want to stay and invest. Development plans occur within a coherent environmental plan, which is developed through consultation with different local groups, supported by a Multi-Sectoral Commission on the Environment, set up in 1987, which draws representatives from different agencies and sectors. There has been long-term political support for this whole approach, exemplified by the fact that six successive mayors have supported it (Díaz and others 1996, Follegati 1999).

All gave more space to low-income groups. This is especially evident in Ilo where improvements in the environment brought multiple benefits to a large section of its low-income population. The environmental plans in Manizales have also sought to fully involve low-income groups in their formulation, implementation and evaluation. But there are obvious limits in the extent to which Local Agenda 21s can address the most pressing concerns of low-income groups. Environmental action plans and programmes often generate employment and, if successful, help to attract new investment but they cannot deliver higher incomes for most low-income households. New environmental plans, however participatory, have to overcome low-income groups' distrust of governments; in her discussion of the local environmental action plan developed for Olivares, the lowest income district in Manizales, Luz Stella Velásquez (1999) points to the long tradition of political clientilism which makes low-income populations distrust new public initiatives. Low-income groups can quite rightly question the role of researchers who ask them to complete questionnaires, as they prepare environmental profiles, wondering whether the research will ever bring them benefits; in Olivares, a sign outside a modest house said 'surveys answered after lunchtime for 5000 pesos' (ibid, page 46). It is also common for Local Agenda 21s to ask too much of low-income groups and their community organizations, especially where local authorities are particularly weak (Wacker and others 1999).

Local NGOs or universities often have important supporting roles. In most of the examples given above of Local Agenda 21s, there was one or more local institution that was not within government and not a private business that made important contributions. For instance, in Ilo, the local NGO Labor and in Chimbote, the local NGO Natura were particularly important. In Manizales, the Institute of Environmental Studies (IDEA) in the local campus of the National University helped to develop, implement and monitor the bioplan and the Local Environmental Action Plans, and has also developed training programmes for staff from other national, regional and local governments and NGOs involved in developing Local Agenda 21s. The innovations in Ilo and Chimbote (and many other Peruvian cities) were also supported by a National 'Cities for Life' Forum organized by a Peruvian NGO, Ecociudad.

Box 7.9 outlines the scope and nature of this national campaign. It is interesting in that it is a small Peruvian non-governmental organization that takes on the role of encouraging and supporting local authorities to develop Local Agenda 21s. This is assumed to be a task for national governments, but in this instance, there was little interest from national government in doing this, or indeed in helping local authorities to address serious environmental problems (Miranda and Hordijk 1998). This NGO has encouraged many local authorities to develop Local Agendas, organized workshops and exchanges to allow such authorities to share their experiences, advised many local authorities on how to develop Local Agenda 21s and developed manuals and other documents to help guide them. It has also developed new courses with universities. In effect, it is doing what national governments should do.

As more Local Agenda 21s become documented, so it will become easier to better understand the kinds of policies and institutions that make them more

---

Box 7.9 *The Peruvian Cities for Life Forum*

In 1996, representatives from several Peruvian cities, grassroots organizations and NGOs, together with staff from universities and local government authorities, decided to establish a national forum to promote and support the implementation of Local Agenda 21s in Peruvian cities. This came to be called the 'Cities for Life' Forum and by 1998, it had brought together representatives from 41 institutions in 18 cities. It also sought from the outset to be a forum for Peruvians, rooted in their knowledge and culture. Those developing this forum also emphasized:

- How it would have been a mistake to develop a single proposal for national development without taking into consideration local characteristics, resources, capacities and political will.
- How environmental management processes must be truly democratic, decentralized and participatory.

This forum developed out of a project to identify 'best practices in urban environmental management' in Peru that were then to be used to design training strategies for building municipal government capacity. An initial seminar helped to form a network of like-minded people and institutions. The process of documenting innovative practices and judging them attracted increasing interest not only from specialist staff but also from politicians and officials from central and local government. Mayors from cities with particularly serious environmental problems took a special interest – for instance the mayors of mining towns such as Cerro de Pasco and La Oroya. There was a great interest in sharing experiences between cities, first in seminars and round tables (which also provided participants with the opportunity to visit other cities), then through courses organized for environmental promoters. A manual to guide local authorities in developing Local Agenda 21s has been developed by Julio Diaz Palacios, a former Mayor of Ilo, who had helped to initiate Ilo's innovative environmental management described earlier.

Source: Miranda, Liliana and Michaela Hordijk (1998), 'Let us build cities for life: the National Campaign of Local Agenda 21s in Peru', *Environment and Urbanization*, Vol 10, No 2, October, pages 69–102.

---

effective. One slightly worrying point is the extent to which much of the innovation is outside large cities and national capitals. For Ilo, its physical distance from Lima, the national capital, and its relatively small size may have been an important protective factor. For large cities, it is obviously more difficult to get an effective city-wide Local Agenda 21 if the city is made up of many municipalities (and usually with different political parties in power in the different municipalities). There are also various potential weaknesses of Local Agenda 21s, including the fact that they are not a substitute for needed political reforms (although they may assist in the reform process) and that the agencies responsible for developing them may have little capacity to ensure that their findings and recommendations are acted on.

CITY-WIDE ENVIRONMENTAL INDICATORS

Indicators are meant to be measures of what we care about.[11] They should provide information about whether chosen goals are being achieved and about problems that need to be addressed. All forms of environmental management have explicit or implicit goals, for instance:

- For air quality management, the reduction of particular air pollutants or air-pollutant combinations below particular thresholds or the reduction in the number of days that official air quality standards are exceeded.
- For water and sanitation, the proportion of households served by piped supplies and sewers and the regularity and quality of the water supply.
- For solid waste, the proportion of households served with a regular collection service and the proportion of waste that is recycled.

As such, they are important for environmental management and, beyond this (as Chapter 8 will describe) for the achievement of sustainable development goals.

Chapter 6 discussed the value of developing indicators on environmental quality or service provision that respond to the priorities of the inhabitants, especially in neighbourhoods or districts with the most serious problems in terms of environmental quality and lack of provision for environmental infrastructure and services. In this section, the concern is more for indicators at a higher level, for instance the district, municipality, city or city-region.

Governments often set environmental (and other) goals towards which progress can be measured. Public and private service providers may set explicit goals and report on progress towards their achievement. The regular reporting by government, private-sector and NGO infrastructure or service providers on the quality and extent of provision has become an accepted feature of any organization committed to transparency and accountability, although it is often difficult for citizens to verify the 'official' statistics since it may only be government statistical services that have the capacity to measure progress or the reported indicators are drawn from private companies' confidential records.

For any goal, it is possible to identify one or more indicator which, if measured, helps to show the extent to which the goal has been achieved. If measured regularly, it helps to map progress over time. For many environmental goals, it is easy to identify relevant indicators – for instance, for environmental health needs within housing and residential neighbourhoods, they would include indicators that show the adequacy of provision for water supplies, sanitation, drainage and solid-waste management, air quality, housing quality, and the extent

---

11 The early part of this section draws on Meadows 1998.

and quality of the provision for recreation and play. But even where it is possible to collect a wide range of data, it is often difficult to get a good match between what should be measured and what is easily measurable. For instance, measures of housing quality should reflect not only information that is relatively easily quantified or measured (for instance rooms per person and the quality of the building structure), but key qualitative aspects such as affordability and dweller security in the sense of dwellers feeling safe and not being at risk from sudden eviction. Ideally, they should also include more subjective aspects such as the level of satisfaction for different household members. For every indicator, inappropriate criteria may be used or the criteria applied in ways that are exclusionary for particular groups, especially low-income groups. For instance, the criteria used to judge whether housing is of adequate quality may deem as 'substandard' much of the housing that serves low-income groups well in terms of location and affordability. Or inappropriate building codes or planning norms may be used to justify the eviction of low-income groups from the homes they had developed on land-sites that government agencies or private interests want for more 'profitable' developments.

The difficulties in reconciling what is measured with what should be measured was described in some detail in Chapter 2 with regard to the provision for water and sanitation. Most official statistics for water and sanitation are inaccurate or misleading because they do not assess the extent to which provision meets human needs. They generally give information only about the presence of a water tap or a latrine, not how easy it is to get to it, how much it costs to do so, its quality and availability. Measures of the provision for recreation and play need to reflect far more than 'open space per person' because it is not only the quantity of open space that matters but also its quality, the ease with which it can be reached, its safety, and the extent to which it is managed to cater for the needs of different groups (including different age groups).

So much basic information about environmental quality at the level of the city is only collected every ten years by censuses. These are the only means by which information is collected for all households on, for instance, housing quality, and infrastructure and service provision. And since it is usually several years after a census that census data become available for individual cities, city authorities are always working with outdated data. They may not receive the census data at the level of detail that is useful for micro-planning or small-area planning. Many city authorities do not even have census data, as in the many (mostly sub-Saharan African) countries that have had no census for more than 15 years. Governments and international donors have often sought to fill this 'data gap' with household surveys, but these only survey a sample of households and, while they may be of great value to national policy-makers, they are of far less value to local authorities since the sample size is too small to allow them to provide relevant statistics for each local government area.

There is also the problem of the biases introduced into policies and public actions by the fact that what is easily measured gets more attention. For instance, we suspect that in many urban centres, ambient air pollution may be getting more attention than it deserves in terms of its health impact, relative to other more pressing environmental hazards. In part, this is because ambient air pollution is more easily measured than (say) the incidence of diarrhoeal diseases or the seriousness of occupational exposures. There are generally other reasons too – for instance because air pollution affects middle- and upper-income groups whereas the impact of diarrhoeal diseases and occupational exposures are more concentrated within lower-income groups. The growing support for air pollution control from international donors is related in part to the fact that the control of air pollution is a priority in their own domestic arena; for some, it is also related to pressure from business interests in their own country that benefit from air pollution control and the systems needed to implement this. We do not want to take attention away from the control of air pollution and, as Chapter 3 described, there are many cities where ambient air pollution has very serious health impacts. But care is needed to ensure that priorities for environmental action in any city are not influenced only by what is measured, what is easily measured or what is measurable by the equipment that is funded by international assistance.

Many indicators do not gauge the adequacy of the environment but are signals of the inadequacy of environmental infrastructure and services or housing quality. Some of the most valuable indicators are age-specific mortality rates, including infant mortality rates (the number of infants who die between birth and 1 year of age per 1000 live births) and child mortality rates (generally the number of children who die between the age of 1 and 5, per 1000 children in this age group). These are powerful indicators of the quality of the environment, since infants and young children are particularly susceptible to many environment-related diseases and injuries. Infant mortality can be further disaggregated into neonatal (aged 0 to 28 days) and post-neonatal (28 days to 1 year) mortality and this is valuable in that neonatal mortality rates are generally linked to problems of reproductive health (including problems of pregnancy and delivery) whereas post-neonatal mortality is linked more to poor quality home environments (Arrossi 1996). Figure 7.1 illustrates how age-specific mortality rates can be mapped by city district to highlight differentials – in this case in Buenos Aires. Not surprisingly, the map fits well with income levels (the high-income municipalities have the lowest infant mortality rates) and with basic service provision (the lowest infant mortality rates are in the local government areas where the lowest proportion of the population has unsatisfied basic needs). This analysis by Silvina Arrossi also mapped the spatial distribution of infant mortality rates by 'avoidable' causes (for instance tetanus, respiratory infections, perinatal jaundice) and by 'partly avoidable' causes (for instance nutritional deficiencies), as well as mapping mortality rates for other age groups and discussing their association with different environmental and non-environmental factors.

This kind of mapping can also be used for any environmental (or other life-threatening or health-threatening) problem for which there is relatively complete information about incidence and geographic location. The data may be available from routine recording systems – for instance particular infectious diseases, murders/homicides or motor vehicle accidents. There are often serious deficiencies in the availability and quality of data about these and other important environmental (and other) health problems. But various studies have

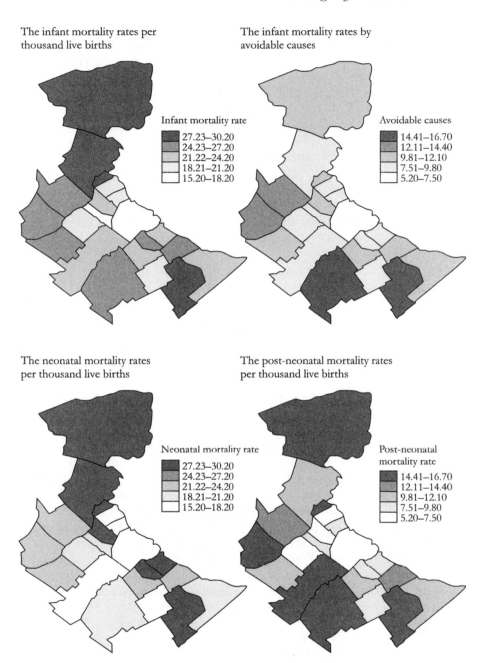

The infant mortality rates per thousand live births

Infant mortality rate

27.23–30.20
24.23–27.20
21.22–24.20
18.21–21.20
15.20–18.20

The infant mortality rates by avoidable causes

Avoidable causes

14.41–16.70
12.11–14.40
9.81–12.10
7.51–9.80
5.20–7.50

The neonatal mortality rates per thousand live births

Neonatal mortality rate

27.23–30.20
24.23–27.20
21.22–24.20
18.21–21.20
15.20–18.20

The post-neonatal mortality rates per thousand live births

Post-neonatal mortality rate

14.41–16.70
12.11–14.40
9.81–12.10
7.51–9.80
5.20–7.50

Source: Arrossi, Silvina (1996), 'Inequality and health in Metropolitan Buenos Aires', *Environment and Urbanization*, Vol 8, No 2, October, pages 43–70.

Figure 7.1 *The distribution of infant mortality among districts in Buenos Aires, 1991*

shown how it is possible to draw on existing data to map different aspects of environmental quality for different neighbourhoods, districts or local government areas within a city, as in the mapping of differentials in socio-environmental quality for Accra and São Paulo (Stephens and others 1994). Here mortality data based on causes of death certificates were the main data source on health. The maps that can be derived from existing data highlight not only poor environmental quality but the very large differentials between districts in environmental quality and in the economic, social and political inequalities that underpin them (Stephens 1996, Stephens and others 1997). Another series of studies showed how household surveys drawing on a carefully selected sample of households can give much more detailed information about the quality of the home and neighbourhood environment in different neighbourhoods of a city; organized by the Stockholm Environment Institute working with local teams, this produced studies in Accra, Jakarta, São Paulo and Port Elizabeth.[12]

One of the difficulties regarding environmental indicators is that their quality and range needs to be expanded in cities where there are great limits on the capacity of city authorities to do so. There are also particular difficulties in developing indicators that monitor environmental conditions and trends outside official municipal boundaries such as measuring the extent to which the city is drawing in regional freshwater resources at levels that can be sustained or the land area of the city's ecological footprint.

Developing an appropriate (and measurable) set of indicators ends up being an intensely local exercise. New models for generating a more appropriate information base have been developed in many cities. In some instances, this is through national agencies responsible for some of these statistics, making these statistics more readily available to city and municipal authorities and other interested bodies – for instance making available to local authorities a larger and more spatially disaggregated range of data drawn from censuses. In other instances, it is initiatives taken by local governments to draw together and analyse key available data or to generate new data if this is not collected. This can include measures that also make this information more accessible to city inhabitants. One example of this is the very comprehensive and detailed environmental atlas produced in Pôrto Alegre, Brazil, which not only serves environmental planning and management in the city and its surrounds, but also is available as an atlas (and an accompanying CD-Rom) to all local schools (Menegat and others 1998). So lessons and courses on environmental issues in Pôrto Alegre have a detailed and accessible local information base on which they can draw. Another example is the urban observatory set up by municipal authorities in Montevideo (Uruguay) that brings together data about the city and its 18 districts from the national censuses and household surveys, the different sectoral ministries and the municipal authorities' own information, and makes it available to government task forces, public agencies, NGOs, companies and the public (Rodé 2000). One non-government example, the Urban Resource Centre in Karachi, was

---

12 Each city study has been published, along with many working papers or articles in journals. McGranahan and others 2001 summarizes the city case studies.

given in Chapter 6. Some city and municipal authorities in Latin America also have substantial statistical offices or data-gathering departments, in response to the fact that the information about their own cities from national censuses often takes too long to be returned to them or it is returned in a form that is too aggregated to be useful for planning and management.

Local processes can help to produce the data, as in the examples given earlier, within cities developing Local Agenda 21s. The indicators programme of Manizales is one of the best known of these. In part, this is because of the ambitious range of social, economic, environmental and ecological indicators that it includes, drawn from a great variety of local, provincial and national bodies (see Velasquez 1998 for a full description of these). But it includes more than this, as it includes an initiative to set up 'observatories' within each district of the city, to involve the inhabitants of each district in defining appropriate indicators and in helping to collect the data and to present back to the public (Velasquez 1998). And as described in Box 7.8, Manizales also developed a set of composite indicators, known as the 'environmental traffic lights', through which progress in each of its 11 communes are tracked with regard to social conditions, community involvement, natural resource use, energy efficiency and waste management, and that show whether things are improving (green), getting worse (red) or are relatively stable (amber). It is possible to critically review the type and range of indicators used in Manizales (or elsewhere) and perhaps identify gaps or question the way that composite indicators are formed, but what such debates can miss is the importance of intense and inclusive local processes within which the concerns of those who suffer the most from environmental hazards get the prominence they deserve. It is important too that local government is fully involved in this, wherever possible, since much of what needs to be done or changed requires their involvement (see for instance Brugmann 1997). But sometimes it falls to citizen groups, NGOs and other actors to start the process, as in Chimbote, where the local government showed little interest in this (see Box 7.8), and as in Karachi with the Urban Resource Centre.

Many national environmental indicators should be based on an aggregation of good local indicators. When they are, they reveal the inadequacies of the previously used nationally collected statistics. As Chapter 2 emphasized, if statistics on water and sanitation were collected in each urban centre (and subject to public scrutiny there), they would certainly change national statistics on the quality and extent of the provision for water and sanitation in urban areas. Perhaps more importantly, they would also allow a far better appreciation of the scope for local action to contribute to national goals. As key local environmental issues, such as deforestation, soil degradation, desertification, urban expansion over farmland and freshwater stress, have become elevated to global environmental concerns so national indicators have been created. Their accuracy is often suspect, because they are not based on an aggregation of accurate local indicators. Perhaps more importantly, addressing these problems within any nation depends largely on local actions in a great variety of localities, each of which must respond to their own very specific local context. It is no wonder then, that much of the discussion about environmental indicators is rooted in discussions of improved local governance.

THE INSTITUTIONAL CONSTRAINTS ON EFFECTIVE ACTION

Constraints at national level

The initiatives outlined in this chapter that have addressed environmental problems within cities represent an incomplete list; many more techniques could be described or case studies given that also cut pollution and wastes and reduce resource use. However, it is not the technical capacity to reduce pollution that is in doubt but the political and institutional will and capacity to act effectively.

Various political and institutional factors inhibit appropriate environmental action at national level. Perhaps the most serious is national (and often local) governments' over-riding concern to attract new investment, often pursued with little consideration given to the cost in terms of pollution or poorly managed natural resource extraction and waste management. There is often a worry in official circles that environmental regulations may discourage new investment. International businesses are also adept at making city and national authorities compete for their new investments and in so doing, getting very large concessions. The main environmental issue may not be the potential pollution of the new facility that government money goes to support, but the concentration of government funding on ensuring that the land and the high-quality infrastructure and services are available for new enterprises or the revenues forgone because of tax concessions, even while half the city's population has no access to land with infrastructure and services for their homes. Yet within a world economy where so much production is mobile, city authorities need to become competitive in attracting new investment. A study of Bangalore by Solomon Benjamin shows how state and national government support to develop this city into India's 'silicon valley' has served the corporate sector and the middle- and upper-income groups associated with it, while ignoring the environmental health needs of most citizens and failing to support the local economies on which much of Bangalore's production and prosperity depend. Power and access to public resources in Bangalore have been taken away from the elected local government and concentrated in state level and national agencies in which there is little or no local representation (Benjamin 2000).

If a government's main concerns are boosting employment and economic growth, or simply the survival of the national economy (and its own survival), new environmental legislation or implementing existing legislation will not be a high priority. National governments will also see the 'national' benefits from industrial production and not their local environmental costs, especially if the local costs are not evident in the capital city. As noted earlier, the citizens of Ilo suffer from very serious air pollution but national government in distant Lima has little interest in enforcing environmental regulations on a copper mine and refinery that generates so much foreign exchange. The fear that enforcing pollution controls creates unemployment is still strong. But in the long term, government policies to promote waste minimization and the recovery and reuse or recycling of wastes from domestic, commercial and industrial wastes are likely to lead to a net gain in employment. A city with a good reputation for a high-quality environment and good governance can also attract a wider range of new investments. However, many nations do have problems with some 'dirty' industries whose survival may be threatened by more stringent pollution standards or the enforcement of existing standards.

There is also the problem of generating the foreign exchange to pay for the import of new 'clean' technologies, whether for industrial production, water purification, sewage and waste-water treatment, power generation or engines for motor vehicles. Few low- and middle-income nations have sufficiently sophisticated capital goods industries to produce most of these new technologies, so most new 'add-on' pollution-control equipment or new 'clean' technologies have to be imported. Foreign exchange is usually very limited and in most nations, machinery and equipment already account for between a quarter and a third of all merchandise imports. In virtually all nations, numerous commodities will be judged of higher priority than such equipment.

Another set of problems arises because of the cumbersome or inappropriate regulatory structures. Many governments have drawn on regulatory or institutional models from high-income nations which are rarely the most appropriate to their own particular circumstances. A review of US waste-management technology and its relevance to lower-income countries noted that the main priorities for waste management should be waste reduction, then ways of recovering materials or using them, then waste treatment or incineration and, as the last resort, secure landfill disposal (Elkington and Shopley 1989). Most regulatory structures promote the reverse. This review also noted the difficulties in developing a regulatory framework which promoted waste reduction. Most existing environmental regulations in low- and middle-income countries are replicas of past regulations in high-income countries and 'have little grounding in local realities and cultures and therefore are largely unenforceable' and 'the agencies responsible for their enforcement are rarely given the authority and the means for enforcement' (Panayatou 1991). It is worth recalling the observation by Arif Hasan noted in Chapter 6 on the many internationally funded studies on solid-waste management in Karachi that failed to recognize the role of the recycling industry which provides a livelihood for some 55,000 families, recovers and recycles or reclaims a large volume of resources and greatly reduces the amount of waste that has to be disposed of (Hasan 1999).

There are also problems with publicly owned facilities. In theory, where power stations, mines and industries are owned and run by public agencies, good environmental performance should be easier to achieve. In practice, publicly owned factories and power stations are often among the worst polluters. In many Latin American and some Asian countries, some of the potentially most polluting industries such as basic metal or petrol-refining industries are either in government hands or in the hands of quasi-government entities (World Bank 1992). Government agencies or parastatals own many polluting industries in sub-Saharan Africa. Government-owned sewage and drainage systems are often serious polluters and contravene environmental legislation (Halter 1991). Where sewage-treatment plants exist, they are often poorly managed and working far below their capacity. Well-managed solid-waste disposal sites are also rare.

Finally, there is the problem noted in previous chapters that the levels of government above city and metropolitan levels do not permit city governments the power and resources they need to address environmental problems and do not ensure that city government structures allow low-income groups sufficient influence on what they do. Although most nations have undergone some form of decentralization over the last 15 years that has affected urban governments, this has not necessarily been accompanied by increased local democracy or by more effective municipal governments. Much of the decision-making and investment in infrastructure and services may remain with the local offices of national ministries.[13] This is often underpinned by political structures at higher levels of government that seek to keep control of power and resource allocations, including control over funding for environmental infrastructure.[14] There are often political conflicts between elected city authorities and higher levels of government, especially where city governments are controlled by different political parties from those in power at higher levels of government. The capacity of national or provincial/state governments to limit the capacity of city governments that are controlled by opposition parties is a recurring theme within most democratic countries.[15] Thus, it cannot be assumed that the introduction of elected municipal authorities and mayors necessarily ensures more effective municipal governments, especially where higher levels of government inhibit effective urban government. Many of the more successful cities succeeded because they had sufficient capacity, including local revenue raising capacity and capacity to develop local partnerships, and so were able to improve environmental conditions, without substantial national government support.

Improving urban environments and protecting rural resources (and inhabitants) from city-generated pollutants requires governments to identify, define and allocate costs and ensure their collection among different producers and consumers. This means charging producers and consumers for the cost of providing basic services and facilities (piped water, drains, disposal sites), strongly penalizing individuals or companies who dispose of their wastes in ways that affect others or damage the environment, and enforcing occupational health and safety standards. At present, in most low- and middle-income nations, much of the benefits of government investment in basic services go to richer households and businesses. They are often paying less than the real cost of provision. Meanwhile, as described earlier, most of the costs fall in lower-income groups in the form of polluted water, air and land sites, and inadequate and no provision of basic services.

The most effective check on the misallocation of public resources and on environmental injustice in terms of who suffers the most serious environmental health burdens is a representative form of government that has sufficient power, resources and trained personnel at city or municipal level to ensure that basic services are provided and environmental legislation enforced, combined

---

13 See for instance the case studies of Kumasi (Devas and Korboe 2000), Mombasa (Rakodi and others 2000), Santiago (Dockemdorff and others 2000) and Bangalore (Benjamin 2000).

14 See contrasts between the case studies in three Indian cities in *Environment and Urbanization*, Vol 12, No 1 – Dutta 2000 (Ahmedabad), Benjamin 2000 (Bangalore) and Amis and Kumar 2000 (Visakhapatnam).

15 See the case studies of Bangalore (Benjamin 2000), Colombo (Russell and Vidler 2000) and Visakhapatnam (Amis and Kumar 2000).

with a legal system that allows rapid redress for those who lose out. The last 25 years have seen virtually all governments set up national environmental agencies but many remain small, weak institutions. A 1996 World Bank report noted how environmental agencies are plagued with problems such as:

- poor information (as monitoring equipment is frequently too poor so compliance with regulations is difficult to assess);
- bureaucratic inefficiency (for instance the units monitoring air and water quality often do not work together and do not share information);
- very limited human and technical resources (including few trained inspectors so it is impossible to monitor most polluting factories); and
- limited political support (as attempts at serious enforcement of existing legislation encounters strong political resistance).

Most examples of governments acting on environmental problems in Africa, Asia and Latin America (as in Europe and North America) owe much to well-organized citizen pressure. They usually occur in societies with representative forms of government. But government action usually consists of ad hoc responses to specific local pressures such as a group of fishermen complaining about industrial effluent damaging their livelihood or citizens complaining about the damage to their homes or farms coming from one particular plant or industrial complex. This is more common than coherent, sustained programmes of incentives, regulations and enforcement. One example of this ad hoc response comes from Taiwan where villagers living near an industrial zone in the south forced local companies to pay around US$35 million compensation for the damage caused by petrochemical plants' waste waters to coastal areas and fishing grounds. But the residents had to invade the industrial zone and force the plants to close down. They had also threatened to cut the supplies of coal to local power plants which would have meant power cuts in the heavy industrialized south (King 1988).

The constraints at city level

Virtually all the environmental measures outlined in this book depend on forms of 'better local practice'. These in turn depend on competent city and (for large cities or metropolitan areas) subcity (municipal/borough/district) government. One returns to the fact that most governments at these levels lack the trained personnel and the financial base and autonomy to provide the needed investments, services and pollution control. This weakness of city governments also makes other changes difficult to implement, from the enforcement of environmental legislation to the efficient collection of waste, management of solid-waste sites and improvement of traffic management. As Carl Bartone at the World Bank has commented, 'the most urgent need is to strengthen (Third World) waste management institutions at the municipal level, to improve their financial base, and then to introduce appropriate waste management technologies – in that order of priority' (quoted in Elkington and Shopley 1989).

City governments in Africa, Asia and Latin America often have one-hundredth or (at their most extreme) one-thousandth of the revenue per capita available to most city or municipal governments in Europe (UNCHS 1996). Yet their range of responsibilities is often comparable. The range of tasks for which urban governments are responsible vary considerably from nation to nation, but in most, they include many tasks that are central to a healthy environment: the regulation of building and land use, and of production (including pollution control); and the provision and maintenance of systems to supply water, sanitation and waste collection and its disposal (even if parts of this are contracted to private enterprises). Most have major responsibilities for traffic management, emergency services, streets and street lighting. Healthcare and schools are usually local responsibilities. Where some of these are the responsibility of central government agencies or are contracted to private companies, local governments usually have important supervisory roles. Most of these responsibilities are inadequately met or not met at all. It is common for local government budgets to have the equivalent of US$20–50 per person per year with most of it spent on recurrent expenditures; in some low-income nations, municipal governments have the equivalent of only a few US dollars per capita per year (UNCHS 1996). Thus, it is rare for local government to have any significant capacity for investment in expanding or extending infrastructure and services.

In addition, in many cities, rapid population growth means that the large deficits in terms of the number of people lacking piped water, sanitation, waste collection, schools, healthcare and emergency services also grow rapidly. In cities made up of different local government areas, it is generally the poorest and weakest local governments on the urban periphery that have the most rapid growth in population. In most cities, there are few (if any) mechanisms to channel funding from richer to poorer local government units.

One of the most critical roles of city and municipal government is providing the institutional means to ensure that the combination of all sectoral policies and actions achieves a balance between social, economic and environmental goals. To take only one example, the attitudes and policies of governments on the use of city resources and wastes is one of the most important factors in achieving such a balance. Dr Furedy has noted that

> *those who make decisions about formal recycling projects are usually not well informed about existing informal practices of waste recovery and recycling in their city and the possible implications of new interventions. Those directly involved (waste gatherers, traders and manufacturers) and those concerned about their health (community workers and informal groups) are rarely listened to* (Furedy 1990a).

Most urban authorities regard waste-pickers and many other waste-related activities as illegal or unhygienic. Some actively suppress and control such activities. Many tolerate it (within limits) since they have little alternative to offer those whose livelihoods depend on this work. Some have recognized that such informal processes can be part of their overall waste-management policy. But rarely do they appreciate the extent of the economic, social and environmental advantages, or the kinds of public provision and support that retain the economic and resource advantages, while reducing health risks and improving incomes for the poorer groups engaged in it. The extent of recycling within a city is also more driven by sectoral concerns than a broader consensus of what is best done (Cointreau and others 1984).

This obstacle of weak, ineffective and unrepresentative urban governments is not easily overcome. The acquisition by local governments of the power to raise substantial funding, the authority to direct private investments (and control pollution) and the financial base to meet their responsibilities for the provision of infrastructure and services is an intensely political issue. Powerful and usually well-organized vested interests oppose such changes, as they did in Europe and North America little more than a century ago. Indeed, in New York (among other cities) it took repeated cholera epidemics before opposition to such basic investments and new powers for municipal authorities could be overcome (Rosenberg 1962). In London, the proponents of piped water supplies and improved sanitation and waste collection in the early 19th century were ridiculed by many people in government and by the most influential newspapers (Wohl 1983).

There is another key constraint, elaborated in a new report on *Municipalities and Community Participation* (Plummer 2000). This source book on how municipalities can build their capacity to support community participation also points to the difficulties in doing so. Many municipal authorities are staffed by administrators and technical professionals who find the concept of community participation irrelevant. This is perhaps especially so in public works departments. Municipal officials have an incomplete knowledge of the potentials and limitations of participatory approaches. Even if they are willing to try participatory approaches, they lack the skills and resources. They also do not appreciate the difficulties in developing effective partnerships with community organizations, or the extent to which their bureaucratic procedures and official norms, codes and regulations inhibit participation. If municipal authorities want to support the kinds of civil-society driven processes outlined in Chapter 6, this will require a transfer of power and decision-making from municipal agencies to community organizations. Many international agencies also fail to recognize that the very nature of the conventional municipality is in conflict with the concept of participation (Plummer 2000).

THE ROLE OF INTERNATIONAL AGENCIES

The lack of interest in cities' environmental problems

Most aid agencies and development banks do not give much attention to cities' environmental problems, especially the problems that impact most on the health and livelihoods of poorer groups. This can be seen in the very low priority they give to, for instance, improving provision for water, sanitation and drainage or to supporting low-income groups in obtaining better quality housing. For many, this is due largely to the low priority they give to urban problems in general. Since the 1970s, many agencies chose to concentrate much of their support for projects in rural areas. Such a rural focus is particularly strong in donor agencies that concentrate most of their funding in the lowest income countries since these are also generally the least urbanized countries and also the countries where most of the poorest groups are in rural areas. A strong rural focus (underpinned by a recognition that donor agencies had previously given inadequate attention to the rural poor) has often been accompanied by an assumption that urban populations are far better provided with basic infrastructure and services than rural populations, including those that are essential for environmental health. This assumption has been supported by official figures on the provision for water and sanitation in rural and urban areas, but as discussed in Chapter 2, these figures greatly overstate the quality and extent of provision in urban areas. There has also been an assumption that a relatively small proportion of each nation's 'poor' lived in urban areas, and this too has been supported by official statistics, although again, the accuracy of these statistics is open to question (see Box 7.10). A widespread 'anti-urban' bias among international agencies also meant little understanding of the importance of well-governed cities and urban systems for more robust national and regional economies. In addition, far too little attention was given to strengthening the capacity of city and municipal governments to addressing environmental (and other) problems and to channelling support direct to low-income groups and their community organizations to support their efforts to improve their environment.

Although this 'anti-urban' bias is changing, many international agencies still have no urban policy and no specialized urban department or division, even though they support urban projects. This implies an assumption that urban projects need no specialist knowledge about urban contexts. And even in the agencies that have developed urban policies, there is still strong opposition from many staff to urban projects. However, growing evidence of the scale and depth of deprivation among urban populations and a recognition that these have been underestimated have encouraged some agencies to increase support for urban projects. Some have developed explicit urban policies and set up urban divisions or departments, usually to advise and support country or regional departments (Milbert with Peat 1999). An interest in urban projects is more evident in international agencies that work in a wide range of low- and middle-income countries (including many that have more than half their population in urban areas). There is also the fact that in many countries, urban populations have increased three- or fourfold since the early 1970s when many aid programmes first recognized their lack of attention to rural poverty and sought to remedy this. In addition, a wider recognition that well-functioning urban centres and systems are important for economic success has encouraged some rethinking of priorities with regard to urban investments.[16] So too has a recognition of the extent to which many low-income households have both rural and urban components to their livelihoods and that poverty-reduction strategies need to recognize this (Tacoli 1998).

---

16 This was a point strongly emphasized by the World Bank in its urban policy of 1993 (see World Bank 1993).

BOX 7.10 *THE UNDERESTIMATION OF THE SCALE AND NATURE OF URBAN POVERTY*

Most national and international estimates of the scale of poverty underestimate the scale and depth of urban poverty, because of unrealistic assumptions about the income level that urban inhabitants need to avoid poverty. Most estimates for the number of 'poor' people or people living in poverty are based on defining a poverty line (an income level that is said to be sufficient to meet a household's consumption needs) and then investigating how many households have incomes below this. Thus the number of 'poor' people is greatly influenced by the income level at which the poverty line is set (and the criteria used in doing so), and governments and international agencies can increase or decrease the number of 'poor' people by changing this income level or the criteria by which it is set.

Many nations still have one poverty line which is applied to all areas within the nation. This assumes that the income needed to avoid poverty is the same wherever someone lives, ie in rural areas, small urban centres or large cities. But in many urban settings, especially in the larger or more prosperous cities, the income level needed to avoid poverty is higher than in most rural areas or in less prosperous smaller centres, especially where official provision for water, sanitation, education, healthcare and public transport are very inadequate, and where the cost of buying, building or renting housing is particularly high (which is often linked to bureaucratic constraints on the increased supply of land for housing).

In most nations, the criteria used to define the poverty line (supposedly the income level needed to avoid poverty) fail to recognize the income that is needed to pay for non-food items. Income-based poverty lines are generally based on estimates of the cost of an 'adequate' diet, with some minor additional amount added for non-food expenditures (for instance a 20–30 per cent upward adjustment from the cost of a 'food-basket' which is considered to constitute an adequate diet). This greatly underestimates the income needed to avoid many of the deprivations that are part of poverty, including the income needed to afford secure and adequate quality accommodation with adequate provision for water, sanitation and waste collection, and also to meet the costs of transport, healthcare and keeping children at school. Renting a room takes 20–30 per cent of poor households' income in many cities, even though the quality of the accommodation is often very inadequate. Or, for city households who seek to keep down housing costs and live in informal settlements in peripheral locations, fares on public transport can take up 10–20 per cent of their income. Many households have such inadequate access to water and sanitation that paying vendors or purchasing water from kiosks or other sources and paying for 'pay-as-you-use' toilets takes up 5–20 per cent of their income (see Chapter 2).

Most poverty lines do not recognize the income that households need to meet the costs of healthcare and to keep their children at school. They often make no allowance for these costs, since they assume that there is public provision for education and healthcare. Yet keeping children at school can represent a high cost for low-income households – for instance having to pay for private provision when there is no public provision or the payments that have to be made even when entry into a government school is free – for instance the cost of uniforms, school meals, school books and exam fees (see for example Kanji 1995) – or the informal payments that are often required from parents because government funding for the school is so inadequate. Payments made for healthcare and medicines can also represent a high cost for low-income households and take up a significant proportion of total income (see for instance Pryer 1993), especially where public provision for healthcare is non-existent or of poor quality (for instance with long queues and such poor treatment that low-income households turn to private provision). And perhaps not surprisingly, poverty lines do not take into account the income needed to pay the bribes and/or informal payments that so many low-income households have to pay to stop their house being demolished or to stop the goods they are selling on the street or in informal (illegal) stores being confiscated.

International poverty lines, such as the World Bank's US$1 a day poverty line, are even more misleading in that these imply that the income needed to avoid poverty is not only the same in all locations within a country but also the same across countries. This leads to a large underestimation as to the scale of urban 'income poverty' since the income level needed to avoid poverty is much higher than US$1 a day in most large and/or prosperous cities.

A reliance only on income-based poverty lines to define and measure poverty also means that many other aspects of urban deprivation are overlooked or underestimated, including:

- *Inadequate, unstable or risky asset bases* (within a recognition that there are different kinds of assets that help people to avoid poverty or its effects, including assets that are important for generating or maintaining income, assets that help low-income people to cope with economic shocks or natural disasters, and avoid the need to take on onerous debt burdens, and assets that limit environmental hazards that can have serious health and economic costs).
- *Limited or no right to make demands within the political system or to get a fair response – 'voicelessness and powerlessness'* – (often within a framework that does not guarantees civil and political rights – for instance the right to have representative government, the right to organize and make demands and to get a fair response, the right to justice, which includes protection against forced eviction, corruption and exposure to environmental hazards).
- *Poor quality/insecure housing and a lack of basic infrastructure*, including insecure tenure and inadequate provision for safe and sufficient water, sanitation and drainage (with the heavy health burden that this imposes and the high economic and other costs this also brings), although

higher incomes generally allow households to find more secure and better quality accommodation.

- *Inadequate basic services*, including good quality education, healthcare, emergency services and protection from crime and violence.
- *Discrimination* in, for instance, labour markets and access to services, political representation and justice. This includes the discrimination that women face in labour markets and access to property, credit and services. It also includes the discrimination faced by people based on their race or caste. Discrimination is often much underestimated as a cause of poverty.

One reason why governments and international agencies use income-based poverty lines is that it appears more politically neutral. It obscures the forces that underlie impoverishment or exclusion, including labour exploitation, discrimination, lack of political influence and absence of a system to guarantee civil and political rights. Defining poverty as a lack of income can also obscure the deprivations that are linked more to weak and ineffective government structures than to income – for instance local government incapacity to ensure cost-effective provision of good quality schools, health centres, land for housing and provision for water, sanitation and drainage. It is common for large sections of those lacking basic infrastructure and services to be able to pay for these; many are already paying more for informal provision than a well-managed official system would cost.

A few agencies such as the World Bank and the Inter-American Development Bank have long had a large and diverse portfolio of urban projects; for the Inter-American Development Bank, these go back to the early 1960s; for the World Bank, to the beginning of the 1970s. More recently, other agencies have developed large urban programmes, perhaps most notably the Overseas Economic Cooperation Fund from Japan (which in 1999 became part of the Japan Bank for International Cooperation). But any attempt to analyse the relative priority given by any agency to 'urban' and 'rural' projects runs into two difficulties. The first is that most projects do not benefit exclusively 'rural' or 'urban' populations. For instance, donor support for building or improving ports and markets in urban areas may be classified as 'urban', but they are often important for supporting agricultural production or increasing agricultural exports. Much of the improved infrastructure and services that stronger local, regional or national economies need will be based in urban areas but will also serve rural production. Donor support for urban-based hospitals may be (and should be) part of a hierarchy of healthcare facilities that include rural healthcare facilities (with urban hospitals also acting as referral centres to which rural health centres send the cases that they cannot treat), while donor support for urban-based secondary schools and higher education institutions should serve both rural and urban populations. (Similarly, many rural projects should bring benefits to urban populations – see Chapter 5).

The second difficulty in analysing the relative priority to 'urban' and 'rural' is that many donor-funded projects include both rural and urban components, as in, for instance, support for the improvement of healthcare or basic education in a particular state or province. Most agencies also have a significant proportion of their funding allocated to 'non-projects' (for instance support for structural adjustment or to help pay for the import of certain commodities or for sectoral policy change as in support for changing the education system) which cannot be classified as 'urban' or 'rural'.

The low priority given to urban environmental problems

In reviewing the current role of international agencies, we have three primary concerns:

1   That most international agencies give a low priority to those interventions that address the environmental health problems that low-income groups face in urban areas and that account for a very large part of the preventable disease and injury burden.
2   That few international agencies give any priority to helping develop the capacity of city and municipal governments to address their environmental (and other) problems.
3   That most international agencies have not developed channels that allow support direct to low-income groups and their community organizations (and thus to support the civil-society driven solutions described in Chapter 6).

In addressing urban environmental problems, our main interest is in the relative priority within total funding flows to three categories:

1   *Improved environmental health in urban areas.* Within this, the analysis will consider the priority given to:
    −   Improved housing for low-income groups (including 'slum' and squatter upgrading programmes, serviced site and core housing schemes and housing finance systems that are meant to serve low-income households).
    −   Improved water supply, sanitation and drainage for urban inhabitants but only including projects with major components to increase or extend provision for city inhabitants; projects that focus only on increasing supply (for instance building reservoirs) or on sewage treatment are classified under urban infrastructure.
    −   Primary healthcare services and the control of infectious and parasitic diseases.
    −   Integrated community development and other measures focused on improving infrastructure, services or livelihoods for low-income urban populations (including social funds and the AGETIP type projects that seek to generate employment and improve public works).
2   *Building or strengthening the capacity of city or municipal authorities.*

3 *Urban pollution control.*
   - Air and water pollution control.
   - Solid waste management.

There is also an interest in the scale and nature of support to public transport, both from the perspective of meeting low-income groups' needs and from an environmental perspective in terms of reducing air pollution and greenhouse gas emissions.

The analyses of selected international agencies' urban funding also looks at the relative priority given to other urban projects, while recognizing the limitations noted above in being able to distinguish between 'urban' and 'rural' projects. It also sees if a low priority to improved environmental health in urban areas is partly explained by a high priority to environmental health in rural areas.

However, it is difficult to give a summary of the involvement in urban development of all international agencies. One problem is the number of such agencies. These agencies can broadly be divided into three categories:

1   The official bilateral aid programmes of governments. Many official bilateral programmes include two or more different agencies. These directly or indirectly fund most aid and technical cooperation, including much of the work done by the agencies in the two categories below. These include not only the bilateral programmes of nations in Europe and North America, and of Japan, Australia and New Zealand, but also those of some high-income Arab nations and some nations that were formerly part of the Soviet Union (although many of these are also major recipients of development assistance). Some middle-income nations also have development assistance agencies.
2   The official multilateral agencies that depend on the bilateral aid programmes to fund the aid or technical cooperation they provide, and these include the World Bank, the regional development banks (the Asian, Inter-American and Caribbean Development Banks), the many United Nations specialized agencies and the multilateral agencies funded by Arab states or nations belonging to the Organization of Petroleum Exporting Countries (OPEC). The World Bank and the regional development banks depend on the bilateral agencies to fund their 'aid' programmes (mostly loans or 'credits' provided with subsidized interest rates), but they also draw a large part of their funding from world capital markets from which they provide 'non-concessional loans' (ie loans that are not considered as aid because they have to be repaid fully). UNICEF is unusual in that it is the only major official multilateral agency that draws a significant part of its funding direct from contributions by the general public.
3   The international NGOs. There are thousands of these, ranging from organizations with annual budgets of hundreds of millions of dollars to those with only a few thousand. Most of the larger international NGOs depend on a combination of funding from official bilateral aid programmes and from private contributions.

Since it is not possible to cover in detail all these agencies (and for many it is impossible to do so since they publish so little detail about their work in urban areas), this summary concentrates on some of the largest agencies. First, a relatively detailed analysis is given for three of the largest agencies: the World Bank, the Asian Development Bank and the former OECF (Overseas Economic Cooperation Fund, Japan). This is followed by some comments about the urban programmes of the main bilateral aid programmes from countries in Europe and North America and some other multilateral agencies and (in the following section) of the international NGOs.

The urban programmes of the World Bank, the Asian Development Bank and the (former) OECF

Tables 7.2–7.4 show the priority given to urban projects for three of the largest international agencies. These are featured here in part because they are among the largest agencies and the ones with among the most influential urban programmes, in part because these are also agencies that publish details of all the projects they fund, so an analysis such as those presented in these tables is possible.[17] Most bilateral agencies do not publish details of all the projects they support so it is impossible to undertake the kind of analysis featured below. Thus comments that follow this section on the priority given by other agencies to urban development and within this to the urban environment are less detailed than for the three agencies considered in this section.

Priority to improved environmental health

Among all agencies, the former OECF gives among the highest priority to urban development projects; over the period 1987–1998, these received 30 per cent of total funding commitments. As Table 7.2 shows, more than half the funding to urban development went to urban infrastructure projects, especially ports, airports, intracity roads and bridges, and water and sanitation projects whose primary focus was not extending or improving supplies to inadequately served city inhabitants. Some 16 per cent of the funding for urban development in these 12 years went to improve environmental health, with nearly all of this going to water and sanitation. Very little went to supporting improved housing (only one small loan was given over the whole period specifically to housing in urban areas, to support housing finance systems in India, although one or two other multi-sector projects may have had small components to improve housing). Very little went to primary healthcare. The agency has long emphasized economic growth and the infrastructure needed to support this, although there are signs of some reconsideration of this emphasis and an acknowledgement that approaches are needed to directly address the situation

---

17 These analyses were undertaken by reviewing descriptions of all the projects funded by these three agencies for the years specified in the tables and identifying all those that conform to the categories in the tables. For more details on the methodology, see Satterthwaite 1997b or contact the Human Settlements Programme at IIED, 3 Endsleigh Street, London WC1H ODD, UK, e-mail: humans@iied.org. Special thanks are due to Åsa Jonnson who helped to undertake the analysis of the OECF.

Table 7.2 *OECF lending to urban development, 1987–1998*

	1987–90	*1990–92*	*1993–95*	*1996–98*	*1987–98*
Annual average total commitments (billion US$ constant value 1990)	7.0	7.1	8.7	8.1	7.7
Per cent of total going to urban development	20.3	24.3	34.5	39.0	30.1
Main priorities for urban lending: Proportion of urban development lending going to:					
Improved environmental health	*18.3*	*11.9*	*19.3*	*15.0*	*16.3*
Improved housing for low-income groups (including housing finance)	0.0	0.4	0.0	0.0	0.1
Improved water supply, sanitation and drainage for city inhabitants	16.7	11.5	17.8	10.4	13.9
Primary health care services	0.0	0.0	0.2	0.2	0.1
Integrated community development and other (including social funds)	1.7	0.0	1.3	4.4	2.1
Urban infrastructure	*48.1*	*53.3*	*64.1*	*51.4*	*55.3*
Airports	3.4	4.5	12.0	14.9	10.3
Electrification/city specific power	5.4	1.9	14.0	3.3	6.8
Ports	22.8	19.5	9.8	7.0	12.6
Water, sanitation, drainage; city level	4.2	10.5	17.5	13.9	12.9
Roads and bridges	6.3	12.5	8.6	11.2	9.8
Gas production and distribution	2.8	0.0	0.6	0.0	0.6
Integrated urban development	2.7	3.8	0.0	1.2	1.5
Other urban infrastructure*	0.6	0.6	1.6	0.0	0.7
Urban pollution control					
Air and water pollution control	0.0	13.7	3.1	13.3	8.1
Solid-waste management	1.0	0.0	0.3	0.1	0.3
Other urban services	*14.2*	*18.8*	*11.4*	*18.5*	*15.6*
Primary/basic education	0.0	2.8	0.0	1.8	1.1
Secondary and Higher education	5.4	2.1	6.3	2.3	4.0
Public transport	7.4	12.3	4.2	13.6	9.4
Hospitals, medical equipment, etc	1.5	1.6	1.0	0.8	1.1
Other urban services	0.0	0.0	0.0	0.0	0.0
Building municipal capacity	*1.8*	*0.0*	*1.4*	*0.7*	*0.9*
*Miscellaneous***	*16.6*	*2.4*	*0.4*	*1.0*	*3.4*

* Including markets and industrial estates.
** These include tourism projects and projects for building materials. The 'miscellaneous' category has a significant proportion of all funding for the first period (1987–1989) due to several large loans to cement factories.

of the poor (OECF 1999). But in summary, this is an agency whose portfolio of urban projects gives a low priority to those projects or programmes that address the environmental health problems of low-income groups.

The World Bank's commitments to urban development provide an interesting contrast. The proportion of total funding commitments going to urban development is less, although substantially higher during the 1990s than in the 1980s; the proportion of the Bank's total commitments allocated to urban development for 1993–1995 was double that of 1981–1983. But the priority given to improved environmental health within its urban projects is much higher than the former OECF and the priority to urban infrastructure much lower. Ironically, although the World Bank is often seen as the agency that promotes 'economic efficiency' above 'improved social provision', at least in its urban development lending, this is less evident than in the urban programmes of most other official development cooperation agencies. Conventional urban infrastructure projects such as ports, airports, city highways and bridges were receiving a very low proportion of the Bank's total funding commitments by the late 1990s. Improved environmental health received more than two-fifths of all the World Bank's commitments to urban development from 1981–1998 while urban infrastructure received 22 per cent. The World Bank is also unusual in comparison with most other development cooperation agencies in allocating a significant (and increasing) priority to primary healthcare. Table 7.3 shows this within its lending to urban development; this increased priority to primary healthcare is also evident in rural areas too. By the late 1990s, more than a seventh of the World Bank's urban development funding was going to urban primary healthcare, compared with 2 per cent in 1981–1983. Table 7.3 also shows how the World Bank has greatly increased the scale of its support to integrated community development projects (which seek to improve a range of infrastructure and services for lower-income groups) and for social funds or other forms of local fund that support improved infrastructure and service provision that are active in urban areas.

The Asian Development Bank's support for urban development is closer to the OECF pattern in that urban infrastructure receives a higher priority than improved environmental health, although the differences are not so dramatic, and by the late 1990s, improved environmental health was receiving more than urban infrastructure. The proportion of the Asian Development Bank's total commitments going to urban development are surprisingly constant during the whole period 1981–1998, despite significant changes in the relative priority given to different aspects of urban development.

Priority to reaching urban-poor groups with improved housing and basic services

Perhaps one of the most notable points arising from Tables 7.2–7.4 is how low a priority is given to projects or programmes that are meant to improve housing for low-income groups. The very low priority to this is particularly notable for the former OECF. The Asian Development Bank also gives this a low priority, although the proportion of its urban funding going to this increased during the late 1990s. The World Bank had given a relatively high priority to this during

Table 7.3 *World Bank lending to urban development, 1981–1998*

	1981–83	*1984–86*	*1987–89*	*1990–92*	*1993–95*	*1996–98*	*1981–98*
Annual average total commitments (billion US$ constant value 1990)	18.0	18.5	21.1	20.9	19.9	19.5	20.7
Per cent of total going to urban development	14.5	17.7	18.4	22.5	28.5	22.2	20.7

Main priorities for urban lending: Proportion of urban development lending going to:

	1981–83	*1984–86*	*1987–89*	*1990–92*	*1993–95*	*1996–98*	*1981–98*
Improved environmental health	*42.6*	*42.9*	*41.5*	*40.9*	*40.8*	*51.4*	*43.3*
Improved housing for low-income groups (including housing finance)	10.6	12.8	16.7	7.5	3.7	2.1	8.2
Improved water supply, sanitation and drainage for city inhabitants	27.9	22.3	16.5	13.2	13.8	12.8	16.6
Primary healthcare services	2.0	5.5	6.4	14.7	13.0	15.4	10.5
Integrated community development and other (including social funds)	2.2	2.3	1.9	5.5	10.4	21.2	8.0
Urban infrastructure	*26.8*	*30.6*	*36.6*	*16.5*	*18.9*	*10.6*	*22.2*
Airports	1.0	0.0	0.0	0.1	0.0	0.0	0.1
Electrification/city specific power	5.9	8.1	10.7	2.6	0.6	4.8	4.9
Ports	9.9	12.3	5.5	2.4	1.3	0.2	4.4
Water, sanitation, drainage; city level	1.1	1.2	5.1	2.6	3.3	1.3	2.6
Roads and bridges	0.0	0.7	0.0	0.4	1.6	1.3	0.8
Gas production and distribution	0.0	0.0	0.0	0.6	0.0	0.0	0.1
Integrated urban development	8.8	8.4	13.7	5.6	10.9	3.0	8.4
Other urban infrastructure*	0.0	0.0	1.7	2.4	1.3	0.0	1.0
Urban pollution control							
Air and water pollution control	0.0	0.0	0.5	1.5	5.4	2.2	2.0
Solid-waste management	0.0	0.0	0.0	0.0	0.1	0.0	0.0
Other urban services	*27.0*	*18.8*	*15.5*	*32.2*	*29.4*	*34.8*	*27.0*
Primary/basic education	5.0	6.0	3.7	13.8	16.7	18.1	11.6
Secondary and higher education	20.2	10.5	6.2	15.3	7.9	7.0	10.6
Public transport	1.6	0.6	5.2	0.8	4.3	4.8	3.1

Table 7.3 *continued*

	1981–83	*1984–86*	*1987–89*	*1990–92*	*1993–95*	*1996–98*	*1981–98*
Hospitals, medical equipment, etc	0.2	1.7	0.4	2.2	0.4	5.0	1.7
Other urban services	0.0	0.0	0.1	0.0	0.1	0.0	0.0
Building municipal capacity	*1.3*	*3.8*	*4.6*	*5.9*	*4.7*	*0.9*	*3.7*
*Miscellaneous***	*2.3*	*3.8*	*1.3*	*3.1*	*0.9*	*0.2*	*1.7*

* Including markets and industrial estates.
** These include tourism projects and projects for building materials.

the 1980s but support declined dramatically during the 1990s. The World Bank had pioneered support for upgrading programmes and serviced site schemes during the 1970s, and support for housing finance systems that were intended to better serve lower-income households in the 1980s. It was one of the few international agencies to give these two areas substantial support. But these were no longer priorities during the mid- and late-1990s.

Priority to strengthening municipal capacity

Many agencies have shifted a significant part of their support for urban development from specific urban projects to what was originally called strengthening the institutional capacity of urban governments and later called supporting 'good governance'. The World Bank was among the first agencies to do so and it became much the largest donor in terms of financial support for this. This can be seen in the increasing scale of funding commitments specifically to increase the institutional capacity of recipient governments to address urban problems and to enhance urban government's capacity to install and maintain infrastructure and services. Between 1970 and 1998, the World Bank made over 50 project commitments to building the institutional and financial capacity of urban governments or to institutions that support urban development. All but two were made since 1983. Although some World Bank urban projects have long had institution building components relating to urban government, it was only in the 1980s that project commitments were made specifically to institution-building for urban areas, training in urban management, local government finance and urban planning. Commitments to building the institutional and financial capacity of urban authorities totalled close to US$2.6 billion between 1983 and 1998, with close to three-quarters of this committed in the years 1988–1995 (with no commitment made during 1996 and relatively small commitments during 1997 and 1998). One reason for this increased support, at least up to 1995, stems from a recognition of the extent to which the new infrastructure or services that the Bank helped to fund can deteriorate or cease to function, without effective local agencies to provide management and maintenance. Another reason for strengthening the capacity of urban authorities is that this will increase the capacity of recipient governments to invest in infrastructure and services, and thus increase their demand for World Bank funding.

Table 7.4 *Asian Development Bank lending to urban development, 1981–1998*

	1981–83	1984–86	1987–89	1990–92	1993–95	1996–98	1981–98
Annual average total commitments (billion US$ constant value 1990)	2.4	2.5	3.3	4.5	4.3	5.9	3.8
Per cent of total going to urban development	21.4	20.3	20.8	22.5	23.7	16.5	22.7

Main priorities for urban lending: proportion of urban development lending going to:

	1981–83	1984–86	1987–89	1990–92	1993–95	1996–98	1981–98
Improved environmental health	34.7	53.6	28.1	12.1	25.8	38.0	30.5
Improved housing for low-income groups (including housing finance)	0.0	3.0	1.7	0.6	0.0	5.6	2.3
Improved water supply, sanitation and drainage for city inhabitants	24.0	27.1	17.0	8.8	19.3	6.7	14.5
Primary health care services	1.9	8.6	9.0	2.6	2.8	3.2	4.1
Integrated community development and other (including social funds)	8.8	14.8	0.4	0.0	3.7	22.4	9.5
Urban infrastructure	29.8	20.7	47.7	57.9	32.4	23.3	35.4
Airports	0.0	0.8	0.4	0.0	7.3	4.9	2.9
Electrification/city specific power	10.8	1.0	19.5	12.8	16.2	2.5	10.0
Ports	7.1	14.9	9.1	15.9	3.4	5.9	8.8
Water, sanitation, drainage; city level	5.6	0.0	0.0	0.0	0.0	3.6	1.6
Roads and bridges	0.0	0.0	0.0	4.8	0.0	0.0	0.9
Gas production and distribution	0.0	0.0	0.0	0.0	0.0	0.0	0.0
Integrated urban development	6.3	4.0	18.6	21.0	5.5	5.4	10.2
Other urban infrastructure*	0.0	0.0	0.1	3.5	0.0	1.0	0.9
Urban pollution control							
Air and water pollution control	0.4	0.0	0.0	6.7	9.3	15.8	7.6
Solid-waste management	0.0	0.0	0.0	0.0	0.0	0.0	0.0
Other urban services	34.3	21.9	23.7	23.0	24.8	18.7	23.3
Primary/basic education	1.3	0.0	4.0	3.7	1.1	7.2	3.7
Secondary and higher education	23.8	19.3	19.6	17.7	23.7	10.8	17.9
Public transport	0.0	0.0	0.0	0.0	0.0	0.0	0.0
Hospitals, medical equipment, etc	9.2	0.0	0.0	1.6	0.0	0.0	1.2

Table 7.4 *continued*

	1981–83	1984–86	*1987–89*	1990–92	*1993–95*	1996–98	*1981–98*
Other urban services	0.0	2.6	0.0	0.0	6.9	0.9	0.5
Building municipal capacity	0.0	2.3	0.0	0.0	6.9	2.6	2.3
*Miscellaneous***	0.8	1.7	0.6	0.3	0.8	1.7	1.0

* Including markets and industrial estates.
** These include tourism projects and projects for building materials.

The World Bank also provided an increasing number of loans to national or municipal institutions responsible for providing funding to local governments, as in loans to support the work of the Cities and Villages Development Bank in Jordan, the Autonomous Municipal Bank in Honduras and the Fonds d'Equipement Communal in Morocco. More loans have provided credit direct to certain urban authorities. These are also examples of the Bank funding intermediary institutions that in turn fund projects, rather than the Bank funding the projects themselves. A Bank document (Kessides 1997) highlights the importance of this shift from 'retailing to wholesaling' of urban development finance, as the Bank gives less attention to developing specific projects, and provides more support to recipient governments that in turn support the development of sub-projects by municipalities or communities. This shift was also evident in water and sanitation as the Bank moved from funding the construction of infrastructure to funding the transformation of recipient government institutions to make them more responsive to low-income communities' preferences and willingness to pay (ibid). This helps to explain the falling proportion of World Bank funding going to urban water and sanitation projects (Table 7.4). This shift means increasing Bank involvement in working with municipal governments and in changing central–local government relations (ibid). Comparable shifts from funding projects to funding institutions that fund projects or funding changes in the institutional structure of sectors are also evident in education and health. By the early 1990s, many sector adjustment loans were for reforms within social services or had within them components for social service reform. An increasing number of structural adjustment loans included provisions to try to widen access to basic social services or to ensure that funding for primary level services did not fall, within overall cuts in government expenditures (Tjønneland and others 1998). Many urban loans were also to support privatization.

The growing interest among donors in municipal government capacity building led to the setting up of the World Bank–United Nations Centre for Human Settlements' Urban Management Programme in the early 1990s, funded by the UNDP and various bilateral donors (with offices in each region) and, most recently, to the Cities Alliance, formed in 1999.

The former OECF gave a much lower priority than the World Bank to building municipal capacity. The Asian Development Bank also gave a lower priority to this than the World Bank, except for the mid- to late-1990s when this received increasing levels of support.

Priority to urban pollution control
Tables 7.2–7.4 show that for all three agencies, urban pollution control suddenly appears as a significant item in their funding commitments in the 1990s. The increase in support for this was particularly notable at the Asian Development Bank where this received virtually no support during the 1980s but received 9 per cent of all commitments to urban development for 1993–1995 and 16 per cent of all commitments for 1996–1998. This support was highly concentrated in China and the Philippines (with three loans focusing on improving air quality in Manila).

Priority to urban public transport
Most large agencies give little or no attention to public transport. For the World Bank, this received only 3 per cent of the funding allocated to urban development for the period 1981 to 1998 and this was heavily concentrated in Latin America (with almost nothing in sub-Saharan Africa); for the Asian Development Bank, public transport received no support at all. Given the importance of a well-functioning public transport system for urban development, the extent to which this can benefit low-income groups and the extent to which in most cities it can be built around buses (and thus not require very expensive metros), this is puzzling. The example of Curitiba's bus-centred public transport system was given earlier. The possibilities of basing a good public transport system on buses and bus-lanes has also been well known for 30 years (see for instance Ward 1976a). Public transport received a higher priority from the OECF, although this is more linked to the export of Japanese technology and construction contracts.

The urban programmes of other official international agencies
Among the multilateral agencies, UNICEF is also an agency with a long history of urban involvement and one of the most interesting and innovative, in terms of addressing the environmental health problems faced by the urban poor. UNICEF's experience is a little paradoxical in that there are many innovative urban projects that received UNICEF support over the last 30 years but the agency itself, especially its headquarters in New York, has been reluctant to support urban initiatives. For most of the 1980s and early 1990s, the official view from headquarters was that urban interventions were too expensive and reached too few people. Yet any broad review of international agency involvement in community-driven urban projects finds many examples of 'urban basic service programmes' supported by UNICEF country offices. UNICEF is far more decentralized than most international agencies since most of its staff are in its country offices in low- and middle-income countries rather than at its headquarters, and many country offices supported urban basic service programmes. Yet these received only a small proportion of all UNICEF funding and country offices usually had a role more as a catalyst for these urban basic service programmes and supporter of other local, national and international agencies than as the main funder. Interviews with UNICEF staff also revealed the difficulties that UNICEF staff faced in supporting urban initiatives.[18]

Among the large official aid agencies from high-income nations, most do not have major urban programmes. Their lack of interest in urban projects (and often a lack of any urban division or department) helps to explain why so few of them publish figures on the proportion of their funds that goes to urban areas. For agencies that do publish figures about their urban programmes, the proportion of their funding going to urban projects is usually between 2 and 12 per cent (Milbert and Peat 1999). But such official statistics are misleading because these figures are generally the proportion of funding being managed by an urban division or classified as 'urban' and it does not include many urban projects being implemented by other divisions or classified in other categories. For instance, staff from the World Bank expressed surprise in our figures for the proportion of World Bank funding going to urban areas since these appeared to be substantially higher than their official figures. But their figures included only the projects that the Bank classifies as urban development, and not the many urban projects that are classified under categories such as Health, Nutrition and Population or Education.

Two reviews of the involvement of development cooperation agencies in urban development (Satterthwaite 1997b, Milbert and Peat 1999) highlight the relatively low priority given by most agencies to urban development but also to the considerable urban programmes of several bilateral agencies. These include the Canadian International Development Agency (although a large part of it is funded through other Canadian institutions), the UK Department for International Development (formerly the Overseas Development Administration), the French Development Fund (formerly CCCE), the US Government's Agency for International Development (mainly through its Urban Environment Credit Programme) and the two largest development cooperation agencies of the German government – GTZ (the main technical cooperation agency) and KfW (the main funder of development projects). Milbert and Peat (1999) note that many of these urban programmes are long established – for instance the credit programme of USAID (United States Agency for International Development) (although this operated as the Housing Guaranty Programme from 1964 to 1993) and the urban programme of French bilateral aid that has long been concentrated in French-speaking Africa.

For those agencies for which there is sufficient published information on their support to 'urban projects', most give a high proportion of their funds to large urban infrastructure projects such as water and sanitation, ports, power stations (and electrification), public transport, hospitals, and secondary or higher education institutions. For many bilateral agency projects, this is in part linked to promoting their exports and contracts for their own companies rather than any explicit policy to improve conditions in urban areas. For instance, in

---

18 This paragraph might be taken as a criticism of UNICEF, yet this is an agency that has long had an intense internal debate about how the relatively modest amount of funding it has in most of its country offices can be spent to the greatest benefit for children. However, for those working in urban areas, the extent to which the institution failed to support the innovation shown by many of its staff members in urban basic service programmes and to draw on their experience in promoting more participatory, community-driven responses to urban deprivation represents a lost opportunity.

the relatively few instances where public transport systems have received substantial support, those sponsored by bilateral agencies tend to mean large civil construction contracts for companies from the donor nation. Projects that directly address the environmental health needs of low-income groups receive a low priority. For instance, few bilateral agencies give a high priority to water, sanitation and basic healthcare (Satterthwaite 1997b, Randel and German 1997, Randel and German 1998). When the OECD Development Cooperation Directorate (the official coordinating body for the large bilateral donors) sought to analyse the scale of funding from bilateral agencies to urban projects in the early 1990s, its figures showed the low priority given to urban development and within this, very little going to housing programmes (including slum and squatter upgrading) and healthcare, and almost nothing to pollution control for the years 1986 to 1990 (OECD 1992). Very little was also going to strengthen the capacity of urban governments. Unfortunately, no more recent figures on the scale of support for urban development have become available.

This focus on large capital projects with little or no attention to strengthening local government capacity has brought many failures. Cities in low- and middle-income nations are littered with projects or capital goods that proved ineffective or inappropriate: buses, refuse-collection trucks and water-treatment plants that could not be maintained; waste incineration or composting plants that do not work or which that produced the anticipated cost-savings; and sophisticated metro systems that do not serve most of the poor areas of the city, yet whose revenues from fares do not even cover their operating costs, let alone the bill for their construction.[19] Our analysis of donor-funded urban projects in the late 1980s and early 1990s found that many were to rehabilitate infrastructure or replace capital goods that had fallen into disrepair, and that had been funded by donor agencies, some years previously.

Urban governments in low- and middle-income countries receive little support for the implementation of other interventions that could help to improve city environments such as: improved solid-waste collection and disposal; more effective pollution control; improved public transport; and land management programmes that ensure a better match between urban needs (especially increasing the supply and reducing the cost of land for housing, and ensuring sufficient open space for children's play and recreation) and the protection of ecological resources (including wetlands, important natural landscapes and agricultural land).

Few aid agencies have a coherent policy for the support they provide to urban development. Decisions about urban projects are made on an ad hoc basis with little attention to how particular projects or investments contribute to developing the capacity and competence of recipient governments to address environmental problems. There is little coordination between donors to ensure some coherence between all the urban projects funded by different donors, although this may reflect recipient governments' reluctance to set up the administrative and managerial structure to promote a more coherent policy.

---

19 With regard to metros, see Ortuzar 1983 and World Bank 1988. For an example of water-treatment plants, see Cohen 1987, and Elkington and Shopley 1989.

It is rare for donor agencies to support projects or programmes to build urban governments' institutional capacity so the local authorities that have responsibility for addressing environmental problems can actually do so. Over the last three decades, as most countries urbanized rapidly, too little attention has been given by donor agencies (or governments) to ensure that city and municipal authorities acquired the power, skills and resources to manage this rapid growth.

However, there is some evidence that this is changing. For instance, several bilateral agencies have rethought their urban programmes and published urban strategies in recent years, including Sida (Swedish International Development Cooperation Agency), Cida (Canadian International Development Agency), DFID (Department for International Development), the Swiss Agency for Development and Cooperation (SDC) and USAID, while a new development cooperation agency was formed within Denmark, DANCED, which has a significant urban programme (and one that concentrates on environmental improvement). In addition, an increasing number of agencies have considerable experience with supporting projects or programmes that are reaching low-income urban households with improved housing and living conditions, even if these still represent a very small proportion of their total funding. These include the slum and squatter upgrading programmes described earlier. The UK government's Department for International Development has funded many upgrading programmes, mainly in India. The Swedish International Development Cooperation Agency has supported various initiatives to reach low-income groups with improved housing and basic services in Latin America, including setting up the Foundation for Low Income Housing (FUPROVI) in Costa Rica and the Programme for Local Development (PRODEL) in Nicaragua (Sida 1997, Stein 2000). The German government's technical cooperation agency GTZ has a long-established and varied programme of support for urban interventions that improve housing and health for low-income groups. Many bilateral donors also support an increasingly significant 'urban' programme through co-funding urban projects implemented by other agencies, especially the World Bank.

One significant innovation in this field has been the channelling of bilateral and multilateral funds to social funds or socially oriented public works programmes. One of the best known is AGETIP in Senegal (the English translation of its name being The Agency for the Implementation of Public Interest Work) which was set up in 1989 with support from various bilateral and multilateral donors. Its objectives were to create jobs in urban areas while also undertaking socially useful tasks. A third of its funds went to urban environment projects (including sanitation, water supplies, drainage, electrification and roads) with 24 per cent to education and 22 per cent to health (MELISSA 1998). Many African countries have AGETIP-like agencies – for instance AGETUR in Benin which has helped to improve the urban environment (Fanou and Grant 2000). The World Bank has increased considerably the scale of its funding to social funds or socially oriented public works programmes in recent years.

The extent to which social funds support projects in urban areas varies considerably; in some nations, they concentrate on rural projects. Such funds also vary greatly in the nature of their relationship with government from autonomous agencies outside regular government bureaucracies to locations within government agencies but operating with varying degrees of independence. They also vary a lot in the extent to which they fund civil society and municipal initiatives. While many have been successful in supporting a large and diverse number of initiatives that have improved infrastructure and services and generated jobs, there are some broader issues that need consideration, including:

- To what extent are they taking attention away from much needed (but more difficult) government reform at national or provincial level, especially in making ministries of health and education more effective?
- To what extent are they helping to increase the competence, capacity and accountability of city and municipal authorities (or are they simply bypassing them)?
- Are they capable of supporting the kinds of civil-society driven processes that were described in Chapter 6 or do they concentrate on quick-to-implement, private-contractor delivered 'solutions'?
- Are they increasing the funding available for poverty reduction or social provision, or are other parts of the government cutting back because the social funds take over their work?
- To what extent are they set up for the convenience of donor agencies, rather than the most effective social response to poverty reduction (Fumo and others 2000).

Many donor agencies are also showing a greater interest in strengthening urban governance.

Given the obvious link between good urban governance and the achievement of development goals (including improved environmental health and poverty reduction), there has been a growing interest among many donors in improving urban management (focusing specifically on improving the competence and capacity of public institutions) or urban governance (with a wider focus, including support for democratization and greater accountability, and support for civil society groups). This should stop the rapid deterioration of so many donor-funded urban infrastructure projects, as it should increase the local capacity to manage and maintain them. It should also make donor-funded urban programmes much easier, as it builds the capacity of recipient government partners to invest in and manage urban infrastructure, and international donors increasingly recognize the difficulties in funding successful interventions without capable and accountable local partners.

This interest in building the capacity of urban authorities to invest in and manage urban development was pioneered by the World Bank as noted earlier and now it has become common for other agencies to support institution building, training in urban management, local government finance and urban planning. For instance, during the 1990s, it became an accepted part of the support provided by USAID and by the Inter-American Development Bank. Many bilateral donors' growing interest in this topic is shown by their contributions to the Urban Management Programme.

These and other initiatives are seeking to involve city authorities more directly in project formulation and implementation. Some bilateral donors have developed channels of support for urban development through local governments and international NGOs within their own country. New international networks have also developed to support city and municipal authorities in low- or middle-income countries or to help them to share their experiences or voice their concerns in international discussions. During the 1980s, mayors and senior municipal officials were essentially ignored; now no international seminar or conference about urban problems is complete without some mayors.

Some international donors have also developed new means of channelling funds direct to local NGOs or CBOs – sometimes because recipient governments recognized that this was the most effective response, sometimes because recipient governments lacked the interest or capacity to address local problems themselves. This includes funds to support organized urban poor groups, although official donors face obvious political difficulties in doing so since all their funding must be approved by recipient governments. It also includes increased funding through local embassies and forms of 'decentralized cooperation' that increase the scope for international NGOs and urban governments from high-income countries to receive support from aid funds for urban projects they manage in low- and middle-income countries. Most official bilateral and multilateral agencies also contract out many urban projects, and, in recent years, there has been a growing use of consultants and/or engineering companies to manage urban projects. This has worrying implications in that this may ensure that projects get implemented (and make the management of urban projects easier for donor agencies), but it usually does little to build the capacity and accountability of urban authorities.

Finally there are a few international agencies that have recognized the need to encourage and support democratic governance in urban areas. For instance, the Urban Management Programme's office for Latin America and the Caribbean has been supporting urban consultations all over the region. Each city consultation facilitates the dialogue between city authorities and community organizations. They help to raise citizen priorities and to develop action plans that enjoy a broader citizen support than conventional municipal plans (PGU/ALC 2000). They also help to document municipal innovations from which others can learn, as in the example of Barra Mansa municipality in Brazil which has involved children and youth throughout the city in defining their priorities and electing their representatives to a council to press their concerns. The children and youth council is allocated a proportion of the municipal budget for which they had responsibility for determining its use; in 1998, this was the equivalent of around US$125,000 (PGU/ALC 2000).

The discussions and debates evident in most international donors about their role in 'urban development' reflects real difficulties in how best to address this topic. Urban development cannot be seen as a sector and all the sectoral divisions within international agencies have projects in urban areas or projects that influence urban development. There are also the multiple interconnections between rural and urban areas, including the extent to which agricultural prosperity can support urban development and urban prosperity can support stronger more diversified employment bases in rural areas. So there is a tension between, on the one hand, building the capacity of a donor agency to identify and support urban projects within a programme that enhances the capacity of urban governments in recipient countries and, on the other to ensure that all country programmes and sectoral departments recognize the 'urban' aspects of their work. Both are important but they are not easily combined within any 'urban' division.

International NGOs

Building the capacity, competence and representative nature of urban governments is only one part of an effective environmental agenda. Another is support for community and/or neighbourhood initiatives in low-income settlements to address their most pressing environmental problems. There are hundreds of innovative urban projects funded and managed by international NGOs that contribute to this. There is also a very large range of international NGOs involved in urban projects and many have annual budgets exceeding US$10 million a year and also receive a significant proportion of their funding from official government bilateral aid programmes. However, many international NGOs, like many bilateral donors, give a very low priority to urban projects and have no coherent urban policy. This too is often based on questionable assumptions about where poverty is concentrated.

From the limited information available about the extent of their support for urban projects, those with the most significant urban support programmes include MISEREOR (Germany), Cordaid (The Netherlands), Plan International and CARE. WaterAid, a UK charity that concentrates on improving water and sanitation and has tended to focus on rural projects, has recently taken steps to increase its involvement in low-income urban communities. A few smaller agencies specialize in supporting community-based initiatives by the urban poor – for instance Homeless International and SELAVIP International. It has also become more common for international NGOs to channel much of their support through local or national NGOs, as illustrated by examples given in the last sections of Chapter 6. So, on occasion, have the large official donors such as the World Bank's support to FUNDASAL in El Salvador and the support of the Swedish International Development Cooperation Agency to FUPROVI in Costa Rica, both innovative NGOs working to improve housing conditions and basic services for low-income households, with a strong emphasis on participatory working methods. UNICEF has also channelled support through local NGOs in many of its urban basic services projects (UNICEF 1988, Etemadi 2000).

There is surprisingly little information available about the urban programmes of international NGOs. In part, this is because many of them do not publish much detail about their work in urban areas and in part, because of the difficulty in gathering information about the work of so many different agencies. This makes it difficult to estimate the scale and significance of such support. However, in most major cities, it is certainly too small to reach more than a few per cent of low-income households. Usually, in a major city, there are various projects or programmes funded by international NGOs in a few of the hundreds of low-income settlements. Many are very sectoral – for instance a healthcare centre but no attention to environmental health problems. But there are also many large cities and thousands of smaller urban centres where no international NGO is working. At least the last 40 years have produced many precedents that show effective, local solutions in which local NGOs had a central role. There are numerous examples of innovative, participatory interventions (Turner 1988, Anzorena and others 1998) that are often more cost-effective and more able to reach the poorest groups with significant improvements than official government projects. But in general, there are two aspects that are lacking. The first is that there is no realistic idea of how to multiply tenfold or a hundredfold the number of communities or neighbourhoods in which participatory action programmes are receiving support. The second is the lack of a city-wide strategy within the cities where they work that provides continuous support to low-income groups and their community organizations and, within this, recognizes the importance of strengthening the capacity of low-income groups and their organizations to negotiate with government agencies. It is no longer adequate for international NGOs (or official development cooperation agencies) to hold up a few examples of successful projects when there are hundreds of thousands of neighbourhoods or districts lacking basic infrastructure and services. In many of the larger cities, there are hundreds of squatter settlements. In the absence of government capacity to deliver and maintain improved infrastructure and services, and to support other actions to improve environmental health, support is needed in each neighbourhood for neighbourhood-level actions.

Going to scale in supporting community initiatives

Most international agencies worry about 'going to scale' in the sense of ensuring that their funding reaches a significant proportion of those in need. But there has been little institutional innovation among the official bilateral or multilateral aid agencies about how to channel technical and financial support to hundreds of neighbourhood-level actions where the inhabitants and their organizations have any significant influence on what is funded, or to go beyond this and fund a diverse, continuous and coherent programme of support for community-directed initiatives within many different low-income nations. Most decisions about what is funded remain centralized in the international agency. Most international agencies retain cumbersome procedures through which applications for funding have to go; even applications for very small sums may have to go through long and complex procedures before decisions are made. This also means long delays before a particular neighbourhood knows whether it can go ahead with an initiative it has planned and for which it has sought funding. It is very discouraging for any low-income community that has developed a plan to improve conditions through, for instance, a communal water tank or building a small day-care centre to have to wait many months (or even years) to find out whether the few thousand dollars they requested have been granted. Each international agency also has its own particular criteria for what can be funded, which may not match the priorities in different neighbourhoods. Most international agencies are also reluctant to fund the institutional processes by which low-income groups organize and develop their own plans and programmes – for instance through support for the salaries of community organizers and for the staff of local NGOs to whom they turn for support.

Most international funding agencies also fail to appreciate the need to support a constant process in most low-income neighbourhoods. Ironically, many withdraw support from a city after a 'successful' project, when one successful project should have laid the basis for expanding the scale and extending the scope of their work. It is not so much that large amounts of funding are needed in each neighbourhood but that a constant flow of support is needed, so that each action can build on the experience of the previous one. Initiating a neighbourhood programme in which the inhabitants are fully involved and that works in ways that best suit local circumstances often takes a long time. But once a momentum has been built up, one successful community-based action (for instance the construction and running of a mother-and-child centre) can lead to another and then another. Most poor neighbourhoods have a multiplicity of environmental problems that have to be addressed. In addition, their capacity to work together develops with each successful intervention and this also allows more complex and ambitious actions to be undertaken. It is support for this continuous process by which the inhabitants of a particular neighbourhood develop their capacity to work together and to negotiate with other actors (for instance the municipal authorities and the state or national government agencies) that is much needed. But most international funding agencies pose limits on the time they provide support to a particular community, or will only support one project (or one particular type of project), and assume that their role ceases when the project is completed. Almost none have understood that building effective community responses to a lack of piped water, sanitation, drainage, paved roads, street lighting, schools, healthcare, child care, play facilities, etc is a long-term process over which the inhabitants themselves must have influence and which involves recurrent costs. Virtually all aid agencies seek to be participatory. But in most instances, there is very little possibility of those who are meant to receive aid to influence these agencies' priorities, including not only what funds they might receive and for what, but also the way that funds are provided (including the conditions attached to them). New channels must be found if aid is to be effective in supporting a vast diversity of initiatives at neighbourhood level to permit low-income groups and the community or neighbourhood associations they form to address their environmental priorities. This is a point to which we return in Chapter 9.

Chapter 8

Sustainable Development and Cities

Carrying recyclable material on a bicycle rickshaw in New Delhi, India
Photo © Janet Jarman, all rights reserved

INTRODUCTION

Previous chapters have concentrated on environmental problems in cities in terms of their impact on human health, natural resources, local ecosystems and global 'life-support' systems, and on policies to address these. This chapter considers how these environmental problems and policies fit within a wider debate about sustainable development. The concept of sustainable development is useful because it brings together most of the concerns raised in earlier chapters. It highlights key links between different sectors and between geographic scales (the local, regional and global). It also highlights potential synergies and conflicts between different goals.

At its core, the concept of sustainable development is about reconciling 'development' (which implies the use of resources and the generation of wastes) with 'environment' (which implies finite limits on the use of many resources and on the capacity to absorb or break down wastes or render them harmless) at local, regional and global scales. If development implies the ever-increasing use of resources and the generation of wastes, eventually it must conflict with local or global systems with finite resources and capacities to assimilate wastes. There is good evidence that such conflicts are occurring in more and more localities, and also that the richest localities have overcome local constraints by drawing on the resources and sinks of other localities to the point where some resources and ecological processes are threatened both in these localities and globally (Rees 1995). So the concept of sustainable development makes us think about the environmental (or ecological) implications of any human activity or artefact – a product, waste, project, programme or policy – both where it takes place (ie in a particular locality or region) and elsewhere (for instance the regional impact or contribution to global problems). What are the environmental costs and who is affected by these costs, both now and in the future? Will the increased draw on groundwater resources to better meet freshwater demands in a city deplete or degrade groundwater resources so that less are available in the future? Will the new residential or commercial developments on the city periphery increase the city average for greenhouse gas emissions per person or deplete natural forests or wetlands whose multiple productive and protective ecological roles are then lost? Are city wastes being managed in such a way as to minimize environmental costs passed on to the future (for instance to avoid contributing to the accumulation of toxic wastes)? Are city enterprises or consumers using timber or timber products that are from forests with sound environmental management (probably not, since only a small fraction of the world's natural forests are subject to such management – see Mayers and Bass 1999).

So a consideration of sustainable development raises many questions. For some, answers are uncertain – for instance the actual current (and future) impact on human health and ecosystem functioning of many persistent chemicals or the exact extent and precise impact within each region of global warming. There is also considerable uncertainty regarding the response of natural systems to increased resource use and waste generation, and this response may include sudden changes, once critical thresholds have been breached with very serious consequences (Rees 1995). For some key natural resources, there is little data or the data that exists is of poor quality, as in accurate assessments of the state of soils in many countries or the sustainable levels for freshwater resource use within many localities. It is also very difficult to protect many essential ecological resources or processes within market economies because economic transactions allocate them no value. For instance, every time we use a car, turn on a light, heat or cool a room or cook food, we generate carbon dioxide and so contribute to global warming.[1] But we do not 'pay' anything towards the costs that global warming will bring, including poten-

---

1 Except where renewable energy sources are used, but at present, these provide only a very small percentage of energy used for these tasks.

tially catastrophic costs for hundreds of millions of people (although some governments are now beginning to consider how to adjust fossil fuel pricing to address this). There are also the natural resources or ecosystem functions that we do not know enough about to be able to understand their value. Thus, there is a fundamental conflict between sustaining the ecological integrity of local and global systems and the logic of what Rees (1995) calls the expansionist world view in which individuals, enterprises and nations are encouraged to maximize their use of resources and seek to get rid of their wastes in ways that minimize their costs.

There are also all the debates about 'What is development?' which complicates any discussion of the links between the environment and development, although, as discussed later, these have helped to reveal how much real wealth can be delinked from increased material use. *But within all the complications, confusions and uncertainties, the core concept of the need to achieve developmental goals within a recognition of (local, regional and global) environmental limits remains relatively simple.* For cities, sustainable development is about developing systems of governance that can reconcile meeting 'developmental' goals (and their use of resources and generation of wastes) with 'the environment'. This means ensuring that the needs of city dwellers are met while keeping to a minimum the environmental costs passed on by city-dwellers' consumption and city-based enterprises' production to other people, other ecosystems and global 'life-support' cycles, both now and into the future. It has to include a consideration of each city's contribution to regional and global environmental problems. Thus, this chapter has to go beyond its focus on Africa, Asia, and Latin America and the Caribbean to also consider the extent to which cities in other regions pass on environmental costs to other people, other ecosystems or into the future, especially cities in Europe, North America and Japan where much of the world's highest levels of resource use, waste generation and greenhouse gas emissions are concentrated.

Although the concept of sustainable development has great importance for forcing a consideration of the complementarities and conflicts between different (environmental and developmental) goals and for demanding a recognition of the finite nature of many natural resources and systems, the term 'sustainable development' is used so loosely and given so many different meanings that we considered dropping it altogether. When a multinational like IBM can appropriate the concepts and language of sustainable development with a corporate slogan 'Sustainable solutions for a small planet', the key concept has become devalued.[2] And as later sections in this chapter will describe, many international agencies have also devalued the term by applying it to their particular concerns that have little to do with reconciling environmental and developmental goals. They have often used the term sustainable development with no environmental considerations at all. Even when they do incorporate some environmental goals,

---

2 The stress on the environmental limits of a 'small planet' goes back at least to the 1960s and became a key slogan for environmental concerns – for instance in Frances Moore Lappe's book *Diet for a Small Planet* first published in 1971, in the 1972 book by Barbara Ward and Rene Dubos *Only One Earth: Care and Maintenance of a Small Planet*, in Barbara Ward's 1979 book *Progress for a Small Planet* and in the 1992 book *Policies for a Small Planet* (Holmberg 1992).

they fail to understand the different forms that environmental degradation takes or they confuse 'environmental degradation' and 'environmental hazards'. Other international institutions (or professional groups) have used the term 'sustainable development' to focus only on ecological sustainability with no consideration given to meeting human needs. But despite this, we need some phrase to remind us about the need to reconcile 'development' with 'environment' at local, regional and global scales, and at present, sustainable development is the term most widely used for this. And, as will be described in a later section, this is also the original meaning given to the term when it was first used in the 1970s by the IIED and by other groups.

Why is Sustainable Development Important for Cities?

Although there is a large and diverse literature about 'sustainable development' that goes back more than 20 years, only in the last 10 years or so has this included a growing proportion that considers sustainable development with regard to cities (or to urban systems). As Graham Haughton and Colin Hunter comment in their book on *Sustainable Cities*, this is probably because so many of those who write on environmental issues have long regarded cities with disdain (Haughton and Hunter 1994). This is surprising for at least three reasons:

1 A large and growing proportion of the world's population lives in cities (as described in Chapter 1) and in general, the countries with the highest levels of resource use, waste generation and greenhouse gas emissions per person are also the countries with the highest proportion of their populations living in urban areas.
2 It is within urban areas that most of the world's resource use and waste generation are concentrated. Worldwide, urban consumers and urban-based production account for most fossil fuel and other non-renewable resource consumption and most greenhouse gas emissions, largely because of the concentration of the world's industries and of middle- and upper-income households in urban centres.
3 Urban policies have very serious implications with regard to future levels of greenhouse gas emissions and the use of most resources in each nation which is related both to the design and construction of urban buildings and to the spatial form that cities and urban systems take. Urban policies that encourage good practice in energy-efficient buildings (for instance through appropriate building and planning norms, codes and regulations) and energy-efficient production units (through appropriate regulation and incentives) and that also ensure urban forms that are not increasingly dependent on high levels of private car use (for instance through appropriate transport and land-use policies) have a major role in delinking high living standards from high greenhouse gas emissions. Thus, urban policies, plans and regulations should have a central role in any national strategy that promotes sustainable development, and city and municipal governments will be important actors in any successful strategy. It is therefore surprising

that much of the literature on 'sustainable development' and many national strategies for sustainable development include little or no discussion about urban policy.

However, it is important to clarify that it is not cities that are responsible for most resource use, waste, pollution and greenhouse gas emissions but particular industries and commercial and industrial enterprises (or corporations), and middle- and upper-income groups with high-consumption lifestyles. These may be concentrated in cities but by and large it is not their concentration in cities that is environmentally destructive but their level of resource use and waste generation. They would be equally destructive if they were dispersed in rural areas, or even more so, because of a greater need for motorized transport. In high-income countries and in the wealthier cities or regions in middle-income countries, it is the middle- or upper-income household with two or three cars living in rural areas or small towns or low-density outer suburbs of cities that generally has the highest consumption of resources – generally much more so than those with similar incomes living within cities.

How a Concern for Sustainable Development Arose

It is in mapping the growth in concern for 'sustainable development' over the last 30 years that the widely diverging opinions as to what the term means and how it should be applied become evident. Mapping this concern also emphasizes how long the core concepts that underpin the term sustainable development have been around.[3] Among the first detailed considerations of the conflict at global level between 'development' (in terms of ever increasing resource use and waste generation) and 'environment' was the report *Limits to Growth* published by the Club of Rome (Meadows and others 1974). While this may have overstated the constraints arising from the availability of mineral resources when discussing the natural limits to exponential growth, it was an important precursor to the sustainable development debate. This can be seen in its emphasis that it is possible to 'establish a condition of ecological and economic stability that is sustainable far into the future' (page 24) and that this could be designed 'so that the basic material needs of each person on earth are satisfied' (page 24). One can see in these words key elements of what later became the most widely used summary of the goal of sustainable development – meeting 'the needs of the present generation without compromising the ability of future generations to meet their own needs' from the report *Our Common Future* published in 1987 (page 8) by the World Commission on Environment and Development (also known as the Brundtland Commission). *Limits to Growth* also emphasized how there were no material limits to many of the most desirable and satisfying human activities '... education, art, music,

---

3 This section is not intended as a detailed or comprehensive review of the key works that contributed to the concept of sustainable development but as a reminder that most works which claim to review how the concept developed miss or give inadequate attention to works from the late 1960s and early 1970s.

religion, basic scientific research, athletics, and social interactions…' (page 175). Thus, there was a recognition right at the outset of the debate about sustainability that many of the most important aspects of human development did not depend on an increasing use of resources.

The importance of understanding and acting to reduce the conflicts between a finite environment and development was also stressed in the book *Only One Earth: Care and Maintenance of a Small Planet* (Ward and Dubos 1972). Written to bring the latest environmental knowledge to a popular audience (with the authors advised by a great range of specialists), the book describes the concerns that had led to the 1972 UN Conference on the Human Environment in Stockholm. This is one of the first books in which discussions about natural resource use and pollution are linked to those of meeting developmental goals (or meeting human needs). It drew together a concern for the 'care and maintenance' of the environment with a concern to meet human needs and eliminate poverty. This was one of the first books to stress that current human needs must be met while also not compromising the needs of future generations. The 1987 definition of the goals of sustainable development by the Brundtland Commission noted above also drew from this 1972 publication which states that the 'charge of the United Nations to the (Stockholm) Conference was to clearly define what should be done to maintain the earth as a place suitable for human life not only now, but also for future generations' (page 25). Our own institute, the International Institute for Environment and Development (IIED), was formed in 1973 to develop and help apply this concept with one of the co-authors of this book, Barbara Ward, as its first president. But the book *Only One Earth* in turn drew on earlier works and publications – for instance some of the authors who contributed to the September 1970 issue of *Scientific American* on 'The Biosphere' raised worries about the disturbances that human activities were introducing to natural systems, and even in this 1970 publication, one finds a chart showing the rapid measured (and projected) increase in atmospheric carbon dioxide, drawing on a monitoring programme that had begun in the late 1950s (Bolin 1970). Barbara Ward's published work throughout the 1970s developed the theme of how to combine the meeting of human needs without compromising the planet's ecological limits.[4] The term sustainable development was already in use by the second half of the 1970s, based on this theme – see for instance the elaboration of the term 'sustainable development' (page 7) and the discussion about what a commitment to sustainable development implies for development agencies (page 134) in the IIED study *Banking on the Biosphere* published in 1979 (Stein and Johnson 1979).

This growing interest in sustainable development was fuelled by the growing popular concern about the environmental implications of human activities. Such concerns had become important political issues in the 1960s, for example, in the protests by citizens, environmental groups and some consumer groups in Europe and North America as to the environmental damage done by intensive farming, industrial production and high-consumption lifestyles. The potential dangers arising from the accidental release of radioactive materials by nuclear

---

4 See for instance Ward and Dubos 1972; Ward 1974; Ward 1976a and 1976b; and Ward 1979.

(fission) power stations and by other activities associated with nuclear power (for instance the wastes generated, the facilities needed for producing and reprocessing the fuel, and the links between the nuclear industry and nuclear weapons) also spurred the growth of the environment movement. Oil price rises in the 1970s made the public (and governments) aware of the possible impact of global natural resource scarcity, even if the price rises were not a result of scarcity. The 'environment movement' gradually widened its focus and its initial concentration on risks to the environment in the richer nations and began to look at comparable problems in Africa, Asia and Latin America.

The concern for the environment in these regions soon developed clear links with the concern for development – for instance in identifying the link between soil erosion and the inadequate size of poorer groups' land holdings and the link between community impoverishment and the appropriation by powerful vested interests of land and forest resources that had previously been a common property (or open access) resource (see for instance Centre for Science and Environment 1982, Lee-Smith and Trujillo 1992, *The Ecologist* 1992). In these regions, NGOs and CBOs became more active on environmental issues both at local level (for instance organizing opposition to a dam, indiscriminate logging or high pollution levels arising from particular factories) and at national level (for instance lobbying their governments for changes in legislation and its enforcement) (Centre for Science and Environment 1987). Some also came to be key influences within international debates. It also became more common for environmental groups to find common ground with groups fighting for social and political rights, especially where much of the population (and the poorest groups within it) relied on access to land, forests and water for their livelihoods. In addition, alliances between some environmentalists and those with a concern for development strengthened, as environmental concerns gave more attention to environmental health (and not just to resource use and waste emissions). Concern for the environment also helped to forge international links between groups in high- and low-income countries. International networks began to bring political pressures to bear on multinational companies, industrial concerns, finance institutions and intergovernmental agencies (including the largest development assistance agencies and development banks) to give more consideration to the environmental impacts of their activities. Most multinational corporations and intergovernmental agencies have had to develop environmental policies or at least to seek to justify their actions in the face of criticism from environmental groups. Some multinational corporations even came to use the slogans of environmental movements, as illustrated by the example of IBM's slogan, noted earlier.

The second half of the 1970s and the first half of the 1980s saw an increased awareness of the finite nature of certain non-renewable resources worldwide and the vulnerability of some global life-support systems to pollution arising from human activities.[5] Although most had been identified as potential problems many

---

5 See for instance Mesarovic and Pestel 1974, 'The Cocoyoc Declaration' adopted by the participants of the UNEP/UNCTAD symposium on 'Pattern of Resource Use, Environment and Development Strategies' in 1974, republished in *World Development*, Vol 3, Nos 2 and 3, February–March 1975; Ward 1976; Bariloche Foundation 1976; Council on Environmental Quality and the Department of State 1979, Brandt Commission 1980.

years previously, they were perceived as uncertain threats. If the concerns about the environment and development today are compared with those in the mid-1970s, there are at least three changes in emphasis. The first is the much increased concern about damage arising from human activities to global systems. The depletion of the stratospheric ozone layer and atmospheric warming are now recognized as far more serious (and much better documented) threats than was the case in the early 1970s. The scale of species extinction and the multiple threats that a loss of biodiversity brings (both within each locality and globally) is also better understood. The second is the change in emphasis regarding resource depletion from a concern about the depletion of non-renewable mineral resources which has, to some extent, receded to a greater concern about the finite nature of many renewable resources (especially fertile soil, forests, fisheries and freshwater resources). The third is the wider acceptance among many environmentalists of the need for economic growth within many nations and regions (especially the poorest ones) to provide the economic base to allow needs to be met. Rather than recommend 'no growth', it has become more common to hear reference to 'green growth', ie economic growth that seeks to keep intact environmental capital and minimize ecological damage.

However, despite this growing knowledge about environmental limits during the late 1970s and early 1980s, the discussions of 'development' generally ignored them. During the 1980s, development debates came to be dominated by how to respond to debt repayment crises and economic stagnation within a political context that emphasized the downsizing of government and a greater importance given to market forces and export-driven 'development'. Environmental aspects were forgotten. Even the greater emphasis given within development to 'directly meeting human needs' during the late 1970s was reversed – in part because it was seen as too state-oriented, in part because economic stagnation or decline in so many nations focused attention on the macro-conditions for economic stability and prosperity. The importance of the publication of *Our Common Future* in 1987 was not so much in the originality of its content but in its rescuing of key environmental concerns that development had to consider (and also re-emphasizing that development should centre on meeting people's needs). It did not invent the term sustainable development; as noted above, the term had been in use for at least 10 years before this report's publication. And the report's definition of sustainable development was based on definitions that preceded it by 15 or more years. But it got the term and the key concept that underlies it back into the discussions of governments and international agencies. It forced international agencies to take the concept more seriously and, unlike most considerations of sustainable development at that time, it even included a chapter on urban issues which highlighted the main concerns of this book.

Our Common Future also helped to emphasize how many global trends (including some associated with urbanization) were not contributing to development or to ecological sustainability. In Africa and much of Asia, Latin America and the Caribbean, the problem centred on the scale of poverty in both rural and urban areas and the failure of five decades of 'development planning' and of development assistance from international agencies to ensure that basic human needs are met. Earlier chapters described the inadequacies in the provision for water, sanitation and drainage in urban areas and the other easily preventable environmental health hazards to which large sections of the urban population are exposed. They also noted the growth in the numbers of urban (and rural) dwellers facing multiple deprivations. *Our Common Future* also highlighted worrying trends in much of Africa, Asia, Latin America and the Caribbean in terms of unsustainable levels of use for many resources, for instance through deforestation, soil erosion, depletion or pollution of freshwater sources, loss or degradation of valuable ecosystems and loss of biodiversity. This and other reports emphasized that meeting the needs of poorer groups in all nations does not imply an unsustainable level of resource use, but it is also clear that extending the levels of resource consumption and waste generation currently enjoyed by the rich minority to an increasing proportion of the world's population almost certainly does (WHO 1992a, Rees 1992).

If the publication of reports about sustainable development indicates real changes in policies and practice towards sustainable development goals, then the 1990s could be judged to have brought considerable progress. There is also the evidence of increasing international interest in global environmental issues in the new intergovernmental bodies (for instance the UN Commission on Sustainable Development and the Intergovernmental Panel on Climate Change) and in the many international discussions – for instance those on climate change, biodiversity, forests, persistent organic pollutants, etc. For urban areas, there was the second UN Conference on Human Settlements in Istanbul in 1996 (also called the City Summit) whose massive 'Habitat Agenda' includes a strong stress on sustainable development.

But within all this prominence suddenly given to sustainable development, those whose primary concern was 'the environment' tended to ignore development concerns, while those whose primary concern was 'development' ignored environmental issues, or misunderstood the many different dimensions of avoiding the depletion of environmental capital. The term 'sustainable development' came to be increasingly used, without specifying what was meant by it. There is also the ambiguity in both the words that make up the term, and there is no consensus as to what is meant by 'development' or what is meant by 'sustainable' (or what it is that sustainable development is meant to sustain). The term sustainable development also came to be used to describe (or legitimize) goals and activities that bear little relation to its original meaning. Vested interests always seek fashionable or popular words or phrases to help to justify or legitimize their interests or obscure their real intent. Even when the term sustainable development is used with reference to the Brundtland Commission definition, it is still possible to have very different emphases – for instance stressing conservation to avoid 'compromising the ability of future generations to meet their own needs' rather than meeting 'the needs of the present generation'. It is also worth recalling the very different emphases that can be termed 'environmental' as discussed in Chapter 1. Before suggesting what we believe to be the most appropriate way to develop a sustainable development framework for cities, short sections outline how some groups emphasize sustainability and forget development, while others emphasize development and forget ecological sustainability. There is also a section discussing the ambiguities about what is to be sustained.

EMPHASIZING SUSTAINABILITY; FORGETTING DEVELOPMENT

Perhaps the most common distortion of the concept of sustainable development is to ignore the 'development' aspects altogether. Much of the discussions on sustainable development (and most of the literature on the subject) concentrate on ecological sustainability. Many authors who discuss what they term 'sustainable development' do not include a discussion of 'development goals' at all. Their concerns are with sustainability, not sustainable development. In such literature, it is common to find the terms 'sustainable development' and 'sustainability' used interchangeably with no recognition that the two mean or imply different things.

The exclusive concentration of many authors on 'ecological sustainability' as the only goal of sustainable development is one reason why it has proved difficult to engage the interest of development practitioners in environmental issues. There is much discussion under the heading of 'sustainable development' about the actions needed to sustain the global resource base (soils, biodiversity, mineral resources, freshwater resources, fisheries, forests) and about limiting the disruption to global cycles as a result of human activities, especially greenhouse gas emissions and the depletion of the stratospheric ozone layer. Such discussion tends to forget two other critical environmental issues or to downplay their importance. The first is the very large environmental health burden suffered by hundreds of millions of people in both rural and urban areas because they lack access to safe and convenient supplies of water for drinking and domestic use, and also adequate provision for sanitation, drainage and prevention-focused primary health care (as described in Chapter 2). The second are the hundreds of millions of households that have unmet needs and who depend for part or all of their livelihood on raising crops or livestock. Their poverty (and the malnutrition and ill health that generally accompanies it) are the result of inadequate access to water and fertile land. This lack of access to land and water for crop cultivation or livestock underlies the poverty of around a fifth of the world's population (Jazairy and others 1992). Yet many discussions about 'sustainability' with regard to soil erosion and deforestation give little or no consideration to the needs of these people. Some of this literature may indeed (inaccurately) portray these people as 'the problem', despite the fact that their poverty is caused by them having access to so little of the resource base for whose degradation they are blamed.[6]

Although we believe that the most important role that the term sustainable development has is to encourage 'development' to consider its ecological implications, it can be used in ways that inhibit development. As soon as 'sustainable development' comes to include a concern for meeting human needs, it must consider why so many people's needs are currently unmet, and this means considering the underlying economic, social and political causes of poverty and deprivation. Most of the literature on sustainable development does not do so. It does not question the current distribution of power and the ownership of resources, except where these are considered a factor in 'unsustainable

---

6 See Chapter 5.

practices'. It assumes that national conservation plans or national sustainable development plans can be implemented within existing social and political structures. Much of the literature assumes that the integration of conservation and development will meet people's needs which, as Adams 1990 points out, is disastrously naive.

There is also the fact that an exclusive concentration on ecological sustainability could judge poverty to be 'valuable'. It is the poverty of such a high proportion of the world's population that has helped to limit the threat to ecological unsustainability; if the two billion poorest people in the world (the vast majority of whom are in Africa, Asia and Latin America) acquire levels of resource use and waste generation comparable with those that are common in high-income countries, the scale of resource use, waste generation and greenhouse gas emissions worldwide would increase manyfold. It may even be that some of the reluctance of governments from high-income nations to address structural issues that limit economic growth among lower income nations is linked to the fact that keeping them poor also keeps down greenhouse gas emissions.

The discussions of ecological sustainability often include discussions of the need to slow or stop population growth, with a strong stress on the need to do so in Africa, Asia and Latin America. This discussion often exaggerates the speed of population growth, failing to notice that there have been very large reductions in the rates of natural increase in many countries and the extent to which demographic projections for future national (and global) populations have been revised downwards. It also assumes that it is the number of people that is the critical factor in determining ecological impact. But what threatens ecological sustainability is not the number of people but the level of use of particular resources, the poor quality of natural resource management and the scale and nature of waste generation. There are huge differentials between individuals in terms of resource use and waste generation. The point was made earlier that many low-income urban dwellers draw hardly at all on the planet's natural resource base and generate very little waste. The same is true for most low-income smallholders. If one constructed an index to compare their contribution per person with local or global ecological unsustainability with those of high-income groups, the differentials would run into the millions. A rich, high-consumption household with several cars, more than one house (and each reliant on high levels of heating/cooling) and high levels of air travel is likely to contribute more to ecological unsustainability than millions of low-income, low-consumption households. Many low-income households might not even register on such an index. Box 8.1 elaborates on such an index.

The relative priority given to ecological sustainability or to human needs within a commitment to sustainable development has major implications for any urban policy. For cities, a stress only on ecological sustainability would imply large investments in reducing the use of fossil fuels (especially coal and, for wealthier cities, private car use), decreasing the throughput of fresh water and non-renewable resources, and controlling air and water pollution. It might include draconian measures to prevent people from moving to urban centres (although the extent to which this would actually serve 'sustainability' goals are in doubt). Such policies

Box 8.1 *THE TRUMP INDEX FOR ASSESSING THE DIFFERENTIALS IN INDIVIDUALS' CONTRIBUTIONS TO ECOLOGICAL UNSUSTAINABILITY*

It is not so much each person's level of resource use and waste generation that defines their contribution to ecological unsustainability but the level of use of particular resources and the level of the generation of particular wastes. An accurate index for measuring each person's individual contribution to ecological unsustainability would need to take this into account. For instance, for food consumption, it is not so much the quantity of food eaten but the ecological costs of producing and delivering it, including the amount of land and the quantity of energy and ecologically damaging chemicals used to do so. For resource use in general, an accurate index of contributions to ecological unsustainability would need to measure the extent to which each person's consumption was products from ecosystems that were being degraded or threatened by overexploitation or products whose fabrication had serious ecological implications. For waste generation, it would need to reflect the large differences in the ecological impact of different wastes – for instance taking due note of those wastes that contribute most to ecological damage or disruption of global systems. Many low-income households in Africa, Asia and Latin America would hardly figure at all on waste generation as they generate so little waste (in part because of low-consumption levels, in part because of high levels of reuse or recycling) and most of the waste they do generate is biodegradable.

If data were available to construct an accurate index for assessing each person's contribution to ecological unsustainability, we suspect that the differentials it would show would greatly reinforce the point that it is the high-consumption lifestyles of most high-income and many middle-income groups and the production systems that serve (and stimulate) their demands that threatens ecological sustainability. Perhaps careful research into the consumption and waste-generation pattern of one prominent individual over the last ten years might serve to initiate the use of this index, and Donald Trump would make an interesting example – hence the suggested name for such an index. One wonders how the use of ecologically damaging resources and the generation of ecologically damaging wastes that arise from his lifestyle over the last ten years would compare with those of low-income urban dwellers in (for instance) India over the same period. One Trump's contribution to ecological unsustainability being comparable with that of many millions of low-income Indian urban dwellers?

would do little for most poorer groups and in many instances may exacerbate their problems. And 'environmental measures' can discriminate against them, as in, for instance, exemption from controls on private vehicle use for those with catalytic converters so that those who are able to afford these avoid the controls (as discussed by Connolly 1999 for Mexico City).

THE AMBIGUITIES IN WHAT IS TO BE SUSTAINED

One of the main ambiguities in the term 'sustainable development' or 'sustainability' is what is to be sustained. For instance, is it particular natural resources, particular areas (or ecosystems) or particular human activities or institutions that are to be sustained. The term sustainable development has even been used to refer to the need to sustain profits/returns to capital investment. Within these, it is worth distinguishing between two different uses of the term 'sustainable development' – its use where the stress is on ecological sustainability and its use where the stress is on sustaining human activities.

The term 'sustainable' is most widely used with reference to ecological sustainability, ie in terms of whether the draw on natural resources by a specific project or broader programme of human activities and the other environmental impacts (for instance the generation of wastes) can be sustained. The use of the term is premised on the understanding that there are ecological limits, for instance to the natural resources that are necessary to economic development (both for production and consumption) and to natural systems whose functioning is affected by buildings and infrastructure, and by the discharge of wastes from production and consumption. Human activities (or the wastes/pollutants they generate) can cause one of three kinds of environmental degradation:

1   Depletion of the natural resource (ie a reduction in the quality and/or quantity of the resource available for use).
2   Disruption of the ecological processes and/or damage to natural resources, for instance through acid rain or through biodegradable liquid wastes dumped into water bodies which exceed their capacity to break it down.
3   The loss of some types of resource altogether, for instance a loss of species and a consequent reduction in biodiversity (Leach and Mearns 1991).

The importance of avoiding the overexploitation of natural resources and the disruption of natural systems has led to an emphasis on the need to maintain 'natural' or 'environmental' capital. Natural capital is the stock of natural assets that includes renewable resources (living species and ecosystems), non-renewable resources (for instance fossil fuels) and the waste-assimilation capacities of ecosystems and of the whole planet. But some care is needed in the use of this concept in that characterizing 'the environment' as capital highlights only its economic value for production. Ecosystems and natural cycles provide many functions that are difficult to value, including those that are essential life-support systems or that provide protective functions or contribute to resilience (see for instance Rees 1995).

One of the main areas of debate within discussions of ecological sustainability is the extent to which natural capital can be substituted by other forms of capital. If sustainability is taken to mean no overall depletion in capital assets – so future generations should receive the same resource endowments as we have – is this endowment only in 'natural capital' or in some combination of natural and other forms of capital (for instance social and human capital)? Thus 'sustainability' might be taken to be a constant stock of some aggregation of all forms of 'assets' or a constant stock of environmental (or natural) assets (Pearce and others 1989).

However, there is little or no scope for substituting many aspects of natural capital with other forms of capital since they are essential for ecosystem functioning or for maintaining stability or resilience. As William Rees stresses, the structural integrity of the ecosphere depends on complex interdependent relationships linking the system's major components and it is difficult to know at what point the erosion of ecosystems and the disruption to the ecosphere begin to interfere with its capacity for self production. '... only the foolhardy would trust in markets and technology to find substitutes for such eco-essentials as photosynthesis and climate regulation, the ozone layer and natural biodiversity' (Rees 1995, page 350). In addition, we know that there are limits to the exploitation of key renewable resources (soils, freshwater resources, forests) and the capacity of ecosystems and global systems to 'render harmless' human wastes but often not what these limits are. For instance, we know with some certainty that a failure to control greenhouse gas emissions will bring very large human costs and ecological disruption but we are not certain as to the best relatively 'safe' limit to set as the basis for controlling greenhouse gas emissions. Such uncertainty is used by the powerful vested interests who want to avoid controls to argue against controls or to promote the setting of limits that are less stringent than those recommended by the scientific community. (These vested interests are also promoting unjust and inequitable measures by which to keep down the growth in greenhouse gas emissions, including those that transfer most of the costs of reducing greenhouse gas emissions to others and that do little to move human activities away from the carbon-based fuels that are the main cause of global warming – see Agarwal and others 1999c). There are also various other threats to ecological systems arising from human activities which an emphasis on natural capital misses – for instance the ecological disruption caused by the accumulation of persistent organic pollutants and the ecological risks from biotechnology.

So it is difficult to know what limits to set and what criteria to apply. For instance, does sustainability require the conservation of a specific type of forest and/or forest landscape, a capacity to sustain biomass production, or simply a continuing ability to grow trees (Svedin 1988)? Many discussions of sustainable development are also unclear about at what scale sustainability is sought, eg is it for local projects, cities, nations or the sum of all activities globally. This issue of scale is particularly important for cities since, as Chapter 5 described, the aggregate 'sustainable development' performance of a city (or rather of all the production and consumption concentrated within its boundaries) in terms of its draw on local and regional natural resources and systems may improve by drawing more heavily on the products and waste-assimilating capacities of distant ecosystems. 'Local' sustainability can be achieved at the expense of 'global sustainability'.

Thus, this characterization of natural resources and natural waste sinks as 'natural capital' is useful in that it is a reminder that they can be depleted and it allows a basis for judging the ecological sustainability of particular projects or policies. But there are also important environmental issues that these do not capture fully, including the present or future ecological disruption caused by the aggregate impact of all projects and policies, the erosion of ecological resilience and the damage to life-support systems.

The concept of 'sustainability' is also used with reference to specific kinds of human activity – for instance for discussions of 'sustainable industrial development' or 'sustainable agricultural development'. One of the most important has been the stress given to 'sustainable livelihoods' in rural areas from the mid-1980s onwards by Robert Chambers and Gordon Conway. Conway (1987) suggests that agricultural sustainability should be defined as the ability to maintain agricultural productivity, whether of a field or farm or nation, in the face of stress or shock. This was further developed in terms of livelihoods in Chambers and Conway (1992): 'a livelihood is sustainable when it can cope with and recover from stresses and shocks and maintain or enhance its capabilities and assets both now and in the future while not undermining the natural resource base'. The need for both ecological sustainability and livelihood sustainability was stressed.

The concept of 'sustainable livelihoods' comes out of this discussion as it seeks to balance ecological sustainability with the achievement of development goals. The stress on ecological sustainability had particular importance since much of the work was with rural households with very limited agricultural land holdings or who relied on common property resources where common property resource-management systems were breaking down or resources that were previously common property were being appropriated by governments or businesses. However, with the term 'sustainable livelihoods' now being applied in urban contexts, where most livelihoods are not dependent directly on access to natural resources, the ambiguity with regard to what the 'sustainable' refers to arises once more.

EMPHASIZING HUMAN ACTIVITIES; FORGETTING ECOLOGICAL SUSTAINABILITY

Although the term 'sustainable development' was coined originally to emphasize the need for ecological sustainability within development, many writers and institutions choose to use it to emphasize the need to sustain different aspects of development – for instance sustaining economic growth or 'human' development, or achieving social or political sustainability. Thus a discussion of sustainable development might consider how to sustain a person's livelihood, a development project, a policy, an institution, a business, a society or some subset of a society (eg a 'community'). It might also consider how to sustain culture or economic growth (in general or for some specific country). Here too, there is often little clarity as to the scale at which sustainability is being sought.

In the preparations for the UN Conference on Environment and Development (also called the Earth Summit) in 1992, an increasing number of UN agencies, bilateral aid agencies and other international organizations began to discuss 'sustainable development'. But many chose to use it with reference only to their projects and without reference to ecological sustainability (or even to their environmental impact). Sustainable development was often used to refer to the goal that development projects should continue to operate and meet development objectives when these agencies' external support was cut off at the 'end of the project'. In this sense, 'sustainability' was far more about operation and maintenance (or 'institutional and managerial sustainability') than about any concept of ecological sustainability. In some instances, project sustainability and project success were used almost interchangeably. So the term 'sustainable development' came to be used to highlight a problem that international development agencies had long encountered (their funding of capital projects which then ceased to operate effectively because of poor management and maintenance) with little or no recognition of the term's origin and original meaning.

A further extension of the term 'sustainability' has been its use in relation to social relations and customs. But there is no consensus as to what 'social sustainability' means. For instance, some consider social sustainability as the social preconditions for sustainable development while others imply that it is the need to sustain specific social relations, customs or structures. But the achievement of sustainable development in terms of meeting human needs without compromising the ability of future generations to meet their needs (its original meaning and also the one emphasized by *Our Common Future*) implies major changes in social relations and structures both within and between nations. In addition, when judged by the length of time for which they were sustained, some of the most 'successful' societies were also among the most exploitative, where the abuse of human rights was greatest and development goals were ignored. These are not societies we would want to 'sustain'. There are also many aspects of human society that we do not want to sustain – for instance high crime rates, widespread drug and alcohol abuse, high levels of political and interpersonal violence, discrimination, abuse of human rights, rising homelessness, etc. Development has at its base strong and explicit social objectives and achieving the development goals within sustainable development demands social change, not 'sustainability' in the sense of 'keeping them going continuously'. Indeed, the achievement of most of the social, economic and political goals that are part of 'sustainable development' requires changes to social structures, including changes to government institutions and, in many instances, to the distribution of assets and income. This can hardly be equated with 'social sustainability'.

Discussions on 'social sustainability', when defined as the social conditions that are necessary to support ecological sustainability, are valuable in so far as they stress that natural resources are used within a social context, and it is the rules and values associated with this context that determine both the distribution of resources within the present generation and between the future generations and the present. Discussions of 'social sustainability' that stress the value of social capital or the social conditions that allow or support the meeting of human needs are also valuable. Our avoidance of the term 'social sustainability' is both because it can invite confusion with the other interpretations and because it can imply that there is only one way to achieve ecological sustainability, whereas there is generally a range of possible options.

There has also been some discussion of 'cultural sustainability' because of the need within human society to develop shared values, perceptions and attitudes that help to contribute to the achievement of sustainable development. It is clear that development should include as a critical component a respect for cultural patrimony. Culture implies knowledge and a vast wealth of traditional knowledge of relevance to sustainable natural resource use (and to development) is ignored or given scant attention in development plans. But the term 'cultural sustainability' seems rather imprecise for the need to recognize the importance of culture and respect it within development. Culture is never static; to argue that it should be sustained is to deny an important aspect, its changing and developing nature.

A FRAMEWORK FOR CONSIDERING SUSTAINABLE DEVELOPMENT AND CITIES

While wanting to encourage a greater attention within discussions about sustainable development to the needs, rights and priorities of low-income groups, or of other groups whose needs and priorities are ignored, we do not think that it is appropriate to discuss this under 'sustainability'. We chose to use the concept of sustainability only with regard to ecological sustainability both because of the lack of consensus as to what sustainability might mean when applied to human activities and institutions, and because we believe the term has been inappropriately applied. Ensuring that human needs are met, human rights are respected and that people have a right to express their own needs and to influence the ways in which they are fulfilled more clearly falls within the 'development' component of sustainable development.

This means that governments and international agencies that wish to move from a concern with development to a concern with sustainable development need to add to their existing development goals the requirement that their achievement minimizes the depletion of natural capital both locally and globally. This allows one to avoid the confusions inherent in such concepts as social or cultural sustainability. Thus desired economic, social or political goals at community, city, regional or national level are best understood within the 'development' part of sustainable development, while the 'sustainable' component is with regard to ecological sustainability.

Figure 8.1 summarizes the multiple goals that are within any commitment to sustainable development, based on its original meaning (and the one taken up by the Brundtland Commission): meeting the needs of the present generation without compromising the ability of future generations to meet their own needs. The development component is the performance of each city and its institutions in meeting its inhabitants' development needs; as previous chapters have stressed, this has an important environmental component since the quality of the home, work, neighbourhood and city environment, and the extent to which the inhabitants are protected from biological pathogens and chemical pollutants in the water, air, soil or food or other environmental hazards has a major influence on the health and well-being of the population (WHO 1992a).

Meeting the needs of the present, the 'development' component of sustainable development, requires consideration of whose needs are to be met, what needs, who defines needs and who obtains more power and resources to ensure that they are met. These obviously include economic, social, cultural, health and political needs as outlined in Figure 8.1.

Many city authorities have the fulfilment of many of these needs and rights as part of their official responsibilities. Many of these are also contained in the UN Universal Declaration of Human Rights, ie meeting each person's right to a standard of living that is adequate for health and well-being, including food, clothing, housing and medical care and the necessary social services.[7] This Declaration, subsequent UN documents and *Our Common Future* all stress that developmental goals should include the right to vote within representative government structures. Perhaps the most relevant debate within this is the long-established discussion as to whether existing structures and institutions will ever improve their performance in ensuring that human needs are met. For instance, there is much more discussion about 'governance' at city and municipal level and this is not only among community organizations, NGOs and other parts of 'civil society' but also among governments and international agencies (see for instance UNCHS 1996). This is also not only about city and municipal authorities having more power and resources to enable them to better meet their responsibilities but also about the need for them to be more accountable, transparent and democratic, and to give more responsibility and resources to community-based or neighbourhood-based organizations, NGOs and other voluntary sector groups (ibid). The discussions about the changes in social structure that are needed to achieve sustainable development goals are also becoming more explicit. As an official UN report states, 'strategies for achieving social equity, social integration and social stability are essential underpinnings of sustainable development' (ibid).

The sustainability component is concerned largely with minimizing the depletion or degradation of the four types of natural capital listed in the lower box of Figure 8.1. These are considered in more detail in the two following sections. However, the lower box of Figure 8.1 also includes a mention of social/human capital since this has important implications for the ability of future generations to meet their own needs.

Cities and renewable sources and sinks

Renewable resources are the first of the four kinds of natural capital listed in Figure 8.1. Human use of some renewable resources (eg the direct use of solar power or its indirect use through wind or wave power) does not deplete the resource. But many renewable resources that are essential to a city's existence such as fresh water and the soils and forests within which food, other agricultural crops and forest products are produced are renewable within finite limits set by the ecosystems within which they are located. Soil is a renewable resource in that good farming practices and pasture management maintain its structure and fertility, and production can be sustained with no loss of the resource base,

7 See the Universal Declaration of Human Rights, Article 25 (1), United Nations.

Meeting the Needs of the Present...

- *Economic needs* – includes access to an adequate income/livelihood or productive assets; also economic security when unemployed, ill, disabled or otherwise unable to work.
- *Environmental needs* – includes accommodation that is healthy and safe with adequate provision for piped water, sanitation and drainage. Also a home, workplace and living environment protected from environmental hazards, including air and water pollution. Provision for recreation and for children's play. Shelters and services must meet the specific needs of children and of adults responsible for most child-rearing (usually women).
  Social, cultural and health needs – includes healthcare, education, transport. Needs related to people's choice and control – including homes and neighbourhoods that they value and where their social and cultural priorities are met – are also important.
- *Political needs* – includes freedom to participate in national and local politics and in decisions regarding management and development of one's home and neighbourhood – within a broader framework that ensures respect for civil and political rights and the implementation of environmental legislation.

Achieving the above implies a more equitable distribution of income between nations and, in most, within nations.

... Without Compromising the Ability of Future Generations to Meet Their Own Needs

- *Minimizing use or waste of non-renewable resources* – includes minimizing the consumption of fossil fuels in housing, commerce, industry and transport, plus substituting renewable sources where feasible. Also, minimizing waste of scarce mineral resources (reduce use, reuse, recycle, reclaim). There are also cultural, historical and natural assets within cities that are irreplaceable and thus non-renewable, for instance, historic districts and parks and natural landscapes that provide space for play, recreation and access to nature.
- *Sustainable use of finite renewable resources* – cities drawing on freshwater resources at levels that can be sustained (with efficient use, recycling and reuse promoted). Keeping to a sustainable ecological footprint in terms of land area on which city-based producers and consumers draw for agricultural and forest products and biomass fuels.
- *Biodegradable wastes not overtaxing the capacities of renewable sinks* (eg the capacity of a river to break down biodegradable wastes without ecological degradation).
- *Non-biodegradable wastes/emissions not overtaxing the (finite) capacity of local and global sinks to absorb or dilute them without adverse effects* (eg especially persistent organic pollutants, greenhouse gases and stratospheric ozone-depleting chemicals).
- *Social/human capital* that future generations need, including institutional structures that support human rights and good governance, and more generally the passing on intact of knowledge, experience and each nation's or social group's rich cultural heritage.

Source: Developed from Mitlin and Satterthwaite 1994.

Figure 8.1 *The multiple goals of sustainable development as applied to cities*

but the whole resource base can be depleted or degraded through soil erosion, salinization, deforestation, desertification, pollution and conversion of soil to urban or other uses. Seeing soils, forests and freshwater resources (including ground and surface water) as capital assets reminds one that they can only sustain the production of their 'income' (food and other agricultural crops, forest products, fresh water) if the assets themselves are not depleted or degraded.

The 'renewable sink capacity' of ecosystems around cities is another important form of natural capital for this breaks down the large volume of biodegradable wastes that are generated by city populations and businesses. Most wastes arising from production and consumption are biodegradable, but as early chapters stressed, there are ecological limits. For instance, each water body has a finite capacity to break down biodegradable wastes without itself becoming degraded (and ultimately dead). There are also conflicts between protecting some renewable resources and using sinks, especially for freshwater as the disposal of wastes into fresh water resources (for instance industries dumping their wastes into rivers or down wells) reduces their quality and/or availability for human use.

An examination of the use made by city consumers and businesses of renewable resources and sinks, and the scale and complexity of their linkages with rural producers and ecosystems within their own region and beyond highlights how 'sustainable urban development' and 'sustainable rural development' cannot be separated. As Chapter 5 emphasized, the rural–urban linkages can be positive in both developmental and environmental terms. Demand for rural produce from city-based enterprises and households can support prosperous farms and rural settlements, where environmental capital is not being depleted. Few governments appreciate the extent to which productive, intensive agriculture can support development goals in both rural and urban areas, in part because no professional group or government institution has the responsibility to understand and support this. Increasing agricultural production can also support urban development within or close to the main farming areas, the two supporting each other.[8]

There are also many examples of less ecologically damaging interactions between city wastes and surrounding areas. Some were mentioned in Chapter 7 – for instance organic solid and liquid wastes that originate from city-based consumers or industries being returned to soils – which demonstrate alternatives to the heavy use of artificial fertilizers and to the disregard of nutrients within city wastes. However, Chapter 5 also highlighted the negative aspects that rural–urban links can have – for instance as agricultural land is lost as cities' built-up areas expand without control and land speculation on urban fringes drives out cultivators.

Thus if citizens and city governments are committed to sustainable development, they should be concerned about the ecological health of the resources and ecosystems that are around the city, even though most of these are gener-

---

8 To do so usually requires a relatively equitable land-owning structure and a concentration of relatively small farms, each producing good livings for those farming them based on relatively high-value crops; see Chapter 9 of Hardoy and Satterthwaite 1989, and Satterthwaite and Tacoli 2001.

ally outside the official city boundaries. As noted in Chapter 7, a good Local Agenda 21 for any city includes a consideration of this, and seeks to develop the institutional means to ensure that such considerations are acted on. But this is not to say that this is easy. For instance, consider the importance of protecting trees, woods and forests in the region around cities. Forests have key local ecological roles in protecting watersheds (and preventing soil erosion), regulating water flows (and preventing floods), maintaining local biodiversity and moderating climatic extremes.[9] A great range of forest products are important for city consumers and producers, especially in regions where fuel wood or charcoal are still widely used as fuels by urban households. Other important forest derivatives include timber and 'a variety of foods including bushmeat ... framing, panelling and thatching materials, and a range of other goods including berries, nuts, fruit, wild animals, honey, resins, oils, rattan and medical products' (Rietbergen 1989). Forests form a key part of the natural landscapes to which city dwellers want access for recreation. Around cities forests are also part of a national resource, and the rich ecological diversity of tropical forests may include important sources of new plants, potentially useful as a source of drugs. Forests also have key global roles within the carbon cycle and with maintaining global biodiversity.

Deforestation or forest depletion is likely to have a number of effects on urban centres. Perhaps the most serious impact will be the loss of employment, income and consumption goods for urban centres in areas where forest exploitation is a major part of the local economy. There is also the increasing difficulty experienced by those living in such settlements in obtaining fuel. The ecological effects of deforestation, including changes in run-off and subsequent erosion, may add to the risk of small floods, reduce the capacity of hydro-electric stations (whose electricity is usually destined for urban consumers or enterprises) and reduce the productivity of agriculture. Deforestation of river catchment areas and associated soil erosion may be a contributory factor in floods that devastate large areas downstream, including cities or city-districts built alongside rivers (Bhatt 1990). All this highlights the need for good forest protection and management in and around cities, within governance structures that ensure that such management is not oriented only to the needs of powerful groups. But as Chapter 5 described, this usually does not happen, in part because the areas in most need of good management fall outside the boundaries of city authorities, and in part because of the incapacity or unwillingness of government agencies to control private developments that cause deforestation.

The need for much improved management of coastal areas provides another example of the institutional difficulties. A large proportion of the world's population (and many of its largest cities) are in coastal areas. Hundreds of millions of people depend, directly or indirectly, on coastal and marine ecosystems for their livelihoods, including not only fishing but also tourism.[10] A great range of resources are drawn from such ecosystems, in part

---

9 This discussion of forests and forest products draws on Mayers and Bass 1999.
10 This paragraph draws on IIED and others 1999.

because of the high productivity of near-shore waters and mangroves. Coastal areas are also widely used as sources of building materials and as dumping grounds for sewage, storm and surface run-off, industrial effluents (often including toxic wastes) and rubbish. In most coastal areas, there is little provision to protect key resources such as mangroves and coral reefs with their multiple productive and protective functions. The result is that, like so many resources, they are generally being used and degraded or polluted by powerful economic interests to the detriment not only of the environment, but also to the livelihoods of large numbers of low-income groups. Take, for instance, the case of mangroves. They have important protective roles (for instance preventing coastal erosion) and productive roles as they are among the world's most productive ecosystems: they trap fallen leaves and silt, and are used as feeding and breeding grounds by crabs, shrimps, many fish and shellfish, birds, mammals and reptiles (Hamilton and Snedaker 1984, Bennett and Reynolds 1993). There are a great range of mangrove products ranging from palm-sugar and honey to tanning materials, charcoal, wood-alcohol and water-resistant poles, and these can support small-scale, continuous harvesting without damaging the mangrove ecosystem. It is possible to envisage good management that protects their key ecological and productive roles, but it is less easy to see how it can be put in place within current institutional structures (IIED and others 1999).

Consideration of a city's use of renewable resources and sinks must also take into account the ecological impacts of its demand for resources in distant regions. Chapter 5 described how many cities now draw on the freshwater resources of distant ecosystems, as their demand for fresh water exceeded local capacities. It also described the concept developed by William Rees of cities' 'ecological footprints' through which it is possible to examine the draw on renewable resources and sinks that cities have in 'distant elsewheres' (Rees 1992; Wackernagel and Rees 1995). The demands for renewable resources by city-based consumers and producers in high-income nations are often being met in low- and middle-income nations in regions with little or no environmental management, and so are accompanied by deforestation and soil erosion.

Cities and non-renewable resources and sinks

Per capita consumption of non-renewable resources such as metals and fossil fuels in the richest nations and cities of the world has reached unprecedented levels. In 1996, average commercial energy use per person in high-income nations was more than 8 times higher than that in low-income nations (see Figure 8.2). Most high-income nations had levels of commercial energy consumption per person that were 20 to 30 times that in many low-income nations.

The average per capita consumption of steel within OECD nations is 450 kg compared with 43 kg in the low- and middle-income nations (OECD 1991). Comparable contrasts exist between per capita consumption in rich and poor nations for most other non-renewable resources.

There are fewer figures comparing city populations' non-renewable resource consumption, but those that do exist also reveal an enormous disparity between high- and low-income nations. Petrol use per capita in cities such as Houston, Detroit and Los Angeles, which are among the world's highest consumption levels, are likely to be between 100 and 1000 times those of most cities in low-income nations (Newman and Kenworthy 1989). By the late 1980s, the average waste generation for each urban citizen in North America was 826 kg compared with 394 kg for Japan and 336 kg for the European OECD nations; the average for low-income countries is between 150 and 200 kg a year and in many cities (or poor city districts) the average can be as low as 50 kg per person per year (OECD 1991, Cointreau 1982). The disparities in terms of the amount of non-renewable resources thrown away as rubbish (especially metals) are much higher because of the higher proportion of metals discarded as wastes in cities in high-income nations.

In one sense, the comparisons of per capita non-renewable resource consumption between nations or between cities are misleading, as the discussion on the development of a Trump index earlier in this chapter suggested. Worldwide, it is the middle- and upper-income groups that account for most resource use and most generation of household wastes; this only becomes a high-income–low-income country issue (or a North–South issue) because most of the world's middle- and upper-income people with high-consumption lifestyles live in Europe, North America and Japan. High-income households in cities such as Lagos, São Paulo and Bangkok may have levels of non-renewable resource use comparable with high-income households in Los Angeles or Houston; it is the fact that there are so many fewer of them within the city population that keeps city averages much lower.

But levels of household wealth alone are insufficient to explain the disparities between cities in terms of per capita resource use. In 1980, petrol use per capita in cities such as Houston, Detroit and Los Angeles was five to seven times that of cities with similar per capita incomes, including three of Europe's most prosperous and attractive cities: Amsterdam, Vienna and Copenhagen (Newman and Kenworthy 1989). A study of the differences in petrol use between cities suggested that larger vehicles, greater wealth and cheaper fuel in the United States explains only between 40 and 50 per cent of the variation; other key factors were urban density and the pattern of land use which in turn were linked to public transport performance and the level of traffic restraint (ibid). The influence of density on per capita petrol use can also been seen in the comparisons made between the core, inner suburbs and outer suburbs of Toronto: on average, each person in the outer suburbs had twice the fuel consumption of each person in the core because of the greater use of cars (and less use of public transport) and the greater number of cars per head of population (Gilbert 1990). The disparities are even larger in New York: those in the outer area averaged five times the petrol use per person of those in the central city (mainly Manhattan).

The dates at which the price of non-renewable resources will begin to rise rapidly, reflecting depletion of their stocks, may have been overstated in the various reports produced during the 1970s, but the finite nature of non-renewable resource stocks is not in doubt. There may be sufficient non-renewable resources to ensure that 9–10 billion people on earth, late in the next century,

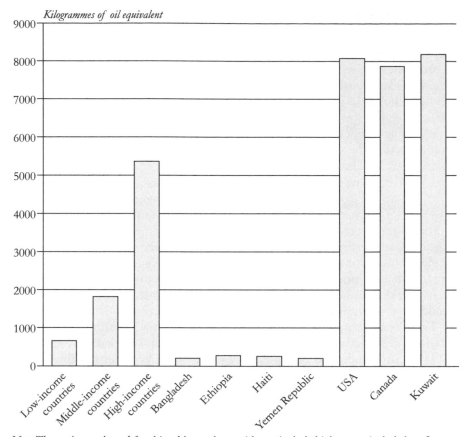

Note: The nations selected for this table are those with particularly high or particularly low figures, to illustrate the scale of the differentials between them.

Source: Table 10 of 'Selected World Development Indicators' in World Bank (1999), *Entering the 21st Century: World Development Report 1999/2000*, Oxford University Press, Oxford and New York, pages 248–249.

Figure 8.2 *Contrasts in commercial energy use per person in 1996 between regions and between selected nations*

have their needs met. But it is unlikely that the world's resource base could sustain a world population of 9 or 10 billion with a per capita consumption of non-renewable resources similar to those enjoyed by the richest households today or even the average figure for cities such as Houston and Los Angeles. There are many middle-income households living in cities with good transport who are committed to environmental issues and can serve as examples of how a high quality of life can be combined with a much more modest use of resources, and who have personal 'ecological footprints' that are sustainable, even when extended to the majority of the world's population. One returns to the great potential that cities have to provide high-quality living standards with lower levels of resource use and waste that was noted in Chapter 1.

Cities and global systems

Discussions with regard to the impact of human activities on global life-support systems tend to centre on their contribution to reducing the stratospheric ozone layer and to atmospheric warming. Chapter 5 outlines the likely direct and indirect consequences for cities of global warming. The disparities in greenhouse gas emissions per person between countries or cities in high-income and low-income countries are as striking as those outlined earlier in terms of non-renewable resource use. Consider average emissions per person for carbon dioxide. Cities such as Canberra, Chicago and Los Angeles have between 6 and 9 times the carbon dioxide emissions per person of the world's average and 25 or more times that of cities such as Dhaka (Nishioka and others 1990). There are comparable disparities between averages per person for nations – for instance, average carbon dioxide emissions per person in high-income nations were more than 8 times those of low-income nations in 1996. The differentials were even more dramatic for particular nations. For instance, for many low-income nations, average emissions of carbon dioxide in 1996 were 0.1 metric tonnes per person or less; the average for high-income nations was over 100 times higher (12.3 metric tonnes per person), with figures for the United States being some 200 times higher.

There is also the issue not only of who is currently contributing most to global warming but who historically contributed most. One estimate suggests that Western Europe and North America alone have been responsible for 61 per cent of all emissions since 1800, although they only contain 10 per cent of the world's population (Agarwal and others 1999c).

Before the international measures taken to control their use, the per capita disparities for the consumption of chlorofluorocarbons and halons (the main cause of stratospheric ozone depletion) were just as striking; figures for 1986 show that most high-income countries had per capita consumptions of 1 or more kilograms per year, with Switzerland having 1.30 and the United States 1.37; most low- and middle-income countries for which data were available had per capita consumptions below 0.1 kilograms per year, while many had figures far below this. For instance, per capita figures for India and Indonesia were for 0.01 – around one-hundredth the average figure for wealthy nations (UNEP 1991).

This discussion of the interaction between city-based production and consumption, and resources and sinks from beyond the city boundaries is a reminder that the goal is not sustainable cities but cities that contribute to sustainable development goals within their boundaries, in the region around them and globally. A concentration on 'sustainable cities' focuses too closely on achieving ecological sustainability within increasingly isolated 'eco-regions' or 'bio-regions'. Seeking 'sustainable cities' implies that each city has to meet the resource needs of the population and enterprises located there from its immediate surrounds. But the goals of sustainable development are the meeting of human needs within all cities (and rural areas) with a level of resource use and waste generation within each region and within the nation and the planet that is compatible with ecological sustainability. It is unrealistic to demand that major cities should be supported by the resources produced in their immediate

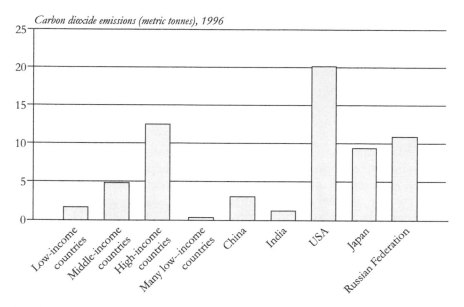

Note: Many low-income nations have figures of 0.1 or less including Benin, Burkina Faso, Ethiopia, Haiti, The Lao People's Democratic Republic, Madagascar, Malawi, Mozambique, Nepal, Niger, Rwanda, Tanzania and Uganda.

The other nations selected are those that are responsible for the largest volume of carbon dioxide emissions that year.

Source: Table 10 of 'Selected World Development Indicators' in World Bank (1999), *Entering the 21st Century: World Development Report 1999/2000*, Oxford University Press, Oxford and New York, pages 248–249.

Figure 8.3 *Contrasts in carbon dioxide emissions per person in 1996 between regions and between selected nations*

surrounds, but entirely appropriate to require that consumers and producers in high-consumption, high-waste cities reduce their level of resource use and waste, and reduce or halt the damaging ecological impacts of their demands for fresh water and other resources on their surrounds.

Although the discussions and recommendations about 'sustainable cities' have much of relevance to reduce the depletion of environmental capital caused by production and consumption in cities in high-income nations, they concentrate too much on individual city performance. What is more important for sustainable development is the local, national and international frameworks needed to ensure the achievement of sustainable development goals world-wide, including the appropriate frameworks for cities.

What sustainable development implies for city authorities

A commitment to sustainable development by city or municipal authorities means adding additional goals to those that are the traditional concerns of local authorities. Meeting development goals have long been among their main responsibilities. They generally include attracting new investment, better social conditions (and fewer social problems), basic services, adequate housing and (more recently) better environmental standards within their jurisdiction. This does not imply that city and municipal authorities need to be major providers of basic services, and they can act as supervisors and/or supporters of private or community provision.

A concern for 'sustainable development' retains these conventional concerns but with two more added. The first is a concern for the environmental impact of city-based production and consumption on the needs of all people, not just those within their jurisdiction. The second is an understanding of the finite nature of many natural resources (or the ecosystems from which they are drawn) and of the capacities of natural systems in the wider regional, national and international context to absorb or break down wastes. Historically, these have not been considered within the remit of city authorities. Indeed, many cities in high-income nations have only made considerable progress in achieving sustainable development goals within their own boundaries (ie reducing poverty, ensuring high-quality living environments, protecting local ecosystems, and developing more representative and accountable government) by drawing heavily on the environmental capital of other regions or nations and on the waste-absorption capacity of 'the global commons' (Rees 1992). But in the long term, all cities will suffer if the aggregate impact of all cities' production and their inhabitants' consumption draws on global resources at unsustainable rates and deposits wastes in global sinks at levels that disrupt the functioning of ecosystems and global cycles.

Adding a concern for 'ecological sustainability' on to existing development concerns means setting limits on the rights of city enterprises or consumers to use scarce resources and to generate non-biodegradable wastes. This has many implications for citizens, businesses and city authorities. Perhaps the most important for cities in high-income nations and for the more prosperous cities in middle-income nations is the role of city and municipal authorities in promoting the needed delinking of high standards of living/quality of life from high levels of resource use and waste generation.

The different environmental emphases that can be given within any 'sustainable development policy' is made clear by Graham Haughton's unpicking of the different aspects of environmental equity. He suggests that we think of sustainable development as seeking to reconcile five different dimensions of environmental equity (see Box 8.2). Many proponents of 'sustainable development' concentrate on only one or two of these aspects and may indeed promote actions that go against the other dimensions, as in forcing local populations off land they have long utilized (and may even own) to create 'wildlife' reserves or 'green belts'.

However, while Figure 8.1 and the checklist in Box 8.2 with its five different aspects of environmental equity are useful for governments in developing policies to contribute towards sustainable development goals, the actual policies and the priorities must be developed locally, so they respond to local circumstances, including local opportunities and constraints. Given the diversity of cities in terms of their size and population growth rates and of their economic, social, political, cultural and ecological underpinnings, it is difficult to consider

---

Box 8.2 *THE FIVE DIFFERENT DIMENSIONS OF ENVIRONMENTAL EQUITY*

- Intragenerational equity (as measured by equity in access to basic services such as water supply, sanitation and primary healthcare and in protection from environmental hazards, especially flooding, landslides and high levels of air pollution).
- Intergenerational equity (measured by the extent to which there are effective policies to help conserve soils and forests, make efficient use of freshwater resources, reduce non-biodegradable wastes and keep down greenhouse gas emissions).
- Geographical or trans-boundary equity (measured by the extent to which environmental cost transfers from city-based production or consumption are minimized, as in damage to local water bodies from liquid and solid wastes, and control of air pollution which causes acid rain).
- Procedural equity – ie the extent to which legal and political systems treat all sections of the population equally (measured by the extent to which different stakeholders benefit from public investments and policies, and the extent to which they are involved in developing and implementing local environmental plans).
- Interspecies equity (measured by the extent to which preserving ecosystem integrity and areas of particular importance for biodiversity are integrated into environmental plans).

Source: Haughton, Graham (1999), 'Environmental justice and the sustainable city', *Journal of Planning Education and Research*, Vol 18, No 3, pages 233–243.

'urban policy and management' for sustainable development in general terms. In most cities there are contradictions between sustainability and development: most of the cities that can be judged positively by development criteria (ie where social, economic and political goals are met) have among the highest per capita draws on environmental capital (ie use of non-renewable resources, draw on watersheds, forests, agricultural systems and ecosystems' waste-absorption capacities and per capita emissions of greenhouse gases). Most of the world's cities with the least draw on environmental capital are the ones that perform worst in development terms with high proportions of their population lacking safe and sufficient water, sanitation, good quality housing, access to healthcare, secure livelihoods and, in many, basic civil and political rights.

Priorities in a move towards sustainable development are going to differ greatly from city to city. For cities (or urban systems) with high levels of non-renewable resource use, the priority must be to reduce fossil fuel use and waste generation (through reducing waste levels and more recycling), while maintaining a productive, stable and innovative economy and a better record in reaching disadvantaged groups. Some clues as to how this can be achieved might be found in the cities that currently have among the world's best living standards but a relatively small draw on environmental capital – and this is not simply the result of a less energy-intensive economic base. Examples of cities such as Copenhagen and Amsterdam with one-seventh of the per capita consumption of petrol of Detroit and Houston were cited earlier. There are also several studies that show how major reductions in resource use and waste generation are possible in high-income nations without declines in the quality of life.[11]

For cities with low levels of non-renewable resource use and waste generation (which usually implies a relatively low-income city), the priority is the achievement of social, economic and political goals, but within a commitment to minimizing the call on environmental capital. In terms of non-renewable resource use, many cities in low- and middle-income countries are among the most resource-conserving cities in the world. Per capita consumption levels are much lower and every item of waste from households or businesses that has some value is reclaimed for reuse or recycled. As described in Chapter 5, this process is generally driven by the poverty of so many citizens; thousands of households can depend for their survival on a meagre income derived from selling materials obtained by sifting through rubbish at the local/city dump, or on industrial sites or other places where wastes are aggregated (Furedy 1990a).

In the longer term, if low- and middle-income nations develop more stable and prosperous economies, they will make increased use of non-renewable resources and their greenhouse gas emissions per capita are also likely to increase. The extent of this growth in the use of environmental capital will depend not only on the level of wealth created and its distribution but also on the extent to which provisions are made now and in the immediate future to promote the efficient use of resources and the minimization of wastes. For example, in rapidly growing cities, measures to encourage fuel-efficient buildings and land-use patterns that respond to citizens' priorities for easy access to employment and services within fuel-efficient transport systems can, over time, bring increasingly large savings in the use of fossil fuels (and thus also in the emissions of greenhouse gases) relative to wealth (Gore 1991, Lowe 1991).

BUILDING SYNERGIES, AVOIDING CONFLICTS?[12]

When city governments consider how to apply a sustainable development framework to their operations, and their urban policies and projects (or national governments and international agencies seek to support them in doing so), there are obvious tensions between different goals within the two boxes in Figure 8.1 and also between the different equity goals noted above. Most centre on the extent to which projects or investments justified for their contribution to expanding production (which in turn is meant to increase incomes and help meet human needs) contribute to the depletion of one or more aspect of natural capital – for instance fossil-fuelled power stations or much expanded

11 See Leach et al 1979 and many subsequent national studies for details of how increasing prosperity need not imply increased fossil fuel use; also Von Weizsäcker and others 1997.
12 This section draws on McGranahan and Satterthwaite 2000.

highway systems that will increase motor-vehicle use and therefore greenhouse gas emissions. Within environmental policies, there are obvious conflicts between what is often termed 'the brown agenda', that concentrates on environmental health, and 'the green agenda', that concentrates on the contribution of urban-based production, consumption and waste generation to ecosystem disruption, resource depletion and global climate change. There are also 'rural' versus 'urban' conflicts as in, for instance, large hydro-electric dams whose construction involves flooding large areas of agricultural land and forest with most of their electricity destined for urban enterprises or consumers. Expanding urban areas inevitably draw more on the resources of their wider region; increasingly prosperous urban areas almost inevitably draw more heavily on non-renewable resources and create more wastes.

In part, it is only when the different goals are pursued independently that there are serious conflicts. If pursued in tandem, important complementarities can be found between safer, healthier city environments and reduced depletion of natural capital. Such complementarities include:

- Systems for the management of liquid and solid wastes that reduce environmental hazards for city dwellers and also reduce non-renewable resource use (through promoting waste minimization, reuse and recycling) and the ecological damage that previously arose from polluted surface run-off.
- Improvements to public transport that better meet the transport needs of most citizens (especially lower-income groups), reduce physical hazards and keep down air pollution and greenhouse gas emissions.

There are often more complementarities between contrasting agendas than might initially appear to be evident. For instance, the priority of those espousing the brown agenda to expand the number of households connected to piped water systems (which implies increased household consumption for those who previously relied on public standpipes or vendors) seems to conflict with those espousing a green agenda who want to keep down the use of fresh water (to avoid depleting groundwater reserves or drawing water from more distant watersheds) and who recommend increasing water prices to encourage conservation. But both agendas can be served by better water management. As noted already, support for water conservation and better maintenance of piped water systems can often free up sufficient 'new' water supplies to allow piped supplies to be extended to unserved households with no overall increase in water use. In addition, the cost of extending water supplies can be met in part by charging the enterprises and households who are connected to the system more realistic prices, with tariff structures that penalize high consumption levels.

Although there will still be trade-offs – for instance, the cheapest or most robust buses may not be the best performers in terms of polluting emissions and fuel use – decisions made within an awareness of such trade-offs and with procedural equity should considerably reduce the conflicts between the environment and development. One of the more controversial aspects is with regard to the choice of systems to improve sanitation, but health and ecological concerns can be combined (see Box 8.3).

In conclusion, it is possible to envisage the development of prosperous, healthy cities that have a much reduced draw on natural capital in comparison with those that are common today.

Avoiding the conflicts between global and local sustainability

How can a concern for global sustainability be reconciled with the need for locally determined development? There need to be international agreements to set limits for each national society's consumption of resources and use of the global sink for their wastes. But most action to achieve sustainable development has to be formulated and implemented locally. The fact that each city and its interaction with local and regional ecosystems is unique implies the need for optimal use of local resources, knowledge and skills. This demands a considerable degree of local self-determination, since centralized decision-making structures have great difficulty in developing policies that respond appropriately to such diversity.

National governments inevitably have the key role in linking local and global sustainability. Internationally, they have the responsibility for reaching agreements to limit each nation's call on the world's environmental capital. Nationally, they are responsible for providing the framework to ensure that local actions can meet development goals without compromising local and global sustainability.

At the level of city and municipal government, there are at least four key policy areas to secure both development and sustainability:

1   Respond to citizens' demands for a safe and healthy living and working environment which includes ensuring the availability of shelter and the provision of basic infrastructure and services, and ensuring that there is an effective legislative and regulatory system to protect citizens from exploitation by landlords and employers, and from environmental hazards.
2   Penalize polluters (ie establish appropriate mechanisms and enforce them), give further incentives to encourage innovative ways to reduce pollution and conserve resources (especially reductions in air pollution and fuel consumption of road vehicles), and encourage waste reduction, reclamation, reuse and recycling of both non-renewable and renewable waste materials.
3   Manage urban growth to promote minimal use of environmental capital while meeting social and economic goals.
4   Identify and support the development of new economic activities that enhance both the urban centre's economic base and its environment.

But city or municipal governments may fulfil these roles while no modifications are made to ensure that the consumers and producers within their boundaries contribute to regional or global sustainable development. While meeting development goals must remain the priority in most cities in low- and middle-income nations, this does not mean that 'sustainable' goals should be excluded. Their most obvious role is in planning, guiding and regulating the built environment – building-material production, construction, building design

BOX 8.3 *COMBINING ECOLOGICAL AND HEALTH CONSIDERATIONS
FOR CITY SANITATION*

Water-borne sewers, when well managed, provide a very safe and convenient way by which households can dispose of their human wastes. From
an environmental health perspective, they are very effective. Although
considered to be 'expensive' solutions for the poor, there are also examples
of where costs were kept down to the point where little or no subsidy was
needed in providing low-income households with sewers, as described in
Chapter 6. However, from an ecological perspective, sewer systems generally require high levels of freshwater use, and by collecting all the wastes
within a single system, they can present serious problems with regard to
what can be done with the large volume of sewage. Sewage can be treated,
but going beyond primary treatment is expensive. Disposing of sewage
sludge is also a problem, especially for large sewer systems.

However, potential conflicts can be minimized, if decisions about
which sanitation system best addresses the needs and resources of the
inhabitants of a city or settlement are made within an awareness of the
short- and long-term ecological consequences. There are many sewer
systems and toilets in operation that keep down the volume of water
needed. There are also systems where treatment is decentralized and the
ecological impacts of the whole sewer and drainage system are much
reduced. There are many examples of 'sewage farming' and sewage-fed
aquaculture that make use of the nutrients in sewage and act as 'treatment',
although care must be taken to minimize the health risks for those working
in this and ensure no health risk to those who consume the products of
sewage farming. There are also sanitation systems that require little or no
water. It is important that the full range of potential solutions to sanitation
problems in any city or city district are considered, but with the needs and
priorities of those whose sanitation is most in need of improvement also
having a central role. In pursuing sanitation systems with less ecological
impact, there is a danger of promoting systems that bring inconvenience,
higher maintenance costs and greater environmental risks to the users, or
of simply producing latrines that the population do not use.

and performance, site and settlement planning, etc. Goals relating to local or
global ecological sustainability can be incorporated into the norms, codes and
regulations that influence the built environment and whose aim (in theory) is to
promote development goals.

But city and municipal government cannot be expected to take the lead
role in addressing such issues as the reduction of greenhouse gas emissions, a
steady increase in fuel efficiency among road vehicles and domestic appliances,
the promotion of more sustainable international trade practices and other
essential elements of sustainable development. National or state government
must provide the legislative, regulatory and fiscal framework within which urban

government can operate and meet its own local and regional sustainable development agenda, and at the same time contribute to meeting national and international goals. It also remains the task of national government to consider the social and environmental impacts of their macro-economic and sectoral policies that may be contributing to the very problems that their sustainable development policies are seeking to avoid.

THE NATIONAL FRAMEWORK FOR CITY ACTION ON SUSTAINABLE DEVELOPMENT

Among the high-income nations, which have much the largest 'ecological footprint' per person, no national government has set up the institutional, regulatory and incentive structure to ensure that the aggregate impact of their nation's economic activities and their citizens' consumption is in accordance with global sustainability. Most have taken some steps towards doing so, as in commitments to lower greenhouse gas emissions and measures to implement international agreements to stop the international trade in toxic and hazardous wastes, and to reduce emissions for chemicals that are depleting the stratospheric ozone layer. But the incompleteness and inadequacies of their responses hardly encourages governments in low- and middle-income nations to take action.

Developing a national framework that encourages and requires action by city authorities for sustainable development is obviously a critical part of achieving national goals for sustainable development. For instance, it will need innovation and good environmental planning and management within all urban governments to be able to deliver the reduction in greenhouse gas emissions that are needed from higher-income nations and to keep down the growth in greenhouse gas emissions in lower-income countries as they develop more prosperous economies. But in most low- and middle-income nations, governments have also denied city and municipal governments the power and resources they need to promote development.

The achievement of urban development goals that also seek to promote ecological sustainability (or at least to minimize the contribution of city-based activities to unsustainability) requires both supportive and regulatory structures. The first are needed to encourage the private sector and community initiatives to contribute to sustainable development. For instance, promoting a greater commitment among companies to waste minimization and recycling generally needs national action. The second are needed so that the workings of the market are not such that the weak and vulnerable are exploited (so development goals are not met), and air and water quality damaged, natural capital depleted and global systems disrupted (so sustainability goals are not met).

The policy options can be subdivided into three broad areas: regulatory controls that use penalties enforceable by sanctions; market incentives (either taxes or subsidies) to influence choices made; and the allocation of property rights, such that externalities are 'internalized' and become one of the set of market decisions. In practice, no one method is used by governments and each has particular advantages and disadvantages associated with it, and so is useful in different circumstances.

There is much discussion as to the relative advantages and disadvantages of regulatory controls and market incentives. Traditionally, what are today the high-income countries used regulation as the basic tool for carrying out environmental policy (OECD 1989). Legislation exists to enforce controls and whatever pollution remains after its enforcement is dealt with by local authorities. But such an approach requires effective city and municipal authorities and agencies since the controls have to be enforced; much of air, water and land pollution in or around cities in Africa, Asia and Latin America arises not from a lack of legislation but from inadequate or no enforcement. Only a small proportion of city and municipal governments in these regions have sufficient power and resources to enforce controls, and have a sufficient revenue base to cover the costs of an effective enforcement agency and pay for the facilities needed to dispose of residual pollution.

In the last two decades, regulation has been viewed less favourably and government intervention has often been criticized for being costly and inefficient. New methods, using market incentives, have become more popular. There are several different ways in which market incentives can be used. One of the most popular is through the use of taxes on activities that are polluting or are costly in their use of natural resources. In some cases such charges are intended to have a major effect on behaviour, in other cases they are largely treated as an additional source of revenue (perhaps to pay for compensating measures). Such charges are justified because the market does not operate to include all social and environmental costs incurred in producing or consuming a product and therefore an efficient market requires some price adjustment. For example, local governments may decide to charge motorists according to how often they choose to drive in busy locations during peak periods. In other cases, governments may choose to subsidize certain kinds of behaviour in order to encourage people to act in an environmentally friendly way. It is common for city governments in Europe to subsidize their public transport networks. In addition to imposing taxes and subsidies, governments can create private markets for environmental 'goods' and 'bads'.

One advantage of market incentives is the flexibility with which such intervention can be applied. For example, taxes dependent on the level of polluting emissions means that companies with a more limited ability to change to cleaner processes may continue to pollute the area (and pay the charge), but those for which alternatives are available will switch to cleaner processes. But such schemes may be hard to operate in certain markets in low- and middle-income nations, particularly those made up of many small buyers and sellers. In such circumstances, the cost of enforcing a charge would exceed several times the amount collected. Leach and Mearns (1989) consider the feasibility of a tax on wood to ensure that forest resources are not exploited as a free good. They note that 'as long as taxes on urban traders are small, they are likely to have little if any effect on curbing forest use ... If, on the other hand, the taxes are large, there will be even stronger incentives than now for the transporters and traders to evade them' (page 224).

Neither regulation nor market incentives can offer an alternative to efficient and effective local government (Winpenny 1991). Regulations and incentives require that local government has the resources to identify environmental damage that is occurring and to develop an understanding of local conditions so it can intervene effectively. Governments need the resources to monitor and enforce whatever environmental policies are chosen, with the necessary powers and penalties for effective prosecutions. Policy-makers also need to consider the broader impacts of such policies. Charges imposed through market intervention policies and additional costs incurred by regulations that discourage certain types of behaviour may increase inflation. Charges that increase the cost of basic necessities may impact particularly heavily on low-income groups and have undesirable redistributional implications. More stringent pollution control may simply encourage polluting enterprises to set up elsewhere, such as outside the municipality, region or nation where the controls are being implemented.

A third option open to governments is the allocation of property rights. This can result in the creation of new markets, for example a market in the right to pollute, with companies being allocated pollution rights that they can trade with other companies. This may have radical impacts on the distribution of resources. For example, if pollution rights are retained by companies, then pollution will continue if it is poorer groups living or working nearby who suffer, since they cannot afford to pay to prevent or reduce such pollution. But if pollution rights are owned by the poor, then the industrialist can afford to pay them to allow some pollution. Even if, in the worst case from the environmental perspective, the industrialist pays so that pollution continues at the previous level, the poor are considerably better off because they have the income generated by the sale of their environmental asset (Pezzey 1989). Pezzey argues that the 'allocative effects of redistributing environmental property rights from rich to poor people ... might be an effective way of simultaneously improving the lot of the poor and improving the environment. But the political difficulties of such redistribution should never be underestimated, since they will certainly limit the pace at which redistribution can proceed' (Pezzey 1989).

Finally, a word is needed about the kinds of indicators that can expand the environmental concerns of the local, city and region to the global. Meadows 1999 describes how indicators are needed at four different levels: natural capital (ultimate means), built capital, human and social capital, and well-being (ultimate ends). Indicators are needed to monitor the ways in which natural capital (the stocks and flows in nature – 'ultimate means' since all life and economic transactions depend on this) are drawn on by 'built capital' (the production structure that produces economic output) and 'human and social capital' (that includes knowledge, wealth, health, trust, fair and democratic political and legal systems) to address well-being ('ultimate ends' that includes happiness, fulfilment, self-respect). Most economic and social indicators concentrate only on built capital, and human and social capital. As Meadows (1999) notes, sustainable development is a call to expand the economic calculus to include natural capital and to ensure that well-being is the ultimate end rather than 'adequate' per capita incomes or levels of consumption that are necessary but not sufficient conditions for well-being. The three most basic aggregate measures of sustainable development are:

1   the sufficiency with which well-being ('ultimate ends') are realized for all people;
2   the efficiency with which natural capital ('ultimate means') are translated into ultimate ends; and
3   the sustainability of use of natural capital (Meadows 1999). This then provides the framework for the indicators themselves.

ENABLING LOCAL ACTION

Much of what has been discussed above stresses the concept of central government as an enabler, developing the laws, institutions and policies that support and encourage individuals, households, communities, enterprises and local governments to undertake economic or social activities with a high proportion of government plans, policies and actions determined and implemented at local level.

The discussion of government as an 'enabler' has a long history. Within the evolution of development theory, it is perhaps through discussions of appropriate housing policies that the importance of an enabling policy has been stressed and its form made more explicit. The origins of the idea that government actions with regard to housing should concentrate on 'enabling' and supporting the efforts of citizens and their community organizations to develop their own housing goes back at least to the 1950s and perhaps earlier.[13] The concept of enablement has also spread to many other sectors – for instance in the organization of agricultural extension services (with the shift to participatory learning and action) and in the construction, organization and management of many forms of infrastructure and services at the 'community' or 'neighbourhood' level (for instance for healthcare services, water supplies and provision for sanitation).

The concept of enablement is based on the understanding that most human investments, activities and choices that influence the achievement of development and sustainability goals take place outside 'government'. Most are beyond the control of governments (or at least of democratic governments) even where governments seek some control. In cities in Africa and much of Asia and Latin America, the point is particularly valid since most homes, neighbourhoods, jobs and incomes are created outside government and often in contravention of official rules and regulations (Hardoy and Satterthwaite 1989; UNCHS 1996). There is the understanding – expressed so clearly by Adam Smith some 200 years ago – that inappropriate government controls and regulations discourage and distort the scale and vitality of individual, family and community investments and activities. But there is also recognition that, without controls and regulations that are scrupulously enforced, individuals,

---

13 See for instance Mangin 1968, and Turner 1966 and 1969.

communities and enterprises can impose their externalities on others. The wave of 'environmental-health' centred reforms of city and municipal governments in Europe and North America in the late 19th and early 20th centuries developed systems of urban governance to ensure better provision in the supply of water and the disposal of liquid and solid wastes. Similar reforms were also evident in many Latin American countries. Environmental legislation in the second half of the 20th century has centred on government control of air and water pollution, and solid-waste generation and disposal because these had imposed costs on urban citizens and on the citizens and ecosystems beyond the city boundaries. In each instance, central government had to provide the framework for action and it was generally city and municipal governments that had to act; successful government enablement is always a careful balance between encouragement and control.

The application of 'enabling policies' has received considerable support from the growing recognition that democratic and participatory government structures are not only important goals of development but also important means for achieving development goals. Participation and enablement are inseparable since popular priorities and demands will be a major influence on the development of effective and flexible enablement. The concept of government policies, actions and institutions as rooted in enablement has a much wider relevance since it is important to the promotion of greater ecological sustainability as well as development. It would be politically unacceptable in most societies for governments to substantially restrict individual consumption levels, but sustainable development worldwide is impossible without national frameworks that promote substantially lower levels of demand by wealthy households on the world's environmental capital.

IMPLEMENTING SUSTAINABLE DEVELOPMENT IN CITIES

The regulations and incentives needed to support the achievement of development goals, within a framework that promotes local and global ecological sustainability, is relatively easy to conceive as an abstract exercise. The poverty suffered by the minority of urban dwellers in richer nations and the majority in poorer nations can be drastically reduced without a large expansion in resource use (and waste generation). The economic and ecological costs of providing safe and sufficient water supplies, provision for sanitation, waste removal and healthcare, and ensuring safe, secure shelters are often overstated. The quality of life of wealthy (generally high-consumption) individuals and households need not diminish and in certain aspects may indeed improve within a long-term programme to cut their draw on the world's environmental capital (see Von Weizsäcker and others 1997). The prosperity and economic stability that poorer nations need to underpin secure livelihoods for their populations and the needed competence at national and local government could be achieved without a much increased call on environmental capital.

But translating this into reality within nations and globally is another issue. Powerful vested interests oppose most of the needed policies and priorities –

for instance as reducing the resource use and greenhouse gas emissions of middle- and upper-income groups implies less profits for them. It is also in the richest nations where changes are most needed for at least three reasons:

1   These are the nations with the highest current and historic contributions to greenhouse gases.
2   These nations have no moral basis for demanding more resource conserving (less greenhouse gas emitting) patterns of development among lower-income nations unless they (and their wealthiest citizens) set an example of how to combine high-quality lives with much lower resource use and waste generation.
3   Low-income nations that need to develop a stronger and more prosperous economic base will generally need to increase their greenhouse gas emissions, and only by reducing emissions per person in the richer nations can this be possible, within a commitment to restrict global greenhouse gas emissions.

Cutting greenhouse gas emissions within the richest countries will bring higher costs, especially to those who currently consume the most. Technological change can help to limit the rise in costs – for instance, moderating the impact of rising petrol prices through the relatively rapid introduction of increasingly fuel-efficient cars and moderating the impact of higher electricity prices (especially where these are generated by fossil-fuelled power stations) through more efficient electrical appliances and better designed and managed buildings that restrict the need for space heating or cooling. Many industries can also limit the impact of higher fossil fuel prices by increasing the efficiency with which fuel is used. In addition, a steady increase in the price of fossil fuels also brings growing possibilities to replace them with renewable energy sources or electricity derived from such sources (and here technological change is also reducing the cost of tapping renewable energy resources). The scope for using renewable energy resources for space heating and cooling is also much increased in energy-efficient buildings. But if combating atmospheric warming does demand a rapid reduction in greenhouse gas emissions in high-income nations, this may require limitations in middle- and upper-income groups' right to use private cars and to have unlimited air travel that cannot be met by new technologies and alternative ('renewable') fuels – at least at costs that will prove politically possible. In addition, so many existing commercial, industrial and residential buildings and urban forms (for instance low-density suburban developments and out-of-town shopping centres) have high levels of energy use built into them and these are not easily or rapidly changed (Gore 1991).

At the same time, in Africa, Asia and Latin America, the achievement of development goals that minimize the call on local and global environmental capital demands a competence and capacity to act by city and municipal government that is currently very rarely present. As noted by one of the most experienced specialists on issues of urban governance, in a review of African cities:

> *ultimately, solutions to problems of urban finance, housing, public transport, the siting and standards of urban infrastructure, public health and public cleansing services, water, electricity and numerous other urban amenities must be formulated locally, by local people, on the basis of local experience and information* (Stren 1989, page 66).

So one returns once again to the need for competent, effective, accountable local governments. They are essential for the meeting of development goals, but also for ensuring sustainable patterns of natural resource use and keeping down greenhouse gas emissions. Adding a concern for sustainability on to existing development concerns strengthens further the rationale for strong, effective, accountable government institutions at local level.

Local governments cannot take on these roles without a strong financial base, the support of national government and an appropriate legislative, regulatory and incentive structure. The laws, norms and regulations set by national government must have considerable flexibility, otherwise they inhibit rather than enable local action and the best use of local resources. There is also the need for mechanisms to allow inter-local government area resource transfers, otherwise only local governments in more prosperous areas will have the resources to address development and sustainability goals.

Chapter 6 also stressed how the capacity of local government to work in partnership with community organizations, non-governmental organizations, non-profit foundations and private sector enterprises is also central to the achievement of development goals, and this is especially true where economic circumstances limit the investment capacity of local government. A stress on 'enablement' at local level is to provide the support and advice that will encourage community initiatives and multiply manyfold the number that start and succeed. Such policy directions imply the need for new kinds of 'enabling' institutions that are widely distributed within each nation to provide funding and technical advice (see Chapter 6). Chapter 7 included a discussion of how Local Agenda 21s can become the means by which local action can include policies and investments that address local, regional and global environmental goals. It also noted how it would need national support and international agreements to ensure that national and global goals become incorporated into local plans. This is the focus of the next section.

THE GLOBAL CONTEXT FOR SUSTAINABILITY AND DEVELOPMENT

Citizen pressure has often helped to persuade city and municipal governments to pursue more sustainable patterns of resource use and waste minimization, where the ecological impacts are local or regional or (on occasion) national. This can be seen in the environmental movements and in the role taken by environmental issues in election campaigns. But most of these have been driven by citizen concern for their own health and quality of life. As Graham Haughton points out, nearly everyone is an environmentalist in the sense of wanting a good environment for themselves. But so much environmental pressure is by groups with power that want to protect or improve their environment at the expense of others (Haughton 1998). For instance:

- Keep parks and nature reserves, so don't allow low-income groups land on which to develop their own homes.
- Middle-class pressure ensuring that dirty industries or facilities are located in low-income areas.
- Cities exporting their environmental problems.

There is less citizen pressure on city and municipal governments pressing for changes in production and consumption patterns that have their most serious ecological impacts 'overseas' or on global cycles. Yet the achievement of sustainable development depends on city residents, businesses and governments reducing the ecological damage to which they contribute far beyond the city boundaries, as well as reducing greenhouse gas emissions.

There are some important signs of change. For example, what is termed 'green consumerism', where consumers choose goods whose fabrication or use has less damaging environmental consequences, supported by 'eco-labelling', has put pressure on many manufacturers to address the environmental implications of their products' fabrication, use and disposal. 'Fair trade' campaigns and the sale of 'fair-trade' goods have helped to raise issues such as the wages and/or working conditions of those who make the goods or the human rights records of their governments. These have put pressure on producers and retailers to take what is usually termed 'ethical sourcing' more seriously – for instance, to avoid the use of goods produced in countries or by companies with poor human rights or environmental records. Many companies' unethical investments or products or poor environmental performance have been exposed by campaigns – for instance to promote consumer boycotts of their products – or by environmental or human rights campaigners purchasing some shares and bringing pressure on the company at shareholder meetings. There are examples of companies (including multinational corporations) that have made explicit commitments to improve environmental performance or to provide better wages and working conditions for their workforce or for those working in major subcontractors. There are even some that allow independent audits to check on their claims. There are examples of governments that have promoted or supported eco-labelling, and the control of certain imports for ethnical or environmental reasons. All these have importance as they show ways of lessening the human and environmental costs of production in 'distant elsewheres'.

But the extent to which this can become sufficiently effective on a global scale is in doubt. 'Eco-labelling' can influence a proportion of the market but is unlikely to influence enough of it to make the needed difference. Then there are the vast imbalances in power between multinational companies and their chains of production, distribution, sale and promotion, and the citizens' groups that raise these issues. The people who are currently affected most by the international transfer of environmental costs – the workforce exposed to dangerous working conditions, the inhabitants suffering from high air pollution levels and other environmental impacts – have no direct political influence on the governments of the nations into which the goods they helped to produce are imported. They often face difficulties within their own nations as they risk losing their livelihood if they are part of any protest against wages, working conditions or environmental abuses. It is perhaps difficult for those of us living in high-income countries to appreciate this, but it is often politically dangerous to protest. Two of the Peruvians who helped to launch the campaign against pollution in Chimbote (Peru) and to develop the Local Agenda 21 described in Chapter 7 were imprisoned for 13 months, falsely accused of being terrorists, and it was only after a strong national and international campaign that they were released (Foronda 1998). Meanwhile, national and city governments desperate to attract new investment and to boost exports so often do not support citizens' environmental concerns. And if the key needs and priorities of so much of the present generation cannot be protected from international production and trading systems, how much less are the needs and priorities of future generations likely to be protected.

There is some international action to prevent the most obvious and blatant international transfers of environmental costs, as in the controls on the export of hazardous wastes or on the trade in endangered species or products derived from them. But the interests of many of the world's most powerful companies and corporations would be threatened if action extended to address all such transfers – for instance, through governments in Europe and North America only permitting imports from countries where good standards of occupational health and safety were maintained. Or where the import of goods produced by multinational companies was only permitted if the company and its main subcontractors met agreed standards for good environmental practice in the use of resources and the generation and management of wastes in all its operations in different countries, with independent groups allowed to monitor their performance. Sustainable development depends on effective measures to reduce the local and international transfer of environmental costs to other people, other ecosystems or global cycles, but we are a very long way from getting the effective means to achieve this accepted by business interests and rich world governments. Meanwhile, the initiatives to promote green consumerism and fair trade can have only a limited impact if the goods they promote have to compete with those whose lower price reflects the inadequate wages and poor working conditions of those who made them and the avoidance of costs through no attention to pollution control and waste management.

Thus, one is faced with the fact that the global context for sustainability can only be achieved by international agreements in which the governments of the world's wealthiest nations agree to limits that will be opposed by most of their higher-income groups and many of their enterprises. One of the key international issues for the next few decades will be whether it is politically possible to combine the pursuit of increased wealth and development by national societies (most of whose members have strong preferences for minimal constraints on their consumption levels) with a recognition of the ecological and material limits of the biosphere.

The actual means to achieve sustainable development are much easier to envisage than the political processes within nations that accept the international agreements that its achievement needs. This was demonstrated at the 1992 UN Earth Summit with the watering down of the Global Climate Change Convention and the refusal of the United States government to even discuss limits on the right of US consumers and businesses to consume in ways that deplete environmental capital. The Summit's sustainable development action plan, Agenda 21, can only encourage and persuade. While it includes many practical recommendations to help governments to move towards sustainable development, it relies on governments who approved to implement it. Neither the text nor the institutions that supervise its implementation have sanctions against governments who do not. The same is true for many of the recommendations within the Habitat Agenda that came out of the 1996 UN Cities Summit (although this, perhaps deliberately, avoided the issue of controlling greenhouse gas emissions). As in all the global summits and conferences in which government representatives formally endorse far-reaching recommendations for development and the environment, perhaps they only do so because they know that there are no procedures to hold them to account for failing to implement them.

The issue of global warming can be seen as a 'test case' in that this is likely to be the first global environmental problem whose resolution depends on significant changes in consumption patterns in the richest and most powerful nations. International agreements have been achieved that limit the call of each national society on global or other nation's environmental capital – for instance the reductions in the use of chlorofluorocarbons (CFCs) and the Basel Convention on the Control of Transboundary Movements of Hazardous Wastes and their Disposal. But these did not imply significant changes in the consumption patterns of the wealthy. The work of the Intergovernmental Panel on Climate Change has stressed how quite stringent controls are needed to keep global warming within 'safe' limits. These imply large constraints on the richest nations' and people's consumption levels.

There are also potential conflicts between limiting global warming (and the ecological disruptions it will bring) and promoting development. A more prosperous and economically stable Africa, Asia and Latin America does imply increases in per capita fossil fuel use (and thus greenhouse gas emissions). The question then becomes what limits are set on greenhouse gas emissions and how the rights to use fossil fuels (or to undertake other activities that generate greenhouse gases) are allocated between countries. The global discussions at the Earth Summit and ever since have been characterized not by fairness and considerations of equity but by the self-interest of the richest nations (Agarwal and others 1999c). Powerful vested interests have also made use of the scientific uncertainty regarding how much emissions levels would have to be controlled and how quickly. A 'safe' level would be a 'contribution to global warming' per person which, if extended to all inhabitants, still implied that total greenhouse gas emissions worldwide should be kept below certain limits. There is uncertainty as to what a 'safe' level is, as can be seen in the international discussions about what level to set as a target for maximum greenhouse gas concentrations in the atmosphere. But what is perhaps more worrying is the difference between the scientific and the political discussions of the 'safe' limit (Houghton 1999). The governments of the richest nations are unlikely to accept the limits suggested by the best scientific evidence (and recommended by the Intergovernmental Panel on Climate Change), since achieving the 'safe' limit implies what they regard as politically unacceptable reductions in emissions. But this implies continued warming (with all the risks that this brings) and even larger reductions required in the future (Houghton 1999, Agarwal and others 1999c).

There are also all the difficulties in translating any agreement on global limits into limits for each nation and the controversies over which criteria to use in doing so. This includes the issue of whether the historic contributions of the wealthiest nations to the greenhouse gases that are now in the atmosphere (and a major contributor to human-induced climate change) should be taken into consideration in setting limits on their future greenhouse gas emissions. From the point of view of equity, it is difficult to see how these can be ignored; these are also the countries with the greatest resources and capacities to support changes. It will also be difficult to promote more resource-efficient, less ecologically disruptive development paths for low- and middle-income nations unless high-income nations demonstrate their commitment to this. But the governments of high-income nations are unlikely to accept the inclusion of their historic emissions in any setting of their emission limits.

Finally, there is the issue of whether (or to what extent) tradable permits can be used. The cheapest way for the wealthiest countries of 'reducing' their emissions is by purchasing the unused emission rights of other nations, mostly from lower-income nations. But this allows high-income nations to make minimal modifications to their production and consumption systems. As such, it does very little to move the world economy and the consumption patterns of middle- and upper-income groups away from high greenhouse gas-emitting patterns (Agarwal and others 1999c).

The concerns to limit global warming among the governments of higher-income nations but also to limit controls on the emissions in their own countries may mean major changes in international development assistance. Aid budgets (and development assistance from the multilateral agencies that the high-income nations control such as the World Bank) may increasingly be influenced by measures to minimize greenhouse gas emissions in low- and middle-income nations. This implies an even lower priority than is evident today in helping to meet human needs for adequate livelihoods, water, sanitation, health care and education, and in strengthening the capacity of recipient governments to do so. It also implies an increasing concentration of development assistance in those nations that are major net greenhouse gas emitters, and away from many of the poorest nations. It might even be questioned as to whether this could be termed development assistance in that most of the benefits will accrue outside the boundaries of the country receiving the assistance.

Thus it is not only the achievement of the 'ecologically sustainable' component of sustainable development that requires international agreements; so too does the meeting of human needs. Most low- and many middle-income nations cannot meet development goals and very few are likely to meet sustainability goals without changes in the world market and in the way that development assistance is provided. A government seeking to resolve a debt crisis and reliant for most foreign exchange on the export of natural resources cannot address longer-term sustainability issues. It is also difficult to see the moral basis for demanding that poorer nations whose economies have made very little demand on finite resources or contributed little to the pollution or disruption of the global commons must now be denied the use of the cheapest energy sources because the rich world made such a high demand on the global commons in the process of becoming rich. In addition, a more sustainable basis for trade in natural commodities is needed, with changes in the relationships between the world's major consumer markets (Europe, North America, Japan) and the nations in Africa, Asia and Latin America that are the major producers of natural resources.

Chapter 9

Conclusions

**'Street samba': girls dance in the street in a favela called Bom Jardim
on the periphery of Fortaleza, Brazil**

INTRODUCTION

There is a growing concern that large cities are reaching a size where the benef-
icence of nature is being surpassed in terms of providing fresh water, breaking
down the pollution loads generated by city-based activities (or through dilution,
rendering them less hazardous), providing all the raw materials that city producers and consumers use, and yielding cheap and easily exploitable energy sources.
The preceding pages have noted many examples of local ecosystems' carrying
capacities being exceeded: freshwater withdrawals exceeding aquifers' natural
rate of recharge; levels of organic pollutants from industries, sewers and urban
run-off exceeding the capacities of rivers and estuaries to break them down;

and city-based demands for wood-fuel, timber and bricks exacerbating deforestation, soil erosion and loss of agricultural land. Urban areas often expand
over prime agricultural land; so too do waste dumps to cope with the increasing
volume of solid wastes generated by city-based producers and consumers. In
many cities, there are problems of acid rain that damages soils, trees and crops
in surrounding areas.

Ambient air pollution is also receiving increasing attention. In many cities
or particular city districts, the combination of air pollutants from motor
vehicles, industries, power stations and (in some instances) household stoves or
fires has reached levels where dangerous concentrations persist, especially when
high emissions coincide with particular atmospheric conditions. There is
growing concern about the increasing role of city-based production and
consumption in greenhouse gas emissions. These concerns for ambient air
quality, greenhouse gas emissions and natural resource consumption or degradation have much in common with city concerns in Europe and North
America.

But such a list of environmental problems is very incomplete and in some
senses misleading. It concentrates on chemical pollution and damage to natural
resources and ecosystems. It gives too little attention to two critical environmental problems: the health risks to which city dwellers are exposed each day
from biological pathogens and physical hazards; and people's access to natural
resources (especially fresh water and safe land sites for housing). The main
reasons for biological pathogens being present are contaminated and inadequate quantities of water, inadequate provision for sanitation and the disposal
of solid and liquid wastes; inadequate measures to control disease vectors
(especially insects); poor quality, overcrowded housing; inadequate health
services; and inadequate environmental and occupational health legislation (or
lax enforcement). The main reasons for physical hazards are, again, poor quality,
overcrowded housing, inadequate provision for infrastructure (including
drainage), and the fact that large sections of the population can only find land
for housing on dangerous sites such as steep slopes or sites that are often
flooded. In many cities, the rising use of motor vehicles combined with poor
management of roads, pavements and traffic has led to large increases in traffic
accidents. Such factors underlie millions of preventable deaths every year. They
also contribute to serious ill health or disablement for hundreds of millions
annually. In most cities, between one-third and two-thirds of the population
cannot afford safe and healthy housing. As Chapter 2 described, a very large
section of the urban population lack safe and sufficient water supplies and
provision for sanitation – far more than international statistics suggest. These
are the environmental problems that deserve a high priority. Since there is a
growing interest among governments in the problems of managing and disposing of 'toxic wastes', it would seem appropriate to classify human excrement as
much the most serious 'toxic waste' because of its health impact as a result of
the inadequacies in the provision for sanitation. It is also one whose safe
disposal is relatively cheap. Below, we elaborate on points first raised in Chapter
1 with regard to a new environmental agenda for cities.

ENVIRONMENTAL PROBLEMS; POLITICAL SOLUTIONS

Most environmental problems have underlying economic or political causes. It can even be misleading to refer to many of the most pressing environmental problems as 'environmental' since they arise not from some particular shortage of an environmental resource (eg land or fresh water) but from economic or political factors that prevent poorer groups from obtaining them and from organizing to demand them. The severe shortages of water that much of the urban population face might be considered a serious environmental problem but rarely is its cause environmental; in most cities, it is not a shortage of fresh-water resources but governments' refusal to give a higher priority to water supply (and the competent organizational structure that its supply, maintenance and expansion requires). In many cities, there are serious constraints on expanding freshwater supplies, as the size of the city and its production base has grown to exceed the capacity of local freshwater resources to supply it on a sustainable basis, but even here, providing adequate supplies to poorer groups may demand less water than that saved by better maintenance of the existing system and more realistic charges for the larger industrial water users. The same is true for land; most cities or metropolitan areas have sufficient unused or underutilized land sites within the current built-up area to accommodate most if not all the low-income households currently living in very overcrowded conditions. The many poor households who live in settlements on dangerous sites (for instance flood-plains or steep slopes) choose such sites not in ignorance of the dangers but because the authorities fail to plan for and allocate more suitable sites. Again, there are cities with critical land shortages because of special site characteristics but even here, governments could do much more to support low-income groups' access to safe sites and to reduce risks for those in hazard-prone areas. Perhaps not surprisingly, one paper discussing the linkages between poverty and the urban environment in Asia was subtitled 'access, empowerment and community-based management' (Douglass 1992). Ensuring that low-income groups can obtain access to safe and secure housing (or land sites on which such housing can be built) and environmental infrastructure and services is central to an improved urban environment.

A failure of government can be said to underlie environmental problems – government failures to control industrial pollution and occupational exposure, to promote environmental health, to ensure that city dwellers have the basic infrastructure and services essential for health and a decent living environment (whether the providers are private, NGO, community-based or public sector), to plan in advance to ensure that sufficient land is available for housing developments for low-income groups and to implement preventive measures to limit risks from, for instance, traffic and extreme weather events. This is not meant to imply that government agencies should undertake all these tasks; often their role is to provide the framework within which private or community land developers and infrastructure and service providers can operate, or to take measures to ensure more public accountability by industries for their emissions and waste management; or to provide frameworks to make markets work, as in, for instance, ensuring a competitive market among private water suppliers, bus companies, land developers and building material suppliers. In large part, it is also a failure of governance in that the inadequacies of government relate to its lack of accountability to its citizens for its policies and expenditures (including a lack of transparency in the way that decisions are made and resources allocated), the lack of democratic structures and the failure of the judiciary to allow citizens to hold it to account. For many countries, the multiple failures or limitations of government can be partly explained by the national economy's weakness; effective government action in ensuring a healthy environment for citizens is much more difficult without a stable and reasonably prosperous economy. In many countries, it is also related to the limited powers and resources allowed to urban governments by higher levels of government.

It is remedying these failures of government within cities and city districts and addressing the reasons that underlie them that should be central to any new urban environmental agenda. This may not parallel the contemporary urban agenda in Europe and North America, although it certainly parallels the urban agenda there a century or less in the past when provision of infrastructure and services, and control of pollution and occupational health hazards were as inadequate as they are today in most cities in Africa, Asia and many in Latin America. In effect, most cities in these regions need the 'environmental health' revolution that most European and North American cities underwent in the last few decades of the 19th and first few decades of the 20th centuries, as well as action on the environmental concerns raised in the 1960s and 1970s. Some cities in Latin America and Asia also underwent an 'environmental health' revolution in the first few decades of this century but the momentum was never maintained. Some cities in Latin America and Asia have also achieved this environmental health revolution in the past few decades. Strengthening the capacity of city and municipal governments to address the lack of sanitation, drains, piped water supplies, refuse collection and health services is generally a precondition for building the institutional capacity to address air and water pollution, protect natural resources and reduce greenhouse gas emissions.

At present, the pressure for environmental action in urban areas of Africa, Asia and Latin America which comes from many research and activist groups and some donor agencies in Europe and North America is neglecting the 'environmental health' agenda. Measures to prevent or limit the transmission of diarrhoeal diseases and other water-borne (or food-borne), water-washed or water-based diseases, or acute respiratory infections and TB, or vector-borne diseases such as malaria, dengue fever and yellow fever, have critical environmental components. So too do measures to reduce accidental injuries and deaths. These must remain at the centre of the urban environmental agenda, along with measures to ensure rapid treatment of environment-related diseases and injuries, where prevention is not possible.

Another example of the transfer of 'rich-world' perceptions is the stress on the loss of agricultural land to urban sprawl. This is often cited as one of the most serious environmental problems in cities in Africa, Asia and Latin America (see for instance Lowe 1991). While this can be judged a serious problem in certain nations with very limited agricultural land, in most nations, urban areas cover only 1 or 2 per cent of the national territory. In addition, urban planning can be made to minimize their encroachment on productive land (for instance by ensuring that vacant plots within the urbanized areas are developed). And as Chapter 6 noted, there are also many examples of cities that have, within their boundaries, large areas with intensive production of crops and livestock. Indeed, the intensity and variety of urban agriculture in many urban centres might even mean that production per unit area for the whole urban centre exceeds that of many agricultural areas. City-based demand for crops and other agricultural goods also underpins so many rural livelihoods. This is not to imply that agricultural land should not be protected from urban sprawl, where possible, but where it is given more attention than such critical environmental problems as water-borne and vector-borne diseases, this does imply an inappropriate set of priorities.

The growing pressure for action on urban environmental problems must press for action in all urban centres. Most of the literature on urban environmental problems is about a handful of large cities, typically Mexico City, São Paulo, Lagos, Bangkok, Calcutta, Cairo, Jakarta, Mumbai/Bombay, Delhi and Karachi. Yet only a small proportion of the urban population lives in large cities; as Chapter 1 noted, the 'mega-cities' of ten million plus inhabitants house a very small proportion of the population in Africa, Asia and Latin America, and this proportion is unlikely to rise very much. Improved water supplies, sanitation, solid- and liquid-waste management, control of disease vectors, the capacity to plan and manage new commercial, industrial and residential developments and preventive-focused health services are needed in virtually all urban areas, including the tens of thousands of small and intermediate sized urban centres in which a high proportion of the urban population lives.

Building the basis for a new environmental agenda for urban centres should focus on six aspects:

1   institutional change within governments and new roles of aid agencies;
2   a shift from improving urban management to 'good governance';
3   a more effective framework of support for citizens' groups and NGOs within more accountable and transparent government structures;
4   a more explicit linking of 'environmental improvement' with poverty reduction;
5   locally driven agendas within each urban centre that respond to the specifics of each location, society and culture within national frameworks that reward good 'global' practice; and
6   new professional attitudes.

INSTITUTIONAL CHANGE AND THE ROLE OF AID AGENCIES

The long-term solution to any city's environmental problems depends on the development within that city of a competent local government that responds to its citizens' needs and is accountable to them for its policies, actions and expenditures. Lessons drawn from 40 years' experience of national or international agencies demonstrate that most local problems need local institutions. Outside agencies, whether national ministries or international agencies, often misunderstand the nature of the problem and the range of options from which to choose the most appropriate solutions. They also fail to appreciate local resources and capacities.

The acquisition by city and municipal governments of the capacity and power to ensure adequate provision and maintenance to all their populations of water supply, sanitation, drainage, refuse collection, healthcare and other essential elements of a good urban environment involves complex political changes. Powerful and well-organized vested interests will oppose such changes, as was the case in Europe and North America. This includes vested interests within governments; as many examples in the text have highlighted, national or state-level governments so often retain control over capital investment in cities and major development decisions. Substantial institutional changes are needed in most countries – for instance, despite recent decentralization programmes in many Asian nations, the comment by Douglass (1992) that most governments in Asia remain highly centralized and that the highly centralized power structures are least able to provide support to local institutions still remains valid. The same is true for much of Africa, with national power struggles so often preventing the development of competent, accountable urban authorities.

Each city (and smaller urban centre) has to develop and implement an action programme, based on a careful evaluation of its own problems and of the resources it can mobilize. Even if current levels of international aid to urban environmental problems were multiplied many times, most urban centres would still never receive substantial amounts and for most of those that do, the amounts would never be more than a useful supplement to their own resources. This book recommends that more attention should be paid by governments and international agencies to environmental problems in urban areas, but this does not necessarily mean a diversion of resources from rural to urban areas. In most countries, too little attention is also given to the environmental problems that impact most on the health and livelihoods of poor rural dwellers (and to addressing their causes). What is recommended is a far higher priority to a better use of existing resources which includes increasing the capacity of city and local governments to tackle both short- and long-term environmental problems, and channelling more funds direct to CBOs and the local NGOs with whom they choose to work.

The political changes by which the capacities of city and municipal government are increased and made more accountable to their citizens are often opaque to outside agencies. Interventions by aid agencies and development banks who seek the efficient implementation of 'their' project may even inhibit this change. Innovative local solutions that are cheaper and more appropriate may be ignored in favour of far more expensive but less effective solutions funded and supported by external aid and designed by foreign consultants.[1] As

---

1 See Hasan 1999 for some recent examples in Karachi where the government initially sought a large loan from the Asian Development Bank to improve sewerage. But the Research and Training Institute of the Orangi Pilot Project demonstrated that the design was faulty and that there were far cheaper and more effective ways of tackling the problems that did not need an international loan. Many governments could considerably reduce the foreign borrowing needed to tackle urban environmental problems by supporting the capacity of urban authorities, community organizations and local specialists to develop cheaper and more appropriate solutions.

noted in Chapter 8, international agencies put great stress on the need to ensure that the capital projects they fund continue to function (and have even appropriated the term 'sustainable development' to describe this). But their need to spend their funding (or increase the amount of capital on loan) often conflicts with the most 'sustainable' solutions which are to keep down costs, maximize the mobilization and use of local resources, and minimize the need for external funding. Ironically, the most 'sustainable' solution in financial terms would be one that does not need their funding. In addition, international agencies can never stay in a city to guarantee the maintenance and expansion of the new water or sanitation or refuse collection systems that they helped to fund.

Box 9.1 contrasts the characteristics of many successful municipal and community-based projects to improve environmental health with the characteristics that make implementation easier for external funding agencies; the difficulties in reconciling the two are obvious.

Basic infrastructure and services, such as piped water systems, provision for sanitation and drains, regular rubbish collection, healthcare and emergency services, cannot be adequately provided to poorer groups without effective local institutions. Yet most aid agencies and development banks operate on a 'project-by-project' basis when what is needed is a long-term process within each city to strengthen institutional capacity, overseen by democratic governance. There may be potential for private sector enterprises to provide some of the needed improvements in particular kinds of infrastructure and services, but as Chapter 6 discusses, most of the literature on privatization overstates this potential and often forgets that effective privatization needs strong, competent and representative local government to set the conditions, oversee the quality and control prices charged, especially in those services that are a natural monopoly. After at least a decade in which privatization has been strongly promoted by many international donors as one of the key solutions for improving the environmental infrastructure and services, the documented successes are modest and not so numerous, especially in the nations with the most serious environmental health problems in their urban areas.

FROM URBAN MANAGEMENT TO IMPROVED GOVERNANCE

The shift in thinking from supporting 'government' to 'governance' has helped to highlight the critical role of civil society in ensuring (and developing) more appropriate responses to environmental (and other) problems. It has also encouraged external agencies to consider how they can support 'civil society' groups that are outside government. All international agencies need local implementors for the work they fund. Although it is common for international agencies to talk or write about the projects they implement, very few implement projects; they oversee the implementation of projects to which they contribute funding.[2] For instance, it is not the staff of these international

---

2 There are some exceptions, especially in disaster relief, but this generalization holds true in most instances.

Box 9.1 *THE MOST IMPORTANT AID PROJECT CHARACTERISTICS FROM TWO DIFFERENT VIEWPOINTS*

Characteristics of many successful initiatives	*Project characteristics which make implementation easy for an outside funding agency*
Modest external funding available to many initiatives in different neighbourhoods	Large capital sum provided to one project; managing many cheap projects is too costly in staff time
Multi-sectoral (addressing multiple needs of low-income groups)	Single sector because managing multi-sectoral project implies coordinating different sections in the donor agency and different government agencies or departments within the project which is too time-consuming
Implementation over many years – less of a project and more of a longer-term process to improve housing and living conditions and to improve relations between low-income communities and external agencies (including local government)	Rapid implementation (internal evaluations of staff performance in funding agencies are often based on the volume of funding supervised and the speed of implementation)
Substantial involvement of local people (and usually their own community organizations) in defining priorities, developing project design and implementation	Project designed by agency staff (usually in offices in Europe or North America) or by consultants from the funding agency's own nation
Project implemented collaboratively with CBOs, often local NGOs, local government and often various agency government or ministries	Project implemented by one construction company or government agencies
High ratio of staff costs to total project cost (in part because project sought to keep down costs and to mobilize resources locally)*	Low ratio of staff costs to total project cost
Difficult to evaluate using conventional cost-benefit analysis	Easy to evaluate
Little or no direct import of goods or services from abroad	High degree of import of goods or services from funding agency's own nation

Note: * This is not always the case and careful preparation may indeed mean a low proportion of staff costs to total costs, especially if the initiative grows.

agencies who dig the ditches, install the water pipes and provide the connections to households. The scope and potential success of any international
agency's projects are thus dependent on the quality and capacity of their local
implementor.

The whole international aid/development assistance structure from the
late 1940s onwards was set up on the assumption that capital made available to
national governments allied with technical advice would deliver 'development'.
The limitations of this quickly became apparent as most 'recipient' governments were unable to be effective implementors or they simply had other
priorities.[3] Such limitations have long been recognized, as can be seen in the
debates about the failure of aid to reach poorer groups and to support social
development that go back at least to the late 1960s (see for instance United
Nations 1971). But it has proved very difficult to change the institutional structure of development assistance agencies in response to this. It is also difficult
politically for the official aid agency of a government from a high-income
nation to steer aid to other local 'implementors' without the approval of the
recipient government. The same is even more so for multilateral agencies; after
all, the large multilateral agencies are partly 'owned' by recipient governments
(even if they lack much voting power, as in the boards of the development
banks). For the large multilateral funding agencies such as the World Bank and
the regional development banks, and the bilateral agencies such as the Japan
Bank for International Cooperation (into which the former OECF is incorporated), or the German government's KfW that provides loans, it is the national
government that has to guarantee that the loans will be repaid. No national
government in Africa, Asia or Latin America is going to sanction increasing
funding flows over which they have little control, or, even 'worse', to fund
citizen groups or NGOs that do not support them or even oppose them. Even
where external funding is intended to other government bodies, especially city
and municipal governments, national governments are inevitably loath to lose
control over which cities and which sectors should receive funding, or to have
international donors fund municipal authorities governed by opposition parties
– for nations with democratically elected national and city governments.

We have sought to stress in this book how improved urban environments
depend on good urban governance, not only in what urban governments fund
and regulate but also in how they encourage and support the efforts and investments of households, citizens' groups, NGOs and the private and non-profit
sector. We have also stressed how this in turn requires a political, legal and institutional framework that guarantees citizens' civil and political rights and access
to justice. Given the lack of interest among so many national governments in
addressing the most critical constraint on improving urban environments – the
limited capacity of most city and municipal governments and, for many, their
lack of democratic structures (and transparency in decisions about resource
use) – it would be a great mistake to continue channelling most external support
through national governments. After all, it is the failure of these governments

---

3 Of course this is not to claim that there were not many other factors that inhibited the effectiveness of international institutions including self-interest, political objectives, etc.

that underlies the most serious environmental problems. In addition, it is low-income individuals, households and communities working outside government that have been responsible for building most new housing units in urban areas and for a large proportion of all investments in housing and infrastructure and services (Hardoy and Satterthwaite 1989, Arrossi et al 1994).

The two critical agents of better urban environmental conditions are urban governments and urban civil society. For international agencies, whether official agencies or international NGOs, the extent to which urban governments are the most useful potential partners obviously depends on their capacity, structure and representative nature. The possibilities for international donors to be effective in supporting the environment and development policies in any urban area is obviously far greater if there is a relatively well-resourced, competent, local authority headed by an elected government that has the support of most of the local population than if there is a weak, poorly resourced local authority controlled by people appointed by higher levels of government with little scope for (or interest in) action. Table 9.1 is a reminder of just how much the local government context varies between nations. But the urban policies and support programmes of most international donors are not agile enough to adjust to such key differences. In nations where decentralization and democratic reforms have made urban governments more accountable, there is much greater scope for external agencies to help to strengthen their capacity to address the failures noted above. Where urban governments remain undemocratic and unaccountable, more attention is needed to support the community processes that are building the city 'from the bottom up'. This is also not in conflict with strengthening local government in that strong, well-organized, democratic community organizations are an essential part of developing strong and effective local democracies.

A NEW FRAMEWORK OF SUPPORT FOR CITIZENS' GROUPS AND NGOS

It is worth distinguishing between two different kinds of civil society organization that are active on environmental issues. The first is one whose primary purpose is working at grassroots level to improve the environment – for instance community organizations or savings and credit schemes formed by the residents of a low-income neighbourhood and the local NGOs that work with them. More support should be channelled to help fund the choices they make and the actions they plan. This can mean not only more cost-effective action than through the state; it can also strengthen citizen and community movements, which in turn are central to building more democratic and accountable state structures. The second is one that concentrates on documenting environmental problems and using this as the basis for demanding action – for instance documenting the 'state of the environment' in a city or highlighting the extent to which air pollution standards are being violated and who are the main contributors to this.

Both kinds of organization were important in driving environmental reform in Europe, North America and Japan, both for 'sanitary reform' from

Table 9.1 *The different roles for external agencies working to address low-income groups'*
needs within the different extremes in terms of local government structures

The continuum in terms of resources available to public institutions	The continuum in terms of local government structure, accountability and representative nature	
	From democratic and accountable local government structures	... to undemocratic, unaccountable and often clientelist local government structures
From relatively well-resourced local government institutions responsible for ensuring the provision of infrastructure and services, land management and pollution control	External funding and support for local government having a major role in infrastructure and service provision, pollution control and land management. For services that are privatized, government capacity to enforce quality and value for money from privatized service providers. Legal and institutional structure in place to guarantee people's civil, political and environmental rights	To meet low-income groups' needs, external agencies have to give priority to strengthening and supporting civil/community organizations that are pressing for changes in government provision and accountability, and in the legal–institutional means of ensuring this. Also supporting provision outside state structures (eg community, NGO), etc
... to poorly resourced local government institutions unable to provide these or to put in place the framework ensuring provision by private, NGO or community enterprises	External agencies helping build capacity of local governments, especially to work with and support a wide range of civil society groups (including CBOs and NGOs) in infrastructure and service provision and in guaranteeing rights. Less local capacity to use privatization well	Similar to the above, although with higher levels of support directed from outside to strengthening and supporting community-level provision and institutions. Here the need is to support the community processes that are building the city 'from the bottom up'. Many community-level initiatives need support outside of traditional government structures. But there is also the need for long-term commitment to making public sector institutions more accountable and effective

the middle of the 19th century onwards and for the environmental reforms from the 1960s onwards. Only through well-organized citizen action and protest sustained over many years did governments begin to act on the environmental problems created by industries and motor vehicles. Citizens' groups did much to document the scale and nature of the problems and to alert people to the dangers. Citizens' groups and what today we would call NGOs also had a major role in driving the political and institutional changes that greatly improved the quality of the urban environment in what are today the highest-income nations in the late 19th and early 20th centuries (see for instance Wohl 1983 and Jones 1991).

Now, as then, there are obvious links between democracy and citizens' action on environmental issues. Most of the examples of local and city action towards improved environments given in earlier chapters are within democratic countries. These include many that moved or returned to democracy in the last 20 years and where city and municipal authorities were made more accountable and acquired more scope for action. The innovations described in places such as Ilo, Manizales and Pôrto Alegre were rooted in strong local democracy. The story of Cubatao in Brazil (Chapter 3) is also a reminder of what local and multinational firms can get away with in terms of no pollution control, toxic emissions and wastes, and very poor quality occupational health, within undemocratic nations; the problems only came to light with the return to democracy in Brazil and democratic pressures were key in getting these problems addressed. It is also from democratic nations that this book drew most of its examples of NGOs with key roles in working with low-income groups on improving home and neighbourhood environments – from those in India, South Africa and Thailand that work with and support federations of low-income groups to acquire and develop their own homes and neighbourhoods (Chapter 6), to those that help develop innovative Local Agenda 21s (Chapter 7). It is also NGOs from democratic nations that have grown not only to pressure their own governments but also to question the priorities of governments and NGOs from high-income nations, as in the example of the Centre for Science and Environment in India which has not only been at the forefront of documenting environmental problems in India but also in demanding a fair voice for the concerns of low- and middle-income countries (and of their lower-income citizens) within global environmental negotiations and institutions (see for instance Agarwal and Narain 1991; Agarwal and others 1999c).

These examples give some clues about how external agencies can help to mobilize action. Outside agencies wanting to stimulate more action on environmental problems in cities should consider providing support direct to citizens' groups and NGOs within these cities, both to implement projects and to help document the problems. Each city needs a citizen-driven process that identifies the key problems and their causes, and that helps to develop the most appropriate solutions. For instance, as Chapter 2 showed, new methods and means are obviously needed to document the inadequacies in the provision for water, sanitation and drainage in each city and these must include assessments that draw on extensive local consultations. There are fewer environmental NGOs in most lower-income nations, especially those that concentrate on the most pressing environmental problems and that affect poorer groups the most. Those that exist often work in much more difficult circumstances. For instance, funding is less easy to find and government legislation to control pollution is less clear. In many instances, such NGOs suffer from harassment or repression from government.

Some care is needed in channelling support to local NGOs in that they may have agendas that hardly accord with the most pressing environmental problems. Indeed, they may be promoting the same distorted priorities as many NGOs from high-income nations, as they represent the priorities of middle- and upper-income groups. Inevitably, many opportunistic NGOs have been formed within recipient countries to tap into the greater enthusiasm from donors for funding NGOs. Even where they have 'pro-poor' agendas that appear to address pressing problems such as inadequate water and sanitation, they may operate in ways that are unaccountable to low-income groups and their community organizations. NGOs are often insensitive to political and power struggles within communities and may find it convenient to support traditional leaders who do not reflect the needs and priorities of many community members (Mitlin 1999). NGOs are often reluctant to delegate power and responsibility to community organizations. They may also impose their own professionally driven means of addressing problems and their own implementation timetables. If these NGOs rely on international donors, it is often difficult for them to avoid doing so, since this is in part the result of them having to follow the procedures and meet the criteria of the donor agencies, and having to generate enough funds to cover their staff salaries.

New channels of international support must also be developed for community-based action: for instance for squatter settlements whose inhabitants have no chance of public support for a piped water supply, drains and a child health centre. This would usually mean support to associations formed by low-income groups, including savings and credit groups, self-help groups and neighbourhood associations. Although there are many examples of highly cost-effective projects in squatter settlements funded by external agencies, the scale of the support remains small and generally ad hoc. Decisions about what to fund and who to fund remain firmly centralized in the capitals of North America, Europe and Japan. The scale of the funding and the conditions under which it is available remain more appropriate to the funding base and accounting procedures of the institutions providing the funding than the needs of those to whom it is provided. Chapters 6 and 7 stressed the need to develop channels to support funds for community-level initiatives set up in individual cities in Africa, Asia and Latin America where decisions about what is funded are made locally and where accountability is to local institutions and citizens. Even the most flexible institutional structure within an external donor cannot support hundreds of community-based initiatives if all decisions about funding and all monitoring and evaluation is concentrated in the donor's office in Europe, North America or Japan. Box 9.2 outlines a possible form for a Fund for Community Initiatives to channel loans, technical advice and additional support to low-income households and their community organizations for income generation, improved infrastructure and services, shelter upgrading and improved environmental health. Aid agencies wishing to support community-level initiatives could channel their support through such funds. Four critical features are worth highlighting:

1   Decisions about what is funded are made locally with a minimum gap between the request and its consideration. When community-based groups apply for funding to donors in Europe or North America, it often takes six months before a decision is reached; it can take two years. With a locally-based Fund for Community Initiatives, it should be cut to a small fraction of this, ie a question of one or two weeks.

2　The application procedures and decision-making processes are kept completely transparent so all groups in a city know who applies for funds, who receives funds and why.

3　Very small funding requests can be managed. A request for a few hundred dollars is not worth making to most international donors. Many would be horrified to receive such a small request because processing and managing it would take as much staff time as a much larger amount. Yet in many instances, it is small amounts that are needed, to cover the cost that locally generated funds cannot or to complement the support being received from the local authority.

4　A substantial part of the funding is made available as a loan with further loans available in part dependent on performance in loan repayment schedules and with loan repayments recycled into funding further local initiatives.

There has been some experimentation with this idea of supporting local funds for community initiatives. Chapter 6 included the example of a loan programme of the Thai government's Urban Community Development Office (funded by the Thai government) and its small-grants programme (supported by funding from DANCED). The UK Department for International Development is experimenting with a Fund for Community Initiatives (called the C3 Challenge Fund) in Uganda and Zambia. The UNDP has sought to support local environmental initiatives through its LIFE programme. But the institutional problems that donors may face in supporting such an approach were illustrated by our experience with the European Commission. In 1994, we were approached by staff from the European Commission to help them to develop a series of funds for community initiatives in different African cities. After much preparation and enthusiastic support from many European Commission staff members, the whole idea was dropped because of the complaint of European Union country representatives within some of the countries concerned that such a fund implies that they no longer have a key role in influencing what is funded. Here lies one of the key institutional (and political) constraints – that any real decentralization implies decentralization of power. A fund for community initiatives can only work if decisions about what are to be funded are made locally in ways that respond to the priorities of low-income groups and that are accountable to the population of that city. The key principle on which the fund should be based was the one that made it unacceptable to some senior staff for the donor agency concerned.

LINKING ENVIRONMENTAL IMPROVEMENT WITH POVERTY REDUCTION

This book has highlighted the multiple links between environmental improvement and reducing deprivation. The links between poverty reduction and environmental improvements have long been obscured by the tendency for poverty to be defined and measured by income levels. Chapter 7 highlighted how the conception and measurement of poverty as 'inadequate income' has

Box 9.2 *A CITY-BASED FUND FOR COMMUNITY INITIATIVES*

If the scale of funding to support community-level initiatives to improve environmental health is to increase substantially, new institutional channels are needed. Existing funding agencies cannot cope with a large increase in requests for small projects. One possibility would be a Fund for Community Initiatives set up within each major city, accepting funds from external donors but managed by a small board made up of people based in that city. These board members would have to be acceptable to community groups and would usually include some NGO staff that were already working with low-income groups and community organizations. It could include some locally-based staff from external donors.

Functioning of the fund. Low-income groups could apply for funding for projects and also for support for developing projects. The procedures by which application has to be made for funds and the decision-making process has to be kept simple, with a capacity to respond rapidly. These would also have to be completely transparent with information publicly available about who applied for funds, for what, who got funded and why. For funding provided as loans, the loan conditions and their repayment implications could have to be made clear and explicit, including repayment period, grace period (if any), interest rate and subsidy element.

Kinds of projects that could be supported. Health (for example support for the construction of sanitary latrines or improved water supplies; campaigns to promote personal and household hygiene and preventive health measures, including mother-and-child immunization; the setting up or expansion of community-based health centres); education (for example special programmes for children or adolescents who left school early; literacy programmes); housing (building material banks, loans to community-based savings and credit schemes through which members could access loans to upgrade their homes or purchase land and build their own home); environment (site drainage, improved water supplies) or employment (support for micro-enterprises, local employment exchanges; skill training, etc).

Funding. Between US$500 and US$50,000 to be made available to any group or community organization formed by low income individuals. The first loan provided would generally be small, with further loans available if the project (and any planned cost recovery) proceeds to plan. Some level of counterpart funding would generally be expected (although this could be in the form of labour contribution).

Terms. Total or close to total cost recovery sought where feasible – with allowance made for inflation and for the cost of borrowing funds – with funding recovered shown publicly to be recycled back into supporting other community initiatives. For most projects, a short period of grace would be permitted before the loan repayment had to begin (typically three months to a year) so that income generated or expenditure savings are partially realized before repayments begin. The Fund for Community Initiatives would also provide a range of support services – for instance, assistance to community organizations in developing proposals and technical and managerial support in project implementation. Grants or soft loans could be made available for certain specific interventions where cost recovery is difficult to achieve (either because funding cannot easily be collected or because incomes are too low).

meant too little attention being paid to other aspects of deprivation, including inadequate assets, abuse of civil and political rights, and inadequate or no access to safe housing with basic infrastructure and services. This and other chapters also highlighted how the underlying causes of these deprivations were not necessarily (or only) inadequate incomes but also discrimination, undemocratic political structures, incompetent local authorities and judicial structures that do not provide low-income groups with access to justice. The multiple deprivations suffered by low-income urban dwellers and the multiple entry-points by which deprivation can be reduced are now more widely accepted.

Earlier chapters have described the many links between environmental problems and poverty, including the very serious health and economic burdens caused by environmental hazards and the extent to which low-income groups face much higher risks and have fewer resources with which to cope with the consequences. Table 9.2 highlights some of the environmental actions that can help to reduce poverty or the deprivations associated with it. It emphasizes not only the improved health that such actions can bring but also other aspects of poverty reduction such as:

- the reduction in costs for those currently paying high prices for water and sanitation;
- the reduction in physical effort and the time freed up; and
- the protection of low-income urban households' assets.

There is also considerable employment potential in addressing the most serious environmental health problems, and also important synergies between employment creation and well-managed solid-waste management schemes where waste reduction and recycling, reuse and reclamation are promoted (as described in Chapter 7).

Thus many environmental improvements not only improve health, but enhance incomes because they reduce expenditures on purchasing water, access to latrines and paying for health care, and reduce the time that income-earners lose from being sick, collecting water, disposing of waste and nursing sick family members. They also protect low-income households' assets by reducing the risks of their homes (and the goods stored within them) being damaged by

Table 9.2 *Examples of how environmental actions can help to reduce poverty or the deprivations associated with it*

Environmental actions	Direct effects	Other effects
Improved provision for water and sanitation	Large reduction in health burdens from water-related infectious and parasitic diseases and some vector-borne diseases, and also in premature death (especially for infants and young children). Safe disposal of excreta from home and neighbourhood environment a great health bonus	For income earners, increased income from less time off work from illness or from nursing sick family members and less expenditure on medicines and on health care. Better nutrition (eg less food lost to diarrhoea and intestinal worms). Less time and physical effort needed in collecting water. Lower overall costs for those who, prior to improved supplies, had to rely on expensive water vendors
Less crowded, better quality housing, through supporting low-income groups to build, develop or buy less crowded, better quality housing	Large reduction in household accidents (often a major cause of serious injury and accidental death in poor quality, overcrowded housing) and remove the necessity for low-income groups to occupy land sites at high risk from floods, landslides or other hazards. Can also help to reduce indoor air pollution	Lower risk for low income groups to lose their homes and other capital assets to accidental fires or disasters. Secure, stimulating indoor space an enormous benefit for children's physical, mental and social development
Improved provision for storm and surface water drainage	Reduced flooding and reduced possibilities for disease vectors breeding bring major health benefits. Safer sites (flooding often spreads excreta everywhere) mean less risk of infection for the inhabitants, especially children	Lowered risk of floods that can damage or destroy housing which is often low-income households' main capital asset and also where they store other assets
Avoidance of hazardous land sites for settlements	Reduces number of people at risk from floods, landslides or other hazards. The damage or destruction of housing and other assets from, for instance, floods or landslides can be the 'shock' which pushes low-income households into absolute poverty	Sites within cities that may be hazardous for settlements are often well-suited to parks or wildlife reserves, and may also be well suited to helping in flood protection and groundwater recharge

Promotion of cleaner household fuels	Reductions in respiratory and other health problems through reduced indoor and outdoor air pollution	Reduced contribution of household stoves to city air pollution
Improved provision for solid-waste management	Removes rubbish from open sites and ditches in and around settlements. Reduces risk of many animal and insect disease vectors and stops waste from blocking drains	Reduces time and physical effort for previously unserved households. Considerable employment opportunities in well-managed solid-waste collection systems where recycling, reuse and reclamation are promoted
Support for community action to improve local environment	If well managed, many low-cost ways to reduce environmental hazards and improve environmental quality in informal settlements	Employment creation; minimum incomes help households to avoid poverty. Can reduce sense of social exclusion
Support for more participatory plans	Low-income groups with more possibilities of influencing city authorities' priorities on environmental policy and investment	Precedents set in participatory Local Agenda 21s and other action plans can lead to low-income groups getting greater influence in other sectors
Improved public transport	Cheap, good quality public transport keeps down time and money costs for income earners of low-income groups getting to and from work; also enhances access to services	Can reduce air pollution and its health impacts. Can reduce the disadvantages of living in peripheral locations and help to keep down house prices

Source: Satterthwaite, David (1999), *The Links Between Poverty and the Environment in Urban Areas of Africa, Asia and Latin America,* paper prepared for UNDP, New York.

floods, landslides and accidental fires. As governments and international agencies develop poverty-reduction programmes that recognize and respond to the multiple deprivations that most poor people face, so the key 'environmental' aspects can be incorporated.

A CITY-SPECIFIC ENVIRONMENTAL AGENDA

Another constant theme in this book is that each city has its own unique mix of environmental problems, in part linked to its own unique local environmental context, in part linked to the factors that shaped its development, and in part linked to its existing demographic, economic, social and cultural base. Where resources are limited, these problems can only be addressed with a knowledge of local resources (and how these can be mobilized), a knowledge of local constraints (and how these can be overcome) and the use of approaches that reduce capital requirements. The fact that capital is limited demands a more profound knowledge of the nature of environmental problems and their causes to allow limited resources to be used to best effect; only with large capital resources can conventional solutions be implemented, applying uniform standards to serve all citizens (McGranahan 1991). Potential solutions will need to be discussed locally and influenced by local citizens' own needs and priorities. Many 'cheap solutions' may be unacceptable; it is only through real community dialogue drawing in all interests that the trade-offs can be decided between quality, convenience and cost. Many upgrading packages simply offer a 'standard solution' that in keeping down costs provided something that was unpopular and unmaintainable. The book has mentioned various partnerships between municipal authorities, local non-governmental organizations and community organizations formed by low-income groups within particular neighbourhoods that have demonstrated how these can prove more cost effective than conventional approaches. This implies a different agenda and a different means of organization (or, more accurately, of governance) from the path taken by European or North American governments towards environmental policies during the 1970s and 1980s. One obvious difference is the level of wealth and prosperity and the different challenges this brings (McGranahan and others 2001). But four other differences need stressing:

1   Most national and regional economies, employment patterns and foreign exchange earnings are more dependent on natural resource exploitation. In Europe and North America, a very small proportion of the labour force depends on farming or forestry, so a decision to put controls on farming or forest exploitation to protect the beauty of a rural landscape or a site of particular scientific interest by putting controls on farming or forestry hardly affects the balance of payments or the scale of economic activities or employment opportunities. The impact of comparable controls is much greater in nations where a substantial proportion of foreign exchange earnings and jobs depends on farming and forestry. In many low- and middle-income nations, the most profound environmental (and political)

conflicts are centred on who has the right to own or use forests, freshwater resources and fertile land. And worldwide, tens of millions of low-income rural households are losing the right to use natural resources that have long formed the basis of their livelihoods (Agarwal and Narain 1992, Lee-Smith and Trujillo 1992).

2   Most nations in Africa and many in Asia and Latin America lack the institutions and the infrastructure on which to base effective actions to address urban environmental problems. In Europe and North America, when the 'environmental movement' began to grow and acquire increasing influence in the early 1960s, the basic infrastructure to deliver good environmental health was already in place – the piped water systems and water-treatment plants, the storm and surface drains and sewers (and at least some sewage-treatment plants), the landfill sites – even if more investment was needed to improve the quality of sewage treatment and solid-waste disposal. Perhaps more importantly, the institutional structure to implement it was also in place, especially the local government structure overseen by elected representatives and an established system to fund local government investments and expenditures. Governments in most of Africa, Asia and Latin America cannot implement comparable environmental policies with weak institutional structures (especially at local government level), very inadequate capital budgets, large backlogs in basic infrastructure and economies that are far less able to generate the capital needed to address the backlog.

3   There are the obvious differences in the nature of government. In West Europe and North America, action on environmental problems was almost always citizen led; citizens' groups and NGOs provided the lobby that eventually produced changes in government policy. This required representative government structures. Many nations in Africa and Asia and some in Latin America do not have representative governments; many of those that have established (or returned to) democratic rule at national level still retain relatively undemocratic structures at local level. These are unlikely to implement environmental policies, except those that benefit the richer and more powerful members of society, unless democratic pressures are allowed to push them in these directions. There has been no shortage of citizen groups pressing strongly for water, sanitation, healthcare and the right to live in cities without the constant fear of eviction, but in many nations this has not been permitted to have much impact on the housing and health policies of their governments. These causes have rarely been supported by middle-class professionals or indeed even by unions and religious bodies. There are now many more examples of 'good urban governance' underpinning more effective responses to environmental problems than there were evident ten years ago, when we completed the previous edition of this book, as the examples given in earlier chapters show. But they are still the exceptions, not the rule.

4   Much of the environmentalism in Europe and North America in recent decades has been driven by middle- and upper-income groups whose health or access to natural landscapes was being impaired. Most of the environmental problems they highlighted could be addressed without changes in

the distribution of income and assets. This is not the case for many environmental problems in Africa, Asia and Latin America, since they are rooted in the current global and local distribution of assets, income and rights to use resources (Gadgil and Guha 1992).

Chapter 3 highlighted how much the scale, range and relative importance of environmental problems differ between urban centres, influenced by (among other things) the size, per capita income, economic base, local ecological context and competence of local authorities. It stressed how the most serious environmental problems for most urban centres in most low-income and many middle-income nations are those associated with poor environmental health. Such urban centres do not have high levels of resource use, waste generation and greenhouse gas emissions (and so have small ecological footprints). Thousands of small urban centres in Africa, Asia and Latin America fall into this category, where the urban centre itself is 'sustainable' in the sense of a very limited draw on regional, national or global resources and sinks, but very unhealthy and with a high proportion of its inhabitants surviving with below poverty line incomes.

NEW PROFESSIONAL ATTITUDES

One reason for the lack of attention by professionals to the most pressing environmental problems can be attributed to the sectoral nature of government and of professional disciplines. As Richard Stren (1992) pointed out in the final chapter of a book on 'Sustainable Cities', most environmental problems are multidimensional, interconnected, interactive and dynamic which makes appropriate actions difficult for conventional government structures. The architects, planners and engineers who work for departments of housing or public works know very little about the environmental health problems faced by those they are meant to serve. Their training may not even consider this as an issue, especially if the curriculum for their training is based on Western models. Where a Ministry or Department of the Environment is set up, these problems may also fall outside its brief. Peter Kolsky (1992) has illustrated the problems posed by professional and administrative boundaries in relation to drainage. Sewerage, drainage and solid-waste services (including street cleaning) are often the responsibility of different agencies, yet their design, implementation and management should be carefully coordinated. Drainage systems cannot work in most cities without solid-waste management which keeps drains clean. Drainage networks need coordinated action at household, neighbourhood and city level, and beyond the city to maintain water quality for those living 'downstream' of the city, yet rarely do their design and operation take account of this fact. There is also the separation between those who design and those who run these systems; professionals who design sewerage, drainage and solid-waste management systems are rarely from the public agencies who are responsible for their operation and maintenance.

There is a need for new attitudes among professionals whose training also equips them to work cooperatively with low-income households and the community organizations they form. If, as many specialists have recommended, more support is to be channelled to citizen-directed community-level initiatives, professionals need to learn how to work cooperatively at community level. As a report by a WHO Expert Committee on *Environmental Health in Urban Development* states, there is also a need for community-oriented environmental health workers who are analogous to primary healthcare workers who can serve as a bridge between public-sector services and community residents as promoters and organizers of community efforts (WHO 1990).

Professional resistance to innovative local solutions remains a major constraint virtually everywhere. Architects are loath to cede to low-income groups the right to develop the house design and room layout they want. Planners do not want their zoning structures or subdivision regulations questioned. The kinds of community-driven house modelling and participatory settlement mapping exercises described in Chapter 6 are very much the exception. Transport engineers don't want to negotiate with each low-income settlement about the amount of space to be allocated to roads, and thus to have their regulations and methodologies for calculating space allocations to roads questioned. Water engineers don't want to engage in discussions about the depth of trenches and size of pipes with community organizations, even if this has large cost implications for the members of these organizations. In large part, of course, this is linked to the more fundamental constraint posed by official rules and regulations, including building codes, infrastructure standards and planning norms. A four-decade long discussion of their inappropriateness and how, for many nations, they are still rooted in inappropriate foreign (often colonial) models has not produced much change.

There is no lack of case studies showing how the most pressing environmental problems can be greatly reduced at a relatively modest cost, especially where local groups and institutions take a central role in developing solutions. Major improvements can be made to poorer groups' living environments at relatively modest per capita costs through six interventions: water piped into (or if not very near to) the home of each inhabitant; systems installed to remove and safely dispose of human excreta; a higher priority to the installation and maintenance of drains and services to collect rubbish; primary healthcare systems available to all (including a strong health prevention component which is so central in any primary healthcare system); house sites available to poorer groups that are not on land prone to flooding, landslides, mudslides or any other site-related hazard; and the implementation of existing environmental legislation. The cost constraints of applying these measures appear to be overstated; as Chapter 6 noted, work on alternatives to conventional water, sanitation, drainage and refuse collection systems have shown a range of cheap options while poorer groups' willingness and ability to pay for improved services (if these match their own priorities) is often underestimated. In many cities, it is not so much a lack of demand for water, sanitation, healthcare and waste collection that is the problem (with demand used here in the economic sense of willingness to pay), but a combination of an institutional incapacity to deliver cheap and effective services and a reluctance of professionals to permit innovative (non-standard) local solutions.

New tools and methods are also needed for community-based actions that guide professionals in how to work with low-income groups and their community organizations in identifying problems and their underlying causes, and developing appropriate solutions. This will include a better understanding of the needs and priorities of women in low-income communities, which are so often ignored or misunderstood (see Box 9.3).

In rural areas, what was called PRA (participatory rural appraisal) and is now more commonly referred to as PLA (participatory learning and action) has helped to transform professional attitudes about how to work with low-income groups and their own organizations in agriculture, natural resource management and social issues in villages. In the previous edition of this volume, we suggested that a comparable transformation was needed for professionals in urban areas. The last ten years have brought considerable innovation in this as described in Chapter 6.

CITY PROBLEMS WITHIN A GLOBAL PERSPECTIVE

The differing environmental interests of the high-income nations and the rest of the world became apparent at the first global governmental discussion of the issue – the UN Conference on the Human Environment in Stockholm in 1972. Large differences remain, even if the focus of international concerns has changed – for instance as the worries about mineral resource shortages have receded and the worries about global climate change have much increased. But as was the case in 1972, the international environmental issues that dominate discussions in Europe, Japan and North America are still rarely the environmental issues that pose the most serious risks to most citizens' health and livelihood in Africa, Asia and Latin America. It is not surprising that issues relating to the modification of the global climate have come to the top of the environmental agenda of both governments and environmental groups in high-income nations, given the estimates for the cost to their economies that could result from a sustained atmospheric warming (even if it is generally low-income countries that will face far more serious costs). But in general, in global environmental discussions, the large and powerful nations seek deals that best serve the interests of their large and powerful vested interests (Agarwal and others 1999c).

In high-income nations, most of the regional, city, neighbourhood and housing-related environmental problems described in earlier chapters have been addressed. Public memories there are too short to recall just how dangerous and unhealthy their city environments were only 100 or so years ago and how this was the result of damp and overcrowded housing, contaminated water, a lack of sewers, drains and provision for rubbish collection and street cleaning, no pollution control and ineffective (and corrupt) local government. Diarrhoeal diseases, typhoid, pneumonia and TB were major causes of death in London just 100 years ago, while in poor, crowded districts, more than one child in five

---

Box 9.3 *Gender aspects of environmental improvement in cities*

Improving provision for water supplies, sanitation, healthcare and other essential forms of infrastructure and services must be based on an understanding of the needs and priorities of those who, within households, are responsible for water collection, sanitation, laundry, disposing of household wastes, child rearing, caring for the sick and other daily necessities. In most instances, these are responsibilities that fall on women. For households engaged in urban agriculture, it is generally women who take on most of the responsibility for growing crops or raising livestock.

But women are rarely consulted about their needs, when plans are drawn up for improving infrastructure and services in squatter settlements or for new residential developments for poorer households. They are rarely consulted about their preferences for the form and content of services – for instance, health clinics and ante- and post-natal services are often open at times that working women cannot attend. Public transport provision is often timed to serve primary income earners and rarely considers the transport needs of secondary income earners or adults who work at home. The provision of a water supply rarely considers the needs of those who are responsible for washing, household hygiene and laundry or the time implications for those responsible for collecting water, although these have important health implications. When basic infrastructure and services are not provided, it is generally women who have to give extra time and effort. The low priority given to crèches and child-care centres is often a reflection of choices made with little or no involvement of those primarily responsible for child care – women. Residential zoning may prohibit the kinds of informal productive activities in which women commonly engage within their homes.

Designs for housing and settlements must take into account the special needs and responsibilities of women. For instance, if women's needs are taken into account, the size and design of house plots in serviced site schemes may be changed to take into account women's priorities for space for income-earning activities within the home. Easy access to clinics, child-care centres, markets and schools would get a higher priority, if those responsible for child care and housework were allowed more influence in settlement design.

Government programmes for low-cost housing, for housing finance and for skill training must ensure that they do not exclude women. To date, many such programmes have explicitly or implicitly excluded women – for instance through only accepting applications from 'male heads of household' or through 'proof of formal employment' when 40 per cent or more of all households are women-headed households, most of whom cannot work in the formal sector. Application forms for low-cost housing, housing finance or skill training are often complex and this discriminates against women, if women already suffer discrimination in access to education. Self-help housing projects must also recognize the limitations faced by women-headed households in allocating time to self-help activities.

Policies and programmes to protect common or public lands must help to protect the rights of the poorer groups who currently use such lands for foraging, firewood collection and livestock grazing. Since it is often poor women who are responsible for foraging and firewood collection, a failure to protect such common resources from appropriation by private interests or to protect their productivity often hits women hardest.

Government programmes to support community actions to improve housing and living conditions or to encourage resource conservation must be framed with an understanding of the role of women and their own networks within communities. Women are likely to be more responsive than men to programmes that really do bring direct benefits to those who are responsible for child rearing, maintaining the house and nursing the sick.

Sources: Drawn from various chapters in Moser, Caroline O N and Linda Peake (editors) (1987), *Women, Human Settlements and Housing,* Tavistock Publications, New York and London, from different papers on the special issue of *Environment and Urbanization* edited by Diana Lee-Smith and Ann Schlyter on 'Women in Environment and Urbanization' (Vol 3, No 2, October 1991) and from Songsore, Jacob and Gordon McGranahan (1998), 'The political economy of household environmental management: gender, environment and epidemiology in the Greater Accra Metropolitan Area', *World Development,* Vol 26, No 3, pp 395–412.

died before its first birthday (Wohl 1983), as is common in poor districts in cities in Africa and much of Asia and Latin America today. What is also forgotten is the essential role that more effective, accountable and democratic urban governance took in transforming the quality of the urban environment.

The continued stress by groups from high-income nations of the links between environmental degradation and 'over-population' where the poor (and their governments) are seen as the guilty party is also divisive. And as Chapter 7 described, the accuracy of such a stress is questionable when it is the high-consumption lifestyles of the relatively well-off, most of them in high-income nations with little or no population growth, that accounts for most non-renewable resource consumption, most of the generation of toxic and hazardous wastes, most of the greenhouse gases currently in the atmosphere and a considerable proportion of the pressure on soils, forests and freshwater resources.

If a growing proportion of a growing urban population in Africa, Asia and Latin America acquire levels of resource consumption comparable with those in Europe and North America, then global environmental problems will be much exacerbated. But what is far more significant for 'sustainable development' is that high standards of health and good quality environments in cities (and rural areas) can be achieved without high levels of resource consumption and environmental degradation (WHO 1992a). It is possible to combine a 'brown' agenda of much improved environmental health with a 'green' agenda of ecological sustainability (McGranahan and Satterthwaite 2000). In addition, improved water supplies, sanitation, drainage, disease-vector control and other elements of healthier living environments for poorer groups are likely to contribute significantly to lowering population growth rates.

Most citizens in Africa, Asia and Latin America find it difficult to share the environmental concerns of the high-income world. Questions of survival 20 or more years into the future have little relevance to those concerned with survival today. Attempts by the governments of high-income nations (or the UN system) to obtain agreement on controls of greenhouse gas emissions should have as a pre-condition that support be available for low- and middle-income societies to develop their capacity to tackle the environmental problems which daily affect the health and livelihoods of poorer groups, and this includes the economic prosperity and stability on which effective governance may depend. The rich world should not hope to promote global agreements on important long-term perspectives for maintaining the integrity of global systems when such a high proportion of the citizens within this global system are suffering from such enormous short-term environmental health problems and when so many governments face seemingly insurmountable economic problems.

There is a danger that both governments and environmental groups in low- and middle-income countries will dismiss the global concerns promoted by high-income nations for two reasons. The first is the obvious question of who will pay; the measures needed to limit greenhouse gas emissions will be expensive to implement, especially for countries that are industrializing rapidly, and have cheap coal. The second is that the high-income countries have shown little interest in helping low- and middle-income nations to resolve the environmental problems that most directly affect their citizens; indeed, certain multinational corporations with their headquarters in Europe, North America or Japan are seen as major contributors to their environmental problems.

Perhaps global concerns such as atmospheric warming provide low- and middle-income nations with a power in global negotiations that they have never enjoyed, except for OPEC's relatively short-lived power with regard to oil prices. Of course, high-income nations will generally seek ways to maximize the benefits and minimize the costs for themselves of any global agreement to reduce greenhouse gas emissions. They will seek measures that impose little or no constraints on production and consumption within their own countries. At present, they are not prepared to allow the cumulative contribution of their citizens and businesses to current greenhouse gas concentrations to be counted in allocating responsibilities for controlling future emissions. They are also seeking 'flexible' solutions that are based on buying emission quotas from lower-income nations, but this allows them to avoid taking the actions needed to reduce their own emissions and inhibits the needed delinking between high standards of living and high greenhouse gas emissions (Agarwal and others 1999c). But it still remains an interesting prospect, whether low- and middle-income nations could once again raise demands for a less unequal world market and for more aid (and new channels for it) to address their most pressing environmental problems in return for joint agreement to reduce the threats of global warming.

A joint programme to address environmental problems must have the long-term goal of building the capacity within each society to identify, analyse and act on their own environmental (and other) problems. Building such a capacity in turn demands action on such international issues as the unrealistic debt repayment levels that most low- and many middle-income nations face. Stagnant economies and heavy debt burdens do not provide an appropriate economic base from which to develop good governance. More prosperous, stable economies in Africa, Asia and Latin America with their citizens no longer suffering constantly from environment-related (and usually easily preventable) diseases, disablement and premature deaths should be preconditions for global agreements. These also provide a more realistic basis from which to advance other important development goals, not least among these being stronger democracies and more effective, accountable local governments. And more effective and accountable local authorities are also needed to delink development from increasing greenhouse gas emissions.

One particular concern of this book has been the impact of urban environmental problems on the health and well-being of low-income groups. This too is an aspect given inadequate attention in high-income nations. Researchers there tend to focus too much on the presence of some pollutant or pathogen and too little on how and why they are there and on whom they impact most severely. In considering environmental problems, one must consider who is suffering from the problem. Even where estimates are made regarding the 'health costs of pollution', there is generally little discussion of whose health is impaired and who benefits from the lack of pollution control.

Thus, cities' environmental problems are wider in scope that those conventionally considered by environmental groups in high-income nations. The housing environments of lower-income groups in most cities and smaller urban centres in Africa, Asia and Latin America rank as among the most life-threatening and unhealthy living environments that exist. When confronted with statistics such as one child in three dying before the age of five, as is the case in some of the worst served illegal settlements, the seriousness of the problem becomes apparent. The need for more documentation, monitoring and pressure for action is acute and should be encouraged by the fact that an enormous reduction in these problems is relatively easy to achieve, even with limited investments.

The effectiveness of environmental and citizens' groups can be enhanced with support from high-income nations. Environmental groups there have considerable experience in organizing well-targeted lobbying and publicity campaigns. Working together on the most immediate and serious environmental problems, including those in cities, would lay an appropriate foundation for joint action on global concerns. Only through joint actions to tackle the environmental problems that impact most on poorer citizens are they able to share wealthier citizens' longer-term environmental concerns. Only through a redistribution of decision-making powers and resources in their favour, both within and between nations, will they be able to act effectively on both.

References

Abaleron, Carlos Alberto (1995), 'Marginal urban space and unsatisfied basic needs: the case of San Carlos de Bariloche, Argentina', *Environment and Urbanization*, Vol 7, No 1, April.

Abantanga, F A and C N Mock (1998), 'Childhood injuries in an urban area of Ghana: a hospital-based study of 677 cases', *Pediatric Surg International*, Vol 13, No 7, pages 515–518.

Abelson, Peter (1996), 'Evaluation of slum improvements: case study in Visakhapatnam, India', *Third World Planning Review*, Vol 13, No 2, pages 97–108.

Abers, Rebecca (1998), 'Learning democratic practice: distributing government resources through popular participation in Pôrto Alegre, Brazil', in Mike Douglass and John Friedmann (editors), *Cities for Citizens*, John Wiley & Sons, West Sussex, pages 39–65.

Achar, K T V and others (forthcoming), 'Organization and management of water needs in slums – case studies', in Shenk, H (editor), *Living in Bangalore's Slums*, quoted in Benjamin 2000.

Acho-Chi (1998), 'Human interference and environmental instability: addressing the environmental consequences of rapid urban growth in Bamenda, Cameroon', *Environment and Urbanization*, Vol 10, No 2, pages 161–174.

Adams, W M (1990), *Green Development: Environment and Sustainability in the Third World*, Routledge, London and New York.

Adedoyin, M and S Watts (1989), 'Child health and child care in Okele: an indigenous area of the city of Ilorin, Nigeria', *Social Science and Medicine*, Vol 29, No 12, pages 1333–1341.

African Medical Relief Fund (AMREF) and Office of the Vice-President/Ministry of Planning and National Development (1997), *The Second Participatory Assessment Study – Kenya, Vol 1*, Nairobi.

Afsar, Rita (1999), 'Rural–urban dichotomy and convergence: emerging realities in Bangladesh', *Environment and Urbanization*, Vol 11, No 1, pages 235–246.

Agarwal, Anil (1983), 'The poverty of nature: environment, development, science and technology', *IDRC Report No 12*, Ottawa, Canada, pages 4–6.

Agarwal, Anil and Sunita Narain (1991), *Global Warming in an Unequal World – a Case of Environmental Colonialism*, Centre for Science and Environment, Delhi.

Agarwal, Anil and Sunita Narain (1992) 'Towards green villages: a strategy for environmentally sound and participatory rural development in India', *Environment and Urbanization*, Vol 4, No 1, April, pages 53–64.

Agarwal, Anil and Sunita Narain (1997), *Dying Wisdom: Rise, Fall and Potential of India's Traditional Water-harvesting Systems*, Centre for Science and Environment, New Delhi.

Agarwal, Anil, Sunita Narain and Srabani Sen (editors) (1999a), *State of India's Environment: The Citizens' Fifth Report*, Centre for Science and Environment, New Delhi.

Agarwal, Anil, Sunita Narain and Srabani Sen (editors) (1999b), *State of India's Environmnent: The Citizens' Fifth Report, Part II: Statistical Databases*, Centre for Science and Environment, New Delhi.

Agarwal, Anil, Sunita Narain and Anju Sharma (editors) (1999c), *Green Politics: Global Environmental Negotiations 1,* Centre for Science and Environment, New Delhi.

Agyemang, O and others (1997), *An Environmental Profile of the Greater Lusaka Area: Managing the Sustainable Growth and Development of Lusaka*, Lusaka City Council, Lusaka.

Aina, Tade Akin (1989), *Health, Habitat and Underdevelopment – with Special Reference to a Low-Income Settlement in Metropolitan Lagos*, IIED Technical Report, London.

Aksoy, Muzaffer, Sakir Erdem and Guncag Dincol (1976), 'Types of leukaemia in a chronic benzene poisoning: a study of thirty-four patients', *Acta haematologica*, Vol 55, pages 65–72.

Alder, Graham (1995), 'Tackling poverty in Nairobi's informal settlements: developing an institutional strategy', *Environment and Urbanization*, Vol 7, No 2, October, pages 85–107.

Ali, Mansoor (1997), *Integration of the Official and Private Informal Practices in Solid Waste Management*, unpublished thesis.

Alimuddin, Salim, Arif Hasan and Asiya Sadiq (2000), *The Work of the Anjuman Samaji Behbood and the Larger Faisalabad Context*, IIED Working Paper, London.

Altaf, Mir Anjum and Jeffrey A Hughes (1994), 'Measuring the demand for improved water and sanitation services: results form a contingent valuation study in Ouagadougou, Burkina Faso, *Urban Studies*, Vol 31, No 10, pages 1763–1776.

Amis, Philip (1992), *Urban Management in Uganda: Survival Under Stress*, The Institutional Framework of Urban Government: Case Study No 5, Development Administration Group, INLOGOV, University of Birmingham, Birmingham.

Amis, Philip and Sashi Kumar (2000), 'Urban economic growth, infrastructure and poverty in India: lessons from Visakhapatnam', *Environment and Urbanization*, Vol 12, No 1, pages 185–197.

AMIS 1998, quoted in Smith and Akbar 1999.

Amuzu, A T and Josef Leitmann (1994), 'Accra urban environmental profile', *Cities*, Vol 11, No 1, pages 5–9.

Anand, P B (1999), 'Waste management in Madras Revisited', *Environment and Urbanization*, Vol 11, No 2, pages 161–176.

Anandalingam, G and Mark Westfall, 'Hazardous waste generation and disposal: options for developing countries', *Natural Resources*, Vol 11, No 1, February 1987, pages 37–47.

ANAWIM (1992), published by the Share and Care Apostolate for Poor Settlers, Vol IV, No 4.

Anderson, Ian (1987), 'Dangerous technology dumped on Third World', report of a paper by Nabiel Makarim presented at a conference in Melbourne, Australia, on the trade in hazardous machinery or technologies, *New Scientist*, 7 March, 1992.

Anderson, Ian, 'Isotopes from machine imperil Brazilians', *New Scientist*, 15 October 1987, page 19.

Anzorena, Jorge, Joel Bolnick, Somsook Boonyabancha, Yves Cabannes, Ana Hardoy, Arif Hasan, Caren Levy, Diana Mitlin, and others (1998), 'Reducing urban poverty: some lessons from experience', *Environment and Urbanization*, Vol 10, No 1, pages 167–186.

Arar, Nedal Hamdi (1998), Cultural responses to water shortage among Palestinians in Jordan: the water crisis and its impact on child health, *Human Organization*, Vol 57, No 3 (autumn) pages 284–91.

Arévalo T, Pedro (1997), 'May hope be realized: Huaycan self-managing urban community in Lima', *Environment and Urbanization*, Vol 9, No 1, April, pages 59–79.

Arrossi, Silvina (1996), 'Inequality and health in Metropolitan Buenos Aires', *Environment and Urbanization*, Vol 8, No 2, October, pages 43–70.

Arrossi, Silvina, Felix Bombarolo, Jorge E Hardoy, Diana Mitlin, Luis Perez Coso and David Satterthwaite (1994), *Funding Community Initiatives*, Earthscan Publications, London.

Arroyo Moreno, Jorge, Francisco Rivas Ríos and Inge Lardinois (1999), *Solid Waste Management in Latin America: The Role of Micro-and Small Enterprises and Cooperatives*, IPES, ACEPESA and WASTE.

Asian Coalition for Housing Rights (1989), 'Evictions in Seoul, South Korea', *Environment and Urbanization*, Vol 1, No 1, April, pages 89–94.

Asian Coalition for Housing Rights (1999), *Face to Face*, Newsletter of the Asian Coalition for Housing Rights, Bangkok.

Asian Development Bank (1997), Second Water Utilities Data Book, Asian and Pacific Region, edited by Arthur C McIntosh and Cesar E Y[n]iguez, ADB, Manila.

AtKisson, Alan (1996), 'Developing indicators of sustainable community: lessons from Sustainable Seattle', *Environmental Impact Assessment Review*, Vol 16, Nos 4–6, July–November, pages 337–350.

Azandossessi, A (2000), 'The struggle for water in urban poor areas of Nouakchott, Mauritania', *WATERfront*, Issue 13, January, UNICEF, New York.

Bachmann, Gunter and Max Hammerer (1984), '80 per cent of losses come from 20 per cent of leaks', *World Water*, October.

Bai, Xuemei and Hidefumi Imura (2000), *Towards Sustainable Urban Water Resource Management: A Case Study in Tianjin, China*, Institute for Global Environmental Strategies, Tokyo.

Bairoch, Paul (1988), *Cities and Economic Development: From the Dawn of History to the Present*, Mansell, London.

Bangladesh Bureau of Statistics (1996), *Progotir Pathey Achieving the Mid Decade Goals for Children in Bangladesh*, Ministry of Planning, Government of the People's Republic of Bangladesh (with assistance from UNICEF), January.

Banuri, Tariq (1997), 'If you torture the data long enough: the case of the Environmental Kuznets Curve', draft, December.

Banuri, Tariq (1999), 'Sustainable development and climate change', Policy Matters, IUCN Commission on Environmental, Economic and Social Policy, pages 1, 4–7.

Barbosa, Ronnie, Yves Cabannes and Lucia Moraes (1997), 'Tenant today, posseiro tomorrow', *Environment and Urbanization*, Vol 9, No 2, October, pages 17–41.

Bariloche Foundation (1976), *Catastrophe or New Society: The Bariloche Model*, International Development Research Centre, Ottawa.

Barraza, Ernesto (1987), 'Effectos del terremoto en la infraestructura de vivienda', in 'El terremoto del 10 de octubre de 1986', a special issue of *La Universidad*, Nino CXII, No 5, San Salvador, January–March.

Barten, Françoise, Suzanne Fustukian and Sylvia de Haan (1998), 'The occupational health needs of workers: the need for a new international approach', in Christopher Williams (editor), *Environmental Victims*, Earthscan Publications, London, pages 142–156.

Bartlett, Sheridan (2000), 'The problem of child accidents and injuries in the South: a brief review of the literature', mimeo, IIED.

Bartlett, Sheridan, Roger Hart, David Satterthwaite, Ximena de la Barra and Alfredo Missair (1999), *Cities for Children: Children's Rights, Poverty and Urban Management*, Earthscan, London.

Bartone, Carl R (1990), 'Sustainable responses to growing urban environmental crises', Urban Development Division, the World Bank, mimeo.

Bartone, Carl, Janis Bernstein, Josef Leitmann and Jochen Eigen (1994) *Towards Environmental Strategies for Cities: Policy Considerations for Urban Environmental Management in Developing Countries*, UNDP, UNCHS and World Bank Urban Management Program No 18, World Bank, Washington, DC.

Baumann, Ted, Joel Bolnick and Diana Mitlin (2001), *The Age of Cities and Organizations of the Urban Poor: The Work of the South African Homeless People's Federation and the People's Dialogue on Land and Shelter*, IIED Working Paper on Poverty Reduction in Urban Areas, IIED, London.

Beall, Jo and Caren Levy (1994), *Moving Towards the Gendered City*, overview paper prepared for the Preparatory Committee for Habitat II, Geneva, 11–22 April.

Beall, Jo, Owen Crankshaw and Susan Parnell (2000a), *Urban Governance, Partnership and Poverty: Johannesburg*, Urban Governance, Partnership and Poverty Working Paper 12, International Development Department, University of Birmingham, Birmingham.

Beall, Jo, Owen Crankshaw and Susan Parnell (2000b), 'Local government, poverty reduction and inequality in Johannesburg', *Environment and Urbanization*, Vol 12, No 1, pages 107–122.

Beg, M Arshad, Ali S Naeem Mahmood, Sitwat Naeem and A H K Yousufzai (1984), 'Land based pollution and the marine environment of the Karachi coast', *Pakistan Journal of Science, Industry and Resources*, Vol 27, No 4, August, pages 199–205.

Benjamin, Solomon (2000), 'Governance, economic settings and poverty in Bangalore', *Environment and Urbanization*, Vol 12, No 1, pages 35–56.

Benjamin, Solomon and R Bhuvaneshari (2000), *Urban Governance, Partnership and Poverty: Bangalore*, Urban Governance, Partnership and Poverty Working Paper 15, International Development Department, University of Birmingham, Birmingham.

Bennett, E L and C J Reynolds (1993), 'The value of a mangrove area in Sarawak', *Biodiversity and Conservation*, Vol 2, pages 359–375.

Bentinck, Johan (2000), *Unruly Urbanization on Delhi's Fringe: Changing Patterns of Land Use and Livelihood*, Netherlands Geographical Studies 270, Utrecht/Groningen.

Bertaud, A and M Young (1990), 'Geographical pattern of environmental health in Tianjin, China', *Research/Sector Paper*, ASTIN, World Bank, Washington, DC.

Bhatt, Chandi Prasad (1990), 'The Chipko Andolan: forest conservation based on people's power', *Environment and Urbanization* Vol 2, No 1, April pages 7–18.

Bibars, Imam (1998), 'Street children in Egypt: from the home to the street to inappropriate corrective institutions', *Environment and Urbanization*, Vol 10, No 1, pages 201–216.

Birley, M H and K Lock (1998), 'Health and peri-urban natural resource production', *Environment and Urbanization*, Vol 10, No 1, pages 89–106.

Blue, Ilona (1996), 'Urban inequalities in mental health: the case of São Paulo, Brazil', *Environment and Urbanization*, Vol 8, No 2, October.

Bogrebon Allan, J (1997), 'Household demand for improved sanitation', in John Pickford and others (editors), *Water and Sanitation for All Partnership and Innovations*, Proceedings of the 23rd WEDC Conference, Durban, South Africa.

Bolin, Bert (1970), 'The carbon cycle', in *The Biosphere: A Scientific American Book*, W H Freeman and Company, San Francisco, which reproduced this paper from the September 1970 issue of *Scientific American*.

Bolnick, Joel (1993), 'The People's Dialogue on land and shelter: community driven networking in South Africa's informal settlements', *Environment and Urbanization*, Vol 5, No 1, October, pages 91–110.

Bolnick, Joel (1996), 'uTshani Buyakhuluma (The grass speaks); People's Dialogue and the South African Homeless People's Federation, 1993–1996', *Environment and Urbanization*, Vol 8, No 2, October, pages 153–170.

Bolnick, Joel and Sheela Patel (1994), 'Regaining Knowledge: an Appeal to Abandon Illusions', *RRA Notes*, No 21, pages 22–27.

Boonyabancha, Somsook (1996), *The Urban Community Development Office*, IIED Paper Series on Poverty Reduction in Urban Areas, IIED, London.

Boon, Ronald, Nancy Alexaki Herrera and Ernesto Becerra (2001), 'The role of air quality monitoring in strengthening the environmental management process of Ilo', *Environment and Urbanization*, Vol 13, No 1

Boonyabancha, Somsook (1999), 'The Urban Community Environmental Activities Project, Thailand', *Environment and Urbanization*, Vol 11, No 1, April, pages 101–115.

Bradley, David, Carolyn Stephens, Sandy Cairncross and Trudy Harpham, *A Review of Environmental Health Impacts in Developing Country Cities*, Urban Management Program Discussion Paper No 6, The World Bank, UNDP and UNCHS (Habitat), Washington, DC, 1991.

Brandon, Carter and Kirsten Homman (1995), *The Cost of Inaction: Valuing the Economy-wide Cost of Environmental Degradation in India*, World Bank, Washington, DC.

Brandt Commission (1980), *North-South: A Programme for Survival*, MIT Press, Cambridge, Mass.

Briceno-Leon, Roberto (1990), *La Casa Enferma: Sociologia de la Enfermedad de Chagas*, Consorcio de Ediciones, Capriles C A Caracas.

Briscoe, John (1986), 'Selected primary health care revisited', in Joseph S Tulchin (editor), *Health, Habitat and Development*, Lynne Reinner, Boulder, Colorado.

Browder, John D and Brian J Godfrey (1997), *Rainforest Cities: Urbanization, Development and Globalization of the Brazilian Amazon*, Columbia University Press, New York and Chichester.

Brown, Lester (1974), *In the Human Interest*, W W Norton & Co, New York.

Brugmann, Jeb (1997), 'Is there a method in our measurement? The use of indicators in local sustainable development planning', *Local Environment*, Vol 2, No 1, pages 59–72.

Bryceson, Deborah (1983), *Urbanization and Agrarian Development in Tanzania with special reference to Secondary Cities*, IIED, London.

Budd, William W (1999), 'Hazardous Waste', in David E Alexander and Rhodes W Fairbridge (editors), *Encyclopedia of Environmental Sciences*, Kluwer Academic Publishers, Dordrecht, pages 311–312.

Cairncross, Sandy (1990), 'Water supply and the urban poor', in Jorge E Hardoy and others, (editors), *The Poor Die Young: Housing and Health in Third World Cities*, Earthscan Publications, London.

Cairncross, Sandy and E A R Ouano (1990), *Surface Water Drainage in Low-income Communities*, WHO, Geneva.

Cairncross, Sandy and Richard G Feachem (1983), *Environmental Health Engineering in the Tropics: An Introductory Text*, John Wiley & Sons, Chichester.

Cairncross, Sandy and Richard G Feachem (1993), *Environmental Health Engineering in the Tropics: An Introductory Text (second edition)*, John Wiley & Sons, Chichester.

Cairncross, Sandy, Jorge E Hardoy and David Satterthwaite (1990), 'The urban context', in Jorge E Hardoy, Sandy Cairncross and David Satterthwaite (editors), *The Poor Die Young: Housing and Health in Third World Cities*, Earthscan Publications, London.

Caldeira, Teresa (1996), 'Building up walls: the new pattern of spatial segregation in São Paulo', *International Social Science Journal*, No 147, March.

Caputo, Maria G, Jorge E Hardoy and Hilda Herzer (compilers) (1985), *Desastres Naturales y Sociedad en America Latina*, CLACSO, Buenos Aires.

CARE Tanzania (1998), *Dar-es-Salaam Urban Livelihood Security Assessment*, Summary Report, June, Dar-es-Salaam.

CASE (1998), *Investigating Water and Sanitation in Informal Settlements in Gauteng*, Report prepared for Rand Water, Johannesburg.

CASSAD (1995), *Urban Poverty in Nigeria: Case Study of Zaria and Owerri*, Centre for African Settlement Studies and Development, Ibadan.

Castleman, B I (1979), 'The export of hazardous factories to developing countries', *International Journal of Health Sciences*, Vol 9, No 4, pages 569–597.

Castleman, Barry I (1987), 'Workplace health standards and multinational corporations in developing countries', in Charles S Pearson (editor), *Multinational Corporation, the Environment and the Third World*, Duke University Press, Durham, USA, pages 149–172.

Castonguay, Gilles (1992), 'Steeling themselves with knowledge', reporting on the work of Cristina Laurell, *IDRC Reports*, Vol 20, No 1, April, Ottawa, pages 10–12.

Central Statistics Office (1997), *Living Conditions Monitoring Survey Report 1996*, Lusaka.

Centre for Science and Environment (1982), *The State of India's Environment: A Citizen's Report*, New Delhi.

Centre for Science and Environment (1985), *The State of India's Environment: A Second Citizen's Report*, New Delhi.

Centre for Science and Environment (1987), *The Fight for Survival*, New Delhi.

Centre for Science and Environment (2000), *A Citizens' Guide to Fight Air Pollution*, New Delhi.

Chambers, Robert (1989), 'Editorial introduction: vulnerability, coping and policy', in 'Vulnerability: How the Poor Cope', *IDS Bulletin*, Vol 20, No 2, April, pages 1–7.

Chambers, Robert and Gordon Conway (1992), *Sustainable Rural Livelihoods: Practical Concepts for the 21st Century*, Discussion Paper 296, Institute of Development Studies, University of Brighton.

Chandler, Tertius (1987), *Four Thousand Years of Urban Growth: An Historical Census*, Edwin Mellen Press, Lampeter, UK.

Chandler, Tertius and Gerald Fox (1974), *3000 Years of Urban Growth*, Academic Press, New York and London.

Changhua, W, M Gottlieb and D Davis (1998), China's environment and health, in *World Resources 1998–1999*, World Resources Institute, Washington, DC, pages 120–122.

Chaplin, Susan E (1999), 'Social Exclusion and the Politics of Sanitation in Urban India', *Environment and Urbanization*, Vol 11, No 1, April, pages 145–158.

Chawla, Louise (1992), 'Childhood place and attachments', in I Altman and S Low (editors), *Place Attachment*, Plenum, New York.

Choguill, C L (1994), 'Implementing urban development projects: a search for criteria for success', *Third World Planning Review*, Vol 16, No 1.

Clapham, David (1996), 'Water and sanitation problems in Lima, Peru', *Water & Health*, No 19/96, North West Water Ltd, Warrington, UK.

Clarke, Robin (editor) (1999), *Global Environment Outlook 2000*, Earthscan Publications, London.

Cocoyoc Declaration (1974) Declaration adopted by the participants of the UNEP/UNCTAD symposium on 'Pattern of Resource Use, Environment and Development Strategies' republished in *World Development*, Vol 3, Nos 2 and 3, February–March 1975.

Cohen, Michael A, 'Macroeconomic adjustment and the city', *Cities*, Vol 7, No 1, February 1987, pages 49–59.

Cohen, Larry and Susan Swift (1993), 'A public health approach to the violence epidemic in the United States', *Environment and Urbanization*, Vol 5, No 2, October, pages 50–66.

Cointreau, Sandra (1982), *Environmental Management of Urban Solid Waste in Developing Countries*, Urban Development Technical Paper No 5, The World Bank, Washington, DC.

Cointreau, Sandra Johnson, Charles G Gunnerson, John M Huls and Neil N Seldman (1984), 'Recycling from Municipal Refuse: a State of the Art Review and Annotated Bibliography', World Bank Technical Paper No 30, UNDP Project Management Guide No 1, World Bank, Washington, DC.

Connolly, Priscilla (1999), 'Mexico City: our common future?', *Environment and Urbanization*, Vol 11, No 1, April, pages 53–78.

Constance, Paul (1999), 'What price for water? Why people in some of the poorest communities would rather pay more', *IDBAMÉRICA*, July–August, pages 3–5.

Consumer Information and Documentation Centre, *Consumer Currents*, International Organization of Consumers Unions March, April 1988, pages 5–6.

Conway, Gordon R (1987), 'The Properties of Agrosystems', *Agricultural Systems*, Vol 24, No 2, pages 95–117.

Conway, Gordon R and Jules N Pretty (1991), *Unwelcome Harvest*, Earthscan Publications, London.

Corbett, Jane (1989), 'Poverty and sickness: the high costs of ill-health', in 'Vulnerability: How the Poor Cope', *IDS Bulletin*, Vol 20, No 2, April, pages 58–62.

Council on Environmental Quality and the Department of State (1979), *The Global 2000 Report to the President: Entering the Twenty-First Century*, Vol 1, Washington, DC.

Crewe, Emma (1995), 'Indoor air pollution, household health and appropriate technology; women and the indoor environment in Sri Lanka', in Bonnie Bradford and Margaret A Gwynne (editors), *Down to Earth: Community Perspectives on Health, Development and the Environment*, Kumarian Press, West Hartford, pages 94–95.

Cropper, M L, N B Simon, A Alberini and A Sharma (1997), *The Health Effects of Air Pollution in Delhi, India*, PRD Working Paper 1860, World Bank, Washington, DC.

Cuenya, Beatriz, Diego Armus, Maria Di Loreto and Susana Penalva (1990), 'Land invasions and grassroots organization: the Quilmes settlement in Greater Buenos Aires, Argentina', *Environment and Urbanization*, Vol 2, No 1, April, pages 61–73.

Cuny, Frederick C (1987), 'Sheltering the urban poor: lessons and strategies of the Mexico City and San Salvador earthquakes', *Open House International*, Vol 12, No 3, pages 16–20.

Damián, Araceli (1992), 'Ciudad de México: servicios urbanos en los noventas' *Vivienda, Vol 3*, No 1, January–April, pages 29–40.

Daniere, Amrita (1996), Growth, inequality and poverty in South-east Asia: the case of Thailand, *Third World Planning Review*, Vol 18, No 4, pages 373–395.

Dasgupta, Nandini (1997), 'Problems and opportunities in providing appropriate assistance to green small recycling firms', *Environment and Urbanization*, Vol 9, No 2, October, pages 289–305.

Dasgupta, Susmita, Hua Wang and David Wheeler (1997), 'Surviving Success: Policy Reform and the Future of Industrial Pollution in China', PRDEI, World Bank, Washington, DC.

Datta, Kavita (1996), 'The organization and performance of a low-income rental market: the case of Gabarone, Botswana', *Cities*, Vol 13, No 4, pages 237–245.

De Cuentro, Stenio and Dji Malla Gadji (1990), 'The collection and management of household garbage', in Sandy Cairncross, Jorge E Hardoy and David Satterthwaite (editors), *The Poor Die Young: Housing and Health in Third World Cities*, Earthscan Publications, London, pages 169–188.

Devas, Nick (1999), *Who Runs Cities? The Relationship Between Urban Governance, Service Delivery and Poverty*, 'Urban Governance, Partnership and Poverty', Working Paper 4, International Development Department, University of Birmingham, Birmingham.

Devas, Nick and David Korboe (2000), 'City governance and poverty: the case of Kumasi', *Environment and Urbanization*, Vol 12, No 1, pages 123–135.

Development Workshop (1995), *Water Supply and Sanitation and its Urban Constraints: Beneficiary Assessment for Luanda*.

Development Workshop (1999), *Community Based Solid Waste Management in Luanda's Musseques: A Case Study*, Development Workshop, Guelph.

di Pace, Maria J, Sergio Federovisky, Jorge E Hardoy and Sergio A Mazzucchelli (1992), *Medio Ambiente Urbano en la Argentina*, CEAL, Buenos Aires.

di Pace, Maria J, Sergio Federovisky, Jorge E Hardoy, Jorge H Morello and Alfredo Stein (1992), 'Human Settlements and Sustainable Development – the Latin American Case', in Stren, Richard E and Rodney White (editors), *Sustainable Cities*, Westview Press, Boulder, Colorado, pages 205–227.

Díaz, Doris Balvín, José Luis López Follegatti and Micky Hordijk (1996), 'Innovative urban environmental management in Ilo, Peru', *Environment and Urbanization*, Vol 8, No 1, April, pages 21–34.

Díaz, Andrés Cabanas, Emma Grant, Paula Irene del Cid Vargas and Verónica Sajbin Velásquez (2000), 'El Mezquital – a community's struggle for development in Guatemala City', *Environment and Urbanization*, Vol 12, No 1, pages 87–106.

Dizon, A M and S Quijano (1997), *Impact of Eviction on Children*, Urban Poor Associates/Asian Coalition for Housing Rights/UN ESCAP

Dockemdorff, Eduardo, Alfredo Rodríguez and Lucy Winchester (2000), 'Santiago de Chile: metropolization, globalization and inequity', *Environment and Urbanization*, Vol 12, No 1, pages 171–183.

Douglas, Ian (1983), *The Urban Environment*, Edward Arnold, London.

Douglas, Ian (1986), 'Urban Geomorphology', in P G Fookes and P R Vaughan (editors), *A Handbook of Engineering Geomorphology*, Surrey University Press (Blackie & Son) Glasgow, pages 270–283.

Douglas, Ian (1989), 'The rain on the roof: a geography of the urban environment', in Dick Gregory and Rex Walford (editors), *Horizons in Human Geography*, Barnes & Noble, New Jersey, pages 217–238.

Douglass, Mike (1987), 'The future of cities on the Pacific Rim', Discussion Paper No 3, Department of Urban and Regional Planning, University of Hawaii, July.

Douglass, Mike (1989) 'The environmental sustainability of development – coordination, incentives and political will in land-use planning for the Jakarta metropolis', *Third World Planning Review*, Vol 11, No 2, May, pages 211–238.

Douglass, Mike (1992), 'The political economy of urban poverty and environmental management in Asia: access, empowerment and community-based alternatives', *Environment and Urbanization*, Vol 4, No 2, October, pages 9–32.

Douglass, Mike (1998), 'A regional network strategy for reciprocal rural–urban linkages: an agenda for policy research with reference to Indonesia', *Third World Planning Review*, Vol 20, No 1.

Down to Earth (2000a), 'For clean air', 15 September, pages 14–15.

Down to Earth (2000b), 'The curse of poor sanitation', 15 September, pages 14–15.

Duhl, Leonard J (1990), *The Social Entrepreneurship of Change*, Pace University Press, New York, 159 pages.

Dutta, Shyam S (2000), 'Partnerships in urban development: a review of Ahmedabad's experience', *Environment and Urbanization*, Vol 12, No 1, pages 13–26.

Dutta, Shyam and Richard Batley (2000), *Urban Governance, Partnership and Poverty: Ahmedabad*, Working Paper 16, International Development Department, University of Birmingham, Birmingham.

Ecologist, The (1992), *Whose Common Future: Reclaiming the Commons*, Earthscan Publications, London.

Edet, E E (1996), 'Agent and nature of childhood injury and initial care provided at the community level in Ibadan, Nigeria', *Central African Journal of Medicine*, Vol 42, No 12, pages 347–349.

Edgerton, Lynne (1990), 'Warmer temperatures, unhealthier air and sicker children', in James McCulloch (editor), *Cities and Global Climate Change*, Climate Institute, Washington, DC, pages 145–148.

Ekblad, Solvig and others (1991), *Stressors, Chinese City Dwellings and Quality of Life*, D12, Swedish Council for Building Research, Stockholm.

El-Hinnawi, Essam (1981), 'Three environmental issues', *Mazingira*, Vol 5, No 4, pages 26–35.

El Raey, M, S Nasr and O Frihy (1990), 'National assessment of the impact of greenhouse induced sea level rises on the northern coastal regions of Egypt', in S P Leatherman (editor), *National Assessments of Sea-level Rise Vulnerability*, Centre for Global Change, University of Maryland, Maryland.

El Sammani, Mohamed O, Mohamed El Hadi Abu Sin, M Talha, B M El Hassan and Ian Haywood (1989), 'Management problems of Greater Khartoum', in Richard E Stren and Rodney R White (editors), *African Cities in Crisis*, Westview Press, Boulder, Colorado, pages 246–275.

El Sayed, M K (1989), 'Implications of relative sea level rise on Alexandria', in R Frassetto (editor), *Cities on Water: Proceedings of the First International Meeting of Sea level Rise on Cities and Regions*, Venice, December.

Elkington, John and Jonathan Shopley (1989), *Cleaning Up: U S Waste Management Technology and Third World Development*, WRI Papers, World Resources Institute, Washington, DC.

Ellepopa, Ramani (1999), 'A case study of urban air quality management early stages (Sri Lanka), in Gordon McGranahan and Frank Murray (editors), *Health and Air Pollution in Rapidly Developing Countries*, Stockholm Environment Institute, Stockholm, pages 159–168.

Elsom, Derek (1996), *Smog Alert: Managing Urban Air Quality*, Earthscan, London.

EMPLASA (1994), Plano Metropolitan da Grande Sao Paulo; 1993/2010, Empresa Metropolitana de Planejamento da Grande Sao Paulo SA, Sao Paulo, 1994.

Escobar, Jairo (1988), 'The south-east Pacific', *The Siren*, No 36, April, pages 28–29.

Esrey, Steve, Jean Gough, Dave Rapaport, Ron Sawyer, Mayling Simpson-Hebert, Jorge Vargas and Uno Winblad (editors) (1989), *Ecological Sanitation*, Department for Natural Resources and the Environment, Sida (Swedish International Development Cooperation Agency), Stockholm.

Esrey, S A and R G Feachem (1989), *Interventions for the Control of Diarrhoeal Disease: Promotion of Food Hygiene*, WHO/CDD/89 30, World Health Organization, Geneva.

Etemadi, Felisa U (2000), 'Civil society participation in city governance in Cebu City', *Environment and Urbanization*, Vol 12 No 1, pages 57–72.

Etemadi, Felisa (2000), *Urban Governance, Partnership and Poverty: Cebu*, Urban Governance, Partnership and Poverty, Working Paper 13, International Development Department, University of Birmingham, Birmingham.

Fanou, Blandine with Ursula Grant (2000), *Poverty Reduction and Employment Generation: The Case of AGETUR, Benin*, Working paper from the Urban Governance, Partnership and Poverty Research Project, University of Birmingham, Birmingham.

Ferguson, Bruce (1996), 'The environmental impacts and public costs of unguided informal settlement: the case of Montego Bay', *Environment and Urbanization*, Vol 8, No 2, October, pages 171–193.

Ferguson, Bruce and Crescencia Maurer (1996), 'Urban management for environmental quality in South America', *Third World Planning Review*, pages 117–154.

Fernando, Austin, Steven Russell, Anoushka Wilson and Elizabeth Vidler (2000), *Urban Governance, Partnership and Poverty: Colombo*, Urban Governance, Partnership and Poverty, Working Paper 9, International Development Department, University of Birmingham, Birmingham.

Fiori, Jorge, Liz Riley and Ronaldo Ramirez (2000), *Urban Poverty Alleviation through Environmental Upgrading in Rio de Janeiro: Favela Bairro*, Development Planning Unit, University College London, London.

Firmo, J O A, Maria Fernanda Lima e Costa, Henrique L Guerra, and Roberto S Rocha (1996), 'Urban schistosomiasis: morbidity, socio-demographic characteristics and water contact patterns predictive of infection', *International Journal of Epidemiology*, Vol 25, No 6, pages 1292–1300.

Follegatti, Jose Luis López (1999), 'Ilo: a city in transformation', *Environment and Urbanization*, Vol 11, No 2, October, pages 181–202.

Foronda F, Maria Elena (1998), 'Chimbote's Local Agenda 21: initiatives to support its development and implementation ', *Environment and Urbanization*, Vol 10, No 2, October, pages 129–147.

Friedmann, John, *Domination and Resistance: The Politics of an Alternative Development*, UCLA/GSUAP, manuscript, 1990.

Fumo, Claudia, Arjan de Haan, Jeremy Holland and Nazneen Kanji (2000), *Social Fund: An Effective Instrument to Support Local Action for Poverty Reduction?*, Social Development Department Working Paper No 5, Department for International Development, London.

Furedy, Christine (1990a), 'Social aspects of solid-waste recovery in Asian cities', *Environmental Sanitation Reviews,* No 30, ENSIC, Asian Institute of Technology Bangkok, pages 2–52.

Furedy, Christine (1990b), 'Urban wastes and sustainable development: a comment on the Brundtland Report', in Nicolas Polunin and John H Burnett (editors), *Maintenance of the Biosphere,* Proceedings of the 3rd International Conference on Environmental Future, Edinburgh University Press, Edinburgh, 1990, pages 213–218.

Furedy, Christine (1992), 'Garbage: exploring non-conventional options in Asian cities', *Environment and Urbanization,* Vol 4, No 2, October, pages 42–61.

Furedy, Christine (1994), 'Socio-environmental initiatives in solid-waste management in Southern cities: developing international comparisons', in M Huysman, B Raman and A Rosario (editors), *Proceedings of the Workshop on Linkages in Urban Solid Waste Management,* Karnataka State Council for Science and Technology, Bangalore.

Gadgil, Madhav and Ramachandra Guha (1992), 'Interpreting Indian environmentalism', paper presented at the UNRISD Conference on the Social Dimensions of Environment and Sustainable Development, Valletta, Malta, April.

Gakenheimer, Ralph and C H J Brando, (1987), 'Infrastructure Standards', in Lloyd Rodwin (editor), *Shelter, Settlement and Development,* Allen & Unwin, Boston and London, pages 133–150.

Garza, Gustavo (1996), 'Social and economic imbalances in the metropolitan area of Monterrey', *Environment and Urbanization,* Vol 8, No 2, October, pages 31–41.

Germain, Adrienne, Sia Nowrojee and Hnin Hnin Pyne (1994), 'Setting a new agenda: sexual and reproductive health and rights', *Environment and Urbanization,* Vol 6, No 2, October, pages 133–154

Girardet, Herbert (1992), *The Gaia Atlas of Cities,* Gaia Books, London.

Ghosh, A, S S Ahmad and Shipra Maitra (1994), *Basic Services for Urban Poor: A Study of Baroda, Bhilwara, Sambalpur and Siliguri,* Urban Studies Series No 3, Institute of Social Sciences and Concept Publishing Company, New Delhi.

Gibb (Eastern Africa) Ltd (1995), *Sewerage, Drainage and Sanitation Studies Strategy Study, Appendix E, Sanitation Options and Strategies,* report for the National Water Conservation and Pipeline Corporation as part of the Second Mombasa and Coastal Water Supply Engineering and Rehabilitation Project, Nairobi.

Gilbert, Richard (1990), 'Cities and global warming', in James McCulloch (editor), *Cities and Global Climate Change,* Climate Institute, Washington, DC, pages 182–190.

Giles, Harry and Bryan Brown (1997), 'And not a drop to drink ' Water and sanitation services to the urban poor in the developing world', *Geography,* Vol 82, No 2, pages 97–109.

Goldstein, Greg (1990), 'Access to life saving services in urban areas', in Sandy Cairncross, Jorge E Hardoy and David Satterthwaite (editors), *The Poor Die Young: Housing and Health in Third World Cities,* Earthscan Publications, London, pages 213–227.

Gomes Pereira, M (1989), 'Characteristics of urban mortality from Chagas' disease in Brazil's Federal District' *Bulletin of the Pan American Health Organization,* Vol 18, No 1.

Gore, Charles (1991), *Transport and Sustainable Development,* mimeo, 1991, and *Policies and Mechanisms for Sustainable Development: The Transport Sector,* mimeo, 1991.

Greenway, D R (1987), 'Vegetation and slope instability', in M E Anderson and K S Richards (editors), *Slope Stability,* John Wiley & Sons, Chichester.

Guimaraes, J J and A Fischmann (1985), 'Inequalities in 1980 infant mortality among shanty town residents and non-shanty town residents in the municipalities of Pôrto Alegre, Rio Grande do Sul, Brazil', *Bulletin of the Pan American Health Organization,* Vol 19, No 3, pages 235–251.

Gupta, Joyeeta (1990), 'A partnership between countries and cities on the issue of climate change with special reference to the Netherlands', in James McCulloch (editor), *Cities and Global Climate Change,* Climate Institute, Washington, DC, pages 66–89.

Halter, Faith (1991), 'Towards more effective environmental regulation in developing countries', in Denizhan Erocal (editor), *Environmental Management in Developing Countries,* Development Centre, OECD, Paris, pages 223–254.

Hamilton, L S and S C Snedaker (1984) *Handbook for Mangrove Area Management,* Environment and Policy Institute, East–West Centre, Honolulu, Hawaii, USA.

Hamza, Ahmed (1989), 'An appraisal of environmental consequences of urban development in Alexandria, Egypt', *Environment and Urbanization*, Vol 1, No 1, April, pages 22–30.

Hanley, Nick, Jason F Shogren and Ben White (1997), *Environmental Economics in Theory and Practice*, MacMillan Press, Basingstoke.

Hardoy, Ana and Ricardo Schusterman (1999), 'Las privatizaciones de los servicios de agua potable y saneamiento y lost pobres urbanos' *Medio Ambiente y Urbanizacion*, No 54, December, pages 63–76.

Hardoy, Ana and Ricardo Schusterman (2000), 'New models for the privatization of water and sanitation for the urban poor', *Environment and Urbanization*, Vol 12, No 2, pages 63–75.

Hardoy, Jorge E (1975), 'Two thousand years of Latin American urbanization', in J E Hardoy (editor), *Urbanization in Latin America: Approaches and Issues*, Anchor Books, New York.

Hardoy, Jorge E and David Satterthwaite (1987), 'Housing and health in the Third World – do architects and planners have a role?', *Cities*, Vol 4, No 3, Butterworth Press, pages 221–235.

Hardoy, Jorge E and David Satterthwaite (1989), *Squatter Citizen: Life in the Urban Third World*, Earthscan Publications, London.

Harpham, T (1994), 'Urbanization and mental health in developing countries: a research role for social scientists, public health professionals and social psychiatrists', in *Social Science and Medicine*, Vol 39, No 2, pages 233–245.

Harpham, Trudy, Paul Garner and Charles Surjadi (1990), 'Planning for child health in a poor urban environment: the case of Jakarta, Indonesia', *Environment and Urbanization*, Vol 2, No 2, October, pages 77–82.

Harpham, Trudy and Ilona Blue (editors) (1995), *Urbanization and Mental Health in Developing Countries*, Avebury, Aldershot.

Harpham, Trudy and Sassy Molyneux (2000), Paper on Urban Health presented to the US National Academy of Science's Panel on Urban Population Dynamics, South Bank University, London.

Hartmann, Betsy (1998), 'Population, environment and security: a new trinity', *Environment and Urbanization*, Vol 10, No 2, pages 113–127.

Hasan, Arif (1990), 'Community organizations and non-government organizations in the urban field in Pakistan', *Environment and Urbanization*, Vol 2, No 1, April, pages 74–86.

Hasan, Arif (1997), *Working with Government: The Story of the Orangi Pilot Project's Collaboration with State Agencies for Replicating its Low Cost Sanitation Programme*, City Press, Karachi.

Hasan, Arif (1999), *Understanding Karachi: Planning and Reform for the Future*, City Press, Karachi.

Hasan, Samiul and M Adil Khan, (1999) 'Community-based environmental management in a megacity, considering Calcutta', *Cities*, Vol 16, No 2, pages 103–110.

Haughton, Graham (1998), Background paper for the Development Assistance Committee, OECD, Urban Environment Resource Book, DFID, *mimeo.*

Haughton, Graham (1999a), 'Environmental justice and the sustainable city', *Journal of Planning Education and Research*, Vol 18, No 3, pages 233–43.

Haughton, Graham (1999b), 'Information and participation within environmental management', *Environment and Urbanization*, Vol 11, No 2, pages 51–62.

Haughton, Graham and Colin Hunter (1994), *Sustainable Cities*, Regional Policy and Development series, Jessica Kingsley, London.

Heft, H (1987), 'The physical environment and the development of the child', in D Stokols and I Altman (editors), *Handbook of Environmental Psychology*, Wiley, New York.

Heller, Léo (1999), 'Who are really benefited from environmental sanitation in cities: an intra-urban analysis in Betim, Brazil', *Environment and Urbanization*, Vol 11, No 1, pages 133–144.

Henderson, M (2000), 'Sanitation and child rights in urban poor Harare', *WATERfront*, UNICEF, New York.

Hernández, Orlando, Barbara Rawlins and Reva Schwartz (1999), 'Voluntary recycling in Quito: factors associated with participation in a pilot programme', *Environment and Urbanization*, Vol 11, No 2, pages 145–159.

Hettelingh, J P, M Chadwick, H Sverdrup and D Zhao (1995), Chapter 6 in *RAINS-ASIA: An Assessment Model of Acid Deposition in Asia*, The World Bank, Washington, DC.

Hinrichsen, Don (1998), *Coastal Waters of the World: Trends, Threats, and Strategies*, Island Press, Washington, DC.

Hobson, Jane (2000), 'Sustainable sanitation: experiences in Pune with a municipal–NGO–community partnership', *Environment and Urbanization*, Vol 12, No 2, pages 53–62.

Hofmaier, V A (1991), *Efeitos de poluicao do ar sobre a funcao pulmonar: un estudo de cohorte em criancas de Cubatão*, Sao Paulo School of Public Health (doctoral thesis).

Holmberg, Johan (editor) (1992), *Policies for a Small Planet*, Earthscan Publications, London.

Honghai, Deng (1992), 'Urban agriculture as urban food supply and environmental protection subsystems in China', Paper presented to the international workshop on 'Planning for Sustainable Urban Development', University of Wales.

Hordijk, Michaela (1999), 'A dream of green and water: Community-based formulation of a Local Agenda 21 in peri-urban Lima, Peru', *Environment and Urbanization*, Vol 11, No 2, October, pages 11–29.

Houghton, Richard A (1999), 'Greenhouse effect', in David E Alexander and Rhodes W Fairbridge (editors), *Encyclopedia of Environmental Sciences*, Kluwer Academic Publishers, Dordrecht, pages 303–306.

Hughes, Bob (1990), 'Children's play – a forgotten right', *Environment and Urbanization*, Vol 2, No, 2, October 1990, pages 58–64.

Hunt, Caroline (1996), 'Child waste pickers in India: the occupation and its health risks', *Environment and Urbanization*, Vol 8, No 2, October, pages 111–118.

Huysman, Marijk (1994), 'Waste picking as a survival strategy for women in Indian cities', *Environment and Urbanization*, Vol 6, No 2, October, pages 155–174.

IIED (1996), *The Sustainable Paper Cycle*, IIED, London and WBCSD, Geneva.

IIED–AL, with CEA and GASE (1992), 'Sustainable development in Argentina', *Environment and Urbanization*, Vol 4, No 1, April, pages 37–52.

IIED, ODI, MRAG AND WCMC (1999), 'The Present Position: The Challenge in regard to protection and better management of the environment', Background paper for the Department for International Development, IIED, London.

ILO (1996), *Child Labour: Targeting the Intolerable*, International Labour Office, Geneva.

International Centre for the Prevention of Crime (ICPC), Workshop on urban violence, IXth UN Congress on Crime Prevention, Cairo, February 1995.

International Federation of Red Cross and Red Crescent Societies (1998), *World Disasters Report 1998*, Oxford University Press, Oxford.

IPCC (1990), *Potential Impacts of Climate Change: Report to IPCC from Working Group II*, World Meteorological Organization and the United Nations Environment Programme.

Islam, Nazrul, Nurul Huda, Francis B Narayan and Pradumna B Rana (editors) (1997), *Addressing the Urban Poverty Agenda in Bangladesh, Critical issues and the 1995 Survey Findings*, The University Press, Dhaka.

Izeogu, C Z, 'Urban development and the environment in Port Harcourt', *Environment and Urbanization*, Vol 1, No 1, April 1989, pages 59–68.

Jacobi, Pedro, Denise Baena Segura and Marianne Kjellén (1999), 'Governmental responses to air pollution: summary of a study of the implementation of 'Rodízio', in São Paulo', *Environment and Urbanization*, Vol 11, No 1, pages 79–88.

Jacobs, Jane, *The Death and Life of Great American Cities*, Pelican, London, 1965.

Jarzebski, L S (1991), 'Case Study of the Environmental Impact of the Non-Ferrous Metals Industry in the Upper Silesian Area', Paper prepared for the WHO Commission on Health and the Environment.

Jazairy, Idriss, Mohiuddin Alamgir and Theresa Panuccio (1992), *The State of World Rural Poverty: An Inquiry into its Causes and Consequences*, IT Publications, London.

Jimenez, Rosario D and Sister Aida Velasquez (1989), 'Metropolitan Manila: a framework for its sustained development', *Environment and Urbanization*, Vol 1, No 1, April, pages 51–58.

Jimenez Diaz, Virginia (1992),'Landslides in the squatter settlements of Caracas: towards a better understanding of causative factors', *Environment and Urbanization*, Vol 4, No 2, October, pages 80–89.

Johnstone, Nick, Libby Wood and Robert Hearne (1999), *The Regulation of Private Sector Participation in Urban Water Supply and Sanitation: Realizing Social and Economic Objectives in Developing Countries*, Discussion Paper 99–01, Environmental Economics Programme, IIED, London.

Jones, Gavin W (1983), 'Structural change and prospects for urbanization in Asian countries', Papers of the East–West Population Institute, No 88, East–West Centre, Honolulu, August.

Jones, Kathleen (1991), *The Making of Social Policy in Britain, 1830–1990*, Athlone Press, London and New Jersey.

Jopling, John and Herbert Girardet (1996), *Creating a Sustainable London*, Sustainable London Trust, London.

Kaferstein, Fritz K. (1997), 'Food safety: fourth pillar in strategy to prevent infant diarrhea', *Voices from the City*, Vol 8, page 3.

Kagan, A R and L Levi, 'Health and environment: psycho-social stimuli – a review', in L Levi (editor), *Society, Stress and Disease – Childhood and Adolescence*, Oxford University Press, 1975, pages 241–260.

Kalbermatten, John M, DeAnne S Julius and Charles C Gunnerson, *Appropriate Technology for Water Supply and Sanitation: Technical and Economic Options*, The World Bank, Washington, DC, 1980.

Kaneez Hasna, Mahbuba (1995), 'Street hydrant project in Chittagong low-income settlement', *Environment and Urbanization*, Vol 7, No 2, October, pages 207–218.

Kanji, Nazneen (1995), 'Gender, poverty and structural adjustment in Harare, Zimbabwe', *Environment and Urbanization*, Vol 7, No 1, April, pages 37–55.

Kebe, Moctar (1988), 'The West and Central African Action Plan', Interview in *The Siren* No 37, July, pages 31–34.

Kellett, Peter and A Graham Tipple (2000), 'The home as workplace: a study of income generating activities within the domestic setting', *Environment and Urbanization*, Vol 12, No 1, pages 203–213.

Kelly, Philip F (1998), 'The politics of urban-rural relationships: land conversion in the Philippines', *Environment and Urbanization*, Vol 10, No 1, pages 35–54.

Kessides, Christine (1997), *World Bank Experience with the Provision of Infrastructure Services for the Urban Poor: Preliminary Identification and Review of Best Practices*, Transport, Water and Urban Development Department, TWU-OR8, World Bank.

Khan, Akhter Hameed (1991), *Orangi Pilot Project Programs*, Orangi Pilot Project, Karachi.

Kibel, M A and L A Wagstaff (editors) (1995), *Child Health for All: a Manual for Southern Africa*, Oxford University Press, Cape Town and New York.

King, Bob (1988), 'Taiwan's industrial pollution bills mount', *Financial Times*, 8 November.

Kirango, Jasper and Maria S Muller (1997), 'MAPET: a service for the collection of latrine sludge from households in Dar es Salaam, Tanzania', in Maria S Muller (editor), *The Collection of Household Excreta: The Operation of Services in Urban Low-income Neighbourhoods*, WASTE and ENSIC, Gouda, pages 19–27.

Kishk, M A (1986), 'Land degradation in the Nile Valley', *Ambio*, Vol XV, No 4, pages 226–230.

Kolsky, Peter J (1992), 'Water, health and cities: concepts and examples' Paper presented at the international workshop on Planning for Sustainable Urban Development, University of Wales, July.

Kone, Sidiki (1988), 'Stop Africa from becoming the dumping ground of the world', *The Siren*, No 37, July, UNEP, Nairobi, pages 2–3.

Korboe, David, Kofi Diaw and Nick Devas (2000), *Urban Governance, Partnership and Poverty: Kumasi*, Urban Governance, Partnership and Poverty, Working Paper 10, International Development Department, University of Birmingham.

Kreimer, Alcira, Thereza Lobo, Braz Menezes, Mohan Munasinghe and Ronald Parker (editors), (1993), *Towards a Sustainable Urban Environment: The Rio de Janeiro Study*, World Bank Discussion Papers No 195, World Bank, Washington, DC.

Krupa, S V and W J Manning (1988), 'Atmospheric ozone: formation and effects on vegetation' *Environmental Pollution*, Vol 50, pages 101–137.

Kulaba, Saitiel (1989), 'Local government and the management of urban services in Tanzania', in Stren, Richard E and Rodney R White (editors), *African Cities in Crisis*, Westview Press, Boulder, Colorado, pages 203–245.

Kumar, Sashi with Philip Amis (1999), *Urban Governance, Partnership and Poverty in Visakapatnam*, Urban Governance, Partnership and Poverty Working Paper, International Development Department, University of Birmingham, Birmingham.

Lafferty, William M and Katarina Eckerberg (editors) (1998), *From the Earth Summit to Local Agenda 21: Working Towards Sustainable Development*, Earthscan, London.

Lamba, Davinder (1994), 'The forgotten half: environmental health in Nairobi's poverty areas', *Environment and Urbanization*, Vol 6, No 1, April, pages 164–173.

Landin, Bo (1987), A film on air pollution produced by the Television Trust for the Environment as part of the series 'Battle for the Planet'

Landwehr D, S M Keita, J M Ponnighaus and C Tounkara (1998), 'Epidemiological aspects of scabies in Mali, Malawi, and Cambodia', *International Journal of Dermatology*, Vol 37, No 8, pages 588–90.

Leach, Gerald and others (1979), *A Low Energy Strategy for the United Kingdom*, Science Reviews Ltd, London.

Leach, Gerald and Robin Mearns (1989), *Beyond the Woodfuel Crisis – People, Land and Trees in Africa*, Earthscan Publications, London.

Leach, Melissa and Robin Mearns (1991), *Poverty and Environment in Developing Countries: An Overview Study*, Institute for Development Studies, University of Sussex.

Lee, James A (1985), *The Environment, Public Health and Human Ecology*, The World Bank, Johns Hopkins University Press, Baltimore and London.

Lee, Kyu Sik (1988), 'Infrastructure Investment and Productivity: the case of Nigerian Manufacturing – a framework for policy study', Discussion paper, Water Supply and Urban Development Division, the World Bank.

Lee-Smith, Diana, Mutsembi Manundu, Davinder Lamba and P Kuria Gathuru (1987), *Urban Food Production and the Cooking Fuel Situation in Urban Kenya*, Mazingira Institute, Kenya.

Lee-Smith, Diana and Catalina Hinchey Trujillo (1992), 'The struggle to legitimize subsistence: Women and sustainable development', *Environment and Urbanization*, Vol 4, No 1, April, pages 77–84.

Lee-Wright, Peter (1990), *Child Slaves*, Earthscan Publications, London.

Lemos, Maria Carmen de Mello (1998), 'The politics of pollution control in Brazil: state actors and social movements cleaning up Cubatão', *World Development*, Vol 26, No 1, pages 75–87.

Leonard, H Jeffrey (1984), 'Confronting Industrial Pollution in Rapidly Expanding Industrializing Countries – Myths, Pitfalls and Opportunities', Conservation Foundation, Washington, DC.

Levett, Roger (1998), 'Footprinting: a great step forward, but treat carefully – a response to Mathis Wackernagel', *Local Environment*, Vol 3, No 1, pages 67–74.

Linn, Johannes F (1982), 'The costs of urbanization in developing countries', *Economic Development and Cultural Change*, Vol 30, No 3, pages 625–648.

Lippmann, M (1999), 'Air pollution and health-studies in North America and Europe', in Gordon McGranahan and Frank Murray (editors), *Health and Air Pollution in Rapidly Developing Countries*, Stockholm Environment Institute, Stockholm, pages 29–41.

Lopez, Jose Manuel (1988), 'The Caribbean and Gulf of Mexico', *The Siren*, No 36, April, pages 30–31.

Losada, H H, Martínez, J Vieyra, R Pealing, R Zavala and J Cortés (1998), 'Urban agriculture in the metropolitan zone of Mexico City: changes over time in urban, suburban and periurban areas', *Environment and Urbanization*, Vol 10, No 2, pages 37–54.

Lowe, Marcia D (1991), *Shaping Cities: the Environmental and Human Dimensions*, Worldwatch Paper 105, Washington, DC, October.

Lungo Ucles, Mario (1987), 'El terremoto de octubre de 1986 y la situacion habitacional de los sectores populares', in 'El terremoto del 10 de octubre de 1986', a special issue of *La Universidad*, Nino CXII, No 5, San Salvador, January–March.

Lungo Ucles, Mario (1988), 'San Salvador: el habitat despues del terremoto', *Medio Ambiente y Urbanizacion*, No 24, September, pages 46–52.

Lyonnaise des Eaux (1998), 'Alternative Solutions for Water Supply and Sanitation in Areas with Limited Financial Resources', Suez Lyonnaise des Eaux, Nanterre.

Mahfouz A A, H el-Morshedy, A Farghaly and S Khalil A (1997), 'Ecological determinants of intestinal parasitic infections among pre-schoolchildren in an urban squatter settlement of Egypt, *Journal of Tropical Paediatrics*, Vol 43, No 6, pages 341–344.

Makil, Perla Q (1982), 'Slums and squatter settlements in the Philippines', *Concerned Citizens of the Urban Poor*, Series No 3, Manila.

Manciaux, M and C J Romer (1986), 'Accidents in children, adolescents and young adults: a major public health problem', *World Health Statistical Quarterly*, Vol 39, No 3, pages 227–231.

Mangin, William (1967), 'Latin American squatter settlements; a problem and a solution', *Latin American Research Review*, Vol, 2, No 3, Summer, pages 65–98.

Mani, Muthukumara and David Wheeler (1997), *In Search of Pollution Havens? Dirty Industry in the World Economy, 1960–1995*, World Bank Working Paper; PRDEI, April, World Bank, Washington, DC.

Manzanal, Mabel and Cesar Vapnarsky (1986), 'The Comahue Region, Argentina', in Hardoy, Jorge E and Satterthwaite, David (editors), *Small and Intermediate Urban Centres; Their Role in National and Regional Development in the Third World*, Hodder & Stoughton, London, and Westview Press, Boudler, Colorado.

Mara, Duncan and Sandy Cairncross (1990), 'Guidelines for the Safe Use of Wastewater and Excreta in Agriculture and Aquaculture', World Health Organization, Geneva.

Marvin, Simon and Nina Laurie (1999), 'An emerging logic of urban water management, Cochabamba, Bolivia', *Urban Studies*, Vol 36, No 2, pages 341–257.

Matte, T D, J P Figueroa, S Ostrowski, G Burr and others (1989), 'Lead poisoning among household members exposed to lead-acid battery repair shops in Kingston, Jamaica (West Indies)', *International Journal of Epidemiology*, Vol 18, pages 874–881.

Mayers, J and S Bass (1999), *Policy that works for forests and people*, Series Overview, IIED, London.

Mbuyi, Kankonde (1989), 'Kinshasa: problems of land management, infrastructure and food supply', in Richard E Stren and Rodney R White (editors), *African Cities in Crisis*, Westview Press, Boulder, Colorado, pages 148–175.

McCarney, Patricia L (editor) (1996), *Cities and Governance: New Directions in Latin America, Asia and Africa*, Centre for Urban and Community Studies, University of Toronto, Toronto.

McCormick, John (1997), *Acid Earth: The Politics of Acid Pollution*, Earthscan, London.

McGee, T G (1987), 'Urbanization or Kotadesasi: the emergence of new regions of economic interaction in Asia', working paper, East–West Center, Honolulu, June.

McGranahan, Gordon (1991), *Environmental Problems and the Urban Household in Third World Countries*, The Stockholm Environment Institute, Stockholm.

McGranahan, Gordon and Jacob Songsore (1994), 'Wealth, health and the urban household; weighing environmental burdens in Accra, Jakarta and Sao Paulo', *Environment*, Vol 36, No 6, July/August, pages 4–11 and 40–45.

McGranahan, Gordon, Jacob Songsore and Marianne Kjellén (1996), 'Sustainability, poverty and urban environmental transitions', in Cedric Pugh (editor), *Sustainability, the Environment and Urbanization*, Earthscan Publications, London, pages 103–134.

McGranahan, Gordon and Åsa Gerger (1999), 'Participation and environmental assessment in Northern and Southern cities, with examples from Stockholm and Jakarta', *International Journal of Environment and Pollution*, Vol 11, No 3, pages 373–394.

McGranahan, Gordon and David Satterthwaite (2000), 'Environmental Health or Ecological Sustainability? Reconciling the Brown and Green Agendas in Urban Development', in Cedric Pugh (editor), *Sustainable Cities in Developing Countries*, Earthscan, London.

McGranahan, G, P Jacobi, J Songsore, C Surjadi and M Kjellén (2001), *Citizens at Risk: From Urban Sanitation to Sustainable Cities*, Earthscan Publications, London.

McMichael, A J, A Haines, R Sloof and S Kovats (1996), *Climate Change and Human Health*, WHO, Geneva.

Meadows, Donella (1998), *Indicators and Information Systems for Sustainable Development, A Report to the Balaton Group*, Sustainability Institute, Hartland.

Meadows, Donella H, Dennis L Meadows, Jorgen Randers and William Behrens III (1974), *The Limits to Growth*, Pan Books Ltd, London.

Meekyaa, Ude James and Carole Rakodi (1990), 'The neglected small towns of Nigeria', *Third World Planning Review*, Vol 12, No 1, February, pages 21–40.

Mega, Voula (1996a), *Innovations for the Improvement of the Urban Environment: Austria, Finland, Sweden*, European Foundation for the Improvement of Living and Working Conditions, Office for Official Publications of the European Communities, Luxembourg.

Mega, Voula (1996b), 'Our city, our future: Towards sustainable development in European cities', *Environment and Urbanization*, Vol 8, No 1, April, pages 133–154.

Mehlwana, Mongameli Anthony (1999), 'The anatomy of a disaster: case studies of fuels-use problems in the shack areas of Greater Cape Town, *Urban Development and Health Bulletin*, Vol 2, No 3, September, pages 29–37.

Meith, N (1989), *High and Dry: Mediterranean Climate in the 21st Century*, United Nations Environment Programme, Athens.

MELISSA (1998), Managing the Environment Locally in Sub-Saharan Africa, '97 KERN Forum Proceedings, Dakar.

Menegat, Rualdo (main coordinator) (1998), *Atlas Ambiental de Pôrto Alegre*, Universidade Federal do Rio Grande do Sul, Prefeitura Municipal de Pôrto Alegre and Instituto Nacional de Pesquisas Espaciais, Pôrto Alegre.

Mesarovic, Mihajlo and Eduard Pestel (1974), *Mankind at the Turning Point*, E P Dutton, New York.

Michaels, David, Clara Barrera and Manuel Gacharna (1985), 'Economic development and occupational health in Latin America: new directions for public health in less developed countries', *American Journal of Public Health*, Vol 85, No 5, pages 536–542.

Milbert, Isabelle with Vanessa Peat (1999), *What Future for Urban Cooperation?*, Swiss Agency for Development and Cooperation.

Miranda, Liliana and Michaela Hordijk (1998), 'Let us build cities for life: the National Campaign of Local Agenda 21s in Peru', *Environment and Urbanization*, Vol 10, No 2, October, pages 69–102.

Misra, Harikesh (1990), 'Housing and health problems in three squatter settlements in Allahabad, India', in Jorge E Hardoy and others (editors), *The Poor Die Young: Housing and Health in Third World Cities*, Earthscan Publications, London.

Mitlin, Diana (1992), 'Sustainable development: a guide to the literature', *Environment and Urbanization*, Vol 4, No 1, April, pages 111–124.

Mitlin, Diana (1997), 'Building with credit: housing finance for low-income households', *Third World Planning Review*, Vol 19, No 1, February, pages 21–50.

Mitlin, Diana (1999), *Civil Society and Urban Poverty, Urban Governance, Partnership and Poverty*: Working Paper 5, International Development Department, University of Birmingham, Birmingham.

Mitlin, Diana and John Thomson (editors) (1994), *RRA Notes 21*: Special Issue on Participatory Tools and Methods in Urban Areas, IIED Sustainable Agriculture Programme, London.

Mitlin, Diana and David Satterthwaite (1994), *Cities and Sustainable Development*, Background paper for Global Forum '94, Manchester City Council, Manchester.

Mitlin, Diana and David Satterthwaite (1996), 'Sustainable development and cities', in Cedric Pugh (editor), *Sustainability, the Environment and Urbanization*, Earthscan Publications, London, pages 23–61.

Modak, Prasad (1998), *Case Studies of Cleaner Production*, Environmental Management Centre, Mumbai.

Montiel, René Pérez and Françoise Barten (1999), 'Urban governance and health development in León, Nicaragua', *Environment and Urbanization*, Vol 11, No 1, April, pages 11–26.

Morris, Saul S, Carol Levin, Margaret Armar-Klemesu, Daniel Maxwell and Marie T Ruel (1999), *Does Geographic Targeting of Nutrition Interventions Make Sense in Cities? Evidence from Abidjan and Accra*, FCND Discussion Paper No 61, IFPRI, Washington, DC.

Moser, Caroline O N (1987), 'Women, human settlements and housing: a conceptual framework for analysis and policy-making', in Caroline O N Moser and Linda Peake (editors), *Women, Housing and Human Settlements*, Tavistock Publications, London and New York, pages 12–32.

Moser, Caroline O N (1996), 'Confronting Crisis: A Summary of Household Responses to Poverty and Vulnerability in Four Poor Urban Communities, Environmentally Sustainable Development Studies and Monographs Series', No 7, The World Bank, Washington, DC.

Moser, Caroline O N (1998), 'The asset vulnerability framework: reassessing urban poverty reduction strategies', *World Development*, Vol 26, pages 1–19.

Moser, Caroline O N and Cathy McIlwaine (1999), 'Participatory urban appraisal and its application for research on violence', *Environment and Urbanization*, Vol 11, No 2, pages 203–226.

Mueller, Charles C (1995), 'Environmental problems inherent to a development style: degradation and poverty in Brazil', *Environment and Urbanization*, Vol 7, No 2, October, pages 67–84.

Muhtab, F U (1989), *Effect of Climate Change and Sea level Rise on Bangladesh*, Report prepared for the Commonwealth Expert Group on Climate Change and Sea Level Rise, Commonwealth Secretariat, London.

Muller, Maria S (1997) 'Understanding the collection of human excreta as part of urban waste management', in Maria S Muller (editor), *The Collection of Household Excreta: The Operation of Services in Urban Low-income Neighbourhoods*, WASTE and ENSIC, Gouda, pages 63–70.

Mupedziswa R and Perpetua Gumbo (1998), *Structural Adjustment and Women Informal Sector Traders in Harare, Zimbabwe*, Research Report No 106, Nordiska Afrikainstitutet, Uppsala.

Murphy, Denis (1990), *A Decent Place to Live – Urban Poor in Asia*, Asian Coalition for Housing Rights, Bangkok.

Murray, C J and A D Lopez (1996), *The Global Burden of Disease: A Comprehensive Assessment of Mortality and Disability from Diseases, Injuries, and Risk Factors in 1990 and Projected to 2020*, Harvard School of Public Health on behalf of the World Health Organization and the World Bank, Cambridge, Mass.

Mwangi, Samson W (1998), 'Partnerships in urban environmental management: an approach to solving environmental problems in Nakuru, Kenya', *Environment and Urbanization*, Vol 12, No 2, pages 77–92.

Myers, Robert, *The Twelve Who Survive: Strengthening Programmes of Early Child Development in the Third World*, Routledge, London and New York, 1991.

Needleman, Herbert L, Alan Schell, David Bellinger, Alan Leviton and Elizabeth N Allred, 'The long-term effects of exposure to low doses of lead in childhood: an eleven-year follow-up report', *The New England Journal of Medicine*, Vol 322 No 2, January 1991, pages 83–88.

Newman, Peter (1996), 'Reducing automobile dependence', *Environment and Urbanization*, Vol 8, No 1, April, pages 67–92.

Newman, Peter W G and Jeffrey R Kenworthy (1989), *Cities and Automobile Dependence: An International Sourcebook*, Gower Technical, Aldershot.

Newman, Oscar, *Defensible Space: Crime Prevention through Urban Design*, MacMillan, New York, 1972.

Ngom, Thiecouta (1989), 'Appropriate standards for infrastructure in Dakar', in Richard E. Stren and Rodney R White (editors), *African Cities in Crisis*, Westview Press, Boulder, Colorado, pages 176–202.

Nishioka, Shuzo, Yuichi Noriguchi and Sombo Yamamura (1990), 'Megalopolis and climate change: the case of Tokyo', in James McCulloch (editor), *Cities and Global Climate Change*, Climate Institute, Washington, DC, pages 108–133.

NIUA (1997), 'The Right to Privacy: Individual Toilets, Bathing Area', *Urban Poverty*, April–June 1997, page 11, article from Women and Sanitation: the Urban Reality Experiences of Government Programmes/NGOs/CBOs, Rena Khosla, Training Co-ordinator, NIUA National Workshop on Women, Children & Sanitation, April 10–11 1997, New Delhi.

Nunan, Fiona and David Satterthwaite (1999), *The Urban Environment*, Theme Paper 6, Urban Governance, Partnership and Poverty, University of Birmingham, Birmingham.

Nurick, Robert and Victoria Johnson (1998), 'Towards community-based indicators for monitoring quality of life and the impact of industry in South Durban', *Environment and Urbanization*, Vol 10, No 1, pages 233–250.

Odero, Wilson (1996), 'Road traffic accidents in Kenya and the effects of location', in S Atkinson, J Songsore and E Werna (editors), *Urban Health Research in Developing Countries: Implications for Policy*, CAB International, Wallingford, pages 161–174.

OECD (1989), *Economic Instruments for Environmental Protection*, Paris, OECD.

OECD (1990), *Urban Environmental Policies for the 1990s*, OECD, Paris.

OECD (1991), *The State of the Environment*, Organization for Economic Cooperation and Development, Paris.

OECD (1992), *Cities and New Technologies*, OECD, Paris.

OECF (1999), *Annual Report 1999*, The Overseas Economic Cooperation Fund, Tokyo.

Ogu, Vincent Ifeany (1998), 'The dynamics of informal housing in a traditional West African City: the Benin City example', *Third World Planning Review*, Vol 20, No 4, pages 419–439.

Ogu, Vincent Ifeanyi (2000) 'Private Sector Participation and Municipal Waste management in Benin City, Nigeria', *Environment and Urbanization*, Vol 12, No 2, pages 103–117.

Okoli E I and A B Odaibo (1999), 'Urinary schistosomiasis among schoolchildren in Ibadan, an urban community in south-western Nigeria', *Tropical Medicine & International Health*, Vol 4, No 4, pages 308–15.

O'Riordan, Timothy (1999), 'Environment and environmentalism', in David E Alexander and Rhodes W Fairbridge (editors), *Encyclopedia of Environmental Science*, Kluwer Academic Publishers, Dordrecht, pages 192–193.

Ortuzar, S, 'Santiago's metro', *Cities*, Vol 1, No 2, November 1983, pages 113–116.

Ouayoro, Eustache (1995), 'Ouagadougou low-cost sanitation and public information programme', in Ismail Serageldin, Michael A Cohen and K C Sivaramakrishnan (editors), *The Human Face of the Urban Environment*, Environmentally Sustainable Development Proceedings Series, No 6, World Bank, Washington, DC, pages 154–159.

Özerdem, Alpaslan (1999), 'Tiles, Taps and Earthquake-proofing: lessons for disaster management in Turkey', *Environment and Urbanization*, Vol 11, No 2, October, pages 177–179.

Pacheco, Margarita (1992), 'Recycling in Bogota: developing a culture for urban sustainability', *Environment and Urbanization*, Vol 4, No 2, October, pages 74–79.

PAHO (1988), 'Research on Health Profiles: Brazil 1984', *Epidemiological Bulletin of the Pan American Health Organization*, Vol 9, No 2, pages 6–13.

Panayotou, Theodore (1991), 'Economic incentives in environmental management and their relevance to developing countries', in Denizhan Erocal (editor), *Environmental Management in Developing Countries*, Development Centre, OECD, Paris, pages 83–132.

Parry, Martin (1992), 'The urban economy', presentation at Cities and Climate Change, a conference at the Royal Geographical Society, 31 March.

Patel, Sheela (1990), 'Street children, hotel boys and children of pavement dwellers and construction workers in Bombay: how they meet their daily needs', *Environment and Urbanization*, Vol 2, No 2, October, pages 9–26.

Patel, Sheela and Kalpana Sharma (1998), 'One David and three Goliaths: avoiding anti-poor solutions to Mumbai's transport problems', *Environment and Urbanization*, Vol 10, No 2, pages 149–159.

Patel, Sheela, Joel Bolnick and Diana Mitlin (forthcoming 2001), 'Squatting on the global highway' in Michael Edwards and John Gaventa (editors), *Global Citizen Action*, Earthscan, London and Lynne Rienner Publishers, Boulder, Colorado.

Patel, Sheela and Diana Mitlin (2001), *The work of SPARC and its partners Mahila Milan and the National Slum Dwellers Federation in India*, IIED Paper on Poverty Reduction in Urban Areas.

Pathak, Bindeshwar (1999), 'Sanitation is the key to healthy cities: a profile of Sulabh International', *Environment and Urbanization*, Vol 11, No 1, April, pages 221–229.

Pearce, David, Anil Markandya and Edward B Barbier (1989), *Blueprint for a Green Economy*, London, Earthscan Publications.

Pearson, Charles S (1987), 'Environmental standards, industrial relocation and pollution havens', in Charles S Pearson (editor) *Multinational Corporations, the Environment and the Third World*, Duke University Press, Durham, pages 113–128.

Peattie, Lisa (1990), 'Participation: a case study of how invaders organize, negotiate and interact with government in Lima, Peru', *Environment and Urbanization*, Vol 2, No 1, April, pages 19–30.

Pelling, Mark (1997), 'What determines vulnerability to floods; a case study in Georgetown, Guyana', *Environment and Urbanization*, Vol 9, No 1, April, pages 203–226.

Pepall, Jennifer (1992), 'Occupational poisoning', Reporting the work of Mohamad M Amr in IDRC Reports, Vol 20, No 1, April, Ottawa, page 15.

Pescod, M B (1992), *Wastewater Treatment and Use in Agriculture*, Report 47, Food and Agriculture Organization, Rome.

Pezzey, John (1989), *Economic Analysis of Sustainable Growth and Sustainable Development*, Environment Department Working Paper, No 15, World Bank, Washington, DC.

PGU – Programa de Gestión Urbana (2000), *Consultas Urbanas: Hacia una Gestion Urbana Participativa en Ciudades Latinoamericanas y del Caribe*, PGU/ALC, Quito.

Phantumvanit, Dhira and Wanai Liengcharernsit (1989), 'Coming to terms with Bangkok's environmental problems', *Environment and Urbanization*, Vol 1, No 1, April 1989, pages 31–39.

Phantumvanit, Dhira and Suthawan Sathirathai (1986), 'Promoting clean technologies in developing countries', *Industry and Environment*, Vol 9, No 4, October, pages 12–14.

Pickford, John (1995), *Low-cost Sanitation: A Survey of Practical Experience*, Intermediate Technology Publications, London.

Pimenta, J C P (1987), 'Multinational corporations and industrial pollution control in Sao Paulo, Brazil', in Charles S Pearson (editor), *Multinational Corporations, Environment and the Third World: Business Matters*, Duke University Press, Durham.

Pio, A (1986), 'Acute respiratory infections in children in developing countries: an international point of view', *Pediatric Infectious Disease Journal*, Vol 5, No 2, pages 179–183.

Plummer, Janelle (2000), *Municipalities and Community Participation: A Sourcebook for Capacity Building*, Earthscan Publications, London.

Postel, Sandra (1992), *The Last Oasis; Facing Water Scarcity*, Worldwatch Environmental Alert Series, Earthscan Publications, London.

Potts, Deborah (1995), 'Shall we go home? Increasing urban poverty in African cities and migration processes', *The Geographic Journal*, Vol 161, Part 3, November, pages 245–264.

Pryer, Jane (1989), 'When breadwinners fall ill: preliminary findings from a case study in Bangladesh', in 'Vulnerability: How the Poor Cope', *IDS Bulletin*, Vol 20, No 2, April, pages 49–57.

Pryer, Jane (1993), 'The impact of adult ill-health on household income and nutrition in Khulna, Bangladesh', *Environment and Urbanization*, Vol 5, No 2, October, pages 35–49.

Puerbo, Hasan (1991) 'Urban solid waste management in Bandung: towards an integrated resource recovery system', *Environment and Urbanization*, Vol 3, No 1, April, pages 60–69.

Rabbani, Fauziah (1999), 'A view of the city's health from the Aga Khan University, Karachi', *Urban Health and Development Bulletin*, pages 99–111.

Rabinovitch, Jonas (1992), 'Curitiba: towards sustainable urban development', *Environment and Urbanization*, Vol 4, No 2, October, pages 62–77.

Rahman, A, H K Lee and M A Khan (1997), 'Domestic water contamination in rapidly growing megacities of Asia: case of Karachi, Pakistan', *Environment Monitoring and Assessment*, Vol 44, Nos 1–3, pages 339–60.

Rai, Usha, 'Escalating violence against adolescent girls in India', *Urban Age*, Vol 1, No 4, Summer 1993, pages 10–11.

Rakodi, Carole, Rose Gatabaki-Kamau and Nick Devas (2000), 'Poverty and political conflict in Mombasa', *Environment and Urbanization*, Vol 12, No 1, pages 153–171.

Randel, Judith and Tony German (editors) (1997), *The Reality of Aid*, Earthscan, London.

Randel, Judith and Tony German (editors) (1998), *The Reality of Aid: An Independent Review of Poverty Reduction and Development Assistance*, Earthscan, London.

Rees, William E (1992), 'Ecological footprints and appropriated carrying capacity: what urban economics leaves out', *Environment and Urbanization*, Vol 4, No 2, October, pages 121–130.

Rees, William E (1995), 'Achieving sustainability: reform or transformation?', *Journal of Planning Literature*, Vol 9, No 4, May, pp 343–361.

Reichenheim, M and T Harpham (1989), 'Child accidents and associated risk factors in a Brazilian squatter settlement', *Health Policy and Planning*, Vol 4, No 2, pages 162–167.

Revi, Aromar and Manish Dube (1999), 'Indicators for urban environmental services in Lucknow – process and methods', *Environment and Urbanization*, Vol 11, No 2, pages 227–246.

Rietbergen, Simon (1989), 'Africa', in Poore, Duncan, *No Timber without Trees*, Earthscan Publications, London.

Roberts, Ian (2000), 'Leicester environment city: learning how to make Local Agenda 21, partnerships and participation deliver', *Environment and Urbanization*, Vol 12, No 2, pages 9–26.

Robins, Nick and Rita Kumar (1999), 'Producing, Providing, Trading: Manufacturing Industry and Sustainable Cities', *Environment and Urbanization*, Vol 11, No 2, pages 75–93.

Robotham, Don (1994), 'Redefining urban health policy in a developing country: the Jamaica case', in S Atkinson, J Songsore and W Werna (editors), *Urban Health Research in Developing Countries: Implications for Policy*, CAB International, Wallingford, pages 31–42.

Rocky Mountain Institute (1991), *Water Efficiency: A Resource for Utility Managers, Community Planners and other Decision Makers*, The Water Program, Rocky Mountain Institute, Snowmass.

Rodé, Patricio (2000), 'The Montevideo Urban Observatory', *Habitat Debate*, Vol 6, No 1, page 25.

Rodriguez, Alfredo, Lucy Winchester and Ben Richards (1999), *Urban Governance, Partnership and Poverty in Santiago*, Urban Governance, Partnership and Poverty, Working Paper 14, International Development Department, University of Birmingham, Birmingham.

Rohde, J E (1983), 'Why the other half dies: the science and politics of child mortality in the Third World', *Assignment Children*, 61/62, pages 35–67.

Romieu, Isabelle, Henyk Weitzenfeld and Jacobo Finkelman (1990), 'Urban air pollution in Latin America and the Caribbean: Health perspectives', *World Health Statistics Quarterly*, Vol 23, No 2, pages 153–167.

Romieu, I, F Meneses, S Ruiz, J Huerta, J J Sienra, M White, R Etzel and M Hernandez (1997), 'Effects of intermittent ozone exposure on peak expiratory flow and respiratory symptoms among asthmatic children in Mexico City', *Architecture and Environmental Health*, Vol 52, No 5, pages 368–376.

Romieu, Isabelle and Mauricio Hernandez (1999), 'Air pollution and health in developing countries: review of epidemiological evidence', in Gordon McGranahan and Frank Murray (editors), *Health and Air Pollution in Rapidly Developing Countries*, Stockholm Environment Institute, Stockholm, pages 43–56.

Rosenberg, Charles E (1962), *The Cholera Years*, University of Chicago Press, Chicago.

Rossi-Espagnet, A, G B Goldstein and I Tabibzadeh (1991), 'Urbanization and health in developing countries; a challenge for health for all', *World Health Statistical Quarterly*, Vol 44, No 4, pages 186–244.

Rothenburg, Stephen J, Lourdes Schnaas-Arrieta, Irving A Perez-Guerrero and others, 'Evaluacion del riesgo potencial de la exposition perinatal al plombo en el Valle de Mexico' *Perinatologia y Reproduccion Humana*, Vol 3, No 1, 1989, pages 49–56.

Royston, Michael G (1977), *Residues or Riches: Technologies for a Conserver Society*, background paper prepared for Barbara Ward for the book *Progress for a Small Planet*, Geneva.

Russell, Steven and Elizabeth Vidler (2000), 'The rise and fall of government–community partnerships for urban development: grassroots testimony from Colombo', *Environment and Urbanization*, Vol 12, No 1, pages 73–86.

Safi, Mohammed Afzal (1998), 'An integrated approach to sanitation and health in Kabul', in John Pickford (editor), *Sanitation and Water for All*, Proceedings of the 24th WEDC Conference, Islamabad, Pakistan.

Sahil (1988), 'Marine pollution and the Indus Delta', Vol 1 (house journal of the National Institute of Oceanography, Karachi, Pakistan), pages 57–61.

Saksena, Sumeet and Kirk R Smith (1999), 'Indoor air pollution', in Gordon McGranahan and Frank Murray (editors), *Health and Air Pollution in Rapidly Developing Countries*, Stockholm Environment Institute, Stockholm, pages 111–125.

Sanbergen, Loes-Schenk (forthcoming), 'Women, water and sanitation in the slums of Bangalore: a case study of action research', in Schenk, H (editor), *Living in Bangalore's Slums*, quoted in Benjamin 2000.

Sanderson, David (1997), 'Reducing risk as a tool for urban improvement: the Caqueta ravine, Lima, Peru', *Environment and Urbanization*, Vol 9, No 1, April, pages 251–261.

Sani, S (1987), 'Urbanization and the atmospheric environment in Southeast Asia', in *Environment, Development, Natural Resource Crisis in Asia and the Pacific*, Sahabat Alam Malaysia, 1987.

Sapir, D (1990), *Infectious Disease Epidemics and Urbanization: a Critical Review of the Issues*, Paper prepared for the WHO Commission on Health and Environment, Division of Environmental Health, WHO, Geneva.

Satterthwaite, David (1996), *The Scale and Nature of Urban Change in the South*, IIED Working Paper, IIED, London.

Satterthwaite, David (1997a), 'Environmental transformations in cities as they get larger, wealthier and better managed', *The Geographic Journal*, Vol 163, No 2, July, pages 216–224.

Satterthwaite, David (1997b), *The Scale and Nature of International Donor Assistance to Housing, Basic services and Other Human Settlements Related Projects*, WIDER, Helsinki.

Satterthwaite, David (1998), 'Cities and sustainable development; what progress since *Our Common Future*', in Softing, Guri Bang, George Benneh, Kjetil Hindar, Larse Walloe and Anders Wijkman, *The Brundtland Commission's Report – 10 years*, Scandinavian University Press, Oslo.

Satterthwaite, David (1999), *The Links Between Poverty and the Environment in Urban Areas of Africa, Asia and Latin America*, Paper prepared for UNDP, New York.

Satterthwaite, David (2000), 'Seeking an understanding of poverty that recognizes rural–urban differences and rural–urban linkages', paper presented at the World Bank's Urban Forum on Urban Poverty Reduction in the 21st Century, Washington, DC.

Satterthwaite, David, Roger Hart, Caren Levy, Diana Mitlin, David Ross, Jac Smit and Carolyn Stephens (1996), *The Environment for Children*, Earthscan and UNICEF, London.

Satterthwaite, David and Cecilia Tacoli (2001), 'Seeking an understanding of poverty that recognizes rural–urban differences and rural-urban linkages', in Carole Rakodi (editor), *Sustainable Urban Livelihoods*, book prepared for the Department for International Development (DFID).

Schaeffer, B, 'Home and health – on solid foundations?', *World Health Forum*, Vol 11, 1990, pages 38–45.

Schmidheiny, Stephan with the Business Council for Sustainable Development (1992), *Changing Course: A Global Business Perspective on Development and the Environment*, The MIT Press, Cambridge.

Schmidt-Bleek, F (1993), 'MIPS revisited', *Fresenius Environmental Bulletin*, Vol 2, No 8, pages 407–412.

Schofield, C J, R Briceno-Leon, N Kolstrup, D J T Webb and G B White (1990), 'The role of house design in limiting vector-borne disease', in Jorge E Hardoy and others (editors), *The Poor Die Young – Housing and Health in Third World Cities,* Earthscan Publications, London, pages 189–212.

Schusterman, Ricardo and Ana Hardoy (1997), 'Reconstructing social capital in a poor urban settlement: the Integrated Improvement Programme, Barrio San Jorge', *Environment and Urbanization*, Vol 9, No 1, April, pages 91–119

Schusterman, Ricardo, Florencia Almansi, Ana Hardoy, Cecilia Monti and Gastón Urquiza (1999), Reducción de la pobreza en acción; planificación participativa en San Fernando, *Medio Ambiente y Urbanizacion*, No 54, December.

Schwela, Dietrich (1999), 'Local ambient air quality management', in Gordon McGranahan and Frank Murray (editors), *Health and Air Pollution in Rapidly Developing Countries*, Stockholm Environment Institute, Stockholm, pages 57–75.

Scott, Michael J (1994), draft paper on human settlements – impacts/adaptation, IPCC Working Group II, WMO and UNEP.

Scott, Michael J and others (1996), 'Human settlements in a changing climate: impacts and adaptation', in Robert T Watson, Marufu C Zinwowera and Richard H Moss (editors), *Climate Change 1995; Impacts, Adaptations and Mitigation of Climate Change: Scientific-Technical Analyses*, published for the Intergovernmental Panel on Climate Change by Cambridge University Press, Cambridge, pages 399–426.

Secrett, Charles (1988), 'Deadly offer poor countries find hard to refuse', *The Guardian*, July.

Sestini, G, L Jeftic and J D Milliman (1990), *Implications of Expected Climatic Changes in the Mediterranean Region: An Overview*, UNEP Regional Seas Reports and Studies, No 103, UNEP, Nairobi.

Sharma, Anju and Anumita Roychowdhury (1996), *Slow Murder: The Deadly Story of Vehicular Pollution in India*, Centre for Science and Environment, New Delhi.

Shelter Associates (1999), *Primary Survey*, Pune.

Shenkut, M (1998), 'Measures to alleviate sanitation and health problems', in John Pickford (editor) *Sanitation and Water for All*, proceedings of the 24th WEDC Conference, Islamabad, Pakistan, 1998.

Shrivastav, P P (1982), 'City for the citizen or citizen for the city: the search for an appropriate strategy for slums and housing the urban poor in developing countries – the case of Delhi', *Habitat International*, Vol 6, Nos 1–2, pages 197–207.

Sida (1997), 'Seeking more effective and sustainable support to improving housing and living conditions for low income households in urban areas: Sida's initiatives in Costa Rica, Chile and Nicaragua', *Environment and Urbanization*, Vol 9, No 2, pages 213–231.

Sidel, J (1995), *Coercion, Capital and the Post-colonial State: Bossim in the postwar Philippines*, unpublished PhD thesis, Cornell University.

Silas, Johan (1992), 'Environmental management in Surabaya's Kampungs', *Environment and Urbanization*, Vol 4, No 2, October, pages 33–41.

Silas, Johan (1994), 'Population and urbanization trends in Indonesia', Background Paper for the UN Global Report on Human Settlements, 1996.

Sinnatamby, Gehan (1990), 'Low cost sanitation', in Jorge E Hardoy, Sandy Cairncross and David Satterthwaite (editors), *The Poor Die Young: Housing and Health in Third World Cities*, Earthscan, London.

Smil, Vaclav (1984), *The Bad Earth: Environmental Degradation in China*, M E Sharpe, New York and Zed Press, London.

Smil, Vaclav (1995), *Environmental Problems in China: Estimates of Economic Costs*, East-West Centre Special Report No 5, East–West Center, Honolulu.

Smit, Barrie (1990), 'Planning in a climate of uncertainty', in James McCulloch (editor), *Cities and Global Climate Change*, Climate Institute, Washington, DC, 1990, pages 3–19.

Smit, Jac and Joe Nasr (1992), 'Urban agriculture for sustainable cities: using wastes and idle land and water bodies as resources', *Environment and Urbanization*, Vol 4, No 2, October, pages 141–152.

Smit, Jac, Annu Ratta and Joe Nasr (1996), *Urban Agriculture: Food, Jobs and Sustainable Cities*, Publication Series for Habitat II, Volume One, UNDP, New York.

Smith, K R (1990), 'Dialectics of improved stoves', in L Kristoferson and others (editors), *Bioenergy:, Contribution to Environmentally Sustainable Development*, Stockholm Environment Institute, Stockholm.

Smith, K.R., M.G. Apte, Y.Q. Ma, W. Wongsekiarttirat and A. Kulkarni (1994), 'Air pollution and the energy ladder in Asian Cities', *Energy* Vol 19, No 5, pages 587–600.

Smith, Kirk R and Sameer Akbar (1999), 'Health-damaging air pollution: a matter of scale', in Gordon McGranahan and Frank Murray (editors), *Health and Air Pollution in Rapidly Developing Countries*, Stockholm Environment Institute, Stockholm, pages 15–27.

Solo, Tova Maria (1999), 'Small-scale entrepreneurs in the urban water and sanitation market', *Environment and Urbanization*, Vol 11, No 1, April, pages 117–131.

Songsore, Jacob (1992), *Review of Household Environmental Problems in the Accra Metropolitan Area, Ghana*, Working Paper, Stockholm Environment Institute, Stockholm.

Songsore, Jacob and Gordon McGranahan (1993), 'Environment, wealth and health: towards an analysis of intra-urban differentials within Greater Accra Metropolitan Area, Ghana', *Environment and Urbanization*, Vol 5, No 2, pages 10–24.

Songsore, Jacob and Gordon McGranahan (1998), 'The political economy of household environmental management: gender, environment and epidemiology in the Greater Accra Metropolitan Area', *World Development*, Vol 26, No 3, pages 395–412 .

SPARC (1996), 'SPARC and its work with the National Slum Dwellers Federation and Mahila Milan, India', IIED Paper Series on Poverty Reduction in Urban Areas, IIED, London.

SPP (1984), *Programa de Desarrollo de la ZMCM y de la Region Centrale*, Mexico,.

Stein, Robert E and Brian Johnson (1979), *Banking on the Biosphere?*, Lexington Books, D C Heath and Company, Lexington and Toronto.

Stein, Alfredo (1996), 'Decentralization and Urban Poverty Reduction in Nicaragua: The Experience of the Local Development Programme (PRODEL)', IIED Paper Series on Poverty Reduction in Urban Areas, IIED, London.

Stein, Alfredo (2000), *Participation and Sustainability in Social Projects: The Experience of the Local Development Programme (PRODEL) in Nicaragua*, IIED case study prepared with DFID support, IIED, London.

Stephens, Carolyn (1996), 'Healthy cities or unhealthy islands: the health and social implications of urban inequality', *Environment and Urbanization*, Vol 8, No 2, October, pages 9–30.

Stephens, Carolyn and Trudy Harpham (1992), *The Measurement of Health in Household Environmental Studies in Urban Areas of Developing Countries: Factors to Be Considered in the Design of Surveys*, Urban Health Programme, London School of Hygiene and Tropical Medicine, London.

Stephens, Carolyn, Ian Timaeus, Marco Akerman, Sebastian Avle, Paulo Borlina Maia, Paulo Campanerio, Ben Doe, Luisiana Lush, Doris Tetteh and Trudy Harpham (1994), *Environment and Health in Developing Countries: an Analysis of Intra-urban Differentials*, London School of Hygiene and Tropical Medicine, London.

Stephens, Carolyn, Marco Akerman, Sebastian Avle, Paulo Borlina Maia, Paulo Campanareio, Ben Doe and Doris Tetteh (1997), 'Urban equity and urban health: using existing data to understand inequalities in health and environment in Accra, Ghana and Sao Paulo, *Environment and Urbanization*, Vol 9, No 1, April, pages 181–202.

Stephens, C and M Gupta (1996), 'Ignorance or lack of control?', in *WHO Environmental Health Newsletter*, Vol 25, page 10.

Stren, Richard E (1989), 'Administration of urban services', in Richard E Stren and Rodney R White (editors), *African Cities in Crisis*, Westview, Boulder, Colorado.

Stren, Richard (1992), 'Conclusions' in Richard Stren, Rodney White and Joseph Whitney (editors), *Sustainable Cities: Urbanization and the Environment in International Perspective*, Westview Press, Boulder, Colorado, pages 307–315.

Surjadi, Charles (1988), *Health of the Urban Poor in Indonesia*, Urban Health Problems Study Group paper No 29, Atma Jaya Research Centre, Jakarta.

Surjadi, Charles (1993), 'Respiratory diseases of mothers and children and environmental factors among households in Jakarta', *Environment and Urbanization*, Vol 5, No 2, October, pages 78–86.

Surjadi, Charles, L Padhmasutra, D Wahyuninsih, G McGranahan and M Kjellén (1994), *Household Environmental Problems in Jakarta*, Stockholm Environment Institute, Stockholm.

Svedin, Uno (1988), 'The Concept of Sustainability', in Stockholm Studies in Natural Resource Management, No 1, *Perspectives of Sustainable Development – Some Critical Issues Related to the Brundtland Report*, Stockholm Group for Studies on Natural Resources Management.

Swilling, Mark (editor) (1997), *Governing Africa's Cities*, Witwatersrand University Press, Johannesburg.

Swyngedouw, Erik A (1995), 'The contradictions of urban water provision a study of Guayaquil, Ecuador', *Third World Planning Review*, Vol 17, No 4, pages 387–405.

Tacoli, Cecilia (1998), *Bridging the Divide: Rural-Urban Interactions and Livelihood Strategies*, Gatekeeper Series, No 77, IIED Sustainable Agriculture and Rural Livelihoods Programme, London.

Tadesse, Yared (1996), 'Solid waste management in peri-urban areas of Ethiopia', *Water and Sanitation News*, Vol 3 (September–December), page 5.

TARU Leading Edge (1998), *Bangalore Water Supply and Sewerage Master Plan: A Situation Analysis*, prepared for AUS AID, New Delhi, December.

Tchounwou, P B, D M Lantum, A Monkiedje, I Takougang, and P H Barbazan (1997), 'The urgent need for environmental sanitation and safe drinking water supply in Mbandjock, Cameroon', *Archives of Environmental Contamination and Toxicology*, Vol 33, No 1, pages 17–22.

The Economist, 13 May 2000, page 146.

Thompson, John, Ina T Porras, Elisabeth Wood, James K Tumwine, Mark R Mujwahuzi, Munguti Katui-Katua and Nick Johnstone (2000), 'Waiting at the tap: changes in urban water use in East Africa over three decades', *Environment and Urbanization*, Vol 12, No 2, October, pages 37–52.

Tischner, Ursula and Friedrich Schmidt-Bleek (1993), 'Designing goods with MIPS', *Fresenius Environmental Bulletin*, Vol 2, No 8, pages 479–484.

Tjønneland, Elling N, Henrik Harboe, Alf Morten Jerve and Nazneen Kanji with contributions from Wycliffe R Chilowa, Niki Jazdowska, Adrianne Madaris, Archie Mafeje, David Satterthwaite, Neo Simutanyi and Else Øyen (1998), *The World Bank and Poverty in sub-Saharan Africa: A Study of Operationalizing Policies for Poverty Reduction*, Chr Michelsen Institute in cooperation with CROP.

Turner, Bertha (editor) (1988), *Building Community – A Third World Case Book*, Habitat International Coalition, London.

Turner, John F C (1966), *Uncontrolled Urban Settlements: Problems and Policies*, Report for the United Nations seminar on Urbanization, Pittsburg.

Turner, John F C (1968), 'Housing priorities, settlement patterns and urban development in modernizing countries', *Journal of the American Institute of Planners*, Vol 34.

Turner, John F C (1976), *Housing By People – Towards Autonomy in Building Environments*, Ideas in Progress, Marion Boyars, London.

Turner, John F C (1996), 'Seeing tools and principles within "best practices"', *Environment and Urbanization*, Vol 8, No 2, pages 198–199.

Turner, R K, P M Kelly and R C Kay (1990), *Cities at Risk*, BNA International, London.

Tuts, Raf (1998), 'Localizing Agenda 21 in small cities in Kenya, Morocco and Vietnam', *Environment and Urbanization*, Vol 10, No 2, pages 175–189.

United Nations (2000) *World Urbanization Prospects: The 1999 Revision*, Population Division, Department of Economic and Social Affairs, ESA/P/WP.161.

UNCHS (1988), *Refuse Collection Vehicles for Developing Countries*, HS/138/88E, UNCHS (Habitat), Nairobi, Kenya, 1988.

UNCHS (1993), *Report of the Regional Workshop on the Promotion of Waste Recycling and Reuse in Developing Countries*, Nairobi.

UNCHS (1995), *Human Settlement Interventions Addressing Crowding and Health Issues*, United Nations Centre for Human Settlements (Habitat), Nairobi.

UNCHS (1996), *An Urbanizing World: Global Report on Human Settlements, 1996*, Oxford University Press, Oxford and New York.

UNCHS (1997), *Analysis of Data and Global Urban Indicators Database 1993*, UNCHS Urban Indicators Programme, Phase 1: 1994–6, Nairobi.

UNDP (1996), *Human Development Report 1996*, Oxford University Press, Oxford.

UNEP (1988), 'Cover Story', *The Siren* No 38, UNEP, Nairobi, October.

UNEP (1991), *Environmental Data Report, 1991–2*, GEMS Monitoring and Assessment Research Centre, Blackwell, Oxford and Massachusetts.

UNEP and UNICEF (1990), *Children and the Environment, The State of the Environment 1990*; United Nations Environment Programme and United Nations Children's Fund, E.90.XX.USA.2, Geneva.

UNEP and WHO (1988), *Assessment of Urban Air Quality*, Global Environment Monitoring Service, United Nations Environment Programme and World Health Organization.

UNICEF (1988), *Improving Environment for Child Health and Survival*, Urban Examples, No 15, UNICEF, New York.

UNICEF (1991), *The State of the World's Children 1991*, Oxford University Press, Oxford.

UNICEF (1992), *Environment, Development and the Child*, Environment Section, Programme Division, New York.

UNICEF (1996), Multi Indicator Cluster Surveys in India 1995–96, Urban Slums, UNICEF, India.

UNICEF–Bangladesh and others (1997), *The Dancing Horizon Human Development Prospects for Bangladesh*, Dhaka.

UNICEF–Nigeria (1997), Profile of the Urban Local Governments of Ibadan, Planning Baseline Data, prepared by Oyo State Government and UNICEF B Zonal Office, Ibadan.

United Nations (1971) 'Report of the 1969 meeting of exports on social policy and planning', *International Social Development Review*, No 3.

United Nations (1980), *Urban, Rural and City Population, 1950–2000, as assessed in 1978*, ESA/P/WP 66, June, New York.

United Nations (1998), *World Urbanization Prospects: the 1996 Revision*, Population Division, Department of Economic and Social Affairs, United Nations.

USAID (1990), *Ranking Environmental Health Risks in Bangkok*, Office of Housing and Urban Programs, Washington, DC.

Valsiner, J (1987), *Culture and the Development of Children's Action*, Wiley, New York.

Vanderschueren, Franz (1996), 'From violence to justice and security in cities', *Environment and Urbanization*, Vol 8, No 1, October, pages 93–112.

Velásquez, Luz Stella (1998), 'Agenda 21: a form of joint environmental management in Manizales, Colombia', *Environment and Urbanization*, Vol 10, No 2, pages 9–36.

Velásquez , Luz Stella (1999), 'The local environmental action plan for Olivares bio-comuna in Manizales', *Environment and Urbanization*, Vol 11, No 2.

Velásquez , Luz Stella and Margarita Pacheco (1999), 'Research-management as an approach to solving environmental conflicts in metropolitan areas: a case study of the Manizales-Villamaría conurbation, Colombia', in Adrian Atkinson, Julio D Dávila, Edésio Fernandes and Michael Mattingly (editors), *The Challenge of Environmental Management in Urban Areas*, Ashgate, Aldershot.

Vimal, O P (1982), 'Recycling of organic residues – status and trends in India', *UNEP Industry and Environment*, April–June, pages 7–10.

Vincentian Missionaries (1998), 'The Payatas Environmental Development Programme: micro-enterprise promotion and involvement in solid waste management in Quezon City', *Environment and Urbanization*, Vol 10, No 2, pages 55–68.

VMSDFI (2000), 'Destigmatizing Patayas', paper by the Vincentian Missionaries Social Development Foundation, mimeo.

von Schirnding, Y D Bradshaw, R Fuggle and M Stokol (1990), 'Blood lead levels in inner-city South African children', *Environmental Health Perspectives*, Vol 94, pages 125–130.

Von Weizsäcker, Ernst Amory B Lovins and L Hunter Lovins (1997), *Factor Four: Doubling Wealth, Halving Resource Use*, Earthscan, London.

Wacker, Corinne, Alain Viaro and Markus Wolf (1999), 'Partnerships for urban environmental management: roles of urban authorities, researchers and civil society', *Environment and Urbanization*, Vol 11, No 2, pages 113–125.

Wackernagel, Mathis and William Rees (1995), *Our Ecological Footprint: Reducing Human Impact on the Earth*, New Society Publishers, Gabriola (Canada).

Waller, Robert E (1991), 'Field investigations of air', in W W Holland, R Detels and G Knox (editors), *Oxford Textbook of Public Health*, Vol 2, (second edition), Oxford University Press, Oxford and New York, pages 435–450.

Walsh, Michael P (1999), 'Motor vehicle pollution and its control in Asia', in Gordon McGranahan and Frank Murray (editors), *Health and Air Pollution in Rapidly Developing Countries*, Stockholm Environment Institute, Stockholm, pages 127–145.

Wang, Jia-Xi and Yong-Mei Bian (1985), 'Fluoride effects on the mulberry-silkworm system' *Environmental Pollution*, Vol 52, pages 11–18.

Wangwongwatana, Supat (1992), 'Bangkok metropolis and its air pollution problems', paper presented at the International Workshop on Planning for Sustainable Urban Development, Cardiff, 13–17 July.

Ward, Barbara (1974), *Human Settlements: Crisis and Opportunity*, Ministry of Urban Affairs, Information Canada, Ottawa.

Ward, Barbara (1976a), *The Home of Man*, W W Norton, New York.

Ward, Barbara (1976b), *The Inner and the Outer Limits*, The Clifford Clark Memorial Lectures 1976, *Canadian Public Administration*, Vol 19, No 3, Autumn, pages 385–416.

Ward, Barbara (1979), *Progress for a Small Planet*, Penguin, London (later republished by Earthscan Publications, London).

Ward, Barbara and René Dubos (1972), *Only One Earth: The Care and Maintenance of a Small Planet*, André Deutsch, London.

Warner, D B and L Laugeri (1991), 'Health for all: the legacy of the water decade', *Water International*, Vol 16, pages 135–141.

Water Newsletter (1996), IRC, International Water and Sanitation Centre, WHO Collaborating Center, November, page 2.

Wegelin-Schuringa, Madeleen and Teresia Kodo (1997), 'Tenancy and sanitation provision in informal settlements in Nairobi: revisiting the public latrine option', *Environment and Urbanization*, Vol 9, No 2, October, pages 181–190.

White, Gilbert F, David J Bradley and Anne U White (1972), *Drawers of Water: Domestic Water Use in East Africa*, University of Chicago Press, Chicago.

White, Rodney R (1992), 'The international transfer of urban technology: does the North have anything to offer for the global environmental crisis?', *Environment and Urbanization*, Vol 4, No 2, October, pages 109–120.

White, Rodney and Joe Whitney (1992), 'Human settlements and sustainable development: an overview', in Richard Stren, Rodney White and Joseph Whitney (editors), *Sustainable Cities Urbanization and the Environment in International Perspective*, Westview Press, Boulder, Colorado, pages 8–52.

Whittington, D and D Lauria (1990), *Household Demand for Improved Sanitation Services: A Case Study of Kumasi, Ghana*, UNDP–World Bank Water and Sanitation Program, Program Report 3, World Bank, Washington, DC.

Wilkinson, Richard G (1996), *Unhealthy Societies*, Routledge, London.

WHO (1986), *Intersectoral Action for Health*, World Health Organization, Geneva.

WHO (1990), *Environmental Health in Urban Development*, Report of a WHO Expert Committee, WHO, Geneva.

WHO (1991), *Global Estimates for Health Situation Assessments and Projections 1990*, Division of Epidemiological Surveillance and Health Situation and Trend Analysis, WHO, WHO/HST/90 2, Geneva.

WHO (1992a), *Our Planet, Our Health*, Report of the Commission on Health and Environment, Geneva.

WHO (1992b), *Reproductive Health: A Key to a Brighter Future*, WHO Special Programme of Research Development and Research Training in Human Reproduction, Geneva.

WHO (1992c), *Report of the Panel on Industry*, WHO Commission on Health and Environment, WHO/EHE/92 4, WHO, Geneva.

WHO (1994), *Facts and Figures on Women's Health*, fact sheet prepared for the United Nations Fourth Conference on Women, WHO, Geneva.

WHO (1995), *The World Health Report 1995: Bridging the Gaps*, WHO, Geneva, 118 pages.

WHO (1997), *Health and Environment in Sustainable Development: Five Years after the Earth Summit*, WHO, Geneva.

WHO (1999), 'Creating healthy cities in the 21st Century', Chapter 6 in David Satterthwaite (editor), *The Earthscan Reader on Sustainable Cities*, Earthscan Publications, London.

WHO (2000), Guidelines for Air Quality, WHO, Geneva, drawn from http://www.who.int/peh/

WHO/UNICEF (1994), *Water Supply and Sanitation Sector Monitoring Report 1994*, Water Supply and Sanitation Collaborative Council, WHO and UNICEF, Geneva.

Winblad, Uno and Wen Kilama (1985), *Sanitation without Water*, Macmillan, Basingstoke.

Wing, Steve Gary Grant, Merle Green and Chris Stewart (1996), 'Community based collaboration for environmental justice: south-east Halifax County environmental re-awakening', *Environment and Urbanization*, Vol 8, No 2, October, pages 129–140.

Winpenny, J T (1991) *Values for the Environment: A Guide to Economic Appraisal*, HMSO, London.

Wohl, Anthony S (1983), *Endangered Lives: Public Health in Victorian Britain*, Methuen, London.

World Bank (1988), *World Development Report, 1988*, Oxford University Press, Oxford.

World Bank (1989), 'Adult health in Brazil: adjusting to new challenges', Report No 7808-BR, Brazil Department, Washington, DC, November.

World Bank (1990), *World Development Report – 1990: Poverty*, Oxford University Press, Oxford.

World Bank (1991), *Urban Policy and Economic Development: An Agenda for the 1990s*, The World Bank, Washington, DC.

World Bank (1992), *World Development Report 1992*, Oxford University Press, Oxford.

World Bank (1993), *World Development Report 1993: Investing in Health*, published for the World Bank by Oxford University Press, Oxford.

World Bank (1997), *Environment Matters: Towards Environmentally and Socially Sustainable Development*, The World Bank, Washington, DC.

World Bank (1999a), *World Development Report 1999*, Oxford University Press, Oxford and New York.

World Bank (1999b), *Greening Industry: New Roles for Communities, Markets and Governments*, Oxford University Press, Oxford and New York.

World Commission on Environment and Development (1987), *Our Common Future*, Oxford University Press.

World Resources Institute (1990), *World Resources 1990–91: A Guide to the Global Environment*, Oxford University Press, Oxford.

World Resources Institute, in collaboration with the United Nations Development Programme, the United Nations Environment Programme and the World Bank (1998), *World Resources 1998–99; Environmental Change and Human Health*, Oxford University Press, Oxford and New York.

Yach, D and D Harrison (1996), *Inequalities in Health Determinants and Status in South Africa*, Medical Research Council, Pretoria.

Yacoob, May and Margo Kelly (1999), *Secondary Cities in West Africa: The Challenge of Environmental Health and Prevention*, Occasional Paper Series: Comparative Urban Studies, No 21, Woodrow Wilson International Center for Scholars, Washington, DC.

Yapi-Diahou, Alphonse (1995), 'The informal housing sector of the metropolis of Abidjan, Ivory Coast', *Environment and Urbanization*, Vol 7, No 2, October, pages 11–29.

Yhdego, Michael (1991), 'Urban environmental degradation in Tanzania', *Environment and Urbanization*, Vol 3, No 1, April, pages 147–152.

Zaba, Basia and Ndalahwa Madulu (1998), 'A drop to drink Population and water resources: illustrations from northern Tanzania', in Alex de Sherbinin and Victoria Dompka (editors), *Water and Population Dynamics: Case Studies and Policy Implications*, American Association for the Advancement of Science (AAAS), Washington, DC, pages 49–86.

Zhao, D and J Xiong (1988), 'Acidification in southwestern China', in H Rohde and R Herrera (editors), *Acidification in Tropical Countries*, SCOPE Report No 36, John Wiley & Sons, Chichester.

Zhongmin, Yan (1988), 'Shanghai: the growth and shifting emphasis of China's largest city', in Victor F S Sit (editor), *Chinese Cities: The Growth of the Metropolis Since 1949*, Oxford University Press, Hong Kong, pages 94–127.

Zorrilla, Silvia and Maria Elena Guaresti (1986), *Sector Agua Potables y Saneamiento: Lineamientos para una Estrategia Nacional*, PNUD (UN Development Programme), Buenos Aires.

Further Reading

Recommendations for further reading are organized under the following headings:

- General (books and journals).
- Environmental problems in the home, workplace and neighbourhood.
- The city environment – air and water pollution, solid wastes, toxic and hazardous wastes.
- The rural, regional and global impacts of cities.
- Tackling environmental health problems.
- Tackling city-wide problems.
- Sustainable development and cities.

GENERAL: BOOKS AND JOURNALS

Books with a broad coverage of urban environmental problems:

McGranahan, G, P Jacobi, J Songsore, C Surjadi and M Kjellén (2001), *Citizens at Risk: From Urban Sanitation to Sustainable Cities*, Earthscan Publications, London. Available from bookstores or direct from Earthscan, http://www.earthscan.co.uk

WRI (1996), *World Resources 1996–1997: The Urban Environment*, The World Resources Institute, Oxford University Press, Oxford and New York, 365 pages, ISBN: 0 19 521161 8.

Haughton, Graham and Colin Hunger (1994), *Sustainable Cities*, Regional Policy and Development Series 7, Jessica Kingsley Publishers, London, 357 pages.

Douglas, Ian (1983), *The Urban Environment*, Edward Arnold, London, 229 pages. A large format book with many maps, figures and illustrations; although published nearly 20 years ago, this is still one of the most interesting and relevant introductions to the physical environment of urban areas.

Harvey, David (1996), *Justice, Nature and the Geography of Difference*, Blackwell Publishers, Oxford and New York, 468 pages – a more radical geography perspective.

For a broad overview of urban change and the links with economic, social, political and environmental changes, see UNCHS (Habitat) (1996), *An Urbanizing World: Global Report on Human Settlements 1996*, Oxford University Press, Oxford and New York, 557 pages.

For a general discussion of the multiple links between environment and health with special sections on urban areas and industry, see World Health Organization (1992) *Our Planet, Our Health*, Report of the WHO Commission on Health and Environment, 282 pages. Available from WHO Publications, WHO, 1211 Geneva 27, Switzerland.

The Centre for Science and Environment (CSE) in India produces publications with among the most detailed descriptions of the scale and range of urban (and rural) environmental problems. The most recent is Agarwal, Anil, Sunita Narain and Srabani Sen (editors) (1999*), State of India's Environment: The Citizens' Fifth Report*, CSE, New Delhi, 300 pages. Available from CSE, 41 Tughlakabad Institutional Area, New Delhi 110 062, India; email: sales@cseindia.org. There is also a companion statistical volume to this. These can also be ordered through CSE's web page: www.cseindia.org (which also has many interesting articles and features).

Hasan, Arif (1999), *Understanding Karachi: Planning and Reform for the Future*, City Press, Karachi, 171 pages, includes descriptions of environmental problems and measures taken to address them within its broader discussion of Karachi. ISBN: 969 8380 28 0. Available from City Press, 316 Madina City Mall, Abdullah Haroon Road, Saddar, Karachi 74400, Pakistan; email: city_press@email.com. This book can be ordered through the web: http://www.pakistanibooks.com

The United Nations University Press has a series of books on urban problems, including Rakodi, Carole (editor) (1997), *The Urban Challenge in Africa*, Lo, Fu-chen and Yue-man Yeung (editors) (1997), *Emerging World Cities in Pacific Asia* and Gilbert, Alan (editor) (1997), *The Mega-city in Latin America*. See: http://brook.edu/press/books/clientpr/unulist.htm

Journals

Environment and Urbanization is a journal that concentrates on urban environmental issues for Africa, Asia and Latin America and the Caribbean, so many recommendations for further reading come from it. (This journal is also edited and published by the research programme that produced this book.) ISSN 0956 2478. Published by the Human Settlements Programme, IIED, 3 Endsleigh Street, London WC1H ODD, UK, e-mail: humans@iied.org, web: http://www.iied.org/eandu. Many papers in *Environment and Urbanization* are available on the web at http://www.catchword.com/titles/09562478.htm

For the urban environment in Latin America, there is *Medio Ambiente y Urbanizacion* published twice a year by IIED-America Latina, Av General Paz 1180, (1429) Buenos Aires, Argentina.

Down to Earth, the fortnightly international journal which provides a detailed and lively coverage of urban and rural environmental issues, mainly with a focus on Asia. Available from *Down to Earth*, 41, Tughlakabad International Area, New Delhi 110 062, India. For more details, see its web page at http://www.cseindia.org

Five journals often have papers on urban environmental issues in Africa, Asia and Latin America:

Local Environment, ISSN: 1354-9839, published by Carfax, at
  http://www.tandf.co.uk/journals/alphalist.html
Urban Studies, ISSN: 0042-0980, published by Carfax; at
  http://www.tandf.co.uk/journals/alphalist.html
Third World Planning Review, Liverpool University Press, at
  http://www.liverpool-unipress.co.uk/third.html
Industry and Environment, ISSN 0378-9993, published by the UN Environment Programme, at
  http://www.unepie.org/publi/4rvpubli.html
Habitat International, ISSN: 0197-3975, published by Pergamon, at
  http://www.elsevier.com/locate/habitatint/

ENVIRONMENTAL PROBLEMS IN THE HOME, WORKPLACE AND NEIGHBOURHOOD

McGranahan, G, P Jacobi, J Songsore, C Surjadi and M Kjellén (2001), *Citizens at Risk: From Urban Sanitation to Sustainable Cities*, Earthscan Publications, London. Available from bookstores or direct from Earthscan at http://www.earthscan.co.uk

For water and sanitation and related health issues, see Cairncross, Sandy and Richard G. Feachem (1993), *Environmental Health Engineering in the Tropics: An Introductory Text (second edition)*, John Wiley & Sons, Chichester.

The Environmental Health Project has many publications on water, sanitation, indoor air pollution and other aspects of environmental health, many of which are available electronically from its website at http://www.ehproject.org/

See also:

Thompson, John, Ina T Porras, Elisabeth Wood, James K Tumwine, Mark R Mujwahuzi, Munguti Katui-Katua and Nick Johnstone (2000), 'Waiting at the tap: changes in urban water use in East Africa over three decades', *Environment and Urbanization*, Vol 12, No 2, pages 37–52.

Johnstone, Nick and Libby Wood (editors) (2001), *Private Firms and Public Water: Realizing Social and Environmental Objectives in Developing Countries*, Edward Elgar, Cheltenham, 239 pages.

The April 2000 issue of *Environment and Urbanization* (Vol 12, No 1) on the theme of 'Poverty Reduction and Urban Governance' includes 12 city case studies with details of the quality and extent of provision for environmental infrastructure and services.

The October 1996 issue of *Environment and Urbanization* (Vol 8, No 2) on the theme of city inequality includes many papers describing and discussing inequality in access to services and exposure to environmental hazards.

The 1997 issues of *Environment and Urbanization* (Vol 9, Nos 1 and 2) were on housing problems; the first was on the struggle for shelter, the second on addressing the needs of tenants.

THE CITY ENVIRONMENT – AIR AND WATER POLLUTION, SOLID WASTES, TOXIC AND HAZARDOUS WASTES

For air pollution, see:

Elsom, Derek (1996), *Smog Alert: Managing Urban Air Quality*, Earthscan, London, 226 pages. Available from bookstores or direct from Earthscan at http://www.earthscan.co.uk

WHO (2000), Guidelines for Air Quality, World Health Organization, Geneva, drawn from http://www.who.int/peh/

McGranahan, Gordon and Frank Murray (editors) (1999*), Health and Air Pollution in Rapidly Developing Countries*, Stockholm Environment Institute, Stockholm.

For case studies, see:

Lemos, Maria Carmen de Mello, 'The politics of pollution control in Brazil: state actors and social movements cleaning up Cubatão', *World Development*, Vol 26, No 1, pages 75 87.

Connolly, Priscilla (1999), 'Mexico City: our common future?', *Environment and Urbanization*, Vol 11, No 1, pages 53–78.

For case studies of environmental problems in smaller cities, see Browder, John D and Brian J Godfrey (1997), *Rainforest Cities: Urbanization, Development and Globalization of the Brazilian Amazon*, Columbia University Press, New York and Chichester, 429 pages, and Agarwal, Anil, Sunita Narain and Srabani Sen (editors) (1999*), State of India's Environment: The Citizens' Fifth Report*, Centre for Science and Environment, New Delhi, 300 pages. This second publication can be ordered through CSE's web page at http://www.cseindia.org

THE RURAL, REGIONAL AND GLOBAL IMPACTS OF CITIES

For further reading on ecological footprints, see Wackernagel, Mathis and William Rees (1995), *Our Ecological Footprint – Reducing Human Impact on the Earth*, New Society Publishers. Available from New Society Publishers, PO Box 189, Gabriola Island, BC Canada V0R 1X0.

For further reading on water, see Anton, Danilo J. (1993), *Thirsty Cities: Urban Environments and Water Supply in Latin America*, IDRC, Ottawa, 197 pages.

For case studies of city-region interactions, see:

Douglass, Mike (1989), 'The environmental sustainability of development – coordination, incentives and political will in land use planning for the Jakarta metropolis', *Third World Planning Review*, Vol 11, No 2, pages 211–238.

Kreimer, Alcira, Thereza Lobo, Braz Menezes, Mohan Munasinghe and Ronald Parker (editors) (1993), *Towards a Sustainable Urban Environment: The Rio de Janeiro Study*, World Bank Discussion Papers No 195, World Bank, Washington, DC.

Kelly, Philip F (1998), 'The politics of urban-rural relationships: land conversion in the Philippines', *Environment and Urbanization*, Vol 10, No 1, pages 35–54.

For more details of the environmental impact of urban pollution on agriculture, see Conway, Gordon R and Jules N Pretty (1991), *Unwelcome Harvest*, Earthscan Publications, London, 645 pages.

For further reading on Cities and Global Warming, see:

McMichael, A J, A Haines, R Sloof and S Kovats (1996), *Climate Change and Human Health*, World Health Organization, Geneva, 297 pages. Available from WHO, 1211 Geneva 27, Switzerland (WHO/EGH/96.7). Although not specifically on cities, this contains a wealth of information about the climate system and the possible effects of climate change on (among other things) temperature, air pollution, disease-causing agents, food production, extreme weather events and sea-level rise.

Agarwal, Anil, Sunita Narain and Anju Sharma (editors) (1999), *Green Politics: Global Environmental Negotiations*, 1, Centre for Science and Environment, New Delhi, 409 pages. This is also not specifically about cities but has an accessible and detailed coverage of global warming. Available from CSE, 41 Tughlakabad Institutional Area, New Delhi 110 062, India; e-mail: sales@cseindia.org. This can also be ordered through CSE's web page at www.cseindia.org

Watson, Robert T, Marufu C Zinwowera and Richard H Moss (editors) (1996), *Climate Change 1995: Impacts, Adaptations and Mitigation of Climate Change: Scientific-Technical Analyses*, published for the Intergovernmental Panel on Climate Change by Cambridge University Press, Cambridge. See especially Scott, Michael J and others, 'Human settlements in a changing climate: impacts and adaptation', Chapter 12 (pages 399–426). During 2001, the Intergovernmental Panel on Climate Change will be publishing a new assessment that includes a chapter on human settlements.

TACKLING ENVIRONMENTAL HEALTH PROBLEMS

With regard to water, sanitation and drainage, see:

Hasan, Arif (1997), *Working with Government: The Story of the Orangi Pilot Project's Collaboration with State Agencies for Replicating its Low Cost Sanitation Programme*, City Press, Karachi, 1997.

Cairncross, Sandy (1990), 'Water supply and the urban poor', Sinnatamby, Gehan (1990), 'Low cost sanitation' and other chapters in Jorge E Hardoy and others (editors), *The Poor Die Young: Housing and Health in Third World Cities*, Earthscan Publications, London.

Hardoy, Ana and Ricardo Schusterman (2000), 'The privatization of water and sanitation and the urban poor in Buenos Aires', *Environment and Urbanization*, Vol 12, No 2, pages 63–75.

Solo, Tova Maria (1999), 'Small scale entrepreneurs in the urban water and sanitation market', *Environment and Urbanization*, Vol 11, No 1, April, pages 117–131.

With regard to refuse collection and management, see:

Arroyo Moreno, Jorge, Francisco Rivas Ríos and Inge Lardinois (1999), *Solid Waste Management in Latin America: The Role of Micro- and Small Enterprises and Cooperatives*, IPES, ACEPESA and WASTE, 214 pages.

Anand, P B (1999), 'Waste management in Madras Revisited', *Environment and Urbanization*, Vol 11, No 2, pages 161–176.

Vincentian Missionaries (1998), 'The Payatas Environmental Development Programme: micro-enterprise promotion and involvement in solid waste management in Quezon City', *Environment and Urbanization*, Vol 10, No 2, pages 55–68.

With regard to upgrading, see:

Schusterman, Ricardo and Ana Hardoy (1997), 'Reconstructing social capital in a poor urban settlement – the Integrated Improvement Programme, Barrio San Jorge', *Environment and Urbanization,* Vol 9, No 1, April, pages 91–119.

Fiori, Jorge, Liz Riley and Ronaldo Ramirez (2000), *Urban Poverty Alleviation through Environmental Upgrading in Rio de Janeiro: Favela Bairro,* Development Planning Unit, University College London, London, 154 pages, at http://www.ucl.ac.uk/dpu/

With regard to community-based actions to address environmental problems, see:

Douglass, Mike (1992), 'The political economy of urban poverty and environmental management in Asia: access, empowerment and community-based alternatives', *Environment and Urbanization,* Vol 4, No 2, October, 1992, pages 9–32.

For case studies of participatory tools and methods in urban areas, see:

RRA Notes 21: Special Issue on Participatory Tools and Methods in Urban Areas, Diana Mitlin and John Thomson (editors), IIED, 1994, 100 pages.

Hordijk, Michaela (1999), 'A dream of green and water: community-based formulation of a Local Agenda 21 in peri-urban Lima, Peru', *Environment and Urbanization,* Vol 11, No 2, October, pages 11–29.

Revi, Aromar and Manish Dube (1999), 'Indicators for urban environmental services in Lucknow: process and methods', *Environment and Urbanization,* Vol 11, No 2, pages 227–246.

See also:

Plummer, Janelle (2000), *Municipalities and Community Participation: A Sourcebook for Capacity Building,* Earthscan Publications, London. Available from bookstores or direct from Earthscan at http://www.earthscan.co.uk

With regard to the roles for NGOS and CBOS, see:

Mitlin, Diana (1999), *Civil Society and Urban Poverty,* 'Urban Governance, Partnership and Poverty', Working Paper 5, available from the International Development Department, University of Birmingham, Birmingham B15 2TT, UK.

Díaz, Andrés Cabanas, Emma Grant, Paula Irene del Cid Vargas and Ver[o]nica Sajbin Velásquez (2000), 'El Mezquital – a community's struggle for development in Guatemala City', *Environment and Urbanization,* Vol 12, No 1, pages 87–106.

Boonyabancha, Somsook (1999), 'The Urban Community Environmental Activities Project, Thailand, *Environment and Urbanization,* Vol 11, No 1, pages 101–115. See also UCDO (2000), *Urban Community Development Office Update No 2,* 32 pages. This has a detailed account of the work of this office, including its support for environmental improvements. Published by and available from UCDO, 2044/31-33 New Petchburi Road, Khet Huay Khwang, Bangkok 10320, Thailand, e-mail: ucdo@ucdo.thai.com, web: http://www.ucdo.thai.com

ACHR (2000), *Face to Face: Notes from the Network on Community Exchange,* Asian Coalition for Housing Rights, 32 pages. This gives more detail about the community exchanges described in Chapter 7. Available from ACHR, 73 Soi Sonthiwattana 4, Ladprao Road Soi 110, Bangkok 10310, Thailand, email: achrsec@email.ksc.net

During 2001, IIED is publishing a series of case studies of poverty reduction in urban areas that include papers on the work of: SPARC, the National Slum Dwellers Federation and Mahila Milan in India; People's Dialogue and the South African Homeless People's Federation; The Local Development Programme (PRODEL) in Nicaragua; The Anjuman Samaji Behbood in Community Driven Water and Sanitation in Faisalabad, Pakistan; Community organizations in El Mezquital (Guatemala City); IIED–America Latina in participatory Planning in San Fernando, Buenos Aires; and local non-profit organizations in Cali, Colombia. All include as a major focus improved housing and provision for environmental infrastructure and services. These can be obtained from IIED, 3 Endsleigh Street, London WC1H ODD, UK; http://www.iied.org

TACKLING CITY-WIDE PROBLEMS

Leitmann, Josef (1999*), Sustaining Cities: Environmental Planning and Management in Urban Design*, McGraw-Hill, New York.

Bartone, Carl, Janis Bernstein, Josef Leitmann and Jochen Eigen (1994), *Towards Environmental Strategies for Cities; Policy Considerations for Urban Environmental Management in Developing Countries*, 115 pages. Published by and available from the UNDP/UNCHS/World Bank Urban Management Program, 1818 H Street NW, Washington, DC, 20433, USA.

For further reading on industrial pollution control, see:

Robins, Nick and Rita Kumar (1999), 'Producing, Providing, Trading: Manufacturing Industry and Sustainable Cities', *Environment and Urbanization*, Vol 11, No 2, pages 75–93.

World Bank (1999), *Greening Industry: New Roles for Communities, Markets and Governments*, Oxford University Press, Oxford and New York. Available from the web at http://www.world-bank.org/nipr (which also has many other publications with a World Bank perspective on pollution control).

Von Weizsäcker, Ernst, Amory B Lovins and L Hunter Lovins (1998), *Factor Four: Doubling Wealth, Halving Resource Use*, Earthscan, London. Available from bookstores or direct from Earthscan at http://www.earthscan.co.uk

For more detail on improving environmental health, see Vol 11, No 1 of *Environment and Urbanization* on '*Healthy Cities, Neighbourhoods and Homes*' (April 1999) which included a description of the Healthy Cities movement and case studies of city programmes.

For case studies of city-wide environmental action plans, there have been four issues of *Environment and Urbanization* on 'Sustainable Cities' and these include many case studies of innovative Local Agenda 21s. For instance: case studies of Curitiba and Surabaya (Vol 4, No 2, 1992); Manizales, Chimbote and the National Campaign of Local Agenda 21s in Peru (Vol 10, No 2, 1998); Ilo (Vol 11, No 1, 1999) and Leicester (Vol 12, No 2, 2000).

New case studies of Local Agenda 21s in Durban (South Africa), Jinja (Uganda), Rufisque (Senegal) and Penang (Malaysia) are also available from the Human Settlements Programme, IIED, 3 Endsleigh Street, London WC1H ODD, UK, email: humans@iied.org, web: http://www.iied.org

With regard to children's needs and priorities, see Bartlett, Sheridan and others (1999), *Managing Cities as if Children Mattered: Children's Rights, Poverty and the Urban Environment*, Earthscan, London, 272 pages. Available from bookstores or direct from Earthscan at http://www.earthscan.co.uk

For further reading on tools and methods for environmental planning and management, see Haughton, Graham (1999), 'Information and participation within environmental management', *Environment and Urbanization*, Vol 11, No 2.

For further reading on transport and sustainability, see Newman, Peter and Jeffrey Kenworthy (1999), *Sustainability and Cities: Overcoming Automobile Dependence*, Island Press, Washington, DC, 442 pages.

SUSTAINABLE DEVELOPMENT AND CITIES

Satterthwaite, David (editor) (1999), *The Earthscan Reader in Sustainable Cities*, Earthscan, 471 pages, brings together 20 papers on different aspects of 'sustainable development and cities', including many of the papers recommended in this section. Available from bookstores or direct from Earthscan at http://www.earthscan.co.uk

On sustainable cities in general, see:

Haughton, Graham (1999) 'Environmental justice and the sustainable city', *Journal of Planning Education and Research*, Vol 18, No 3, 1999, pages 233–243 (also reprinted in *The Earthscan Reader on Sustainable Cities*).

Rees, William E (1995) 'Achieving sustainability: reform or transformation?', *Journal of Planning Literature*, Vol 9, No 4, May, pp 343–361 (also reprinted in *The Earthscan Reader on Sustainable Cities*).

Pugh, Cedric (editor) (1996), *Sustainability, the Environment and Urbanization*, Earthscan, London, and Cedric Pugh (editor) (2000), *Sustainable Cities in Developing Countries*, Earthscan, London, 256 pages. Both are available from bookstores or direct from Earthscan at http://www.earthscan.co.uk

Haughton, Graham and Colin Hunger (1994), *Sustainable Cities*, Regional Policy and Development Series 7, Jessica Kingsley Publishers, London, 1994. A comprehensive and accessible overview of the subject.

On urban agriculture, see Smit, Jac, Annu Ratta and Joe Nasr (1996), *Urban Agriculture: Food, Jobs and Sustainable Cities*, 302 pages. Publication series for Habitat II, Vol 1, UNDP, New York. Available from United Nations Publications, through their distributors within each country or region, or from UN Publications, 2 UN Plaza DC-2-853, New York, NY 10017, USA. A new, revised edition was due for publication in 2000.

For a paper considering the health implications of urban agriculture, see Birley, M H and K Lock (1998) 'Health and peri-urban natural resource production', *Environment and Urbanization*, Vol 10, No 1, pages 89–106.

For a discussion of the issues regarding sustainable development and cities within a city-wide and a community-level context, see Pezzoli, Keith (1998), *Human Settlements and Planning for Ecological Sustainability: The Case of Mexico City*, MIT Press, Boston and London, 437 pages.

The International Council for Local Environmental Initiatives (ICLEI) has various general publications of relevance to sustainable development and cities, as well as case studies of innovative local government action and guides to local government action. See ICLEI's web page at http://www.iclei.org or write to ICLEI at City Hall, West Tower, 16th Floor, Toronto, Ontario M5H 2N2, Canada.

For a stimulating discussion about 'sustainability' and its role within sustainable development, see Marcuse, Peter (1998), 'Sustainability is not enough', *Environment and Urbanization*, Vol 10, No 2, pages 103–111.

Subject Index

accidents 2, 119, 396
  to children 163–4
  in the home 71–2, 121
  industrial 122
  occupational 73–5, 165–6
  road 111–12, 277
accountability 271–3, 353, 406
Acho-chi 141, 175, 176
acid precipitation 173, 188–9, 190
acute respiratory infections 2, 9, 20, 68, 69, 72,
  104, 152, 163, 203, 383
Agarwal, Anil 216, 280, 281
age-specific mortality rates 304, 305
AGETIP 318, 330
Agenda 21 289–93, 294, 377
agricultural land, loss to cities 176, 177, 178–9,
  180, 284–5, 383–4
aid 329–30, 378–9
aid agencies *see* international agencies
aid projects 386, 387
air pollution 87, 89, 123, 150, 188–91, 303–4,
  397
  health impacts 90, 91, 92, 94–5, 98, 101–7
  indoor 72–3, 107, 163, 168
  level of risk 101, 102
  reduction 274–80
  sources 89–92
air quality 93–8, 99–100
aquaculture 284, 367
aquifers 7, 83, 122, 180, 182–4, 204, 380
asbestos 73, 112–114, 116, 117
Asian Coalition for Housing Rights 255
Asian Development Bank 320, 325–6, 326–7
asthma 73, 95, 101, 103–5, 156, 203, 282
atmospheric warming *see* global warming

Bamenda (Cameroon) 141, 175–6
Barrio San Jorge 225–7, 243
Bartone, Carl 311
Basel Convention 119, 377
beaches 3, 184, 186, 204, 205, 299
benzene 74, 92, 96, 97, 113, 114
biodiversity 19, 192, 298, 343, 344, 345, 348,
  349, 356, 363
Bradley, David 39
brown agenda 365, 404
Brundtland Commission *see* World Commission
  on Environment and Development

building codes 201, 208, 261, 287, 303, 339, 401

cadmium 96, 97, 104, 108, 112–6, 187, 189
Cairncross, Sandy 6, 216
cancer 94, 104, 113, 114, 116, 154, 162, 203
capacity building 321, 324–6, 330, 331, 390,
  405–6
carbon dioxide 96, 97, 192, 196, 197, 200, 201,
  337, 341, 360, 361
carbon monoxide 90–3, 95, 98, 99, 162, 190, 274,
  275, 279
carcinogens 73, 92
catalytic converters 274, 278, 347
Cavite (Philippines) 178–9
CBOs (community-based organizations) 7, 10, 13,
  14, 164, 170, 217, 219, 243, 245, 287, 298,
  333, 353, 382, 385, 386, 390, 392, 394
  partnerships with local government and NGOs 13,
  242–50, 268, 398
centralized governments 309–10, 385
Centre for Science and Environment (India) 109,
  140, 141, 280, 281, 391
CFCs 96, 377
child development 164–5
children 131, 157, 214, 215, 222
  accidents to 112, 163–4
  effect of maternal health 161–2
  occupational hazards 165–6
  vulnerability to environmental hazards 161–6
Chimbote (Peru) 297, 298–9, 300, 376
cholera 9, 40, 70, 71, 108, 121, 122, 184, 260,
  313
chromates 114
cities 2–4, 17–20, 22, 28–9, 398–400
  Agenda 21 289–93, 294
  demand for rural resources 177–83, 193
  ecological impacts 191–6, 198–200
  encroachment on agricultural land 176, 177,
  178–9, 180, 284–5, 383–4
  environmental management 19, 287–8
  environmental opportunities 20–4
  environmental problems 11–13, 143–8, 380–1,
  406
  impact on global commons 196–201
  impact of global warming 201–8
  impact on greenhouse gas emissions 197–200,
  201, 339, 340
  new environmental agenda 8–14, 384–402

physical expansion 174–7
population growth 24–36
population growth rates 33–5, 404
regional environmental impacts 172–3, 186–90
smaller cities 30–1
sub-Saharan Africa 34–5
'sustainable' 361–2
sustainable development 339–40, 353–4,
    361–4, 365–6, 366–8, 372–4
see also local government; urban centres; urban
    development; urbanization
Cities Alliance 326
citizen groups 389–91, 399, 406
citizen pressure 280, 281–2, 297, 299, 311, 374–6,
    399
Civic Exnora 228
civil society 4, 13, 19, 251, 252, 254, 256, 268,
    313, 318, 331, 535, 386, 389
clean industry 107, 118, 271, 272, 274, 278, 279
climate change 197, 201–8
    see also global warming
coal 72, 89, 90, 91, 93, 94, 97, 100, 101, 114,
    116, 133, 139, 145, 163, 168, 180, 189,
    198–200, 250, 274, 286, 311, 346, 405
coastal areas 357
community based organizations see CBOs
communities 242, 260–5, 267–9
community exchanges 254, 255–6
community facilities 3, 76, 150
community-based organizations see CBOs
community-based projects 242–50, 254–6, 335,
    387, 391–3, 394–5, 397
commuting 183, 185
Connolly, Priscilla 111, 279
consumption patterns 197–201
coordination 175, 186, 191
credit 248–9, 251, 252
crime 128–30
Cubatão (Brazil), industrial pollution 104–7, 139,
    142, 271–2
'cultural sustainability' 352
Curitiba (Brazil) 274, 276–7
cyclones 119, 120, 121, 122, 125, 204

Dakar (Senegal) 182–3, 184
DANCED 249, 330, 393
death rates 6, 17, 151–2, 161, 304, 305
debt 379, 405–6
decentralization 30, 310
deforestation 83, 177–9, 186, 197, 199, 307, 344,
    345, 356–7
demand-side management 291
democracy 13, 296, 332, 389, 391, 406
democratic processes 10, 38
dengue fever 2, 8, 9, 41, 42, 46, 62, 82, 83, 103,
    207, 383
density of population 20–3, 28, 69, 82, 134, 155,
    174, 212, 358, 373
Department for International Development
    (DFID), UK 328, 330, 393
deprivation 393–5
    see also poverty

development 342–3, 374–9
    see also sustainable development
development assistance 378–9
development banks *see* international agencies
diarrhoeal diseases 2, 8, 9, 40, 42, 43, 45, 62, 69,
    70, 71, 76, 82, 84, 85, 103, 108, 120, 134,
    136, 152, 161, 163, 203, 212, 260, 261, 263,
    304, 383, 396, 402
dirty industries, relocation 116–8
disasters 1–2, 21, 78, 119–25, 158–61
disease vectors 2, 8, 15, 42, 43, 46, 62, 75, 79, 82,
    83, 132, 185, 188, 203, 207, 232, 261, 286,
    381, 384, 396, 397
diseases 2, 9, 207, 396
    association with overcrowding 68–70
    environment-related 6–7, 152, 163
    excreta-related 57, 59, 62
    food-related 70–1
    occupational 73–4
    water-related 39–43, 57, 59, 62
Douglas, Ian 14, 173
drainage 44, 45, 46, 82–4, 109, 132–9
Drawers of Water/Drawers of Water II 52
dust 5, 73, 74, 88, 90, 96, 97, 234
dysentery 8, 103, 125, 135, 184

earthquakes 13, 21, 77, 119–122, 125, 159, 160,
    208
East Africa, water supplies 52–7
Ecociudad 300
eco-labelling 375
ecological footprints, cities 192–3, 194–5, 196,
    198–200
ecological impacts, cities 191–6
ecological sustainability 8, 345, 346–50, 352, 379
economic growth 343
effluents 22, 47, 89, 97, 106, 109, 110, 140,
    186–8, 357
elderly people 70, 90, 101, 104, 156, 158, 162,
    206
El Niño 206
emergency services 20, 120, 125, 126, 132, 152,
    157, 159, 160, 170, 198, 265, 312, 317, 386
enablement 371–2, 374
environment 12
    impact on well-being 84–6, 126–32
    links with health 8–9, 12–13, 393–8
    see also environmental degradation;
        environmental hazards; environmental
        problems; health impacts
environment movement 341–2, 399–400, 406
environmental action, constraints 308–13
environmental agencies, national 311
environmental audit procedures 291
environmental capital 3, 348–50, 353, 354
environmental costs, transfers 191–2, 376
environmental degradation 7, 12–13, 197, 198,
    348
environmental equity 362–3
environmental hazards 12–13, 198
    correlation with incomes 149–51
    home environments 71–3, 85–6, 121, 163–4

house sites 75–8, 159, 160–1, 396
  susceptibility to 152–7, 161
  vulnerability to 152–8
  see also disasters; hazards; health impacts
environmental health 209–10, 383
  burdens 84–5, 170, 345, 396
  improvements 211–12, 320–2, 323, 325, 403–4
environmental impact
  industries 96–7
  urban development 5–6
environmental impact assessment 291
environmental improvement 401–2
  links with health 393–8
  links with poverty reduction 393–8
environmental indicators 302–7
environmental management 2, 19, 287–8, 290–2
environmental opportunities 20–4
environmental planning 287–8, 290–2
environmental problems 15–16
  cities 11–13, 142–8, 380–1, 406
  global context 402–6
  impact of national wealth 142–8
  political roots 10, 382–3
  urban agriculture 286–7
  urban expansion 4–7
  see also environmental hazards; pollution
environmental quality 8, 304–6
environmental risks 198
  high-risk groups 158–69
  intra-city differentials 151–2, 153–5, 171
environmental transitions 142–8
epidemics 121–2, 125
equity 353, 362, 363–365, 377, 378
erosion 5, 84, 88, 96, 97, 123, 141, 175, 177, 180,
    181, 186, 199, 204, 286, 287, 342, 344, 245,
    349, 350, 355, 356, 357, 381
ethical sourcing 375
evictions 72, 77, 105, 165, 169, 170, 175, 221,
    222, 255, 264, 303, 316, 399, 408
excreta-related diseases 57
external agencies *see* international agencies
extreme weather events 119, 202, 206, 382

fair trade 375, 376
favelas 277, 380
filariasis 41, 43, 45, 57, 62, 82, 83, 207, 261
fires 38, 71, 72, 85, 96, 97, 119–23, 150, 163,
    164, 168, 200, 208, 262, 381, 396, 398
fish-farming 7, 13, 107, 177, 183, 184, 187, 207,
    231, 284–6, 343, 345
fisheries, pollution 184, 187
flooding 7, 77, 120–1, 125, 162, 175–6, 396
  reducing vulnerability 160
  result of global warming 205–6
  result of inadequate drainage 45, 46
fluorides 97, 114, 188–190
food-related diseases 70–1
forests 356–7
fossil fuels 3, 23, 24, 89–91, 114, 146, 184,
    190–2, 195–7, 199, 200, 204, 230, 274, 338,
    339, 346, 348, 354, 357, 363, 364, 373, 377
freshwater, shortages of 7, 10, 21, 111, 122, 180,

    187, 205, 207, 213, 215, 241, 286, 343, 382
fuelwood 177–9, 180, 186, 197
funding, community-based projects 391–3, 394–5
FUPROVI 330, 333
Furedy, Christine 232, 312

gender aspects 130, 167, 168, 403, 404
Global Climate Change Convention 377
Global Climate Coalition 250
global negotiations 405–6
global warming 3, 14, 122, 197, 200, 349, 360–1,
    378, 405
  and development 377–9
  impact on cities 201–8
  see also greenhouse gas emissions
good governance 3–4, 6, 19–20, 148, 170–1,
    241–2, 388
governance 8, 142, 267–8, 307, 331, 339, 353
  failures 7–8, 382–3
  good governance 3–4, 6, 19–20, 148, 170–1,
    241–2, 388
government–community partnerships 260–5,
    267–9
governments 310, 366, 368, 388–9
  centralized 309–10, 385
  failures 170, 382–3, 388–9
  representative 10–11, 310–11, 353, 354, 389,
    399
  see also governance; local government
green agenda 365
green consumerism 375–6
greenhouse gas emissions 349, 360–1, 364, 404,
    405
  impact of cities 197–200, 201, 339, 340
  see also global warming
  groundwater 5, 46, 47, 61, 109, 110, 180,
    182–4, 204, 205, 337, 365, 396

Habitat Agenda 344, 377
Habitat II, Second UN Conference on Human
    Settlements 1996 (Istanbul) 295, 296
Hasan, Arif 76, 309
Haughton, Graham 292, 339, 362, 374
hazardous wastes 112–16, 118–19, 232
hazards
  occupational 73–5, 165–6
  risks 123–5
health
  implications of urban expansion 83
  links with environment 8–9, 12–13, 393–8
health burdens 84–5, 170, 345, 396
health impacts
  air pollution 90, 91, 92, 94–5, 98, 101–7
  climate change 203
  hazardous sites 77–8
  inadequate sanitation 39
  inadequate water supplies 39–43
  noise pollution 125
  overcrowding 39, 68–70, 71–2
  toxic waste 113, 114, 115–16
  urban expansion 4–6, 6–7, 83
healthcare 7, 69, 72, 403

Healthy Cities programme 268
heat islands 206
heavy metals 112, 113, 114, 115–16, 188
Homeless International 333
homes
  environmental hazards 71–3, 75, 85–6, 121,
    163–4
  see also health; housing
homeworkers 75
homicides *see* murders
household wastes 78–82, 132, 135, 225–30, 233
  see also solid wastes
housing
  and environmental health 38–9
  hazardous sites 75–8, 159, 160–1, 396
  improvements 321, 322–4, 325
  low-income groups 10, 77, 382
housing deficit 220
human rights 351, 352–354, 375
Hurricane Mitch 78, 206

IBM 388, 342
IIED 26, 183, 320, 339, 341
IIED-America Latina 225, 227
Ilo (Peru) 243, 252, 268, 308
immunization programmes 69, 72
income levels, and environmental risks 151–2,
    153–5
India 10, 31, 58–9, 109, 110
indicators 302–7, 370–1
indoor air pollution 72–3, 107, 163, 168
industrial accidents 119, 122, 166
industrial pollution 87–9, 96–7, 112–19, 139–41
  control 271–4
  Cubatão (Brazil) 104–7, 139, 142, 271–2
  see also air pollution; water pollution
industries
  environmental impacts 96–7
  relocation 116–18
industry, sustainable 271, 272
inequality 152, 155, 305
infant mortality rates 6, 17, 151–2, 161, 304,
    305
informal settlements 20–1, 77, 174–5, 209–10
information-gathering measures 257–67
infrastructure, shared 216–18
injuries 2, 6, 7, 9, 72–4, 78, 85, 108, 111, 112,
    119–122, 124, 145, 156, 159, 163, 164, 168,
    170, 203, 206, 232, 265, 304, 383
Institute of Environmental Studies (IDEA),
    Colombia 300
institutional change 384–6
institutional constraints 308–13, 393, 399
Inter–American Development Bank 317, 331
international agencies 63, 296, 318–20, 327–32
  'anti-urban' bias 313–14, 318, 328
  Fund for Community Initiatives 392–3, 394–5
  'going to scale' 334–5
  roles 385–9, 390, 391
  underestimation of urban poverty 314, 315–17
  urban projects 314–17
  withdrawal 335

  see also Asian Development Bank; OECF; World
    Bank
intestinal parasites 8, 9
investment 308
ISO 14001 273

Jakarta (Indonesia) 179–80, 181–2
Japan Bank for International Cooperation 317,
    388
Jockin 10, 280
joint action 406

Kampung improvement programme (Indonesia)
    224
Kolsky, Peter 400
Kuznets curve 142, 143

lakes 3, 79, 107–9, 124, 158, 173, 184, 186, 187,
    216
land 21–3, 382
landfill 106, 147, 162, 210, 230–233, 309, 399
landslides 1, 6, 38, 75, 78, 84, 105, 119–124, 127,
    150, 154, 159, 169, 175, 169, 175, 205, 206,
    264, 297, 298, 363, 396, 398, 401
large cities 2, 26–31, 33, 34, 36, 51, 64, 98, 109,
    120, 124, 133, 144, 176, 196, 230, 301, 311,
    315, 334, 380, 384
largest cities (in the world) 11, 23, 26, 27, 30, 31,
    34–6, 93, 101, 123, 124, 140, 141, 186, 205,
    356
latrines 22, 43–6, 54–7, 59, 61, 65, 68, 84,
    133–135, 144, 212–4, 235, 244, 245, 270,
    367, 394, 395
lead 73, 74, 89, 90, 92, 95–99, 103, 104, 108,
    112–116, 140, 162, 163, 189, 274, 278
leptospirosis 40, 82, 125
life expectancies 17
  see also mortality rates
Limits to Growth 340
liquid wastes 173, 186–8, 212, 214
livestock 168, 182, 185, 189, 191, 197, 257, 280,
    283–286, 345, 384, 403, 404
loans 248–9, 251, 252
Local Agenda 21s 288–302, 374, 396
local government 241–2, 297, 311–13, 370, 374,
    388–9, 390
  action to achieve sustainability and development
    366–8
  capacity building 321, 324–6, 330, 331, 384–5,
    390
  partnerships with CBOs and NGOs 13,
    242–50, 268, 374, 398
local institutions 384–6
low-income groups 10, 77, 149–53, 198, 406
  housing trade-offs 169–70
  and private enterprises 236–8
  see also susceptibility; vulnerability

malaria 2, 8, 9, 41, 42, 62, 77, 82, 83, 134, 135,
    136, 152, 161–163, 207, 261, 383
malnutrition 49, 69, 73, 203, 345
Manizales (Colombia) 296–7, 298, 300, 307

market incentives 369–70
material intensity 196
McGranahan, Gordon 143, 306, 364
McMichael, Tony 156
measles 42, 69, 163
mega-cities 27–9, 30, 31, 33, 384
mercury 73, 96, 97, 108, 112–117, 162, 181
Mexico City 109–11, 278–80
Mexico City's Clean Air Policy 278, 279
migration to cities 183, 185, 186
million-cities 27–9
MISEREOR 333
mortality rates 6, 17, 151–2, 161, 304, 305
mosquitoes 42, 43, 77, 79, 82, 83, 214, 261, 286
motor vehicle accidents 111, 304
motor vehicle use 23
multinational corporations 117, 342, 375, 405
municipal government *see* local government
murders 128, 304

national frameworks, sustainable development 15,
    361, 368–71, 372, 384
National Slum Dwellers Federation (India) 10,
    217, 218, 253, 254, 257
natural capital 3, 348–50, 353, 354
natural disasters 14, 21, 122, 125, 150, 316
natural hazards, interaction with human actions
    76–7
natural monopolies 237, 241
negotiations, global 405–6
neighbourhood environments 75–84, 85–6
NGOs (non–governmental organizations) 250–3,
    254–6, 300–1, 332, 385, 389–92, 399
    international 319, 333–4
    partnerships with local government and CBOs
        13, 242–50, 253, 268, 398
nitrogen oxides 92, 93, 141, 188, 279
noise pollution 125–6
non-governmental organizations *see* NGOs
non-renewable resources 196, 199, 358–60
nuclear power 116, 342

occupational hazards 73–5, 165–6
OECF (Overseas Economic Cooperation Fund)
    320–2, 326, 327
official statistics 59–68, 303, 314
Only One Earth 338, 341
Orangi Pilot Project (Karachi) 13, 217, 236,
    242–3, 244–5
Our Common Future (World Commission on
    Environment and Development 1987) 340,
    343–4, 351
overcrowding 39, 68–70, 71–2, 150
Overseas Economic Cooperation Fund *see* OECF
ozone 189, 190, 206–7

Pampas de San Juan 259
participation 13, 252–7, 296, 313, 335, 372, 397
participatory methods 256–67, 402
particulate matter 72, 88, 90–94, 96–103, 105,
    112, 141, 274
PCBs 96, 97, 112, 114, 162

People's Dialogue on Land and Shelter (South
    Africa) 253, 254, 257
pesticides 110, 114, 162–4, 181
photochemical smog 89, 90, 92, 190
pilot projects 253–4
piped water 43, 50–7
pit latrines *see* latrines
PM_{10} 91, 93, 98, 99, 102, 104–6, 275, 279
pneumonia 42, 68, 69, 105, 152, 163, 402
poisoning 72, 73, 85, 114, 115, 181, 187
pollutants 37, 89–92, 96–7, 107–9
pollution
    by publicly-owned facilities 309
    water 87, 89, 96–7, 107–9, 186–8
    see also air pollution; industrial pollution
pollution control 270–80, 321, 323, 325, 327
    citizen action 280, 281–2
pollution inventory 275
population growth, cities 24–36
population growth rates, cities 33–5, 404
Pôrto Alegre (Brazil) 4, 17, 306
poverty 13, 198, 344, 345, 346, 382, 393–5
    and environmental degradation 198, 199–200
    underestimation in urban areas 314, 315–17
poverty lines 315–17
poverty reduction 393–8
power stations 23, 90, 91, 110, 116, 189, 192,
    193, 197, 199, 200, 205, 274, 281, 309, 328,
    342, 364, 373, 381
premature deaths 2, 6, 101, 103, 111, 406
privatization 235–42, 269, 386
PRODEL 330
professional attitudes 13–14, 400–2
project sustainability 351
PROPER (Programme for Pollution Control,
    Evaluation and Rating) 272, 273
property rights 370, 398–9
psychosocial disorders 127–8, 130–1, 169
    see also violence
public amenities 3, 76, 150
public transport 7, 23, 327, 396, 397
    Curitiba 240, 274, 276–7
publicly-owned facilities 309

quality of life 3, 24, 182, 259, 359, 362, 364, 372,
    374

radioactive wastes 116, 192
rats 79, 82, 261
recreation 126, 177, 180, 186, 216, 263, 287, 303,
    329, 354, 356
recycling 230–2, 233–5, 277, 309, 312–13
redistribution 370, 406
Rees, William E 173, 192, 195, 296, 338, 349,
    357
regulatory controls 309, 368–9
relocation, dirty industries 116–18
renewable resources 199–200, 355–7
renewable sinks 355–7
representative governments 10–11, 310–11, 353,
    354, 389, 399
resource consumption, inequities 404